W9-CBZ-112

NOTHING BUT THE TRUTH

AN ANTHOLOGY OF NATIVE AMERICAN LITERATURE

John Purdy
Western Washington University

James Ruppert
University of Alaska, Fairbanks

Prentice
Hall

Upper Saddle River, New Jersey 07458

SIENA COLLEGE LIBRARY

Library of Congress Cataloging-in-Publication Data

Nothing but the truth: an anthology of Native American literature / [selected by]
John Purdy, James Ruppert.
    p. cm.
  Includes bibliographical references and index.
  ISBN 0-13-116424-
    1. American literature—Indian authors. 2. Indians of North America—Literary
collections. I. Purdy, John. II. Ruppert, James, 1947-III. Title.

PS508.I5 N67 2000
810.8'0897—dc21   00-027700

Editor in Chief: Leah Jewell
Senior Acquisitions Editor: Carrie Brandon
Editorial Assistant: Sandy Hrasdzira
VP, Director of Production and Manufacturing: Barbara Kittle
Managing Editor: Mary Rottino
Production Editor: Randy Pettit
Prepress and Manufacturing Manager: Nick Sklitsis
Prepress and Manufacturing Buyer: Sherry Lewis
Marketing Director: Beth Gillett Mejia
Marketing Manager: Rachel Falk
Interior Design: Ximena Tomvakopoulos
Cover Design Director: Jayne Conte
Cover Design: Robert Farrar-Wagner
Cover Photo: Sandy Hrasdzira

For permission to use copyrighted material, grateful acknowledgment is made to
the copyright holders listed on page 633–637, which is considered an extension of
this copyright page.

This book was set in 10/12 Garamond by Carlisle Communications, Ltd. and printed
and bound by R.R. Donnelley & Sons Company.
The cover was printed by Phoenix Color Corp.

© 2001 by Prentice-Hall Inc.
A Division of Pearson Education
Upper Saddle River, New Jersey 07458

All rights reserved. No part of this book may be
reproduced, in any form or by any means,
without permission in writing from the publisher.

Printed in the United States of America
10 9 8 7 6 5 4 3 2 1

ISBN 0-13-011642-4

Prentice-Hall International (UK) Limited, London
Prentice-Hall of Australia Pty. Limited, Sydney
Prentice-Hall Canada Inc., Toronto
Prentice-Hall Hispanoamerica, S.A., Mexico
Prentice-Hall India Private Limited, New Delhi
Prentice-Hall of Japan, Inc., Tokyo
Pearson Education Asia Pte. Ltd., Rio de Janeiro

PS
508
.IS
N67
2001

There can be only one dedication for this collection, and it is to those who have produced it: the authors and poets who have enriched our lives in countless and often unacknowledged ways. We hope that, in some small way, this may honor you. Good thoughts in all things.

CONTENTS

FICTION   190

POETRY   412

DRAMA 591

SELECTIONS BY AUTHOR

PREFACE

As the old saying goes, necessity is the mother of invention, and necessity certainly drove the creation of this anthology. As any educator will tell you, one of the difficult duties we face year after year, semester after semester, is the selection of texts for classes. Even in the case of literature courses that cover the writings of "dead white guys" who no longer produce literary works, there is still a continuous stream of secondary books about them and myriad analyses of their writings. In the area of writings by American Indians, this task is even more difficult because of the growing body of secondary sources, of course, but also because of the tremendous increase in the numbers of pieces of literature produced by writers of Native American descent. It is a perplexing quandary when one tries to choose from such a wonderfully rich selection.

Such difficulties also arise when one tries to compile an anthology, and there are some very good examples in print today. Some try to provide the widest coverage: an expansive array of writings from as many nations and tribal groups as possible. Some try to provide an all-inclusive sense of history: coverage from the late eighteenth century to the present. Others center on specific thematic concerns—identity issues, political policies—and thus narrow their scope. Some simply opt for the editors' favorites.

This present endeavor, however, cuts across the various attempts of the past, and it has one simple, perhaps obvious, guiding principle. It was our intention to compile the pieces of literature that our colleagues who teach Native American literature use time and time again. To accomplish this task, we surveyed our colleagues around the globe and asked them to give us a list of their "core" texts. The questionnaires—sent by post and also posted on the Internet—covered all genres and eras. Our only stipulation was that we were looking for complete works of literary art and not "excerpts," that is, sections of longer works, like novels, which rarely stand as discrete units of art. (There are short stories included here that became novel chapters later.) The response was wonderful, and although there were some obviously central authors listed on significant numbers of questionnaires, there was also a great diversity in the recommendations they made.

This may seem to be a very self-serving effort: to create the anthology we always wanted to have. To a degree, this is true, but primarily this book is an attempt to construct an effective introductory collection to written Native literature. In our questionnaire, we asked for lists of pieces used most often because "they work." We did not get into a lengthy attempt to define this vague qualifier, believing that every educator knows when something has a profound, productive effect on a class, an audience. We simply wanted to bring together literary pieces that have this effect, because we also realize that the students who read these pieces of literature in the myriad courses our colleagues teach at a wide array of public and private institutions around the globe constitute the reading public itself; they come from every element of society, cutting across every group distinction employed in the world today: class, gender, race, and political ideology, to name just a few. Nonetheless, the literature speaks personally and compellingly to them, and that is a remarkable achievement.

We truly hope it speaks to you, the current reader, as well.

Acknowledgments

We want to thank all the people who have made this anthology possible, including all our colleagues around the world who took the time to answer our survey and thus provided the list of works they find most useful in their courses. We would also like to thank Steven Beech, who tracked these works down, and our editor, Carrie Brandon, for helping us realize our goal. Finally, however, our greatest appreciation goes to the Native American writers and storytellers who have made such remarkable contributions to the literary arts and enriched our society with their myriad voices and their illuminating insights.

We would also like to thank the reviewers of our manuscript for their input on this anthology: Jacquelyn Kilpatrick, Ph.D., Governors State University; Gloria Lynn Larrieu, Southwestern Indian Polytechnic Institute; Louis Roma-Deeley, Paradise Valley Community College; Patrick Clark Smith, University of New Mexico; and Norma Clark Wilson, University of South Dakota.

—John Purdy,
James Ruppert

INTRODUCTION

A Little Publication History

Early twentieth-century Native American writers struggled to efface the stereotyped, damaging images of Indian peoples. Writers like Charles Eastman (Sioux), Pauline Johnson (Mohawk), Luther Standing Bear (Sioux), and Gertrude Bonin (Sioux) wrote to show the natural decency of Native people faced with a misunderstanding white world ready to do away with them for once and for all. Though Native Americans held progressive attitudes, they were not willing to accept assimilation without some sense of cultural pride and some appreciation of the value of Native cultures. This was no easy task in the first quarter of the century. During these years, Wild West shows were crisscrossing the United States and Europe, reducing the history of the American West and the lives of Native peoples to caricatures. Still, there was a popular interest in Native Americans. Indeed, at this moment in history the first anthology of Native American poetry (really songs) was published, and many non-Native writers were exploring Native literatures and cultures. In 1926, an anthropologist-turned-novelist, Oliver LaFarge, won the Pulitzer Prize for fiction with his novel *Laughing Boy,* which grew from his experiences on the Navajo reservation. Whether this interest grew out of modernism's fascination with "the primitive" or from a renewed sense of American uniqueness depended on the writers themselves. However, the Great Depression of the 1930s created other imperatives, and thus the "interest" in Indians gave way to economic concerns.

During the 1930s, 1940s, and 1950s, Native writers had difficulty finding an audience. Writers like D'Arcy McNickle (Métis-Salish), Mourning Dove (Salish), John Oskison (Cherokee), and Joseph Matthews (Osage) published but did not discover wide fame or fortune. The Depression, World War II, and the determined conformity of the postwar era worked together to enforce an invisibility on Native peoples and silence their voices, at least from the viewpoint of the dominant society. Indeed, the 1950s saw an organized governmental policy of terminating reservations and relocating reservation dwellers into large cities so the final mass cultural assimilation could be quietly effected. The effort was spearheaded by Dillon Myer, who was appointed head of the Bureau of Indian Affairs after the tenure of the progressive commissioner John Collier. Previously, during World War II, Myer had supervised the relocation of Japanese-Americans to internment camps.

Like the oppressive practices of the past, termination and relocation met with resistance, including literary resistance. The Native cultural (re)awakenings and empowerment movements (such as the American Indian Movement) of the 1960s launched what has come to be known as the Native American Renaissance, a phenomenon usually dated to the publication of N. Scott Momaday's *House Made of Dawn* in 1968. This Pulitzer Prize–winning novel proved tremendously influential for Native writers and, along with the republication of *Black Elk Speaks* (an as-told-to autobiography of the Sioux elder originally published in the 1930s), primed a broad general interest in American Indian peoples and cultures, indicative of an ebb and flow of general public attention to Native cultures and issues noted by a number of writers, most notably Vine Deloria, Jr. (Sioux), and Geary Hobson (Chickasaw).

Partly, this popularity can certainly be attributed to an expanded audience comprising the "baby boom" generation; this postwar tidal wave of youth came of age (through the era of Walt Disney) in the fifties and sixties when counterculture movements were searching for alternative ways to live in this world. As a result, well-established and influential publishers brought out collections of transcribed oral materials such as *The Winged Serpent* and *The Sky Clears,* as well as reprintings of George Cronyn's *The Path on the Rainbow* and Natalie Curtis's *The Indian's Book.* Mostly, though, the growing appreciation of Native literatures and awareness of the issues they engage must be attributed to the power of the writing of a new generation of Native authors. An expanded audience is receptive only if the words speak to them in compelling ways, and these words speak eloquently. Moreover, the small-press movement of the era began to publish work by a variety of Native writers and new voices that rose from all over the country. In the 1970s, Harper & Row started a high-profile publication series that brought a number of Native writers to prominence.

Many novels, books of poetry, and anthologies were published over the next ten years, including the much acclaimed *Winter in the Blood* (1974) by Gros Ventre/Blackfeet writer James Welch, *Darkness in Saint Louis Bearheart* (1978) by Anishinaabe (Chippewa) author Gerald Vizenor, *Ceremony* (1977) by Leslie Marmon Silko (Laguna Pueblo), and *Love Medicine* (1984) by Louise Erdrich (Anishinaabe). While the small press movement lost momentum (and National Endowment for the Arts grants) during the 1980s, Native writers continued to write and were able to open up more venues with commercial and university publishers. Popular interest might have waned some in the early 1980s but for the growth of the New Age movement, which was yet another attempt to revise (and thus essentialize) contemporary lifeways through a connection with cultures other than one's own. By the late 1980s, the public interest in "Indian" was blossoming again. Indeed, Michael Dorris (Modoc) and Louise Erdrich received an unprecedented advance of over a million dollars for writing their quincentennial Columbus novel, *The Crown of Columbus.*

The 1990s have seen the maturation of established writers and the growth of a new generation of writers unsatisfied with the approaches and themes of the last generation. In her introduction to *Song of the Turtle,* Paula Gunn Allen (Laguna/Sioux) referred to this group as the third wave of Native writers. She sees them as more concerned with articulating contemporary Native experience as it is lived than with busting stereotypes or creating "authenticity," which were the directives of earlier writings. The new millennium will witness the steady growth of Native writers and a continuation of postmodern variety: Joy Harjo (Creek) will continue playing the saxophone, Sherman Alexie (Spokane/Coeur d'Alene) will continue appearing on PBS and writing screenplays for movies, and N. Scott Momaday will continue painting. The arts flourish.

A Little Literary History

Many scholars date the beginning of the field of Native American literary studies to the Modern Language Association/National Endowment for the Humanities curriculum development seminar in Flagstaff, Arizona, in 1977. Certainly, critical notice had been taken of Native American literatures long before this, but this first meeting of scholars and Native writers (such as Silko and Gunn Allen) forged a common purpose that spawned books, magazines, scholarly articles, and conference sessions. Faced with a disbelieving academic system and a marginal position in mainstream American thought, those who sought to promote Native American literatures because of convictions of cultural relativism and social criticism tended to praise first and ask questions later. Often, early criticism tried to show the worth of Native materials by comparing them to classics of the American and other Western traditions. This missionary zeal is understandable, given the social conditions of the times, but much of the early criticism it generated was impressionistic, personal, explanatory, laudatory, and unsophisticated. Very little negative criticism was published, as Arnold Krupat has been quick to point out. In keeping with this orientation, scholars pursued historical and ethnographic critical perspectives. One of the strengths of these approaches was that the real lives of people and their communities were central to literary insight.

While the nineties introduced Native American literary criticism to postmodern theories, the best scholarship still retains a central focus. Those who work with this growing canon of literature see it as a vital and, at times, tumultuous discourse, deeply concerned with issues of self-determination (in both communal and personal senses) and cultural continuance. The tensions between lived experience and academic realities have driven much of the critical output since the early 1990s, and some Native literary texts as well. In other words, this continuing discourse is yet another indication of the evolution of a canon of literature.

A Little Academic History

Many ethnic studies and Native American studies departments date to the late 1960s and early 1970s before contemporary Native American literature had established itself as a field of inquiry in American institutions of higher education. Its efforts to inform and broaden academic offerings gave Native American literatures an opening into many academic settings. However, for much of the 1980s, departments only grudgingly established courses dedicated to literature by American Indians, and it was not until the 1990s that Native and other ethnic literatures found widespread inclusion in "mainstream" (i.e. American survey) and required courses. While these literatures have moved away from "the margin," as the distinctions between margin and "center" become diffuse the tension generated by contested issues of canon formation and publication history remain central to academic discourse. Native American literary studies increasingly find themselves situated in the debate over education, power, and ethnicity. Too often, Western civilization is placed in opposition to multiculturalism, with little realization that it is the interface between them that creates the nature of our modern society and the richness of much of today's art. The center and margin are in flux and are renegotiated as each new generation of readers comes into dialogue with literary texts that expand their reading horizons.

The editors hope their readers will engage these social discourses, exploring not only their understandings of the literary works that follow, but also how such discourses can aid their approaches to meaning in contemporary life. In the first decade of the twenty-first century, the universities will continue to see a profusion of multiethnic/multicultural and diverse perspectives, and they will be faced with the task of seeing negotiations as progressive and not (simplistically) oppositional.

We see a future of transformation and change spreading before us, and we know the writers in this book have something very provocative to say about that future and our shared society.

NONFICTION

The interweavings of language and community emerge through these essays, from the cries above the Hotchkiss guns at Wounded Knee to the quiet questions that follow cigarette smoke inside a car parked beside Crater Lake. The pieces in this nonfiction section reflect a spectrum of topics in Native American literatures. Among these are concerns with postmodernism, nationalism, humor, the Ghost Dance, symbolism in oral traditions, language and imagination, authenticity, identity, logics of orality, cultural property, and the power of stories. Personal and professional issues mix honestly as the writers carefully blend subjective or objective voices. They bring incisive intellectual perspectives to bear on questions in which their hearts and their bodies are entwined. Thus we read simultaneously of ethics and aesthetics, politics and poetry, history and myth, identity and community.

From a number of perspectives, nonfiction is a non-category in Native American literatures. Aside from the more general fact that Native American writers so frequently choose to blur European genres, including the foundational Western genres of orality and literacy, their nonfiction covers a wide array of forms. There is a romantic view of Native expression which claims that forms such as poetry, oratory, and plays are more indigenous than either fiction or nonfiction. Yet, as A. LaVonne Brown Ruoff has suggested, "The major genre written by American Indian authors in the late eighteenth and nineteenth centuries was nonfiction prose. In addition to writing autobiographies, Indian authors wrote sermons, protest literature, tribal histories, and travel accounts. They hoped that their prose would make their white audiences recognize Indians' humanity as a people and the significance of their tribal cultures and history. Their efforts paralleled the political developments, such as the Indian Removal Bill of 1830, that threatened the sovereignty of Indian peoples" (Ruoff 62). The essays and excerpts in this collection, entirely from the twentieth century, are a continuation of more than two centuries of a tradition of nonfiction protest literature.

After centuries of Native writing and publishing in colonial languages and colonial genres, it is no longer possible to say that Euroamerican forms such as poetry, short stories, novels, essays, or plays are not Native American forms. When Montaigne (1533–92) was inventing *le essai* in France and writing about the superiority of cannibals, Guaman Pomo de Ayala in Peru was writing a long essay explaining to King Philip of Spain about the savagery of colonialists. The fact that Native writers have been reimagining

European forms to argue for recognition of tribal cultures and sovereignties for so long confirms the notion in Joy Harjo's and Gloria Bird's recent compilation entitled *Reinventing the Enemy's Language.* The reappropriation of English and other colonial languages is an ongoing process, however, always beset with cultural hazards. As Louis Owens has written, "the assimilation of 'alien' discourse by an oppressed people" raises ideological questions about the authority with which Native writers speak of cultural continuity and change. Thus "'Language' indissolubly fused with its authority—with political power—is a central concern of Native writers" (*Other Destinies* 12,13). This issue of authority in Native voices has often been translated through the ethnographic lens as an issue of authenticity, and several of the writers in this collection address "authenticity" directly. For instance, Susan Perez Castillo discusses "the real" in relation to Leslie Marmon Silko's and Louise Erdrich's juxtaposed representations of Native American experience; Carter Revard maps a different structure of identity as an explicitly "Indian" ethos; and Simon Ortiz harnesses a basic humanism in the struggle for nationalism as a foundational authenticity. These discussions seek to explain Indian authenticity to both Indians and non-Indians, to open up Euroamerican conceptual spaces by tracing different trajectories of such fundamental human longings as identity and community.

If for the past centuries the audience for Native American writers was primarily non-Native, now in the last generation it has become largely Native, with profound effects. Craig Womack's recent study of Native literature, *Red on Red: Native American Literary Separatism,* affirms a Native-to-Native dialogue around literary politics from a Creek perspective, and some Native poets are publishing in their untranslated tongues. Yet the pieces in this collection take more of a cross-cultural approach, where even Elizabeth Cook-Lynn, a forceful voice here for Native literary nationalism, addresses white audiences: "It is the challenge of modern thinkers and critics to find out what these nativist ideals mean in terms of the function of literature."

The challenge of political and cultural content is often driven by rhetorical and sometimes lyrical skill that animates much of this prose. Scott Momaday is of course a lyrical master of prose and poetry, and his classic "Man Made of Words" is a tour de force: "And all at once everything seemed suddenly to refer to that name. The name seemed to humanize the whole complexity of language. All at once, absolutely, I had the sense of the magic of words and of names." With similar layering of emotion and history, Simon Ortiz writes, "And it is that reason—the struggle against colonialism—which has given substance to what is authentic." Or we may read the persuasive power in Susan Perez Castillo's pure concision, when she writes, "In the field of Native American studies, one pernicious effect of regarding individual groups in a somewhat idealized fashion as threatened bastions of authenticity is that it often results in a reverential, sycophantic approach to Native American texts." This nonfiction section is focused precisely on a less idealized view of Native American literary dynamics.

Native writers are often explicit about reshaping English structures to their own patterns and purposes. As Leslie Marmon Silko explains to her readers in "Language and Literature from a Pueblo Perspective," " . . . I want you to *hear* and to experience English in a structure that follows patterns from the oral tradition. For those of you accustomed to being taken from point A to point B to point C, this presentation may be somewhat difficult to follow." Silko is not here speaking for the other writers in this section, some of whom may use more of a linear logic than the "spider's web" form of expression which she summons. However, the point comes clear from reading these pieces that each writer makes choices from among a variety of linguistic strengths, mixing description, narration, analogy, analysis, personal voice, or irony to acute effect.

So let's look briefly at those effects. This collection offers the student of Native American literatures a representative sampling of vital issues in Indian country. We might summarize them through Gerald Graff's notion of "teaching the conflicts" or the questions which most concern Native scholars today. Each essay raises particular issues, perhaps overlooks others, or opens up questions for further discussion.

Susan Pérez Castillo's essay, "Postmodernism, Native American Literature and the Real: The Silko-Erdrich Controversy," tackles one of the more emotionally charged problems in the field. Along with Paula Gunn Allen's 1990 article, "Special Problems in Teaching Leslie Marmon Silko's *Ceremony*," Silko's own 1986 critique of Louise Erdrich's *The Beet Queen* has evoked the pedagogical paranoia of professors. Castillo finds in Silko's "acerbic critique" of Erdrich a "genuine concern about issues related to postmodern fiction and its relation to the real which are of great relevance in the interpretation of Native American texts." In a nuanced comparison and contrast between Native texts and postmodern theories about the crisis of representing "the real," Pérez Castillo suggests that when Silko "characterizes Erdrich's text as lacking in political commitment" to issues of race and gender, she is "underrating Erdrich's subtlety." Castillo refers to what she calls "misunderstandings related to a limited concept of ethnicity and an essentialist, logocentric view of referentiality." These issues are of crucial importance to the millions of readers of Native literatures. Castillo juxtaposes a common, "limited concept of ethnicity" as "an ideal mystified category" versus ethnicity as "a discursive construct." (Again we return to the power of language.) "Surely it is more productive," Castillo claims, "in the evaluation of so-called 'ethnic' texts, to view ethnicity not as a static entity but rather as a dynamic, historically constructed process." This suggestion of ethnicity as discourse might approach Momaday's notion "that an Indian is an idea" of self, or Allen's emphasis on understanding literature "in terms of the culture from which it springs." Texts which build such "discursive constructs" can affirm resistant differences while they celebrate ongoing change.

Her discussion certainly sets the stakes, whether or not Castillo sets the terms, and we shall see how the other writers in this selection approach questions of ethnicity in representing Native experience. In the Dakota writer Elizabeth Cook-Lynn's breakthrough essay, "The American Indian Fiction Writers: Cosmopolitanism, Nationalism, the Third World, and First Nation Sovereignty," she takes a more historical approach and includes a discussion of the essay referred to above, Paula Gunn Allen's critical essay on Silko's *Ceremony*. Cook-Lynn raises the vital challenge of exploring what the literature says differently to Native and non-Native readers. She claims that in readings of Native literatures, tribal specificity is being overlooked too often by an effort to thematize general colonialism. She faults Native fiction writers themselves for this "cynical absorption into the 'melting pot.'" In a counterclaim to Native literary nationalism, she abjures Native writers' "pragmatic inclusion in the canon, and involuntary unification of an American national literary voice." Again the issue of authentic representation underlies the debate. "Ironically," she writes, "much of the criticism and fiction published today contributes to the further domination of modern nations and individualism, all the while failing in its own implied search for sovereignty and tribalism."

Cook-Lynn's Sioux compatriot, Vine Deloria, Jr., is the most influential and wide-ranging Native voice for legal sovereignty to have published on the subject. Indeed, Ruoff refers to him as "The most prolific Indian writer of nonfiction prose. . . ," and much of his voluminous output, from theology to legal theory, has focused on this "search for sovereignty and tribalism." The selection here on "Indian Humor," from his 1969 best-seller, *Custer Died for Your Sins,* articulates the comic logic underlying so much of his writing. "In humor life is redefined and accepted. . . . Satirical remarks often circumscribe problems so that possible solutions are drawn from the circumstances that would not make sense if presented in other than a humorous form." Deloria here describes a comic strategy of alterity and boundary-breaking which resonates with Gerald Vizenor's more recent "trickster discourse." Deloria affirms the central trick of the comic rather than tragic view of Indian experience: "Humor, all Indians will agree, is the cement by which the coming Indian movement is held together. When a people can laugh at themselves and laugh at others and hold all aspects of life together without letting anybody drive them to extremes, then it seems to me that that people can survive."

Another Sioux master of prose, Charles Eastman (Ohiyesa), returns us directly to one of the most tragic moments in American history with his chapter on Wounded Knee and "The Ghost Dance War," out of his autobiographical book, *From the Deep Woods to Civilization* (1917). With little room for humor beyond some domestic pleasantries, he describes in direct, chiseled prose his own circumstances as a young medical doctor around the incidents of the 1890 massacre on the Pine Ridge reservation. "Many were frightfully torn by pieces of shells, and the suffering was terrible. . . . All this was a severe ordeal for one who had so lately put all his faith in the Christian love and lofty ideals of the white man. Yet I passed no hasty judgment, and was thankful that I might be of some service and relieve even a small part of the suffering." Remarkably, the parallel narrative of his engagement to the white schoolteacher, Elaine Goodale, "a woman whose sincerity was convincing and whose ideals seemed very like my own," frames the tragic tale in an understated Victorian romance. Structurally, Eastman's cross-cultural personal affirmation softens the political and bloody conflict. With spring returning to the prairies as the tragic chapter ends, Eastman concludes, "and our wedding day was set for the following June." This narrative shift is a remarkable turn for one so intensely involved, but of course it did not mark the end of Eastman's marital or historical concerns. By including his personal narrative, he never eclipses the history, as when he quotes Red Cloud to Bishop Whipple: "Which God is our brother praying to now? Is it the same God whom they have twice deceived, when they made treaties with us which they afterward broke?" Such was the crisis of representation in Eastman's day, when the whites indeed found too much "hermeneutical flexibility," to use Pérez Castillo's term, in their reading of the treaties. Certainly Eastman's history is part of the reason that Cook-Lynn favors intra- rather than inter- cultural readings of texts.

The Laguna-Sioux-Lebanese scholar, poet, and novelist Paula Gunn Allen is a key figure among those who in the 1970s founded the field of Native American literary studies in the academy. Her essay, "The Sacred Hoop: A Contemporary Perspective," helped to lay the groundwork of issues and questions. While the piece has been criticized for generalizations that lack in tribal specificity, and for broad statements about both Native and European cultures, those form the context for her insights about oral traditions and contemporary Native literatures. Allen's comparative discussions about two Native aesthetics in particular, repetition and symbolic systems, remain invaluable in reading Native texts. Presaging Elizabeth Cook-Lynn's manifesto for literary nationalism, Allen begins by affirming that, "The significance of a literature can be best understood in terms of the culture from which it springs, and the purpose of literature is clear only when the reader understands and accepts the assumptions on which the literature is based." She proceeds to analyze repetition and symbolism from inside what she describes as "the American Indian universe" and "the unitary nature of reality." Without making Western dualistic divisions between material and spiritual, American Indian thinkers recognize all things as conscious or intelligent. "The Indian does not regard awareness of being as an abnormality peculiar to one species, but, because of a sense of relatedness to (instead of isolation from) what exists, the Indian assumes that this awareness is a natural by-product of existence itself." Aside from the larger categories of ceremonial and popular literature in the oral tradition, Allen traces "The two forms basic to American Indian literature" as ceremony and myth. "The ceremony is the ritual enactment of a specialized perception of a cosmic relationship, while the myth is a prose record of that relationship." Within this ceremonial context, we can understand repetition and symbolism in a Native American aesthetic. Dismissing ethnographers' and linguists' readings of repetition as mnemonic devices or as childish paranoia striving to control a threatening universe, Allen returns repetition to its ceremonial purpose, "to integrate: to fuse the individual with his or her fellows, the community of people with that of the other kingdoms, and this larger communal group with the worlds beyond this one." Repetition thus "has an entrancing effect." It is "oceanic," diffusing the participants' attention from "the distractions of ordinary life" so that they can be "redirected and integrated into a ceremonial context" and feel "the greater awareness." By repetition, "they lose consciousness of mere individuality and share the consciousness that characterizes most orders of being." Yet at the same time "repetition operates like the chorus in Western drama, serving to reinforce the theme and to focus the participants' attention on central concerns while intensifying their involvement with the enactment."

Certainly Allen's discourse breaks academic strictures built on Enlightenment rationality, as when she claims, "American Indian thought is essentially mystical and psychic in nature," but she does so by an explicit critique of the Freudian or socio-anthropological readings that have dominated ethnographic approaches to Native literatures. Certain Native writers I have spoken with carefully avoid terms like "mystical" because of the overloaded connotations, both negative and positive, of that word in the "New Age." However, Allen's essay is groundbreaking in making this point: "The failure of folklorists to comprehend the true metaphysical and psychic nature of structural devices such as ceremonial repetition is a result of the projection of one set of cultural assumptions onto another culture's customs and literature."

Her related analysis of "symbolism in American Indian ceremonial literature" is even more far-reaching, as it suggests a semiotic system different from the Western dualism of sign and signified. As she writes, Native symbolism is "not symbolic in the usual sense; that is, the four mountains in the Mountain Chant [of the Navajo] do not stand for something else. They are those exact mountains perceived psychically, as it were, or mystically." The ostensible sign or symbol has value itself as the thing signified or symbolized. If this is so, then the dream of poets to create literary *experience* resides in this use of language. The intriguing question remains how much or how little Allen is describing what Susan Pérez Castillo refers to as "the nostalgic desire to return to a pre-lapsarian world in which there existed an immutable, one-to-one correspondence between sign and referent." Castillo's healthily skeptical tone contrasts with Allen's healthy sense of mystery, but the real mystery might be how these two perspectives on symbolism might coexist.

The grand master of the mystery and power of words must be N. Scott Momaday (Kiowa), whose essay, "The Man Made of Words" is a classic of Native American literary nonfiction. Echoing the sermon on "the Word" by the "Priest of the Sun" in his Pulitzer Prize-winning novel, *House Made of Dawn,* Momaday's piece ranges from the foundational question of authenticity, "What is an American Indian?" to language itself as representing "the only chance of survival." Perhaps, indeed, Momaday does bridge the gap between Allen and Castillo by celebrating language as the extent of our experience, in the man *made* of words. If the gap between sign and signified is the gap between language and experience, then Momaday affirms the blending or blurring or balancing of that gap. "Then it was that that ancient, one-eyed woman Ko-sahn stepped out of the language and stood before me on the page." Yet he is precise in making distinctions further on: "We are concerned here not so much with an accurate representation of actuality, but with the realization of the imaginative experience." Like the power of stories which Silko evokes in one of her selected pieces, Momaday links this "realization of the imaginative experience" to survival, a real cultural ability to continue. Speaking of "the year the stars fell" in 1833, Momaday writes, "The terrified Kiowas, when they had regained possession of themselves, did indeed imagine that the falling stars were symbolic of their being and their destiny. . . . Only by means of that act could they bear what happened to them thereafter. . . . The imagination of meaning was not much, perhaps, but it was all they had, and it was enough to sustain them." The imaginative use of language reshapes their world. Thus Momaday meditates with us on what he calls "the questions which interest me most" "Who is the storyteller? Of whom is the story told? What is there in the darkness to imagine into being? What is there to dream and to relate? What happens when I or anyone exerts the force of language upon the unknown?" As with Allen's disavowal of ethnographers' condescending characterizations of Native repetition as a childish controlling device, Momaday's affirmation of these questions and his delight in the subtle dynamics of "the force of language upon the unknown" opens the reader to a participation in Native texts.

Simon Ortiz (Acoma) takes this question of "What is an Indian?" and the authenticity of Native representations into an entirely different arena, or rather, he yokes another discourse to this long conversation. The current political terminology would say "sovereignty," but Ortiz's 1981 publication makes a remarkable move by equating cultural authenticity with "a celebration of the human spirit and the Indian struggle for liberation." A general human tendency in "a nationalistic impulse to make use of foreign ritual, ideas, and material in their own—Indian—terms," constitutes an authenticity which grows and changes, as the Acoma dancers, for instance, incorporate colonial heroes and villains into their ceremonies. Rather than anything static, authenticity is a kind of dynamic sovereignty, "the creative ability of Indian people to gather in many forms of the socio-political colonizing force which beset them and to make these forms meaningful in their own terms." Thus Ortiz suggests that the power of Native literatures is a humanistic one, to integrate experience into one's own language. Iconoclastically, Ortiz points out that it is this "primary element," rather than any secondary cultural practice, which drives Native expression. "Nevertheless, it is not the oral tradition as transmitted from ages past alone which is the inspiration and source for contemporary Indian literature. It is also because of the acknowledgement by Indian writers of a responsibility to advocate" for their people. What is most "culturally authentic" is "fundamental to human dignity, creativity, and integrity." And in this mapping, Ortiz expresses a stunning trust in the fundamental goodness of America whose "racism, political and economic oppression, sexism, supremacism, and the needless and wasteful exploitation of land and people" he has just recounted. Yet he sees in a creative nationalism, "this character which will prove to be the heart and fibre and story of an America which has heretofore too often feared its deepest and most honest emotions of love and compassion. It is this story, wealthy in being without an illusion of dominant power and capitalistic abundance, that is the most authentic." Ortiz envisions an America that might face its own fear of him, an American Indian. Underneath the catalog of oppressions, Ortiz sees a fear of the other, or more precisely, a fear of the vulnerability which would honestly love the American other, the Native American. It is a remarkable claim, and it opens the non-Native audience to a reading experience quite beyond voyeurism. In writing about authenticity and nationalism, Ortiz, in passing, gives America a lesson in its own authentic nationalism.

Carter Revard's essay, "History, Myth, and Identity among Osages and Other Peoples," then offers another exact analysis of what authentic Indian identity structures look like. Starting with Geronimo's autobiography, Revard (Osage) clarifies how, "In his story, the notions of cosmos, country, self, and home are inseparable." Addressing Eastman, Revard explores how "the Santee system of names for animals and plants . . . tied his sense of personal identity to his sense of tribal identity and relationship to the world of other-than-human 'natural' beings." Revard shows us how a "sense of linguistic 'authority'" in Eastman's oral society has a participatory quality "where spoken language came from authorities present and known." The child is encouraged to name birds and plants himself, and then his efforts are merged with the tribal traditions. Revard contrasts this Santee catechism with English language acquisition where the etymological authority of words is so far removed from personal identity. He continues to, "Look now at two other tribes, Pawnee and Osage, to observe in more detail how the *land-orientation* of a family and individual created an Indian identity among Pawnees, and how the *naming ceremony* (for persons) helped create Indian identity among Osages." And here Revard is explicit, where Paula Gunn Allen was implicit, in claiming "it is an *Indian* and not just an *Apache* or *Santee* 'identity' we are looking at. The sample, admittedly, is limited, but it seems to me cautious inferences can be drawn from it." Furthermore, he describes this Indian identity in terms similar to Allen's as well: "that way's ceremonies *embodied a unified way of life:* what was Indian was the seamlessness of human life, in which it would not make sense to speak of religion on the one hand, and warfare on the other, of hunting here and naming a new chief there, of the Creation of the Universe on this side and the Naming of a Child on that." Revard affirms that "'History' and 'Myth' and 'Identity' are not three separate matters, here, but three aspects of one human being."

Greg Sarris's essay "The Woman Who Loved a Snake: Orality in Mabel McKay's Stories" further exemplifies certain dynamics of that oral society which Revard articulates, as the essay itself embodies the nondualistic symbolism which Allen describes. Sarris is himself a member of the Pomo tribe. In an academic friend's inability to comprehend McKay's storytelling device of melding a woman's human paramour with an actual snake, Sarris juxtaposes literate and oral differences. When the elderly and astute McKay at one moment referred to the paramour as a man and at other moments as a snake, the doctoral student asked for clarification which was never forthcoming. (A famous literary parallel is in the trial scene in Momaday's *House Made of Dawn* where the protagonist claims not to have killed a man, but a witch snake, a *culebra,* and Father Ortiz tries in vain to explain, "I believe that this man was moved to do what he did by an act of imagination so compelling as to be inconceivable to us.") Sarris's writing style, infusing the personal voice into this complex narrative analysis, also effects the erasure of objective and subjective realities in cross-cultural perceptions. By following the process of miscommunication between the academic and the oral storyteller, Sarris explores "the ways Mabel's talk counters literate tendencies to close the oral context in which oral communication takes place. . . . So much depends on the interlocutor." Again the challenge to the reader is "so compelling as to be inconceivable to" many.

Leslie Marmon Silko's essay, "Language and Literature from a Pueblo Indian Perspective," is another offer to the general reader to reshape their thinking. "My task is a formidable one," she writes. "I ask you to set aside a number of basic approaches that you have been using and probably will continue to use, and, instead, to approach language from the Pueblo perspective, one that embraces the whole of creation and the whole of history and time." Like Sarris's "holistic approach to American Indian texts," or Revard's "unified way of life," or Allen's "unitary nature of reality," Silko affirms a representational boundary crossing where art and reality do not constitute separate realms: "we do not differentiate or fragment stories and experiences." Like Momaday's "imagination of meaning" which sustains the Kiowas, Silko describes the community's nourishment in language: "Keeping track of all the stories within the community gives us all a certain distance, a useful perspective, that brings incidents down to a level we can deal with. If others have done it before, it cannot be so terrible. If others have endured, so can we." Indeed, according to Silko, "language *is* story," where "many individual words have their own stories," and "one story is only the beginning of many stories and the sense that stories never truly end."

Yet this limitlessness of language and story does not mean that the culture is an infinite "trackless waste" ripe for the taking by those outside the community. Silko's second piece in this nonfiction collection, "An Old-time Indian Attack Conducted in Two Parts," draws a line in the sand about cultural appropriation. The underlying value is the link between language and community. Those outside the community cannot lay claim to the stories.

This rallying piece takes "ethnopoets" to task for assuming "that the white man, through some innate cultural or racial superiority, has the ability to perceive and master the essential beliefs, values, and emotions of persons from Native American communities." Silko is outlining the intellectual colonialism which accompanies its more overt economic forms, and she turns to economic terminology by claiming "that the prayers, chants, and stories weaseled out by the early white ethnographers, which are now collected in ethnological journals" are not "public property." She goes further, to suggest that the efforts of white writers who follow these "racist assumptions" are "pathetic evidence that in more than two hundred years, Anglo-Americans have failed to create a satisfactory identity for themselves." Readers might return to Simon Ortiz's compassionate affirmation of "an America which has heretofore too often feared its deepest and most honest emotions of love and compassion," for a hint at both the improper and proper boundaries that Silko is suggesting for her readers. She writes that Gary Snyder, for instance, in his appropriation of Native voices, "is headed in the same unfortunate direction as other white pioneers have gone, a direction which avoids historical facts which are hard to swallow: namely, that at best, the Anglo-American is a guest on this continent; and at the worst, the United States of America is founded upon stolen land." Yet exposure of historical theft of continental proportions is not the end of "the story." Silko suggests that Snyder and the rest of her readers, "come to terms with these facts, and his own personal, ancestral relation to them. . . ." That painful prospect may be the other story in these pages.

—David L. Moore

Susan Pérez Castillo

Postmodernism, Native American Literature and the Real: The Silko-Erdrich Controversy

When Leslie Silko's acerbic critique of Louise Erdrich's novel *The Beet Queen* was published in *Impact/Albuquerque Journal* magazine,[1] many readers might have been forgiven for diagnosing an acute case of New Kid on the Block Syndrome. It would be easy to leap to the conclusion that the tone of Silko's remarks might represent disgruntlement at a talented newcomer's challenging her literary turf; both Silko and Erdrich are gifted Native American writers whose work has received a great deal of critical acclaim. It seems to me, however, that in texts such as *Ceremony* and *Storyteller* Silko reveals a generosity of spirit which is hardly compatible with sentiments of petty envy, and that the vehemence of her critique of Erdrich stems from a genuine concern about issues related to post-modern fiction and its relation to the real which are of great relevance in the interpretation of Native American texts.

Therefore, in this article I would like to analyze some of the issues Silko raises in her review of *The Beet Queen*. In view of the fact that her differences with Erdrich are apparently rooted in a restrictive view of ethnicity and an essentialist, logocentric concept of textual representation, I shall examine these concepts in some detail, in the light of recent contributions to post-structuralist critical theory.

Silko's review of *The Beet Queen* opens with praise for Erdrich's prose style, which she describes as "dazzling" and "sleek," "a poet's prose"; she also refers favorably to Erdrich's vivid descriptions, such as that of the interior of Aunt Fritzie's butcher shop, as seen by the newly abandoned Mary Adare. But then she goes on to characterize Erdrich's writing as the product of "academic, postmodern, so-called experimental influences," which foreground the interaction of words and de-emphasize their referential dimension. According to Silko, the auto-referential text has "an ethereal clarity and shimmering beauty because no history or politics intrudes to muddy the well of pure necessity contained within the language itself." This sort of writing is, in Silko's perspective, radically different from the Native American oral tradition, which is by definition a shared, communal experience. The postmodern literary aesthetic (exemplified, for Silko, by *The Beet Queen*) would

---

[1]Leslie Silko, "Here's an Odd Artifact for the Fairy-Tale Shelf," rev. of *The Beet Queen,* by Louise Erdrich, *Impact/Albuquerque Journal* 8 Oct. 1986: 10–11. This review was later reprinted in *Studies in American Indian Literatures,* Vol. 10, 1986: 177–184. Subsequent notes will refer to the *SAIL* reprint.

thus reflect the fragmentation of contemporary society as portrayed by the alienated Western writer, whose only link to other human beings is through language (Silko, "Artifact," 178–79).

Silko goes on to affirm that the autoreferential text is singularly well-suited to depict the labyrinthine world of the subconscious mind, or to evoke complicated relationships between tormented characters. It is worth noting that the adjectives "labyrinthine" and "complicated" are used in a pejorative sense. Her most devastating thrust, however, comes when she attacks what she perceives as Erdrich's ambivalence about her Indian origins, manifested by the uneasy relationship between text and context existing in *The Beet Queen*. She ends her review with the verbal equivalent of a hand grenade:

> *The Beet Queen* is a strange artifact, an eloquent example of the political cli-
> mate in America in 1986. It belongs on the shelf next to the latest report from
> the United States Civil Rights Commission, which says black men have made
> tremendous gains in employment and salary. This is the same shelf that holds
> *The Collected Thoughts of Edwin Meese on First Amendment Rights* and
> Grimm's *Fairy Tales*. (Silko, "Artifact," 179)

Silko is probably being unfair when she dismisses Erdrich's stylistic virtuosity as the product of an alienated, postmodern sensibility. Many critics have characterized Erdrich as an extraordinarily gifted writer, and it is significant that they have evaluated her writing not merely as an "ethnic" curiosity but in terms of the so-called mainstream canonical tradition.[2] Nonetheless, Silko does bring up some relevant points, which I would like to examine more closely.

According to Silko, some of the uglier realities of North Dakota in the Depression years are suppressed in *The Beet Queen*. As she points out, in the racist, homophobic atmosphere of rural North Dakota in 1932, being white or Indian, straight or gay, made a great deal of difference; and yet the marginal status of these characters in relation to the rest of the town is never attributed to political or social factors but rather to internal psychological conflicts. Many of the characters of *The Beet Queen* are apparently outsiders; Celestine is of Indian ancestry, Karl is bisexual, and Wallace is gay. Silko points out that it is never clearly stated whether Karl and Mary are of Indian descent, and whether this might be one of the motives that led Adelaide, their mother, to flee into the clouds with a glamorous aviator at the county fair; Erdrich merely mentions Mary's "stringy black hair," which would seem to imply Indian blood. Russell, the only character who actually lives on the Chippewa reservation, is a scarred, much-decorated war veteran whose

---

[2]See Josh Rubin's untitled review of *The Beet Queen* in *The New York Review of Books*, 15 Jan. 1987: 14–15.

opacity contrasts with the rich inner life of Mary, Karl and Celestine; but even Mary and Celestine are seen through a white European lens as dark, substantial and unattractive, while Sita, who is blonde and fragile, is perceived as beautiful (Silko, "Artifact," 181–82).

These are valid points to raise, and one can understand why Silko does so. The insidious thing about discrimination, however, is that it does not fit into neat categories. When, for example, a Native American woman writer is excluded from so-called mainstream literary anthologies, it is often difficult to determine whether the motives underlying this exclusion are related to her status as a woman, or a Native American, or both. It also seems to me that Silko, when she characterizes Erdrich's text as lacking in political commitment, is underrating Erdrich's subtlety: surely it is significant that Russell is trotted out by the white Establishment of Argus to display his scars at patriotic parades. What Silko characterizes as his "opacity" may simply be the apparent incapacity to feel which is the product of great pain. Silko herself has movingly described the figure of the Indian war veteran in her portrayal of Tayo in *Ceremony;* but it must be said that Tayo, like Russell, is somewhat unidimensional. As Marxist theorists like Pierre Macherey have demonstrated, a text is linked to ideology by its silences as well as by that which it explicitly states.[3] Erdrich's silences are often very eloquent indeed, and are perhaps more politically effective than overt sloganeering.

Silko, however, seems to be implying in this review that Erdrich is ambivalent about her own Indianness, and that she is skirting issues which, although often messy and inaesthetic, are vital ones in the texts of so-called ethnic writers. While I share Silko's concern with these issues, it is possible that some of her differences with Erdrich arise from misunderstandings related to a limited concept of ethnicity and an essentialist, logocentric view of referentiality.

In the first place, it would seem that Silko's view of ethnicity is a restricted one. Scholars like Werner Sollers have pointed out how difficult it is in today's America to classify a writer as belonging exclusively to one ethnic group, given the existing degree of cultural synchretism.[4] Silko herself is a case in point, with her Anglo-American and Mexican (as well as Laguna) forebears; and this multicultural background is without a doubt one of the sources of the power and conceptual richness of her writing. It is also significant that she grew up in a tribe which is almost unique in that it has succeeded to a notable degree in maintaining its collective identity while adapting to change. Erdrich, however, is a member of the Chippewa tribe, which

---

[3]See Terry Eagleton, *Marxism and Literary Criticism* (Berkeley: U of California P, 1986), 34–36.

[4]Werner Sollers, "Introduction: The Invention of Ethnicity," *The Invention of Ethnicity,* ed. Werner Sollers (New York: Oxford UP, 1989), xv.

for historical and geographic reasons has suffered the effects of acculturation on a far greater scale. While it is true that she has German-American as
well as Chippewa blood, the fact that she chooses to focus on this facet of
her ancestry in *The Beet Queen* can hardly be construed as a betrayal of her
Chippewa roots. Paradoxically, the cultural ambivalence reflected in *The
Beet Queen* may be mimetic in character, mirroring the fragmented ontological landscape in which many Native Americans exist today, shuttling between radically diverse realities. This diversity can be seen, however, not
only as potentially alienating, but also as a source of creative ferment and
positive historical change.

When Silko characterizes ethnicity (defined as membership in an ethnic group) as a stable, unchanging category, it would seem that she is falling
into the same ahistoricism of which she accuses Erdrich. In *The Invention
of Ethnicity,* Werner Sollers has convincingly demystified the concept of ethnicity as a natural, immutable category with essentialist characteristics. Describing ethnic groups as existing within history, and, as such, highly un-
stable and pliable entities which are constantly interacting and redefining
themselves, Sollers characterizes ethnicity as "widely shared, though intensely debated, collective fictions that are continually reinvented" (Sollers,
"Invention," xi). This description, predictably, has been the source of intense
polemic; many readers have interpreted the words "invention" and "fiction"
as signifying *unreality*. It should be pointed out, however, that Sollers is using these words in a postmodern context. It is undeniable that ethnic groups
exist in the so-called real world; but it is important to remember that our
perception of these groups (and of ourselves as members of one group and
not another) is a discursive construct and not an ideal mystified category. In
the field of Native American studies, one pernicious effect of regarding individual groups in a somewhat idealized fashion as threatened bastions of
authenticity is that it often results in a reverential, sycophantic approach to
Native American texts. I strongly believe that texts by Silko and Erdrich, to
name only two of many excellent writers, can stand up to tough critical
scrutiny, and that anything else is patronizing and demeaning to the texts in
question. Surely it is more productive, in the evaluation of so-called "ethnic"
texts, to view ethnicity not as a static entity but rather as a dynamic, historically constructed process.

Silko is certainly not alone in her concern with ethical issues related to
post-structuralist theory and textual referentiality. The links between the
world of fiction and world of so-called objective reality have been hotly debated since Aristotle's *Poetics*. The Aristotelian idea of fiction as heterocosm,
as radically other in nature, has its limitations, however, in that the real often interpenetrates the world of fiction; real historical individuals (such as
Henry VIII or Theodore Roosevelt) and real places (Pearl Harbor, Mississippi, Portugal) are often incorporated into the fictional domain. As theorists
like Roman Ingarden have pointed out, diverse levels of ontological stratifi-

cation exist in the literary text.[5] It is thus misleading as well as naive to suggest that the text is an immutable mirror of a static reality, and that a rigid one-to-one relationship must exist between the referent and its corresponding sign, verbal or otherwise. Silko herself implies the need for hermeneutical flexibility in *Ceremony* when she describes the vital, mutable capacity of discursive practices like storytelling to shape reality. In the words of Betonie, the shaman with Navajo and Mexican blood who cures Tayo,

> "At one time, the ceremonies as they had been performed were enough for the way the world was then. But after the white people came, elements in the world began to shift; and it became necessary to create new ceremonies. I have made changes in the rituals. The people mistrust this greatly, but only this growth keeps the ceremonies strong. . . . She [his grandmother] taught me this above all else; things which don't shift and grow are dead things."[6]

It should also be observed that Silko's classification of *The Beet Queen* as an autoreferential text is highly debatable. She is not alone, however, in attacking postmodern fiction as alienated from objective reality, or, worse yet, as active accomplice in the creation of an alienated reality. Gerald Graff raises a relevant point in *Literature Against Itself* when he observes that literature can demystify reified structures only when we are able to distinguish between the mythical and the non-mythical, the real and the unreal.[7] Graff is right in implying that much of contemporary literature (and much poststructuralist criticism) is autistic in character, but it seems to me that this sort of statement often masks a nostalgic desire to return to nineteenth-century aesthetic standards, as if nineteenth-century realism were the only sort of realism there is.

One of the most common accusations made against post-structuralist criticism is that it negates extratextual reality. In this context, the words of Jacques Derrida, "there is nothing beyond the text,"[8] have often been interpreted as a neo-Berkelian anti-materialist attack on the real world beyond the text. There is indeed a solipsistic and self-indulgent side to American deconstruction; but the hermeneutical conservatives of present-day American criticism seem almost willfully to misunderstand Derrida's affirmation. It is obvious that we apprehend reality through verbal categories; but most poststructuralists would agree that to deny that there *is* a material reality "out

---

[5]See Roman Ingarden, *Das Literarische Kunstwerk,* trans. Albin E. Beau (Lisbon: Calouste Gulbenkian Foundation, 1965).

[6]Leslie Silko, *Ceremony* (New York: Penguin, 1977), 126.

[7]Gerald Graff, *Literature Against Itself* (Chicago: U of Chicago P, 1979), 27.

[8]Jacques Derrida, *Of Grammatology,* trans. Gayatri Spivak (Baltimore: Johns Hopkins UP, 1976), 158.

there" is to relegate literary studies to total irrelevance. In any case, the existence of objective material reality is a matter of everyday common sense. The literary critic, for example, is free to interpret, contextualize, or decode the word "stool." The ontological status of an actual stool, however, is not affected by the textual character of the word, and even the most sincere deconstructionist, if she trips over a stool on her way to the word processor, will suffer the extratextual consequences of her action, and probably react in irate verbal (though perhaps unprintable) terms. Texts do of course have referents in the world of the real; texts about Native Americans, for example, often have referents who existed and suffered extratextually, but their pain is no less real for that. What is naive is to insist that we can somehow accede to their suffering without recourse to language, and that resistance to hegemonic or totalitarian systems of discourse which have excluded or attempted to diminish them can be carried out beyond discourse itself. Rather than yielding to the nostalgic desire to return to a pre-lapsarian world in which there existed an immutable, one-to-one correspondence between sign and referent, it might be more productive to analyze the discursive systems that authorize some representations and suppress others.

Another controversial point in Silko's review is her characterization of postmodern literature. In his book *Postmodernist Fiction,* Brian McHale describes the emergence of a postmodern literary aesthetic. Using Jakobson's concept of the dominant (defined as the focusing component of the work of art, which rules, determines and transforms the remaining components), McHale characterizes this transition as the shift from a modernist foregrounding of epistemology to a postmodern poetics of ontology: paradoxically, post-modernism uses representation itself to subvert representation, problematizing and pluralizing the real.[9] Thus the text emerges, not as a passive mirror of reality, but as a space in which two or more distinct and often mutually exclusive worlds battle for supremacy. The desire for mastery over a chaotic universe (imposed, needless to say, by the perception of a white male European subject) which characterized so many modernist texts has given way to an aesthetic of discontinuity, heteroglossia, and difference.

Although Leslie Silko would probably reject the label "postmodern" in no uncertain terms, it is interesting to note that we can observe this sort of ontological flicker in *Ceremony.* The reader is thrust into contact with two widely divergent worlds, namely that of the Laguna oral tradition and that of the sordid reality of the Laguna reservation in the years after World War II. This ontological disparity functions in two ways: by highlighting the coalescence between the mythical and the profane worlds, it gives vividness and universality to the narrative, but at the same time it points out the gap between the extraordinary richness of Laguna mythology and the cultural impoverishment and alienation which characterize so much of contemporary reservation life.

---

[9]Brian McHale, *Postmodernist Fiction* (New York: Methuen, 1987), 26–40.

In Erdrich's writing, we can observe a similar sort of ontological instability. In *The Beet Queen,* we encounter the Reservation more as absence than presence, more as latency than as statement, in contrast to the arid reality of the small town of Argus, North Dakota. However, in *Tracks,* her most recent novel, this ontological flicker between two radically different realities is far more pronounced. One of the most interesting features of the novel is Erdrich's recourse to a dual narrative perspective, alternating between the viewpoint of the wily old survivor Nanapush, a tribal elder, whose name and attributes resemble those of the Chippewa trickster Nanabozho and a young girl called Pauline, whose descent into madness is hastened by religious fanaticism and a fragmented sense of cultural identity.

In an interview given to the *New York Times,* Erdrich revealed recently that the idea of using a dual narrative perspective came out of a conversation with her husband and collaborator Michael Dorris. According to Erdrich, *Tracks* is based on a 400-page manuscript which had been lying around for ten years, and which had become stalled. When Michael Dorris made a comment about the language of the Athabaskan Indians of Alaska, in which there is no word for "I" but only for "we," this in turn suggested the concept of multiple narration, which would allow Erdrich (like Silko) to recover the collective perspective which characterized traditional Chippewa oral narratives and simultaneously to highlight the spiritual fragmentation of her tribe.[10] In the dialectic between the two radically diverse realities of Nanapush and Pauline, there emerges a narrative firmly anchored in (often grim) extratextual reality. Pauline is a victim of accelerated acculturation. Her loss of cultural and personal identity becomes apparent in her frenzied attempts to identify with white European ideals, and her growing religious fanaticism emerges as a response to an alienated reality. Even her sinister activity of laying out the dead represents an attempt to mediate between her people and the dominant culture:

> "I saw the people I had wrapped, the influenza and consumption dead whose hands I had folded. They traveled, lame and bent, with chests darkened from the blood they coughed out of their lungs. . . . I saw their unborn children hanging limp or strapped to their backs, or pushed along in front hoping to get the best place when the great shining doors, beaten of air and gold, swung open on soundless oiled fretwork to admit them all.
>
> Christ was there, of course, dressed in glowing white.
> 'What shall I do now?' I asked. 'I've brought you so many souls!'
> And He said to me gently:
> 'Fetch more.'"[11]

---

[10]Deborah Stead, "Unlocking the Tale," *The New York Times Book Review,* 2 Oct. 1988: 41.

[11]Louise Erdrich, *Tracks* (New York: Henry Holt, 1988), 140.

Pauline thus becomes, in Erdrich's words, "death's bony whore" (*Tracks,* 86), representing death as the only space of refuge for her oppressed people. Nanapush, on the other hand, is a survivor. He has also known suffering and death, but rather than becoming bitter, he responds with vitality and, incredibly enough, humor. We can observe, for example, the enormous differences in the attitudes of these two characters to sex. While Pauline denies and represses her own sexuality by religious mortification, often with masochistic overtones (this often reaches absurd proportions, as when she wears her shoes on the wrong feet, causing Nanapush to remark caustically, "God is turning this woman into a duck!" (*Tracks,* 146) Nanapush, in spite of the fact that he is not a young man, loves ribald stories and "keeps company" with Margaret Kashpaw, a tough old survivor like himself. One could argue that the differences between Nanapush and Pauline are primarily epistemological, but it seems to me that they are far more radical in character. *Tracks* is a highly effective, politicized text in which the reader shuttles between, not two different perceptions of reality, but two diametrically different realities: that of a people in the grip of disease, death and spiritual despair, and that of a group of courageous and irreverent survivors. Somewhere in the middle of these two realities emerges the world of the Chippewa in all its power and complexity.

With the publication of *Tracks,* it seems reasonably safe to affirm that any doubts about Erdrich's commitment to the portrayal of extratextual reality have been put to rest. In the future, rather than focusing on issues which divide Silko and Erdrich, it would be far more productive for students of Native American literature to analyze the many points these two gifted writers have in common. Both offer us a fascinating glimpse into the world of Native American oral tradition. Both describe the emptiness and self-destructiveness which characterize much of contemporary reservation life. Perhaps most importantly, both describe Native Americans, not as Noble Savage victims or as dying representatives of a lost authenticity, but as tough, compassionate people who use the vital capacity of discourse to shape—and not merely reflect—reality.

Elizabeth Cook-Lynn (Crow Creek, Dakota)

The American Indian Fiction Writers
Cosmopolitanism, Nationalism, the Third World, and First Nation Sovereignty

Cosmopolitanism

One of the observations made by Third World literary decolonization theoreticians like Homi K. Bhabha (Sussex), Timothy Brennan (Purdue), and perhaps a dozen other scholars even lesser known in the United States is that there are particular modern writers whose origins are not Euro-American, such as Salman Rushdie, Vargas Llosa, and perhaps Isabelle Allende and V. S. Naipaul, and (according to the Asian-American critic and novelist Frank Chin) even Amy Tan and Maxine Hong Kingston, who have moved away from the expected nationalistic affiliations towards an acquired "cosmopolitanism." In the process of doing so, it is argued, they have contributed to the confusion about cultural authority in the Third World literary voice.

Little of analytical importance has been published about this confusion in cultural authority as it concerns the American Indian fiction writer, though in off-the-record discourse among scholars it is a critical interest. This essay begins by addressing what that observation means in terms of contemporary American Indian literatures and moves toward a broader analysis of nationalism in American Indian fiction. Explored within the contexts of Third World literary criticism will be the work of fiction writers who claim to be American Indians, those who are enrolled members (i.e. citizens) of existing tribal nations, and those who live in the United States and write in English.

Third World intellectuals in discourse on nationalistic literatures, the theory of decolonizations in general, and cosmopolitanism in particular, argue that cosmopolitanism becomes the enemy of "resistance literatures" specifically because its criteria arise from Western tastes, or in other words, for aesthetic reasons. Specifically, according to Timothy Brennan, those criteria are as follows:

1. the preference, first of all, for novels (an imported genre), which sell better than poetry, testimonials, and plays even though the latter forms make up the majority of what is actually written in the Third World;

2. the tendency to privilege writing in European languages even though (in Asia and the Middle East particularly) there are developed, continuous, and ancient literary traditions in such languages as Urdu, Bengali, Chinese, and Arabic;

3. the attraction to writing that thematizes colonialism but that does not do so from a strident point of view; and (in a way related to the last point),

4. the attraction to writing that is aesthetically "like us," that displays the complexities and subtleties of all "great art."

We may discuss the extent to which editors, publishers, and critics are involved in these preferences and attractions; however, the answer does not matter, for the writers themselves ultimately take responsibility for these trends. This means, of course, that the dialogue leading to the best understanding of the reality of fiction must be author-centered, a phenomenon not always evident in Native American literary studies and one which raises the questions of where these dialogues take place and for what audiences. For some world literatures, the *New York Times* occasionally offers examples of how helpful author-centered discussions concerning intent and responsibility can be. Recently it reported a conversation between Haruki Murakami and Jay McInerney in which Murakami says,

> Yes, there is a sense of non-nationality about the story "Wind Up Bird and Tuesday's Woman," but it's not as though I depict Japanese society through that aspect of it that could just as well take place in New York or San Francisco. You might call it Japanese nature that remains only after you have thrown out, one after another, all those parts that are altogether too Japanese.

He is talking about cultural aesthetics; thus his intent in that context can then be explored. The fact that he writes fiction in the Japanese language does not make his authorial intent any more or any less a reality than it is for the American Indian writer who writes in English, except to make the odd point that Japanese is more accessible to critics, scholars, and readers than any Indian language in America. The reason it is not so easy for Native American writers to express intent in such discussions is that their work is almost always perceived as oriented toward a contrived "mainstream" (a function of colonialism) not only in publishing and editing but in critical analysis as well.

There is probably not an American Indian writer today who has not had questions of taste rather than intent posed as a prelude to publishing, such as "How can you make this story more accessible to the 'general American reader' "? (an agent's query) and "How and why is it that you use an Indian language word or phrase at certain places in your narrative, and don't you think you should have a glossary at the end of the manuscript?" (an editor's query). Such questions suggest that there is, in reality, an existing methodology which imposes a Euro-American cast upon the literary works of American Indian writers. "Stridency" in the native voice is also used to justify editorial intrusion, and comments like "editors took exception to your tone: far too much anger, sarcasm, and cynicism" are not unusual.

Native American writers, as a result of editorial and agented assistance in getting their manuscripts accepted, assume that under such strict circumstances their own efforts toward the recovery of memory through writing seem thwarted, selective, and narrowly interpreted within the imposed context of Western knowledge and aesthetics. Perhaps this is always the case in cross-cultural dialogue, but for American Indians whose work presumably stems from an obscure and "other" tribal perspective, any kind of postcolonial dialogue seems to be either of little interest to the mainstream or too strident.

A number of Native American writers have achieved broad readership either with or without this editorial intrusion. In light of this achievement and based on the preceding criteria, it is conceivable that Native American literary critics might ask whether successful American Indian writers, most notably Louise Erdrich, educated at Dartmouth College and a participant in the Johns Hopkins University Writing Program, and her husband, creative writer Michael Dorris (who make up the most popular writing team of the current era), as well as the nationally known Gros-Ventre/Blackfeet novelist James Welch, the Kiowa intellectual N. Scott Momaday, and Laguna writer Leslie Marmon Silko may also have moved away from nationalistic concerns in order to gain the interest of mainstream readers. A number of lesser luminaries come to mind.

Few or perhaps none of these writers have ever claimed a major place as Third World thinkers, but they do speak out on issues both political and intellectual and are often considered experts in the field of Native American Studies and related topics, though some actively dislike that assumption by the non-Indian reading public. Close readings of their works by critics who are not interested in decolonization theories often suggest that these writers have an implied intimacy with the American Indian tribal experience.

These same critics, in assessing the work from a pedagogical standpoint, often claim for these writers a deeply authoritative cultural voice, a phenomenon which, in my view, clouds issues of intent and responsibility for Native American writers in the Third World lexicon. Thus, it appears that professors in Native American literatures, mostly white and male, have the capacity to rearrange native intellectualism in dubious ways. University of Montana professor Dr. William W. Bevis, for example, though perhaps not claiming to be a major pedagogue in the field, said in a recent article in the popular *Washington Post* publication *The World And I,* that Erdrich might be compared to William Faulkner, yet at the same moment tells us that she "sets the pace" as a foremost Native American Indian writer. In doing so, he unintentionally illustrates the confused status in critical theory and pedagogy of the nationalistic/cosmopolitan role as it applies to specific literary works. For those who have accepted the idea that Americans have a common literature, there is no problem. For those who want to pose the dialectics of difference, and that includes many American Indian writers, there are no options. Critics like Bevis, who want to have it both ways, are rarely challenged.

To be sure, Third World literary theorists are troubled by the lack of clear distinction between the nationalistic and cosmopolitan literary voice as a beginning point in the discussion of Native literatures because the strategy of ignoring and obscuring authorial intent lends itself to the pitting of pedagogical concerns and theoretical uses of literature against one another. The confusion largely stems from subject matter, the significant function of pedagogy. Because of what Erdrich writes about, says Bevis, and also because she is "Indian first and writer second," he claims for Erdrich and, by implication, for all others, a difference "from the mainstream American notion of defining ourselves by our vocation: a writer writes and can make any subject his own." The result is, Bevis posits, "that Indian writers are more like Third World writers, inherently political, marginal and social: serving their people." Being "like" Third World writers is, according to Bevis, as far as Erdrich goes.

Bevis's interest in the fact that Indian writers, including Erdrich, "don't even trespass on each other's tribes," much less attempt the range of material that most successful white writers take for granted as part of being "professional," suggests a "marginality" that is probably in no way an accurate assessment of the influence, popularity, and financial success of Erdrich and Dorris, especially considering the tribelessness of Dorris's *Yellow Raft In Blue Water,* and the sheer commercialism of *Crown of Columbus.*

To the extent that American Indian writers work with themes which might be said to be comparable to the themes of their contemporaries in the Third World, such as oppression, diaspora and displacement, colonization, racism, cultural conflict, exile, resistance, and other assorted experiences, their fiction brings several contingent arguments into focus not only for the writer and reader but for the critic as well. *Intent* is a large part of the failed discourse. Erdrich says unabashedly, "I am probably an Easterner who mistakenly grew up in the Midwest," thereby dismissing the essential notion of Native American intellectual knowledge, that is the reality of race memory as it is connected to environment and geography. How can one be a tribal nationalist and "set the pace" if one claims no connection to the land either in one's personal life or in one's fiction? One can't even say that this is a sentiment of the "exile," so pervasive in the writing of American Indians (for whom the journey theme is primary), nor of Third Worldists driven from their homelands.

This observation from a writer who is often thought by the scholarly public, perhaps mistakenly, to be doing nation-centered or tribal-centered (Chippewa) work adds to the confusion over defining the political realities of the function of Native literatures. The tacit worry that Native American writers are thought by critics and readers to be in some important way representative of modern tribal nationalistic perspective and the failure to be clear about authorial intent suggest several things about tribal sovereignty or First Nation status: that the tribes are not nations, that they are not part of the Third World perspective vis-à-vis colonialism, and that, finally, they are simply "colonized" enclaves in the United States, some kind of nebulous sociological phenomena. It is crucial to understand that such an assessment is in direct opposition not only to the historical reality of Indian nations in America, but also to the contemporary work being done by tribal governmental officials and activists, politicians, and grassroots intellectuals to defend sovereign definition in the new world.

Thus, the violation of nationalistic or Third World models in fiction and criticism should be of legitimate concern to scholars and should become part of the discourse in literary theory as it is applied to the works of Native American writers. While the writers themselves may disclaim any responsibility, and even while the critical, scholarly discussion is nonexistent or misdirected, the existence of such postcolonial incoherence on the part of writers who claim to be indigenous people can only contribute to the confusion about the role of minority intellectuals within the United States and, more important, their influence. Scholarship and art must say something about the real world, mustn't they? As Vine Deloria, Jr., asked the anthropologists in 1970, "Where were you when we needed you?" Indians may now ask of their writers, two decades later, "Where were you when we defended ourselves and sought clarification as sovereigns in the modern world?"

In addition to authorial intent, themes of invasion and oppression so familiar to colonized peoples throughout the world that are taken up by American Indian writers serve as proof for the argument that major concerns of Third World theorists must be crucial analytical components of anything that might be said about the current literary trends in American Indian voice. These are themes about which mainstream critics can no longer be ignorant nor silent.

Themes and Aesthetics

In spite of Momaday's Pulitzer Prize and Erdrich's American Book Award, it is safe to say that the comparison of the success of these writers to the success of a global writer like Salman Rushdie, whose work has drawn the international spotlight, or Naipaul, one of the most prolific writers of our time, may seem inappropriate. Yet, their themes share a concern with the anticolonial struggle, intended or not. Thus, thematic similarities as well as tendencies toward European language and literary tastes would suggest that Brennan's "cosmopolitan" model, demonstrated by Rushdie in particular (perhaps not the best example, but surely a useful one) and described earlier in this essay, might have the same results if taken up by American Indian writers: first, the further obfuscation of the already confusing issues in the debate concerning the need for decolonization, that is, whether or not writers who claim to be indigenes are committed to the need for resistance; second, the relegation of the native writer to the status of an outsider, or even of a "traitor" (e.g., Rushdie); and third, the shying away of native writers from legitimate Third World points of view simply because they fear that their work will be labeled "strident," or lacking "artfulness," or "aesthetically flawed."

Without further examination of these literary realities, it is quite possible that American Indian writers will accept the notion that they can, and perhaps should, with impunity become cosmopolitans, serving as translators of materials into an already existing mode, or that they can and should legitimize "hybridity," or that they can and should transcend national affiliations, or that they can and should simply serve as "exotica." There seems to be evidence already that such influence is at work or thought to be at work in the public and scholarly assessment of the highly visible work of Erdrich and Dorris, *Crown of Columbus,* the publication so excellently planned and timed to coincide with the quincentennial of the "discovery" of America. The writers have been accused of everything from pandering to not living up to someone's expectations of them—comments which, first of all, suggest an unhealthy determinism but, more important, lead us away from discussions of decolonization in contemporary Native American Literatures.

Politics

The significance of the study of aesthetics and politics cannot be overemphasized, since American Indian fiction writers, clearly, have been instrumental, intentionally or not, in legitimizing the struggle to open up the American literary canon to include minority literatures, as though that were the major function of Third World writers. This effort may be appealing to some, especially in the face of the Bennett/Bloom hysteria that such an effort simply attempts to abolish the idea of canon altogether in American schools and is, therefore, almost treasonous. Even if the open-canon movement were to succeed, however, there remain for American Indian (First Nation) scholars two issues over which they will have little influence: first, opening up the canon is a little like opening world trade markets: exploitation abounds—a few legends here, a myth there. Seattle's famous oration, some poetry, and Momaday's "Man Made of Words" essay are inserted between the Age of Romanticism and T. S. Eliot just to illustrate some cross-cultural interest and fairness.

The second worry for the nativist is the question of whether or not opening up the American literary canon to include native literary traditions and contemporary works will have much relevance, given its own set of unique aims—the interest in establishing the myths and metaphors of sovereign nationalism; the places, the mythological beings, the genre structures and plots of the oral traditions; the wars and war leaders, the treaties and accords with other nations as the so-called gold standard against which everything can be judged. These are the elements of nationalism which have always fueled the literary canon of tribal peoples and their literary lives. In my own tribal literary traditions, there is a fairly long list of Dakota/Lakota writers and storytellers as well as a huge body of ritual and ceremony against which everything may be compared. Reference to the body of nationalistic myths, legends, metaphors, symbols, historical persons and events, writers and their writings must form the basis of the critical discourse that functions in the name of the people; the presence of the Indian nation as cultural force is a matter of principle.

The unfortunate truth is that there are few significant works being produced today by the currently popular American Indian fiction writers which examine the meaningfulness of indigenous or tribal sovereignty in the twenty-first century. Seemingly overwhelmed by violence, self-hate, romanticism, blame, mournfulness, loss, or anger, the writers seem to suggest that there is little room for liberation literature, little use for nationalistic/tribal resistance. Frank Chin's observation that in the case of Asian works, history was nearly destroyed by Christian missionaries and is now being faked by writers continuing in that tradition must be taken up by Native American critics as a cause-and-effect probability.

The Christian-oriented apocalyptic vision of Erdrich's rich prose, the anguished dismissal of the nationhood of the Blackfeet by James Welch, the ambiguity concerning the Indian rights struggle of politics and land in my own novel, the mythic self-absorption of Scott Momaday, perhaps even the feeling that "whoever wants to be tribal can join the tribe" of Gerald Vizenor (and we could, perhaps, name a dozen more) collectively seem to leave American Indian tribal peoples in this country stateless, politically inept, and utterly without nationalistic alternatives. The idea that Indians lacked political skills, which may now have found its way into contemporary fiction written by Indians, is a stereotype which has been used by historians for a century to dismiss and distort early Indian/white relations. Though Gerald Vizenor has described my recent long fiction, *From the River's Edge,* as a novel which "celebrates the honorable conditions of tribal sovereignty and survivance," there is an intellectual uncertainty in its whole which is an appalling and unexpected flaw in the imaginative work of a daughter of tribal politicians, men and women for whom there was no ideological ambivalence concerning nationhood. In characterization, at least, I simply tell you about a believer; Tatekeya has faith. He believes, and because faith is complete in itself, he cannot respond to secular divisiveness. He has no rules for modern politics, only a degree of faith. While Tatekeya may be attempting to say how it is that he may return to a moral world, the reality of our real lives as tribal people is that without effective politics, such a return can be at best temporary.

Nationalism

At a time when nationalism seems to be asserting itself in the world in new and puzzling ways, the most obvious example being the breakaway republics of the former U.S.S.R., the people of America's First Nations find themselves struggling with the myths of their own national status against a long history of enforced denationalization. Yet the American Indian writers who have achieved successful readership in mainstream America seem to avoid that struggle in their work and present Indian populations as simply gatherings of exiles, emigrants, and refugees, strangers to themselves and their lands, pawns in the control of white manipulators, mixed-bloods searching for identity—giving support, finally, to the idea of nationalistic/ tribal culture as a contradiction in terms.

The work of traditional native thinkers like the Lakota religious leader Arvol Looking Horse, Sioux attorneys Mario Gonzalez and Vine Deloria Jr., politicians such as Birgil Kills Straight, members of the Grey Eagles Society, Alex White Plume, and countless other individuals and institutions with First Nation status suggest otherwise. The organizers of the 1985–1990 Big Foot Ride Centennial from Fort Yates, North Dakota, to Wounded Knee, South Dakota (in ceremonial grieving of the death of over three hundred unarmed Lakotas), the ever-present tribal orators who concern themselves with healing the Sioux Nation's wounds, and the hundreds of others involved in such continuing tribal activities throughout the country illustrate the historical interest in decolonization and the revival of nationalistic paradigms necessary for the return of the spirit and the journey into the twenty-first century.

These matters are often looked upon as the fanciful emergence of empire building which exists isolated from the literary voice of the people, or else they are dismissed as mere political action for political gain and dangerous authoritarianism. However, if they are examined as essentially literary events, actions, and ideas, it may be that the incorporation of such concrete praxis can affect canon theory and literary theory (as it always has in oral societies) by challenging intellectual orthodoxies which do not appreciate—indeed, negate and omit—a nationalistic approach to the development and interpretation of any works, including contemporary fiction.

In this current movement of critical thought away from Europeanism, native traditionalists are telling scholars it is time to abandon the idea that without pope or emperor nationhood has never been achieved, that, on the contrary, national affiliations are a part of the urgency of contemporary thought and writing for American Indians, whose own national histories have never been appropriately defined in reality-based, historical contexts. It is the challenge of modern thinkers and critics to find out what these nativist ideals mean in terms of the function of literature.

Many of today's scholars are willing to make that move, though they may not know how, and their freedom to do so may be stifled by a body of inchoate reasoning called empirical criticism. This means that they are often fearful of exacting a decolonizing focus and thus refuse to enter the discourse wholeheartedly. Writer and critic Raymond Williams, for example, in his very interesting and forward-looking book, *The Year 2000,* though drifting toward a global focus rather than a tribal one, unintentionally reasserts the native view in this limited way: " 'Nation' as a term is radically connected with native. We are born into relationships which are typically settled in a place. This form of primary and 'placeable' bonding is of quite fundamental human and natural importance."

American Indians couldn't agree more. However, Williams concludes that the jump from that to anything like the modern nation-state is entirely artificial. His refusal to take up the function of the indigenous myths of origin on this continent, which are irrevocably tied to place and tribal nationalism, makes his conclusion seem both racist and nonfunctional. He further asserts the colonist view in America and does little to clarify the reality of national existence as it has applied to the modern treaty-status tribes (the First Nation) in the United States and Canada for at least a hundred years and, traditionally, for thousands more.

While intellectual antagonists have always existed in the fight for American Indian nationhood, tribal bonding with geography as the most persistent native nationalistic sentiment is often dismissed as a major criterion for nationhood in the modern world. Recognition of the need for decolonization inherent in a people's spiritual connection to the land rises from history and mythology, two components of literature; yet, scholarly awareness of the corrupt thinking which disavows this criterion emerges from wildly dissimilar theorists. Ernest Renan, for example, the nineteenth-century French philosopher, surely removed from the experience of the natives in the so-called wilds of America, delivered a lecture at the Sorbonne in 1882 in which he defined a nation in this way:

> A nation is a soul, a spiritual principle. Two things, which in truth are but one, constitute this soul or spiritual principle. One lies in the past, one in the present. One is the possession in common of a rich legacy of memories; the other is present day consent, the desire to live together, the will to perpetuate the value of the heritage that one has received in an undivided form. Man does not improvise. The nation, like the individual, is the culmination of a long past of endeavors, sacrifices, and devotions.

This lecture was delivered as the Indian nations of North America were in the final stages of a bloody war in defense of their lands and sovereign rights. On the northern plains and throughout much of America, the wars ended in peace treaties signed between sovereigns. Much of Renan's argument is found in all of the works of American Indians then and now, and it may even constitute part of the rationale for the common trait Bevis points out when he says of American Indian writers today, "They don't even trespass upon each other's tribes." Surely, there is a sense of loyalty to that ideal in all of the writers mentioned in this discussion (for some more than others).

Unfortunately, Renan's discourse turns out to be an argument for colonization rather than the nationalism which indigenous peoples have imagined and asserted for generations, for he goes on to dismiss race, language, religion, and geography as anything more than natural considerations: "It is no more soil than it is race which makes a nation. The soil furnishes the substratum, the field of struggle and of labor; man furnishes the soul. Man is everything in the formation of this sacred thing which is called a people."

The indigenous view of the world—that the very origins of a people are specifically tribal (nationalistic) and rooted in a specific geography (place), that mythology (soul) and geography (land) are inseparable, that even language is rooted in a specific place—makes Renan's considerations antagonistic to the kind of discourse on nationalism desired by American Indian intellectuals.

The broad acceptance of Renan's one-sided arguments in American intellectual thought has lessened the tensions for American Indian writers (themselves constantly subjected to colonization and assimilation forces), and the result is they may no longer feel hostile nor isolated from modernity and cosmopolitanism. They begin to feel that decolonization may be both ridiculous and irrelevant besides being impossible and futile. They no longer know what the Hunkpapa Sioux Chieftain Sitting Bull meant when he said, "God made me an Indian and he put me here, *in this place.*" It seems to them very much like Mormonism, perhaps, or any cultish view. The term *nationalism,* then, takes on a pejorative definition except to such unique critics as the Osage professor of English and Native Studies, Dr. Robert Warrior, who says that the work of criticism is not to pronounce judgments but to "go beyond merely invoking categories and engage in careful exploration of how those categories impact the process of sovereignty."

Euro-American scholars have always been willing to forgo discussion concerning the connection between literary voice and geography and what that means to Indian nationhood. It is with regard to this failure that Warrior's challenge is particularly meaningful.

Reality of the Third World and Tribal Sovereignty

What Third Worldists, then, have in common is the question of what their fictive mythmaking has to do with the reality of their postcolonial conditions as *nations* of people. For those writers who are called American Indians, the question of whether the myth of nationhood is a cultural force is often unanswerable in their works. The idea that a national culture exists for them is obliterated by ideas of minority status in the United States, temporality, dysfunction, Indian-ness. The sovereign rights and obligations of citizens of the First Nation of America as modern concepts seem less important to today's writers than stories of loss, exile, identity, and degeneration.

If it is true, as the Palestinian critic Professor Edward W. Said asserts, that the " 'nationalistic mood' is aesthetically and socially more strongly felt in the emergent societies of the world today" (and, therefore, one assumes, in the struggling colonized societies), the question for native writers of fiction becomes, To what extent does my specific contemporary tribal voice mirror that strongly felt idea? And, specifically, how does that passion realize itself within the content or plot of a given novel? or does it? or need it? The question for critics is, Have we shown a lack of interest in this urge, and have we failed to apply Third World critical methodology to major works?

Perhaps the most ambitious novel yet published by an American Indian fiction writer which fearlessly asserts a collective indigenous retrieval of the lands stolen through colonization is Leslie Marmon Silko's *Almanac of the Dead,* published in 1991. The idea of decolonization, Silko tells us, is dependent upon writing that has "living power within it, a power that would bring all the tribal peoples in the Americas together to retake the land." She obviously clings to the idea that the imagination plays a functional role in political and social life, an idea which most of the native traditionalists I have known have always held.

Silko's new novel seems to stand alone in creating a fictionalized pantribal nationalism, an event which provides an interesting, antagonistic, rebellious moment in contemporary literary development. In that light, it seems difficult to explain the hostile reaction to her critical analysis of the work of other writers. Her assessment of Louise Erdrich's work, in particular, is seen by some as an attack, rather than as a sincere effort to understand the forces which have served to displace the discussion of the nation as a cultural force in literature. Louis Owens, in *Other Destinies,* charges Silko with an "attack" upon Erdrich's *Beet Queen,* which she calls "a strange artifact, an eloquent example of the political climate in America in 1986." Owens says,

> Oddly, in attacking the book for its refusal to foreground the undeniably bitter racism toward Indians in America's heartland Silko seems to be demanding that writers who identify as Indian, or mixedblood, must write rhetorically and polemically, a posture that leaves little room for the kind of heterogeneous literature that would reflect the rich diversity of Indian experiences, lives and cultures . . . and a posture Silko certainly does not assume in her own fiction.

If a native artist's effort to examine forms of narrative which do or do not express the ideology of the modern nation, which is a major concern of Third World criticism and the real focus of Silko's comments on Erdrich's work, is labeled as an "attack" by presumably knowledgeable critics, then the ability of American Indians to create new forms of living and writing is seriously jeopardized.

Owens is quite wrong about Silko's posture, at least as far as it applies to her most recent novel, *Almanac of the Dead,* for it is the foremost Indian novel in which we see the clear and unmistakable attempt to describe Indian nationalism in what she sees as modern terms. That diagnosis of native nationalism, which appears in terms of economics, power, and numbers, however troubling to the moralists among us, attempts to redefine the boundaries of the Western hemisphere, and is strangely familiar to the militants of the last decades and haunting to anyone who understands the longing of a tribal nation for its homelands.

Retribution, a major part of that nationalism, is obviously a matter of utmost importance to Silko, to indigenous peoples everywhere and, in particular, to people like the citizens of the Sioux Nation who are presently engaged in the longest legal struggle for the return of stolen lands (the Paha Sapa) in the history of the United States. You need only look at the current and historical legislative efforts of tribal people, the contemporary speeches of people like Royal Bull Bear, Arvol Looking Horse, and the now-deceased Fools Crow (Eagle Bear); you need only look at the body of oratory by American Indians in history, the continued ritual life in native communities, and the work of the International Indian Treaty Organizations to understand that the political reality of the imagination, as Silko's work suggests, is a major component of nationalism.

Silko's novel, however, in describing America's worst nightmare, that is, the triumph of the indigenes as tidal waves of South and North American Indians wipe out borders and reclaim lands, does not answer all of the prayers of the First Nation purists just named. These purists, by and large, have not moved away from the traditional stance of their own tribal legacies, nor from the 1970s "awakening" spoken of by Said when Third Worldists had not yet been labeled "people of color" in lieu of their own nationalistic/tribal titles and definitions. Thus, the unanswered questions of a privileged Third World author, separated from the realities she describes (a condition found almost everywhere in the Third World), support two tendencies in nation-centered fiction: they temper but do not refute the sweeping claims of her fiction that imagination is the source of history, an ambiguity of some importance to scholars. More important, they reassure readers and critics that the process of authenticating cultural interpretation for American Indians is ongoing. Both of these tendencies must be acknowledged in the critical work which will inevitably accompany the developing body of contemporary American Indian fiction.

While what has happened in critical discourse may be confusing and inappropriate, the pedagogical debate centered upon multiculturalism in the United States is no less chaotic. In practice, multicultural education has not and will not cast much light on the centuries-long struggle for sovereignty faced by the people of the First Nation of America. Its very nature, ironically, is in conflict with the concept of American Indian sovereignty, since it emphasizes matters of spirituality and culture, anthropology and sociology.

Laguna author, critic, and professor Paula Gunn-Allen has taken up the issue of literature and notions of tribal sacred reality and privacy as related to pedagogy in her recent essay, "Special Problems in Teaching Leslie Marmon Silko's *Ceremony*" though she, too, avoids the discussion of nation-centered scholarship in that essay. Gunn-Allen says she tends to "non-teach" *Ceremony* because she finds it particularly troublesome:

> I focus on the story, the plot and action. I read the novel quite differently from how it is read by many, I believe. I could no more do (sanction) the kind of ceremonial investigation of *Ceremony* done by some researchers than I could slit my mother's throat. Even seeing some of it published makes my skin crawl. I have yet to read one of those articles all the way through, my reaction is so pronounced.

I teach the novel as being about a half-breed, in the context of half-breed literature from *Cogewea* on. Certainly, that is how I read the novel the first time I read it, as a plea for inclusion by a writer who felt excluded and compelled to depict the potential importance of breeds to Laguna survival. The parts of the novel that set other pulses atremble largely escaped me. The long poem text that runs through the center has always seemed to me to contribute little to the story or its understanding. Certainly, the salvation of Laguna from Drought is one of its themes, but the Tayo stories which, I surmise, form their own body of literature would have been a better choice if Silko's intentions were to clarify or support her text with traditional materials.

Tayo is the name of one of the dramatic characters around Keres-land. Perhaps in some story I am unfamiliar with, he is involved with Fly or Reed Woman. But, the story she lays alongside the novel is a clan story and is not told outside the clan.

I have long wondered why she did so. Certainly, being raised in greater proximity to Laguna Village than I, she must have been told what I was, that we don't tell those things outside. Perhaps her desire to demonstrate the importance of breeds led her to do this, or perhaps no one ever told her why the Lagunas and other Pueblos are so closed about their spiritual activities and the allied oral tradition.

Putting these matters in the context of pedagogy as Gunn-Allen does suggests very clearly the heretofore unspoken risks of omission and distortion in the opening up of the canon, in some ways resembling the contradictory role played by Salman Rushdie's literary contributions to global and American fiction.

The opening up of the canon, an American democratic ideal so vigorously pursued by scholars, writers, and professors like Dr. Paul Lauter whose interests in open admissions policies, women's studies, and black studies have fostered in the last two decades a movement of great force, unintentionally belittles the very real conflict between what Third Worldists call "national form" and "anticolonial liberalism," which is really at the heart of the Rushdie tragedy. Gunn-Allen's comments here on Silko illustrate the dilemma for American Indians.

While the point about pedagogy that Gunn-Allen makes concerning *Ceremony* might also be true of Silko's earlier works (for example, the short fiction *Tony's Story,* in contrast to the Simon J. Ortiz rendering of the same event in *The Killing of a State Cop*), the real issue here is that canon theory and critical theory rise out of pedagogy, not the other way around, as some have suggested, thereby magnifying issues of cultural authenticity. Since, in general, the faculties in departments where these works are taught are often the last places to draw in any great numbers of Native scholars, it is quite likely that conflicting and minority views will be dismissed, distorted, or unknown.

Whatever may be said about Silko's earlier works, *Almanac of the Dead* engages in and insists upon the nationalist's approach to historical events and in the process seems to put any so-called pandering ordinarily required of the storyteller in its place. Her effort here in her new work is to create a pan-Indian journey toward retribution, not to appeal to nonindigenous mainstream readership nor to tell tribal secrets.

While this is a heartening focus, it too fails in this nationalistic approach, since it does not take into account the specific kind of tribal/nation status of the original occupants of this continent. There is no apparatus that allows the tribally specific treaty-status paradigm to be realized either in Silko's fiction or in the pan-Indian approach to history. The explanation for that in tribal terms may be that Laguna falls under the Treaty of Guadalupe Hidalgo—very different circumstances from the Plains Indian Treaty paradigm. Nonetheless, if it is true that the definition of a nation is historically determined, then Silko's vision might seem unworkable or even offensive to those nation-states that insist upon the accuracy of their own specific histories. Her gallant effort, though, makes us realize that the theories, both literary and spiritual, about the world in which American Indians find themselves are not to be abandoned by the literati.

The pedagogical problems referred to by Gunn-Allen take many forms, and they most often have to do with discussion of the intent of the works themselves and the intent of their traditions. It seems sensible to point out in an instance or two what happens when interpretations of the literature of the Sioux, for example, are almost always rendered in English by non-Sioux scholars in the pedagogical mode. The continuous overtracing of personal histories within the *tiospaye* concept (defined as a societal/cultural/tribal organizational construct), which is based upon blood and ancestral ties and lineage and is so much a part of the storytelling process for the Sioux, is never put into the Third World theoretical lexicon simply because the professors are not much interested or are uninformed. The result is the diminishment or alteration of the *tiospaye* concept *as a nationalistic forum* for the people, in spite of the fact that the appropriate interpretation of traditional literatures suggests that nationalism is a major reason for their existence. Pedagogical models rising out of anthropology departments and literary/humanistic study centers are almost entirely responsible for this phenomenon. Since pedagogical models are rarely criticized within the Third World theoretical framework, the literatures themselves are rarely conceptualized as foundations for native political insight and action, and the result is that the study of their own literatures by tribal people becomes irrelevant to their lives.

One example of the lack of critical sensitivity for Third World concerns is Julian Rice's work on the Ella Deloria materials in Sioux literatures. Deloria's *Dakota Texts,* translation studies in language and literature first published in the early decades of this century, an exemplary tribal work by a tribal scholar, has become the basis for much subsequent scholarship in Lakota/Dakota/Nakota (i.e., Sioux) literatures.

Rice, in his work *Lakota Storytelling* (1989), embellishes the notion of Dr. Raymond DeMallie, considered a foremost scholar in Sioux religions, that "real kinship" (which is a major function of the *tiospaye*) was not narrowly defined by the Lakotas in biological terms, but was defined, rather, by behavior. "Even today, among the Lakotas," DeMallie asserts, "relatives are people who act like relatives and consider themselves to be related." There is little understanding that while this is, of course, accepted as a philosophical idea, behavior alone does not make one a Lakota. One cannot be a Lakota unless one is related by the lineage (blood) rules of the *tiospaye*. While it is true that the narrow definition of biology was not accepted by the Lakotas, since they are also related to the animal world, spirit world, and everything else in the world, biology is *never* dismissed categorically. On the contrary, it is the overriding concern of the people who assiduously trace their blood ties throughout the generations.

This ambiguity, further asserted through the literary studies of Rice, seems to extend anthropological theories which may define the Lakota as a sociological phenomenon rather than in terms of the political lexicon of the nationhood of people who know their citizenship to be based upon the blood kinship rules of lineage inherent in the *tiospaye*. They are citizens of a sovereign nation that signed treaties with the United States of America and, before that, defended and allied themselves throughout history with the citizens of other tribal nations.

The implication of these mostly pedagogical studies by the foremost white male scholars in the field is profoundly disturbing. The idea that *if you act like a Lakota you are a Lakota,* seeming to emerge from their genuine if misguided interest in putting Ella Deloria's work to good classroom use, is patently absurd to the people who call themselves Lakotas. The end result is even more devastating, since the sincere pedagogical efforts to bring this material into contemporary classrooms seem to have resulted in the creation of a body of critical work which renders the literature useless to the people from whom it originates. It is particularly ironic that Rice uses the Blood-Clot stories, essential as origin stories of the people, to demonstrate his obvious thesis, which is as follows:

> As a microcosm of a family united in strength and natural affection rather than by "blood," they can unregretfully leave prideful individualism, the wife's elder sister, to her limited routine of "taking out the ashes."

Nowhere in his examination of the Deloria work, in which he also discusses Black Elk and Fools Crow materials, does he clarify this oversimplified position. In addition to being simply absurd, the question of what such omissions might be contributing to the current controversies concerning the New Age "becoming Indian" fad so offensive to Indian populations remains to be answered. Rice's work, originally published by subsidiary presses, is now being taken up and published by other more orthodox university presses.

While this discussion does not intend to present Rice's work as totally corrupt, it is used here to illustrate how ludicrously inappropriate much scholarship is to the nationhood status of Indian America. When white scholars articulate a private vision with little or no interest in understanding the national conscience, their voices seem shamefully inauthentic. This fact, however, is rarely perceived by other, similarly uninformed scholars, readers, and professors.

Some of Rice's other conclusions are equally astonishing, even in studies of a less esoteric mode such as the contemporary oratory of the Sioux. He misinterprets the unifying motif of a speech by Fools Crow as "giving." Listening to the speech, Lakota, on the other hand, believe the unifying motif to be "sharing." This is a long-standing issue in interpretation made public in preliminary studies of others who precede Dr. Rice, namely the work of Dr. John Bryde, a former priest, who wrote on Indian values and attempted to clarify them some two decades ago when he taught courses in Indian psychology at the University of South Dakota. Lakota listeners, supposing a past in which the nation has suffered and that any understanding requires a common effort, know that nationhood for the Lakota is based on sharing, of which giving is only a part. To claim otherwise is to misunderstand the nationalistic function of oratory as a literary genre in the study of native literatures and reciprocity as a major principle of the *tiospaye* concept.

In conclusion, then, I suggest that pedagogical works in tribal literatures be critiqued within Third World theoretical considerations more than they are at present. The interest in decolonization goes back to the Mayan resistance narratives of the 1500s and has always played an important role in political and social life.

Tribal scholars like my fellow tribeswoman Ella Deloria, as well as all the subsequent fiction writers and scholars mentioned in this article and many others not mentioned, have stumbled into this remarkable debate about society and culture. The climate in which these debates occur is fraught with risk because it appears that much of what is called contemporary American Indian fiction and scholarship is validated as such by non-Indian publishers, editors, critics, and scholars for reasons which have very little to do with the survival into the twenty-first century of the First Nation of America.

Because of flaws in pedagogy and criticism, much modern fiction written in English by American Indians is being used as the basis for the cynical absorption into the "melting pot," pragmatic inclusion in the canon, and involuntary unification of an American national literary voice. Ironically, much of the criticism and fiction published today contributes to the further domination of modern nations and individualism, all the while failing in its own implied search for sovereignty and tribalism. To succumb to such an intellectual state is to cut one's self off as a Native American writer from effective political action. It severs one's link not only to the past but to the present search by one's native compatriots for legitimate First Nation status.

Vine DeLoria, Jr. (Sioux)
Indian Humor

One of the best ways to understand a people is to know what makes them laugh. Laughter encompasses the limits of the soul. In humor life is redefined and accepted. Irony and satire provide much keener insights into a group's collective psyche and values than do years of research.

It has always been a great disappointment to Indian people that the humorous side of Indian life has not been mentioned by professed experts on Indian Affairs. Rather the image of the granite-faced grunting redskin has been perpetuated by American mythology.

People have little sympathy with stolid groups. Dick Gregory did much more than is believed when he introduced humor into the Civil Rights struggle. He enabled non-blacks to enter into the thought world of the black community and experience the hurt it suffered. When all people shared the humorous but ironic situation of the black, the urgency and morality of Civil Rights was communicated.

The Indian people are exactly opposite of the popular stereotype. I sometimes wonder how anything is accomplished by Indians because of the apparent overemphasis on humor within the Indian world. Indians have found a humorous side of nearly every problem and the experiences of life have generally been so well defined through jokes and stories that they have become a thing in themselves.

For centuries before the white invasion, teasing was a method of control of social situations by Indian people. Rather than embarrass members of the tribe publicly, people used to tease individuals they considered out of step with the consensus of tribal opinion. In this way egos were preserved and disputes within the tribe of a personal nature were held to a minimum.

Gradually people learned to anticipate teasing and began to tease themselves as a means of showing humility and at the same time advocating a course of action they deeply believed in. Men would depreciate their feats to show they were not trying to run roughshod over tribal desires. This method of behavior served to highlight their true virtues and gain them a place of influence in tribal policy-making circles.

Humor has come to occupy such a prominent place in national Indian affairs that any kind of movement is impossible without it. Tribes are being brought together by sharing humor of the past. Columbus jokes gain great sympathy among all tribes, yet there are no tribes extant who had anything to do with Columbus. But the fact of white invasion from which all tribes have suffered has created a common bond in relation to Columbus jokes that gives a solid feeling of unity and purpose to the tribes.

SIENA COLLEGE LIBRARY

The more desperate the problem, the more humor is directed to describe it. Satirical remarks often circumscribe problems so that possible solutions are drawn from the circumstances that would not make sense if presented in other than a humorous form.

Often people are awakened and brought to a militant edge through funny remarks. I often counseled people to run for the Bureau of Indian Affairs in case of an earthquake because nothing could shake the BIA. And I would watch as younger Indians set their jaws, determined that they, if nobody else, would shake it. We also had a saying that in case of fire call the BIA and they would handle it because they put a wet blanket on everything. This also got a warm reception from people.

Columbus and Custer jokes are the best for penetration into the heart of the matter, however. Rumor has it that Columbus began his journey with four ships. But one went over the edge so he arrived in the new world with only three. Another version states that Columbus didn't know where he was going, didn't know where he had been, and did it all on someone else's money. And the white man has been following Columbus ever since.

It is said that when Columbus landed, one Indian turned to another and said, "Well, there goes the neighborhood." Another version has two Indians watching Columbus land and one saying to the other, "Maybe if we leave them alone they will go away." A favorite cartoon in Indian country a few years back showed a flying saucer landing while an Indian watched. The caption was "Oh, no, not again."

The most popular and enduring subject of Indian humor is, of course, General Custer. There are probably more jokes about Custer and the Indians than there were participants in the battle. All tribes, even those thousands of miles from Montana, feel a sense of accomplishment when thinking of Custer. Custer binds together implacable foes because he represented the Ugly American of the last century and he got what was coming to him.

Some years ago we put out a bumper sticker which read "Custer Died for Your Sins." It was originally meant as a dig at the National Council of Churches. But as it spread around the nation it took on additional meaning until everyone claimed to understand it and each interpretation was different.

Originally, the Custer bumper sticker referred to the Sioux Treaty of 1868 signed at Fort Laramie in which the United States pledged to give free and undisturbed use of the lands claimed by Red Cloud in return for peace. Under the covenants of the Old Testament, breaking a covenant called for a blood sacrifice for atonement. Custer was the blood sacrifice for the United States breaking the Sioux treaty. That, at least originally, was the meaning of the slogan.

Custer jokes, however, can barely be categorized, let alone sloganized. Indians say that Custer was well-dressed for the occasion. When the Sioux found his body after the battle, he had on an Arrow shirt.

Many stories are derived from the details of the battle itself. Custer is said to have boasted that he could ride through the entire Sioux nation with his Seventh Cavalry and he was half right. He got half-way through.

One story concerns the period immediately after Custer's contingent had been wiped out and the Sioux and Cheyennes were zeroing in on Major Reno and his troops several miles to the south of the Custer battlefield.

The Indians had Reno's troopers surrounded on a bluff. Water was scarce, ammunition was nearly exhausted, and it looked like the next attack would mean certain extinction.

One of the white soldiers quickly analyzed the situation and shed his clothes. He covered himself with mud, painted his face like an Indian, and began to creep toward the Indian lines.

A Cheyenne heard some rustling in the grass and was just about to shoot.

"Hey, chief," the soldier whispered, "don't shoot, I'm coming over to join you. I'm going to be on your side."

The warrior looked puzzled and asked the soldier why he wanted to change sides.

"Well," he replied, "better red than dead."

Custer's Last Words occupy a revered place in Indian humor. One source states that as he was falling mortally wounded he cried, "Take no prisoners!" Other versions, most of them off color, concentrate on where those **** Indians are coming from. My favorite last saying pictures Custer on top of the hill looking at a multitude of warriors charging up the slope at him. He turns resignedly to his aide and says, "Well, it's better than going back to North Dakota."

Since the battle it has been a favorite technique to boost the numbers on the Indian side and reduce the numbers on the white side so that Custer stands out as a man fighting against insurmountable odds. One question no pseudo-historian has attempted to answer, when changing the odds to make the little boy in blue more heroic, is how what they say were twenty thousand Indians could be fed when gathered into one camp. What a tremendous pony herd must have been gathered there, what a fantastic herd of buffalo must have been nearby to feed that amount of Indians, what an incredible source of drinking water must have been available for fifty thousand animals and some twenty thousand Indians!

Just figuring water-needs to keep that many people and animals alive for a number of days must have been incredible. If you have estimated correctly, you will see that the Little Big Horn was the last great *naval* engagement of the Indian wars.

The Sioux tease other tribes a great deal for not having been at the Little Big Horn. The Crows, traditional enemies of the Sioux, explain their role as Custer's scouts as one of bringing Custer where the Sioux could get at him! Arapahos and Cheyennes, allies of the Sioux in that battle, refer to the time they "bailed the Sioux out" when they got in trouble with the cavalry.

Even today variations of the Custer legend are bywords in Indian country. When an Indian gets too old and becomes inactive, people say he is "too old to muss the Custer anymore."

The early reservation days were times when humorous incidents abounded as Indians tried to adapt to the strange new white ways and occasionally found themselves in great dilemmas.

At Fort Sisseton, in Dakota territory, Indians were encouraged to enlist as scouts for the Army after the Minnesota Wars. Among the requirements for enlistment were a working knowledge of English and having attained twenty-one years of age. But these requirements were rarely met. Scouts were scarce and the goal was to keep a company of scouts at full strength, not to follow regulations from Washington to the letter.

In a short time the Army had a company of scouts who were very efficient but didn't know enough English to understand a complete sentence. Washington, finding out about the situation, as bureaucracies occasionally do, sent an inspector to check on the situation. While he was en route, orders to disband the scouts arrived, and so his task became one of closing the unit and making the mustering-out payments.

The scouts had lined up outside the command officer's quarters and were interviewed one by one. They were given their choice of taking money, horses, or a combination of the two as their final severance pay from the Army. Those who could not speak English were severely reprimanded and tended to get poorer horses in payment because of their obvious disregard of the regulations.

One young scout, who was obviously in violation of both requirements, was very worried about his interview. He quizzed the scouts who came from the room about the interview. To a man they repeated the same story: "You will be asked three questions, how old you are, how long you have been with the scouts, and whether you want money or horses for your mustering-out pay."

The young scout memorized the appropriate answers and prepared himself for his turn with the inspector. When his turn came he entered the room, scared to death but determined to do his best. He stood at attention before the man from Washington, eager to give his answers and get out of there.

The inspector, tired after a number of interviews, wearily looked up and inquired:

"How long have you been in the scouts?"

"Twenty years," the Indian replied with a grin.

The inspector stopped short and looked at the young man. Here was a man who looked only eighteen or twenty, yet he had served some twenty years in the scouts. He must have been one of the earliest recruits. It just didn't seem possible. Yet, the inspector thought, you can't tell an Indian's age from the way he looks, they sure can fool you sometimes. Or was he losing his mind after interviewing so many people in so short a time? Perhaps it was the Dakota heat. At any rate, he continued the interview.

"How old are you?" he continued.

"Three years."

A look of shock rippled across the inspector's face. Could this be some mysterious Indian way of keeping time? Or was he now delirious?

"Am I crazy or are you?" he angrily asked the scout.

"Both" was the reply and the scout relaxed, smiled, and leaned over the desk, reaching out to receive his money.

The horrified inspector cleared the window in one leap. He was seen in Washington, D.C., the following morning, having run full speed during the night. It was the last time Indian scouts were required to know English and applications for interpreter were being taken the following morning.

The problems of the missionaries in the early days provided stories which have become classics in Indian country. They are retold over and over again wherever Indians gather.

One story concerns a very obnoxious missionary who delighted in scaring the people with tales of hell, eternal fires, and everlasting damnation. This man was very unpopular and people went out of their way to avoid him. But he persisted to contrast heaven and hell as a carrot-and-stick technique of conversion.

One Sunday after a particularly fearful description of hell he asked an old chief, the main holdout of the tribe against Christianity, where he wanted to go. The old chief asked the missionary where *he* was going. And the missionary replied that, of course, he as a missionary of the gospel was going to heaven.

"Then I'll go to hell," the old chief said, intent on having peace in the world to come if not in this world.

On the Standing Rock reservation in South Dakota my grandfather served as the Episcopal missionary for years after his conversion to Christianity. He spent a great deal of his time trying to convert old Chief Gall, one of the strategists of Custer's demise, and a very famous and influential member of the tribe.

My grandfather gave Gall every argument in the book and some outside the book but the old man was adamant in keeping his old Indian ways. Neither the joys of heaven nor the perils of hell would sway the old man. But finally, because he was fond of my grandfather, he decided to become an Episcopalian.

He was baptized and by Christmas of that year was ready to take his first communion. He fasted all day and attended the Christmas Eve services that evening.

The weather was bitterly cold and the little church was heated by an old wood stove placed in the center of the church. Gall, as the most respected member of the community, was given the seat of honor next to the stove where he could keep warm.

In deference to the old man, my grandfather offered him communion first. Gall took the chalice and drained the entire supply of wine before returning to his seat. The wine had been intended for the entire congregation and so the old man had a substantial amount of spiritual refreshment.

Upon returning to his warm seat by the stove, it was not long before the wine took its toll on the old man who by now had had nothing to eat for nearly a day.

"Grandson," he called to my grandfather, "now I see why you wanted me to become a Christian. I feel fine, so nice and warm and happy. Why didn't you tell me that Christians did this every Sunday. If you had told me about this, I would have joined your church years ago."

Needless to say, the service was concluded as rapidly as possible and attendance skyrocketed the following Sunday.

Another missionary was traveling from Gallup to Albuquerque in the early days. Along the way he offered a ride to an Indian who was walking to town. Feeling he had a captive audience, he began cautiously to promote his message, using a soft-sell approach.

"Do you realize," he said, "that you are going to a place where sinners abound?"

The Indian nodded his head in assent.

"And the wicked dwell in the depths of their iniquities?"

Again a nod.

"And sinful women who have lived a bad life go?"

A smile and then another nod.

"And no one who lives a good life goes there?"

A possible conversion, thought the missionary, and so he pulled out his punch line: "And do you know what we call that place?"

The Indian turned, looked the missionary in the eye, and said, "Albuquerque."

Times may have changed but difficulties in communications seem to remain the same. At Santee, Nebraska, the people tell of a full blood who had a great deal of trouble understanding English. He used the foreign tongue as little as possible and managed to get along. But he knew only phrases of broken English, which he used when bargaining for his necessities of life.

One day he approached a white farmer and began bargaining for a fine rooster that the farmer owned. The old timer had brought two large bags filled with new potatoes and he motioned to the farmer that he wanted to trade them for the rooster.

Pointing from one to the other, he anxiously inquired, "potato rooster, potato rooster?" Soon the white farmer got the message and decided that it would be a good trade.

"Sure, chief," he replied, "I'll trade you."

So the Indian picked up the rooster, looked at it with satisfaction, tucked the rooster under his arm, and started to walk away.

As he was leaving, the white farmer began to think about the exchange. Obviously the rooster would be of little value without some hens for it. The potatoes were more than adequate to pay for a number of chickens, so he called after the Indian:

"Chief, do you want a pullet?"

The Indian turned around, tucked the rooster tighter under his arm, and said, "No, I can carry it."

In the Southwest, Indians like to talk about a similar play on words. One favorite story concerns a time when the Apaches and the settlers were fighting it out for control of Arizona territory. The chief of one Apache band was the last one needed to sign the peace treaty. Scout after scout had urged him to sign so the territory could have peace. But to no avail.

One day the chief took sick and, because he realized his days were numbered, he called his three sons together and made them pledge not to make peace unless all three signed the treaty. Soon after that the old man died and his three sons, Deerfoot, Running Bear, and Falling Rocks, all left to seek their fortunes with portions of the original band.

Scouts quickly found Deerfoot and Running Bear and convinced them they should sign the treaty. But they were unable to find Falling Rocks. Years went by and everyone in the territory sought the missing band so the treaty could be concluded. Falling Rocks was not to be found.

Eventually everyone gave up except the state highway department. They continued looking for him. And that is why today as you drive through the mountain passes in Arizona you will see large signs that read, "Look out for Falling Rocks."

The years have not changed the basic conviction of the Indian people that they are still dealing with the United States as equals. At a hearing on Civil Rights in South Dakota a few years ago a white man asked a Sioux if they still considered themselves an independent nation. "Oh, yes," was the reply, "we could still declare war on you. We might lose but you'd know you'd been in a terrible fight. Remember the last time in Montana?"

During the 1964 elections Indians were talking in Arizona about the relative positions of the two candidates, Johnson and Goldwater. A white man told them to forget about domestic policies and concentrate on the foreign policies of the two men. One Indian looked at him coldly and said that from the Indian point of view it was all foreign policy.

The year 1964 also saw the emergence of the Indian vote on a national scale. Rumors reached us that on the Navajo reservation there was more enthusiasm than understanding of the political processes. Large signs announced, "All the Way with LJB."

The current joke is that a survey was taken and only 15 percent of the Indians thought that the United States should get out of Vietnam. Eighty-five percent thought they should get out of America!

One of the most popular topics of Indian humor is the Bureau of Indian Affairs. When asked what was the biggest joke in Indian country, a man once said, "the BIA." During the years of termination, no matter how many tribes were being terminated the BIA kept adding employees. Since the thrust of termination was to cut government expenditures, the continual hiring of additional people led Indians to believe that such was not the real purpose. The rumor began that the BIA was phasing out Indians and would henceforth provide services only for its own employees.

A favorite story about the BIA concerns the time when Interior tried to merge the Standing Rock and Cheyenne River Sioux agencies in an economy move. A Sioux from Cheyenne River told an investigating committee the following story.

One day an Indian went to the Public Health Service because he had a bad headache. The PHS doctor decided to operate on him and he cut the Indian's head open and took out the brain to examine it.

Just then a man came in the door and shouted, "Joe, your house is on fire."

Joe, lying on the operating table, urged the doctor to sew up his head so that he could go and fight the fire. The doctor did as requested and Joe headed for the door.

"Wait, Joe," the doctor yelled, "you forgot your brain."

"I don't need any brain," Joe answered as he went out the door. "Afer I get the fire out, I'm going to work for the BIA."

An additional story about the BIA concerns the Indian who wanted a new brain. He walked into the PHS clinic and asked for an operation whereby he could exchange his brain for a better one.

The doctor took him into a room that contained many shelves upon which were rows of jars containing brains. Each jar had a price tag on it. A doctor's brain sold for ten dollars an ounce, a professor's brain sold for fifteen dollars an ounce. Similar brains from professional people ranged higher and higher until, at the very end of the back row of jars, there was a jar marked one thousand dollars an ounce.

The Indian asked why that type of brain was so expensive and wanted to know what kind of brain it was. The doctor said that the jar contained brains of the BIA, and added, "You know, it takes so many of them to make an ounce."

In 1967 we had a conference on manpower at Kansas City. One panel on employment had a well-known BIA representative moderating it. He made an excellent presentation and then asked for questions. For a long time the assembled delegates just sat and looked at him. So again he asked for questions, mentioned a few things he thought were important, and waited for response from the audience. Nothing.

Finally he said, "I really didn't want any discussion. I just wanted to show that the BIA can come to a conference and stand here without saying anything."

"You proved that during your speech," one of the Indians retorted.

Perhaps the most disastrous policy, outside of termination, ever undertaken by the Bureau of Indian Affairs was a program called Relocation. It began as a policy of the Eisenhower administration as a means of getting Indians off the reservation and into the city slums where they could fade away.

Considerable pressure was put on reservation Indians to move into the cities. Reservation people were continually harassed by bureau officials until they agreed to enter the program. Sometimes the BIA relocation officer was so eager to get the Indians moved off the reservation that he would take the entire family into the city himself.

But the Indians came back to the reservation as soon as they learned what the city had to offer. Many is the story by BIA people of how Indians got back to the reservations before the BIA officials who had taken them to the city returned.

When the space program began, there was a great deal of talk about sending men to the moon. Discussion often centered about the difficulty of returning the men from the moon to earth, as reentry procedures were considered to be very tricky. One Indian suggested that they send an Indian to the moon on relocation. "He'll figure out some way to get back."

Chippewas always tease the Sioux about the old days when they ran the Sioux out of Minnesota. It was, they claim, the first successful relocation program. In turn, the tribes that were pushed aside by the Sioux when they invaded the plains are ribbed about the relocation program which the Sioux conducted.

One solution to the "Indian problem" advocated in the Eisenhower years was closing the rolls of Indians eligible to receive federal services. Instead of federal services, each Indian would receive a set per capita share of the total budget. As each Indian died off, the total budget would be reduced. When all of the eligible Indians died off, that would be the end of federal-Indian relationships.

This plan was the favorite solution of Commissioner Glenn Emmons, who was heading the bureau at that time. But try as he might, he couldn't sell the program to anyone.

An agency superintendent from the Rosebud Sioux reservation in South Dakota had to go to Washington on business and so he decided to drive. As long as he was going he decided to take an old full blood with him to let the old man see the nation's capital.

The old man was very excited to be going to Washington and he made up his mind to see the Commissioner when he arrived there. So the superintendent began to suggest that the old man might have some solution to the Indian problem that he could share with the Commissioner. The old Indian discussed several ideas but admitted that they would probably be rejected.

Finally the superintendent outlined Emmons' plan to distribute the federal budget being spent on Indians among those then eligible for services. The old man pondered the idea for some time. Then he said, "That's the craziest idea I ever heard of. If I said something like that to the Commissioner, he would have me thrown out of his office."

Later the superintendent said he had always wished that the old man had suggested the plan to Emmons. "I always wanted," he told me, "to see the look on Emmons' face when an uneducated full blood suggested his own plan to him. I'd bet my last dollar that things would have changed at the BIA."

Frequently, without intending any humor, Indians can create a situation that is so funny that it is nearly impossible to believe. At the Manpower Conference in Kansas City in 1967 a series of events set up a hilarious incident. At least, looking back at it, Indians still chuckle over the results of the conference.

In 1966, after Philleo Nash had been Commissioner and had been fired for protecting the tribes, Udall gathered all of his top people and began to plan for a massive new program for "his" Indians. The administration also planned a comprehensive survey of Indian problems, perhaps realizing that Interior would once again draw a blank.

All of 1966 a secret Presidential Task Force surveyed Indian Affairs. By late December of that year they had compiled their report which, among other things, advocated a transfer of the Bureau of Indian Affairs from Interior to Health, Education and Welfare. Rumors began to fly in Indian country about the impending transfer and so the administration sent John Gardner, then Secretary of HEW, to Kansas City to present the idea to the assembled tribes.

In spite of all we could do to get HEW to advance the idea to a series of small conferences made up of influential tribal leaders, HEW insisted on presenting the idea to the entire group of assembled tribes—cold. So Gardner embarked for Kansas City with the usual entourage of high officialdom to present the message.

The tribal chairmen were greatly concerned about the possible loss of treaty rights which might occur during the transfer. When Gardner finished his presentation he opened the floor for questions, and the concerned chairmen began.

The first man wanted to know if all treaty rights would be protected. The Secretary of HEW assured him that treaty rights would be protected by law. The second man said that he had had such assurances before and now he wanted Gardner to give him his personal assurance so he could go back and talk with his people. Gardner gave him the personal assurances he wanted.

The next chairman wanted Gardner's assurance that nothing would be changed in the method of operations. The third wanted Gardner's assurance that no part of the existing structure would be changed, but that only the name plates would be different. The man following again wanted assurance that nothing would be changed, absolutely nothing. Wearily Gardner explained that *nothing* would be changed, everything would remain the same, all personnel would remain the same.

Eight straight chairmen questioned Gardner, asking for assurances that the basic structure would remain absolutely as it had been under Interior. Not a jot or tittle, according to Gardner, would be changed at all. There was no possible way that anything could be changed. Everything was to remain just as it was.

The ninth questioner brought down the house. "Why," he inquired, "if there are to be no changes at all, do you want to transfer the bureau to HEW? It would be the same as it is now," he concluded.

It suddenly occurred to everyone that the chairmen had successfully trapped Gardner in a neat box from which there was no escape. Suffice it to say, there was no transfer.

Not only the bureau, but other agencies, became the subject of Indian humor. When the War on Poverty was announced, Indians were justly skeptical about the extravagant promises of the bureaucrats. The private organizations in the Indian field, organized as the Council on Indian Affairs, sponsored a Capital Conference on Poverty in Washington in May of 1966 to ensure that Indian poverty would be highlighted just prior to the passage of the poverty program in Congress.

Tribes from all over the nation attended the conference to present papers on the poverty existing on their reservations. Two Indians from the plains area were asked about their feelings on the proposed program.

"Well," one said, "if they bring that War on Poverty to our reservation, they'll know they've been in a fight."

At the same conference, Alex Chasing Hawk, a nationally famous Indian leader from Cheyenne River and a classic storyteller, related the following tale about poverty.

It seemed that a white man was introduced to an old chief in New York City. Taking a liking to the old man, the white man invited him to dinner. The old chief hadn't eaten a good steak in a long time and eagerly accepted. He finished one steak in no time and still looked hungry. So the white man offered to buy him another steak.

As they were waiting for the steak, the white man said, "Chief, I sure wish I had your appetite."

"I don't doubt it, white man," the chief said. "You took my land, you took my mountains and streams, you took my salmon and my buffalo. You took everything I had except my appetite and now you want that. Aren't you ever going to be satisfied?"

At one conference on urban renewal, an Indian startled the audience when he endorsed the program. All day he had advocated using the poverty program to solve Indian problems on the reservation. Then, when the discussion got around to urban renewal, he abruptly supported the program.

He was asked why he wanted the program. It was, he was assured, perfectly natural for black and Mexican people to support urban renewal because so many of their people lived in the cities. But it didn't make sense to the conference participants what good an urban program would do for reservation Indians.

"I know," the Indian replied, "that a great many blacks and Mexicans want the program because so many of their people live in the cities and these cities must be rebuilt to give them a better life. But the program would also mean a better life for my people. You see, after the cities are rebuilt and everyone is settled there, we are going to fence them off and run our buffalo all over the country again."

People are always puzzled when they learn that Indians are not involved in the Civil Rights struggle. Many expect Indians to be marching up and down like other people, feeling that all problems of poor groups are basically the same.

But Indian people, having treaty rights of long standing, rightly feel that protection of existing rights is much more important to them. Yet intra-group jokes have been increasing since the beginning of the Civil Rights movement and few Indians do not wryly comment on movements among the other groups.

An Indian and a black man were in a bar one day talking about the problems of their respective groups. The black man reviewed all of the progress his people had made over the past decade and tried to get the Indian inspired to start a similar movement of activism among the tribes.

Finally the black man concluded, "Well, I guess you can't do much, there are so few of you."

"Yes," said the Indian, "and there won't be very many of you if they decide to play cowboys and blacks."

Another time, an Indian and a black man were talking about the respective races and how they had been treated by the white man. Each was trying to console the other about the problem and each felt the other group had been treated worse.

The Indian reminded the black man how his people had been slaves, how they had not had a chance to have a good family life, and how they were so persecuted in the South.

The black man admitted all of the sufferings of his people, but he was far more eloquent in reciting the wrongs against the Indians. He reviewed the broken treaties, the great land thefts, the smallpox infected blankets given to the tribes by the English, and the current movement to relocate all the Indians in the cities, far from their homelands.

Listening to the vivid description, the Indian got completely carried away in remorse. As each wrong was recited he nodded sorrowfully and was soon convinced that there was practically no hope at all for his people. Finally he could stand no more.

"And do you know," he told the black man, "there was a time in the history of this country when they used to shoot us *just to get the feathers!*"

During the riots, an Indian and a black man were talking about the terrible things going on. The black man said that the Indians could have prevented all of this grief if they had only stopped the white men at the Allegheny Mountains in the early days. Then there would have been no expansion of white influence and perhaps even slavery would not have been started. Why, the black man wanted to know, hadn't the Indians stopped the white man when it was possible for them to do so.

"I know, I know," the Indian answered, "but every time we tried to attack their forts, they had 'Soul Brother' painted on them, and so we never got the job done."

Because there is so little communication between minority communities, inter-group jokes always have the great danger of being misunderstood. In 1966, beside the Custer cards, we put out a card which read "We Shall Overrun," which, at least to us, harked to the scenes in Western movies where a small group of Indians mysteriously grows as it is outlined along the rim of a canyon until it appears as if several thousand warriors have sprung from the initial group of a dozen.

When we showed the card to various blacks in the Civil Rights movement, they didn't know how to take it and several times there was a tense situation until the card was explained.

Such is not the case when tribes tease each other. Then everything is up for grabs. Sioux announce that safe-conduct passes are available to Chippewas at the registration desk. Chippewas retort that if the Sioux don't behave they will relocate them again. Southwestern tribes innocently proclaim that their chili is very mild when in reality they are using asbestos pottery to serve it in. And the northern tribes seem always to take large helpings, which they somehow manage to get down amid tears and burnt mouths.

In the old days, after the buffalo were gone, the Sioux were reduced to eating dogs to keep alive. They had no meat of any kind and rabbits on the reservation were rare. Other tribes keep up the ribbing by announcing that the chef has prepared a special treat for the Sioux present at the annual banquet through the special cooperation of the local dog pound.

In 1964, Billy Mills, a Sioux from Pine Ridge, South Dakota, won the ten thousand meter run at the Olympics in Tokyo. Justly proud of Billy, the Sioux went all out to inform other tribes of his achievement. One day we were bragging about Billy's feat to the Coeur d'Alenes of Idaho, who politely nodded their heads in agreement.

Finally the wife of the chairman, Leona Garry, announced that Mills' running ability did not really surprise the Coeur d'Alenes. "After all," she said, "up here in Idaho, Sioux have to run far, fast, and often if they mean to stay alive." That ended the discussion of Sioux athletic ability for the evening.

Clyde Warrior, during his time, was perhaps the single greatest wit in Indian country. One day he announced that the bureau was preparing a special training program for the other tribes. When quizzed about how it differed from other programs in existence, he noted that it had a restriction of only a half-hour lunch period. "Otherwise," Clyde said, "they would have to be retrained after lunch."

Providing information to inquisitive whites has also proved humorous on occasion. At a night club in Washington, D.C., a group of Indians from North Dakota were gathered, taking the edge off their trip before returning home. One man, a very shy and handsome Chippewa, caught the eye of one of the entertainers. She began to talk with him about Indian life.

Did Indians still live in tents, she inquired. He admitted shyly that he sometimes lived in a tent in the summer time because it was cooler than a house. Question after question came and was answered by the same polite responses. The girl took quite a fancy to the Chippewa and he got more and more embarrassed at the attention.

Finally she wanted to know if Indians still raided wagon trains. He said no, they had stopped doing that a long time ago. She was heartbroken at hearing the news. "I sure would like to be raided by you," she said, and brought down the house.

Louie Sitting Crow, an old timer from Crow Creek, South Dakota, used to go into town and watch the tourists who traveled along Highway 16 in South Dakota to get to the Black Hills. One day at a filling station a car from New York pulled up and began filling its tank for the long drive.

A girl came over to talk with Louie. She asked him a great many questions about the Sioux and Louie answered as best he could. Yes, the Sioux were fierce warriors. Yes, the Sioux had once owned all of the state. Yes, they still wished for the old days.

Finally the girl asked if the Indians still scalped people. Louie, weary of the questions, replied, "Lady, remember, when you cross that river and head west, you will be in the land of the fiercest Indians on earth and you will be very lucky to get to the Black Hills alive. And you ask me if they still scalp. Let me tell you, it's worse than that. Now they take the whole head."

As Louie recalled, the car turned around and headed east after the tank was full of gas.

Southwestern Indians can get off a good one when they are inspired. A couple of years ago I was riding a bus from Santa Fe to Albuquerque late at night. The bus was late in leaving Santa Fe and seemed like it was taking forever to get on its way.

Two old men from one of the pueblos between the two cities were aboard and were obviously feeling contented after their night in town. They filled the time we were waiting for the bus to depart telling stories and as the bus got under way they began to make comments on its snail's pace.

The bus driver was in no humor to withstand a running commentary on the speed of the bus that night and so he turned around and said, "If you don't like the speed we're making, why don't you get out and walk?"

"Oh, we couldn't do that," one of the men said. "They don't expect us home until the bus gets in."

An Indian in Montana was arrested for driving while intoxicated and he was thrown in jail for the night. The following morning he was hauled before the judge for his hearing. Not knowing English very well, the Indian worried about the hearing, but he was determined to do the best he could.

The judge, accustomed to articulate, English-speaking people appearing before him, waited for the man to make his plea. The Indian stood silently waiting for the judge to say something. As the two looked at each other the silence began to become unbearable and the judge completely forgot what the man was being tried for.

Finally he said, "Well, speak up, Indian, why are you here?"

The Indian, who had been planning to plead not guilty, was also completely off balance. He gulped, looked at the judge, and said, "Your honor, I was arrested for driving a drunken car."

One-line retorts are common in Indian country. Popovi Da, the great Pueblo artist, was quizzed one day on why the Indians were the first ones on this continent. "We had reservations," was his reply. Another time, when questioned by an anthropologist on what the Indians called America before the white man came, an Indian said simply, *"Ours."* A young Indian was asked one day at a conference what a peace treaty was. He replied, "That's when the white man wants a piece of your land."

The best example of Indian humor and militancy I have ever heard was given by Clyde Warrior one day. He was talking with a group of people about the National Indian Youth Council, of which he was then president, and its program for a revitalization of Indian life. Several in the crowd were skeptical about the idea of rebuilding Indian communities along traditional Indian lines.

"Do you realize," he said, "that when the United States was founded, it was only 5 percent urban and 95 percent rural and now it is 70 percent urban and 30 percent rural?"

His listeners nodded solemnly but didn't seem to understand what he was driving at.

"Don't you realize what this means?" he rapidly continued. "It means we are pushing them into the cities. Soon we will have the country back again."

Whether Indian jokes will eventually come to have more significance than that, I cannot speculate. Humor, all Indians will agree, is the cement by which the coming Indian movement is held together. When a people can laugh at themselves and laugh at others and hold all aspects of life together without letting anybody drive them to extremes, then it seems to me that that people can survive.

Charles Eastman Ohiyesa (Sioux)
The Ghost Dance War

A religious craze such as that of 1890–91 was a thing foreign to the Indian philosophy. I recalled that a hundred years before, on the overthrow of the Algonquin nations, a somewhat similar faith was evolved by the astute Delaware prophet, brother to Tecumseh. It meant that the last hope of race entity had departed, and my people were groping blindly after spiritual relief in their bewilderment and misery. I believe that the first prophets of the "Red Christ" were innocent enough and that the people generally were sincere, but there were doubtless some who went into it for self-advertisement, and who introduced new and fantastic features to attract the crowd.

The ghost dancers had gradually concentrated on the Medicine Root creek and the edge of the "Bad Lands," and they were still further isolated by a new order from the agent, calling in all those who had not adhered to the new religion. Several thousand of these "friendlies" were soon encamped on the White Clay creek, close by the agency. It was near the middle of December, with weather unusually mild for that season. The dancers held that there would be no snow so long as their rites continued.

An Indian called Little had been guilty of some minor offense on the reservation and had hitherto evaded arrest. Suddenly he appeared at the agency on an issue day, for the express purpose, as it seemed, of defying the authorities. The assembly room of the Indian police, used also as a council room, opened out of my dispensary, and on this particular morning a council was in progress. I heard some loud talking, but was too busy to pay particular attention, though my assistant had gone in to listen to the speeches. Suddenly the place was in an uproar, and George burst into the inner office, crying excitedly "Look out for yourself, friend! They are going to fight!"

I went around to see what was going on. A crowd had gathered just outside the council room, and the police were surrounded by wild Indians with guns and drawn knives in their hands. "Hurry up with them!" one shouted, while another held his stone war-club over a policeman's head. The attempt to arrest Little had met with a stubborn resistance.

At this critical moment, a fine-looking Indian in citizen's clothes faced the excited throng, and spoke in a clear, steady, almost sarcastic voice.

"Stop! Think! What are you going to do? Kill these men of our own race? Then what? Kill all these helpless white men, women and children? And what then? What will these brave words, brave deeds lead to in the end? How long can you hold out? Your country is surrounded with a network of railroads; thousands of white soldiers will be here within three days. What ammunition have you? what provisions? What will become of your families? Think, think, my brothers! this is a child's madness."

It was the "friendly" chief, American Horse, and it seems to me as I recall the incident that this man's voice had almost magic power. It is likely that he saved us all from massacre, for the murder of the police, who represented the authority of the Government, would surely have been followed by a general massacre. It is a fact that those Indians who upheld the agent were in quite as much danger from their wilder brethren as were the whites, indeed it was said that the feeling against them was even stronger. Jack Red Cloud, son of the chief, thrust the muzzle of a cocked revolver almost into the face of American Horse. "It is you and your kind," he shouted, "who have brought us to this pass!" That brave man never flinched. Ignoring his rash accuser, he quietly reëntered the office; the door closed behind him; the mob dispersed, and for the moment the danger seemed over.

That evening I was surprised by a late call from American Horse, the hero of the day. His wife entered close behind him. Scarcely were they seated when my door again opened softly, and Captain Sword came in, followed by Lieutenant Thunder Bear and most of the Indian police. My little room was crowded. I handed them some tobacco, which I had always at hand for my guests, although I did not smoke myself. After a silence, the chief got up and shook hands with me ceremoniously. In a short speech, he asked my advice in the difficult situation that confronted them between the ghost dancers, men of their own blood, and the Government to which they had pledged their loyalty.

Thanks to Indian etiquette, I could allow myself two or three minutes to weigh my words before replying. I finally said, in substance: "There is only one thing for us to do and be just to both sides. We must use every means for a peaceful settlement of this difficulty. Let us be patient; let us continue to reason with the wilder element, even though some hotheads may threaten our lives. If the worst happens, however, it is our solemn duty to serve the United States Government. Let no man ever say that we were disloyal! Following such a policy, dead or alive, we shall have no apology to make."

After the others had withdrawn, Sword informed me confidentially that certain young men had threatened to kill American Horse while asleep in his tent, and that his friends had prevailed upon him and his wife to ask my hospitality for a few days. I showed Mrs. American Horse to a small room that I had vacant, and soon afterward came three strokes of the office bell—the signal for me to report at the agent's office.

I found there the agent, his chief clerk, and a visiting inspector, all of whom obviously regarded the situation as serious. "You see, doctor," said the agent, "the occurrence of to-day was planned with remarkable accuracy, so that even our alert police were taken entirely by surprise and readily overpowered. What will be the sequel we can not tell, but we must be prepared for anything. I shall be glad to have your views," he added.

I told him that I still did not believe there was any widespread plot, or deliberate intention to make war upon the whites. In my own mind, I felt sure that the arrival of troops would be construed by the ghost dancers as a threat or a challenge, and would put them at once on the defensive. I was not in favor of that step; neither was Mr. Cook, who was also called into conference; but the officials evidently feared a general uprising, and argued that it was their duty to safeguard the lives of the employees and others by calling for the soldiers without more delay. Sword, Thunder Bear, and American Horse were sent for and their opinions appeared to be fully in accord with those of the agent and inspector, so the matter was given out as settled. As a matter of fact, the agent had telegraphed to Fort Robinson for troops before he made a pretense of consulting us Indians, and they were already on their way to Pine Ridge.

I scarcely knew at the time, but gradually learned afterward, that the Sioux had many grievances and causes for profound discontent, which lay back of and were more or less closely related to the ghost dance craze and the prevailing restlessness and excitement. Rations had been cut from time to time; the people were insufficiently fed, and their protests and appeals were disregarded. Never was more ruthless fraud and graft practiced upon a defenseless people than upon these poor natives by the politicians! Never were there more worthless "scraps of paper" anywhere in the world than many of the Indian treaties and Government documents! Sickness was prevalent and the death rate alarming, especially among the children. Trouble from all these causes had for some time been developing, but might have been checked by humane and conciliatory measures. The "Messiah craze" in itself was scarcely a source of danger, and one might almost as well call upon the army to suppress Billy Sunday and his hysterical followers. Other tribes than the Sioux who adopted the new religion were let alone, and the craze died a natural death in the course of a few months.

Among the leaders of the malcontents at this time were Jack Red Cloud, No Water, He Dog, Four Bears, Yellow Bear, and Kicking Bear. Friendly leaders included American Horse, Young Man Afraid of His Horses, Bad Wound, Three Stars. There was still another set whose attitude was not clearly defined, and among these men was Red Cloud, the greatest of them all. He who had led his people so brilliantly and with such remarkable results, both in battle and diplomacy, was now an old man of over seventy years, living in a frame house which had been built for him within a half mile of the agency. He would come to council, but said little or nothing. No one knew exactly where he stood, but it seemed that he was broken in spirit as in body and convinced of the hopelessness of his people's cause.

It was Red Cloud who asked the historic question, at a great council held in the Black Hills region with a Government commission, and after good Bishop Whipple had finished the invocation, "Which God is our brother praying to now? Is it the same God whom they have twice deceived, when they made treaties with us which they afterward broke?"

Early in the morning after the attempted arrest of Little, George rushed into my quarters and awakened me. "Come quick!" he shouted, "the soldiers are here!" I looked along the White Clay creek toward the little railroad town of Rushville, Nebraska, twenty-five miles away, and just as the sun rose above the knife-edged ridges black with stunted pine, I perceived a moving cloud of dust that marked the trail of the Ninth Cavalry. There was instant commotion among the camps of friendly Indians. Many women and children were coming in to the agency for refuge, evidently fearing that the dreaded soldiers might attack their villages by mistake. Some who had not heard of their impending arrival hurried to the offices to ask what it meant. I assured those who appealed to me that the troops were here only to preserve order, but their suspicions were not easily allayed.

As the cavalry came nearer, we saw that they were colored troopers, wearing buffalo overcoats and muskrat caps; the Indians with their quick wit called them "buffalo soldiers." They halted, and established their temporary camp in the open space before the agency enclosure. The news had already gone out through the length and breadth of the reservation, and the wildest rumors were in circulation. Indian scouts might be seen upon every hill top, closely watching the military encampment.

At this juncture came the startling news from Fort Yates, some two hundred and fifty miles to the north of us, that Sitting Bull had been killed by Indian police while resisting arrest, and a number of his men with him, as well as several of the police. We next heard that the remnant of his band had fled in our direction, and soon afterward, that they had been joined by Big Foot's band from the western part of Cheyenne River agency, which lay directly in their road. United States troops continued to gather at strategic points, and of course the press seized upon the opportunity to enlarge upon the strained situation and predict an "Indian uprising." The reporters were among us, and managed to secure much "news" that no one else ever heard of. Border towns were fortified and cowboys and militia gathered in readiness to protect them against the "red devils." Certain classes of the frontier population industriously fomented the excitement for what there was in it for them, since much money is apt to be spent at such times. As for the poor Indians, they were quite as badly scared as the whites and perhaps with more reason.

General Brooke undertook negotiations with the ghost dancers, and finally induced them to come within reach. They camped on a flat about a mile north of us and in full view, while the more tractable bands were still gathered on the south and west. The large boarding school had locked its doors and succeeded in holding its hundreds of Indian children, partly for their own sakes, and partly as hostages for the good behavior of their fathers. At the agency were now gathered all the government employees and their families, except such as had taken flight, together with traders, missionaries, and ranchmen, army officers, and newspaper men. It was a conglomerate population.

During this time of grave anxiety and nervous tension, the cooler heads among us went about our business, and still refused to believe in the tragic possibility of an Indian war. It may be imagined that I was more than busy, though I had not such long distances to cover, for since many Indians accustomed to comfortable log houses were compelled to pass the winter in tents, there was even more sickness than usual. I had access and welcome to the camps of all the various groups and factions, a privilege shared by my good friend Father Jutz, the Catholic missionary, who was completely trusted by his people.

The Christmas season was fast approaching, and this is perhaps the brightest spot in the mission year. The children of the Sunday Schools, and indeed all the people, look eagerly forward to the joyous feast; barrels and boxes are received and opened, candy bags made and filled, carols practiced, and churches decorated with ropes of spicy evergreen.

Anxious to relieve the tension in every way within his power, Mr. Cook and his helpers went on with their preparations upon even a larger scale than usual. Since all of the branch stations had been closed and the people called in, it was planned to keep the Christmas tree standing in the chapel for a week, and to distribute gifts to a separate congregation each evening. I found myself pressed into the service, and passed some happy hours in the rectory. For me, at that critical time, there was inward struggle as well as the threat of outward conflict, and I could not but recall what my "white mother" had said jokingly one day, referring to my pleasant friendships with many charming Boston girls, "I know one Sioux who has not been conquered, and I shall not rest till I hear of his capture!"

I had planned to enter upon my life work unhampered by any other ties, and declared that all my love should be vested in my people and my profession. At last, however, I had met a woman whose sincerity was convincing and whose ideals seemed very like my own. Her childhood had been spent almost as much out of doors as mine, on a lonely estate high up in the Berkshire hills; her ancestry Puritan on one side, proud Tories on the other. She had been moved by the appeals of that wonderful man, General Armstrong, and had gone to Hampton as a young girl to teach the Indians there. After three years, she undertook pioneer work in the West as teacher of a new camp school among the wilder Sioux, and after much travel and study of their peculiar problems had been offered the appointment she now held. She spoke the Sioux language fluently and went among the people with the utmost freedom and confidence. Her methods of work were very simple and direct. I do not know what unseen hand had guided me to her side, but on Christmas day of 1890, Elaine Goodale and I announced our engagement.

Three days later, we learned that Big Foot's band of ghost dancers from the Cheyenne river reservation north of us was approaching the agency, and that Major Whiteside was in command of troops with orders to intercept them.

Late that afternoon, the Seventh Cavalry under Colonel Forsythe was called to the saddle and rode off toward Wounded Knee creek, eighteen miles away. Father Craft, a Catholic priest with some Indian blood, who knew Sitting Bull and his people, followed an hour or so later, and I was much inclined to go too, but my fiancée pointed out that my duty lay rather at home with our Indians, and I stayed.

The morning of December 29th was sunny and pleasant. We were all straining our ears toward Wounded Knee, and about the middle of the forenoon we distinctly heard the reports of the Hotchkiss guns. Two hours later, a rider was seen approaching at full speed, and in a few minutes he had dismounted from his exhausted horse and handed his message to General Brooke's orderly. The Indians were watching their own messenger, who ran on foot along the northern ridges and carried the news to the so-called "hostile" camp. It was said that he delivered his message at almost the same time as the mounted officer.

The resulting confusion and excitement was unmistakable. The white teepees disappeared as if by magic and soon the caravans were in motion, going toward the natural fortress of the "Bad Lands." In the "friendly" camp there was almost as much turmoil, and crowds of frightened women and children poured into the agency. Big Foot's band had been wiped out by the troops, and reprisals were naturally looked for. The enclosure was not barricaded in any way and we had but a small detachment of troops for our protection. Sentinels were placed, and machine guns trained on the various approaches.

A few hot-headed young braves fired on the sentinels and wounded two of them. The Indian police began to answer by shooting at several braves who were apparently about to set fire to some of the outlying buildings. Every married employee was seeking a place of safety for his family, the interpreter among them. Just then General Brooke ran out into the open, shouting at the top of his voice to the police: "Stop, stop! Doctor, tell them they must not fire until ordered!" I did so, as the bullets whistled by us, and the General's coolness perhaps saved all our lives, for we were in no position to repel a large attacking force. Since we did not reply, the scattered shots soon ceased, but the situation remained critical for several days and nights.

My office was full of refugees. I called one of my good friends aside and asked him to saddle my two horses and stay by them. "When general fighting begins, take them to Miss Goodale and see her to the railroad if you can," I told him. Then I went over to the rectory. Mrs. Cook refused to go without her husband, and Miss Goodale would not leave while there was a chance of being of service. The house was crowded with terrified people, most of them Christian Indians, whom our friends were doing their best to pacify.

At dusk, the Seventh Cavalry returned with their twenty-five dead and I believe thirty-four wounded, most of them by their own comrades, who had encircled the Indians, while few of the latter had guns. A majority of the thirty or more Indian wounded were women and children, including babies in arms. As there were not tents enough for all, Mr. Cook offered us the mission chapel, in which the Christmas tree still stood, for a temporary hospital. We tore out the pews and covered the floor with hay and quilts. There we laid the poor creatures side by side in rows, and the night was devoted to caring for them as best we could. Many were frightfully torn by pieces of shells, and the suffering was terrible. General Brooke placed me in charge and I had to do nearly all the work, for although the army surgeons were more than ready to help as soon as their own men had been cared for, the tortured Indians would scarcely allow a man in uniform to touch them. Mrs. Cook, Miss Goodale, and several of Mr. Cook's Indian helpers acted as volunteer nurses. In spite of all our efforts, we lost the greater part of them, but a few recovered, including several children who had lost all their relatives and who were adopted into kind Christian families.

On the day following the Wounded Knee massacre there was a blizzard, in the midst of which I was ordered out with several Indian police, to look for a policeman who was reported to have been wounded and left some two miles from the agency. We did not find him. This was the only time during the whole affair that I carried a weapon; a friend lent me a revolver which I put in my overcoat pocket, and it was lost on the ride. On the third day it cleared, and the ground was covered with an inch or two of fresh snow. We had feared that some of the Indian wounded might have been left on the field, and a number of us volunteered to go and see. I was placed in charge of the expedition of about a hundred civilians, ten or fifteen of whom were white men. We were supplied with wagons in which to convey any whom we might find still alive. Of course a photographer and several reporters were of the party.

Fully three miles from the scene of the massacre we found the body of a woman completely covered with a blanket of snow, and from this point on we found them scattered along as they had been relentlessly hunted down and slaughtered while fleeing for their lives. Some of our people discovered relatives or friends among the dead, and there was much wailing and mourning. When we reached the spot where the Indian camp had stood, among the fragments of burned tents and other belongings we saw the frozen bodies lying close together or piled one upon another. I counted eighty bodies of men who had been in the council and who were almost as helpless as the women and babes when the deadly fire began, for nearly all their guns had been taken from them. A reckless and desperate young Indian fired the first shot when the search for weapons was well under way, and immediately the troops opened fire from all sides, killing not only unarmed men, women, and children, but their own comrades who stood opposite them, for the camp was entirely surrounded.

It took all of my nerve to keep my composure in the face of this spectacle, and of the excitement and grief of my Indian companions, nearly every one of whom was crying aloud or singing his death song. The white men became very nervous, but I set them to examining and uncovering every body to see if one were living. Although they had been lying untended in the snow and cold for two days and nights, a number had survived. Among them I found a baby of about a year old warmly wrapped and entirely unhurt. I brought her in, and she was afterward adopted and educated by an army officer. One man who was severely wounded begged me to fill his pipe. When we brought him into the chapel he was welcomed by his wife and daughters with cries of joy, but he died a day or two later.

Under a wagon I discovered an old woman, totally blind and entirely helpless. A few had managed to crawl away to some place of shelter, and we found in a log store near by several who were badly hurt and others who had died after reaching there. After we had dispatched several wagon loads to the agency, we observed groups of warriors watching us from adjacent buttes; probably friends of the victims who had come there for the same purpose as ourselves. A majority of our party, fearing an attack, insisted that some one ride back to the agency for an escort of soldiers, and as mine was the best horse, it fell to me to go. I covered the eighteen miles in quick time and was not interfered with in any way, although if the Indians had meant mischief they could easily have picked me off from any of the ravines and gulches.

All this was a severe ordeal for one who had so lately put all his faith in the Christian love and lofty ideals of the white man. Yet I passed no hasty judgment, and was thankful that I might be of some service and relieve even a small part of the suffering. An appeal published in a Boston paper brought us liberal supplies of much needed clothing, and linen for dressings. We worked on. Bishop Hare of South Dakota visited us, and was overcome by faintness when he entered his mission chapel, thus transformed into a rude hospital.

After some days of extreme tension, and weeks of anxiety, the "hostiles," so called, were at last induced to come in and submit to a general disarmament. Father Jutz, the Catholic missionary, had gone bravely among them and used all his influence toward a peaceful settlement. The troops were all recalled and took part in a grand review before General Miles, no doubt intended to impress the Indians with their superior force.

In March, all being quiet, Miss Goodale decided to send in her resignation and go East to visit her relatives, and our wedding day was set for the following June.

Paula Gunn Allen (Laguna Pueblo, Sioux)

The Sacred Hoop
A Contemporary Perspective

Literature is one facet of a culture. The significance of a literature can be best understood in terms of the culture from which it springs, and the purpose of literature is clear only when the reader understands and accepts the assumptions on which the literature is based. A person who was raised in a given culture has no problem seeing the relevance, the level of complexity, or the symbolic significance of that culture's literature. We are all from early childhood familiar with the assumptions that underlie our own culture and its literature and art. Intelligent analysis becomes a matter of identifying smaller assumptions peculiar to the locale, idiom, and psyche of the writer.

The study of non-Western literature poses a problem for Western readers, who naturally tend to see alien literature in terms that are familiar to them, however irrelevant those terms may be to the literature under consideration. Because of this, students of traditional American Indian literatures have applied the terms "primitive," "savage," "childlike," and "pagan" to these literatures. Perceiving only the most superficial aspects of American Indian literary traditions, Western scholars have labeled the whole body of these literatures "folklore," even though the term specifically applies only to those parts of the literatures that are the province of the general populace.

The great mythic[1] and ceremonial cycles of the American Indian peoples are neither primitive, in any meaningful sense of the word, nor necessarily the province of the folk; much of the literature, in fact, is known only to educated, specialized persons who are privy to the philosophical, mystical, and literary wealth of their own tribe.

Much of the literature that was in the keeping of such persons, engraved perfectly and completely in their memories, was not known to most other men and women. Because of this, much literature has been lost as the last initiates of particular tribes and societies within the tribes died, leaving no successors.

Most important, traditional American Indian literature is not similar to Western literature because the basic assumptions about the universe and,

---

[1]*Mythic:* 1. narratives that deal with metaphysical, spiritual, and cosmic occurrences that recount the spiritual past and the "mysteries" of the tribe; 2. sacred story. The *Word* in its cosmic, creative sense. This usage follows the literary meaning rather than the common or vernacular meaning of "fictive" or "not real narrative dealing with primitive, irrational explanations of the world." 3. translational.

therefore, the basic reality experienced by tribal peoples and by Western peoples are not the same, even at the level of folklore. This difference has confused non-Indian students for centuries. They have been unable or unwilling to accept this difference and to develop critical procedures to illuminate the materials without trivializing or otherwise invalidating them.

For example, American Indian and Western literary traditions differ greatly in the assumed purposes they serve. The purpose of traditional American Indian literature is never simply pure self-expression. The "private soul at any public wall" is a concept alien to American Indian thought. The tribes do not celebrate the individual's ability to feel emotion, for they assume that all people are able to do so. One's emotions are one's own; to suggest that others should imitate them is to impose on the personal integrity of others. The tribes seek—through song, ceremony, legend, sacred stories (myths), and tales—to embody, articulate, and share reality, to bring the isolated, private self into harmony and balance with this reality, to verbalize the sense of the majesty and reverent mystery of all things, and to actualize, in language, those truths that give to humanity its greatest significance and dignity. To a large extent, ceremonial literature serves to redirect private emotion and integrate the energy generated by emotion within a cosmic framework. The artistry of the tribes is married to the essence of language itself, for through language one can share one's singular being with that of the community and know within oneself the communal knowledge of the tribe. In this art, the greater self and all-that-is are blended into a balanced whole, and in this way the concept of being that is the fundamental and sacred spring of life is given voice and being for all. American Indian people do not content themselves with simple preachments of this truth, but through the sacred power of utterance they seek to shape and mold, to direct and determine, the forces that surround and govern human life and the related lives of all things.

An old Keres song says:

I add my breath to your breath
That our days may be long on the Earth
That the days of our people may be long
That we may be one person
That we may finish our roads together
May our mother bless you with life
May our Life Paths be fulfilled.

In this way one learns how to view oneself and one's tradition so as to approach both rightly. Breath is life, and the intermingling of breaths is the purpose of good living. This is in essence the great principle on which all productive living must rest, for relationships among all the beings of the universe must be fulfilled; in this way each individual life may also be fulfilled.

This idea is apparent in the Plains tribes' idea of a medicine wheel[2] or sacred hoop.[3] The concept is one of singular unity that is dynamic and encompassing, including all that is contained in its most essential aspect, that of life. In his introduction to Geronimo's autobiography, Frederick Turner III incorrectly characterizes the American Indian cultures as static.[4] Stasis is not characteristic of the American Indians' view of things. As any American Indian knows, all of life is living—that is, dynamic and aware, partaking as it does in the life of the All Spirit and contributing as it does to the continuing life of that same Great Mystery. The tribal systems are static in that all movement is related to all other movement—that is, harmonious and balanced or unified; they are not static in the sense that they do not allow or accept change. Even a cursory examination of tribal systems will show that all have undergone massive changes while retaining those characteristics of outlook and experience that are the bedrock of tribal life.[5] So the primary assumptions tribespeople make can be seen as static only in that these people acknowledge the essential harmony of all things and see all things as being of equal value in the scheme of things, denying the opposition, dualism, and isolation (separateness) that characterize non-Indian thought. Christians believe that God is separate from humanity and does as he wishes without the creative assistance of any of his creatures, while the non-Christian tribal person assumes a place in creation that is dynamic, creative, and responsive. Further, tribal people allow all animals, vegetables, and minerals (the entire biota, in short) the same or even greater privileges than humans. The Indian participates in destiny on all levels, including that of creation. Thus this passage from a Cheyenne tale in which Maheo, the All Spirit, creates out of the void four things—the water, the light, the sky-air, and the peoples of the water:

> "How beautiful their wings are in the light," Maheo said to his Power, as the birds wheeled and turned, and became living patterns against the sky.
>
> The loon was the first to drop back to the surface of the lake. "Maheo," he said, looking around, for he knew that Maheo was all about him, "You have made us sky and light to fly in, and you have made us water to swim in. It sounds ungrateful to want something else, yet still we do. When we are tired of swimming and tired of flying, we should like a dry solid place where we could walk and rest. Give us a place to build our nests, please, Maheo."

---

[2] Hyemehosts Storm, *Seven Arrows* (New York: Harper and Row, 1972), p. 4.

[3] John G. Neihardt, *Black Elk Speaks* (Lincoln: University of Nebraska Press, 1961), p. 35.

[4] Frederick Turner III, Introduction, *Geronimo: His Own Story,* by Geronimo, ed. S. M. Barrett (New York: Ballantine, 1978), p. 7.

[5] D'Arcy McNickle, *Native American Tribalism: Indian Survivals and Renewals* (New York: Oxford University Press, 1973), pp. 12–13.

"So be it," answered Maheo, "but to make such a place I must have your help, all of you. By myself, I have made four things. . . . Now I must have help if I am to create more, for my Power will only let me make four things by myself."[6]

In this passage we see that even the All Spirit, whose "being was a Universe,"[7] has limited power as well as a sense of proportion and respect for the powers of the creatures. Contrast this spirit with the Judeo-Christian God, who makes everything and tells everything how it may and may not function if it is to gain his respect and blessing and whose commandments make no allowance for change or circumstance. The American Indian universe is based on dynamic self-esteem, while the Christian universe is based primarily on a sense of separation and loss. For the American Indian, the ability of all creatures to share in the process of ongoing creation makes all things sacred.

In Paradise, God created a perfect environment for his creatures. He arranged it to their benefit, asking only that they forbear from eating the fruit of one particular tree. In essence, they were left with only one means of exercising their creative capacities and their ability to make their own decisions and choices. Essentially, they were thus prevented from exercising their intelligence while remaining loyal to the creator. To act in a way that was congruent with their natural curiosity and love of exploration and discovery, they were forced to disobey God and thus be exiled from the perfect place he had made for them. They were severely punished for exercising what we might call liberty—Eve more than Adam, for hers was the greater sin (or so the story goes):

And the Lord God commanded the man, saying, Of every tree of the garden thou mayest freely eat:

But of the tree of the knowledge of good and evil, thou shalt not eat: for in the day that thou eatest thereof thou shalt surely die. (Gen. 2:16–17)

The Cheyennes' creator is somewhat wiser. He gives his creatures needs so that they can exert their intelligence and knowledge to satisfy those needs by working together to solve common problems or attain common goals. Together Maheo, the creator, and the water beings create the earth, and with the aid of these beings, Maheo creates first man and first woman and the creatures and environment they will need to live good and satisfying lives. These creation stories demonstrate the basic ordering principles

---

[6]Alice Marriott and Carol K. Rachlin, *American Indian Mythology* (New York: New American Library, 1972), p. 39.

[7]Marriott and Rachlin, *American Indian Mythology,* p. 39.

of two different cultures. The Judeo-Christian view is hierarchical. God commands first; within the limits of those commands, man rules; woman is subject to man, as are all the creatures, for God has brought them to Adam for him to name (Gen. 2:18–24, 3:16). In this scheme, the one who is higher has the power to impose penalties or even to deny life to those who are lower:

> And the Lord God said, Behold, the man is become as one of us, to know good and evil; and now, lest he put forth his hand, and take also of the tree of life, and eat, and live for ever;
> Therefore, the Lord God sent him forth from the garden of Eden to till the ground from whence he was taken. (Gen. 3:22–23)

The sin Adam and Eve committed in the Garden of Eden was attempting to become knowledgeable. Their attempt opened the further possibility that, with knowledge, they might become immortal. This, apparently, was not acceptable, not because knowledge and immortality were sinful but because the possession of them by human beings would reorder the hierarchical principles on which the Judeo-Christian universe is posited. Those reared in a Christian society are inclined to perceive social relationships—and literary works—in this context; they order events and phenomena in hierarchical and dualistic terms. Those reared in traditional American Indian societies are inclined to relate events and experiences to one another. They do not organize perceptions or external events in terms of dualities or priorities. This egalitarianism is reflected in the structure of American Indian literature, which does not rely on conflict, crisis, and resolution for organization, nor does its merit depend on the parentage, education, or connections of the author. Rather, its significance is determined by its relation to creative empowerment, its reflection of tribal understandings, and its relation to the unitary nature of reality.

The way the loon prays in the Cheyenne creation story is indicative of that difference. The loon looks around him as he addresses Maheo, "for he knew that Maheo was all about him," just as earlier in the story the snow-goose addressed Maheo in these words: "I do not know where you are, but I know you must be everywhere."[8]

Another difference between these two ways of perceiving reality lies in the tendency of the American Indian to view space as spherical and time as cyclical, whereas the non-Indian tends to view space as linear and time as sequential. The circular concept requires all "points" that make up the sphere of being to have a significant identity and function, while the linear model assumes that some "points" are more significant than others. In the one, significance is a necessary factor of being in itself, whereas in the other,

---

[8]Natalie B. Curtis, *The Indians' Book: Songs and Legends of the American Indians* (New York: Dover, 1968), pp. 8, 7.

significance is a function of placement on an absolute scale that is fixed in time and space. In essence, what we have is a direct contradiction of Turner's notion about the American Indian universe versus that of the West: the Indian universe moves and breathes continuously, and the Western universe is fixed and static. The Christian attitude toward salvation reflects this basic stance: one can be "saved" only if one believes in a Savior who appeared once and will not come again until "the end of time." The idea "once a saint, always a saint" is another expression of the same underlying perception and experience.

The notion that nature is somewhere over there while humanity is over here or that a great hierarchical ladder of being exists on which ground and trees occupy a very low rung, animals a slightly higher one, and man (never woman)—especially "civilized" man—a very high one indeed is antithetical to tribal thought. The American Indian sees all creatures as relatives (and in tribal systems relationship is central), as offspring of the Great Mystery, as cocreators, as children of our mother, and as necessary parts of an ordered, balanced, and living whole. This concept applies to what non-Indian Americans think of as the supernatural, and it applies as well to the more tangible (phenomenal) aspects of the universe. American Indian thought makes no such dualistic division, nor does it draw a hard and fast line between what is material and what is spiritual, for it regards the two as different expressions of the same reality, as though life has twin manifestations that are mutually interchangeable and, in many instances, virtually identical aspects of a reality that is essentially more spirit than matter or, more correctly, that manifests its spirit in a tangible way. The closest analogy in Western thought is the Einsteinian understanding of matter as a special state or condition of energy. Yet even this concept falls short of the American Indian understanding, for Einsteinian energy is believed to be unintelligent, while energy according to the Indian view is intelligence manifested in yet another way.

Many non-Indians believe that human beings possess the only intelligence in phenomenal existence (often in any form of existence). The more abstractionist and less intellectually vain Indian sees human intelligence as rising out of the very nature of being, which is of necessity intelligent in and of itself, as an attribute of being. Again, this idea probably stems from the Indian concept of a circular, dynamic universe in which all things are related and are of one family. It follows that those attributes possessed by human beings are natural attributes of *all* being. The Indian does not regard awareness of being as an abnormality peculiar to one species, but, because of a sense of relatedness to (instead of isolation from) what exists, the Indian assumes that this awareness is a natural by-product of existence itself.

In English, one can divide the universe into two parts: the natural and the supernatural. Humanity has no real part in either, being neither animal nor spirit—that is, the supernatural is discussed as though it were apart from people, and the natural as though people were apart from it. This necessarily forces English-speaking people into a position of alienation from the world they live in. Such isolation is entirely foreign to American Indian thought. At base, every story, every song, every ceremony tells the Indian that each creature is part of a living whole and that all parts of that whole are related to one another by virtue of their participation in the whole of being.

In American Indian thought, God is known as the All Spirit, and other beings are also spirit—more spirit than body, more spirit than intellect, more spirit than mind. The natural state of existence is whole. Thus healing chants and ceremonies emphasize restoration of wholeness, for disease is a condition of division and separation from the harmony of the whole. Beauty is wholeness. Health is wholeness. Goodness is wholeness. The Hopi refer to a witch—a person who uses the powers of the universe in a perverse or inharmonious way—as a two-hearts, one who is not whole but is split in two at the center of being. The circle of being is not physical, but it is dynamic and alive. It is what lives and moves and knows, and all the life forms we recognize—animals, plants, rocks, winds—partake of this greater life. Acknowledgment of this dynamic unity allows healing chants such as this from the Night Chant to heal (make a person whole again):

Happily I recover.
Happily my interior becomes cool.
Happily I go forth.
My interior feeling cool, may I walk.
No longer sore, may I walk.
As it used to be long ago, may I walk.
Happily, with abundant dark clouds, may I walk.
Happily, with abundant showers, may I walk.
Happily, with abundant plants, may I walk.
Happily, on a trail of pollen, may I walk.
Happily, may I walk.[9]

Because of the basic assumption of the wholeness or unity of the universe, our natural and necessary relationship to all life is evident; all phenomena we witness within or "outside" ourselves are, like us, intelligent manifestations of the intelligent universe from which they arise, as do all things of earth and the cosmos beyond. Thunder and rain are specialized aspects of this universe, as is the human race. Consequently, the unity of the whole is preserved and reflected in language, literature, and thought, and arbitrary divisions of the universe into "divine" and "worldly" or "natural" and "unnatural" beings do not occur.

Literature takes on more meaning when considered in terms of some relevant whole (like life itself), so let us consider some relationships be-

---

[9]From a prayer of the Night Chant of the Navajo people.

tween specific American Indian literary forms and the symbols usually found in them. The two forms basic to American Indian literature are the ceremony and the myth. The ceremony is the ritual enactment of a specialized perception of a cosmic relationship, while the myth is a prose record of that relationship. Thus, the wiwanyag wachipi (sun dance) is the ritual enactment of the relationship the Plains people see between consecration of the human spirit and Wakan Tanka as manifested as Sun, or Light, and Life-Bestower. Through purification, participation, sacrifice, and supplication, the participants act as instruments or transmitters of increased power and wholeness, which bestows health and prosperity, from Wakan Tanka.

The formal structure of a ceremony is as holistic as the universe it purports to reflect and respond to, for the ceremony contains other forms such as incantation, song (dance), and prayer, and it is itself the central mode of literary expression from which all allied songs and stories derive. The Lakota view all the ceremonies as related to one another in various explicit and implicit ways, as though each were one face of a multifaceted prism. This interlocking of the basic forms has led to much confusion among non-Indian collectors and commentators, and this complexity makes all simplistic treatments of American Indian literature more confusing than helpful. Indeed, the non-Indian tendency to separate things from one another—be they literary forms, species, or persons—causes a great deal of unnecessary difficulty with and misinterpretation of American Indian life and culture. It is reasonable, from an Indian point of view, that all literary forms should be interrelated, given the basic idea of the unity and relatedness of all the phenomena of life. Separation of parts into this or that category is not agreeable to American Indians, and the attempt to separate essentially unified phenomena results in distortion.

For example, to say that a ceremony contains songs and prayers is misleading, for prayers are one form of address and songs are another. It is more appropriate to say that songs, prayers, dances, drums, ritual movements, and dramatic address are compositional elements of a ceremony. It is equally misleading to single out the wiwanyag wachipi and treat it as an isolated ceremony, for it must of necessity include the inipi (rite of purification) and did at one time contain the hanblecheyapi (vision quest), which was how the Lakota learned about it in the first place.[10] Actually, it might best be seen as a communal vision quest.

The purpose of a ceremony is to integrate: to fuse the individual with his or her fellows, the community of people with that of the other kingdoms, and this larger communal group with the worlds beyond this one. A raising or expansion of individual consciousness naturally accompanies this

---

[10]I am making this inference from the account of the appearance of White Buffalo Cow Woman to Kablaya as recounted by Black Elk in *The Sacred Pipe: Black Elk's Account of the Seven Rites of the Oglala Sioux,* ed. Joseph Eyes Brown (Baltimore: Penguin, 1971), pp. 67–100.

process. The person sheds the isolated, individual personality and is restored to conscious harmony with the universe. In addition to this general purpose, each ceremony has its own specific purpose. This purpose usually varies from tribe to tribe and may be culture-specific. For example, the rain dances of the Southwest are peculiar to certain groups, such as the Pueblos, and are not found among some other tribes, while war ceremonies, which make up a large part of certain Plains tribes' ceremonial life, are unknown among many tribes in California.[11] But all ceremonies, whether for war or healing, create and support the sense of community that is the bedrock of tribal life. This community is not made up only of members of the tribe but necessarily includes all beings that inhabit the tribe's universe.

Within this context the dynamic characteristics of American Indian literature can best be understood. The structures that embody expressed and implied relationships between human and nonhuman beings, as well as the symbols that signify and articulate them, are designed to integrate the various orders of consciousness. Entities other than the human participants are present at ceremonial enactments, and the ceremony is composed for their participation as well as for that of the human beings who are there. Some tribes understand that the human participants include members of the tribe who are not physically present and that the community as a community, not simply the separate persons in attendance, enact the ceremony.

Thus devices such as repetition and lengthy passages of "meaningless" syllables take on significance within the context of the dance. Repetition has an entrancing effect. Its regular recurrence creates a state of consciousness best described as "oceanic," but without the hypersentimental side effects implied by that term. It is hypnotic, and a hypnotic state of consciousness is the aim of the ceremony. The participants' attention must become diffused. The distractions of ordinary life must be put to rest and emotions redirected and integrated into a ceremonial context so that the greater awareness can come into full consciousness and functioning. In this way the participants become literally one with the universe, for they lose consciousness of mere individuality and share the consciousness that characterizes most orders of being.

In some sense repetition operates like the chorus in Western drama, serving to reinforce the theme and to focus the participants' attention on central concerns while intensifying their involvement with the enactment. One suits one's words and movements (if one is a dancer) to the repetitive pattern. Soon breath, heartbeat, thought, emotion, and word are one. The repetition integrates or fuses, allowing thought and word to coalesce into one rhythmic whole, which is not as jarring to the ear as rhyme.

Margot Astrov suggests that this characteristic device stems from two sources, one psychic and one magical:

---

[11]T. Kroeber and Robert F. Heizer, *Almost Ancestors: The First Californians,* ed. F. David Hales (San Francisco: Sierra Club, 1968), pp. 28–30.

. . . this drive that forces man to express himself in rhythmic patterns has its ultimate source in psychic needs, for example the need of spiritual ingestion and proper organization of all the multiform perceptions and impressions rushing forever upon the individual from without and within. . . . Furthermore, repetition, verbal and otherwise, means accumulation of power.[12]

Astrov finds evidence that the first, the need to organize perception, predominates in the ceremonies of some tribes, such as the Apaches, and that the second, a "magically creative quality," is more characteristic of others, such as the Navajo. In other words, some tribes appear to stress form while others stress content, but either way a tribe will make its selection in terms of which emphasis is most likely to bring about fusion with the cosmic whole in its group and environment. This fusion depends on the emphasis that is most congenial to the aesthetic and psychic sense of the tribe.

One should remember, when considering rhythmic aspects of American Indian poetic forms, that all ceremony is chanted, drummed, and danced. American Indians often refer to a piece of music as a dance instead of a song because song without dance is very rare, as is song without the use of a drum or other percussion instrument. One must also note that the drum does not "accompany" the song, for that implies separation between instrument and voice where no separation is recognized. Words, structure, music, movement, and drum combine to form an integral whole, and accompaniment per se is foreign to the ceremony, though it is common in Western music. The ceremony may be enacted before people who are neither singing nor dancing, but their participation is nevertheless assumed. Participation is a matter of attention and attunement, not of activity.

Repetition is of two kinds, incremental and simple. In the first, variations will occur. A stanza may be repeated in its entirety four times—once for each of the directions—or six times—once for each lateral direction plus above and below—or seven times—once for each direction plus the center "where we stand." Alternatively, the repetition may be of a phrase only, as in the Yei be chi, or of a phrase repeated four times with one word—the ceremonial name for each of four mountains, say, or the names of significant colors, animals, or powers—inserted in the appropriate place at each repetition, as in this Navajo Mountain Chant:

Seated at home behold me,
Seated amid the rainbow;
Seated at home behold me,

---

[12]Margot Astrov, *American Indian Prose and Poetry* (New York: Capricorn, 1962), p. 12.

Lo, here, the Holy Place!
    Yea, seated at home behold me.
At Sisnajinni, and beyond it,
    Yea, seated at home behold me;
The Chief of Mountains, and beyond it,
    Yea, seated at home behold me;
In Life Unending, and beyond it,
    Yea, seated at home behold me;
In Joy Unchanging, and beyond it,
    Yea, seated at home behold me.

Seated at home behold me,
Seated amid the rainbow;
Seated at home behold me,
Lo, here, the Holy Place!
    Yea, seated at home behold me.
At Tsodschl, and beyond it,
    Yea, seated at home behold me;
The Chief of Mountains, and beyond it,
    Yea, seated at home behold me;
In Life Unending, and beyond it,
    Yea, seated at home behold me;
In Joy Unchanging, and beyond it,
    Yea, seated at home behold me.

Seated at home behold me,
Seated amid the rainbow;
Seated at home behold me,
Lo, here, the Holy Place!
    Yea, seated at home behold me.
At Doko-oslid, and beyond it,
    Yea, seated at home behold me;
The Chief of Mountains, and beyond it,
    Yea, seated at home behold me;
In Life Unending, and beyond it,
    Yea, seated at home behold me;
In Joy Unchanging, and beyond it,
    Yea, seated at home behold me.

Seated at home behold me,
Seated amid the rainbow;
Seated at home behold me,
Lo, here, the Holy Place!
    Yea, seated at home behold me.
At Depenitsa, and beyond it,
    Yea, seated at home behold me;

The Chief of Mountains, and beyond it,
    Yea, seated at home behold me;
In Life Unending, and beyond it,
    Yea, seated at home behold me;
In Joy Unchanging, and beyond it,
    Yea, seated at home behold me.[13]

Some critics have said that this device results from the oral nature of American Indian literature, that repetition ensures attention and makes the works easy to remember. If this is a factor at all, however, it is a peripheral one, for nonliterate people have more finely developed memories than do literate people. The child learns early to remember complicated instructions, long stories—often verbatim—multitudes of details about plants, animals, kinship and other social relationships, privileges, and responsibilities, all "by heart." For a person who can't run to a bookshelf or a notebook to look up either vital or trivial information, reliance on memory becomes very important in everyday life. This highly developed everyday memory is not likely to fail on ceremonial occasions, so the use of repetition for ease of memorization is not significant.

Astrov, in her discussion of the "psychic" basis of the device, touches on another reason folklorists give for the widespread use of repetition in oral ceremonial literature:

> A child repeats a statement over and over for two reasons. First, in order to make himself familiar with something that appears to him to be threateningly unknown and thus to organize it into his system of familiar phenomena; and, second, to get something he wants badly.[14]

Astrov implies that repetition is childish on two counts: that it (rather than rational thought) familiarizes and defuses threat and that the person, irrationally, believes that oral repetition of a desire will ensure its gratification. Let us ignore the obvious fact that shamans, dancers, and other adult participants in the ceremony are not children and concentrate on actual ceremonies to see whether they contain factors that are or might appear "threatening" to the tribe or whether they simply repeat wishes over and over. Nothing in the passages quoted so far could be construed as threatening, unless beauty, harmony, health, strength, rain, breath, life unending, or sacred mountains can be so seen. Nor are any threatening unknowns mentioned in the songs and chants Astrov includes in her collection; there are

---

[13]Curtis, *Indians' Book*, p. 356. I have reproduced this part of the chant in its entirety, although the Curtis version has only one stanza with a note regarding the proper form.

[14]Astrov, *American Indian Prose*, p. 12.

threats implicit in death or great powers, but while these constitute un-knowns to many civilized people, they are familiar to the tribes. And, by As-trov's own admission, the works approach death or severe illness in posi-tive ways, as in this death song:

> From the middle
> Of the great water
> I am called by the spirits.[15]

"Light as the last breath of the dying," she comments, "these words flutter out and seem to mingle with the soft fumes and mists that rise from the river in the morning"—hardly a threatening description. She continues:

> It is as though the song, with the lightness of a bird's feather, will carry the departing soul up to where the stars are glittering and yonder where the rain-bow touches the dome of the sky.[16]

Nowhere in her discussion of Indian songs does Astrov indicate that the singers feel threatened by the chants. Instead, she points out that they ex-press serenity and even joy in the face of what might seem frightening to a child. Nor do there appear any passages, in her extensive collection, that are the equivalent of "Lord, Won't You Buy Me a Color TV," and the absence of such material weakens the childhood-magic theory of repetition. In fact, the usual American Indian perception of humanity (collectively, not individu-ally) as cocreator discourages the people from perceiving the deity as a sort of cosmic bellhop who alone is responsible for their personal well-being. This perception simultaneously discourages people from setting themselves up as potentates, tyrants, dictators, or leaders of any other kind.

The failure of folklorists to comprehend the true metaphysical and psy-chic nature of structural devices such as ceremonial repetition is a result of the projection of one set of cultural assumptions onto another culture's cus-toms and literatures. People of the Western cultures, particularly those in professions noted for their "objectivity" and intellectual commitment to Freudian tenets, are likely not to interpret psychic components of ceremo-nial literature in its extramundane sense but rather in its more familiar psychological sense. The twin assumptions that repetition serves to quiet childish psychological needs and to assure participants in a ceremony that they are exerting control over external phenomena—getting something they want badly—are projections. The participants do indeed believe that they can exert control over natural phenomena, but not because they have child-

---

[15]Astrov, *American Indian Prose*, p. 50.

[16]Astrov, *American Indian Prose*, p. 50.

ishly repeated some syllables. Rather, they assume that all reality is internal in some sense, that the dichotomy of the isolate individual versus the "out there" only appears to exist, and that ceremonial observance can help them transcend this delusion and achieve union with the All Spirit. From a position of unity within this larger Self, the ceremony can bring about certain results, such as healing one who is ill, ensuring that natural events move in their accustomed way, or bringing prosperity to the tribe.

The Westerner's bias against nonordinary states of consciousness is as unthinking as the Indian's belief in them is said to be. The Westerner's bias is the result of an intellectual climate that has been carefully fostered in the West for centuries, that has reached its culmination in Freudian and Darwinian theories, and that only now is beginning to yield to the masses of data that contradict it. This cultural bias has had many unfortunate side effects, only one of which is deep misunderstanding of tribal literatures that has for so long marked the learned and popular periodicals that deal with tribal culture.

In his four-volume treatise on nonordinary reality, Carlos Castaneda has described what living in the universe as a shaman is like. Unfortunately, he does not indicate that this experience is rather more common to ordinary than to extraordinary people, that the state of consciousness created through ceremony and ritual and detailed in mythic cycles is exactly that of the "man of knowledge," or sage. He makes the whole thing sound exotic, strange, beyond the reach of most persons, yet the great body of American Indian literature suggests quite a different conclusion. This literature can best be approached as a psychic journey. Only in the context of the consciousness of the universe can it be understood.

American Indian thought is essentially mystical and psychic in nature. Its distinguishing characteristic is a kind of magicalness—not the childish sort described by Astrov but rather an enduring sense of the fluidity and malleability, or creative flux, of things. This is a reasonable attitude in its own context, derived quite logically from the central assumptions that characterize tribal thought. The tribal person perceives things not as inert but as viable and alive, and he or she knows that living things are subject to processes of growth and change as a necessary component of their aliveness. Since all that exists is alive and since all that is alive must grow and change, all existence can be manipulated under certain conditions and according to certain laws. These conditions and laws, called "ritual" or "magic" in the West, are known to American Indians variously. The Sioux refer to them as "walking in a sacred manner," the Navajo as "standing in the center of the world," and the Pomo as "having a tradition." There are as many ways of referring to this phenomenon as there are tribes.

The symbolism in American Indian ceremonial literature, then, is not symbolic in the usual sense; that is, the four mountains in the Mountain Chant do not stand for something else. They are those exact mountains perceived psychically, as it were, or mystically. The color red, as used by the

Lakota, doesn't stand for sacred or earth, but it is the quality of a being, the color of it, when perceived "in a sacred manner" or from the point of view of the earth itself. That is, red is a psychic quality, not a material one, though it has a material dimension, of course. But its material aspect is not its essential one. As the great metaphysician Madame Blavatsky put it, the physical is not a principle; or, as Lame Deer the Lakota shaman suggests, the physical aspect of existence is only representative of what is real:

> The meat stands for the four-legged creatures, our animal brothers, who gave of themselves so that we should live. The steam [from the stewpot] is living breath. It was water; now it goes up to the sky, becomes a cloud again. . . .
>
> We Sioux spend a lot of time thinking about everyday things, which in our mind are mixed up with the spiritual. We see in the world around us many symbols that teach us the meaning of life. We have a saying that the white man sees so little, he must see with only one eye. We see a lot that you no longer notice. You could notice if you wanted too, but you are usually too busy. We Indians live in a world of symbols and images where the spiritual and the commonplace are one. To you symbols are just words, spoken or written in a book. To us they are part of nature, part of ourselves, even little insects like ants and grasshoppers. We try to understand them not with the head but with the heart, and we need no more than a hint to give us the meaning.[17]

Not only are the "symbols" statements of perceived reality rather than metaphorical or poetic statements but the formulations that are characterized by brevity and repetition are also expressions of that perception. One sees life as part of oneself; a hint as to which particular part is all that is needed to convey meaning. This accounts for the "purity" and "simplicity" that apparently characterize traditional American Indian literatures. The works are simple in that they concern themselves with what is known and familiar, not in that they are childlike or unsophisticated.

In a sense, the American Indian perceives all that exists as symbolic. This outlook has given currency to the concept of the Indian as one who is close to the earth, but the closeness is actual, not a quaint result of savagism or childlike naiveté. An Indian, at the deepest level of being, assumes that the earth is alive in the same sense that human beings are alive. This aliveness is seen in nonphysical terms, in terms that are perhaps familiar to the mystic or the psychic, and this view gives rise to a metaphysical sense of reality that is an ineradicable part of Indian awareness. In brief, we can say that the sun or the earth or a tree is a symbol of an extraordinary truth.

This attitude is not anthropomorphic. No Indian would regard personal perception as the basic, or only, unit of universal consciousness. Indians believe that the basic unit of consciousness is the All Spirit, the living fact of intelligence from which all other perceptions arise and derive their power:

---

[17]John (Fire) Lame Deer and Richard Erdoes, *Lame Deer: Seeker of Visions* (New York: Touchstone, 1972), pp. 108–109.

I live, but I will not live forever.
Mysterious moon, you only remain,
Powerful sun, you alone remain,
Wonderful earth, you remain forever.
All of us soldiers must die.[18]

This attitude is not superstitious, though it can degenerate into super-
stition when the culture disintegrates. It is based very solidly on experience,
and most members of the tribe share that experience to some degree. The
experience is verified by hundreds and thousands of years of experience
and is a result of actual perception—sight, taste, hearing, smell—as well as
more indirect social and natural phenomena. In the West, if a person points
to a building and says, "There is a building," and if other people looking in
the direction indicated agree, and if that building can be entered, walked
through, touched, then the building is said to be really there.

In the same way, traditional American Indians encounter and verify
metaphysical reality. No one's experience is idiosyncratic. The singer who
tells of journeying to the west and climbing under the sky speaks of a journey that many have taken in the past and will take in the future. Every traveler will describe the same sights and sounds and will enter and return in
like fashion.

Generations of Western observers have noticed this peculiarity of psychic travel, and many attempt to explain it in psychoanalytic terms, referring
to Jung's "collective unconscious," for example, or to Freud's notion of the
projection of repressed conflict. Nevertheless, the evidence, however one
interprets it, suggests that the psychic life of all humanity is the same. Western sophisticates presume that the experiences—sights, sounds, and beings
encountered on psychic journeys—are imaginary and hallucinatory; they are
equally inclined to presume that thoughts are idiosyncratic events of no real
consequence. Nowhere in the literature on ceremonialism have I encountered a Western writer willing to suggest that the "spiritual and the commonplace are one."[19] Many argue that these "hallucinations" are good, others that they are the product of diseased minds,[20] but none suggests that one
may *actually* be "seated amid the rainbow."

Symbols in American Indian systems are not symbolic in the usual sense
of the word. The words articulate reality—not "psychological" or imagined
reality, not emotive reality captured metaphorically in an attempt to fuse
thought and feeling, but that reality where thought and feeling are one,

---

[18]Crazy Dog Society song of the Kiowa people. This version appears in Alice Marriott, *Kiowa
Years: A Study in Culture Impact* (New York: Macmillan, 1968), p. 118.

[19]Lame Deer and Erdoes, *Lame Deer,* p. 115.

[20]Sigmund Freud, *Totem and Taboo,* trans. James Strachey (New York: Norton, 1952), p. 14.

where objective and subjective are one, where speaker and listener are one, where sound and sense are one.

The many kinds of American Indian literature can be categorized in various ways, but, given the assumptions behind the creation and performance of the literature, a useful division might be along functional lines rather than along more mechanical ones.

It might be said that the basic purpose of any culture is to maintain the ideal status quo. What creates differences among cultures and literatures is the way in which the people go about this task, and this in turn depends on, and simultaneously maintains, basic assumptions about the nature of life and humanity's place in it. The ideal status quo is generally expressed in terms of peace, prosperity, good health, and stability. Western cultures lean more and more heavily on technological and scientific methods of maintenance, while traditional cultures such as those of American Indian tribes tend toward mystical and philosophical methods. Because of this tendency, literature plays a central role in the traditional cultures that it is unable to play in technological ones. Thus, the purpose of a given work is of central importance to understanding its deeper significance.

We can divide traditional literature into two basic genres: ceremonial and popular, as opposed to the Western prose and poetry distinction. Ceremonial literature includes all literature that is accompanied by ritual actions and music and that produces mythic (metaphysical) states of consciousness and/or conditions. This literature may appear to the Westerner as either prose or poetry, but its distinguishing characteristic is that it is to some degree sacred. The word *sacred,* like the words *power* and *medicine,* has a very different meaning to tribal people than to members of technological societies. It does not signify something of religious significance and therefore believed in with emotional fervor—"venerable, consecrated, or sacrosanct," as the Random House dictionary has it—but something that it is filled with an intangible but very real power or force, for good or bad. Lame Deer says in his discussion of symbolism:

> *Four* is the number that is most wakan, most sacred. Four stands for Tatuye Tope—the four quarters of the earth. One of its chief symbols is Umane, which looks like this:

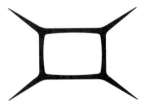

> It represents the unused earth force. By this I mean that the Great Spirit pours a great unimaginable amount of force into all things—pebbles, ants, leaves, whirlwinds—whatever you will. . . .

This force is symbolized by the Umane. In the old days men used to have an Umane altar made of raised earth in their tipis on certain special occasions. It was so *wakan* you couldn't touch it or even hold your hand over it.[21]

Lame Deer is not saying that one was forbidden to touch the altar; he is saying that one *could not* touch it. The Umane does not represent the power; it *is* the power. *Sacred, power,* and *medicine* are related terms. Having power means being able to use this extra force without being harmed by it. This is a particular talent that human beings possess to greater or lesser degree, and *medicine* is a term used for the personal force through which one possesses power. Medicine is powerful in itself, but its power can be used only by certain persons, under certain conditions, and for certain purposes.

Ceremonial literature is sacred; it has power. It frequently uses language of its own: archaisms, "meaningless" words, or special words that are not used in everyday conversation. It can be divided into several subcategories, some of which appear in some tribes but not in others, and others that can be found throughout Indian America. Ceremonial literature includes songs for many occasions: healing; initiation; planting, harvesting, and other agricultural pursuits; hunting; blessing new houses, journeys, and undertakings. There are also dream-related songs; war songs; personal power songs; songs for food preparation, purification, and vision seeking. The subjects of the major ceremonial cycles include origin and creation, migration, celebration of new laws, and commemoration of legendary or mythic occurrences. Each serves to hold the society together, create harmony, restore balance, ensure prosperity and unity, and establish right relations within the social and natural world. At base the ceremonials restore the psychic unity of the people, reaffirm the terms of their existence in the universe, and validate their sense of reality, order, and propriety. The most central of these perform this function at levels that are far more intense than others, and these great ceremonies, more than any single phenomenon, distinguish one tribe from another.

Every tribe has a responsibility to the workings of the universe; today as yesterday, human beings play an intrinsic role in the ongoing creation. This role is largely determined by the place where the tribe lives, and the role changes when the tribe moves. In the Southwest, for example, the Zuñi dance Shalako every winter at the solstice so that the sun will turn in its course and move once again toward summer. Cosmic cycles such as Shalako or Wúwuchim relate to life processes on earth and, by virtue of natural relationship, within the universe. They aim toward forces far bigger than the community or the individual, though each is inescapably dependent on the other— "circles within circles," as Lame Deer says, "with no beginning and no end."[22]

---

[21]Lame Deer and Erdoes, *Lame Deer,* p. 115.

[22]Lame Deer and Erdoes, *Lame Deer,* p. 112.

The greater and lesser symbols incorporated into the ceremonies take their meaning from the context of the ceremony—its purpose and its meaning. Attempts to understand ceremonial literature without knowledge of this purpose often have ludicrous results. The symbols cannot be understood in terms of another culture, whether it be that of Maya or of England, because those other cultures have different imperatives and have grown on different soil, under a different sky within the nexus of different spirits, and within a different traditional context. "Owl" in one situation will have a very different significance from "owl" in another, and a given color—white or blue—will vary from place to place and from ceremony to ceremony in its significance, intensity, and power. In other words, the rules that govern traditional American Indian literatures are very different from those that govern Western literature, though the enormity of the difference is, I think, a fairly recent development. Literature must, of necessity, express and articulate the deepest perceptions, relationships, and attitudes of a culture, whether it does so deliberately or accidentally. Tribal literature does this with a luminosity and clarity that are largely free of pretension, stylized "elegance," or show. Experiences that are held to be the most meaningful—from those that completely transcend ordinary experience to those that are commonplace—are celebrated in the songs and ceremonial cycles of the people.

The more commonplace experiences are celebrated in popular tales and songs, which may be humorous, soothing, pedagogical, or entertaining. In this category are lullabies, corn-grinding and ditch-digging songs, jokes, pourquoi tales, "little" stories, and stories with contemporary settings. Included here, too, are those delightful dances called '49s.[23] All but the '49s appear in collections of Indian lore, sometimes masquerading as true myths or simple songs. This masquerade, of course, does little to clear up misunderstandings regarding American Indian literature, for frequently those "myths" that seem childlike are forms developed for children and bear only a slight resemblance to the true mythic chants from which they derive.

Between the trivial, popular forms and the ceremonial works are songs and stories such as various games; incantations and other simple forms of magic; prose cycles such as the Trickster tales recorded by Paul Radin; and some journey- and food-related songs and legends.

Individual songs may be difficult to classify, though the level of symbolism they contain and the amount of prescribed ritual and associated ceremony, the number and special qualifications of the celebrants, and the physical setting and costume can help distinguish one kind from another. To

---

[23]'49 songs were sung (danced) just before a war party went out. They are widely enjoyed today after a powwow has officially ended after midnight. One '49 song goes like this:

> When the dance is ended sweetheart
> > I will take you home.
> > *He-ya he-he-ya*
> > *He-ya he-he-ya.*

classify any given song, though, one needs more than a nodding acquaintance with the locality and the tribe whose song or story is under consideration.

Another important factor to consider in classification of a song is the relative secrecy of parts or all of the ceremony, especially when tourists, cameras, or tape recorders are present. The amount of secrecy will vary to some extent from tribe to tribe, some being more open than others, but some secrecy is nearly always the rule.

Another such indicator, particularly valuable for classroom work, is the source of the song or story. Only very erudite tomes are likely to have much that is really sacred, and even those have usually been altered in some way. Popular books are likely to carry mainly popular literature, with a few selections from the next more powerful category. It would be well to mention, in this connection, that the use of really sacred materials by ordinary mortals and publishers is generally forbidden. Also, these works do not make good classroom materials for a variety of reasons: they are arcane; they are usually taboo; they tend to confuse non-Indian students; they may cause resentment among Indian students; and they create questions and digressions that are usually beyond the competence of the teacher or of the academic setting. Frequently they lead to ridicule, disrespect, and belittlement; non-Indian students are not inclined by training or culture to view the sacred as that which has power beyond that of economics, history, or politics.

Underlying all their complexity, traditional American Indian literatures possess a unity and harmony of symbol, structure, and articulation that is peculiar to the American Indian world. This harmony is based on the perceived harmony of the universe and on thousands of years of refinement. This essential sense of unity among all things flows like a clear stream through the songs and stories of the peoples of the Western hemisphere. This sense is embodied in the words of an old man:

> There are birds of many colors—red, blue, green, yellow—yet it is all one bird. There are horses of many colors—brown, black, yellow, white—yet it is all one horse. So cattle, so all living things—animals, flowers, trees. So men: in this land where once were only Indians are now men of every color—white, black, yellow, red—yet all one people. That this should come to pass was in the heart of the Great Mystery. It is right thus. And everywhere there shall be peace.[24]

So Hiamove said, more than fifty years ago. It remains for scholars of American Indian literature to look at this literature from the point of view of its people. Only from this vantage can we understand fully the richness, complexity, and true meaning of a people's life; only in this way can we all learn the lessons of the past on this continent and the essential lesson of respect for all that is.

---

[24]Curtis, *Indians' Book*, p. x.

N. Scott Momaday (Kiowa)

The Man Made of Words

I want to try to put several different ideas together this morning. And in the process, I hope to indicate something about the nature of the relationship between language and experience. It seems to me that in a certain sense we are all made of words; that our most essential being consists in language. It is the element in which we think and dream and act, in which we live our daily lives. There is no way in which we can exist apart from the morality of a verbal dimension.

In one of the discussions yesterday the question "What is an American Indian?" was raised.

The answer of course is that an Indian is an idea which a given man has of himself. And it is a moral idea, for it accounts for the way in which he reacts to other men and to the world in general. And that idea, in order to be realized completely, has to be expressed.

I want to say some things then about this moral and verbal dimension in which we live. I want to say something about such things as ecology and storytelling and the imagination. Let me tell you a story:

One night a strange thing happened. I had written the greater part of *The Way to Rainy Mountain*—all of it, in fact, except the epilogue. I had set down the last of the old Kiowa tales, and I had composed both the historical and the autobiographical commentaries for it. I had the sense of being out of breath, of having said what it was in me to say on that subject. The manuscript lay before me in the bright light. Small, to be sure, but complete, or nearly so. I had written the second of the two poems in which that book is framed. I had uttered the last word, as it were. And yet a whole, penultimate piece was missing. I began once again to write.

During the first hours after midnight on the morning of November 13, 1833, it seemed that the world was coming to an end. Suddenly the stillness of the night was broken; there were brilliant flashes of light in the sky, light of such intensity that people were awakened by it. With the speed and density of a driving rain, stars were falling in the universe. Some were brighter than Venus; one was said to be as large as the moon. I went on to say that that event, the falling of the stars on North America, that explosion of meteors which occurred 137 years ago, is among the earliest entries in the Kiowa calendars. So deeply impressed upon the imagination of the Kiowas is that old phenomenon that it is remembered still; it has become a part of the racial memory.

"The living memory," I wrote, "and the verbal tradition which transcends it, were brought together for me once and for all in the person of Ko-sahn." It seemed eminently right for me to deal, after all, with that old woman. Ko-sahn is among the most venerable people I have ever known.

She spoke and sang to me one summer afternoon in Oklahoma. It was like a dream. When I was born she was already old; she was a grown woman when my grandparents came into the world. She sat perfectly still, folded over on herself. It did not seem possible that so many years—a century of years—could be so compacted and distilled. Her voice shuddered, but it did not fail. Her songs were sad. An old whimsy, a delight in language and in remembrance, shone in her one good eye. She conjured up the past, imagining perfectly the long continuity of her being. She imagined the lovely young girl, wild and vital, she had been. She imagined the Sun Dance:

There was an old, old woman. She had something on her back. The boys went out to see. The old woman had a bag full of earth on her back. It was a certain kind of sandy earth. That is what they must have in the lodge. The dancers must dance upon the sandy earth. The old woman held a digging tool in her hand. She turned towards the south and pointed with her lips. It was like a kiss, and she began to sing:

We have brought the earth.
   Now it is time to play.

As old as I am, I still have the feeling of play. That was the beginning of the Sun Dance.

By this time I was back into the book, caught up completely in the act of writing. I had projected myself—imagined myself—out of the room and out of time. I was there with Ko-sahn in the Oklahoma July. We laughed easily together; I felt that I had known her all of my life—all of hers. I did not want to let her go. But I had come to the end. I set down, almost grudgingly, the last sentences:

It was—all of this and more—a quest, a going forth upon the way of Rainy Mountain. Probably Ko-sahn too is dead now. At times, in the quiet of evening, I think she must have wondered, dreaming, who she was. Was she become in her sleep that old purveyor of the sacred earth, perhaps, that ancient one who, old as she was, still had the feeling of play? And in her mind, at times, did she see the falling stars?

For some time I sat looking down at these words on the page, trying to deal with the emptiness that had come about inside of me. The words did not seem real. I could scarcely believe that they made sense, that they had anything whatsoever to do with meaning. In desperation almost, I went back over the final paragraphs, backwards and forwards, hurriedly. My eyes fell upon the name Ko-sahn. And all at once everything seemed suddenly to refer to that name. The name seemed to humanize the whole complexity of language. All at once, absolutely, I had the sense of the magic of words and of names. Ko-sahn, I said, and I said again KO-SAHN.

Then it was that that ancient, one-eyed woman Ko-sahn stepped out of the language and stood before me on the page. I was amazed. Yet it seemed entirely appropriate that this should happen.

"I was just now writing about you," I replied, stammering. "I thought—forgive me—I thought that perhaps you were . . . that you had . . ."

"No," she said. And she cackled, I thought. And she went on. "You have imagined me well, and so I am. You have imagined that I dream, and so I do. I have seen the falling stars."

"But all of this, this imagining," I protested, "this has taken place—is taking place in my mind. You are not actually here, not here in this room." It occurred to me that I was being extremely rude, but I could not help myself. She seemed to understand.

"Be careful of your pronouncements, grandson," she answered. "You imagine that I am here in this room, do you not? That is worth something. You see, I have existence, whole being, in your imagination. It is but one kind of being, to be sure, but it is perhaps the best of all kinds. If I am not here in this room, grandson, then surely neither are you."

"I think I see what you mean," I said meekly. I felt justly rebuked. "Tell me, grandmother, how old are you?"

"I do not know," she replied. "There are times when I think that I am the oldest woman on earth. You know, the Kiowas came into the world through a hollow log. In my mind's eye I have seen them emerge, one by one, from the mouth of the log. I have seen them so clearly, how they were dressed, how delighted they were to see the world around them. I must have been there. And I must have taken part in that old migration of the Kiowas from the Yellowstone to the Southern Plains, near the Big Horn River, and I have seen the red cliffs of Palo Duro Canyon. I was with those who were camped in the Wichita Mountains when the stars fell."

"You are indeed very old," I said, "and you have seen many things."

"Yes, I imagine that I have," she replied. Then she turned slowly around, nodding once, and receded into the language I had made. And then I imagined I was alone in the room.

Once in his life a man ought to concentrate his mind upon the remembered earth, I believe. He ought to give himself up to a particular landscape in his experience, to look at it from as many angles as he can, to wonder about it, to dwell upon it. He ought to imagine that he touches it with his hands at every season and listens to the sounds that are made upon it. He ought to imagine the creatures that are there and all the faintest motions in the wind. He ought to recollect the glare of noon and all the colors of the dawn and dusk.

The Wichita Mountains rise out of the Southern Plains in a long crooked line that runs from east to west. The mountains are made of red earth, and of rock that is neither red nor blue but some very rare admixture of the two like the feathers of certain birds. They are not so high and mighty as the mountains of the Far West, and they bear a different relationship to the land around them. One does not imagine that they are distinctive in themselves, or indeed that they exist apart from the plain in any sense. If you try to think of them in the abstract they lose the look of mountains. They are preeminently in an expression of the larger landscape, more perfectly organic than one can easily imagine. To behold these mountains from the plain is one thing; to see the plain from the mountains is something else. I have stood on the top of Mt. Scott and seen the earth below, bending out into the whole circle of the sky. The wind runs always close upon the slopes, and there are times when you can hear the rush of it like water in the ravines.

Here is the hub of an old commerce. A hundred years ago the Kiowas and Comanches journeyed outward from the Wichitas in every direction, seeking after mischief and medicine, horses and hostages. Sometimes they went away for years, but they always returned, for the land had got hold of them. It is a consecrated place, and even now there is something of the wilderness about it. There is a game preserve in the hills. Animals graze away in the open meadows or, closer by, keep to the shadows of the groves: antelope and deer, longhorn and buffalo. It was here, the Kiowas say, that the first buffalo came into the world.

The yellow grassy knoll that is called Rainy Mountain lies a short distance to the north and west. There, on the west side, is the ruin of an old school where my grandmother went as a wild young girl in blanket and braids to learn of numbers and of names in English. And there she is buried.

> Most is your name the name of
> this dark stone.
> Deranged in death, the mind to
> be inheres
> Forever in the nominal unknown,
> Who listens here and now to
> hear your name.
> The early sun, red as a hunter's
> moon,
> Runs in the plain. The mountain
> burns and shines;
> And silence is the long approach
> of noon
> Upon the shadow that your name
> defines—
> And death this cold, black
> density of stone.

I am interested in the way that a man looks at a given landscape and takes possession of it in his blood and brain. For this happens, I am certain, in the ordinary motion of life. None of us lives apart from the land entirely; such an isolation is unimaginable. We have sooner or later to come to terms with the world around us—and I mean especially the physical world; not only as it is revealed to us immediately through our senses, but also as it is perceived more truly in the long turn of seasons and of years. And we must come to moral terms. There is no alternative, I believe, if we are to realize and maintain our humanity; for our humanity must consist in part in the ethical as well as the practical ideal of preservation. And particularly here and now is that true. We Americans need now more than ever before—and indeed more than we know—to imagine who and what we are with respect to the earth and sky. I am talking about an act of the imagination essentially, and the concept of an American land ethic.

It is no doubt more difficult to imagine in 1970 the landscape of America as it was in, say, 1900. Our whole experience as a nation in this century has been a repudiation of the pastoral ideal which informs so much of the art and literature of the nineteenth century. One effect of the Technological Revolution has been to uproot us from the soil. We have become disoriented, I believe; we have suffered a kind of psychic dislocation of ourselves in time and space. We may be perfectly sure of where we are in relation to the supermarket and the next coffee break, but I doubt that any of us knows where he is in relation to the stars and to the solstices. Our sense of the natural order has become dull and unreliable. Like the wilderness itself, our sphere of instinct has diminished in proportion as we have failed to imagine truly what it is. And yet I believe that it is possible to formulate an ethical idea of the land—a notion of what it is and must be in our daily lives—and I believe moreover that it is absolutely necessary to do so.

It would seem on the surface of things that a land ethic is something that is alien to, or at least dormant in, most Americans. Most of us in general have developed an attitude of indifference toward the land. In terms of my own experience, it is difficult to see how such an attitude could ever have come about.

Ko-sahn could remember where my grandmother was born. "It was just there," she said, pointing to a tree, and the tree was like a hundred others that grew up in the broad depression of the Washita River. I could see nothing to indicate that anyone had ever been there, spoken so much as a word, or touched the tips of his fingers to the tree. But in her memory Ko-sahn could see the child. I think she must have remembered my grandmother's voice, for she seemed for a long moment to listen and to hear. There was a still, heavy heat upon that place; I had the sense that ghosts were gathering there.

And in the racial memory, Ko-sahn had seen the falling stars. For her there was no distinction between the individual and the racial experience, even as there was none between the mythical and the historical. Both were realized for her in the one memory, and that was of the land. This landscape, in which she had lived for a hundred years, was the common denominator of everything that she knew and would ever know—and her knowledge was profound. Her roots ran deep into the earth, and from those depths she drew strength enough to hold still against all the forces of chance and disorder. And she drew strength enough to hold still against all the forces of change and disorder. And she drew therefrom the sustenance of meaning and of mystery as well. The falling stars were not for Ko-sahn an isolated or accidental phenomenon. She had a great personal investment in that awful commotion of light in the night sky. For it remained to be imagined. She must at last deal with it in words; she must appropriate it to her understanding of the whole universe. And, again, when she spoke of the Sun Dance, it was an essential expression of her relationship to the life of the earth and to the sun and moon.

In Ko-sahn and in her people we have always had the example of a deep, ethical regard for the land. We had better learn from it. Surely that ethic is merely latent in ourselves. It must now be activated, I believe. We Americans must come again to a moral comprehension of the earth and air. We must live according to the principle of a land ethic. The alternative is that we shall not live at all.

Ecology is perhaps the most important subject of our time. I can't think of an issue in which the Indian has more authority or a greater stake. If there is one thing which truly distinguishes him, it is surely his regard of and for the natural world.

But let me get back to the matter of storytelling.

I must have taken part in that old migration of the Kiowas from the Yellowstone to the Southern Plains, for I have seen antelope bounding in the tall grass near the Big Horn River, and I have seen the ghost forests in the Black Hills. Once I saw the red cliffs of Palo Duro Canyon. I was with those who were camped in the Wichita Mountains when the stars fell. "You are very old," I said, "and you have seen many things." "Yes, I imagine that I have," she replied. Then she turned slowly around, nodding once, and receded into the language I had made. And then I imagined that I was alone in the room.

Who is the storyteller? Of whom is the story told? What is there in the darkness to imagine into being? What is there to dream and to relate? What happens when I or anyone exerts the force of language upon the unknown?

These are the questions which interest me most.

If there is any absolute assumption in back of my thoughts tonight, it is this: We are what we imagine. Our very existence consists in our imagination of ourselves. Our best destiny is to imagine, at least, completely, who and what, and *that* we are. The greatest tragedy that can befall us is to go unimagined.

Writing is recorded speech. In order to consider seriously the meaning of language and of literature, we must consider first the meaning of the oral tradition.

By way of suggesting one or two definitions which may be useful to us, let me pose a few basic questions and tentative answers:

(1) What is the oral tradition?

The oral tradition is that process by which the myths, legends, tales, and lore of a people are formulated, communicated, and preserved in language by word of mouth, as opposed to writing. Or, it is a *collection* of such things.

(2) With reference to the matter of oral tradition, what is the relationship between art and reality?

In the context of these remarks, the matter of oral tradition suggests certain particularities of art and reality. Art, for example . . . involves an oral dimension which is based markedly upon such considerations as memorization, intonation, inflection, precision of statement, brevity, rhythm, pace, and dramatic effect. Moreover, myth, legend, and lore, according to our definitions of these terms, imply a separate and distinct order of reality. We are concerned here not so much with an accurate representation of actuality, but with the realization of the imaginative experience.

(3) How are we to conceive of language? What are words?

For our purposes, words are audible sounds, invented by man to communicate his thoughts and feelings. Each word has a conceptual content, however slight; and each word communicates associations of feeling. Language is the means by which words proceed to the formulation of meaning and emotional effect.

(4) What is the nature of storytelling? What are the purposes and possibilities of that act?

Storytelling is imaginative and creative in nature. It is an act by which man strives to realize his capacity for wonder, meaning and delight. It is also a process in which man invests and preserves himself in the context of ideas. Man tells stories in order to understand his experience, whatever it may be. The possibilities of storytelling are precisely those of understanding the human experience.

(5) What is the relationship between what a man is and what he says— or between what he is, and what he thinks he is?

This relationship is both tenuous and complicated. Generally speaking, man has consummate being in language, and there only. The state of human *being* is an idea, an idea which man has of himself. Only when he is embodied in an idea, and the idea is realized in language, can man take possession of himself. In our particular frame of reference, this is to say that man achieves the fullest realization of his humanity in such an art and product of the imagination as literature—and here I use the term "literature" in its broadest sense. This is admittedly a moral view of the question, but literature is itself a moral view, and it is a view of morality.

Now let us return to the falling stars. And let me apply a new angle of vision to that event—let me proceed this time from a slightly different point of view:

In this winter of 1833 the Kiowas were camped on Elm Fork, a branch of the Red River west of the Wichita Mountains. In the preceding summer they had suffered a massacre at the hands of the Osages, and Tai-me, the sacred Sun Dance Doll and most powerful medicine of the tribe, had been stolen. At no time in the history of their migration from the north, and in the evolution of their plains culture, had the Kiowas been more vulnerable to despair. The loss of Tai-me was a deep psychological wound. In the early cold of November 13 there occurred over North America an explosion of meteors. The Kiowas were awakened by the sterile light of falling stars, and they ran out into the false day and were terrified.

The year the stars fell is, as I have said, among the earliest entries in the Kiowa calendars, and it is permanent in the Kiowa mind. There was symbolic meaning in that November sky. With the coming of natural dawn there began a new and darker age for the Kiowa people; the last culture to evolve on this continent began to decline. Within four years of the falling stars the Kiowas signed their first treaty with the government; within twenty, four major epidemics of smallpox and Asiatic cholera destroyed more than half their number; and within scarcely more than a generation their horses were taken from them and the herds of buffalo were slaughtered and left to waste upon the plains.

Do you see what happens when the imagination is superimposed upon the historical event? It becomes a story. The whole piece becomes more deeply invested with meaning. The terrified Kiowas, when they had regained possession of themselves, did indeed imagine that the falling stars were symbolic of their being and their destiny. They accounted for themselves with reference to that awful memory. They appropriated it, recreated it, fashioned it into an image of themselves—imagined it.

Only by means of that act could they bear what happened to them thereafter. No defeat, no humiliation, no suffering was beyond their power to endure, for none of it was meaningless. They could say to themselves, "yes, it was all meant to be in its turn. The order of the world was broken, it was clear. Even the stars were shaken loose in the night sky." The imagination of meaning was not much, perhaps, but it was all they had, and it was enough to sustain them.

One of my very favorite writers, Isak Dinesen, said this: "All sorrows can be borne if you put them into a story or tell a story about them."

Some three or four years ago, I became interested in the matter of "oral tradition" as that term is used to designate a rich body of preliterate storytelling in and among the indigenous cultures of North America. Specifically, I began to wonder about the way in which myths, legends, and lore evolve into that mature condition of expression which we call "literature." For indeed literature is, I believe, the end-product of an evolutionary process, a stage that is indispensable and perhaps original as well.

I set out to find a traditional material that should be at once oral only, unified and broadly representative of cultural values. And in this undertaking, I had a certain advantage, because I am myself an American Indian, and I have lived many years of my life on the Indian reservations of the southwest. From the time I was first able to comprehend and express myself in language, I heard the stories of the Kiowas, those "coming out" people of the Southern Plains from whom I am descended.

Three hundred years ago the Kiowa lived in the mountains of what is now western Montana, near the headwaters of the Yellowstone River. Near the end of the seventeenth century they began a long migration to the south and east. They passed along the present border between Montana and Wyoming to the Black Hills and proceeded southward along the eastern slopes of the Rockies to the Wichita Mountains in the Southern Plains (Southwestern Oklahoma).

I mention this old journey of the Kiowas because it is in a sense definitive of the tribal mind; it is essential to the way in which the Kiowas think of themselves as a people. The migration was carried on over a course of many generations and many hundreds of miles. When it began, the Kiowas were a desperate and divided people, given up wholly to a day-by-day struggle for survival. When it ended, they were a race of centaurs, a lordly society of warriors and buffalo hunters. Along the way they had acquired horses, a knowledge and possession of the open land, and a sense of destiny. In alliance with the Comanches, they ruled the Southern Plains for a hundred years.

That migration—and the new golden age to which it led—is closely reflected in Kiowa legend and lore. Several years ago I retraced the route of that migration, and when I came to the end, I interviewed a number of Kiowa elders and obtained from them a remarkable body of history and learning, fact and fiction—all of it in the oral tradition and all of it valuable in its own right and for its own sake.

I compiled a small number of translations from the Kiowa, arranged insofar as it was possible to indicate the chronological and geographical progression of the migration itself. This collection (and it was nothing more than a collection at first) was published under the title *The Journey of Tai-me* in a fine edition limited to 100 hand printed copies.

This original collection has just been re-issued, together with illustrations and a commentary, in a trade edition entitled *The Way to Rainy Mountain*. The principle of narration which informs this latter work is in a sense elaborate and experimental, and I should like to say one or two things about it. Then, if I may, I should like to illustrate the way in which the principle works, by reading briefly from the text. And finally, I should like to comment in some detail upon one of the tales in particular.

There are three distinct narrative voices in *The Way to Rainy Mountain*—the mythical, the historical, and the immediate. Each of the translations is followed by two kinds of commentary; the first is documentary and the second is privately reminiscent. Together, they serve, hopefully, to validate the oral tradition to an extent that might not otherwise be possible. The commentaries are meant to provide a context in which the elements of oral tradition might transcend the categorical limits of prehistory, anonymity, and archaeology in the narrow sense.

All of this is to say that I believe there is a way (first) in which the elements of oral tradition can be shown, dramatically, to exist within the framework of a literary continuance, a deeper and more vital context of language and meaning than that which is generally taken into account; and (secondly) in which those elements can be located, with some precision on an evolutionary scale.

The device of the journey is peculiarly appropriate to such a principle of narration as this. And *The Way to Rainy Mountain* is a whole journey, intricate with notion and meaning; and it is made with the whole memory, that experience of the mind which is legendary as well as historical, personal as well as cultural.

Without further qualification, let me turn to the text itself.

The Kiowa tales which are contained in *The Way to Rainy Mountain* constitute a kind of literary chronicle. In a sense they are the milestones of that old migration in which the Kiowas journeyed from the Yellowstone to the Washita. They recorded a transformation of the tribal mind, as it encounters for the first time the landscape of the Great Plains; they evoke the sense of search and discovery. Many of the tales are very old, and they have not until now been set down in writing. Among them there is one that stands out in my mind. When I was a child, my father told me the story of the arrowmaker, and he told it to me many times, for I fell in love with it. I have no memory that is older than that of hearing it. This is the way it goes:

If an arrow is well made, it will have tooth marks upon it. That is how you know. The Kiowas made fine arrows and straightened them in their teeth. Then they drew them to the bow to see that they were straight. Once there was a man and his wife. They were alone at night in their tipi. By the light of a fire the man was making arrows. After a while he caught sight of something. There was a small opening in the tipi where two hides had been sewn together. Someone was there on the outside, looking in. The man went on with his work, but he said to his wife, "Someone is standing outside. Do not be afraid. Let us talk easily, as of ordinary things." He took up an arrow and straightened it in his teeth; then, as it was right for him to do, he drew it to the bow and took aim, first in this direction and then in that. And all the while he was talking, as if to his wife. But this is how he spoke: "I know that you are there on the outside, for I can feel your eyes upon me. If you are a Kiowa, you will understand what I am saying, and you will speak your name." But there was no answer, and the man went on in the same way, pointing the arrow all around. At last his aim fell upon the place where his enemy stood, and he let go of the string. The arrow went straight to the enemy's heart.

Heretofore the story of the arrowmaker has been the private possession of a very few, a tenuous link in that most ancient chain of language which we call the oral tradition; tenuous because the tradition itself is so; for as many times as the story has been told, it was always but one generation removed from extinction. But it was held dear, too, on that same account. That is to say, it has been neither more nor less durable than the human voice, and neither more nor less concerned to express the meaning of the human condition. And this brings us to the heart of the matter at hand: The story of the arrowmaker is also a link between language and literature. It is a remarkable act of the mind, a realization of words and the world that is altogether simple and direct, yet nonetheless rare and profound, and it illustrates more clearly than anything else in my own experience, at least, something of the essential character of the imagination—and in particular of that personification which in this instance emerges from it: the man made of words.

It is a fine story, whole, intricately beautiful, precisely realized. It is worth thinking about, for it yields something of value; indeed, it is full of provocation, rich with suggestion and consequent meaning. There is often an inherent danger that we might impose too much of ourselves upon it. It is informed by an integrity that bears examination easily and well, and in the process it seems to appropriate our own reality and experience.

It is significant that the story of the arrowmaker returns in a special way upon itself. It is about language, after all, and it is therefore part and parcel of its own subject; virtually, there is no difference between the telling and that which is told. The point of the story lies, not so much in what the arrowmaker does, but in what he says—and indeed that he says it. The principal fact is that he speaks, and in so doing he places his very life in the balance. It is this aspect of the story which interests me most, for it is here that the language becomes most conscious of itself; we are close to the origin and object of literature, I believe; our sense of the verbal dimension is very keen, and we are aware of something in the nature of language that is at once perilous and compelling. "If you are a Kiowa, you will understand what I am saying, and you will speak your name." Everything is ventured in this simple declaration, which is also a question and a plea. The conditional element with which it begins is remarkably tentative and pathetic; precisely at this moment is the arrowmaker realized completely, and his reality consists in language, and it is poor and precarious. And all of this occurs to him as surely as it does to us. Implicit in that simple occurrence is all of his definition and his destiny, and all of ours. He ventures to speak because he must; language is the repository of his whole knowledge and experience, and it represents the only chance he has for survival. Instinctively, and with great care, he deals in the most honest and basic way with words. "Let us talk easily, as of ordinary things," he says. And of the ominous unknown he asks only the utterance of a name, only the most nominal sign that he is understood, that his words are returned to him on the sheer edge of meaning. But there is no answer, and the arrowmaker knows at once what he has not known before; that his enemy is, and that he has gained an advantage over him. This he knows certainly, and the certainty itself is his advantage, and it is crucial; he makes the most of it. The venture is complete and irrevocable, and it ends in success. The story is meaningful. It is so primarily because it is composed of language, and it is in the nature of language in turn that it proceeds to the formulation of meaning. Moreover, the story of the arrowmaker, as opposed to other stories in general, centers upon this procession of words toward meaning. It seems in fact to turn upon the very idea that language involves the elements of risk and responsibility; and in this it seeks to confirm itself. In a word, it seems to say, everything is a risk. That may be true, and it may also be that the whole of literature rests upon that truth.

The arrowmaker is preeminently the man made of words. He has consummate being in language; it is the world of his origin and of his posterity, and there is no other. But it is a world of definite reality and of infinite possibility. I have come to believe that there is a sense in which the arrowmaker has more nearly perfect being than have other men, by and large, as he imagines himself, whole and vital, going on into the unknown darkness and beyond. And this last aspect of his being is primordial and profound.

And yet the story has it that he is cautious and alone, and we are given to understand that his peril is great and immediate, and that he confronts it in the only way he can. I have no doubt that this is true, and I believe that there are implications which point directly to the determination of our literary experience and which must not be lost upon us. A final word, then, on an essential irony which marks this story and gives peculiar substance to the man made of words. The storyteller is nameless and unlettered. From one point of view we know very little about him, except that he is somehow translated for us in the person of an arrowmaker. But, from another, that is all we need to know. He tells us of his life in language, and of the awful risk involved. It must occur to us that he is one with the arrowmaker and that he has survived, by word of mouth, beyond other men. We said a moment ago that, for the arrowmaker, language represented the only chance of survival. It is worth considering that he survives in our own time, and that he has survived over a period of untold generations.

David L. Moore

Decolonializing Criticism

Reading Dialectics and Dialogics in
Native American Literatures

Politics and Epistemology

Readers of American Indian literatures move through a range of ethical responses varying from despair to guilt, from romance to anger, from sanctimonious idealism to righteous indignation. Then there are more pragmatic responses and commitments to cultural continuity and survival. Any response will have its effects, whether in print, in the classroom, in communities, in politics, in the courts. Of course, responses that subtly reinscribe the "vanishing Indian" myth have ethical effects with peculiar political resonance, and professional critics of Indian literature find themselves under unique pressures to elude the intricate forces of that myth.[1]

The colonial, hence racial and ethical, context moves the discussion of ways of reading Native American literatures toward issues of epistemology. If how we know the world begins with how we know the nexus of self and other, then our view of that nexus structures our ethical relations. That epistemological sequence cycles into not only our ethics but our politics and our colonial history as well. Colonial cognitive structures underlie cultural definitions of race and ethnicity, embedded as those definitions are in the economics of colonial history.

The ways in which readers and writers conceive of culture, self and other, knowledge and experience, past and present, determine different relations between reader and text as well as different readings of literary elements. For example, Walt Whitman's 1855 line, "And what I assume you shall assume" ("Song of Myself" 28), inscribes assimilative or absorptive relations, different from Frederick Douglass's contemporary (1857) statement of resistant relations: "The limits of tyrants are prescribed by the endurance of those whom they oppress" ("West India Emancipation Speech" 437). Yet both pronouncements are characterized by a dualistic episteme. Similarly, Whitman's own various references to American Indians reveal an epistemological duality in American identity when he idealizes the "red squaw" in "The Sleepers" (429) but demonizes the "red marauder" in "Song of Myself" (57). Finer comparisons of epistemological structures may be made between, for instance, the choice of Leslie Silko's protagonist in *Ceremony* not

---

[1] See Tobin Seibers' *The Ethics of Criticism* for a cogent description of ethics as inherent to literary studies.

to continue "fighting with the destroyers" (134) and the affirmation of Gerald Vizenor's tricksters in *The Heirs of Columbus,* "We heal with opposition" (176). The one transcends dualistic opposition, the other deconstructs it.

The epistemological point here is that these writers describe different ways of conceiving and negotiating cognitive and epistemological binaries. To map these differences, I will trace ways in which epistemology is linked to ethics and to aesthetic study by what I outline as dualistic, dialectic, and dialogic ways of thinking. Those ways of thinking echo ethical and then political ways of interacting. In the first half of this article, I explore such structures in Tohono O'odham and Omaha literatures; in the second half, I examine selected critical points by David Murray and Arnold Krupat in light of those structures.

A performative dimension frequently emerges in various genres of Native American literature, and this dimension ties Native texts to a vital context of both land-based and pan-tribal communities in at least three important ways. Those communities reside as an audience in the texts, as a tacit chorus for the communal values reflected in those texts, and as a beneficiary of the writers' political performances related to those communal values. This political linkage between text and context establishes a particular dimension of ethical commitment between performance and performer that needs to be carefully described. Further, the communal and political dimensions call for and call into being a readership to participate imaginatively in the performance. The texts thus try to increase a community that understands what I will call dialogical processes by which Native cultures often conceive of their own survival. That process shapes its readers' aesthetic and ethical responses.

Such responses are not prescribed. Readers of Native American literature certainly do not need to follow the pattern of Sol Tax's "action anthropology," which invokes "the need to help as well as to learn" (378). There are of course many kinds of ethical responses. The point is rather that responses may reflect a closer and fuller reading of textual aesthetics insofar as they discover the contextual experience of community which gives the words their vitality. The ethical impulse both "to learn" and "to help" can reflect the ethics of a specific epistemology of exchange in the texts.

James Clifford, in *Predicament of Culture,* has come close to describing that epistemology of exchange. His "Identity in Mashpee" chapter documents the unsuccessful legal effort of the Mashpee, a group of Massachusetts Wampanoags, to gain federal recognition as a tribe. The Mashpees' notion of their own identity remains American Indian after centuries of intermarriage with whites and African American sailors and ex-slaves. Yet the court's decision is that they are not Indian. Clifford's interpretation is especially useful both because it is so suggestive and because, as I will show, it can be misread by the bipolar epistemology it describes and unravels:

> Stories of cultural contact and change have been structured by a pervasive dichotomy: absorption by the other *or* resistance to the other. A fear of lost identity, a Puritan taboo on mixing beliefs and bodies, hangs over the

process. Yet what if identity is conceived not as a boundary to be maintained but as a nexus of relations and transactions actively engaging a subject? The story or stories of interaction must then be more complex, less linear and teleological. What changes when the subject of "history" is no longer Western? How do stories of contact, resistance, and assimilation appear from the standpoint of groups in which exchange rather than identity is the fundamental value to be sustained? (344)

Clifford sets up a tricky set of two categories, one operating in terms of dualities, of absorptions or resistances, and another operating in terms of multiplicities, of a nexus of exchanges. The trick, embedded in his italicized *"or,"* is that only one side denies the other, while the other draws a circle that takes in the denier. That is, Clifford's dual system suggests possibilities of multiplicity outside its own dualistic limitations. The trick is reflected in a jest of popular American oral tradition: "There are two kinds of people in the world: those who think there are two kinds of people, and those of us who don't." If it is a binary, it is not a balanced one, because the one side is closed and the other is open.

Clifford describes Mashpee identity "not as an archaic survival but as an ongoing process, politically contested and historically unfinished" (9). He registers the difficulty of imagining a binary with only one end open to other polarities, conceiving of open-endedness via a language of closed and oscillating oppositions. The closed oscillations may safely be called "dialectics," while the open end I will call "dialogics."[2]

This paper then becomes essentially an examination of dialogic ways of eluding dialectic systems. Two general points are pertinent here as qualifiers. First, as is suggested by a binary with only one open-ended pole, the dialogic never erases the dialectic, though the dialectic ignores the dialogic. The dialectic ignores the dialogic by reducing issues to binaries, while the dialogic continues to "dialogue" with the dialectic by opening up more than binary possibilities. Those who construct their world through dialectical binaries, such as civilization v. wilderness, Euro-American v. Indian, or Euro-American v. African American, miss the blurring of those boundaries that drives the pragmatic unfolding of American identities and differences. Indeed, much of canonical American history has been driven by such dialectics, either at the slave auction or along the frontier. Those, however, who see the world through dialogical interaction, through a nexus of exchange by Clifford's description, continue to negotiate that dialectical history in ways that seem invisible to dialecticians. They are perennially "vanishing Indians" who continue to survive after five hundred years of colonization's dialectical materialism.

---

[2]It would be inaccurate to align Native American with the dialogic and Euro-American with the dialectic sides of this system. Such an alignment, aside from its obvious over-generalizations, would simply reinscribe the dualities that an open-ended dialogism eludes.

Second, the dialogic negotiates the dialectic in two ways, immanent and transcendent. Within dialectical systems such as civilization v. wilderness, a dialogic can deconstruct each binary instead of synthesizing them, dialectically, into oscillating unity. That strategy is an immanent relation of the dialogic to the dialectic. While the dialectic fastens on one polarity in oscillating synthesis, the transcendent relation occurs outside that dialectic binary. The dialogic bears a transcendent relation to the dialectic when it reveals a wider field of intersecting binaries, each altering the others. Any single dialectic is then transcended by that multi-dimensional field.

By these two relations a dialogic eludes dialectics as context both transcends and infuses text. Through a reader's fuller attention to context, the dialogic begins to enter the reading process.[3] Two dialogic texts of Native lives, *Papago Woman*[4] and *The Middle Five: Indian Schoolboys of the Omaha Tribe*, express dialogue within a particular ethical context. In Clifford's terms, these two works suggest complex cultural exchanges instead of binary absorption or resistance between self and other, between tribes, or between Indian and white.

Non-Dialectical Knowing

The idea of Native intercultural exchange has its corollaries, if not its causes, in Native interpersonal and ecological relations. Familiar notions about Native American values of interrelationship have reached the truth value of a cliché. Those overworked notions often assume that the sense of interrelationship does not extend beyond natural and tribal boundaries. Yet the dialogic notion of interrelations renews itself in Ruth Underhill's *Papago Woman,* in which internal values of exchange extend into the dynamics of external cultural contact.

In their annual cactus camp, the Tohono O'odham, as the formerly "Papago" call themselves, brew their cactus wine to drink in communion with the desert plants and to generate a magnetism for rain: "People must all make themselves drunk like the plants in the rain and they must sing for happiness" (40). Not only do they link themselves metaphorically to the plants but, as the following cactus camp song exemplifies, they also perceive themselves as exchanging feelings with the land itself:

Where on Quijotoa Mountain a cloud stands
There my heart stands with it.
Where the mountain trembles with the thunder
My heart trembles with it. (40)

---

[3]For discussions of context in relation to Native American literatures, see Paula Gunn Allen's "Teaching American Indian Oral Literatures" in her *Studies in American Indian Literature* and A. LaVonne Brown Ruoff's "Oral Literatures," "Life History and Autobiography," and "History of Written Literature" in her *American Indian Literatures.*

[4]Concerning *Papago Woman,* I must pass by for now the complex and important questions of translation and editorial mediation by Ruth Underhill of this "autobiography."

This poetic interrelationship with the land finds its parallels on Tohono O'odham cultural soil with Chona's, the protagonist's, expression of their human interrelationships.

> I used to like it in the summertime when all our friends and relatives were around us. . . . The houses were scattered all over the flat land—round brush houses like ours. (34, 53)

Here is a seemingly universal ideal of enclosed community. Yet such a familiar notion of tribal exchange is not usually registered in its relationality across what Westerners conceive of as "enemy" boundaries. Chona, however, expresses just such a transaction between the family of a Tohono O'odham man, a "Slayer," who has killed an enemy in war, and the slain Apache:

> Then they took my father out in the dark before the morning came and bathed him again, and they bathed us too. Then we were purified and we could have the Apache scalp in our family to work for us like a relative. . . . Then it was in our family and it would always help us. (46–47)

This practice suggests something quite different from a dialectical *agon* between conquered and conqueror, between absorption and resistance, winner and loser. Instead, a more complex dialogics emerges where the Tohono O'odham and Apache warriors, their families, and the purifying water, the darkness, the light, the land, even life and death, participate in a delicate exchange of powers that translates giving into taking and enemy into protector in a blurring of categories.

Such a delicate pattern of relations transfers logically, in another family setting, to the history of intercultural contact:

> Then my husband and I and the baby went to the medicine man, and he gave us all white clay to eat as he had given me when I became a maiden. But he did not give my baby a name. We were modern and I let a priest name him, Bastian. (67)

Perhaps the Euro-American priest would consider this episode another coup for some progressive cultural absorption by Christianity of Tohono O'odham practices, a promise of manifest destiny. And possibly the medicine man as well would consider this Christian naming a loss for cultural resistance. But Chona and her husband, who is also a medicine man, make a choice within their circumstances. She clearly sees herself as acting in a nexus of exchange rather than being limited, in Clifford's terms, to either absorption by or resistance to Christianity. Her choices suggest a Tohono O'odham dialogics of culture that matches the value of a dialogics of nature, suggesting further that categories of nature and culture, if they are useful at all, are porous and quite flexible.

Certainly any assumption of boundaries helps to create their effects. When your non-Native enemies do not function by such a system of exchange but instead assume either your absorption in or resistance to the enemy culture, and when the enemies are thus blind to both their own and your participation in exchange, then a different sort of war ensues, and a different sort of tragedy takes over. Yet dialogic cultural exchange occurs even in the midst of dialectic culture wars. To move beyond such a dialectical history requires precisely the recognition of inexorable and mutual, dialogical historical exchange. Chona's text suggests just such a possibility.[5]

In the preface of his turn-of-the-century autobiographical piece, *The Middle Five: Indian Schoolboys of the Omaha Tribe*, Francis La Flesche, an Omaha lawyer and ethnologist, is explicit where Chona's account is implicit about cultural exchange:

> As the object of this book is to reveal the true nature and character of the Indian boy, I have chosen to write the story of my school-fellows rather than that of my other boy friends who knew only the aboriginal life. I have made this choice not because the influences of the school alter the qualities of the boys, but that they might appear under conditions and in an attire familiar to the reader.
>
> . . . So while the school uniform did not change those who wore it, in this instance, it may help these little Indians to be judged, as are other boys, by what they say and do. (v)

La Flesche undoubtedly sees his audience as non-Indian and his theme as a presentation to that audience of Indian lives during his own childhood in the late 1860s, but he immediately complicates—or dialogically clarifies—the representation by claiming that Indian lives can be shown accurately in an intercultural rather than an authentic, pure, or "aboriginal" context.

A dialectical response to his statements might dismiss La Flesche's claim that "the school uniform did not change those who wore it." According to binary structures such as change v. not-change, or civilization v. savage, the uniform itself necessitates "change"—just as the school administrators intended it to help them civilize the savage. Further assumed messages of cultural change in that uniform reside within the dialectic epistemology of those "educators" as well. So what does La Flesche mean by claiming that

---

[5]This notion of the inexorable emergence of dialogics may be understood linguistically through an application of Mikhail Bakhtin's terminology. Michael Holquist defines Bakhtin's use of heteroglossia as "the base condition governing the operation of meaning in any utterance. It is that which insures the primacy of context over text . . . all utterances are heteroglot in that they are functions of a matrix of forces practically impossible to recoup, and therefore impossible to resolve" (Bakhtin 428). Because of the workings of heteroglossia in communication, efforts to reduce communication to monologues are doomed to failure. Similarly, efforts to reduce cultural contact to monocultural domination are doomed to failure, as cultures engage necessarily in a nexus of dialogue.

the uniform "did not change those who wore it"? Perhaps he assumes a biological, essentialist Indian identity in his phrase "the true nature and character of the Indian boy" and in his affirmation that the influences of the school did not alter "the qualities of the boys." But such phraseology must be read in the historical, colonial context of the intercultural contact that produced it. In spite of the romantic discourse available to La Flesche's educated prose in the 1890s, nevertheless he posits a "true nature" here only insofar as it affirms that what is culturally Indian in these boys is capable of negotiating with what is culturally non-Indian in the mission school.

La Flesche's dedication of the book, "To The Universal Boy," certainly suggests a humanist core, which then freely engages in cultural exchanges; but that dedication itself is clearly written as a bridge to his non-Indian audience, and whether the cultural exchange or the universal core is primary remains undefined. (It also remains undefined whether his humanist discourse is a result of his Omaha upbringing or his Euro-American education, or both.)

At the crux of La Flesche's claim are his definitions of "change" itself and of the identity that experiences change. La Flesche's text and context suggest that he operates by a dialogic of *exchange,* wherein identities may exchange cultural goods—such as clothing—without *changing* something called identity. In contrast, the dualistic tendencies of Euro-American cultural dialectics tend to structure change and identity as mutually opposed. In his article "Democratic Social Space," Philip Fisher observes:

> The "Making of Americans" as Gertrude Stein called it occurred first of all by those thousands of negations by which the children of Italian-Americans, German-Americans, and Chinese-Americans erased letter by letter the accent, style of laughter, customs, and costumes of family life, dress, and idiom of the old country so as to be, at last, simply American. (63)

Fisher concludes that "In every American personality there exists a past history of erasure" (63). With "American" change must come erasure of former identity, a process necessary to Euro-American immigrant experience but relatively alien to land-based Native American experience.[6] Thus the multiple tendencies of La Flesche's cultural dialogics acknowledge that the uniform, as a mode of exchange, does not change the boys.

La Flesche scripts an assumption of cultural exchange into the dialogue of Omaha parents of the 1860s as they discuss whether to send their boy to the mission school:

> "We are the only ones in the village who haven't sent any children to the House of Teaching. . . . There must be some good in it; we ought to send one of our boys at least. . . . Before many years have gone, our dealings will be

---

[6]See Philip Fisher, "Democratic Social Space," for a cogent analysis of erasure as part of Euro-American identity and imperialism.

mostly with the white people who are coming to mingle with us; and, to have relations with them of any kind, some of us must learn their language and familiarize ourselves with their customs. That is what these men who send their children to the White-chests are looking forward to, and they love their boys as much as we do ours." (23–24)

As with Chona's priest who named her baby, the Omahas' mission school "teacher and disciplinarian," whom the Omaha boys call "Gray-beard," might read such a dialogue as the first unconscious step down a slippery slope toward victory for Christian civilization. Yet such evangelical glee might be based on a misconception, arising from "a Puritan taboo on mixing beliefs and bodies," that Omaha beliefs must be erased in order to embrace Christian ones. Instead of being limited to either/or cultural options, the Omahas, like the Tohono O'odham, appear to function from a pragmatic standpoint by which, again in Clifford's terms, "exchange rather than identity is the fundamental value to be sustained." Echoing Sitting Bull's famous dictum to his children to take only what is good from the white man, Frank's own father addresses him with these words:

"You . . . have reached the age when you should seek for knowledge. That you might profit by the teachings of your own people and that of the white race, and that you might avoid the misery which accompanies ignorance, I placed you in the House of Teaching of the White-chests, who are said to be wise and to have in their books the utterances of great and learned men. I had treasured the hope that you would seek to know the good deeds done by men of your own race, and by men of the white race, that you would follow their example and take pleasure in doing the things that are noble and helpful to those around you. Am I to be disappointed?" (127–28)

Indeed, Frank's father asserts it as the logic of a specific value of knowledge and survival to engage in cultural exchange. As D'Arcy McNickle explains in *Native American Tribalism,* "Indians remain Indians not by refusing to accept change or to adapt to a changing environment, but by selecting out of available choices those alternatives that do not impose a substitute identity" (10).

Frank's father does not advise his son to erase his own identity and become absorbed in the white culture or to resist the white and entrench his own; rather, he presumes an intercultural process. Such a view is naive only insofar as it is nonviolent. Whether the "enemy" operates by a notion of exchange or of resistance and absorption, the exchange does occur until—and even after—the enemy violates the process by asserting through violence his "Puritan taboo on mixing beliefs and bodies" (Clifford 344).

Indeed, Gray-beard in the narrative does enact that historical, polarizing violence which demonizes the other, thence the self, and which misses the dialogics of cultural exchange. Yet even in the face of the old missionary's brutality, the Omaha schoolchildren, true to the "nature and character of the Indian boy" and dramatically expressing the values inculcated by their parents, remain open to the potential for mutual existence. A charismatic character, Brush, the leader of Frank's gang of boys known in the school as "the middle five," sets the tone early in the narrative by reprimanding his mates for joking about Gray-beard's cough and about his belief in the Devil:

> "Don't make fun of the old man, he is here to help us; he wants to do us good."
>
> "Yes," answered Warren; "I guess he wanted to do you good last week, when he switched your back for you!"
>
> "I think I deserved it." (63)

Brush's magnanimity is enabled by the strength of his position in a cultural system of exchange rather than of absorption or resistance. Only a notion of dialogue could place him in such a subject position with the option to exonerate his attacker.

In terms of the historical context of Gray-beard's violence, it is important to point out that these events take place relatively early in the history of Omaha-white relations, when dispossession had not yet shown its full face. Furthermore, this story takes place on Omaha land filled with tribal tradition, where the mission school is diminished by "the highest hill for miles around. This was known by the Indians as 'the hill on which Um'pa-ton-ga (Big Elk) was buried.' He was one of the greatest chiefs of the Omaha" (10). Such a dominantly Omaha setting further generates a subject position for Brush sufficient to engage in dialogue on equal terms.

Strengthened by the land, that system of cultural exchange operates in the narrative as a microcosm of Omaha-white relations. Even in the face of Gray-beard's enraged beating of a frail and obsequious schoolboy, Brush transforms the situation through the discourse of reciprocity. The scene begins with Frank's description of the violence:

> Catching a firm grip on the hand of the boy, Gray-beard dealt blow after blow on the visibly swelling hand. The man seemed to lose all self-control, gritting his teeth and breathing heavily, while the child writhed in pain, turned blue, and lost his breath. It was a horrible sight. (138)

Frank, who narrowly escapes a similar treatment, remembers the words of the small boy's grandmother: "as she gave the boy to Gray-beard, 'I beg that he be kindly treated; that is all I ask!' And she had told the child that the White-chests would be kind to him" (138). Struggling mentally with Gray-beard's violence, Frank accounts for his own depths of anger:

> As for Gray-beard I did not care in the least about the violent shaking he had given me; but the vengeful way in which he fell upon that innocent boy created in my heart a hatred that was hard to conquer. . . . After supper I slipped away from my companions, and all alone I lay on the grass looking up at the stars, thinking of what had happened that afternoon. I tried to reconcile the act of Gray-beard with the teachings of the Missionaries, but I could not do so from any point of view. (138)

These are predictable feelings as a consequence of such a scene, and they play out the grueling dualisms registered by the teacher's polarizing violence. But La Flesche's narrative makes an important cultural negotiation by going further, registering the possibility of exchange even beyond material polarization. Brush takes the matter in hand, feeling entitled as he does to affirm his position in the exchange. When Frank tells of Gray-beard's violence,

> Brush had been listening to my story without a word; now he arose and said, "Boys, stay here till I come back."
>
> He went into the house and knocked at the superintendent's door.
>
> . . . When Brush had finished, the superintendent sent for Gray-beard. For a long time the two men talked earnestly together. At length Brush returned, and said, as he took his seat among us:
>
> "Boys, that will not happen again. Gray-beard says he's sorry he did it, and I believe him." (140)

This remarkable account climaxes the penultimate chapter with a complex victory. The dialogic triumph then is overshadowed by the final melancholy chapter, in which Brush dies of tuberculosis in the school infirmary. He dies only after he proves himself generously equal to the missionary, not in a belligerent opposition but in a dramatized assumption of equality that derives from a value of exchange.

Ending on loss, La Flesche structures his narrative in recognition of the historical oppositions that engulfed his people, yet he juxtaposes such loss with the non-oppositional pragmatics of cultural exchange which lost the historical struggle and yet survives. It survives both because part of the culture operates outside the terms of that struggle and because dialogic survival, unlike dialectic synthesis, maintains difference within the dynamics of opposition. La Flesche himself, an educated American Indian working as an ethnologist in Washington DC, embodies some of that intercultural dynamic which eludes cultural dualisms. Like *Papago Woman, The Middle Five* suggests a possibility not only of a dialogic mode of reading Native texts but also of reading history.

A postcolonial rather than neocolonial critique must by definition be non-oppositional and heteroglossic, because colonial hegemonies are based on dualistic oppositions. Non-oppositional dialogics does not mean "harmony" or "communication," any more than it means conciliation or complicity. To the extent that Native American authors, since the Sixteenth and Seventeenth Centuries,[7] labor to rewrite the colonial present, their work

---

[7]For instance the Incan, Felipe Guaman Poma de Ayala, wrote a twelve-hundred page letter to King Phillip III of Spain in 1613. Mary Louise Pratt analyzes the letter's complex negotiations of cultural difference in her "Arts of the Contact Zone." See also Louise Burkhart, "The Amanuenses Have Appropriated the Text." Native literary efforts have been chipping away at colonial dialectics for centuries.

becomes postcolonial.[8] It might be possible, however, through the efforts of theoreticians of various backgrounds, catching up with centuries of Native writers, for Native and non-Native readers to approach Native American texts with the assurance that knowing and understanding are processes rather than products. A final product of understanding across cultural differences may be unattainable, while an ongoing process of understanding may remain inescapable.

The Nexus of Exchange

Oversimplifying for the sake of discussion, Clifford's terms of cultural interaction and identity, which we have seen in Tohono O'odham and Omaha cultural texts, may spark the following sequence: Clifford's "resistance" would equal a dualistic pattern; "absorption" would equal a dialectic pattern; and a "nexus" of exchange would equal a dialogic. Thus resistance would be two monologisms in dualistic competition; absorption would be two monologisms in dualistic co-optation; and exchange would be a dialogism of multiple voices in collaboration, not in a utopian sense but in the sense of mutual cultural dynamics rather than hegemonic cultural domination or inertia.

While the limitations of dualism are relatively obvious, the distinctions between dialectics and dialogics are less so. In the discrete conceptual spaces opened up by these two notions there is a difference between their ethical effects in criticism. A dialogic, as in *Papago Woman* and *The Middle Five,* makes visible the possibility of exchange without dominance or co-optation, whereas the dialectic is haunted by the hierarchies of dominance inherent in dualism.

As Gilles Deleuze explains of the Platonic foundations of dialectical analysis,

> The purpose of division then is not at all to divide a genus into species, but, more profoundly, to select lineages: to distinguish pretenders; to distinguish the pure from the impure, the authentic from the inauthentic. (254)

---

[8]Bill Ashcroft et al. in *The Empire Writes Back* provide a useful definition: "We use the term 'post-colonial,' however, to cover all the culture affected by the imperial process from the moment of colonization to the present day. This is because there is a continuity of preoccupations throughout the historical process initiated by European imperial aggression. We also suggest that it is most appropriate as the term for the new cross-cultural criticism which has emerged in recent years and for the discourse through which this is constituted" (2). They go on to include "the literature of the USA" as postcolonial as well, and they specify the uniting features: "What each of these literatures has in common beyond their special and distinctive regional characteristics is that they emerged in their present form out of the experience of colonization and asserted themselves by foregrounding the tension with the imperial power, and by emphasizing their differences from the assumptions of the imperial centre. It is this which makes them distinctively post-colonial" (2). My use of the term emphasizes this latter effort enacted by dialogic strategies against colonial dialectics.

Platonic dualism is vertical rather than horizontal, an epistemological set of assumptions distinguishing truth from appearance. These assumptions take on oppressive force in hegemonic systems of authority and difference, such as civilization and wilderness, which they create. According to Deleuze, philosophy in the Platonic mode

> always pursues the same task . . . and adapts it to the speculative needs of Christianity. . . . Always the selection among pretenders, the exclusion of the eccentric and the divergent, in the name of a superior finality, an essential reality, or even a meaning of history. (260)

The dialectic thus selectively locates a final meaning within the colonial subject of history as against the colonized object. A dialogic emphasizes, however, the changeability of meaning in "both" participants, the colonized and the colonizer, the text and the author, the text and the reader, by showing how they are not aligned dualistically but rather are surrounded by influences in a multiple field. In Native American literature, continuing community is part of that field.

The thesis/antithesis structure of dialectics focuses on the definitions, the "what," of each opposing term in order to effect their synthesis. In addition to "what," the multiple structures of dialogics seek also to locate "where" each term stands in its place in the contextual web. In addition to definition, relation. While a dialectic moves toward definitive synthesis between subject and object, a dialogic moves toward relationality. Instead of dialectic synthesis, dialogic difference. Instead of static and ideal knowledge, dynamic and pragmatic interplay.

The dualistic, dialectic, and dialogic modes thus function as ideologies offering different patterns of information and accordingly generating different epistemological expectations and perceptions. Yet, if Bakhtin is correct, a dialogic heteroglossia is a given element of linguistic systems whether or not its users acknowledge those dialogic dynamics.

A dialogic system generates interactions, oppositions, and alliances in four dimensions. Instead of bipolar lines of force, the dialogic suggests Theodor Adorno's constellations or force-fields: "a relational interplay of attractions and aversions that constitute[d] the dynamic, transmutational structure of a complex phenomenon" (Jay 14). The image is of a sphere of intersecting polarities, each a dialectic interacting dialogically with all the others, while the sphere's circumference and center are constantly changing. Adorno's *Negative Dialectics* conceives further of an immanent shift of dialectics that subverts the Platonic hierarchies from within, resisting synthesis and accepting indeterminacy.

Dialogism acknowledges not only the primacy of context but also the impossibility of textual resolution, a productive indeterminacy, because it simultaneously accounts for a generalized force-field while it acknowledges the specificity of the other in that field. In literary theory, a tendency toward dualistic critique aligns itself hierarchically with self and other, which then, without examining the ethics of a colonial context, projects various unfortunate forms of the "noble savage" onto the colonized other. That dualistic epistemology can produce a politics of exoticism, an "orientalism," on the economics of mercantilism and commodification, reading the text for academic lucre. A more common dialectic operates in between these modes, suggesting the changeability or indeterminacy of dialogism but never moving beyond the objectizing and commodification inherent in the self-other paradigm of the dualistic mode.

Without expectations of fully "knowing the other," what then would be an alternative purpose for reading and critiquing texts from a cross-cultural position? Implementing Bakhtin's undecidability in the dialogics of language and Clifford's nexus of interactions, I would add to the specular Baconian paradigm of entertainment and information the notion of participation as an ethical response to reading. If non-Native or Native readers cannot finally read Indian texts to "know" the other, or even themselves, they can read to trace a path through the text to context, and thence to participation with textual and extratextual concerns of Indian communities. Thus the telos of reading would be not a cognitive commodity but a pragmatic, incremental, and participatory process. It would become not "the Indian problem" but everyone's responsibility, nor would it be a canon and its exclusions, perhaps not even a set of "American" and "Native American" literatures. Critiques would thus be able to measure themselves against history not only in retrospect but also within the present perspective of ethical relations to community context. The linkage of ethics with epistemology ultimately generates participation rather than information, an epistemology of active exchange, an intersubjective knowledge of how to participate with the other.[9] I will take up specific ways in which that academic participation might express itself in my concluding remarks. Generally, I have tried thus far to suggest how critiques that recognize the dialogics of cultural continuity actually participate in those political processes by visualizing possibilities apart from tragic colonial dialectics. An effort to deconstruct colonial binaries must have ethical effects.

Dialectical Readings of Dialogical Texts

Critiques trailing clouds of colonial dialectics often contrast with the dialogic exchange between cultures expressed in Chona's, La Flesche's, and many other Native texts. Choices by authors, translators, editors, publishers, audi-

---

[9]The contextual logic of the academy expects rigorous and thorough textual research in history and culture as contexts of any text. It does not ultimately expect living, experiential community to intersect that context. In contrast, a contextual logic in Native American texts is suspicious of critics who publish on Native literatures without community experience and investment. In the politics of publication, the logic of academic publishers eclipses the relatively invisible logic of Native American communities concerning texts written about themselves. Dialogic criticism suggests that the Native American context adds extratextual dimensions to critical "research."

ences, critics, and teachers of Native works are framed by assumptions of dialectical or dialogical cultural possibilities. Having described terms of dialogics and dialectics through which Native American literatures often construct their readership, I want to emphasize now the differences between these ways of reading by analyzing some critical oversights in relation to these terms. Dialectical approaches to dialogical texts can miss some of the cultural exchange both described and performed by such texts.

For this essay's focus on the ethical engagement of critics, I limit myself to examples of some specific choices by two professional readers, Arnold Krupat and David Murray, as they do and do not operate by a dialogic nexus of exchange with context. These two are key contributors to the current formative stages of Native American literary studies. Murray and Krupat are especially important in examining this issue of dialectic versus dialogic critique because each makes a careful effort to describe dialogics in Native texts.

It is difficult, if not impossible, in the discourse of this not yet postcolonial world to attain, much less sustain, a dialogical stance. I would be surprised if I am not practicing dialectic oversights of dialogic possibilities in my discussion of these issues. My discussion is a response to Arnold Krupat's own invitations to dialogism, and my critique of some of his and David Murray's critical choices is given in the spirit of dialogue rather than opposition. Krupat, who achieves a remarkable articulation of the foundations of a critical discourse in his *Ethnocriticism: Ethnography, History, Literature,* is quite open to criticism of his provisionary "ethnocriticism," saying that it

> does not yet exist and . . . will only be achieved by means of complex interactions between a variety of Western discursive and analytic modes and a variety of non-Western modes of knowing and understanding. (43–44)

In their distinctive contributions to the criticism of Native literatures, Krupat and Murray both make a conscious point of not naively assuming that they can cross from the colonial self to a full understanding of the colonized or the postcolonial other. Murray marks these concerns as the foundation of his benchmark study, *Forked Tongues: Speech, Writing, and Representation in North American Indian Texts:*

> In trying to avoid the colonialist assumption of an ability to comprehend (in the sense of encompass, as well as understand) Indian cultures and their difference, we could modestly confine ourselves to examining the accounts and representations of Indians, not to judge their accuracy but to reveal what they say about white ideological investments. (3)

For all the modesty in this approach, it threatens a certain cultural solipsism. The ultimate return to the (post) colonial subject as the *telos* of engagement with the other seems unfortunate, not in the sense of lacking completion or finality but precisely in its cessation of ongoing dialogue, its conclusive stasis. Is it not possible to negotiate a reading beyond the traditional one in which, as Roy Harvey Pearce describes it in Cooper, "The interest is not in the Indian as Indian, but in the Indian as a vehicle for understanding the white man . . ." (202)?

The question is the fulcrum of my effort to describe an ethics of criticism of Native American literatures. Certainly Murray sees his reflection on white ideological investments as one step in an ongoing process, although his language tends to erase such a process by the terms: "confine ourselves" to a final focus on "white ideological investments." I am outlining a critical ethics by which further exchange, however incremental, is clearly consistent with the texts. What about the focus of Native American texts for Indian and other non-white readers? Do Indians reading literature by white writers return only to Native American ideological investments?

Such polarized questions derive from Murray's carefully and consciously polarized self-positioning, and as such they suggest the dialectical limits of such a stance. In spite of his critical intentions, his discourse helps to delineate essentialist boundaries. Murray's choice, for all its semiotic logic, is to follow colonial and racial lines of readership, white and Indian, placing himself honestly on the white side of the frontier. But in so doing he follows Clifford's "pervasive dichotomy: absorption by the other *or* resistance to the other," even while Murray's purpose is to avoid absorbing the other. His choices clarify further how the ethics of Native American literary criticism call for different paradigms.

In order to engage in a dialogue with Indian literature, the exchange becomes not merely cognitive but also participatory, not merely textual but also contextual. The knowledge of self and other, of "white ideological investments," may give way to participation in context, in community, an agonistic process in itself. Minimally, critics can perform that participatory knowing by recurring reference to context surrounding text, by visualizing the cultural constellations or force-fields that bend and shape colonial binaries.

Murray's modesty recognizes cultural representations of the other as the central focus of his project, "paying attention to the mediator or interpreter, rather than what he is pointing to" (1), and ostensibly avoiding, as he says, an "essentializing of difference, with all that this politically and culturally entails" (2). Murray's project proves to be one of the most useful applications of post-structural theory to the field so far, clarifying the complexities of colonial representation. However, the political correctness that Murray invokes in the name of modesty can subtly reinvoke the Platonic dualisms built up historically around colonial self and other. By focusing on mediations within the cultural gap, he does not reduce the dualistic tendencies of language. In fact, by magnifying the eclipsing function of mediation, Murray's "other" can slip away further into the dialectic gap of semiotic uncertainty, effectively essentializing difference. The function of a dialectic epistemology is to re-excavate that chasm, and the function of an alternate dialogic epistemology is to elude it.

Murray's reinscriptions of that dualistic paradigm lead him paradoxically to some critical choices that explicitly conflate Native and non-Native writers. Yet Murray's intention is negotiation, or navigation, of that uncertainty, as he explains in concert with Arnold Krupat:

> We must therefore have a view of translation and communication which can take us between the Scylla of universalism, and the Charybdis of absolute relativism. We need as Arnold Krupat puts it, "not to overthrow the Tower of Babel, but, as it were, to install a simultaneous translation system in it; not to homogenize human or literary differences but to make them at least mutually intelligible." (3)

For all the professional care that such statements summon, the defensive use of the phrase "absolute relativism" elides two epistemological points: "absolute relativism" is an oxymoron available only to a universalist, and dualistic, discourse; and a fear of relativism as "absolute" is expressly a fear on the part of a dialectic faced by open-ended dialogism. When such conceptual parameters guide Murray's critical choice to focus on mediation in the name of avoiding naive or colonizing readings, he redefines the options by a continued polarization.

As Murray overlooks a context of dialogic cultural survival, he produces phrases and crucial claims that take a dialectical, specular position in relation to Native American texts. For instance, when he discusses the postcolonial complexity of returning to tribally specific and local rather than universalist and hence dominating cultural identities, his cogent discussion arrives at a claim that seems calculated to startle by its scrupulous honesty. First he summarizes Leslie Silko's 1979 "An Old-Time Indian Attack," an essay that challenges the "cultural arrogance" of Louis Simpson, Gary Snyder, and white ethnopoets in their appropriations of Indian materials. Silko identifies a notion of "universal consciousness" that provides especially white writers with the assumed " 'power' to inhabit any soul, any consciousness" (4). Murray agrees with this critique, writing that this process derives from "universalist assumptions which, given an imbalance of power, effectively mean domination and monoculture" (91). He asserts that "here the issue is what resources can be marshalled against" such dominating assumptions, and he goes on to suggest "the political implications of the recourse to the local" as against the universal, citing parallels in this stress on "the personal and the situational" between "primitive" and postmodern contexts (91–92).

Yet Murray's political focus narrows as he proceeds to draw on De Certeau to assert that Native American identities are

> imposed from the outside—by ethnology—but I would argue that even if this is so, the problem is now that available identities are not—certainly in North America—separable from this cultural one in any straightforward way. (92)

While certainly the colonial gaze must be a key part of Native American identity structures, the underlying problem with Murray's analysis, which shows up below in his further conclusion about Silko, is that he is looking at identities, "imposed from the outside," in dialectic terms—outside versus inside—rather than in terms of a dialogic nexus of exchange. This dialectic becomes nearly paralyzed by paradox: "In particular, to write about Indian experience and be published in English is inevitably to be involved in an ambiguous area of cultural identity" (92). The reality of ambiguity is undeniable, but the direction Murray takes through it is a linear dialectical one, which leads him to his universalizing rejoinder to Silko's "Old-time Indian Attack": Murray asserts that because of that "ambiguous area of cultural identity" constructed by a postmodern world,

> . . . modern Indian writers writing in English are not so very different from the white ethnopoets Silko criticizes, in their relation to Indian cultures. (92)

Murray seems unaffected by the prospect that his ethical critical choice to make this claim ignores other dialogic possibilities, while it presumes to do the forthright work of an honest critique. The unfortunate effect, by simply "returning the fire" of Silko's attack, is to replay the historically racial dialectic it tries to pacify.

The dialectical epistemological structure of Murray's response leads him to claim a "not so very different," absorptive sameness, thus effecting a co-optation. His last phrase, "in their relation to Indian cultures," would seem most unreasonable to a dialogic reading for the following reason: if Indian communities are a context for the Indian texts Silko contrasts with ethnopoetic texts, and if Indian communities speak dialogically in Indian texts, then writers who are part of those communities write with a significantly different context, hence dialogic text, than those who are not part of those communities. In a dialogic reading, the context is inseparable from the text, and the ethics of community in that context are also inseparable. Some white ethnopoets and others, though rarely, do become a welcome part of Indian communities as a function of the nexus of exchange. Yet Murray's equation of Indian and non-Indian writers as "not so very different . . . in their relation to Indian cultures" overlooks that dialogic context in Silko and other Indian writers who write from Indian community in ways that few if any white ethnopoets can. Murray is assuming the dialectical, a contextual, individual voice in both Indian writers and white ethnopoets.

In a similar ethical direction, Murray attempts to restore the work of Carlos Castaneda to the academic "debate of fictional techniques in ethnography" (155). In his last chapter entitled "Dialogues and Dialogics," Murray discusses authenticity as an undercurrent behind what he calls dialogic or reflexive anthropology. He ends his book by claiming that certain criticisms against Carlos Castaneda are founded on a nostalgia for authenticity among those reflexive anthropologists, such as Stephen Tyler and Clifford Geertz, who assume a final, authentic "non-fiction." Such authenticity, they maintain, should not and cannot be fictionalized à la Castaneda:

> . . . for all the talk of fiction, there is throughout postmodern anthropology an implicit assumption that fiction only operates *within* a text already authorized as ethnography and therefore as non-fiction, and that there are professional and unstated parameters of behavior, which Castaneda has violated. (155)

Criticism of Castaneda may certainly be nostalgic, as Murray suggests. Yet that nostalgia may be cut, and the criticism sharpened, by a sense of ethical dialogics that eludes the essentialism, the nostalgia for nonfictional truth, that Murray imputes to those critics.

Murray seems to miss the dialogic issue that what is authentic in Native texts and inauthentic in Castaneda is not an Indian essence, but an historical memory within the nexus of exchange in and between cultures. The point is not that Castaneda lacks some essential Yaqui identity, as the anthropologists, whom Murray criticizes, might indirectly suggest, but that Castaneda lacks a particular historical identity, an ethical context of interrelations that only a Yaqui text can speak. Murray's choice to valorize Castaneda and to place him significantly at the finale of his study of "Indian texts" eclipses that specific dialogic Yaqui history. He reifies cultural absorption, thus missing, along with Castaneda, that contextual difference. Murray's semiotics, emphasizing the dialectical oscillation and distance between representation and reality, between text and context, thus misses the ethical problems of Castaneda's appropriation of Native American representations. A pragmatic dialogic does not pause at that semiotic abyss to wonder at the irony of represented otherness; it moves by the force of material realities not to close that gap but to play around its circumference.

Not unlike Murray's, Krupat's critique of naiveté is central to his crucial work in mapping "ethnocriticism." For instance, he critiques a universalist, "idealistic vein" in Karl Kroeber for describing Indian stories as appealing "to enough common features in human nature to allow us at least entrance to their pleasures" (9). Krupat points out that "Kroeber here replicates the worst aspects of Levi-Straussian idealism" by predicating an "esthetic universalism" (*Ethnocriticism* 180) and "ignoring the particular, different, and other . . . culturally specific modes and codes" (182) of the Native text.

Krupat is rigorous in his ideological critique, as he identifies similar cross-cultural naiveté in Jarold Ramsey's evocation of "vivid feelings within oneself" as a reader's source of appreciation of Nez Perce tales. Taking exception to Ramsey's citation of Nez Perce translator Archie Phinney, Krupat writes,

> As a participant in Nez Perce culture, a speaker of the language, and a fully prepared auditor of mythic stories, Phinney may well judge the effectiveness of any given telling as it does or does not produce "vivid feelings" in him. For

> Ramsey to appropriate Phinney's criteria as so easily available to the Western reader is naive at best, and even then a naiveté perpetuating the worst imperial arrogance. (*Ethnocriticism* 182)

Strong words at least, setting up an oppositional and hence dialectic rather than dialogic critique of a critique.[10] Krupat is direct in acknowledging that his own ethnocritical alternatives "may never fully exist in other than tentative, oxymoronic . . . forms" (43).

Further, Krupat is quite explicit, in *The Voice in the Margin,* to avoid "the sort of criticism which, in the rather mystical—and, indeed, mystifying—old-fashioned way," (12) is written by early and recent scholars with more interest in simply championing Indians than in rigorous critical analysis. His critique addresses apparently naive assumptions of figures as varied as non-Indian scholars Mary Austin or Robin Riddington and Kiowa writer and artist N. Scott Momaday. While Krupat's critical challenge has sharpened the field invaluably, he follows that line through its logical polemics to assert a position that must entrench itself in colonial oppositions. His position apparently misses the alternatives that Clifford proposes. Krupat asserts,

> Nor can anyone who would comment on Native American culture ignore the perspective from which it is produced. But that does not mean that one is "obliged" to adopt that perspective or to insist on the absolute difference of it from the perspectives of the West. (14)

Like Murray's "absolute relativism" above, Krupat's own stance, in his absolute phrasing, sets him in dialectic opposition to a straw man. My discussion of the ways in which an ethics of reading overlaps with aesthetic textual issues does indeed suggest a degree of participation in, though certainly not unanimity with, alternative perspectives. Krupat's resistant hyperbole against being "obliged" to insist on "absolute difference" suggests a defensive stance that wants to circle the wagons against an imagined attack. That attack must be a dialectic projection of the menacing other, one the critical self assumes to be real.

From this more entrenched dualism, Krupat returns in *The Voice in the Margin* to an open suggestion of dialogue that echoes the participatory purposes of my discussion:

> For all these strong words, I would not want to be understood as denying that one might learn from the Indians themselves how to produce a more accurate criticism of Indian literature. (15)

---

[10]Both Ramsey and Kroeber elsewhere critique Krupat's work. It is important to point out, neither in defense of Ramsey or Kroeber nor of naiveté but only toward a clearer sense of dialogic critique between even the texts of scholars, that Ramsey and Kroeber are elsewhere careful in their generalizations, that they are not transparently naive, certainly not uninformed, and that the antidote to any naiveté's imbalanced perspective is not *ad hominem* attack but balanced analysis in dialogue.

Krupat's and Murray's skepticism toward naively universalist assumptions, which are as traditional in American letters as Walt Whitman's amative, imperial selfhood, is certainly a prerequisite to careful negotiation of critical and cultural exchange with texts. Yet it is not naive to suggest that the particular possibilities for intercultural critical participation are multiple, however sensitive. If exchange is possible then acculturation can move in both directions. Without Foucault's view of distributed power, however, a certain cultural hegemony assumes that the non-Native can be only a colonizing agent, whereas a view of alterity suggests that the former colonizer was and is indeed a participant in exchange. A too scrupulous application of the Heisenberg principle without a notion of exchange can lead to a mystified insistence on uncertainty, even to that "Puritan taboo on mixing beliefs and bodies" (Clifford 344), that reinforces the dichotomous Western model of cultural contact with its exotic other. An assessment of naiveté can in fact be an excess of caution that belies certain conceptual dualisms rather than dialogisms. Further, it can be the expression of a failed faith in an epistemology of cognition, where the impossible effort to know, without an alternative participatory epistemology of exchange, simply reinscribes the Native other first as the vanishing sign and then as the vanishing Indian.

An alternative epistemology of exchange logically opens up both perceptions of historically specific Native cultural survival and of academic participation in recognition of that survival. Thus a dialectic critique can miss the political context of dialogic cultural survival in these texts. A dialogic critique, however, might find textual and contextual ways for critical selves to speak neither of nor for the other but rather with the other.

Krupat's ethnocritical project is to "say something about Native Americans as subjects and producers of varieties of American discourse" (*Ethnocriticism* 3). Yet the force of historical and cultural dialectics can lead even one such as Krupat, who so carefully analyzes the "dialogic self"[11] in Native American autobiography, to at times take refuge in dialectical critique. A couple of further instances will serve to mark the ethical intricacy of this territory. The first is a minor one, having the uncomfortable air of a joke turned sour. Krupat's academic witticism, like much humor, functions by caricature, an exaggerated generality. (Which is why so much of literary criticism, trying to get beyond generalities to specificities, seems so humorless. Still I must apologize for the humorlessness of my analysis of his joke.) Problems with the joke are worth pointing out as an analogy of larger contextual problems in some of his critical choices.

---

[11]See, for instance, Chapter 4 of Arnold Krupat's *The Voice in the Margin,* "Monologue and Dialogue in Native American Autobiography," 132–33. Krupat describes the dynamics of Native dialogic selves primarily by textual interactions between informant, translator, and editor. The question remains how that dialogic Native informant's position in "a particular [textual] placement in relation to the many voices without which it could not exist" (133) resonates with extratextual Native cultural patterns of dialogic identities.

The opening salvo of Krupat's important essay on "Post-Structuralism and Oral Literature" begins thus:

> To speak of post-structuralist theory in conjunction with Native American literatures may seem as odd as serving dog stew with *sauce béarnaise*. (113)

Krupat sets up this joke as an objective description of the perceived distance between Native Americanists and critical theorists, and he does so specifically to bridge that gap. But his witticism is unfortunate in that the dualism at the heart of its metaphorical power can so vividly reinforce the terms of a colonial history which it seeks to elude. Clearly the sophisticated humor works only for those in the *sauce béarnaise* crowd, not for the various Plains tribes whose rituals still include ceremonial cooking and eating of dog stew. But how does this backfire?

As a framing statement it selectively aligns cultural images into a comparative set which, within the context of the academic discourse used to describe those images, is unequal. Dog stew, being so far outside the context of academic discourse, must create in most of Krupat's readers a different level of response from *sauce béarnaise,* an image more familiar to the contexts of Krupat's text. This difference parallels those of positive v. negative, superlative v. pejorative, pleasure v. disgust. The effect is to further exoticize a ritual food with cultural significance to Sioux, Kiowa, and other tribes and hence to play into the inauspicious polarizations of colonialism. This is not to say that the phrase "dog stew" itself could not be used in academic discourse, but it does emphasize the dialogic need to establish a context of Indian community ethics surrounding the two-word text, "dog stew."

However much it is Krupat's logical purpose to open with the "unfortunate fact" of a misunderstanding that he intends to resolve, however much he intends to bridge the dualities that dog stew and *sauce béarnaise* represent, and however much his own text indeed speaks explicitly to "signal a change in the situation I have described" (113), the unbalanced contexts of academic and Indian communities clarify the ethical implications of his critical choice to open an essay in those terms. He allows the academic context to interact with his text without the Indian context, a dialectic choice for absorption rather than a dialogic choice for exchange. As my discussion suggests, each of those contexts, academic and Indian community, is a necessary dialogic component of both Krupat's analytical text and the brief text "dog stew," not only in terms of the aesthetic interplay between text and context but also in the ethical interplay of text and reader derived from the interplay of aesthetics and ethics.

A larger issue in relation to dialogic criticism is Krupat's "interest in a frontier perspective" for his critical enterprise (*Ethnocriticism* 5). Krupat's intention is to reappropriate the term "frontier" as a trope for his ethnocriticism. "Central to ethnohistorical work is the concept of the *frontier*" (4):

> Ethnocritical discourse, in its self-positioning at the frontier, seeks to traverse rather than occupy a great variety of "middle grounds," both at home and abroad. (*Ethnocriticism* 25)

In reappropriating the word, he wishes to align himself with modern eth-nohistorians such as James Clifton for whom, as Krupat explains,

> The frontier . . . is not defined in the progressivist-evolutionist manner of Frederick Jackson Turner as the farthest point to which *civilization* has ad-vanced, a series of those points apparently marking a clearly discernible line between "us" and "them." Rather, in a more relativist manner, the frontier is understood as simply that shifting space in which two *cultures* encounter one another. (*Ethnocriticism* 5)

In spite of this careful redefinition, the rationale for recycling the term is not itself clarified in Krupat's discussion, i.e., not only *whether* the frontier can indeed be redefined apart from its historical discursive context, but *why* it should be. Why eclipse that history by attempting to reclaim the word? Not unlike my choice to retain "dialogism" with its dualistic etymology as a ges-ture toward the historical power of dualistic epistemes, Krupat perhaps chooses "frontier" as an ironic gesture toward its historical and popular cur-rency as well. Yet the term "frontier" does not by historical definition offer a dynamic beyond oppositional paradigms. Instead, it matches a dialectic episteme where the interplay is seen in dualistic terms, "in which two cul-tures encounter each other."

The critical choice to reinvest in a term like "the frontier" is made problematic simply by the history of that material dialectic playing it-self out in mercantile and martial contexts. In Leslie Fiedler's words, "Guilt and the Frontier are coupled from the first . . ." (132). As Al-fonso Ortiz writes in his essay "Indian/White Relations: A View from the Other Side of the 'Frontier,' " the notion of the "frontier" is, like the notion of "Western civilization," an "enemy" to "the cause of a mean-ingful Indian history" (3). Indeed, in contrast to Krupat's intentions, Ortiz suggests that ideologically the term "frontier" itself matches pre-cisely the same advance-guard relation to "Western civilization" that it assumes historically. In comparison with "Western civilization," Ortiz writes, the term "frontier"

> has been much more actively harmful to the cause of Indian survival and to the writing of meaningful histories of Indian/white relations, let alone of In-dian tribes themselves. (3)

In making this claim, Ortiz is drawing upon the ethics of context that a dia-logic critique calls for, linking text ethically to context. The text of the word "frontier" evidently contains an historical context to which scholars must make ethical responses.

Certainly the word bristles with images of settlers and Indians aligned in opposition along that dualistic, historic, imaginary dividing line. Follow-ing inevitably on the choice of a contextually unredeemable term, the aca-demic critic of any race and the Native American text must then take their historically constructed oppositional positions, since "the frontier," in Indian country, is always already an alienating term. Moreover, Krupat's "frontier perspective" can exclude not only the communities contextualized in Native texts but also those in the growing community of Native scholars in the academy who avoid the term. (Native scholars are not united in opposition to use of the word "frontier.") If the term is conflicted, why then select that trope?

Krupat himself articulates pragmatic alternatives:

> . . . ethnocriticism wishes to constitute itself as a critical practice in no way condemned to ironic oscillations between Western narratives, but, rather, as freely choosing a commitment to the production of whatever narratives—and it is impossible to predict with any accuracy the forms these will take—may serve to tell the emerging story of culture change. . . . (*Ethnocriticism* 126)

That Krupat's critique might oscillate between open-ended dialogism and more polarized dialectics is a mark itself of that emergence. This is the irony of a dialectic faced with and thus alienated by dialogism, as an imperial *sauce béarnaise* is alienated by a relational dog stew or as so many explorers on the "frontier" were alienated, since 1492, by their own lack of perception of ongoing exchange with Native America.

Critiques of Native American texts can introduce a positive, postcolonial postmodernism that acknowledges new visibilities, new paradigms on the intercultural field. The slightly nostalgic critique to which Krupat, along with Clifford, candidly confesses as "the hope of telling the 'whole' or 'true' story" (*Ethnocriticism* 123) is less willing to see a postmodern nexus as positive. Instead of a paradox of closed "ironic oscillations," where two poles perpetually face each other, a positive postmodernism suggests many poles. Each gazes not only at its own opposite or projection, but toward an openness of positional political or ethical opportunities to act and experience, to know pragmatically. Eluding that epistemological quest for absolute knowledge, Native texts such as La Flesche's and Chona's generate instead both aesthetic and ethical participation. As Krupat says,

> To read Native American literature, to take pleasure in it and try to understand it, can be an end in itself, like going to a museum or a concert. It can also engage us in a struggle for the values that determine our lives. (*Voice* 238)

Decolonializing Criticism

How then can critics participate in a textual context of dialogic cultural survival? Certainly the most direct labor that literary critics can perform is a textual effort. Not only can we avoid, as Anthony Wilden says, "Any scientific theory or position which . . . can be construed as contributing to the psychological, social, or material alienation of any class or group."[12] Critics can affirmatively articulate modes of cultural interaction in the texts that elude domination, assimilation, or co-optation and that make visible possibilities of cultural survival through such processes as a nexus of exchange.

Elaine Jahner suggests in a similar vein that

> the critic must start with the premise that oral forms reflect particular ways of knowing, that they are epistemological realities. They exist both as artifact and as process. (223)

In response to this sense of realities in the text, Jahner envisions a critical approach to the complex field of Native American studies that begins to reflect certain Native American ways:

> . . . cooperation among many critics, writers, folklorists, anthropologists, and art historians, all of whom can publish sensitive descriptions of specific artistic traditions, not in the style of the once-popular "definitive" accounts of "dying" traditions, but in a way that shows both the continuity and the open-endedness of tribal ways. (212)

Beyond Wilden's call to avoid oppressive metaphors, Jahner proposes affirmative descriptions of tribal patterns of survival. Such work would attest to dialogic relations between the academy and Indian communities.

In addition, a dialogical context does offer extratextual responses as well as textual ones in both academic and Indian communities. If the ethics of reading includes community participation by both Native and non-Native scholars, then linking academia to Indian communities (not only west but east of the Mississippi as well)—via teaching and mentoring Native students, via support of tribal college programs, via publication of Native materials, via clarifying cultural dialogics in classrooms to both non-Native and Native students—all could be additional modes of reading the contexts of Native texts. Another complex area in which professionals may reshape colonial epistemologies toward postcolonial ones is the ethical treatment of intellectual and cultural property rights.

One can "give back" in a variety of ways—by teaching, by writing, by round dancing when the invitation goes out at a powwow, by just attending cultural events such as powwows, by bringing food to a wake, or by coming over merely to hang out and visit. Eventually I must leave the question of whether we can move experientially and intellectually outside our own received epistemologies for those who still think we cannot. Certainly critics can build toward a dialogic reading of Native American texts with a perspective that those texts provide.

---

[12]Epigraph by Anthony Wilden in Krupat, *Ethnocriticism,* unnumbered front pages.

Works Cited

Allen, Paula Gunn. "Teaching American Indian Oral Literatures." *Studies in American Indian Literature: Critical Essays and Course Designs.* Ed. Paula Gunn Allen. New York: MLA, 1983. 33–51.

Ardorno, Theodor. *Negative Dialectics.* Trans. E. B. Ashton. New York: Continuum, 1992.

Ashcroft, Bill, et al. *The Empire Writes Back: Theory and Practice in Post-Colonial Literatures.* New York: Routledge, 1989.

Bakhtin, M. M. *The Dialogic Imagination: Four Essays.* Ed. Michael Holquist. Austin: U of Texas P, 1981.

Burkhart, Louise M. "The Amanuenses Have Appropriated the Text." *On the Translation of Native American Literatures.* Ed. Brian Swann. Washington DC: Smithsonian Institution P, 1992. 339–55.

Clifford, James. *The Predicament of Culture.* Cambridge: Harvard UP, 1988.

Deleuze, Gilles. "The Simulacrum and Ancient Philosophy: Plato and the Simulacrum." *The Logic of Sense.* New York: Columbia UP, 1990.

Douglass, Frederick. "West Indian Emancipation." *The Life and Writings of Frederick Douglass II: Pre-Civil War Decade, 1850–1860.* Ed. Philip S. Foner. New York: International, 1950. 426–39.

Fiedler, Leslie. "Montana; or The End of Jean-Jacques Rousseau." *An End to Innocence: Essays on Culture and Politics.* Boston: Beacon, 1955. 131–41.

Fisher, Philip. "Democratic Social Space: Whitman, Melville, and the Promise of American Transparency." *Representations* 24 (Fall 1988): 60–101.

Jahner, Elaine. "A Critical Approach to American Indian Literature." *Studies in American Indian Literature: Critical Essays and Course Designs.* Ed. Paula Gunn Allen. New York: MLA, 1983. 211–24.

Jay, Martin. *Adorno.* Cambridge: Harvard UP, 1984.

Kroeber, Karl. "An Introduction to the Art of Traditional American Indian Narration." *Traditional American Indian Literatures: Texts and Interpretations.* Ed. Karl Kroeber. Lincoln: U of Nebraska P, 1981.

———. *Ethnocriticism: Ethnography, History, Literature.* Berkeley: U of California P, 1992.

———. "Post-Structuralism and Oral Literature." *Recovering the Word: Essays on Native American Literature.* Eds. Brian Swann and Arnold Krupat. Berkeley: U of California P, 1987. 113–28.

———. *The Voice in the Margin: Native American Literature and the Canon.* Berkeley: U of California P, 1989.

Krupat, Arnold. *Ethnocriticism: Ethnography, History, Literature.* Berkeley: U of California P, 1992.

———. *Voice in the Margin: Native American Literature and the Canon.* Berkeley: U of California P, 1989.

La Flesche, Francis. *The Middle Five: Indian Schoolboys of the Omaha Tribe.* 1900. Lincoln: U of Nebraska P, 1978.

McNickle, D'Arcy. *Native American Tribalism: Indian Survivals and Renewals.* New York: Oxford UP, 1973.

Murray, David. *Forked Tongues: Speech, Writing, and Representation in North American Indian Texts.* Bloomington: Indiana UP, 1991.

Ortiz, Alfonso. "Indian/White Relations: A View from the Other Side of the 'Frontier.' " *Indians in American History: An Introduction.* Ed. Frederick E. Hoxie. Arlington Heights, IL: Harlan Davidson, 1988. 1-16.

Pearce, Roy Harvey. *Savagism and Civilization: A Study of the Indian and the American Mind.* 1953. Berkeley: U of California P, 1988.

Pratt, Mary Louise. "Arts of the Contact Zone." *Profession 91.* New York: MLA, 1991. 33-40.

Ruoff, A. LaVonne Brown. *American Indian Literatures: An Introduction, Bibliographic Review, and Selected Bibliography.* New York: MLA, 1990.

Siebers, Tobin. *The Ethics of Criticism.* Ithaca: Cornell UP, 1988.

Silko, Leslie Marmon. "An Old-Time Indian Attack Conducted in Two Parts." *Shantih* 4 (1979): 3-5.

———. *Ceremony.* New York: New American Library, 1977.

Tax, Sol. *Documentary History of the Fox Project, 1948–1959.* Chicago: U of Chicago P, 1960.

Underhill, Ruth M. *Papago Woman.* 1936. New York: Holt, Rinehart and Winston, 1979.

Vizenor, Gerald. *The Heirs of Columbus.* Hanover, NH: UP of New England, 1991.

Whitman, Walt. *Leaves of Grass.* Norton Critical Edition. Eds. Sculley, Bradley and Harold W. Blodgett. New York: Norton, 1973.

Simon J. Ortiz (Acoma, Pueblo)

Towards a National Indian Literature:
Cultural Authenticity in Nationalism

Uncle Steve—Dzeerlai, which was his Acqumeh name—was not a literate man and he certainly was not literary. He is gone now, into the earth and back north as the Acqumeh people say, but I remember him clearly. He was a subsistence farmer, and he labored for the railroad during his working years; I remember him in his grimy working clothes. But I remember him most vividly as he sang and danced and told stories—not literary stories, mind you, but it was all literature nevertheless.

On fiesta days, Steve wore a clean, good shirt and a bright purple or blue or red neckerchief knotted at his tightly buttoned shirt collar. Prancing and dipping, he would wave his beat-up hat, and he would holler, Juana, Juana! Or Pedro, Pedro! It would depend on which fiesta day it was, and other men and younger ones would follow his lead. Juana! Pedro! It was a joyous and vigorous sight to behold, Uncle Dzeerlai expressing his vitality from within the hold of our Acqumeh Indian world.

There may be some question about why Uncle Steve was shouting Juana and Pedro, obviously Spanish names, non-Indian names. I will explain. In the summer months of June, July, and August, there are in the Pueblo Indian communities of New Mexico celebrations on Catholic saints' days. Persons whose names are particular saints' names honor those names by giving to the community and its people. In turn, the people honor those names by receiving. The persons named after the saints such as John or Peter—Juan, Pedro—throw from housetops gifts like bread, cookies, cracker-jacks, washcloths, other things, and the people catching and receiving dance and holler the names. It will rain then and the earth will be sustained; it will be a community fulfilled in its most complete sense of giving and receiving, in one word: sharing. And in sharing, there is strength and continuance.

But there is more than that here. Obviously, there is an overtone that this is a Catholic Christian ritual celebration because of the significance of the saints' names and days on the Catholic calendar. But just as obviously, when the celebration is held within the Acqumeh community, it is an Acqumeh ceremony. It is Acqumeh and Indian (or Native American or American Indian if one prefers those terms) in the truest and most authentic sense. This is so because this celebration speaks of the creative ability of Indian people to gather in many forms of the socio-political colonizing force which beset them and to make these forms meaningful in their own terms. In fact, it is a celebration of the human spirit and the Indian struggle for liberation.

Many Christian religious rituals brought to the Southwest (which in the 16th century was the northern frontier of the Spanish New World) are no longer Spanish. They are now Indian because of the creative development that the native people applied to them. Present-day Native American or Indian literature is evidence of this in the very same way. And because in every case where European culture was cast upon Indian people of this nation there was similar creative response and development, it can be observed that this was the primary element of a nationalistic impulse to make use of foreign ritual, ideas, and material in their own—Indian—terms. Today's writing by Indian authors is a continuation of that elemental impulse.

Let me tell you more about Dzeerlai. I have a memory of him as he and other men sang at one Acqumeh event. He is serious and his face is concentrated upon the song, meaning, and the event that is taking place during this particular afternoon in early September. Santiago and Chapiyuh have come to Acqu. They enter from the south, coming exactly upon the route that Juan de Onate's soldiers took when they razed Acqu in the winter of 1598.

Santiago was the patron saint of the Spanish soldiers, and the name seemed to have been their war cry as well. On this afternoon, as he steps upon the solid stone of Acqu, Santiago is dressed in ostentatious finery. His clothes have a sheen and glitter that anyone can marvel at and envy. He wears a cowboy ten-gallon hat and there are heavy revolvers strapped to his hips. The spurs on his fancy boots jingle and spin as he and his horse prance about. As Santiago waves a white-gloved hand at the crowds of Acqumeh people lining his route and grins ludicrously with a smile painted rigidly on a pink face, the people still marvel but they check their envy. They laugh at Santiago and the hobby horse steed stuck between his legs.

Alongside, and slightly behind to his right, is another figure, Chapiyuh. His name is abrupt in the mouth. He doesn't walk; he stomps as he wears heavy leather thick-soled boots like a storm-trooper. Chapiyuh has a hood over his face with slits cut in it for eyes. He wears the dark flowing robes of a Franciscan priest secured with a rough rope at his waist. In one hand Chapiyuh carries a bullwhip which he cracks or a length of chain, and in the other hand he carries the book, the Bible. As he stomps along heavily, he makes threatening gestures to the people and they shrink away. Children whimper and cling desperately to their mothers' dresses.

There are prayer narratives for what is happening, and there are songs. Uncle Steven and his partners sang for what was happening all along the route that Santiago and Chapiyuh took into Acqu. It is necessary that there be prayer and song because it is important, and no one will forget then; no one will regard it as less than momentous. It is the only way in which event and experience, such as the entry of the Spaniard to the Western Hemisphere, can become significant and realized in the people's own terms. And this, of course, is what happens in literature, to bring about meaning and meaningfulness. This perception and meaningfulness has to happen; otherwise, the hard experience of the Euroamerican colonization of the lands and people of the Western Hemisphere would be driven into the dark recesses of the indigenous mind and psyche. And this kind of repression is always a poison and detriment to creative growth and expression.

As one can see, most of this perception and expression has been possible through the oral tradition which includes prayer, song, drama-ritual, narrative or storytelling, much of it within ceremony—some of it outside of ceremony—which is religious and social. Indeed, through the past five centuries the oral tradition has been the most reliable method by which Indian culture and community integrity have been maintained. And, certainly, it is within this tradition that authenticity is most apparent and evident.

Uncle Steve and his singer-partners were naturally authentic as they sought to make a lesson of history significant, and they did so within the context of the Acqumeh community. There is no question of the authenticity of the ritual drama in that case. But there is more than the context that makes the drama—and any subsequent literary expression of it—authentic. Steve was only one in a long line of storytellers and singers who have given expression to the experience of Indian people in the Americas. Throughout the difficult experience of colonization to the present, Indian women and men have struggled to create meaning of their lives in very definite and systematic ways. The ways or methods have been important, but they are important only because of the reason for the struggle. And it is that reason—the struggle against colonialism—which has given substance to what is authentic.

Since colonization began in the 15th century with the arrival of the Spaniard priest, militarist, and fortune and slave seeker upon the shores of this hemisphere, Indian songmakers and storytellers have created a body of oral literature which speaks crucially about the experience of colonization. Like the drama and the characters described above, the indigenous peoples of the Americas have taken the languages of the colonialists and used them for their own purposes. Some would argue that this means that Indian people have succumbed or become educated into a different linguistic system and have forgotten or have been forced to forsake their native selves. This is simply not true. Along with their native languages, Indian women and men have carried on their lives and their expression through the use of the newer languages, particularly Spanish, French, and English, and they have used these languages on their own terms. This is the crucial item that has to be understood, that it is entirely possible for a people to retain and maintain their lives through the use of any language. There is not a question of authenticity here; rather it is the way that Indian people have creatively responded to forced colonization. And this response has been one of resistance; there is no clearer word for it than resistance.

It has been this resistance—political, armed, spiritual—which has been carried out by the oral tradition. The continued use of the oral tradition today is evidence that the resistance is on-going. Its use, in fact, is what has given rise to the surge of literature created by contemporary Indian authors. And it is this literature, based upon continuing resistance, which has given a particularly nationalistic character to the Native American voice.

Consider Antoine, the boy-character through whose eyes the idea of the novel, *Wind from an Enemy Sky,* by D'Arcy McNickle is realized. Antoine is witness to the tumultous and terrible events that face and cause change among his Little Elk people. McNickle not only has us see through Antoine's immediate youthful eyes but also through the knowledge related by Bull, his grandfather, and other kinfolk. We come to see not only a panorama of the early 20th century as experienced by the Little Elk people but also of the national Indian experience. Antoine, through his actions, thought, and understanding shows what kind of decisions become necessary, and even though the novel ends with no victory for the Little Elk people, we realize that the boy and his people have fought as valorously and courageously as they have been able, and that McNickle, as an Indian writer, has provided us a literary experience of it.

Abel in N. Scott Momaday's novel, *House Made of Dawn,* is unlike Antoine, but he carries on a similar struggle not only for identity and survival but, more, to keep integral what is most precious to him: the spiritual knowledge which will guide him throughout his life as it has guided those before him. It is knowledge of this life source that Momaday denotes as the strength which inspires the resistance of the people from whom Abel comes, and it will be what will help them to overcome. Surely, it is what proves to be the element which enables Abel to endure prison, city life, indignities cast upon him, and finally it is what helps him to return to himself and run in the dawn so that life will go on. Momaday concludes his novel by the affirmation that dawn will always come and renewal of life will be possible through resistance against forces which would destroy life. It is by the affirmation of knowledge of source and place and spiritual return that resistance is realized.

Ceremony, the novel by Leslie M. Silko, is a special and most complete example of this affirmation and what it means in terms of Indian resistance, its use as literary theme, and its significance in the development of a national Indian literature. Tayo, the protagonist in the usual sense, in the novel is not "pure blood" Indian; rather he is of mixed blood, a mestizo. He, like many Indian people of whom he is a reflection, is faced with circumstances which seemingly are beyond his ability to control. After a return home to his Indian community from military service in World War II, Tayo is still not home. He, like others, is far away from himself, and it is only through a tracking of the pathways of life, or rebuilding through ceremony of life, that he is able at last to return to himself and to on-going life. Along the way, Silko, the novelist, has Tayo and other characters experience and describe the forces of colonialism as "witchery" which has waylaid Indian people and their values and prevents return to their sources. But Tayo does return, not by magic or mysticism or some abstract revelation; instead the return is achieved through a ceremony of story, the tracing of story, rebuilding of story, and the creation of story.

It is in this ritual that return and reaffirmation is most realized, for how else can it be. Story is to engender life, and *Ceremony* speaks upon the very process by which story, whether in oral or written form, substantiates life, continues it, and creates it. It is this very process that Indian people have depended upon in their most critical times. Indeed, without it, the oral tradition would not exist as significantly as it does today, and there would likely be no basis for present-day Indian writing, much less Indian people. But because of the insistence to keep telling and creating stories, Indian life continues, and it is this resistance against loss that has made that life possible. Tayo in *Ceremony* will live on, wealthy with story and tradition, because he realizes the use and value of the ritual of story-making which is his own and his people's lives in the making. "It is never easy," Silko writes; it is always a struggle and because it is a struggle for life it is salvation and affirmation.

The struggle to maintain life and the resistance against loss put up by Antoine, Abel, and Tayo, in their separate entities, illustrate a theme, national in character and scope, common to all American native people and to all people indigenous to lands which have suffered imperialism and colonialism. In the decade of the 70's, it has been the predominant subject and theme that has concerned Indian writers. And it has been the oral tradition which has carried this concern in the hearts of Indian people until today it is being expressed not only in the novel but in poetry and drama as well.

Nevertheless, it is not the oral tradition as transmitted from ages past alone which is the inspiration and source for contemporary Indian literature. It is also because of the acknowledgement by Indian writers of a responsibility to advocate for their people's self-government, sovereignty, and control of land and natural resources; and to look also at racism, political and economic oppression, sexism, supremacism, and the needless and wasteful exploitation of land and people, especially in the U.S., that Indian literature is developing a character of nationalism which indeed it should have. It is this character which will prove to be the heart and fiber and story of an America which has heretofore too often feared its deepest and most honest emotions of love and compassion. It is this story, wealthy in being without an illusion of dominant power and capitalistic abundance, that is the most authentic.

Bob Hall in *Southern Exposure* wrote, describing the textile workers struggle in the South, that the themes of family, community, religion, humor, and rage are the most common among the workers in their stories and music. He could have added "most authentic" to common, and he could have been commenting upon Indian people for it is those very themes that Indian literature of today considers. The voice given these themes is the most culturally authentic as these are fundamental to human dignity, creativity, and integrity. This voice is that authentic one that my nonliterary Uncle Steve, wearing a beat-up cowboy hat and bright blue neckerchief, expressed at Acqu as he struggled to teach history, knowledge of our community, and understanding of how life continues. Indeed, like that ceremony at Acqu, depicting Santiago, the conquistador-saint, and Chapiyuh, the inquisitor-missionary, the voice is not a mere dramatic expression of a sociohistorical experience, but it is a persistent call by a people determined to be free; it is an authentic voice for liberation. And finally, it is the voice of countless other non-literary Indian women and men of this nation who live a daily life of struggle to achieve and maintain meaning which gives the most authentic character to a national Indian literature.

Carter Revard (Osage)

History, Myth, and Identity among Osages and Other Peoples

Something strange appears when we look at certain autobiographies of Indian people: the notion of identity, of how the individual is related to world, people, self, differs from what we see in "Euroamerican" autobiography. In "Western Civilization," an *identity* is something shaped between birth and death, largely by tiny molecules called genes, somewhat also by what the child's nervous system undergoes between birth and the first few years thereafter—and with every year past the first one, events become less and less important in shaping that identity[1]. That is not how Geronimo sees his identity in the autobiography he dictated to S. M. Barrett.[2] Nor does Geronimo begin by focusing on what a Euroamerican audience would likely consider the key to his identity: the clash with American soldiers and invaders of the Apache lands.[3] Geronimo does not even get around to mentioning his own birth until the book's third chapter. Instead, he begins the story of his life in this way: "In the beginning the world was covered with darkness. There was no sun, no day. The perpetual night had no moon or stars. There were, however, all manner of beasts and birds. . . . All creatures had power of speech and were gifted with reason. There were two tribes of creatures, the birds and . . . the beasts."[4] Geronimo then tells how the birds wanted light brought into the world, but the beasts would not have it, and there was war. The birds won, admitting light and so allowing humans to live and thrive. But the Dragon continually came down and devoured human children, until one year a son of the Rainstorm was born to the woman, and she hid her son away until he grew up to fight and kill the Dragon.[5] This boy's name was *Apache,* which (Barrett's book says) literally means *Enemy,* and he was the first chief of the people, first to wear the eagle's feathers in sign of justice, wisdom, and power such as the birds had shown in fighting for light. For Apache and his people, *Usen* created a homeland, placing within it, as in each homeland created for a people, all that was best for them: grain, fruits, game, herbs of healing, a pleasant climate, all that they could use for clothing and shelter. Geronimo concludes this opening part of his autobiography by saying, "Thus it was in the beginning: the Apaches and their homes each created for the other by Usen himself. When they are taken from these homes they sicken and die. How long until it is said, there are no Apaches?"[6] It is only after this Genesis-like history of his world's creation, his people's creation and deliverance, of their land's creation, of why they are called *Apaches,* of what it means to be taken from the land created particularly for his people, that Geronimo speaks of himself—of his individual birth into the world: "I was born in No-doyohn Canyon, Arizona, June, 1829."[7]

Whatever the order of importance among such facts might be for a Euroamerican autobiography, Geronimo ranked them from cosmic through geologic to tribal, subtribal, family and then only, last and in full context, the "individual" self that was Geronimo. And every *name* in his narrative, whenever he speaks it, has its symbolic meaning that resonates in this deeper context, can be rightly understood only in light of that part of the people's history which he is then telling. *Apache* does not "mean" only what (in Barrett's version) it "literally says," *Enemy,* but refers to The Enemy of that Dragon who threatens human children, and it is the name of the first great "Culture Hero" (as Euroamericans would call him): that Son of the Rainstorm who killed the Great Destroyer of Humankind.

I doubt that for most Euroamericans our national terms—*English, American, German, European*—resonate thus, because we lack a system of national and personal names that is openly and plainly linked to our mythic history or religious creeds.[8] There is of course the Catholic custom of naming after saints and biblical figures, and the Jewish naming arrangements that preserve religious and ethnic and family histories, and there are certainly subterranean passages between mainstream American personal names and the older familial and ethnic and national histories hidden within them. Yet particularly among Protestants, it seems, Americans have untied their names and individual histories from place and nation to an astonishing extent in the last five hundred years—precisely since the terms *individualism, self, identity* and *civilize* came into the English language in their current meanings.[9]

Now, when Geronimo told his life story, he had been a prisoner of war for twenty years, and a great deal had been done to *civilize* him.[10] As a recent editor of his autobiography puts it, "He took on all the trappings of the white man's civilization, becoming a farmer, a member of the Dutch Reformed Church, a Sunday School teacher, and a tireless promoter of himself, hawking photographs, bows and arrows at various fairs and expositions."[11] Civilized or not, Geronimo at seventy-six years of age (when dictating his life story to Barrett) still had his culture, his hierarchy of values. He knew who he was and where he came from, and he was sure that removal of the Apaches from their *homeland* meant, for him and for all of them, the loss not just of a "way of life" or a "home," but a change in, perhaps a loss of, their *beings*—or, as we might say, their *identities*. In his story, the notions of cosmos, country, self, and home are inseparable.

The result of losing that *homeland* can be seen in another Apache autobiography, though at first it seems to offer counter-evidence on the relation of being to land. This is a book narrated by one of the young Apache men who went with Geronimo on one of the last breakaways into the free Sierra Madre of Mexico—a man named Jason Betzinez, born in 1860 and producing his autobiography in 1958 (he died in 1960, aged 100, from a car crash).[12] Betzinez tells us that in 1902, when the Apache heads of families met with military authorities at Fort Sill, Oklahoma (where they were still prisoners of war), to request once more that they be repatriated to their old homeland in New Mexico, as they had been promised when they surrendered in Mexico, Betzinez himself stood up courageously and said that he wanted to stay in Oklahoma:

> I was born and raised among these Indians. I lived just like they did—a hard life, *homeless and hopeless*. But through a Government school I had a chance to *better myself.* . . . I learned to be a blacksmith. I worked in a steel mill. I learned farming. Now I am being forced to choose between this new, good life and that old, primitive life out west. If I go west to live in a camp as a reservation Indian, all that I have gained, all that I have learned, will be lost. . . . My wish this day is that the Government should give me a house and land and permit me to remain. (p. 190)

Betzinez was clearly a fine person, and I would bet my life he was a good neighbor and friend—but the quoted words make him seem a perfect instance of a "wild" Indian who was "tamed" by the Euroamerican schools. Indeed, rebutting an Arizona senator, Betzinez says this himself: "At the time the removal of the Apaches from Fort Sill was . . . under consideration in Washington. One of the Senators from Arizona said, 'You can no more tame an Apache than you can a rattlesnake.' I think . . . the recent history of our people flings those words back in the worthy gentleman's teeth" (p. 199). At the age of twenty-seven, Jason Betzinez had been put into Carlisle Indian School, taught to speak and write English, converted to Christianity, and brought to be ashamed of and hostile to Apache dances and ceremonies, and now he considered his Apache life as "the old pitiful existence to which I was born" (p. 153).

Consider how different Betzinez's "old" life had been from Geronimo's. Geronimo had been born in 1829 and could grow up both "wild" and "free"; Betzinez, born in 1860 after the U.S. annexed his homeland, was from his teens onward under deadly and constant harassment. As he tells it, "As far back as I remember we had never had a permanent home or a place we could call our own. Some of us were beginning to prefer quiet and security to the ever present worry and fear of being hounded. . . . I think we realized dimly, as we jolted along in these wagons, that even as prisoners our worst troubles might be coming to an end" (p. 141). The episode he refers to here is when the Apaches, having been rounded up in Mexico and Arizona, were being railroaded off to Florida as prisoners of war, in direct violation of the agreement made when they surrendered. What Betzinez says, in effect, is that the prisoners have decided they are only safe in prison. It is meant, of course, as compliment to the jailers.

It is a hard question whether Geronimo or one of the older Apaches, if asked to describe Jason Betzinez when he returned from Carlisle to live at Fort Sill in 1900, would have described him as "Apache." His *identity* was not merely changed from "wild" to "tame," from hunter/warrior to black-smith/farmer. Consider: it was thenceforward impossible for Betzinez to begin his life story with the Apache account of the Creation, for he was now a sincere Christian. It was no longer relevant to his life to name the subtribes of Apaches as Geronimo's autobiography does, for readers of Betzinez's story would be interested only in his being "an Apache." After going to Carlisle, Jason Betzinez had no homeland unless the United States government assigned him one. He had no religion shared with his people, no ceremonies that tied his youth to his age or self to tribe. In short, he had no IDENTITY unless he could reinvent himself in Euroamerican terms.

After 1900, that is, he was cut off completely from his first twenty-six years of life—from cosmos, tribe, homeland, and "values." From that time on, *all that made him Indian was his race*—and the chief test of that, by Euroamerican values, would be whether he could raise his status to be like a "white" man, for that alone would show whether he was racially inferior or could "make it." His sense of worth now depended on how NON-Apache he could act. Yet, of course, skin color and features would "identify" him as "Indian," no matter what his lifestyle became.

Betzinez had kept some attitudes, and he saw clearly how false was some of what Euroamericans wanted him to believe about his people's history. He could see it because he still had, in oral history, Apache truths that were omitted or distorted by printed Euroamerican accounts; he makes this clear at the very beginning of his autobiography (pp. 1–2). He quickly reveals that even though he had come to praise the non-Apache life to which Carlisle had turned him, even though he deplored the wish of "wild" Apaches to return to an existence and home country which, he insisted, was wretched and harassed, yet his feelings and memories of that homeland and existence were not negative. On the contrary, as he says: "We loved this beautiful land. . . . Between . . . 1858, when the Government granted us this reservation 'forever,' and 1876, when that same Government took it away from us forever so that white men seeking gold might have it, we lived there in peace and contentment. We hunted, gathered and traded. . . . For a short time life was . . . a happy one" (p. 25). But the official views expressed as Betzinez concludes his autobiography are very different from those at his beginning. From his Carlisle days, Betzinez had "thrown away" his Apache identity and accepted the Euroamerican self patterned for him by the soldiers at Carlisle whom he came to admire and trust. It is a remarkable and attractive self, clearly that of an unusually strong, courageous and decent man, whose life is told in this book. But it is clearly a Euroamerican self. We may account for its shaping, perhaps, by the imprisonment, penances, and education at Carlisle. If this were a U.S. citizen in 1994 we would presumably call the process brainwashing.

How, then, do we account for the different sense of self or identity in Geronimo's book? Here we have no clear description from Geronimo: he shows us an Apache self, but does not show how it was shaped. We can look into particular books for some idea of the ways Apache education shaped people—for instance, Morris Opler's *Apache Odyssey, Journey Between Two Worlds* tells how a Mescalero Apache "grew to maturity when his people . . . were experiencing defeat, confinement, and profound cultural readjustment."[13] But something more than one tribe's self-shaping is involved here, or so it appears to me from some years of having taught a course in which we read autobiographies of Indians from very different tribal cultures. Not only how Apache but how Indian beings are shaped is what I want to look into, if only a little way, in this chapter. One trail into this great Sierra is the way of naming and using language.

The autobiography that has helped me see how naming and language reflect and shape a sense of identity within the world, both outside and part of an Indian self, is Charles Eastman's *Indian Boyhood*.[14] Eastman was a Santee Sioux born about 1858 and raised, like Geronimo, "wild," but Eastman was then "brought in to the mainstream" as Betzinez was, through education, rather than through capture and imprisonment as Geronimo was. Eastman was just four years old in 1862 when the Santee took part in the great Sioux uprising and massacre in what is now called Minnesota. Eastman's father was captured and sentenced to death, but Eastman's mother and others in the family fled into Canada where Eastman was raised to age sixteen in the old ways, expecting some day to return to the United States to take revenge for the father who, he thought, had been hanged. But his father's sentence had been commuted to life in prison, where he was converted to Christianity, decided to take the white man's road, learned farming, won release on parole, and finally went to Canada looking for his son. One day, wearing white man's clothes, he walked into the Santee village where his nearly grown son was living, and presently walked out again, taking his son back to the United States. The son, given the name Charles Eastman, was put into mission school, then Beloit College, Knox College, and Dartmouth. Graduating with honors in 1887, he went to medical school at Boston University, where he got his M.D. just in time to be sent out to the Pine Ridge Sioux Agency shortly before the 1890 massacre of Sioux by the Seventh Cavalry at Wounded Knee. Eastman writes of trying to save some of the Indian children wounded there by the Hotchkiss machine guns, or the more prosaic carbines used by the troopers as they followed and shot down the women and children trying to flee the slaughter.

Such are the facts. I want to look, however, not at the Cavalry versus Redskins scenario so familiar from movies, but at one aspect of Eastman's *education as a "wild" Indian,* before being *civilized.* That aspect, briefly examined in the previous chapter, is his learning the Santee system of names for animals and plants, and how this system tied his sense of personal identity to his sense of tribal identity and relationship to the world of other-than-human "natural" beings. In his chapter on "An Indian Boy's Training" (pp. 49–56), Eastman points out that the education of Indian children was highly systematic and its customs "scrupulously adhered to and transmitted from one generation to another." While a male child was being carried in its mother's womb, she would keep in mind for him some celebrated figure from the tribe's history and "would gather from tradition all his noted deeds and daring exploits, rehearsing them to herself when alone." After he was born, her lullabies would "speak of wonderful exploits in hunting and in war," and he would be called "the future defender of his people." As he grew older, he would be hearing the hunting songs, and in these, "the leading animals are introduced; they come to the boy to offer their bodies for the sustenance of his tribe. The animals are regarded as his friends and spoken of almost as tribes of people or as his cousins, grandfathers, and grandmothers." What Eastman's account here barely hints when the animals are said to "offer their bodies"[15] may well be what is made explicit in the ceremonies of a related tribe, the Osage, particularly in the *Origin Wi-gi-e of the Buffalo Bull Clan* that might be recited as part of the feast of corn given a year after a child was named.[16] In this recitation, a member of the *Tho-xe* (Buffalo Bull) clan tells of how the Osages came from the mid-heavens, the stars, to become a people on this earth. In this journey they were directed by various powers through three "divisions" of the heavens, where they found no place to become a people, but in the fourth "division" they met "the Man of Mystery, the god of the clouds" (understood to be "Thunder," though all these terms are much more than "literal").[17] He said to them: "I am a person of whom your little ones may make their bodies. *When they make of me their bodies,* they shall cause themselves to become deathless" [emphasis added]. They then went to the Buffalo Bull, who also said they could make their bodies of him, and proceeded to throw himself upon the ground so that there sprang up for their use as medicine and food certain plants—including four kinds of corn.

What the Osage chants show is that when the "clan" animals came to offer their bodies it was not only (as Eastman's printed account seems to say) as willing sacrifices for food and clothing and ceremonial regalia—it was as part of the sacred agreement made at Origin Time between human and non-human beings of this world, between Osage beings on the one hand, and on the other hand beings from Thunder through Mountain Lion and Red Bird "down" (or "up") to the stones of the earth. I believe Eastman's account should be taken as implying that among the Santee the same was true, that when Eastman heard the "hunting songs" he would hear them as part of the Creation Stories and the Origin Stories and the Naming Stories.

Eastman's account does describe what I take to be the telling of Santee creation stories—the "legends of his ancestors and his race" were told and repeated "almost every evening," and whatever story a boy heard one night from parents or grandparents, he himself was "usually required to repeat" the next evening. In this way "his household became the audience by which he was alternately criticized and applauded." It was a schooling without having home and school separated, without creating a clerical class within the tribe.

But what interests me here is the naming system. Let's consider once more Eastman's description of how his uncle "catechized" him on his observation of animals: "It was his custom to let me name all the new birds that I had seen during the day. I would name them according to the color or the shape of the bill or their song or the appearance and locality of the nest—in fact, anything about the bird that impressed me as characteristic. . . . He then usually informed me of the correct name. Occasionally I made a hit and this he would warmly commend." Part of Eastman's Santee identity-sense came from realizing that his own close observation of the birds, and his naming them based on this, might well be at one with his community's choice of names for them. He was adjusting his own verbal creativity to his tribesmen's traditions in a very direct way. The sense of linguistic "authority" in his "oral" society seems just as strong as it is in our "literate" society, but the whole relation of individual to authority must have had a different "feel" in the oral society, where spoken language came from authorities present and known. English speakers have two sets of names for creatures—"common" and "scientific," and in neither set is it apparent to an ordinary speaker *why* a given name is used for a given creature. Our word-roots are buried far out of mind in unknown history.[18] But for Eastman, his language was "transparent," not "opaque" as English is to most of us. English is a melting-pot language, with a priestly language of Latinate terms, and a commoners' language of shorter words, but all of them are opaque so far as animals are concerned.[19] Our words no longer put us in touch with the LAND we live on and from, or the ANIMALS we live among and upon.

So far, we have focused on three autobiographies only—those of Geronimo, Betzinez, and Eastman. We have posited a "wild" sense of identity with its hierarchy from cosmic to personal firmly set, and a "tame" sense dependent on white beneficence and cultural power; and we have touched briefly on how the "wild" sense (as in Eastman) may have been shaped by the language as used by its speakers. Let's look now at two other tribes, Pawnee and Osage, to observe in more detail how the *land-orientation* of a family and individual created an Indian identity among Pawnees, and how the *naming ceremony* (for persons) helped create Indian identity among Osages. We turn to these two distinctly different tribes because they show it is *Indian* and not just an *Apache* or *Santee* "identity" we are looking at. The sample, admittedly, is limited, but it seems to me cautious inferences can be drawn from it.

For the Pawnees we draw mostly upon Gene Weltfish's beautiful book, *The Lost Universe*.[20] Our point is how powerful a force the Pawnee ceremonies were in shaping each Pawnee's sense of identity. Weltfish says: "The thing that made life most worthwhile to the Pawnees was their elaborate round of ceremonies . . . based on a complex philosophy of the creation of the universe and of man and of their ongoing nature. The ceremonies were considered as the means for keeping the cosmic order in its course and the continuance of the earth and its life processes. . . . The ceremonies were more than religious observances. They were the whole focus of Pawnee aesthetic life" (p. 8). Nor were these "ceremonial ways" only dances and songs and recitations. The shape of a Pawnee house, and the place in this house of each inhabitant, were part of an ordered patterning that placed this person in a certain clear relation to kinfolk, to household tasks, to the working areas and the sacred areas—*and to the cosmos*. That is, the circular Pawnee lodge was oriented not just within the village, but within the universe, by the sun and stars:

> Everyone in the house knew his appointed place and where he could go and . . . not go. In the sacred area at the west was an earthen platform. . . . Between the fireplace and the buffalo altar, there was a sacred spot that was invisible—the *wi-haru,* "the place where the wise words of those who have gone before us are resting." Rather than step over this place in order to pass from one side of the house to the other, everyone walked around the entire house by the way of the east. When the heads of the household sat down . . . it was to the west . . . and no one would want to pass in front of them. The house was a microcosm of the universe and as one was at home inside, one was also at home in the outside world. For the dome of the sky was the . . . roof of the universe and the horizon . . . was the circular wall of the cosmic house. Through the roof . . . the star gods poured down their strength from their appropriate directions in a constant stream. In the west was the Evening Star, . . . and in her garden the corn and buffalo were constantly being renewed . . . and in the western part of the house the sacred buffalo skull and the bundle with its ears of corn symbolized this power. In the eastern sky was the Morning Star—god of light, of fire, and of war. As he rose every morning he sent his beam into the long entryway of the house and lit the fire in an act of cosmic procreation, symbolizing his first union with the Evening Star in the times of the great creation [when they begot] the girl that was the first human being. . . . The house was also the womb of a woman, and the household activities represented her reproductive powers. The beds of the women along the circular walls were . . . ranged by age to represent the main stages in a woman's life—the youngest woman near the west where the garden of the Evening Star was located, the mature woman in the middle . . . and the old women near the exit to the east, for at their age they were "on the way out." Being at home was spoken of as being "inside"; *ti-ka,* "he-is-inside"; the house, *a-ka-ru,* "the-inside-place"; the universe, *ka-huraru,* "the-inside-land." . . . Everyone in the house had a clear consciousness of these things as they moved about within it. Now secure in his bed, the boy was also secure in the world. (pp. 63–64)

Naturally, to be oriented to heaven and the stars meant one was oriented in time as well as space, among the seasons and the ceremonies that "marked" the seasons: except that for a Pawnee, a ceremony did not merely mark, it helped in the moving of time.[21] There was, for instance, the "spring awakening": "The first ceremonial act of the year was to awaken the whole earth from its winter sleep. . . . The year began about the time of the spring equinox with the ritual recitation of the creation by the five priests. The position of the stars was an important guide to the time. . . . The earth lodge served as an astronomical observatory and as the priests sat inside at the west, they could observe the stars in certain positions through the smokehole and through the long east-oriented entranceway" (p. 12). Each Pawnee therefore knew from the repeated ceremonies how the Creation began, and saw the ordering of that creation symbolized in the shape and orientation of the house and its inhabitants, saw the seasonal occupations and activities closely tied to the stars, observed that the singing and dancing ceremonies were part of the link between self and tribe and universe, part of a Pawnee being.

From these facts I would argue that the "wild" Indian held quite different opinions from "civilized" Americans around 1880, concerning a person's relation to land, sky, and the creatures therewithin. They differed not only in their notions about property and ownership, or in their political views on voting, taxation, churchgoing, salvation and damnation. Geronimo, in being Apache, was like a Pawnee, or a Santee, or an Omaha, or an Osage: all were *Indian,* not *Euroamerican.* I suggest that for all the anthropologists can say about differences of high importance between cultures of Plains, Pueblo, Woodlands, Coastal and other tribes, groups, nations, there WAS such a thing as an "Indian" way beneath the differences. Succinctly put, that way's ceremonies *embodied a unified way of life:* what was Indian was the seamlessness of human life, in which it would not make sense to speak of religion on the one hand, and warfare on the other, of hunting here and naming a new chief there, of the Creation of the Universe on this side and the Naming of a Child on that. "History" and "village arrangement," "Cosmos" and "lodge architecture," were intimately related through ceremonies as well as stories and art work; the inside of a lodge, as well as placement of houses in the camp, carried historic and cosmic meanings.

The best way to demonstrate this might be a detailed discussion of ways in which, for instance, the Osage ceremonies for naming a child reflect, are linked with, those for naming a new chief, and both ceremonial cycles embody the tribe's history as well as its Genesis-Exodus version. Having discussed the Osage Naming Ceremony at length elsewhere, I will focus here on a few points from Francis La Flesche's account. Himself Omaha and speaking Osage well, La Flesche was the right person at the right time to preserve in print Osage ceremonies that would shortly afterwards be "thrown away." In the Osage *Rite of the Chiefs,* as he notes, are not only the ceremonies for naming a new chief, but (in what we may call allegorical narrative form) the history of the Osage people's becoming a nation. We are told in this rite how they came from the stars and chose bodily forms, how they took the tribal organization that simultaneously represented their history and the form of the universe. In the ceremony one finds, also, explanation of the choosing of certain animals as patrons for their clans, certain foods as the right ones, certain names for individuals as appropriate (and as tied to their mythic and in-time history). In this *Rite of the Chiefs,* therefore, what Europeans would subdivide into "history, religion, social structure, farming, hunting and ethology" are all subsumed. This rite was supplemented by another which La Flesche titles *Hearing of the Sayings of the Ancient Men,* in which we also see expressed "in mythical form, the origin of the people," here envisioned as a begetting of life between "two great fructifying forces—namely the sky and the earth," with life continuing forever to proceed from this begetting. And this notion of a continuous procreating of the universe is embodied in the tribal organization, divided into moieties of Sky and Earth divisions, with men from one of these required to marry women from the other, so that for each Osage marriage arrangement and ceremony there was a reenactment of the tribe's origins and of the cosmic reasons and theory behind this.[22] Further, the version of this origin-story recited by a given clan was modified so as to "conform to that part of nature which the [clan] represented in the tribal and the gentile organizations, for the tribe in its entirety symbolized the visible universe in all its known aspects." Specifically, the Black Bear or Thunder clan would each have its own version, with its particular patron-being giving its special name, powers, and blessing to the clan and the tribe.

Such, then, were the *Rite of the Chiefs* and the *Hearing of the Sayings of the Ancient Men.* When we now look at the Osage rite for naming a child—which as La Flesche puts it "installs the child in his proper place in the tribal organization and entitles him to recognition as a person"—we do not see an isolated and unrelated set of stories and histories. We find instead that the names bestowed in the bringing of a child into a clan reflect the tribal and gentile histories. The name *Nom-peh-wah-the,* for instance, may be literally translated as "Fear-Inspiring," but that is only the surface part of its meaning. Literally, *nom-peh* means "to be afraid," and *wah-the* means "cause or make to be." But the fear referred to in this name, it is understood, is that caused by Thunder: the sacred Thunder of the time before the Osages came to earth, when they sent ahead a messenger to discover how they might become a people, and what they could make their bodies from and what names they might take. The name *Nom-peh-wah-the* therefore embodies and recalls this part of the people's sacred history, as well as that part of its chronicle-history when certain famous men bore this name in the memory of the elders.[23]

Clearly, then, giving a clan-name involved a ceremony that itself was an epicycle on the great cycle of clan-origin, which was part of the universe's wheel that had turned to bring the entire tribe and its world into being. The Osages, we may stress, believed that the universe did move in an order given it by a "silent, invisible creative power . . . named *Wa-kon-dah,* Mysterious Power."[24] Therefore, when the first ceremony in the child-naming ritual was called *Wa-zho-i-ga-the,* "the Taking of Bodies," it was not merely that some incorporeal star-beings decided to come down and incarnate themselves, but that they were moving as part of the universe under Wa-kon-dah's guidance. When they adopted their life-symbols through which they became a people and could live on earth, they addressed these as "grandfather" and "grandmother": Sun, Moon, Morning Star, Evening Star, Dipper, Pleiades, Elk, Bear, Puma, Red Cedar, Buffalo Bull. When (at a later stage of the child-naming) the naming *wi-gi-e* of a clan was recited, the recital was called the *Zha-zhe Ki-ton,* "Taking of Names." The names were given according to a set sequence of possibilities determined in part by the order of birth within a family: first male, second male, third male; first, second, third female—each had its possible set of names.[25]

At the ceremony's end, there would be a special set of instructions for the child's mother. At the later feast (including corn ceremonially planted by the mother) for the *Xo-ka* who had presided over the naming, there might be the recitation by a member of the Buffalo Bull clan of that clan's *wi-gi-e,* telling how the Osages descended from the heavens and—most pertinently—how the Buffalo Bull had brought corn to the Osages. And to recur to the name just mentioned, *Nom-peh-wah-the,* this *wi-gi-e* tells how, when the Osages were trying to come down from stars to earth, their messenger was sent ahead to find a place where they might become a people. Having passed through three divisions of the heavens, the messenger had found no habitation for them, but in the Fourth Division he saw the "Man of Mystery, the god of the clouds"—and turning to his brothers, he said: "Here stands a *fear-inspiring man!* His name, I verily believe, is *Nom-peh-wah-the* ("fear-inspiring")!" Thereupon this mysterious and terrible man addresses the messenger and other Osages: "I am a person of whom your little ones may make their bodies. When they make of me their, bodies, they shall cause themselves to be deathless."[26] He then gives them other personal names that they can use.

The name *Nom-peh-wah-the,* then, would be given in a context which would bring its new bearer into the tribe in a very complete fashion, at least as complete as a Christian or Jewish naming ceremony—and on its religious and cosmic side it would be comparable to such rites. It also referenced the tribal, family, and clan history into which the newly named child would be precisely placed. An Osage child in those "wild" times would thus have had all these placements brought to his awareness not only at the particular time he was given the name, but each time he attended another name-giving, and also when he attended the *Rites of the Chiefs* and other ceremonies.

In short, like Geronimo, or Eastman, or La Flesche, or a Pawnee child, an Osage would have had his personal identity carefully, explicitly, unmistakably linked with that of his people, with the symbolic arrangement of his village, with the marriage arrangements and hunting encampments and choosing of chiefs and war and peace ceremonies, with the animals whom he could hunt or whose feathers he could wear, the plants he would eat, the earth and sky he dwelt within. If we wanted to ask about a "wild" Indian's sense of identity, therefore, we ought to ask also about these "other" matters. The "wild" Indian was tied to land, people, origins and way of life, by every kind of human order we can imagine. "History" and "Myth" and "Identity" are not three separate matters, here, but three aspects of one human being.

Notes

1. Erik Erikson has argued for the importance of much later periods in an individual's life as crucial to shaping and reshaping identity; the long obituary notice in the *New York Times* (Friday, May 13, 1994) gives a very useful and interesting account of his work. It mentions, for instance, that his *Childhood and Society* (1950) was published after he had studied early childhood training of Sioux people and differentiated their children's identity-sense from that of the Yurok Indians whom he also studied. He proposed that humans undergo successive "identity crises" during their lives, and applied this notion to "psychobiographic" studies of Martin Luther and Mahatma Gandhi (1958, 1969). Erikson's having himself been an "in-betweener"—illegitimate child suspended between religions (Lutheran, Jewish), taunted by Nazis as a Jew, rejected at the synagogue as of Nordic appearance—and his studies of non-European identity-formation surely made him sensitive to issues with which one is faced in looking at the "autobiographies" of American Indians with which the present essay is concerned.

2. *Geronimo: His Own Story,* ed. S. M. Barrett, newly ed. by Frederick W. Turner, III (New York: E. P. Dutton, 1970). All kinds of problems are presented to us by this work: to what extent is it an accurate transcription or paraphrase of Geronimo's account, how far does its organization and sequencing reflect Barrett's rearranging of bits and pieces, how much was added or subtracted or altered by the intermediary Apache translators used by Barrett. I cut this Gordian knot by assuming the book as printed is authentic and accurate enough for the purposes of this discussion, expressing reservations only here and there.

3. The 1993 movie called *Geronimo,* for instance, though "sympathizing" with Geronimo, presents him primarily as a larger-than-life Indian warrior fighting American soldiers; and the soldiers are presented as, of course, highly respectful of his courage, of the relatively just causes for which he was fighting, and so on. In the end, that movie asks us to understand Geronimo as "Apache" in only two dimensions: the fierce indomitable warrior, and the man unjustly treated by mean and crooked Mexicans and Americans. There is nothing whatever of Apache cosmology, theology, ideology, customs or ways except in relation to the "war with whites," which is pictured as about a homeland but not about a way of life or world-views.

4. *Geronimo,* p. 61. Barrett's version of Apache "creation time" is probably much distorted, but my point is that Geronimo began by telling some version of the Apache Creation Story as his introduction to the story of Geronimo. One may argue that the Christian Gospel of John distorts the Judaic account of the beginning of things, since it is a late Hellenized version adapted to provide a biography of a man taken by its author to be the Messiah. The Hellenizer, nevertheless, has reasons for providing that reference to the *Genesis* story.

5. "Dragon" of course carries all kinds of European baggage, but so does "Monster," a term more usual for translators of Apache, Navajo, or Pueblo Creation Stories, in which such episodes of "Monster-slaying" set parameters for the world as humans now know it. See, for instance, Paul Zolbrod's edition of the Navajo Creation Story, *Diné Bahané* (Albuquerque: University of New Mexico Press, 1984).

6. *Geronimo,* p. 69. I wonder about the "literal meaning" that in Barrett's account is assigned to *Apache,* and suspect some confusion on Barrett's part.

7. *Geronimo,* p. 70. Could *No-doyohn* be a mistake for *Mogollon?*

8. See the earlier essay in this collection, "Making a Name," for qualifications of this.

9. Though the history of these words sheds light on the attitudes of Europeans toward "Indians" whom they civilized with such genocidal efficiency, there is not space to summarize that history here. A sketch is given in my "Why Shakespeare, Though Not Unselfish, Never Had Any Fun," in E. Cooley, Mervin R. Barnes, and John A. Dunn, eds., *Papers of the Mid-America Linguistics Conference for 1978* (Norman: University of Oklahoma Press, 1979), pp. 478–487.

10. See the entry for *civilise* in the *Oxford English Dictionary.* The word was Anglicized in the early 17th century precisely to justify man's ways to man as the British began to turn the globe a shocking Imperial pink: as Captain John Smith wrote of his experiences in Virginia, it was easier to civilize "them" by the sword than by fair means (to paraphrase the *OED* citation from his 1624 *History of Virginia).*

11. *Geronimo,* p. 49. One of the "fairs and expositions" was the St. Louis World's Fair of 1904, where he was exhibited as prisoner of war. He must have been in its headquarters, the newly built Brookings Hall of Washington University. I teach and have an office across the quadrangle from Brookings. Geronimo perhaps walked round the new-built quadrangle, where Commencement ceremonies now are held.

12. Jason Betzinez, *I Fought With Geronimo,* with W. S. Nye (Harrisburg, Penn.: The Stackpole Company, 1959). (Page references to this book are given parenthetically in the text.)

13. Morris E. Opler, *Apache Odyssey: A Journey between Two Worlds* (New York: Holt, Rinehart and Winston, 1969), p. x.

14. Eastman, *Indian Boyhood,* hereafter in this chapter cited by page number alone. As with Geronimo's autobiography, I leave aside the difficult question of how non-Indian input—in this case, from Eastman's white wife, herself a teacher whom he met while at Pine Ridge where she was teaching Sioux children—may have shaped and colored Eastman's account of his life as it stands in his printed work. I ignore also (for now) the neo-historicist aspects of the case: the shifting vogues and forms of Indian autobiography; the particular and general social tasks assigned by whites to this genre during the period 1890–1940 as part of dealing with post-Wounded Knee Indian

tribal entities and the "Indian question" as a whole; and the ways Eastman himself fitted his autobiographical writing and speaking into such tasks and his own personal and ethnic agenda. The very useful discussions and bibliographic account of Indian autobiographies by scholars, especially Peter Beidler, Kathleen Sands, H. David Brumble and Arnold Krupat, are essential to the full discussion such questions deserve.

15. The account as here cited from *Indian Boyhood* misses the sacred dimension of such songs, which tie intricately into the Creation Stories— though certainly Eastman would have known that dimension well, so it is likely the inadequate understanding of Santee ways by his wife Elaine Goodale Eastman that caused this lacuna in Eastman's account. We can clearly see this sacred dimension in traditional Osage naming ceremonies, as printed in 1928 (with transcription, translation, introduction and detailed commentary) by Francis La Flesche in *The Osage Tribe: Two Versions of the Child-Naming Rite,* Smithsonian Institution, Bureau of American Ethnology Annual Report, no. 43, 1924–1925 (Washington, D.C.: 1928), pp. 23–264. Other Osage ceremonies, which illustrate how members of this Siouan-language tribe were being educated at the time Eastman was growing up, are transcribed and translated by La Flesche as BAE Annual Reports numbers 36, pp. 35–597 (*Rites of the Chiefs, Sayings of the Ancient Men*); 39, pp. 31–630 (*Rite of Vigil*); 45, pp. 529–833 (*Rite of the Wa-xo-be*); and in the 1939 *BAE Bulletin (War Ceremony and Peace Ceremony of the Osage Indians), passim.* Some translations of songs and recital-chants from these ceremonies, and many useful glosses and definitions, are found in La Flesche's 1932 *Dictionary of the Osage Language.* And see, now, Garrick Bailey's account, *The Osage and the Invisible World* (Norman: University of Oklahoma Press, 1995).

16. La Flesche, *Osage Tribe,* pp. 56–58.

17. Ibid., p. 57. In Euroamerican culture, words like *electricity* and *gravity* have "literal," "figurative," and "scientific" sense-clusters. Alert and sensible readers negotiate among these flavors and quarky senses with no particular difficulty, and the same ability to negotiate among ceremonial and everyday, metaphysical and physical word-senses should be recognized among Osages and other Indian peoples. There are actual instances within some of the ceremonial recitations or narratives where the reciter will say things, in referring to the "journey from the stars to this earth," such as "They came to a valley: verily, it was not a valley"—warning the listeners, I believe, that the language being used is special, figurative, mysterious, not everyday.

18. I happened lately to look at the words *chameleon* and *chamomile* in the *American Heritage Dictionary* and was surprised to find the same Greek word is behind the first half of each. A *chameleon* is a "ground-lion," and the herb *chamomile* is a "ground-apple." The *AHD* editors say that behind the Greek *chameleon* is a Babylonian word which itself means "ground-lion," so the Greeks must have thought the Babylonians had a good name for that little reptile, and just translated the name into their own language. As for *chamomile,* it of course is not actually a ground-apple; rather,

as the *AHD* editors say, some varieties *smell* like apples. I have my doubts about this, particularly since *melon* is the Greek word behind the *-mile* part of *chamomile,* and *melon* might refer to some fruit other than what we would call an "apple." Ah well—Sprachgeschmellers differ.

19. Of course, as discussed in "Making a Name," our English is far more transparent where machines and technology are concerned and our speakers are still coining names in spoken as well as literary English: we understand *hatchback* or *Fuzzbuster* or *beeper* to be "tribal" words that are figurative, describing what they refer to.

20. Gene Weltfish, *The Lost Universe: Pawnee Life and Culture* (Lincoln: University of Nebraska Press, 1977); page references are cited in the text. A primary source, given by the Pawnee elder Tahirussawichi through the bilingual Pawnee scholar James Murie, transcribed and translated by Murie and Alice Fletcher, is printed as *The Hako: A Pawnee Ceremony,* Smithsonian Institution, Bureau of American Ethnology Annual Report, no. 22 (Washington, D.C., 1904). Fletcher for years had found no Omaha informants to recite for her the texts and songs of this intertribal ceremony, but at last located a Pawnee elder who knew and would recite it. I assume that since the Hako Ceremony was intertribal, each tribe performed it in its own language and particular format. The ceremony is an "adoption" rite in which two groups become "brothers." That it involves the sacred pipe suggests it may be one of the most important "peace" ceremonies of the pre-Columbian Great Plains tribes. Anglo accounts of Plains Indians seem always to stress their warfare, their hostilities and rivalries—making them sound very like the Europe known to history as a collection of rabidly hostile and murderous peoples always trying to slaughter or conquer or dominate each other. How the Indian nations succeeded in getting along, rather than how they conducted their warring or raiding relationships, is emphasized by Howard Meredith in *Dancing on Common Ground: Tribal Cultures and Alliances on the Southern Plains* (Lawrence: University of Kansas Press, 1995), discussing Southern Plains nations including Wichita, Pawnee, Caddo, Plains Apache, Cheyenne and Arapaho, and Comanche (see, for the annual Pawnee-Wichita Visitation, pp. 20–21, 58–59).

21. The Pawnee images of microcosm/macrocosm ought to be compared to those of the Europeans in about the same time-frame, say 1400–1600 A.D.—there are startling resemblances as well as the expected differences. Work by Chaucer, Spenser, and Shakespeare could be set beside Pawnee texts—though it would outrage Mono-culturists to anthologize *The Faerie Queene* along with *The Hako Ceremony.*

22. La Flesche, B. A. E. *Annual Report No. 36* (1921), p. 48.

23. See La Flesche, *Osage Tribe,* especially pp. 159, 162.

24. Ibid., p. 30.

25. Ibid., p. 31.

26. Ibid., pp. 56–57.

Greg Sarris (Miwok~Pomo)

The Woman Who Loved a Snake
Orality in Mabel McKay's Stories

One day I took a colleague of mine from Stanford University to the Rumsey Wintun Reservation to meet Mabel McKay. "I want to meet this famous Pomo medicine woman," my friend said. "I've heard her talk and I've seen her baskets in the Smithsonian." My friend, Jenny, had heard me talk about Mabel also. I had been recording Mabel's stories for a book about her life. As always, Mabel proved a gracious host. She served us hot buttered toast and coffee and, for lunch, tuna fish sandwiches with pickles and lettuce. As Jenny and I ate, Mabel told about the woman who loved a snake.[1]

"See, her husband, he would work at night. 'Lock the door,' he'd tell her. 'Don't let nobody in.' Every night he'd go off saying that: 'Lock the door, keep everything locked up.' She would fix his dinner, then his lunch." Mabel chuckled to herself. "By lunch I mean what he takes to work. That's what I call lunch when I was working nighttime at the cannery.

"Anyway, this woman, she says 'OK.' And sometimes, after he would leave, she'd stay up for a while. She'd clean up around, maybe do the dishes, get things ready for the morning, for the breakfast. I don't know.

"Then ONE TIME she hears a knock on the back door. 'What is that?' she's thinking. First she thought maybe it was her husband; maybe he was coming home early; maybe he got sick or something. 'But then why doesn't he just come in?' she was saying. Well, then she thought maybe she was hearing things. She just kept working then.

"But it kept on, this knocking. Then she got scared. See in those days no phones up there. And this was far out, up on some white man's place there, where her husband worked. She could not yell, nothing. Nobody to hear her. Maybe she's thinking this to herself. I don't know.

" 'Who is this?' she is saying. Then I don't know what he said. I forgot. Something, anyway. And she opens the door. Just a little bit. He comes in and she stands there looking at him. But she doesn't recognize him.

"Anyway, she fixes some coffee. I don't know. Gives him something to eat. They're talking around there. I don't know what.

---

[1]This story has been produced from tapes, notes, and my memory of my meeting with Mabel McKay on October 15, 1988. My friend—Jenny—did not want her true name revealed.

"Next day, her husband comes home. 'What's this?' he is saying. He's standing there—by the bedroom—and he's looking down in some vase. Something there. It was on the table. 'What are you talking about?' she says. Then she goes and looks where he's looking. And she sees it, too: a snake, a little black snake all coiled up. 'What is this?' he says to her. Then he takes it out and puts it in the brush. He lets it out there.

"Next day, same thing it happens. Then the husband, he gets suspicious of that snake. 'What is this?' he is saying. Then she gets worried; now she knows what the snake is. But she don't say nothing. 'I'm going to kill it,' he says, 'chop it to bits out in the brush.' He's testing her, but she don't say nothing. Then she got REAL worried, seeing him go out with that snake.

"But next day same thing it happens. Maybe she tried talking to that man. I don't know. 'Don't stay around here,' she might said to him. But it's there again, that snake. Now her husband, he shakes her; he knows something is going on. 'What is this?' he's saying. But he had an idea about it anyway. 'You come with me,' he says, 'and watch me kill it.' He starts pulling on her arm, shaking her, but she refuses him. She won't go. She's crying by this time.

"He takes the snake out, same way, coiled around his hand. She just sees him go. Then he comes back. She doesn't know what it happened. Maybe this time he DID kill it. She's crying yet. Her husband, he comes in and says nothing. Just goes to bed.

"But he never did chop that snake up. Maybe he did. I don't know. Anyway, it went on like that . . ."

Jenny, a Ph.D. candidate in English, asked what the snake symbolized. Mabel didn't seem to understand the question. She looked at me then turned to Jenny. "Well, it was a problem, I don't know."

"Why didn't he, I mean the husband, just kill the snake?" Jenny asked.

With an incredulous look on her face, Mabel focused on Jenny. "Well, how could he?" she asked. "This is white man days. There's laws against killing people. That man, he would go to jail, or maybe get the electric chair, if he done that."

Jenny's response to the story, that is, her question, prompted in turn a response from Mabel that exposed what was different about their respective worldviews regarding the story. For Jenny the snake was symbolic of something and, in that sense, supernatural. For Mabel the snake/the man was part of one coexistent reality, a reality that is located in historic time and subject to its strictures. Mabel mentioned that she knew the woman, that she often visited her when she lived in the same area north of Clear Lake. "Then one night I seen that man. He was handsome, too," she chuckled. "It was late. Lakeport grocery was closing and I seen him come out with groceries. He didn't take the road. He went the creek way, north. Then, I say to myself, 'I bet I know where he's going.' "

"Maybe he just carried the snake with him and left it in the vase each morning before he left," Jenny offered. "Like a sign."

Mabel laughed out loud. "Like a sign. That's cute. Why he want to do that?" She lit a cigarette and exhaled a cloud of smoke. "See, I knew he was odd. He's moving in cold, late at night. Snakes don't do that."

"Well, was it man or snake? I mean when you were looking at it?" Jenny was desperate now.

"You got funny ideas," Mabel answered. "Aren't I sitting here?" She tapped her cigarette in the aluminum ashtray on the table. "You do crazy things like Greg. And he's Indian! He gets ideas where he wants to know this or that so he can write it all up for the people. Well, it ain't like that what I am saying."

Jenny told me that for weeks she kept thinking about Mabel and the story. "Hearing that story, just hearing Mabel, I thought more and learned more about myself in one sitting than I have with Shakespeare in ten years," Jenny said. "I've been studying Shakespeare and, well, if my ideas change, and they do, at least the text is the same. With Mabel what is the story? There is so much more than just the story and what was said that *is* the story. I wanted to write it, you know, when I was thinking of things, so I could think about it. But it—whatever it is—wouldn't stay put. Mabel was right: 'It ain't like that what I am saying.' Greg, how are you going to write her stories?"

Once again Mabel confounded her interlocutor. She undermined clear-cut, unqualified answers. She opened the context in which the exchange took place, exposing what made for people talking and listening. Jenny, in retelling "The Woman Who Loved a Snake," will remember that for Mabel the snake/the man was not what it was for Jenny and that the difference spoke of the differences between them. I am reminded of the context, of the world Mabel and I share when talking, every time I try to write something she said.

Writing recreates oral experience in given ways. The transcriptions of American Indian oral literatures, for example, sometimes provide nothing about the context in which the literatures were told and recorded or the manner in which they were translated. In the end we have a story as an object devoid of the context that might suggest something about the story beyond our interaction with it as an independent text. The context of the story consists of story and reader. Based on their biases and purposes for writing, writers select and shape what they experience orally. In the example just cited, editors might decide that a certain story is the whole Indian story. Writing then fixes or makes permanent not only oral experience but what is actually an interpretation of that experience. In this sense, Mabel's talk impedes these literate tendencies for closure by continually opening the world in which oral exchange takes place. "The Woman Who Loved a Snake" is a story not only about the woman in the story but about Jenny and, as I will show in this essay, about me.

Jenny's instinct was literate. "I wanted to write it . . . so I could think about it." She thought if she had a written (fixed) text she would be able to sort out what was in her mind from what was on the page. (Of course Stanley Fish and a host of others have been telling us for some time that such sorting is problematic at best with written texts.) It was not just a matter of what was spoken that made writing the oral story problematic but also what was unspoken. The unspoken that was exposed in the verbal exchange, in this case the different worldviews of Mabel and Jenny regarding the story, became part of the story such that a straight version of "The Woman Who Loved a Snake" (Mabel's narrative without Jenny's presence as a listener) would hardly represent Jenny's experience of the story. Even if Jenny were to write a conventional version, and even if she were to include the brief conversation with Mabel about the story, she would not automatically have a clear picture of her experience and the way she negotiates that experience in time. So much of Jenny's verbal encounter—that which might be transcribed from a tape recorder—had life and significance not only in terms of what was unspoken in the immediate context but in the days and weeks ahead as Jenny kept thinking about the story and her relationship to it. As she said, the story "wouldn't stay put." She told me: "I began to think of snakes differently. People too. All kinds of things came up. I went back to my dissertation on Shakespeare and began to think about Shakespeare's historical period. How was I understanding that period? How was I understanding Shakespeare as a result?"

More and more scholars of oral literatures are looking to the broader contexts in which these literatures live. Specifically, they are considering what lies beyond the spoken word, beyond their perceptual range as listeners and readers, and what that larger context says about their position as literate speakers and writers for and about oral traditions. Concerns regarding context become particularly significant in cross-cultural situations. After struggling with the question as to whether structure or texture generated meaning in Navajo stories, Barre Toelken, with the help of Tacheeni Scott, a Navajo who knew the stories, resolved that

> actually both structure and texture unite to provide an excitement of meaning which already exists elsewhere, in the shared ideas and customs of people raised in an intensely traditional society. . . . Thus, the stories act like "surface structure" in language: by their articulation they touch off a Navajo's deeper accumulated sense of reality. . . . They provide culturally enjoyable correlatives to a body of thought so complicated and profound that vicarious experience in it through entertainment is one of the only access points available to most people.
>
> (110)

Toelken asked the storytellers questions and found that "by seeing the story in terms of any categories [he] had been taught to recognize, [he] had missed the point" (73). Dennis Tedlock notes: "The problem of the mythographer is not merely to present and interpret Zuni myths as if they were objects from a distant place and time and the mythographer were a sort of narrow, one-way conduit, but as events taking place among contemporaries along a frontier that has a long history of crossings" (292). Tedlock is not just talking about Zuni contemporaries. He is stressing the presence of the mythographer who positions the Zuni storytellers in certain ways, and whose interpretation of the situation will partly depend on a subjective interpretation of the stories produced in the context of his presence. After writing about his experience and sense of an oral story-telling event, Tedlock says: "Everything that has been reported here concerning the events of a certain November evening at Zuni, New Mexico, rests finally on conversational and more broadly interactional grounds, and it was there, just there, that it was even possible for me—and now, I hope for us—to understand at least a part of what was going on. . . . Here I say, leewi (all), which means it's someone else's turn" (301).[2]

Without ever directly addressing the question about what is oral in an oral exchange, or what constitutes context, Toelken and Tedlock suggest that in an oral exchange there is much that is unspoken—the histories and varying perspectives of speakers and listeners—which may or may not be evoked verbally in the exchange itself or in continued exchange. Mabel's story and conversation with Jenny—Mabel's talk—reminds us that in oral discourse the context of orality covers the personal territory of those involved in the exchange, and because the territory is so wide, extending throughout two or more personal, and often cultural, worlds, no one party has access to the whole of the exchange. One party may write a story, but one party's story is no more the whole story than a cup of water is the river.

While this may seem obvious, it underscores what it is we do when we tell, transcribe, or write about oral texts. Basically, in whatever form or manner we deal with oral texts, whether orally or literally, we continue their life in very specific ways. This is just as true about an oral exchange within a single culture as it is about an oral exchange that is cross-cultural. No two personal worlds are identical anywhere. This does not mean that

---

[2]Other scholars—linguists and social scientists in particular—have studied differing coherence systems in oral and written communication, an approach that is basically comparative and contrastive and that focuses on the relationship and differences between spoken and written language in human interaction. The works of these scholars, most notably Erickson (1984) and Scollon and Scollon (1984), show that there are different kinds of nonliteracies and that scholars must remember this fact when considering issues of orality and literacy. Scollon and Scollon note: "We feel that this [Northern Athabaskan] oral tradition is strikingly unlike the bard-and-formula oral tradition [i.e., the Homeric tradition studied by Parry and referred to by Ong via Parry] so often advanced as the representative of oral traditions" (182). In Northern Athabaskan storytelling, sense-making is dependent upon audience response as it is for the Chicago-based Afro-American youth (whom Erickson studied) in their general verbal (oral) interactions. Further, Tannen (1982) shows that it is not just a matter of orality vs. literacy but that there is an "interplay in spoken and written discourse in various settings" (4). The work of these scholars focuses primarily on the spoken and written word, and, while this focus is important in a variety of ways, particularly in terms of what it can tell us about different learning styles, their work does not explicitly consider the larger world in which either the oral or the written word lives and is made meaningful as do scholars such as Toelken and Tedlock.

we are not, or cannot be, distanced or critical, for critical response is part of hearing. We sort out what we hear, unconsciously and consciously, and this sorting has to do with our cultural and personal histories and the situation of our hearing.

My discussion here continues the story of "The Woman Who Loved a Snake" in specific ways. Mabel's story, characteristic of her talk, opens the vast territory that is oral and, in so doing, not only suggests the extent of the territory but also lets the territory be talked about and explored. The story reminds me of this and in turn of other stories and experiences. While I am Indian and am familiar with certain aspects of Pomo culture, I am, like Jenny, literate and have specific literate expectations, including the urge to fix, when writing, stories and ideas in given ways.[3] Mabel bucks these literate expectations so that neither she nor any aspect of her world is seen as or reduced to anything other than what it is, in all its complexity and difference; and I am never more reminded of how her talk frustrates such expectations than when I write about something she says. "The Woman Who Loved a Snake" then is as much about orality and interpersonal and intercultural discourse as it is about anything else. You may or may not be able to glean this dimension from a mere transcription of Mabel's narrative. You might, for example, look at the husband's interaction with the snake, the wife's interaction with the snake, or the husband's interaction with his wife, as an encounter with an "other" and then project from the nature and outcome of the encounter. But let me continue my story here of "The Woman Who Loved a Snake" by telling you more of it as I heard it and as it became particularly meaningful for me:[4]

Mabel and I were parked along a road on the south side of Clear Lake, where we had a view of the lake and of Elem Rancheria, the old village site and present-day reservation of the Elem tribe of Pomo Indians. Mabel had been talking about her maternal grandmother, Sarah Taylor, and about how the Elem people initiated her into their dances and cult activities after Sarah's people, the Cache Creek Pomo, had been removed from their land and ceremonial grounds by the non-Indian invaders.

" 'You will find a way, a way to go on even after this white people run over the earth like rabbits. They are going to be everywhere,' he was saying. That's Old Man, I forgot his name. He had only Indian name, Taylor's father, Grandma's grandfather. He's the one saying these things."

Mabel opened her purse, pulled out a cigarette. She lit her cigarette and exhaled a cloud of smoke. Below us, on the narrow peninsula of Elem, smoke rose from the rusted chimney tins of the small, dilapidated houses. A lone dog barked in the distance.

---

[3] Of course a nonliterate audience probably would negotiate Mabel's talk in ways very different from those of us with certain strong literate tendencies.

[4] This story has been produced from tapes, notes, and my memory of my meeting with Mabel McKay on November 20, 1988.

"Well, it was over here, below them hills," Mabel said, gesturing south over her shoulder with her chin. "This things, they come over the hill in a trail, long trail. So much that dust is flying up, like smoke wherever they go. And first to see them this people down there, where you are looking. 'What is this?' the people saying. Things with two heads and four legs, bushy tail, standing here on this hill somewhere, looking down at Elem people.

"Lots of people scared, run off, some far as our place, Cache Creek. They tell what they seen then. All Indians, Indians all over, talking about it then. 'What is it?' they is asking. Nobody knows. People is talking about it all over the place. Lot's scared. I don't know. People say different things.

"Some people somewhere seen them things come apart, like part man, then go back together. Then I guess maybe they knew it was people—white people. I don't know," Mabel said and chuckled. "They Indians dance and pray. I don't know. Then they was saying these things mean, killing Indians and taking Indians."

Mabel drew on her cigarette and leisurely exhaled. "But he seen it in his Dream, Old Man. He said what is coming one day, how this would be."

"So they knew what it was coming down this hill," I ventured.

"Hmm," Mabel said, gazing across the lake. "They knew what he meant by 'white man.' "

"So why did they run? Why all the fuss?"

Mabel rubbed out her cigarette and looked at me as if she had not understood what I said. "If they knew from Old Man's prophecy that white people were coming, why didn't they know what was coming down the hill? Why all the fuss?"

Mabel started chuckling, then exploded with loud, uncontrollable laughter. She caught her breath finally and asked, "How can that be? You ever know white people with four legs and two heads? Maybe you do. You're raised around them—your mother's people. I don't know," she said, chuckling again.

She lit another cigarette, then straightened in her seat. "Sometimes takes time for Dream to show itself. Got to be tested. Now we know what he told about, Old Man. He was told . . . He said lots of things: trails, big trails covering the earth, even going into the sky. Man going to be on moon he was saying."

"But how did HE know that?"

"But sometimes Dream forgets, too. Like them snakes. Old Man come in MY Dream, give me rattlesnake song. 'You going to work with this snakes; they help you,' he is saying. Then, after that, I seen them. All over my house I seen them: porch, closet, in my bathtub when it's hot, all over. Then I say to him, to that spirit, 'This is modern times, better take that song out of me . . . I don't want nothing to happen. People around here might call animal control place.

"You know, peoples around here they don't always understand things like that."

Mabel was not merely making a comment about a gap in understanding between two cultures but also, intentionally or not, pointing up what I had just experienced as a result of my interaction with her. I had been implicated: my own understanding, or lack of understanding, had been exposed. The sentence in context, like the story about intercultural contact in context, pointed beyond itself to the present, opening the story of the two people talking and listening. Here I was busy taking notes and tape-recording her stories for a book about her life, as I had been for the past six months, and, as always, she reminded me of my prejudices and point of view, locating me in the present, turning a story she tells into a story of our exchange. Contact narrative became an instance of culture contact and culture contact a story.[5]

Not new news for Mabel.

Not so ironically I was just laughing a month before at Jenny's question about what the snake symbolized. Non-Indians often ask what this or that symbolizes, as if signs and semiotic systems were transcultural. I was used to stories about snakes. I have heard how rattlesnakes were used by certain medicine people for healing the sick. There are stories of rattlesnake cults in which cult members handled the snakes, asking the snakes for special powers, for guidance. And always there is talk of snakes taking the form of human beings and vice versa. It seems to me that the ways snakes are viewed by the Pomo vary from tribe to tribe and even from person to person within a given tribe. So much depends on the situation, who is in the situation, who is telling about it, and who is listening. Jenny was an outsider, a non-Indian from the university. Suddenly I felt the same way.

Presuppositions that predicated my question about Mabel's story about first contact between natives and non-natives were overturned by her laughter and her question to me, "How can that be? You ever know white people with four legs and two heads?" I had assumed a literal, linear relation between prophecy, or Old Man's Dream, and so-called empirical reality, a relation which posits a kind of fundamental difference between the two states that Mabel may not share. I must begin to consider a worldview in which dream "[g]ot to be tested," as Mabel said later, commenting on both the story and my reaction to it. This difference between Mabel and me is an essential feature of the context in which words are spoken, and that context influences how the words are presented again here, in the way I am now telling the story in this essay.

---

[5]Here I use the term *culture contact* in the broadest sense, as Gregory Bateson says, "not only [in] those cases in which the contact occurs between two communities with different cultures and results in profound disturbance of the culture of one or both groups; but also in cases of contact within a single community. In these cases the contact is between differentiated groups of individuals, e.g. between the sexes, between the young and old. . . . I would even extend the idea of 'contact' so widely as to include those processes whereby a child is molded and trained to fit the culture into which he was born. . . ." (64).

The contact narrative about what the people of Elem encountered is embedded in the longer narrative about Mabel's grandmother, Sarah Taylor, which in turn is embedded in the conversation about Mabel's life as we sat in a car above Clear Lake, which is embedded in our work over the last six months, and so on. The context is ever widening. Still, a dialogical dynamic can be seen in the straight contact narrative just as easily as within the context in which the narrative is told. Mabel made context within the narrative independent of my interjections by commenting on the narrative. Her remarks about Old Man "see[ing] it in his Dream" were interpretive and reveal a dialogue she had with the text about the coming of those "things with two heads and four legs" such that this dialogue made the story. Old Man "seeing what [was] coming one day" is as integral to Mabel's narrative as what the people of Elem saw coming "over the hill in a trail." The story, or the part of it she told, about what the people of Elem saw is likely to be an interpretation rather than a literal retelling on Mabel's part; therefore, it is a comment on another version of the first contact between the natives and the non-natives, in which case we have a comment on a comment, an endless cycle of text becoming interpretation becoming text.[6] Mabel's dialogical dynamic that might otherwise be interior (unspoken) was exposed in the oral presentation of the story.

While such a dynamic may be present in Mabel's narrative independent of my interjections, and while I may be able to talk about the dynamic, I could only gain a sense of its significance for Mabel and of the limits of my own projections with regard to its significance when we talked about it. Mabel's exchange with me, as with Jenny, opened the narrative to new territories, or, more specifically, to the territory of our meeting together in the instance of my hearing a story.

Of course, scholars can excerpt the contact narrative or any part of it from the larger story. Folklorists, for instance, might want to compare various textualized versions of the same tale and attempt to discover the true, or what Hymes calls "authoritative," tale (Hymes 1981, 79–141). So if they were to determine, let's say, that one text, or tale, of what the people of Elem saw was the authoritative Lake County Pomo contact narrative, they would effectively exclude the larger context in which the narrative was told and still lives for the various Pomo of the area and, subsequently, the means for getting an idea of how the narrative might be meaningful for different Pomo beyond the folklorists' interpretations. "A systematic study of variation in performance" (Hymes 1981, 86) of textualized versions of a given tale might show that the so-called true tale is being used or performed in different ways

---

[6]Tedlock has illustrated that when listening to a Zuni storyteller listeners are "in the presence of a performing art, all right, but are getting the criticism at the same time from the same person. The interpreter does not merely play the parts, but is the narrator and commentator as well. . . . At times [listeners] may hear direct quotations from that ["original"] text, but they are embedded in a hermeneutics" (236).

structurally, but that the significance of the difference is understood only in terms of the folklorists' interpretations. Likewise, if scholars were to consider the text proper as only what Mabel says before my interjections, they may be able to discern the dialogical dynamic that I have seen, but they would not have the opportunity to know any story about the text except that of their own invention. Little, if anything, would inhibit their culture-specific projection, which, in turn, can engender further discussion about the projection and spin the discourse further and further from the Indian narrator and her narration.

Again, as I indicated in the last essay, I am not using Mabel's stories and my interaction with her simply to indicate the limits of a text-centered approach to oral literatures or to extol the virtues of contextual studies. "The Woman Who Loved a Snake" and "What the People of Elem Saw" suggest to me, in the ways they come together as one story for me, the territory of orality and a way that territory is opened with Mabel's talk. When Mabel told Jenny about the snake, I saw how I understood Mabel's world; when she told me what the people of Elem saw, I discovered the limits of my understanding of her world. In both instances, I learned there is so much more than just the story and what was said that *is* the story. Mabel's talk not only reminds me of what is at stake when writing, or textualizing, oral experience but also suggests that the writing, as much as possible, should reflect oral tendencies to engage the larger world in which the spoken word lives so that it is seen for what it might or might not be beyond the page. To answer Jenny's question presented at the start of this essay regarding how this is done, specifically how I write Mabel's stories, I offer this same essay as a model of, though not necessarily a model for, writing what Mabel says. Mabel is saying: Remember that when you hear and tell my stories there is more to me and you that *is* the story. You don't know everything about me and I don't know everything about you. Our knowing is limited. Let our words show us as much so we can learn together about one another. Let us tell stories that help us in this. Let us keep learning.

Naturally stories are told differently in different situations, and tellers often do not suggest much about the situation in which they are told or invite further discourse about the stories or the world of the stories. In the last chapter I discussed how Kashaya Pomo scholars Herman James and Essie Parrish in their work with linguist Robert Oswalt used frames to open and close their stories, a use which is likely to reinforce certain literate tendencies that would diminish the larger world of the stories and their tellers. See the following contact narrative told by Essie Parrish to Robert Oswalt:

> This that I am going to tell is what the people thought when they first saw a boat.
> In the old days, before white people came up here, there was a boat sailing on the ocean from the south. Because before that they had never seen a boat, they said, "Our world must be coming to an end. Couldn't we do something? This big bird floating on the ocean is from somewhere, probably from up

high. Let us plan a feast. Let us have a dance." They followed its course with their eyes to see what it would do. Having done so they promised Our Father [a feast] saying destruction was upon them.

When they had done so, they watched [the ship] sail way up north and disappear. They thought that [the ship] had not done anything but sail northwards because of the feast they had promised. They were saying that nothing had happened to them—because of the promise of a feast; because of that they thought it had not done anything. Consequently they held a feast and a big dance.

A long time afterwards, when white men had come up and they saw their boats, they then found out what they had thought was a big bird was otherwise. It wasn't a bird they had seen; they had spied a sailboat. From then on we knew that they hadn't seen a big bird.

This is the end.

(Oswalt, *Kashaya Texts,* 224–47)

The text, as with virtually all of the texts in Oswalt's collection, is effectively framed so that it is closed ("This is the end"), inviting neither further story nor inquiry into the world of the story.

By looking at Mrs. Parrish's contact story, we can further appreciate the ways Mabel does not end or close her story but opens it continually, by the dialogue she has both with it and with the person hearing it. Her story—her talk—counters literate tendencies that would close the vastness of its world and, hence, the complexity of its teller.

In closing I must mention again that Mabel should not be seen as representing a typical Pomo speaker or storyteller. Her talk—her narratives, conversations, responses to questions—seems in many ways unique. I have known other Pomo storytellers who expose internal dialogue they have with a story they are telling. I have also known Pomo storytellers to implicate their listeners in what they are saying. None of the speakers I have known, however, is as consistent in these matters as Mabel. But I have not done a study or comprehensive survey. I have only looked at Mabel's talk in terms of its effect as I have known it, not in terms of the ways it may or may not represent traditional or typical Pomo discourse.

Specifically, I have explored in this essay the ways Mabel's talk counters literate tendencies to close the oral context in which oral communication takes place. Mabel's dynamic is not, I am sure,the only way to break open that immense oral territory, nor is it any guarantee that the territory will be opened. So much depends on the interlocutor. And, as demonstrated with Mrs. Parrish's narrative, some speakers, inadvertently or not, may keep the gates to the territory closed. The territory—all that is oral, spoken and unspoken—is as vast as the culture which it gives life to and from which in turn it takes life. For that reason it is as impossible to generalize about "oral discourse" as it is about "culture." They are inseparable from and specific to particular people, either as the people interact with one another from a shared knowledge base or with groups (or individuals) with a different knowledge base and history. Within a given group or between groups certain kinds of discourse may be aggressive or prompt fear; other kinds may do just the opposite. It depends on the given circumstances in the broadest sense. Mabel's talk, which is oral, provides an opportunity to explore the territory for individuals who may in some ways share her territory, such as myself, and for those who do not at all, such as Jenny. The territory, after all, is not empty, unpeopled.

After Mabel told the story about the people of Elem seeing non-Indian invaders coming "over the hill in a trail," we headed east, back to the Rumsey Reservation. On the way home, Mabel again told the story of "The Woman Who Loved a Snake": "It was across there. Up in them hills where she lived. That time Charlie [Charles McKay, Mabel's husband] running stock up there. By stock I mean the cattle. Charlie always wanted to have the stock. That woman lived there. Sometimes she would come down the road the other side there and talk to me. Anyway, how it happened she was alone at night. Her husband used to go off working, where it was I don't know. I forgot. How it happened she hears this knocking one night, at her door . . ."

I was quieter now, listening.

"Well, you see, I know about them snakes," she said as she finished the story. "They can teach about a lot of things."

Mabel pulled her purse to her lap and began rummaging for her cigarettes. I looked to the cold, damp winter hills. Too cold for snakes, I thought to myself.

"Hmm," she said. "Maybe you'll get some idea about the snakes." I looked at her and she was laughing, holding an unlit cigarette between her fingers. "I know you. You'll . . . you're school way. You'll think about it then write something."

She was right.[7]

Notes

In addition to the sources cited in this section, I would like to acknowledge my indebtedness to the following individuals: Mollie Bishop, Tim Buckley, Juanita Carrio, Violet Chappell, Great-Grandma Nettie, Emiliano Hilario, Rita Hilario-Carter, Mabel McKay, Kathy O'Connor, Old Auntie Eleanor, Essie Parrish, Victoria Kaplan Patterson, Mary Louise Pratt, Anita Silva, Vivien Wilder, numerous unnamed Pomo Elders, family members, and friends, the

---

[7]Portions of this essay have appeared in my "Fieldwork as Cultural Contact and Cultural Critique: Mabel McKay's Model," a paper presented at the 1989 California Indian Conference, Humbolt, California, and in my "Conversations With Mabel McKay: Story as Contact, Contact as Story," a paper presented at the 1989 Association for Study of American Indian Literature (ASAIL) session of the Modern Language Association Convention, Washington, D.C.

Kashaya students at the Kashaya Reservation School at Stewart's Point, California, and the students in my Saddle Lake Summer Course and Writing I class at the University of California at Santa Cruz.

Aginsky, B. W. "The Socio-Psychological Significance of Death among the Pomo Indians." In *Native Californians: A Theoretical Retrospective,* edited by L. J. Bean and T. C. Blackburn, 319–29. Socorro, New Mexico: Ballena Press, 1976.

Allen, Paula Gunn. *The Sacred Hoop.* Boston: Beacon Press, 1986.

Apes, William. *A Son of the Forest. The Experience of William Apes, a Native of the Forest. Comprising a Notice of the Pequot Tribe of Indians. Written by Himself.* New York: published by the author, 1829.

Apess, Mary (variant spelling of Apes, above). "Experience of the Missionary's Consort, Written by Herself." In *Experience of Five Christian Indians of the Pequot Tribe.* Boston: published by William Apess (variant spelling of Apes, above), 1837 [1833].

Bahr, Donald, J. Gregorio, D. I. Lopez, and A. Alvarez. *Pinan Shamanism and Staying Sickness.* Tucson: University of Arizona Press, 1974.

Bakhtin, M. M. *The Dialogic Imagination.* Austin: University of Texas Press, 1981.

Barrett, S. A. *Pomo Myths.* Milwaukee: Bulletin of the Public Museums of the City of Milwaukee 15, 1933.

Barrett, S. M., ed. *Geronimo's Story of His Life.* New York: Duffield, 1906.

Basso, Keith H. "Stalking with Stories: Names, Places, and Moral Narratives among the Western Apache." In *Text, Play, and Story,* edited by Edward M. Bruner, 19–55. Berkeley and Los Angeles: University of California Press, 1984.

Bataille, Gretchen M., and Kathleen Sands. *American Indian Women: Telling Their Lives.* Lincoln: University of Nebraska Press, 1981.

Bateson, Gregory. "Culture Contact and Schismogenesis." In *Steps to an Ecology of Mind.* New York: Ballantine Books/Random House, 1972.

Bauman, Richard. *Verbal Art as Performance.* Prospect Heights, Illinois: Waveland Press, 1984.

Bean, L. J., and D. Theodoratus. "Western Pomo and Northeastern Pomo." In *Handbook of North American Indians,* vol. 8, edited by Robert F. Heizer, 289–305. Washington, D.C.: Smithsonian Institution, 1978.

Ben-Amos, Dan. "Analytical Categories and Ethnic Genres." In *Folklore Genres,* edited by Dan Ben-Amos. Austin: University of Texas Press, 1976.

Benjamin, Walter. "The Work of Art in the Age of Mechanical Reproduction." In *Illuminations.* New York: Schocken Books, 1969.

Berthouex, Susan J., and Robin S. Chapman. "Storytelling: A Way to Teach Non-Native Students." In *Non-Native and Nonstandard Dialect Students,* edited by Candy Carter, 37–43. Urbana: National Council of Teachers of English, 1982.

Bleich, David. "Intersubjective Reading." *New Literary History* 27, no. 3 (1986): 401–21.

Boyarin, Jonathan. "Voices around the Text: The Ethnography of Reading at Mesivta Tifereth Jerusalem." *Cultural Anthropology* (1989): 399–421.

———. "Reading Exodus into History." Unpublished paper, 1991.

Brumble, David H., III. *An Annotated Bibliography of American Indian and Eskimo Autobiographies.* Lincoln: University of Nebraska Press, 1981.

———. *American Indian Autobiography.* Berkeley and Los Angeles: University of California Press, 1988.

Campbell, Maria. *Halfbreed.* Toronto: McClelland and Stewart-Bantam, 1973.

Castaneda, Carlos. *A Separate Reality: Further Conversations with Don Juan.* New York: Simon and Schuster, 1971.

Christian, Chester C., Jr. "The Analysis of Linguistic and Cultural Differences: A Proposed Model." In *Report of the Twenty-First Annual Round Table Meeting on Linguistics and Language Studies,* edited by Chester C. Christian, Jr. Washington, D.C.: Georgetown University Press, 1970.

Clifford, James. "On Ethnographic Authority." *Representations* 1, no. 2 (1983): 118–46.

———. *The Predicament of Culture.* Cambridge: Harvard University Press, 1988.

Colson, Elizabeth, ed. *Autobiographies of Three Pomo Women.* Berkeley: Archeological Research Facility, Department of Anthropology, University of California, 1974 [1956].

Committee on Tolerance and Understanding. *Public Policy—Statements on Native Education.* Edmonton: Government of Alberta, 1984.

Copway, George. *The Life History and Travels of Kah-ge-ga-gah-bowh.* Albany: Weed and Parsons, 1847.

Crapanzano, Vincent. *The Fifth World of Enoch Maloney: Portrait of a Navaho.* New York: Viking, 1969.

———. *The Fifth World of Forster Bennett: Portrait of a Navaho.* New York: Viking, 1972.

———. "The Life History in Anthropological Field Work." *Anthropology and Humanism Quarterly,* no. 2 (1977): 3–7.

DuBois, Cora. "The 1870 Ghost Dance." In *The California Indians,* edited by R. F. Heizer and M. A. Whipple, 496–99. Berkeley and Los Angeles: University of California Press, 1971. (Originally "The 1870 Ghost Dance" was published by University of California Publications: Anthropological Records, 1939.)

Dundes, Alan. "Texture, Text, and Context." *Southern Folklore Quarterly* 29, no. 4 (December 1964): 251–65.

Eakin, Paul John. *Fiction in Autobiography: Studies in the Art of Self-Invention.* Princeton: Princeton University Press, 1974.

Erdrich, Louise. *Love Medicine.* New York: Bantam Books, 1984.

Erickson, Frederick. "Rhetoric, Anecdote, and Rhapsody: Coherence Strategies in a Conversation among Black American Adolescents." In

Coherence in Spoken and Written Discourse, edited by Deborah Tannen, 81–154. Norwood: Ablex Publishing Corporation, 1984.

Fabian, Johannes. *Time and the Other: How Anthropology Makes Its Object.* New York: Columbia University Press, 1983.

Fischer, Michael M. J. "Ethnicity and the Post-Modern Arts of Memory." In *Writing Culture,* edited by James Clifford and George E. Marcus, 194–233. Berkeley and Los Angeles: University of California Press, 1986.

———. *Debating Muslims: Cultural Dialogues in Postmodernity and Tradition.* Madison: University of Wisconsin Press, 1990.

Fish, Stanley. *Is There a Text in This Class? The Authority of Interpretive Communities.* Cambridge: Harvard University Press, 1980.

Freire, Paulo. *Pedagogy of the Oppressed.* New York: Seabury, 1970.

Gleason, William. " 'Her Laugh an Ace': The Function of Humor in Louise Erdrich's *Love Medicine.*" *American Indian Culture and Research Journal* 11, no. 3 (1987): 51–73.

Goffman, Erving. *Frame Analysis.* Cambridge: Harvard University Press, 1974.

Gramsci, Antonio. *The Prison Notebooks: Selections.* Trans. and ed. Quinton Hoare and Geoffrey Nowell Smith. New York: International Publishers, 1971.

Heath, Shirley Brice. *Ways with Words.* New York: Cambridge Univ. Press, 1983.

Hopkins, Sarah Winnemucca. *Life among the Piutes: Their Wrongs and Claims.* New York: G. P. Putman's Sons, 1883.

Hopper, Paul J. "Discourse Analysis: Grammar and Critical Theory in the 1980's." *Profession* 88 (1988): 18–24.

Hymes, Dell. "Breakthrough into Performance." In *Folklore: Performance and Communication,* edited by Dan Ben-Amos and Kenneth Goldstein, 11–74. The Hague: Mouton, 1975. (Later reprinted in Dell Hymes's *In Vain I Tried to Tell You,* 1981.)

———. *In Vain I Tried to Tell You: Essays in Native American Ethnopoetics.* Philadelphia: University of Pennsylvania Press, 1981.

JanMohamed, Abdul R., and David Lloyd. "Toward a Theory of Minority Discourse: What Is to Be Done?" *Cultural Critique* (Fall 1987): 5–17.

Kaplan, Victoria Dickler, et al. *Sheemi Ke Janu (Talk from the Past).* Ukiah, California: Ukiah Title VII Project, Ukiah Unified School District, 1984.

Krupat, Arnold. *For Those Who Come After.* Berkeley and Los Angeles: University of California Press, 1985.

Lavie, Smadar. *The Poetics of Military Occupation: Mzeina Allegories of Bedouin Identity under Israeli and Egyptian Rule.* Berkeley and Los Angeles: University of California Press, 1990.

Leighton, Alexander H., and Dorothea C. Leighton. "The Life Story." In *Gregorio, the Hand-Trembler: A Psychobiological Personality Study of a Navaho Indian,* edited by Alexander H. Leighton and Dorothea C. Leighton. Papers of the Peabody Museum of American Archaeology and Ethnography 40, no. 1 (1949): 45–81.

Lowenthal, Leo. "The Triumph of Mass Idols." In *Literature and Mass Culture*. New Brunswick, New Jersey: Transaction, 1984.

McKenzie, James. "Lipsha's Good Road Home: The Revival of Chippewa Culture in *Love Medicine.*" *American Indian Culture and Research Journal* 10, no. 3 (1986): 53–63.

Majnep, Ian, and Ralph Bulmer. *Birds of My Kalam Country*. Auckland, New Zealand: Auckland University Press, 1977.

Marcus, George E., and Michael M. J. Fischer. *Anthropology as Cultural Critique*. Chicago: University of Chicago Press, 1986.

Momaday, N. Scott. *The Way to Rainy Mountain*. Albuquerque: University of New Mexico Press, 1969.

———. *The Names*. New York: Harper and Row, 1976.

Mooney, James. *The Ghost Dance Religion and the Sioux Outbreak of 1890*. Chicago: University of Chicago Press, 1965.

Murray, David. *Forked Tongues*. Bloomington: Indiana University Press, 1991.

Neihardt, John G., ed. *Black Elk Speaks*. New York: Washington Square Press, 1972 [1932].

Newkirk, Thomas. "Looking for Trouble: A Way to Unmask Our Readings." *College English* 46, no. 8 (December 1984): 756–66.

Occom, Samson. "A Short Narrative of My Life." In *The Elders Wrote: An Anthology of Early Prose by North American Indians, 1768–1931*, edited by Bernd Peyer, 12–18. Berlin: Dietrich Reimer Verlag, 1982.

Ong, Walter. *Orality and Literacy: The Technologizing of the Word*. London: Methuen, 1982.

Oswalt, Robert. *Kashaya Texts*. University of California Publications in Linguistics, vol. 36. Berkeley and Los Angeles: University of California Press, 1964.

Parry, Milman. *The Making of Homeric Verse: The Collected Papers of Milman Parry*. Ed. Adam Parry. Oxford: Clarendon Press, 1971.

Paul, Richard. "The Critical Thinking Movement." *National Forum* (Winter 1985): 1–5.

Pomolita School Title VII students. *Pomo Supernaturals Coloring Book*. Ukiah, California: Ukiah Unified School District, 1983.

Ricoeur, Paul. *Interpretation Theory: Discourse and the Surplus of Meaning*. Fort Worth: Texas Christian University Press, 1976.

Rodriguez, Richard. *Hunger of Memory: The Education of Richard Rodriguez, an Autobiography*. Boston: Godine, 1982.

Roemer, Marjorie Godlin. "Literate Cultures: Multi-Voiced Classrooms." Paper presented at the Modern Language Association, San Francisco, California, December 1987.

Rosaldo, Renato. "Ilongot Hunting as Story and Experience." In *The Anthropology of Experience*, edited by Victor W. Turner and Edward M. Bruner, 97–138. Urbana: University of Illinois Press, 1986.

———. *Culture and Truth*. Boston: Beacon Press, 1989.

Said, Edward W. "Opponents, Audiences, Constituencies and Community." *Critical Inquiry* 9 (1982): 135–59.

———. "Representing the Colonized: Anthropology's Interlocutors." *Critical Inquiry* 15 (Winter 1989): 205–25.

Sarris, Greg. "A Culture under Glass: The Pomo Basket." In *In Writing,* edited by Paul Khoo and others, 44–53. Stanford: Stanford University Press, 1987.

———. "Storytelling in the Classroom: Crossing Vexed Chasms." *College English* 52, no. 2 (1990): 169–85.

Schwab, Gabriele. "Reader-Response and the Aesthetic Experience of Otherness." *Stanford Literature Review* (Spring 1986): 107–36.

Schwartzman, Helen B. "Stories at Work: Play in an Organizational Context." In *Text, Play, and Story: The Construction and Reconstruction of Self and Society,* edited by Edward M. Bruner. Washington, D.C.: American Ethnological Society, 1984.

Scollon, Ron, and Suzanne B. K. Scollon. "Cooking It up and Boiling It Down: Abstracts in Athabaskan Children's Story Retellings." In *Coherence in Spoken and Written Discourse,* edited by Deborah Tannen. Norwood: Ablex Publishing Corporation, 1984.

Shostak, Marjorie. *Nisa: The Life and Words of a !Kung Woman.* New York: Vintage Books, 1983.

Silberman, Robert. "Opening the Text: *Love Medicine* and the Return of the Native American Woman." In *Narrative Chance,* edited by Gerald Vizenor. Albuquerque: University of New Mexico Press, 1989.

Silko, Leslie Marmon. *Ceremony.* New York: Signet Books, 1977.

———. *Storyteller.* New York: Seaver Books, 1981.

Standiford, Lester A. "Worlds Made of Dawn: Characteristic Image and Incident in Native American Imaginative Literature." In *Three American Literatures,* edited by Houston A. Baker, Jr, 168–96. New York: The Modern Language Association of America, 1982.

Swearingen, C. Jan. "Oral Hermeneutics during the Transition to Literacy: The Contemporary Debate." *Cultural Anthropology* 1 (1986): 138–56.

Tannen, Deborah. "The Oral/Literate Continuum in Discourse." In *Spoken and Written Language: Exploring Orality and Literacy,* edited by Deborah Tannen, 1–16. Norwood: Ablex Publishing Corporation, 1982.

Tedlock, Dennis. "The Spoken Word and the Work of Interpretation in American Indian Religion." In *The Spoken Word and the Work of Interpretation.* Philadelphia: University of Pennsylvania Press, 1983.

Theisz, R. D. "The Critical Collaboration: Introductions as a Gateway to the Study of Native American Bi-Autobiography." *American Indian Culture and Research Journal* 5, no. 1 (1981): 65–92.

Toelken, Barre, and Tacheeni Scott. "Poetic Retranslation and the 'Pretty Languages' of Yellowman." In *Traditional Literatures of the American Indian: Texts and Interpretations,* edited by Karl Kroeber, 65–116. Lincoln: University of Nebraska Press, 1981.

Tyler, Stephen A. "Post-Modern Ethnography: From Document of the Occult to Occult Document." In *Writing Culture,* edited by James Clifford and George E. Marcus, 122–40. Berkeley and Los Angeles: University of California Press, 1986.

Velie, A. *Four American Indian Literary Masters: N. Scott Momaday, James Welch, Leslie Marmon Silko, and Gerald Vizenor.* Norman: University of Oklahoma Press, 1982.

Vizenor, Gerald. *Interior Landscapes.* Minneapolis: University of Minnesota Press, 1990.

Wallace, A. F. C. *The Death and Rebirth of the Seneca.* New York: Knopf, 1970.

YA-KA-AMA Indian Education and Development Inc. *"A Description of Slug Woman" and "A Story about the Slug Woman"* (pamphlet). Santa Rosa, Calif.: YA-KA-AMA, 1974.

Leslie Marmon Silko (Laguna Pueblo)

Language and Literature from a Pueblo Indian Perspective

Where I come from, the words most highly valued are those spoken from the heart, unpremeditated and unrehearsed. Among the Pueblo people, a written speech or statement is highly suspect because the true feelings of the speaker remain hidden as she reads words that are detached from the occasion and the audience. I have intentionally not written a formal paper because I want you to *hear* and to experience English in a structure that follows patterns from the oral tradition. For those of you accustomed to being taken from point A to point B to point C, this presentation may be somewhat difficult to follow. Pueblo expression resembles something like a spider's web—with many little threads radiating from the center, crisscrossing one another. As with the web, the structure emerges as it is made, and you must simply listen and trust, as the Pueblo people do, that meaning will be made.

My task is a formidable one: I ask you to set aside a number of basic approaches that you have been using and probably will continue to use, and, instead, to approach language from the Pueblo perspective, one that embraces the whole of creation and the whole of history and time.

What changes would Pueblo writers make to English as a language for literature? I have some examples of stories in English that I will use to address this question. At the same time, I would like to explain the importance of storytelling and how it relates to a Pueblo theory of language.

So I will begin, appropriately enough, with the Pueblo Creation story, an all-inclusive story of how life began. In this story, Tse'itsi'nako, Thought Woman, by thinking of her sisters, and together with her sisters, thought of everything that is. In this way, the world was created. Everything in this world was a part of the original Creation; the people at home understood that far away there were other human beings, also a part of this world. The Creation story even includes a prophecy that describes the origin of European and African peoples and also refers to Asians.

This story, I think, suggests something about why the Pueblo people are more concerned with story and communication and less concerned with a particular language. There are at least six, possibly seven, distinct languages among the twenty pueblos of the southwestern United States, for example, Zuñi and Hopi. And from mesa to mesa there are subtle differences in language. But the particular language being spoken isn't as important as what a speaker is trying to say, and this emphasis on the story itself stems, I believe, from a view of narrative particular to the Pueblo and other Native American peoples—that is, that language *is* story.

I will try to clarify this statement. At Laguna Pueblo, for example, many individual words have their own stories. So when one is telling a story and one is using words to tell the story, each word that one is speaking has a story of its own, too. Often the speakers, or tellers, will go into these word stories, creating an elaborate structure of stories within stories. This structure, which becomes very apparent in the actual telling of a story, informs contemporary Pueblo writing and storytelling as well as the traditional narratives. This perspective on narrative—of story within story, the idea that one story is only the beginning of many stories and the sense that stories never truly end—represents an important contribution of Native American cultures to the English language.

Many people think of storytelling as something that is done at bedtime, that it is something done for small children. But when I use the term *storytelling,* I'm talking about something much bigger than that. I'm talking about something that comes out of an experience and an understanding of that original view of Creation—that we are all part of a whole; we do not differentiate or fragment stories and experiences. In the beginning, Tse'itsi'nako, Thought Woman, thought of all things, and all of these things are held together as one holds many things together in a single thought.

So in the telling (and you will hear a few of the dimensions of this telling), first of all, as mentioned earlier, the storytelling always includes the audience, the listeners. In fact, a great deal of the story is believed to be inside the listener; the storyteller's role is to draw the story out of the listeners. The storytelling continues from generation to generation.

Basically, the origin story constructs our identity—with this story, we know who we are. We are the Lagunas. This is where we come from. We came this way. We came by this place. And so from the time we are very young, we hear these stories, so that when we go out into the world, when one asks who we are or where we are from, we immediately know: we are the people who came from the north. We are the people of these stories.

In the Creation story, Antelope says that he will help knock a hole in the Earth so that the people can come up, out into the next world. Antelope tries and tries; he uses his hooves but is unable to break through. It is then that Badger says, "Let me help you." And Badger very patiently uses his claws and digs a way through, bringing the people into the world. When the Badger clan people think of themselves, or when the Antelope people think of themselves, it is as people who are of *this* story, and this is *our* place, and we fit into the very beginning when the people first came, before we began our journey south.

Within the clans there are stories that identify the clan. One moves, then, from the idea of one's identity as a tribal person into clan identity, then to one's identity as a member of an extended family. And it is the notion of extended family that has produced a kind of story that some distinguish from other Pueblo stories, though Pueblo people do not. Anthropologists and ethnologists have, for a long time, differentiated the types of stories the

Pueblos tell. They tended to elevate the old, sacred, and traditional stories and to brush aside family stories, the family's account of itself. But in Pueblo culture, these family stories are given equal recognition. There is no definite, preset pattern for the way one will hear the stories of one's own family, but it is a very critical part of one's childhood, and the storytelling continues throughout one's life. One will hear stories of importance to the family—sometimes wonderful stories—stories about the time a maternal uncle got the biggest deer that was ever seen and brought it back from the mountains. And so an individual's identity will extend from the identity constructed around the family—"I am from the family of my uncle who brought in this wonderful deer, and it was a wonderful hunt."

Family accounts include negative stories, too; perhaps an uncle did something unacceptable. It is very important that one keep track of all these stories—both positive and not so positive—about one's own family and other families. Because even when there is no way around it—old Uncle Pete *did* do a terrible thing—by knowing the stories that originate in other families, one is able to deal with terrible sorts of things that might happen within one's own family. If a member of the family does something that cannot be excused, one always knows stories about similarly inexcusable things done by a member of another family. But this knowledge is not communicated for malicious reasons. It is very important to understand this. Keeping track of all the stories within the community gives us all a certain distance, a useful perspective, that brings incidents down to a level we can deal with. If others have done it before, it cannot be so terrible. If others have endured, so can we.

The stories are always bringing us together, keeping this whole together, keeping this family together, keeping this clan together. "Don't go away, don't isolate yourself, but come here, because we have all had these kinds of experiences." And so there is this constant pulling together to resist the tendency to run or hide or separate oneself during a traumatic emotional experience. This separation not only endangers the group but the individual as well—one does not recover by oneself.

Because storytelling lies at the heart of Pueblo culture, it is absurd to attempt to fix the stories in time. "When did they tell the stories?" or "What time of day does the storytelling take place?"—these questions are nonsensical from a Pueblo perspective, because our storytelling goes on constantly: as some old grandmother puts on the shoes of a child and tells her the story of a little girl who didn't wear her shoes, for instance, or someone comes into the house for coffee to talk with a teenage boy who has just been in a lot of trouble, to reassure him that someone else's son has been in that kind of trouble, too. Storytelling is an ongoing process, working on many different levels.

Here's one story that is often told at a time of individual crisis (and I want to remind you that we make no distinctions between types of story—historical, sacred, plain gossip—because these distinctions are not useful when discussing the Pueblo *experience* of language). There was a young man who, when he came back from the war in Vietnam, had saved up his army pay and bought a beautiful red Volkswagen. He was very proud of it. One night he drove up to a place called the King's Bar, right across the reservation line. The bar is notorious for many reasons, particularly for the deep arroyo located behind it. The young man ran in to pick up a cold six-pack, but he forgot to put on his emergency brake. And his little red Volkswagen rolled back into the arroyo and was all smashed up. He felt very bad about it, but within a few days everybody had come to him with stories about other people who had lost cars and family members to that arroyo, for instance, George Day's station wagon, with his mother-in-law and kids inside. So everybody was saying, "Well, at least your mother-in-law and kids weren't in the car when it rolled in," and one can't argue with that kind of story. The story of the young man and his smashed-up Volkswagen was now joined with all the other stories of cars that fell into that arroyo.

Now I want to tell you a very beautiful little story. It is a very old story that is sometimes told to people who suffer great family or personal loss. This story was told by my Aunt Susie. She is one of the first generation of people at Laguna who began experimenting with English—who began working to make English speak for us, that is, to speak from the heart. (I come from a family intent on getting the stories told.) As you read the story, I think you will hear that. And here and there, I think, you will also hear the influence of the Indian school at Carlisle, Pennsylvania, where my Aunt Susie was sent (like being sent to prison) for six years.

This scene is set partly in Acoma, partly in Laguna. Waithea was a little girl living in Acoma and one day she said, "Mother, I would like to have some *yashtoah* to eat." *Yashtoah* is the hardened crust of corn mush that curls up. *Yashtoah* literally means "curled up." She said, "I would like to have some *yashtoah*," and her mother said, "My dear little girl, I can't make you any *yashtoah* because we haven't any wood, but if you will go down off the mesa, down below, and pick up some pieces of wood and bring them home, I will make you some *yashtoah*." So Waithea was glad and ran down the precipitous cliff of Acoma mesa. Down below, just as her mother had told her, there were pieces of wood, some curled, some crooked in shape, that she was to pick up and take home. She found just such wood as these.

She brought them home in a little wicker basket. First she called to her mother as she got home, "*Nayah, deeni!* Mother, upstairs!" The Pueblo people always called "upstairs" because long ago their homes were two, three stories, and they entered from the top. She said, "*Deeni! Upstairs!*" and her mother came. The little girl said, "I have brought the wood you wanted me to bring." And she opened her little wicker basket to lay out the pieces of wood, but here they were snakes. They were snakes instead of the crooked sticks of wood. And her mother said, "Oh my dear child, you have brought snakes instead!" She said, "Go take them back and put them back just where you got them." And the little girl ran down the mesa again, down below to the flats. And she put those snakes back just where she got them. They were snakes instead, and she was very hurt about this, and so she said, "I'm not going home. I'm going to Kawaik, the beautiful lake place Kawaik, and drown myself in that lake, *byn'yah'nah* [the 'west lake']. I will go there and drown myself."

So she started off, and as she passed by the Enchanted Mesa near Acoma, she met an old man, very aged, and he saw her running, and he said, "My dear child, where are you going?" "I'm going to Kawaik and jump into the lake there."

"Why?" "Well, because," she said, "my mother didn't want to make any *yashtoah* for me." The old man said, "Oh, no! You must not go, my child. Come with me and I will take you home." He tried to catch her, but she was very light and skipped along. And every time he would try to grab her she would skip faster away from him.

The old man was coming home with some wood strapped to his back and tied with yucca. He just let that strap go and let the wood drop. He went as fast as he could up the cliff to the little girl's home. When he got to the place where she lived, he called to her mother. *"Deeni!"* "Come on up!" And he said, "I can't. I just came to bring you a message. Your little daughter is running away. She is going to Kawaik to drown herself in the lake there." "Oh my dear little girl!" the mother said. So she busied herself with making the *yashtoah* her little girl liked so much. Corn mush curled at the top. (She must have found enough wood to boil the corn meal and make the *yashtoah*.)

While the mush was cooling off, she got the little girl's clothing, her *manta* dress and buckskin moccasins and all her other garments, and put them in a bundle—probably a yucca bag. And she started down as fast as she could on the east side of Acoma. (There used to be a trail there, you know. It's gone now, but it was accessible in those days.) She saw her daughter way at a distance and she kept calling: "Stsamaku! My daughter! Come back! I've got your *yashtoah* for you." But the little girl would not turn. She kept on ahead and she cried: "My mother, my mother, she didn't want me to have any *yashtoah*. So now I'm going to Kawaik and drown myself." Her mother heard her cry and said, "My little daughter, come back here!" "No," and she kept a distance away from her. And they came nearer and nearer to the lake. And she could see her daughter now, very plain. "Come back, my daughter! I have your *yashtoah*." But no, she kept on, and finally she reached the lake and she stood on the edge.

She had tied a little feather in her hair, which is traditional (in death they tie this feather on the head). She carried a feather, the little girl did, and she tied it in her hair with a piece of string; right on top of her head she put the feather. Just as her mother was about to reach her, she jumped into the lake. The little feather was whirling around and around in the depths below. Of course the mother was very sad. She went, grieved, back to Acoma and climbed her mesa home. She stood on the edge of the mesa and scattered her daughter's clothing, the little moccasins, the *yashtoah*. She scattered them to the east, to the west, to the north, to the south. And the pieces of clothing and the moccasins and *yashtoah* all turned into butterflies. And today they say that Acoma has more beautiful butterflies: red ones, white ones, blue ones, yellow ones. They came from this little girl's clothing.

Now this is a story anthropologists would consider very old. The version I have given you is just as Aunt Susie tells it. You can occasionally hear some English she picked up at Carlisle—words like *precipitous*. You will also notice that there is a great deal of repetition, and a little reminder about *yashtoah* and how it is made. There is a remark about the cliff trail at Acoma—that it was once there but is there no longer. This story may be told at a time of sadness or loss, but within this story many other elements are brought together. Things are not separated out and categorized; all things are brought together, so that the reminder about the *yashtoah* is valuable information that is repeated—a recipe, if you will. The information about the old trail at Acoma reveals that stories are, in a sense, maps, since even to this day there is little information or material about trails that is passed around with writing. In the structure of this story the repetitions are, of course, designed to help you remember. It is repeated again and again, and then it moves on.

There are a great many parallels between Pueblo experiences and those of African and Caribbean peoples—one is that we have all had the conqueror's language imposed on us. But our experience with English has been somewhat different in that the Bureau of Indian Affairs schools were not interested in teaching us the canon of Western classics. For instance, we never heard of Shakespeare. We were given Dick and Jane, and I can remember reading that the robins were heading south for the winter. It took me a long time to figure out what was going on. I worried for quite a while about our robins in Laguna because they didn't leave in the winter, until I finally realized that all the big textbook companies are up in Boston and *their* robins do go south in the winter. But in a way, this dreadful formal education freed us by encouraging us to maintain our narratives. Whatever literature we were exposed to at school (which was damn little), at home the storytelling, the special regard for telling and bringing together through the telling, was going on constantly.

And as the old people say, "If you can remember the stories, you will be all right. Just remember the stories." When I returned to Laguna Pueblo after attending college, I wondered how the storytelling was continuing (anthropologists say that Laguna Pueblo is one of the more acculturated pueblos), so I visited an English class at Laguna-Acoma High School. I knew the students had cassette tape recorders in their lockers and stereos at home, and that they listened to Kiss and Led Zeppelin and were well informed about culture in general. I had with me an anthology of short stories by Native American writers, *The Man to Send Rain Clouds*. One story in the book is about the killing of a state policeman in New Mexico by three Acoma

Pueblo men in the early 1950s. I asked the students how many had heard this story and steeled myself for the possibility that the anthropologists were right, that the old traditions were indeed dying out and the students would be ignorant of the story. But instead, all but one or two raised their hands—they had heard the story, just as I had heard it when I was young, some in English, some in Laguna.

One of the other advantages that we Pueblos have enjoyed is that we have always been able to stay with the land. Our stories cannot be separated from their geographical locations, from actual physical places on the land. We were not relocated like so many Native American groups who were torn away from their ancestral land. And our stories are so much a part of these places that it is almost impossible for future generations to lose them—there is a story connected with every place, every object in the landscape.

Dennis Brutus has talked about the "yet unborn" as well as "those from the past," and how we are still *all* in *this* place, and language—the storytelling—is our way of passing through or being with them, of being together again. When Aunt Susie told her stories, she would tell a younger child to go open the door so that our esteemed predecessors might bring their gifts to us. "They are out there," Aunt Susie would say. "Let them come in. They're here, they're here with us *within* the stories."

A few years ago, when Aunt Susie was 106, I paid her a visit, and while I was there she said, "Well, I'll be leaving here soon. I think I'll be leaving here next week, and I will be going over to the Cliff House." She said, "It's going to be real good to get back over there." I was listening, and I was thinking that she must be talking about her house at Paguate village, just north of Laguna. And she went on, "Well, my mother's sister [and she gave her Indian name] will be there. She has been living there. She will be there and we will be over there, and I will get a chance to write down these stories I've been telling you." Now you must understand, of course, that Aunt Susie's mother's sister, a great storyteller herself, has long since passed over into the land of the dead. But then I realized, too, that Aunt Susie wasn't talking about death the way most of us do. She was talking about "going over" as a journey, a journey that perhaps we can only begin to understand through an appreciation for the boundless capacity of language that, through storytelling, brings us together, despite great distances between cultures, despite great distances in time.

An Old-Time Indian Attack Conducted in Two Parts:
Part One: Imitation "Indian" Poems
Part Two: Gary Snyder's *Turtle Island*

Imitation "Indian" Poems

Since white ethnologists like Boas and Swanton first intruded into Native American communities to "collect" prayers, songs and stories, a number of implicit racist assumptions about Native American culture and literature have flourished. The first is the assumption that the white man, through some innate cultural or racial superiority, has the ability to perceive and master the essential beliefs, values and emotions of persons from Native American communities. (This assumption has been applied to non-white communities world-wide.) It is this assumption which, in 1927, allowed Oliver La Farge, New England born, Harvard educated, to write his novel, *Laughing Boy,* which won the Pulitzer Prize in 1929. The novel was written after La Farge spent a number of summer vacations doing ethnological field work on the Navajo Reservation.

I do not disagree with the fact that La Farge cared deeply for the Navajos as well as for other Indian people; he not only had sincere intentions, he actively worked to "better the lot" of Indian people. But as an artist and a writer, La Farge fell victim to the assumption that he could write a novel centered in the consciousness of a Navajo man; a Navajo who by La Farge's own design, had grown up with almost no contact with white people.

In the summer of 1971, the Navajo students in a Southwestern Literature class at Navajo Community College concluded that *Laughing Boy* was entertaining; but, as an expression of anything Navajo, especially with relation to Navajo emotions and behavior, the novel was a failure.[1] And, for the non-Navajo or the non-Indian, it is worse than a failure: it is a lie because La Farge passes off the consciousness and feelings of Laughing Boy as those of Navajo sensibility.

Fifty years later, this racist assumption is thriving; it flourishes among white poets and writers who romanticize their "power" as writers to inhabit souls and consciousness far beyond the realms of their own knowledge or experience. Not long ago, in an Albuquerque bookstore, I found William Eastlake's latest novel, hot off Viking press which also happens to be my publisher. The blurb on the bookcover said that Eastlake was "the only white man who knows enough about Indians" to say the "ir-

---

[1] I was an instructor at Navajo Community College during two summer sessions (1971 and 1972) and during one full year from Fall of 1972 through May of 1973.

reverent" things he says about Indians. Eastlake's "Indian" characters have as much relation to Navajos, as Topsy and Uncle Tom have to Blacks; what disturbs me more, is his presumption to speak for Navajos. In 1973, during a panel discussion in Tempe, Arizona, Eastlake rhapsodized about the good will and generosity of white traders operating trading posts on the Navajo Reservation. His ignorance was remarkable. Within a few months of Eastlake's "knowledgeable" remarks, the Federal Trade Commission filed a report indicating gross illegal conduct by white traders against Navajo people. So much for Bill Eastlake, knowledgeable white spokesman for the Navajos. . . .[2]

If you examine this notion that the writer has the "power" to inhabit any soul, any consciousness, you will find this idea restricted to the white man: the concept of a "universal consciousness" did not occur until sometime in the early Eighteenth century. Ask an older tribal person to attempt to recreate the thoughts and feelings of a white person, and they will tell you that they can't: they will tell you that they can describe *their* observations of whites, even probable responses in whites, but they will tell you they certainly will not pretend to know or understand what is going on *inside* those white people.

The second implicit racist assumption still abounding is that the prayers, chants, and stories weaseled out by the early white ethnographers, which are now collected in ethnological journals, are public property. Presently, a number of Native American communities are attempting to recover religious objects and other property taken from them in the early 1900's that are now placed in museums. Certainly, the songs and stories which were taken by ethnographers are no different. But, among white poets—Rothenberg and Snyder, to mention the most prominent—the idea that these materials should be left to those tribes and their descendants is unthinkable. White poets cash in on the generosity which many tribes have and still practice; white poets delight in saying "Indians believe in sharing," and so they go on "sharing," collecting book royalties on plagiarized materials.

What is an "imitation" Indian poem? Almost certainly, it is a poem labeled by the white poet, a "translation." White poets use the term "translation" very loosely when applied to Asian or Native American material; few, if any, of them, are conversant in the Asian or Native American languages they pretend to "translate." What they do is sit down and rearrange English transcriptions done by ethnologists and then call this a "translation."

---

[2]The panel discussion took place during a meeting of the Coordinating Council of Literary Magazine's November, 1973, meeting held in Tempe, Arizona. Also sitting on the panel was Frank Waters. I was there, and there were other persons who heard Eastlake expound these "facts." My husband worked for the Navajo legal services organization which alerted the Federal Trade Commission to the widespread and grossly illegal practices of white traders in their dealings with Navajos.

In an interview in the Summer, 1975 issue of the *Chicago Review,* Louis Simpson said:

> I think that there are many kinds of Indian poems. There would be the poem which you wrote like an Indian, where you understood how he thought, his magic, his life, his values. Then there's the white man's Indian poem, in which, after all, the Indian is not just the Indian, he is a concept like the "noble savage" which the white man has had in his head for a long time. (page 105)[3]

Simpson's views are interesting for a number of reasons. First, because they evidence that implicit racist assumption that a white man *can* think and feel whatever a Native American thinks and feels. Secondly, Simpson gives an insight into the white "Indian poems" which, along with Li Po "oriental" poems, began to emerge in the early sixties:

> . . . the new poems we were writing in the sixties were a literary construction. We were trying to use the Indian as a means of expressing our feeling about the repressed side of America that should be released. However, if I or anyone were to continue to write Indian poems, we should know more about Indians than we did. I was writing with sympathy and a historical sense of feeling, but to write about Indians you should in a sense become an Indian. (page 105)[4]

Again, the unmitigated egotism of the white man, and the belief that he could "in a sense become an Indian." And finally, the reduction of Native American people to the grossest stereotype of all: the literary device.

But what about the white poets who are knowledgeable, sympathetic, who "feel deeply," who "identify" with beliefs and values of many Native American communities? What about the white poets with Indian friends, surely these special few have "earned" their poetic license to write white "Indian" poems? The answer is complicated.

Above all else, the old people have taught us to value the truth. I value the truth. We are taught to remember who we are: our ancestors, our origins. We must know the place we came from because it has shaped us and continues to make us who we are.

In contrast, the Anglo-American attitude for the past two hundred years has been to cast off familial and geographic ties; to "go West, young man," to change identities as easily as changing shoes. And so, in the early sixties, young white Americans travelled to Japanese monasteries, or studied books of Native American "lore" in an attempt to remake themselves, and to obliterate their white, middle-class ancestry and origins. It was with the attempt

---

[3]*The Chicago Review,* Volume 27, No. 1, Summer, 1975, "A Conversation With Louis Simpson" interviewed by Lawrence R. Smith (pp. 99–109).

[4]*Ibid.*

to cultivate a "new" sensibility and "new" consciousness that imitation "Indian" poems, and "orientalism" in American poetry began to appear.

Ironically, as white poets attempt to cast off their Anglo-American values, their Anglo-American origins, they violate a fundamental belief held by the tribal people they desire to emulate: they deny the truth; they deny their history, their very origins. The writing of imitation "Indian" poems, then, is pathetic evidence that in more than two hundred years, Anglo-Americans have failed to create a satisfactory identity for themselves.

Part Two: Gary Snyder's *Turtle Island*

Without question, Gary Snyder is one of the white poets Louis Simpson was referring to in his remarks about the white "Indian poems" and the "orientalism" of the early sixties. The title *Turtle Island* is itself "borrowed," we are told in the introduction; the concept of the turtle being that the continent was shared by more than one Native American tribe. Still, there is only one poem, "Prayer for the Great Family" which is clearly a "translation"; it appears with the notation "from a Mohawk prayer" (p. 25).[5] What about the other poems in *Turtle Island?*

Although Snyder talks about "harking back again to those roots" in his introductory note, there are actually only two instances in *Turtle Island* where this happens: one is his dedication of the book to his mother and mention of "my Mother's old soft arm" as he helps her up the trail to visit his place ("The Egg," p. 37).[6]

The other instance occurs in the poem "Dusty Braces" where Snyder for the first time acknowledges his own ancestors:

O you ancestors
lumber schooners
    big moustache
long-handled underwear
sticks out under the cuffs
tan stripes on each shoulder
dusty braces
nine bows
nine bows
you bastards

my fathers
   and grandfathers, stiff-necked
punchers, miners, dirt farmers, railroad men
killed off the cougar and grizzly (p. 75)[7]

---

[5]*Turtle Island* by Gary Snyder. New Directions paperback.

[6]*Ibid.*

[7]*Ibid.*

Of course, he has often written about his people, his ancestors; it is just that he seldom acknowledges them as fathers and grandfathers. They are the drivers of logging trucks who hit deer on highway forty-nine; they are cowboys in the Maverick Bar in Farmington where the band played "Okie from Muskokie"; but Snyder has seldom revealed his roots and relationship with this part of his identity although Snyder himself was born in a Texas town, and the last I heard, his mother was living in a housetrailer in Florida.[8] Until *Turtle Island,* we had heard nothing of mothers or fathers and grandfathers; his hide-away in the Sierras underscored this detachment. But now, as he "harkens us back to those roots," maybe we can expect to see the connection made with his own roots and origins. Until this connection is made, Snyder will not be able to complete the philosophical and artistic synthesis he is attempting to make for Anglo-Americans in his *Turtle Island* Manifestos. Since the manifestos are addressed primarily to Anglo-American technocrats, I prefer to deal with things in *Turtle Island* which involve me or the people.

Although Snyder goes on at length about the land, the earth, and the Native Americans' relationship to it, he does not deal with the facts surrounding his ownership or "use," if you prefer, of the acreage in the Sierras. He clearly acknowledges that the land he is occupying is

> the land that was deer and acorn
> grounds of the Nisenan
> branch of Maidu (p. 79)[9]

But he intellectualizes his complicity in the land theft by enthusiastically quoting the pre-Columbian notion that "the land belongs to itself" (p. 80). Snyder reasons that since he doesn't believe in land ownership either, he doesn't really "own" the land (although he apparently purchased it and pays taxes on it), and therefore, he is without guilt. Snyder is, of course, missing the important point: for whatever the different Native American communities have thought or continued to think about their relationship to the earth, Native Americans are very much aware of the occupancy and use rights to the land. We continue to fight bitterly to regain control of the occupancy and use of land that was taken.

In "Control Burn" he writes:

> What the Indians
> here
> used to do, was
> to burn out the brush every year . . .

---

[8]Snyder himself told me this.

[9]*Turtle Island.*

I would like,
with a sense of helpful order,
with respect for laws
of nature,
to help my land
with a burn, a hot clean
burn . . .

And then
it would be more
like,
when it belonged to the Indians

Before.   (p. 19)[10]

Again though, Snyder somehow fails to realize that although he is careful, even reverent with this land he is occupying, it is *not* "his" land, as he erroneously claims; he is occupying stolen property. And even when Anglo-Saxon common law is applied, the fact remains: stolen property, no matter how many times it is sold or changes hands, no matter the "good faith" of the innocent subsequent purchaser, remains stolen property; and at common law, all property rights remained vested in the original legal owner. In this case, legal title still remains with the Maidu people.

It is admirable that Snyder is attempting to make

> the rediscovery of this land and the ways by which we might become natives of the place, ceasing to think and act [after all these centuries] as newcomers and invaders.[11]

as the blurb on the jacket of the book indicates. It is admirable and perhaps even worthy of a Pulitzer Prize. But unless Snyder is careful, he is headed in the same unfortunate direction as other white pioneers have gone, a direction which avoids historical facts which are hard to swallow: namely, that at best, the Anglo-American is a guest on this continent; and at the worst, the United States of America is founded upon stolen land. Unless Snyder comes to terms with these facts, and his own personal, ancestral relation to them, the "rediscovery" which so many Americans are waiting for, will be just another dead-end in more than two hundred years of searching for a genuine American identity.

Gary Snyder once said to me "you must create your own new myths."

That is good advice to follow.

---

[10]*Ibid.*

[11]Blurb on the back of *Turtle Island*.

Brian Swann

Introduction
Only the Beginning

Discovering America

In four World's Fairs held between the Civil War and World War I, writes Frederick E. Hoxie, white attitudes toward Native Americans moved from the social evolutionists' optimism in Philadelphia in 1876, with their belief in the Indians' "progress" and future, to the opinion in San Francisco in 1915 that Indians were "an interesting but limited people whose future was of only marginal concern to their fellow Americans."[1] Indians didn't figure largely in the 1915 Panama-Pacific International Exposition in San Francisco, but the most prominent presentation of native life was the bronze statue by James Earle Fraser, "The End of the Trail": an exhausted Indian slumped in the saddle of a broken-down pony. This statue won a gold medal, and was one of the Exposition's most popular attractions. Today, if the Indians are thought about at all, the general assumption is that they have long since fallen from their ponies and vanished. Today, despite something of a resurrection of interest in the Indians in the 1960s and early 1970s, they are still likely to be seen by most people as victims of inevitable progress, their tribal names used to sell cars and trucks, the heads of their heroes (such as Crazy Horse, who was murdered by whites) used to decorate postage stamps.[2]

D. H. Lawrence wrote that "the real American day" would only dawn when Americans "at last discover America and their wholeness."[3] But America still refuses to look at itself and its history. We still refuse to acknowledge the truth of William Carlos Williams' statement: "History! History! We fools, what do we know or care? History begins for us with murder and enslavement, not with discovery."[4] And today we remain ignorant of the plight of Indians living in cities (more than half of the Native American population) and of life on the reservations that, according to a recent article in the *New York Times* (December 11, 1986), are in terrible shape, with conditions "bad and worsening with no immediate help in sight." As Suzan Harjo, executive director of The National Congress of American Indians, says in the *Times* article: "The situation in Indian country is a national disgrace."[5]

Despite everything, however, the Indian has not disappeared. In fact, more and more Native Americans are now writing about their lives and experiences in fiction, nonfiction, poetry, drama, and autobiography than ever before. There is, indeed, a Native American renaissance in the arts, which we non-Indians ignore to our impoverishment, and even to our peril. If at this late date we still believe in "the real American day," then the writings of Native Americans are a good place to begin to "discover America."

Native American Literature: A Brief Survey

There are approximately two million Native American people in the United States, some one-half of one percent of the total population. In that figure are some of the most interesting poets and writers in the English language—poets and writers present in such numbers, given the tiny percentage, that one can only wonder at their determination, energy, and skill and the power of the tradition and culture that has nurtured them.

In fact, Indians have been writing in English for over two centuries. The earliest autobiographies were produced by Christianized Indians, the first in 1768 by the Reverend Samson Occum, a Mohegan (who also wrote *Choice Collections of Hymns and Spiritual Songs* in 1774), and the second by the Pequot William Apes whose *Son of the Forest* appeared in 1829. Then came books on various subjects by David Cusick (Tuscarora), the Sioux Ohiyesa (Dr. Charles Eastman), Luther Standing Bear (also Sioux), and John Joseph Mathews (Osage). The first fiction (a fictionalized conversion story) was written by the Cherokee Elias Boudinot in 1823, while the first "true" novel, entitled *The Life and Adventures of Joaquín Murieta,* was produced in 1854 by John Rollin Ridge, another Cherokee. The earliest known book of poems by an Indian is *The Ojibway Conquest* (1850) by the Ojibway George Copway (Kah-ge-ga-gah-bowh). Ridge's *Poems,* the second poetry book, appeared in 1868. Other nineteenth and twentieth century poets include the Creek Alex Posey (1873–1908), whose *Collected Poems* was posthumously published in 1910; the Mohawk E. Pauline Johnson (1862–1913), whose *Flint and Feather* came out posthumously in 1917; and the Wyandot Bertrand Walker.[6]

There are many others. Wendy Rose is preparing a multi-genre bibliography of book-length works by Native American and Eskimo authors. She has discovered nearly three hundred books from the 1950s to the present. Still, they are hardly household titles or household names, and they are seldom, if ever, found in standard histories of American literature. In fact, until about the last twenty years, what interest there was in Native American literature (though it wasn't called literature) was concentrated in the fields of anthropology, linguistics, and folklore and on certain poets and writers. These include Mary Austin, Hart Crane, William Carlos Williams, Charles Olsen, Frank Waters, and more recently Jerome Rothenberg and Gary Snyder—the full story is told in Michael Castro's *Interpreting the Indian: Twentieth Century Poets and the Native American* (1984).

The earliest collection of aboriginal poetry appeared in 1918 with George W. Cronyn's *The Path on the Rainbow: An Anthology of Songs and Chants.* There followed Mary Austin's *The American Rhythm: Studies and*

Re-expressions of Amerindian Songs (1932), Margot Astrov's *The Winged Serpent: An Anthology of American Indian Prose and Poetry* (1946), and A. Grove Day's *The Sky Clears: Poetry of the American Indians* (1951).[7] Native Americans were writing poetry, drama, and fiction during the years from 1918 to 1951, notably the Flathead D'Arcy McNickle and the Cherokee Lynn Riggs (one of whose plays was made into the musical "Oklahoma!").

But prior to the 1960s there was little interest in Native American poetry and prose, and it was difficult to find, since it was published mostly in small magazines with small circulations.[8] Then came John Milton's two collections of contemporary Native American poetry, prose, and art in *South Dakota Review* (vol. 7, no. 2, Summer 1969, and vol. 9, no. 2, Summer 1971). In the Summer 1969 issue, for the first time in one place, appeared the poetry of Simon Ortiz and James Welch; the Summer 1971 issue carried the poetry of Duane Niatum, Ray Young Bear, and others. All this took place about the time that N. Scott Momaday won the Pulitzer Prize in 1969 for *House Made of Dawn,* which went far in establishing the worth of Native American literature in the eyes of a mainstream literary audience.

In 1975 *Carriers of the Dream Wheel,* the predecessor of this anthology, made a distinguished appearance as "the first substantial collection of contemporary Native American poetry."[9] It was poetry of mingled roots, drawing on Faulkner, Winters, Vallejo, Hugo, Wright, Roethke, Neruda, and other sources available to late twentieth-century writers, as well as on the native oral tradition and individual vision. Since then, Native American literature has become one of the most lively developments on the American art scene. But it still fights for recognition and acceptance in the curricula of our schools and colleges, and it is still something of a secret.[10] Few large publishing houses have shown serious interest in the phenomenon, preferring to give the world *The Teachings of Don Juan, Rolling Thunder,* or *Hanta Yo.* So Native American poets must still rely on the small presses and magazines as well as some university presses—Illinois, Purdue, Washington, and Massachusetts have recently published volumes by Native American poets. Moreover, in a consistent pattern of omission, contemporary poetry anthologies generally ignore Native American poets. *The Harvard Book of Contemporary American Poets* edited by Helen Vendler (1985), William Heyen's *The Generation of 2000* (1984), *New American Poets of the 80s* edited by John Meyers and Roger Weingarten (1984), and *The Norton Anthology of American Literature* edited by Nina Baym et al. (1985) contain not one Native American poet. Three anthologies contain one Native American poet each. They are Daniel Halpern's *The American Poetry Anthology* (1975) which contains five poems by James Welch, *The Norton Anthology of Poetry* (1983) edited by Alexander W. Allison et al., which contains three poems by Leslie Silko, and *The Morrow Anthology of Younger American Poets* (1985) edited by Dave Smith and David Bottoms, which has four poems by Simon Ortiz. So, while some poets say they don't like the idea of segregated anthologies, they still seem necessary until those who edit major anthologies and publish books of poems abandon their tokenism and parochialism.

What Distinguishes Native American Poetry?

Vine Deloria, Jr., has written that modern Indian poetry can "tell you more about the Indian's travels in historical experience than all the books written and lectures given."[11] Although a poem is an individual response to experience, Deloria's remark is illuminating. More than most poetry being written today, Native American poetry is the poetry of historic witness. It grows out of a past that is very much a present. Anglo-America, in the main, does not believe in history. Things simply turned out the way they did through a natural process, one of whose names is Manifest Destiny. History can be taken for granted, in the way of the conqueror, because things worked out the way they were supposed to. But the Native American poet *is* his or her history, with all its ambiguities and complications. Their history is not something external to be learned, molded, or ignored, though it may be something that has to be acknowledged and recovered. It is embodied and unavoidable because the weight and consequences of that history make up the continuum of the present. This fact gives an urgency to the utterance, a resonance to the art that carries it deeper than much of the poetry one finds today. The poets are still "singing for power."

So what distinguishes Native American poetry? Isn't it simply a sub-branch of Western regional literature, as the chief editor of a reputable publishing house once suggested to me? Or is it just poetry with a variety of themes and techniques that happens to be written by Native Americans? Some of the poets themselves are uneasy with the term. "There is no *genre* of 'Indian literature,' " writes Wendy Rose, "because we are all different. There is only literature written by people who are Indian and who, therefore, infuse their work with their own lives the same way that you do."[12] Duane Niatum, too, asks if there is an "Indian Aesthetic that is different from a non-Indian."[13] He answers that there is not. "Anyone who claims there is encourages a conventional response from both Indians and non-Indians, and as a result actually inhibits the reader's imagination."[14] Jim Barnes doesn't like terms such as "regional writer," "ethnic writer," or "Native American writer" because all are reductive. "The writer is first a writer, second a Native American, a Black, a Chicano."[15]

Of course these poets are right. Too often a classification can reduce attention to what is special; it can be used to pigeonhole and thereby deny full regard. But if we use a term such as "Native American poetry" appropriately, if we use it knowing that such a grouping is only a start, a convenience, an aid to understanding that leads to reinforcement and intensification of attention, then it is useful. It helps us to hold on to something new and distinct. The poets vary widely from each other in many ways, but they are also similar in many ways. One thing is certain: these poets can hold their own on the American literary scene today. They are an integral part of it.

The well-known Luiseño painter Fritz Scholder expands this question of classification to the visual arts. He too objects to arranging artists by race or sex. "Painting, like most of the visual arts, is an individual activity that is completely personal, and can only be developed through one's own unique frame of reference. If one is to make a statement in whatever medium, one must find out who one is and fully accept it."[16] There is a point to be made here, even if we ignore Yeats's dictum that it is out of the *quarrel* with ourselves that we make poetry. It is true that an artist or poet today must achieve an individual voice or vision. But to talk about an individual artistic activity that is "completely personal," capable of being developed through "one's own unique frame of reference" sounds more typically Anglo-American than Native American. The Native American poet seems to work from a sense of social responsibility to the group as much as from an intense individuality. In fact, a poet wrote to me recently, "I have heard Indian critics say, referring to poetry, that it is best if there are no I's in it. I grew up and continue to live among people who penalize you for talking about yourself and going on endlessly about your struggles."[17] And another poet wrote, "My attitude is that it is not my personal life that is important, but the work that comes through me somehow. It is something deeply ingrained and difficult to overcome."[18] The individual voice in Native American literature would seem to be at its strongest when it is not just "individual" (and it is all a matter of degree) but also "representative." Often the individual speaks for, is spoken through. We see this across the spectrum of Native American artists—from traditional singers to the contemporary poet Joy Harjo: "She learned to speak for the ground / the voice coming through her like roots that / have long hungered for water" ("For Alva Benson . . ."). Many Native American poets regard themselves as both distinct individual voices and voices that speak for whatever cannot speak, as in Linda Hogan's poem "Who Will Speak," which desires to speak for the animals and the earth.[19]

If I approach a definition of Native American poetry obliquely and hesitantly it is not simply because of problems such as the foregoing. If one says Native American poetry is poetry written by Native Americans the difficulty might appear to be solved—more on that in a short while. The best way might be to say I'm not really interested in defining this poetry. Its full and generous presence in this volume will *announce* what it is in its own terms, using its own names—"we wonder / whether anyone will ever hear / our own names for things / we do" (Gail Tremblay, "Indian Singing in 20th Century America").

I cannot define "Indian" or "Native American" with any confidence. We whites, from our arrival on this earth on turtle's back, have gotten it all wrong. (Even white insistence on telling the Indians that they migrated over the Bering Strait is contradicted by Indian legend and tradition—legend and tradition more culturally significant than any archaeological proof.) The latest insult is to measure blood. To be enrolled in a tribe, says the Bureau of Indian Affairs (the BIA), one must possess one-quarter Indian blood.[20] The best definition I can arrive at is this: Native Americans are Native Americans if they say they are, if other Native Americans say they are and accept them, and (possibly) if the values that are held close and acted upon are values upheld by the various native peoples who live in the Americas. It would be presumptuous for me to define further. Many questions such as whether a person is Native American if he or she has rejected tribal values and identity I leave to others, for it does not concern us here. All the poets in these pages come from a Native American background and, as James Welch has said, "For the most part an Indian knows who he is."[21] Elizabeth Cook-Lynn's words ring in the ears: "Writing, for me . . . is an act of defiance born of the need to survive. I am me. I exist. I am a Dakotah. I write. It is the quintessential act of optimism born of frustration. It is an act of courage, I think. And, in the end, as Simon [Ortiz] says, it is an act which defies oppression."[22]

Climate of Change: Poetic Emergence

Why and how has Native American poetry achieved such distinction in so few years? One reason is that the intellectual climate changed during the 1960s. These years and their legacy brought about for many a rejection of the supremacy of Western civilization and a rejection of the Western idea of high art. The prevailing ideas of political and artistic hegemony were confronted and the established canon challenged. New beginnings were sought, and Native American writers responded. In addition, while, as we have noted, much remains to be done, channels for Native Americans have opened. Some have studied with famous authors who have encouraged and fostered their work and careers. My own interest in Native American poetry was sparked when I picked up a special supplement of *The American Poetry Review* in 1975 entitled "Young American Indian Poets: Roberta Hill, Ray A. Young Bear, Duane Niatum, James Welch." The supplement was edited by the distinguished poet Richard Hugo, who at the time was teaching at the University of Montana in the Master of Fine Arts Writing Program.

In his introduction, Hugo discusses what attracts him to Native American poetry. He finds it "both imaginative and highly individualistic."[23] He believes that the poets are mining the same seam as major twentieth-century poets such as Eliot and Yeats "who felt we inherited ruined worlds that, before they were ruined, gave man a sense of self-esteem, social unity, spiritual certainty and being at home on the earth."[24] This is due to the fact, Hugo suggests, that Indians come from "a recently destroyed civilization. No other minority group does"[25] (a qualifiable statement). For white poets, Hugo continues, no matter how true this theme of ruined worlds may be, it nevertheless results from "an idealization of a past they never knew."[26] But for the Indians this ruin is fact, a real, known fact. So, says Hugo, the Indian poet is an authentic paradigm of the modern condition. However, if individual isolation is the source of much lyric poetry today, in the Indian poet it is combined with a cultural tradition that is "still a living thing in the memory,"[27] and consists of "establishing personal identity through ritualistic discovery of kinship with objects and creatures of nature."[28] We may want to qualify such statements. The cultural tradition does not just exist in the memory. It exists in act, thought, speech; the "ritualistic discovery of kinship" sounds peculiarly mechanical and quaint. Nevertheless, Hugo renders us a service by directing us toward this new poetry and trying to help us enter its world, even though he discusses it on the whole, not in relationship to contemporary "mainstream" work, but to other "minority" poetry. In comparison with these unnamed other "minority" poets, he finds that Native American poetry "seems most to involve emotional possession of materials."[29] Since he claims that "no audience save the self is presumed,"[30] we may deduce that he sees Native American poetry in contradistinction to the poetry of social and political commitment, presumably mostly Black poetry, being written at the time. He praises Native American poetry "for creating interesting sounds with poetry,"[31] that is, for craft.

For Richard Hugo, then, Native American poetry is thoroughly modern, yet it reaches back to a cultural tradition substantially different from that available to other modern poets. Native American poetry is not overtly, militantly, or stridently political; it has depth of emotion and consciousness of form. Whatever the shortcomings of Hugo's essay (the political and "committed" element in Native American poetry is ignored, although most of it appeared after Hugo's essay), this presentation of younger Native American poets to the larger literary world via a magazine with large circulation and prestige by a well-known and respected poet represented a major advance.

Poetic Themes

What are some of the themes of Native American poetry? Reading this anthology, each of us can come up with answers. I will suggest a few. Both cultural traditions and Native American society itself are under stress. Suicide, alcoholism, unemployment abound. The situation is a national disgrace. The poets have responded to this crisis, and none more powerfully than James Welch in his novels and poems. His well-known poem "Harlem, Montana: Just Off the Reservation," with its place name linking one place of disaffection in Montana with another in New York, indicts a whole country. And yet the anger is never strident. It is dissolved in an irony that infuses all details, from the Indians drinking in the "best" taverns, to "money is free if you're poor enough." Words accrete ironic weight by juxtapositions: "runners" (smugglers of liquor onto reservations), "running for office." Indians are "planted" in the jail by the local farmer/constable. Everything is confused; there is no cultural authenticity for white or Indian. Welch's complex language keeps alive confusion as a series of possibilities; it draws us into the poem but keeps us off balance. How are we to regard the drunk who "bugs the plaster man / on the cross with snakes"? Christ is no savior. The man on the cross is plaster, and the Indian world of animal-human relationships is reduced to something like the DTs with serpents (the serpents also recall the biblical ancient enemy). "Bugs" suggests intense annoyance on the part of the plaster man. In the drunken state, are these imaginary snakes seen as spies (reading "bugs" in the context of surveillance)? What could they hope to learn? It is a world of delirium and paranoia, bits and pieces of meaning. The drunk himself has no identity, or at best a mixed-up one. He is an ex-Methodist who is now a "saint" in the Indian church. We can no longer be sure of point of view. In whose eyes is he a saint? The language shoots out in a number of directions. We catch it as we can. The paradox is that Welch writes with such energy about cultural decay. Yet there is a crazy, surreal energy about the whole town, Indian and white (and Turk), that fights against decay. It is as if the poet were saying this inchoate place still has possibilities; there is still life here. The poem ends with the young bucks inside the shot-up store yelling that they're rich. The Indians have been sucked into a world of perverted values; they identified the ru-ined store with wealth and have shot their way into plenty, trapping them-selves. But their prayer, "Help us, oh God, we're rich," is not just easy, if sharp, irony. They still have the power of prayer, even if only in the form of an exclamation or idiom. The poem certainly does not exactly end on an up beat, but it is not altogether bleak nihilism.[32]

We can see a slightly stronger expression of faith in the tradition in the poetry of Louise Erdrich. The problem for the uprooted drunk Raymond Twobears (in "Family Reunion") is to get home again. The key image is the turtle—a real snapper and not just some useful symbolic entity. And yet the turtle is also cultural *nuomenon,* for this is, after all, the earth on turtle's back ("the old house caulked with mud / sails into the middle of Metagoshe"), and Ray's smell is the "rank beef of fierce turtle pulled dripping from Metagoshe." Ray is a lost soul, unaware of cultural values. He blows off the turtle's head with a cherry bomb, an act of cruel and practical indifference. But the animal is not that easily destroyed. After Ray had gone "to sleep his own head off," the next day, "headless and clenched in his armor," the tur-tle drags himself off. Even though Ray doesn't know it, he and the turtle are still connected, despite the wasteland in the poem. The headless turtle climbs a hill and aims for "a small stream that deepens into a marsh." It has been hauled from the lake, had its head blown off, and now, in a kind of rebirth, finds a stream that will presumably widen into a lake. The cyclic pat-tern is still there. Turtle is not destroyed. "Somehow we find our way back." The line reverberates. But to what? The submerged image of the turtle gives strength. Ray's body pulls him toward home; his hands become "gray fins," and his face has "the calm patience of a child who has always / let bad wounds alone." Ray is clearly in bad shape and, with his weak heart, may be dying. His bad wounds should have been cared for. Yet in the strange world of the poem, realistic yet subliminal, Ray somehow is the turtle. The turtle seems to return to another, deeper existence, as if to grow another head, and Ray has the look of a creature "that has lived / for a long time un-derwater." The poem weaves opposites together, and ends very oddly with "angels," creatures from another range of reference altogether, "lowering their slings and litters" as if they were divine Red Cross workers or refugees from "Swing Low, Sweet Chariot." Does Ray, a being between two worlds (as his name "Twobears" suggests), take refuge in some form of Christianity? The last stanza reads like a hallucination. The poem does not present a conclusion; it simply presents a situation. But the most powerful entity in the poem is the turtle.

Time and time again in Native American poetry we find a picture of raw existence side by side with a refusal to cave in, often with hints of renewal through connection with tradition. In Erdrich's "I Was Sleeping Where the Black Oaks Move," the relentless water that has been dammed (cause of much lost Indian land), uproots the trees with their nests of herons. ("Nests" is a loaded cultural word. We recall Black Elk: "Our tepees were round like the nests of birds, and they were always set in a circle, the nation's hoop, a nest of many nests, where the Great Spirit meant for us to hatch our children."[33]) The forest is pulled through the spillway, and trees surface singly. The scene is fully presented realistically, yet the tenor is almost allegorical. The nation's hoop is broken; we are "below the reservation," after "the long removal." ("Removal" is as loaded a word for Indians as "holocaust" is for Jews.) Grandpa explains: herons are ghosts of people unable to rest. But there is a way back, symbolized by the dream, with its full Native American implication of a creative source:

> Sometimes now, we dream our way back to the heron dance.
> Their long wings are bending the air
> into circles through which they fall.
> They rise again in shifting wheels.
> How long must we live in the broken figures
> their necks make, narrowing the sky?

The fall is really part of the full wing-beat and they rise again. The process is cyclical, circular. The poem ends, not with a question but a statement, almost an exclamation. This part of the circle has to be endured; it is as if it is necessary to live in the broken figures for a time, in the narrowing. As Yeats said, only that which has been broken can be whole.

Voices of the Past: The Oral Tradition

The oral tradition of speech is vital to Native American poets. In the anthology and elsewhere, poets write of how they were *told* what to do and how to be—told stories and legends. Time and again in the anthology one feels the presence of living *voices,* the commitment to orality in the nonoral medium of print, a form "locked in space, inanimate."[34] To be sure, Native American poets are aware of the emphasis in the poetry of the 50s and 60s on "breath"—one recalls the Black Mountain School, and in particular Charles Olson's important essay "Projective Verse" (1960), as well as the Beat poets, Allen Ginsberg especially. But the human voice in these pages—

insistent, animating, animated—I like to think of as the direct descendant, or literary equivalent, of the language of song and chant used to communicate with (and largely derived from) the world of the spirit, the language of the fullest life of being itself. In the oral tradition this language *is* life. As David Guss notes of the Yekuana, a people from the northern Amazon, "words are not simply uttered or sung but infused with the actual spirit of the chanter."[35] Native American poets attempt in their insistent utterances to lessen the distance created by print, to transform the "passive word of the written page" into an "active immediacy."[36] The talking, the singing, the telling, the writing pass on the voice to an anonymous audience and attempt to make a community. The poems do not withdraw into style, but project into life.

We should, then, listen to these poems as well as read them. For, as N. Scott Momaday's Rev. J. B. B. Tosamah in *House Made of Dawn* asserts, when you hold onto things heard you come directly into the presence of mind and spirit. The white man, he says, has taken words and literature for granted. He has "diluted and multiplied the word" and is therefore "sated and insensitive."[37] This is not just another book of poems. We must use the printed word, and go beyond it, go back to its sources.[38]

Reverencing Tradition: Ancestors and Myth

Parents play a major part in Native American poetry, in the passing on of tradition; Momaday has noted in *House Made of Dawn,* the oral tradition is always but one generation from extinction.[39] None of the poets surpasses Simon Ortiz in parent-reverence. We see his father in the poem "A Story of How a Wall Stands," a poem about the oral tradition itself, and in his essay "Song, Poetry, and Language—Expression and Perception," where he gives a full and loving portrait of his father, the "thousand year old man," keeper of ancient traditions.[40] Paula Gunn Allen has described how her mother constantly told her stories, "and in these stories she told me who I was, who I was supposed to be, whom I came from, and who would follow me."[41]

Grandparents play a large part, perhaps because they are felt to be closer to sources. Simon Ortiz was told by his grandfather, medicine man and elder of the kiva, "how we must sacredly concern ourselves with the people and the holy earth."[42] He remembers how his words "were about how we must regard ourselves and others with compassion and love."[43] This belief permeates Ortiz's work. "My grandfather represented for me a link to the past that is important for me to hold in my memory because it is not only memory but knowledge that substantiates my present existence,"[44] Ortiz writes. "He and the grandmothers and grandfathers before him thought about us as they lived, confirmed in their belief of a continuing life, and they brought our present beings into existence by the beliefs they held. The consciousness of that belief is what informs my present concerns with language, poetry and fiction."[45] Such a statement holds true for many Native American writers. Meaningful and continuous contact with the past is a source of great strength in the present and for the future; it "release[s] the energy of the impulse to help my people,"[46] as Ortiz phrases it. Such contact, he continues, constitutes the strength of "the oral tradition of speech, social and religious ritual, elders' counsel and advice, countless and endless stories, everyday event."[47]

Likewise the editor of this volume has written of the spiritual connection·he has maintained with the Klallam land, and the promise he made with his grandfather never to lose touch with his Coast Salish traditions, "never to abandon our cedar roots, never to forget any creature that shares this world, and never to allow or participate in a rape of the earth or the sea."[48] Elizabeth Cook-Lynn, in her poem "Grandfather at the Indian Health Clinic," depicts the old man as having great nobility; he is "averse to / an unceremonious world." In her "Journey," grandmothers are "old partisans of faith" and pass on their wisdom to their daughters. The old ones "go bail" for the present generation. Because of cultural genocide, all the survivors are ironically "sacristans." Yet the faith of the grandparents lives on in ceremonies and prevents total alienation or acculturation, despite the fact that "migration makes / new citizens of Rome."

Time and time again in Native American poetry one senses that grandparents are keepers of the faith, inspirational, powerful beings, symbols of rooted continuity, as in Mary TallMountain's "Matmiya," Gail Tremblay's "To Grandmother on Her Going," and "Night Gives Old Woman the Word" (where she is the Earth itself). They are there again in Robert E. Davis's "At the Door of the Native Studies Director," Wendy Rose's "Loo-wit" (where the old woman is a mountain), in Earle Thompson's "Mythology" (Thompson has said in his earlier biographical note for this volume that "obviously my roots lie in the oral tradition which I learned from listening to my grandfather telling legends"), in Lance Henson's "Grandfather" and "near twelve mile point," in Barney Bush's "The Memory Sire," and so on. This reverence, this presence, stands in stark contrast to non-Indian society with its headlong rush to jettison the past and its largely disjunct and separate generations.[49]

If grandparents are physical links to the past, myth is the eternal contact. In white culture, "myths are simply lies" (Roberta Hill Whiteman, "For Heather, Entering Kindergarten"). But for the Native American artist, myths and traditions are "a shield / against the social and spiritual plague of twentieth century consumer culture."[50] Non-Indians have largely given up on myth, or else have created their own from various sources, something that has been happening since at least the Romantic period. Contemporary poets find Jung congenial because he directs them to archetypes that transcend any culture-specific origin. But the Native American poet has a rich variety of native myth to live in and draw on. He or she can draw upon specific characters, such as Raven, Mink, or Coyote—Coyote is rapidly becoming, in art and literature, a pan-Indian character. Or the poet can refer obliquely, relying on a certain shorthand connection to those in the know. And if, as readers, we are not in the know, we can make the same effort we would have to make if we were reading Greek or Russian literature. We may not need to know stories and myths of people turning into deer, myths of reciprocal obligation, trust, and love (as in "The Man Who Married a Deer Woman" in Leonard Bloomfield's *Menomini Texts*).[51] But such knowledge adds a timeless dimension to Louise Erdrich's timely "feminist" poem "Jacklight." This poem is a story of the need for the violent male principle to be inducted into the deep female woods. (I am not suggesting that Erdrich knew this Menomini version of the myth, though versions are widespread.)

Myth is vital if we are to retain a sense of "the orchestration and recognition of life energies,"[52] Frederick Turner has written. Myths are celebrations in which even dark tides of existence "lend the richness and tone of reality itself."[53] Thus, Turner continues, "living myths must include and speak of the interlocking cycles of animate and vegetable life, of water, sun, and even the stones, which have their own stories. It must embrace without distinction the phenomenal and the numinous. In such ways these vital fictions turn us toward the unchanged realities we must live amidst. They may yet prove to be our most successful response to life on this earth."[54] Native American poetry uses myth vitally, revitalizing it, feeding it from the source. Thus, in Leslie Silko's "Toe'osh: A Laguna Pueblo Coyote Story," the ancient mythic Coyote figure becomes a contemporary resident of Laguna, and in the last stanza is transformed into an Indian poet scattering "white people / out of bars all over Wisconsin."[55] And one of the most visionary, mystic poets today is Ray Young Bear, who creates from the deep base of the native tradition of the dream and from the surrealist alchemy of the unconscious— the "merveilleaux."[56]

Balancing Life: A Journey toward Wholeness

What is striking about Native American poetry is not the bitterness or anger, though they are there. Nor is it the sense of loss, of living divided in two worlds, or alienation, though they are there too. What is impressive is the courage to continue, to write poetry that uses all the resources of the English language, a language clearly loved for its "beauty and poetic power."[57] There is energy and joy in existence; there is song and dance. Scott Momaday sings in his "The Delight Song of Tsoai-Talee," "You see, I am alive, I am alive,"[58] and Joy Harjo reaches way beyond psychic dualism in "She Had Some Horses."[59] She releases her fear in "I Give You Back," and transforms hatred in "Transformations." There is humor and comedy from Louise Erdrich's "Old Man Potchikoo" to Leslie Silko's "Toe'osh." And laughter is needed, because "who would believe / the fantastic and terrible story of all of our survival / those who were never meant / to survive?" (Joy Harjo, "Anchorage"). The poems in this collection reach for balance, for sanity in a mad world, in the face of antagonism, past and present. One sees a desire for wholeness—for balance, reconciliation, and healing—within the individual, the tribe, the community, the nation; one sees an *insistence* on these things, on growth, on rich survival. Gail Tremblay writes: "Change moves relentlessly, / the pattern unfolding despite their planning. / We're always there—singing round dance / songs, remembering what supports / our life—impossible to ignore" ("Indian Singing in 20th Century America"). Coyote may often appear to be dead, but he always seems to survive—part of continuing metamorphosis and energetic change, a cosmic force including everything. As Paula Gunn Allen's mother told her: "Life is a circle, and everything has its place in it."[60] And there is always one more story."[61] The great seas underground "have journeyed through the graveyards / of our loved ones, / turning in their graves / to carry the stories of life to air" (Linda Hogan, "To Light").

If contemporary "mainline" American poetry must have "rubber, coal, uranium, moons, poems"[62] to fuel its voracious engines; and if, "like a shark, it contains a shoe,"[63] and must swim "through the desert / Uttering cries that are almost human,"[64] then Native American poetry is something different. Clearly, it can absorb and digest, though the preferred metaphor is different: "like the spider / we weave new beds around us / when old ones are swept away" (Linda Hogan, "To Light"). It is thoroughly modern. But it is not predatory, self-absorbed. And it is not a shark in the desert; it is not "almost human," but *human*. Its whole thrust is toward completeness of life, even in the desert. As Simon Ortiz writes:

> You see, son, the eagle is a person the way it lives; it means it has to do with paying attention to where it is, not the center of the earth especially, but part of it, one part among all parts, and that's only the beginning.[65]

Notes

1. Frederick E. Hoxie, "Red Man's Burden," *The Antioch Review* 37 (Summer 1979): 340.
2. I recently received through the mail a brochure for videocassettes available from Film for the Humanities (Princeton, NJ). The series was entitled "The West of the Imagination." Here is part of the copy for the episode "The Trail of Tears": "As explorers and pioneers travelled further and further west, the urge and the technological means to expand led inevitably to the seizure of Indian land and the destruction of Indian culture." And this from "The Warpath": "Indians were the major obstacle to westward expansion. The pioneering American spirit overcame all obstacles. . . ." "Inevitably," "obstacles," "pioneering American spirit"—enough said.
3. D. H. Lawrence, *Studies in Classic American Literature* (New York: Viking, 1971), 7.
4. William Carlos Williams, *In The American Grain* (New York: New Directions, 1925), 39.
5. For background on this topic see Larry W. Burt, "Roots of the Native American Urban Experience: Relocation Policy in the 1950s,"

in *The American Indian Quarterly* 10 (Spring 1986): 85–99. See also a number of works cited in the footnotes to Burt's essay. Useful, on a wider scale, is James S. Olson and Raymond Wilson's *Native Americans in the Twentieth Century* (Urbana, IL: University of Illinois Press, 1984), despite qualifications expressed by Vine Deloria, Jr. in the same issue of *The American Indian Quarterly* cited above (pp. 136–37). A national disgrace on a huge scale is now unfolding in Alaska. Native peoples could lose all their land and have their tribal and subsistence way of life destroyed by 1991 if something isn't done soon to undo the Alaska Native Claims Settlement Act of 1971, which is attempting to turn these peoples into corporate businesspeople and shareholders. A powerful book on this is Thomas R. Berger's *Village Journey* (New York: Hill and Wang, 1985).

6. See A. LaVonne Ruoff, "American Indian Authors, 1774–1899," in *Critical Essays on Native American Literature,* ed. Andrew Wiget (Boston, MA: G. K. Hall, 1985), 191–202. Also see Daniel F. Littlefield and James W. Parins's *A Bibliography of Native American Writers, 1772–1924* (Metuchen, NJ: The Scarecrow Press, 1981) and their *Supplement* (Metuchen, NJ: The Scarecrow Press, 1985).

7. For a sharp critique of their approach, particularly A. Grove Day's, see William Bevis's essay, "American Indian Verse Translations," *College English* 35 (March 1974): 693–703.

8. A useful list of publishers today can be found in Kenneth Lincoln's *Native American Renaissance* (Berkeley, CA: University of California Press, 1983), 285–292. Joseph Bruchac provides a "Bibliography and List of Presses" in "American Indians Today," a special issue edited by Elaine Jahner, in *Book Forum* vol. V, no. 3 (1981): 336–342.

9. Andrew Wiget, *Native American Literature* (Boston: Twayne, 1985). (The quote is from the section "Chronology," no page number given.) Despite the appearance of *Carriers of the Dream Wheel,* however, Native American poetry could still be largely ignored by the white "establishment." In a major compilation of essays entitled *The Harvard Guide to Contemporary American Writing,* edited by Daniel Hoffman and issued by Harvard University Press in 1979, more space is devoted to reworkings of Native American texts by David Wagoner, Gary Snyder, and Jerome Rothenberg than to the work of Native American writers. The only Native American poets mentioned are in Hoffman's chapter "Poetry: Schools of Dissidents." Momaday, Niatum, Ortiz, and Bruchac are given a princely half page in a 618-page book! One hopes that with books such as Paul Lauter's *Reconstructing American Literature* published by Feminist Press in 1983, and associated attempts to reorder the canon (including Lauter's forthcoming anthology from D. C. Heath), things will be changed, if only a little.

10. On this subject, see Arnold Krupat's "An Approach to Native American Texts," *Critical Inquiry* 9 (December 1982): 323–338, and "Native American Literature and the Canon," *Critical Inquiry* 10 (September 1983): 145–171. *Studies in American Indian Literature,* ed. Paula Gunn Allen (New York: Modern Language Association, 1983) contains useful essays on teaching and course outlines.

11. Vine Deloria, Jr., "Introduction," in *Voices From Wah'Kon-Tah,* ed. Robert Dodge and Joseph B. McCullough (New York: International Publishers, 1975).

12. Wendy Rose, "American Indian Poets and Publishing," *Book Forum* vol. V, no. 3 (1981): 402.

13. Duane Niatum, "On Stereotypes," *Parnassus* vol. 7, no. 1 (Fall/Winter 1978): 160.

14. Ibid.

15. Jim Barnes, "On Native Ground," in *I Tell You Now: Autobiographical Essays By Native American Writers,* ed. Brian Swann and Arnold Krupat (Lincoln, NE: University of Nebraska Press, 1987). Page numbers unavailable at time of writing.

16. Fritz Scholder, "The Native American and Contemporary Art: A Dilemma," *Book Forum,* vol. V, no. 3. (1981): 423.

17. Quoted in the Introduction to *I Tell You Now.*

18. Quoted in the Introduction to *I Tell You Now.*

19. Linda Hogan, "Who Will Speak," *Shantih* 4 (Summer/Fall 1979): 28–30. This special Native American issue was edited by Roberta Hill [Whiteman] and Brian Swann.

20. The situation is complex. The issue is discussed in Vine Deloria, Jr. and Clifford Lytle's *American Indians, American Justice* (Austin, TX: University of Texas Press, 1983) and *The Nations Within* (New York: Pantheon Books, 1984), as well as in *Indian Lives,* ed. L. G. Moses and Raymond Wilson (Albuquerque: University of New Mexico Press, 1980).

21. James Welch, "The Only Good Indian," *South Dakota Review* 9 (Summer 1971): 54.

22. Elizabeth Cook-Lynn, "You May Consider Speaking About Your Art," in *I Tell You Now,* ed. Brian Swann and Arnold Krupat (Lincoln, NE: University of Nebraska Press, 1987).

23. Richard Hugo, "Introduction," *The American Poetry Review* (November/December 1975).

24. Ibid., 22.

25. Ibid.

26. Ibid.

27. Ibid.

28. Ibid.

29. Ibid.

30. Ibid.

31. Ibid.

32. A similar pattern can be seen in Welch's novel *Winter in the Blood* (New York: Harper & Row, 1974). The world is still bleak and absurd at the end, but there is some possibility of healing "if only a connection could be made between the old people and the young ones" and a reconnection established with the animals—in other words, if there could be a return to tradition. See Carter Revard, "Deer Talk, Coyote Songs, Meadowlark Territory: The Muses Dance to Our Drum Now" (Paper presented at the Modern Language Association Convention, New York, December 1979). I would like to thank Carter Revard for a careful reading of this introductory essay and for some helpful suggestions.

33. John G. Neihardt, *Black Elk Speaks* (New York: Pocket Books, 1959), 165.

34. David Guss, "Keeping It Oral: A Yekuana Ethnology," *American Ethnologist* 13 (August 1986): 423.

35. Ibid.

36. Ibid.

37. N. Scott Momaday, *House Made of Dawn* (New York: Harper & Row, 1977), 88.

38. The oral tradition is based as much on rumor and gossip (entities located lowest on the literary scale and associated with the "ignorant") as much as anything else. "We make no distinctions between the stories—whether they are history, whether they are fact, whether they are gossip," says Leslie Silko in "Language and Literature from a Pueblo Indian Perspective," in *English Literature: Opening Up the Canon,* ed. Leslie A. Fiedler and Houston A. Baker (Baltimore: Johns Hopkins University Press, 1981), 60. The impulse is to leave nothing out, to be inclusive—to create communal truth, not an absolute. See Silko's essay "Landscape, History, and the Pueblo Imagination," *Antaeus* 57 (Autumn 1986).

39. Momaday, *House Made of Dawn,* 90.

40. Simon Ortiz, *Song, Poetry, and Language—Expression and Perception.* Occasional Papers, vol. III (Music and Dance Series), no. 5 (Tsaile, AZ: Navajo Community Press, 1977), 4. In passing, the "thousand year old man" is close to Valéry's definition of the true poet, *un homme très ancien.*

41. Paula Gunn Allen, *The Sacred Hoop: Recovering the Feminine in American Literature* (Boston: Beacon Press, 1986), 46.

42. Simon Ortiz, "The Language We Know," in *I Tell You Now,* ed. Brian Swann and Arnold Krupat (Lincoln, NE: University of Nebraska Press, 1987).

43. Ibid.

44. Ibid.

45. Ibid.

46. Ibid.

47. Ibid.

48. Duane Niatum, "Autobiographical Sketch of Duane Niatum," in *I Tell You Now*, ed. Brian Swann and Arnold Krupat (Lincoln, NE: University of Nebraska Press, 1987).

49. "Grandfather" was an honorific title with religious overtones in many native societies. In *Black Elk Speaks*, for instance, the six grandfathers symbolize Wakan Tanka, the "Great Mysterious," the power of the six directions. "Understood as grandfathers, these spirits were represented as kind and loving, full of years and wisdom," writes Raymond J. Demallie, *The Sixth Grandfather* (Lincoln, NE: University of Nebraska Press, 1984), xix.

50. Niatum, "Autobiographical Sketch," in *I Tell You Now*.

51. Leonard Bloomfield, *Menomini Texts* (New York: AMS Press, 1974), 536–555.

52. Frederick Turner, *Beyond Geography: The Western Spirit Against the Wilderness* (New York: Viking Press, 1980), 18.

53. Ibid., 19.

54. Ibid.

55. In *Songs from this Earth on Turtle's Back*, ed. Joseph Bruchac, (Greenfield Center, NY: Greenfield Review Press, 1983), 229.

56. It would be difficult to demonstrate the effect of a poet's original language on his or her poetry. But, as Joseph Bruchac has noted, "When you speak English / with the memory / of a first tongue / still sweet in your throat / it comes out different." These lines are from "November at Onandaga" in *Entering Onandaga* (Austin, TX: Cold Mountain Press, 1978), 16. Ray Young Bear is one of the few Native American poets who is bilingual in a "first tongue" and English. The jacket notes to Young Bear's *Winter of the Salamander* (New York: Harper & Row, 1980) tell us that the poet "began thinking his poems in his native tongue then translating them verbatim. Through ten years of writing he has refined his technique so that the poems while no longer word-for-word translations, have become, in essence, an authentic Native American experience, finalized in English."

57. Ortiz, "The Language We Know," in *I Tell You Now*.

58. *Songs from This Earth on Turtle's Back*, 158.

59. Joy Harjo discusses this poem with Paula Gunn Allen in the latter's *The Sacred Hoop*, 166.

60. Allen, *The Sacred Hoop*, 1.

61. Simon Ortiz, "Telling," in *A Good Journey* (Berkeley, CA: Turtle Island, 1977), 39. This poem is a good example of the oral tradition at work since it draws on many past stories as well as many in the present. Leslie Silko draws on the poem to make up her own story, "Skeleton Fixer's Story," which first appeared in *Sun Tracks* vol. 4 (1978): 2–3. It is, she says, "a piece of a bigger story they tell around Laguna and Acoma too—from a version told by Simon Ortiz." (In a

recent letter to me, Simon Ortiz, after reading a draft of this essay, asks, "Does Leslie draw on the source I give to make her own Skeleton Fixer story? The answer is that both of us draw upon the traditions we know—and it is a good example of the creative continuing work of the oral tradition." I would like to thank Simon Ortiz for a careful reading of this introductory essay and for some helpful suggestions.

62. Louis Simpson, "American Poetry," in *At the End of the Open Road* (Middletown, CT: Wesleyan University Press, 1963), 25.

63. Ibid.

64. Ibid.

65. Simon Ortiz, "What's Your Indian Name," part of "Four Poems for a Child Son," in *Going For the Rain* (Harper & Row, 1976), 7.

Fiction

On April 6, 1929, the Métis author D'Arcy McNickle, then writing under the name of D'Arcy Dahlberg, received a letter from Harcourt, Brace and Company rejecting his first novel. Despite the rejection, however, a reader for the press waxed enthusiastic about this Indian novel: "The story of an Indian, wandering between two generations, two cultures; excellent. . . . A new territory to be explored; ancient material used for a different end. Perhaps the beginning of a new Indian literature to rival that of Harlem." Five years later, McNickle's much-revised book was rejected one last time before it would finally be published, this rejection paradoxically accompanied by an editor's glowing declaration that "it is becoming easier and easier as time goes on to put across books with the primitive American appeal. I think we could work up a good ballyhoo for this novel."[1]

Raised on the Flathead Reservation in Montana, and adopted into that tribe, McNickle was not the first Native American to publish fiction. He had been preceded by the Cherokee writer John Rollin Ridge, who in 1854 published a subversive, deeply encoded swashbuckling romance titled *The Life and Adventures of Joaquín Murieta, The Celebrated California Bandit.* Also leading the way for McNickle and others who would follow him were Alice Callahan with *Wynema: A Child of the Forest* in 1891, Simon Pokagan with *O-Gî-Mäw-Kwe Mit-I-Gwä-Ki: Queen of the Woods* in 1899, Mourning Dove with *Cogewea, the Half-Blood* in 1921, John Milton Oskison with three novels and a number of stories in the 1920s and 1930s, and John Joseph Mathews with *Sundown,* a powerful depiction of the Osage oil crisis of the twenties in 1934. Among other early Native authors, the Canadian Metís writer Pauline Johnson had also made a name for herself as poet and fiction writer by the first decade of the century. Though not the first in this field, McNickle, with three strong novels, nonfiction works, and a significant number of published short stories, as well as a prominent career in Native American politics and education, was perhaps the seminal early figure in what would become a powerful Native American current in American literature. This new territory to be explored did indeed comprehend both ancient material used for a different end and the beginning of a new Indian literature, and as the publicity fanfare surrounding late-twentieth-century fiction by such writers as Louise Erdrich and Sherman

---

[1]Charles A. Pearce to "Miss D'Arcy Dahlberg," April 6, 1929, and "Manuscript Report," October 23, 1934, author and publisher not identified, McNickle Papers, D'Arcy McNickle Center, Newberry Library.

Alexie demonstrates, publishers have indeed found it possible to "work up a good ballyhoo" for certain, if not many, American Indian fictions.

Native American Indian fiction has come a long way. Until recently, this work seldom found a place in anthologies and even more seldom in the classroom. Until recently, publishers have looked to writing by or about Natives primarily for what McNickle's reader called the "primitive American appeal." Most successful in packaging this highly commodified "appeal," of course, have been non-Native American writers such as James Fenimore Cooper or Oliver LaFarge or, more recently, the best-selling author Tony Hillerman. Rather than catering to this market for the predictable "primitive," Native American authors, as the works in this present anthology amply demonstrate, have consistently sought avenues for other voices, other possibilities, including both a steadfast respect for traditions and an insistence that the Indian, too, is part of the modern world. The heterogeneity of voices and perspectives found in these stories reflects the remarkable diversity of Native cultures and experiences in North America.

The fictions gathered here span nearly a century of Indian publishing and show the range and depth of what we have come to call Native American literature. In "The Hawk Is Hungry," McNickle demonstrates his own insistence that a writer can be Native American and write about anything he chooses. McNickle's narrator in this finely ironic study of human endurance and contrary courage is not obviously Native American, nor are the three women who surround and confound the narrator. This taut and effective story reflects its author's early declaration that he intended to write "of the West, not of Indians primarily, and certainly not the romantic West."[2] Like so many other Native American artists, though he had previously written powerfully about Indian subjects as a determinedly "Indian" author and would do so in the future, in this story McNickle was refusing to be contained within the Euramerican definition of Indianness or within the stock formula of the romantic West. Declining to kowtow to peddlers of the "primitive American appeal," McNickle claims a full range of human experience as the terrain of his art and in doing so defiantly helps to build the foundation of contemporary Native American literature. Decades earlier, in "As It Was in the Beginning," another story in this anthology, the Canadian Métis writer Pauline Johnson had made an even more surprising and subversive move. In this intense piece, Johnson's mixedblood narrator, Esther, claims agency in her own life when, in an extraordinary gesture by the author, Esther's impulsive final act ironically and unexpectedly reinforces the white world's definition of the savage while the protagonist claims her rights not as an Indian but as a woman. Johnson, who dressed in a self-created pastiche "Indian" costume and performed her poetry on stages across North

---

[2]McNickle to John Collier, May 4, 1934, McNickle Papers.

America and in England, was acutely conscious of the performance aspects of her "Indian" art and thus of her audience's expectations. In this shrewd story, she subverts those expectations profoundly and does so precisely by appearing, at first glance, to fulfill them.

In the works collected here, we can find stories of individuals and even communities seemingly lost between generations and cultures, which the first reader of McNickle's novel, above, celebrated. Zitkala-Sa's narrator in "The Soft-Hearted Sioux," the Lamartines in Louise Erdrich's "The Red Convertible," and Pauline Johnson's Esther in "As It Was in the Beginning" all seem to inhabit this precarious space. At times the tensions and instabilities within this transcultural zone, and the radical inequality of Indian and white relations therein, produce deadly results for the Native, as Elizabeth Cook-Lynn demonstrates sharply in "A Good Chance." At times this intensely hybridized world gives birth to heroic survivors, such as the haltingly eloquent Alice in Greg Sarris's "How I Got to Be a Queen." Sarris's Alice is a young mixedblood woman fighting rather desperately for balance and mere survival in a very difficult and extraordinarily intricate life.

Complex voices of resistance emerge out of this fiction, such as those in Mary Tallmountain's subtly crafted story "The Disposal of Mary Joe's Children" and Leslie Marmon Silko's subtly resonant "The Man to Send Rain Clouds." In a different but closely related vein, Carter Revard uses broadly ironical humor to write back against the too often unselfconscious colonizers of the Indian world in "Report to the Nation: Repossessing Europe," while Sherman Alexie merges often dark and flint-edged comedy with bleak vignettes of modern reservation life in both stories from *The Lone Ranger and Tonto Fistfight in Heaven* collected in this anthology. Similarly, Thomas King, the finest and most politically astute humorist among contemporary Native American writers, aims graceful but nonetheless scathing satirical probes at the confused and at best disruptive attitudes of non-Natives toward First Nations people. King's "Borders" depicts a Native family who are very much a part of today's complicated reality but who are led by a mother determined to cross all boundaries with her Indian identity and dignity intact.

More than any other single definable impulse, the fictions collected here underscore what Anishinaabe writer Gerald Vizenor has termed "survivance." Survival, endurance, and the repudiation of dominance characterize these syncretic voices. In "All the Colors of Sunset," for example, Luci Tapahonso presents with extraordinary, understated skill a Navajo community that is intact and subtly nuanced, a reality that stands apart from European America with self-assurance even in the face of great loss and pain. Tapahonso depicts an Indian world that is whole, intact, and certain of the stories that arise from the people and define their world. "I understand now," Tapahonso's narrator says, "that all of life has ceremonies connected with it, and for us, without our memory, our old people, and our children, we would be like lost people in this world we live in, as well as the other worlds in which our loved ones are waiting." Luci Tapahonso's Navajo characters are not lost, not wandering between worlds; they hold to the truths of the ancient stories while they also shop at the local supermarket. In a very different kind of story, Paula Gunn Allen brings the traditional stories of southeastern peoples to life in a modern Oklahoma "stomp dance." Linda Hogan gives us the voice of a young mixedblood woman who is able and willing to stand up against her Oklahoma small-town world. Gordon Henry, in "Sleeping in Rain," goes even further to challenge our very notions not merely of what constitutes an "Indian" story, but of what we define as story.

For too long, the stories Native American readers found in books were someone else's, even when those stories purported to be about something called "Indian." Those stories too often defined vanishing cultures and vanishing peoples, and they incarcerated Native Americans in a static history excluded from the infinite complexities of contemporary human experience. All of us, regardless of what we call ourselves, live within stories that give order to the chaos of existence. Stories tell us where we came from, where we are going, and, most crucially, how to live in this world. Stories can bring into being and they can destroy; stories hold great power. If a people is silenced, denied its own voice, it will be forced to live within stories that others make about it, and it will thus be deprived of the essential power to articulate its own meaning, its own lives. A gathering of Native voices and Native stories such as this constitutes, therefore, an exciting and absolutely necessary moment in American literature. Without such stories, as Luci Tapahonso has written, "we would be like lost people in this world we live in."

—*Louis Owens*

Sherman Alexie (Spokane, Coeur d'Alene)

The Approximate Size of My Favorite Tumor

After the argument that I had lost but pretended to win, I stormed out of the HUD house, jumped into the car, and prepared to drive off in victory, which was also known as defeat. But I realized that I hadn't grabbed my keys. At that kind of moment, a person begins to realize how he can be fooled by his own games. And at that kind of moment, a person begins to formulate a new game to compensate for the failure of the first.

"Honey, I'm home," I yelled as I walked back into the house.

My wife ignored me, gave me a momentary stoic look that impressed me with its resemblance to generations of television Indians.

"Oh, what is that?" I asked. "Your Tonto face?"

She flipped me off, shook her head, and disappeared into the bedroom.

"Honey," I called after her. "Didn't you miss me? I've been gone so long and it's good to be back home. Where I belong."

I could hear dresser drawers open and close.

"And look at the kids," I said as I patted the heads of imagined children. "They've grown so much. And they have your eyes."

She walked out of the bedroom in her favorite ribbon shirt, hair wrapped in her best ties, and wearing a pair of come-here boots. You know, the kind with the curled toe that looks like a finger gesturing *Come here, cowboy, come on over here.* But those boots weren't meant for me: I'm an Indian.

"Honey," I asked. "I just get back from the war and you're leaving already? No kiss for the returning hero?"

She pretended to ignore me, which I enjoyed. But then she pulled out her car keys, checked herself in the mirror, and headed for the door. I jumped in front of her, knowing she meant to begin her own war. That scared the shit out of me.

"Hey," I said. "I was just kidding, honey. I'm sorry. I didn't mean anything. I'll do whatever you want me to."

She pushed me aside, adjusted her dreams, pulled on her braids for a jumpstart, and walked out the door. I followed her and stood on the porch as she jumped into the car and started it up.

"I'm going dancing," she said and drove off into the sunset, or at least she drove down the tribal highway toward the Powwow Tavern.

"But what am I going to feed the kids?" I asked and walked back into the house to feed myself and my illusions.

After a dinner of macaroni and commodity cheese, I put on my best shirt, a new pair of blue jeans, and set out to hitch-hike down the tribal highway. The sun had gone down already so I decided that I was riding off toward the great unknown, which was actually the same Powwow Tavern where my love had escaped to an hour earlier.

As I stood on the highway with my big, brown, and beautiful thumb showing me the way, Simon pulled up in his pickup, stopped, opened the passenger door, and whooped.

"Shit," he yelled. "If it ain't little Jimmy One-Horse! Where you going, cousin, and how fast do you need to get there?"

I hesitated at the offer of a ride. Simon was world famous, at least famous on the Spokane Indian Reservation, for driving backward. He always obeyed posted speed limits, traffic signals and signs, even minute suggestions. But he drove in reverse, using the rearview mirror as his guide. But what could I do? I trusted the man, and when you trust a man you also have to trust his horse.

"I'm headed for the Powwow Tavern," I said and climbed into Simon's rig. "And I need to be there before my wife finds herself a dance partner."

"Shit," Simon said. "Why didn't you say something sooner? We'll be there before she hears the first note of the first goddamned song."

Simon jammed the car into his only gear, reverse, and roared down the highway. I wanted to hang my head out the window like a dog, let my braids flap like a tongue in the wind, but good manners prevented me from taking the liberty. Still, it was so tempting. Always was.

"So, little Jimmy Sixteen-and-One-Half-Horses," Simon asked me after a bit. "What did you do to make your wife take off this time?"

"Well," I said. "I told her the truth, Simon. I told her I got cancer everywhere inside me."

Simon slammed on the brakes and brought the pickup sliding to a quick but decidedly cinematic stop.

"That ain't nothing to joke about," he yelled.

"Ain't joking about the cancer," I said. "But I started joking about dying and that pissed her off."

"What'd you say?"

"Well, I told her the doctor showed me my X-rays and my favorite tumor was just about the size of a baseball, shaped like one, too. Even had stitch marks."

"You're full of shit."

"No, really. I told her to call me Babe Ruth. Or Roger Maris. Maybe even Hank Aaron 'cause there must have been about 755 damn tumors inside me. Then, I told her I was going to Cooperstown and sit right down in the lobby of the Hall of Fame. Make myself a new exhibit, you know? Pin my X-rays to my chest and point out the tumors. What a dedicated baseball fan! What a sacrifice for the national pastime!"

"You're an asshole, little Jimmy Zero-Horses."

"I know, I know," I said as Simon got the pickup rolling again, down the highway toward an uncertain future, which was, as usual, simply called the Powwow Tavern.

We rode the rest of the way in silence. That is to say that neither of us had anything at all to say. But I could hear Simon breathing and I'm sure he could hear me, too. And once, he coughed.

"There you go, cousin," he said finally as he stopped his pickup in front of the Powwow Tavern. "I hope it all works out, you know?"

I shook his hand, offered him a few exaggerated gifts, made a couple promises that he knew were just promises, and waved wildly as he drove off, backwards, and away from the rest of my life. Then I walked into the tavern, shook my body like a dog shaking off water. I've always wanted to walk into a bar that way.

"Where the hell is Suzy Boyd?" I asked.

"Right here, asshole," Suzy answered quickly and succinctly.

"Okay, Suzy," I asked. "Where the hell is my wife?"

"Right here, asshole," my wife answered quickly and succinctly. Then she paused a second before she added, "And quit calling me *your wife*. It makes me sound like I'm a fucking bowling ball or something."

"Okay, okay, Norma," I said and sat down beside her. I ordered a Diet Pepsi for me and a pitcher of beer for the next table. There was no one sitting at the next table. It was just something I always did. Someone would come along and drink it.

"Norma," I said. "I'm sorry. I'm sorry I have cancer and I'm sorry I'm dying."

She took a long drink of her Diet Pepsi, stared at me for a long time. Stared hard.

"Are you going to make any more jokes about it?" she asked.

"Just one or two more, maybe," I said and smiled. It was exactly the wrong thing to say. Norma slapped me in anger, had a look of concern for a moment as she wondered what a slap could do to a person with terminal cancer, and then looked angry again.

"If you say anything funny ever again, I'm going to leave you," Norma said. "And I'm fucking serious about that."

I lost my smile briefly, reached across the table to hold her hand, and said something incredibly funny. It was maybe the best one-liner I had ever uttered. Maybe the moment that would have made me a star anywhere else. But in the Powwow Tavern, which was just a front for reality, Norma heard what I had to say, stood up, and left me.

Because Norma left me, it's even more important to know how she arrived in my life.

I was sitting in the Powwow Tavern on a Saturday night with my Diet Pepsi and my second-favorite cousin, Raymond.

"Look it, look it," he said as Norma walked into the tavern. Norma was over six feet tall. Well, maybe not six feet tall but she was taller than me, taller than everyone in the bar except the basketball players.

"What tribe you think she is?" Raymond asked me.

"Amazon," I said.

"Their reservation down by Santa Fe, enit?" Raymond asked, and I laughed so hard that Norma came over to find out about the commotion.

"Hello, little brothers," she said. "Somebody want to buy me a drink?"

"What you having?" I asked.

"Diet Pepsi," she said and I knew we would fall in love.

"Listen," I told her. "If I stole 1,000 horses, I'd give you 501 of them."

"And what other women would get the other 499?" she asked.

And we laughed. Then we laughed harder when Raymond leaned in closer to the table and said, "I don't get it."

Later, after the tavern closed, Norma and I sat outside on my car and shared a cigarette. I should say that we pretended to share a cigarette since neither of us smoked. But we both thought the other did and wanted to have all that much more in common.

After an hour or two of coughing, talking stories, and laughter, we ended up at my HUD house, watching late-night television. Raymond was passed out in the backseat of my car.

"Hey," she said. "That cousin of yours ain't too smart."

"Yeah," I said. "But he's cool, you know?"

"Must be. Because you're so good to him."

"He's my cousin, you know? That's how it is."

She kissed me then. Soft at first. Then harder. Our teeth clicked together like it was a junior high kiss. Still, we sat on the couch and kissed until the television signed off and broke into white noise. It was the end of another broadcast day.

"Listen," I said then. "I should take you home."

"Home?" she asked. "I thought I was at home."

"Well, my tipi is your tipi," I said, and she lived there until the day I told her that I had terminal cancer.

* * *

I have to mention the wedding, though. It was at the Spokane Tribal Longhouse and all my cousins and her cousins were there. Nearly two hundred people. Everything went smoothly until my second-favorite cousin, Raymond, drunk as a skunk, stood up in the middle of the ceremony, obviously confused.

"I remember Jimmy real good," Raymond said and started into his eulogy for me as I stood not two feet from him. "Jimmy was always quick with a joke. Make you laugh all the damn time. I remember once at my grandmother's wake, he was standing by the coffin. Now, you got to remember he was only seven or eight years old. Anyway, he starts jumping up and down, yelling, *She moved, she moved.*"

Everyone at the wedding laughed because it was pretty much the same crowd that was at the funeral. Raymond smiled at his newly discovered public speaking ability and continued.

"Jimmy was always the one to make people feel better, too," he said. "I remember once when he and I were drinking at the Powwow Tavern when all of a sudden Lester FallsApart comes running in and says that ten Indians just got killed in a car wreck on Ford Canyon Road. *Ten Skins?* I asked Lester, and he said, *Yeah, ten.* And then Jimmy starts up singing, *One little, two little, three little Indians, four little, five little, six little Indians, seven little, eight little, nine little Indians, ten little Indian boys.*"

Everyone in the wedding laughed some more, but also looked a little tense after that story, so I grabbed Raymond and led him back to his seat. He stared incredulously at me, tried to reconcile his recent eulogy with my sudden appearance. He just sat there until the preacher asked that most rhetorical of questions:

"And if there is anyone here who has objections to this union, speak now or forever hold your peace."

Raymond staggered and stumbled to his feet, then staggered and stumbled up to the preacher.

"Reverend," Raymond said. "I hate to interrupt, but my cousin is dead, you know? I think that might be a problem."

Raymond passed out at that moment, and Norma and I were married with his body draped unceremoniously over our feet.

Three months after Norma left me, I lay in my hospital bed in Spokane, just back from another stupid and useless radiation treatment.

"Jesus," I said to my attending physician. "A few more zaps and I'll be Superman."

"Really?" the doctor said. "I never realized that Clark Kent was a Spokane Indian."

And we laughed, you know, because sometimes that's all two people have in common.

"So," I asked her. "What's my latest prognosis?"

"Well," she said. "It comes down to this. You're dying."

"Not again," I said.

"Yup, Jimmy, you're still dying."

And we laughed, you know, because sometimes you'd rather cry.

"Well," the doctor said. "I've got other patients to see."

As she walked out, I wanted to call her back and make an urgent confession, to ask forgiveness, to offer truth in return for salvation. But she was only a doctor. A good doctor, but still just a doctor.

"Hey, Dr. Adams," I said.

"What?"

"Nothing," I said. "Just wanted to hear your name. It sounds like drums to these heavily medicated Indian ears of mine."

And she laughed and I laughed, too. That's what happened.

Norma was the world champion fry bread maker. Her fry bread was perfect, like one of those dreams you wake up from and say, *I didn't want to wake up.*

"I think this is your best fry bread ever," I told Norma one day. In fact, it was January 22.

"Thank you," she said. "Now you get to wash the dishes."

So I was washing the dishes when the phone rang. Norma answered it and I could hear her half of the conversation.

"Hello."

"Yes, this is Norma Many Horses."

"No."

"No!"

"*No!*" Norma yelled as she threw the phone down and ran outside. I picked the receiver up carefully, afraid of what it might say to me.

"Hello," I said.

"Who am I speaking to?" the voice on the other end asked.

"Jimmy Many Horses. I'm Norma's husband."

"Oh, Mr. Many Horses. I hate to be the bearer of bad news, but, uh, as I just told your wife, your mother-in-law, uh, passed away this morning."

"Thank you," I said, hung up the phone, and saw that Norma had returned.

"Oh, Jimmy," she said, talking through tears.

"I can't believe I just said *thank you* to that guy," I said. "What does that mean? Thank you that my mother-in-law is dead? Thank you that you told me that my mother-in-law is dead? Thank you that you told me that my mother-in-law is dead and made my wife cry?"

"Jimmy," Norma said. "Stop. It's not funny."

But I didn't stop. Then or now.

Still, you have to realize that laughter saved Norma and me from pain, too. Humor was an antiseptic that cleaned the deepest of personal wounds.

Once, a Washington State patrolman stopped Norma and me as we drove to Spokane to see a movie, get some dinner, a Big Gulp at 7-11.

"Excuse me, officer," I asked. "What did I do wrong?"

"You failed to make proper signal for a turn a few blocks back," he said.

That was interesting because I had been driving down a straight highway for over five miles. The only turns possible were down dirt roads toward houses where no one I ever knew had lived. But I knew to play along with his game. All you can hope for in these little wars is to minimize the amount of damage.

"I'm sorry about that, officer," I said. "But you know how it is. I was listening to the radio, tapping my foot. It's those drums, you know?"

"Whatever," the trooper said. "Now, I need your driver's license, registration, and proof of insurance."

I handed him the stuff and he barely looked at it. He leaned down into the window of the car.

"Hey, chief," he asked. "Have you been drinking?"

"I don't drink," I said.

"How about your woman there?"

"Ask her yourself," I said.

The trooper looked at me, blinked a few seconds, paused for dramatic effect, and said, "Don't you even think about telling me what I should do."

"I don't drink, either," Norma said quickly, hoping to avoid any further confrontation. "And I wasn't driving anyway."

"That don't make any difference," the trooper said. "Washington State has a new law against riding as a passenger in an Indian car."

"Officer," I said. "That ain't new. We've known about that one for a couple hundred years."

The trooper smiled a little, but it was a hard smile. You know the kind.

"However," he said. "I think we can make some kind of arrangement so none of this has to go on your record."

"How much is it going to cost me?" I asked.

"How much do you have?"

"About a hundred bucks."

"Well," the trooper said. "I don't want to leave you with nothing. Let's say the fine is ninety-nine dollars."

I gave him all the money, though, four twenties, a ten, eight dollar bills, and two hundred pennies in a sandwich bag.

"Hey," I said. "Take it all. That extra dollar is a tip, you know? Your service has been excellent."

Norma wanted to laugh then. She covered her mouth and pretended to cough. His face turned red. I mean redder than it already was.

"In fact," I said as I looked at the trooper's badge. "I might just send a letter to your commanding officer. I'll just write that Washington State Patrolman D. Nolan, badge number 13746, was polite, courteous, and above all, legal as an eagle."

Norma laughed out loud now.

"Listen," the trooper said. "I can just take you both in right now. For reckless driving, resisting arrest, threatening an officer with physical violence."

"If you do," Norma said and jumped into the fun, "I'll just tell everyone how respectful you were of our Native traditions, how much you understood about the social conditions that lead to the criminal acts of so many Indians. I'll say you were sympathetic, concerned, and intelligent."

"Fucking Indians," the trooper said as he threw the sandwich bag of pennies back into our car, sending them flying all over the interior. "And keep your damn change."

We watched him walk back to his cruiser, climb in, and drive off, breaking four or five laws as he flipped a U-turn, left rubber, crossed the center line, broke the speed limit, and ran through a stop sign without lights and siren.

We laughed as we picked up the scattered pennies from the floor of the car. It was a good thing that the trooper threw that change back at us because we found just enough gas money to get us home.

After Norma left me, I'd occasionally get postcards from powwows all over the country. She missed me in Washington, Oregon, Idaho, Montana, Nevada, Utah, New Mexico, and California. I just stayed on the Spokane Indian Reservation and missed her from the doorway of my HUD house, from the living room window, waiting for the day that she would come back.

But that's how Norma operated. She told me once that she would leave me whenever the love started to go bad.

"I ain't going to watch the whole thing collapse," she said. "I'll get out when the getting is good."

"You wouldn't even try to save us?" I asked.

"It wouldn't be worth saving at that point."

"That's pretty cold."

"That's not cold," she said. "It's practical."

But don't get me wrong, either. Norma was a warrior in every sense of the word. She would drive a hundred miles round-trip to visit tribal elders in the nursing homes in Spokane. When one of those elders died, Norma would weep violently, throw books and furniture.

"Every one of our elders who dies takes a piece of our past away," she said. "And that hurts more because I don't know how much of a future we have."

And once, when we drove up on a really horrible car wreck, she held a dying man's head in her lap and sang to him until he passed away. He was a white guy, too. Remember that. She kept that memory so close to her that she had nightmares for a year.

"I always dream that it's you who's dying," she told me and didn't let me drive the car for almost a year.

Norma, she was always afraid; she wasn't afraid.

One thing that I noticed in the hospital as I coughed myself up and down the bed: A clock, at least one of those old-style clocks with hands and a face, looks just like somebody laughing if you stare at it long enough.

The hospital released me because they decided that I would be much more comfortable at home. And there I was, at home, writing letters to my loved ones on special reservation stationery that read: FROM THE DEATH BED OF JAMES MANY HORSES, III.

But in reality, I sat at my kitchen table to write, and DEATH TABLE just doesn't have the necessary music. I'm also the only James Many Horses, but there is a certain dignity to any kind of artificial tradition.

Anyway, I sat there at the death table, writing letters from my death bed, when there was a knock on the door.

"Come in," I yelled, knowing the door was locked, and smiled when it rattled against the frame.

"It's locked," a female voice said and it was a female voice I recognized.

"Norma?" I asked as I unlocked and opened the door.

She was beautiful. She had either gained or lost twenty pounds, one braid hung down a little longer than the other, and she had ironed her shirt until the creases were sharp.

"Honey," she said. "I'm home."

I was silent. That was a rare event.

"Honey," she said. "I've been gone so long and I missed you so much. But now I'm back. Where I belong."

I had to smile.

"Where are the kids?" she asked.

"They're asleep," I said, recovered just in time to continue the joke. "Poor little guys tried to stay awake, you know? They wanted to be up when you got home. But, one by one, they dropped off, fell asleep, and I had to carry them off into their little beds."

"Well," Norma said. "I'll just go in and kiss them quietly. Tell them how much I love them. Fix the sheets and blankets so they'll be warm all night."

She smiled.

"Jimmy," she said. "You look like shit."

"Yeah, I know."

"I'm sorry I left."

"Where've you been?" I asked, though I didn't really want to know.

"In Arlee. Lived with a Flathead cousin of mine."

"Cousin as in cousin? Or cousin as in I-was-fucking-him-but-don't-want-to-tell-you-because-you're-dying?"

She smiled even though she didn't want to.

"Well," she said. "I guess you'd call him more of that second kind of cousin."

Believe me: nothing ever hurt more. Not even my tumors which are the approximate size of baseballs.

"Why'd you come back?" I asked her.

She looked at me, tried to suppress a giggle, then broke out into full-fledged laughter. I joined her.

"Well," I asked her again after a while. "Why'd you come back?"

She turned stoic, gave me that beautiful Tonto face, and said, "Because he was so fucking serious about everything."

We laughed a little more and then I asked her one more time, "Really, why'd you come back?"

"Because someone needs to help you die the right way," she said. "And we both know that dying ain't something you ever done before."

I had to agree with that.

"And maybe," she said, "because making fry bread and helping people die are the last two things Indians are good at."

"Well," I said. "At least you're good at one of them."

And we laughed.

Sherman Alexie (Spokane, Couer d'Alene)

This Is What It Means to Say Phoenix, Arizona

Just after Victor lost his job at the BIA, he also found out that his father had died of a heart attack in Phoenix, Arizona. Victor hadn't seen his father in a few years, only talked to him on the telephone once or twice, but there still was a genetic pain, which was soon to be pain as real and immediate as a broken bone.

Victor didn't have any money. Who does have money on a reservation, except the cigarette and fireworks salespeople? His father had a savings account waiting to be claimed, but Victor needed to find a way to get to Phoenix. Victor's mother was just as poor as he was, and the rest of his family didn't have any use at all for him. So Victor called the Tribal Council.

"Listen," Victor said. "My father just died. I need some money to get to Phoenix to make arrangements."

"Now, Victor," the council said. "You know we're having a difficult time financially."

"But I thought the council had special funds set aside for stuff like this."

"Now, Victor, we do have some money available for the proper return of tribal members' bodies. But I don't think we have enough to bring your father all the way back from Phoenix."

"Well," Victor said. "It ain't going to cost all that much. He had to be cremated. Things were kind of ugly. He died of a heart attack in his trailer and nobody found him for a week. It was really hot, too. You get the picture."

"Now, Victor, we're sorry for your loss and the circumstances. But we can really only afford to give you one hundred dollars."

"That's not even enough for a plane ticket."

"Well, you might consider driving down to Phoenix."

"I don't have a car. Besides, I was going to drive my father's pickup back up here."

"Now, Victor," the council said. "We're sure there is somebody who could drive you to Phoenix. Or is there somebody who could lend you the rest of the money?"

"You know there ain't nobody around with that kind of money."

"Well, we're sorry, Victor, but that's the best we can do."

Victor accepted the Tribal Council's offer. What else could he do? So he signed the proper papers, picked up his check, and walked over to the Trading Post to cash it.

While Victor stood in line, he watched Thomas Builds-the-Fire standing near the magazine rack, talking to himself. Like he always did. Thomas was a storyteller that nobody wanted to listen to. That's like being a dentist in a town where everybody has false teeth.

Victor and Thomas Builds-the-Fire were the same age, had grown up and played in the dirt together. Ever since Victor could remember, it was Thomas who always had something to say.

Once, when they were seven years old, when Victor's father still lived with the family, Thomas closed his eyes and told Victor this story: "Your father's heart is weak. He is afraid of his own family. He is afraid of you. Late at night he sits in the dark. Watches the television until there's nothing but that white noise. Sometimes he feels like he wants to buy a motorcycle and ride away. He wants to run and hide. He doesn't want to be found."

Thomas Builds-the-Fire had known that Victor's father was going to leave, knew it before anyone. Now Victor stood in the Trading Post with a one-hundred-dollar check in his hand, wondering if Thomas knew that Victor's father was dead, if he knew what was going to happen next.

Just then Thomas looked at Victor, smiled, and walked over to him.

"Victor, I'm sorry about your father," Thomas said.

"How did you know about it?" Victor asked.

"I heard it on the wind. I heard it from the birds. I felt it in the sunlight. Also, your mother was just in here crying."

"Oh," Victor said and looked around the Trading Post. All the other Indians stared, surprised that Victor was even talking to Thomas. Nobody talked to Thomas anymore because he told the same damn stories over and over again. Victor was embarrassed, but he thought that Thomas might be able to help him. Victor felt a sudden need for tradition.

"I can lend you the money you need," Thomas said suddenly. "But you have to take me with you."

"I can't take your money," Victor said. "I mean, I haven't hardly talked to you in years. We're not really friends anymore."

"I didn't say we were friends. I said you had to take me with you."

"Let me think about it."

Victor went home with his one hundred dollars and sat at the kitchen table. He held his head in his hands and thought about Thomas Builds-the-Fire, remembered little details, tears and scars, the bicycle they shared for a summer, so many stories.

Thomas Builds-the-Fire sat on the bicycle, waited in Victor's yard. He was ten years old and skinny. His hair was dirty because it was the Fourth of July.

"Victor," Thomas yelled. "Hurry up. We're going to miss the fireworks."

After a few minutes, Victor ran out of his house, jumped the porch railing, and landed gracefully on the sidewalk.

"And the judges award him a 9.95, the highest score of the summer," Thomas said, clapped, laughed.

"That was perfect, cousin," Victor said. "And it's my turn to ride the bike."

Thomas gave up the bike and they headed for the fairgrounds. It was nearly dark and the fireworks were about to start.

"You know," Thomas said. "It's strange how us Indians celebrate the Fourth of July. It ain't like it was *our* independence everybody was fighting for."

"You think about things too much," Victor said. "It's just supposed to be fun. Maybe Junior will be there."

"Which Junior? Everybody on this reservation is named Junior."

And they both laughed.

The fireworks were small, hardly more than a few bottle rockets and a fountain. But it was enough for two Indian boys. Years later, they would need much more.

Afterwards, sitting in the dark, fighting off mosquitoes, Victor turned to Thomas Builds-the-Fire.

"Hey," Victor said. "Tell me a story."

Thomas closed his eyes and told this story: "There were these two Indian boys who wanted to be warriors. But it was too late to be warriors in the old way. All the horses were gone. So the two Indian boys stole a car and drove to the city. They parked the stolen car in front of the police station and then hitchhiked back home to the reservation. When they got back, all their friends cheered and their parents' eyes shone with pride. *You were very brave,* everybody said to the two Indian boys. *Very brave.*"

"Ya-hey," Victor said. "That's a good one. I wish I could be a warrior."

"Me, too," Thomas said.

They went home together in the dark, Thomas on the bike now, Victor on foot. They walked through shadows and light from streetlamps.

"We've come a long ways," Thomas said. "We have outdoor lighting."

"All I need is the stars," Victor said. "And besides, you still think about things too much."

They separated then, each headed for home, both laughing all the way.

Victor sat at his kitchen table. He counted his one hundred dollars again and again. He knew he needed more to make it to Phoenix and back. He knew he needed Thomas Builds-the-Fire. So he put his money in his wallet and opened the front door to find Thomas on the porch.

"Ya-hey, Victor," Thomas said. "I knew you'd call me."

Thomas walked into the living room and sat down on Victor's favorite chair.

"I've got some money saved up," Thomas said. "It's enough to get us down there, but you have to get us back."

"I've got this hundred dollars," Victor said. "And my dad had a savings account I'm going to claim."

"How much in your dad's account?"

"Enough. A few hundred."

"Sounds good. When we leaving?"

* * *

When they were fifteen and had long since stopped being friends, Victor and Thomas got into a fistfight. That is, Victor was really drunk and beat

Thomas up for no reason at all. All the other Indian boys stood around and watched it happen. Junior was there and so were Lester, Seymour, and a lot of others. The beating might have gone on until Thomas was dead if Norma Many Horses hadn't come along and stopped it.

"Hey, you boys," Norma yelled and jumped out of her car. "Leave him alone."

If it had been someone else, even another man, the Indian boys would've just ignored the warnings. But Norma was a warrior. She was powerful. She could have picked up any two of the boys and smashed their skulls together. But worse than that, she would have dragged them all over to some tipi and made them listen to some elder tell a dusty old story.

The Indian boys scattered, and Norma walked over to Thomas and picked him up.

"Hey, little man, are you okay?" she asked.

Thomas gave her a thumbs up.

"Why they always picking on you?"

Thomas shook his head, closed his eyes, but no stories came to him, no words or music. He just wanted to go home, to lie in his bed and let his dreams tell his stories for him.

Thomas Builds-the-Fire and Victor sat next to each other in the airplane, coach section. A tiny white woman had the window seat. She was busy twisting her body into pretzels. She was flexible.

"I have to ask," Thomas said, and Victor closed his eyes in embarrassment.

"Don't," Victor said.

"Excuse me, miss," Thomas asked. "Are you a gymnast or something?"

"There's no something about it," she said. "I was first alternate on the 1980 Olympic team."

"Really?" Thomas asked.

"Really."

"I mean, you used to be a world-class athlete?" Thomas asked.

"My husband still thinks I am."

Thomas Builds-the-Fire smiled. She was a mental gymnast, too. She pulled her leg straight up against her body so that she could've kissed her kneecap.

"I wish I could do that," Thomas said.

Victor was ready to jump out of the plane. Thomas, that crazy Indian storyteller with ratty old braids and broken teeth, was flirting with a beautiful Olympic gymnast. Nobody back home on the reservation would ever believe it.

"Well," the gymnast said. "It's easy. Try it."

Thomas grabbed at his leg and tried to pull it up into the same position as the gymnast. He couldn't even come close, which made Victor and the gymnast laugh.

"Hey," she asked. "You two are Indian, right?"

"Full-blood," Victor said.

"Not me," Thomas said. "I'm half magician on my mother's side and half clown on my father's."

They all laughed.

"What are your names?" she asked.

"Victor and Thomas."

"Mine is Cathy. Pleased to meet you all."

The three of them talked for the duration of the flight. Cathy the gymnast complained about the government, how they screwed the 1980 Olympic team by boycotting.

"Sounds like you all got a lot in common with Indians," Thomas said.

Nobody laughed.

After the plane landed in Phoenix and they had all found their way to the terminal, Cathy the gymnast smiled and waved good-bye.

"She was really nice," Thomas said.

"Yeah, but everybody talks to everybody on airplanes," Victor said. "It's too bad we can't always be that way."

"You always used to tell me I think too much," Thomas said. "Now it sounds like you do."

"Maybe I caught it from you."

"Yeah."

Thomas and Victor rode in a taxi to the trailer where Victor's father died.

"Listen," Victor said as they stopped in front of the trailer. "I never told you I was sorry for beating you up that time."

"Oh, it was nothing. We were just kids and you were drunk."

"Yeah, but I'm still sorry."

"That's all right."

Victor paid for the taxi and the two of them stood in the hot Phoenix summer. They could smell the trailer.

"This ain't going to be nice," Victor said. "You don't have to go in."

"You're going to need help."

Victor walked to the front door and opened it. The stink rolled out and made them both gag. Victor's father had lain in that trailer for a week in hundred-degree temperatures before anyone found him. And the only reason anyone found him was because of the smell. They needed dental records to identify him. That's exactly what the coroner said. They needed dental records.

"Oh, man," Victor said. "I don't know if I can do this."

"Well, then don't."

"But there might be something valuable in there."

"I thought his money was in the bank."

"It is. I was talking about pictures and letters and stuff like that."

"Oh," Thomas said as he held his breath and followed Victor into the trailer.

When Victor was twelve, he stepped into an underground wasp nest. His foot was caught in the hole, and no matter how hard he struggled, Victor couldn't pull free. He might have died there, stung a thousand times, if Thomas Builds-the-Fire had not come by.

"Run," Thomas yelled and pulled Victor's foot from the hole. They ran then, hard as they ever had, faster than Billy Mills, faster than Jim Thorpe, faster than the wasps could fly.

Victor and Thomas ran until they couldn't breathe, ran until it was cold and dark outside, ran until they were lost and it took hours to find their way home. All the way back, Victor counted his stings.

"Seven," Victor said. "My lucky number."

* * *

Victor didn't find much to keep in the trailer. Only a photo album and a stereo. Everything else had that smell stuck in it or was useless anyway.

"I guess this is all," Victor said. "It ain't much."

"Better than nothing," Thomas said.

"Yeah, and I do have the pickup."

"Yeah," Thomas said. "It's in good shape."

"Dad was good about that stuff."

"Yeah, I remember your dad."

"Really?" Victor asked. "What do you remember?"

Thomas Builds-the-Fire closed his eyes and told this story: "I remember when I had this dream that told me to go to Spokane, to stand by the Falls in the middle of the city and wait for a sign. I knew I had to go there but I didn't have a car. Didn't have a license. I was only thirteen. So I walked all the way, took me all day, and I finally made it to the Falls. I stood there for an hour waiting. Then your dad came walking up. *What the hell are you do-ing here?* he asked me. I said, *Waiting for a vision.* Then your father said, *All you're going to get here is mugged.* So he drove me over to Denny's, bought me dinner, and then drove me home to the reservation. For a long time I was mad because I thought my dreams had lied to me. But they didn't. Your dad was my vision. *Take care of each other* is what my dreams were saying. *Take care of each other.*"

Victor was quiet for a long time. He searched his mind for memories of his father, found the good ones, found a few bad ones, added it all up, and smiled.

"My father never told me about finding you in Spokane," Victor said.

"He said he wouldn't tell anybody. Didn't want me to get in trouble. But he said I had to watch out for you as part of the deal."

"Really?"

"Really. Your father said you would need the help. He was right."

"That's why you came down here with me, isn't it?" Victor asked.

"I came because of your father."

Victor and Thomas climbed into the pickup, drove over to the bank, and claimed the three hundred dollars in the savings account.

Thomas Builds-the-Fire could fly.

Once, he jumped off the roof of the tribal school and flapped his arms like a crazy eagle. And he flew. For a second, he hovered, suspended above all the other Indian boys who were too smart or too scared to jump.

"He's flying," Junior yelled, and Seymour was busy looking for the trick wires or mirrors. But it was real. As real as the dirt when Thomas lost altitude and crashed to the ground.

He broke his arm in two places.

"He broke his wing," Victor chanted, and the other Indian boys joined in, made it a tribal song.

"He broke his wing, he broke his wing, he broke his wing," all the Indian boys chanted as they ran off, flapping their wings, wishing they could fly, too. They hated Thomas for his courage, his brief moment as a bird. Everybody has dreams about flying. Thomas flew.

One of his dreams came true for just a second, just enough to make it real.

Victor's father, his ashes, fit in one wooden box with enough left over to fill a cardboard box.

"He always was a big man," Thomas said.

Victor carried part of his father and Thomas carried the rest out to the pickup. They set him down carefully behind the seats, put a cowboy hat on the wooden box and a Dodgers cap on the cardboard box. That's the way it was supposed to be.

"Ready to head back home," Victor asked.

"It's going to be a long drive."

"Yeah, take a couple days, maybe."

"We can take turns," Thomas said.

"Okay," Victor said, but they didn't take turns. Victor drove for sixteen hours straight north, made it halfway up Nevada toward home before he finally pulled over.

"Hey, Thomas, " Victor said. "You got to drive for a while."

"Okay."

Thomas Builds-the-Fire slid behind the wheel and started off down the road. All through Nevada, Thomas and Victor had been amazed at the lack of animal life, at the absence of water, of movement.

"Where is everything?" Victor had asked more than once.

Now when Thomas was finally driving they saw the first animal, maybe the only animal in Nevada. It was a long-eared jackrabbit.

"Look," Victor yelled. "It's alive."

Thomas and Victor were busy congratulating themselves on their discovery when the jackrabbit darted out into the road and under the wheels of the pickup.

"Stop the goddamn car," Victor yelled, and Thomas did stop, backed the pickup to the dead jackrabbit.

"Oh, man, he's dead," Victor said as he looked at the squashed animal.

"Really dead."

"The only thing alive in this whole state and we just killed it."

"I don't know," Thomas said. "I think it was suicide."

Victor looked around the desert, sniffed the air, felt the emptiness and loneliness, and nodded his head.

"Yeah," Victor said. "It had to be suicide."

"I can't believe this," Thomas said. "You drive for a thousand miles and there ain't even any bugs smashed on the windshield. I drive for ten seconds and kill the only living thing in Nevada."

"Yeah," Victor said. "Maybe I should drive."

"Maybe you should."

Thomas Builds-the-Fire walked through the corridors of the tribal school by himself. Nobody wanted to be anywhere near him because of all those stories. Story after story.

Thomas closed his eyes and this story came to him: "We are all given one thing by which our lives are measured, one determination. Mine are the stories which can change or not change the world. It doesn't matter which as long as I continue to tell the stories. My father, he died on Okinawa in World War II, died fighting for this country, which had tried to kill him for years. My mother, she died giving birth to me, died while I was still inside her. She pushed me out into the world with her last breath. I have no brothers or sisters. I have only my stories which came to me before I even had the words to speak. I learned a thousand stories before I took my first thousand steps. They are all I have. It's all I can do."

Thomas Builds-the-Fire told his stories to all those who would stop and listen. He kept telling them long after people had stopped listening.

Victor and Thomas made it back to the reservation just as the sun was rising. It was the beginning of a new day on earth, but the same old shit on the reservation.

"Good morning," Thomas said.

"Good morning."

The tribe was waking up, ready for work, eating breakfast, reading the newspaper, just like everybody else does. Willene LeBret was out in her garden wearing a bathrobe. She waved when Thomas and Victor drove by.

"Crazy Indians made it," she said to herself and went back to her roses.

Victor stopped the pickup in front of Thomas Builds-the-Fire's HUD house. They both yawned, stretched a little, shook dust from their bodies.

"I'm tired," Victor said.

"Of everything," Thomas added.

They both searched for words to end the journey. Victor needed to thank Thomas for his help, for the money, and make the promise to pay it all back.

"Don't worry about the money," Thomas said. "It don't make any difference anyhow."

"Probably not, enit?"

"Nope."

Victor knew that Thomas would remain the crazy storyteller who talked to dogs and cars, who listened to the wind and pine trees. Victor knew that he couldn't really be friends with Thomas, even after all that had happened. It was cruel but it was real. As real as the ashes, as Victor's father, sitting behind the seats.

"I know how it is," Thomas said. "I know you ain't going to treat me any better than you did before. I know your friends would give you too much shit about it."

Victor was ashamed of himself. Whatever happened to the tribal ties, the sense of community? The only real thing he shared with anybody was a bottle and broken dreams. He owed Thomas something, anything.

"Listen," Victor said and handed Thomas the cardboard box which contained half of his father. "I want you to have this."

Thomas took the ashes and smiled, closed his eyes, and told this story: "I'm going to travel to Spokane Falls one last time and toss these ashes into the water. And your father will rise like a salmon, leap over the bridge, over me, and find his way home. It will be beautiful. His teeth will shine like silver, like a rainbow. He will rise, Victor, he will rise."

Victor smiled.

"I was planning on doing the same thing with my half," Victor said. "But I didn't imagine my father looking anything like a salmon. I thought it'd be like cleaning the attic or something. Like letting things go after they've stopped having any use."

"Nothing stops, cousin," Thomas said. "Nothing stops."

Thomas Builds-the-Fire got out of the pickup and walked up his driveway. Victor started the pickup and began the drive home.

"Wait," Thomas yelled suddenly from his porch. "I just got to ask one favor."

Victor stopped the pickup, leaned out the window, and shouted back. "What do you want?"

"Just one time when I'm telling a story somewhere, why don't you stop and listen?" Thomas asked.

"Just once?"

"Just once."

Victor waved his arms to let Thomas know that the deal was good. It was a fair trade, and that was all Victor had ever wanted from his whole life. So Victor drove his father's pickup toward home while Thomas went into his house, closed the door behind him, and heard a new story come to him in the silence afterwards.

Beth Brant (Mohawk)

Swimming Upstream

Anna May spent the first night in a motel off Highway 8. She arrived about ten, exhausted from her long drive—the drive through farmland, bright autumn leaves, the glimpse of blue lake. She saw none of this, only the gray highway stretching out before her. When she saw the signs of a motel she stopped, feeling the need for rest. It didn't matter where.

She took a shower, lay in bed, and fell asleep, the dream beginning again. Her son—drowning in the water, his skinny arms flailing the waves, his mouth opening to scream but no sound coming forth. She, Anna May, moving in slow motion running into the waves, her hands grabbing for the boy and feeling only water run through her fingers. She grabbed and grabbed but nothing held to her hands. She dove and opened her eyes underwater and saw nothing. He was gone. She dove and grabbed, her hands connecting with sand, with seaweed, but not her son. He was gone. Simon was gone.

Anna May woke. The dream was not a nightmare anymore. It had become a companion to her. A friend, almost a lover, reaching for her as she slept; making pictures of her son, keeping him alive while recording his death. In the first days after Simon left her, the dream made her wake screaming, sobbing, arms hitting at the air, legs kicking the sheets, becoming tangled in the material. Her bed was a straitjacket, pinning her down, holding her until the dream ended. She would fight the dream then. Now she welcomed it.

During the day she had other memories of Simon. His birth, his first pair of shoes, his first steps, his first word "Mama," his first book, his first day of school. Now that he was dead, she invented a future for him during the day. His first skating lessons, his first hockey game, his first reading aloud from a book, his first . . . But she couldn't invent beyond that. His six-year-old face and body wouldn't change in her mind. She couldn't invent what she couldn't imagine. The dream became the final video of her imagining.

She hadn't been there when Simon drowned. Simon had been given to her ex-husband by the courts. She was unfit—because she lived with a woman, because a woman, Catherine, slept beside her, because she had a history of alcoholism. The history was old. Anna May had stopped drinking when she became pregnant with Simon, and she had stayed dry all those years. She couldn't imagine what alcohol tasted like after Simon came. He was so lovely, so new—the desire for drink evaporated every time Simon took hold of her finger, or nursed from her breast, or opened his mouth in a toothless smile. She had marveled at his being, this gift that had come from her own body. This beautiful being who had formed inside her, had come with speed through the birth canal to welcome life outside her; his face red with anticipation, his black hair sticking straight up as if electric with hope, his little fists grabbing, his pink mouth finding her nipple and holding on for dear life. She had no need for alcohol—there was Simon.

Simon was taken away from them. But they saw him on weekends, Tony delivering him on a Friday night, Catherine discreetly finding someplace else to be when his car drove up. They still saw Simon, grateful for the two days out of the week they could play with him, they could delight in him, they could pretend with him. They still saw Simon, but the call came that changed all that. The call from Tony saying that Simon had drowned when he fell out of the boat as they were fishing. Tony sobbing, "I'm sorry. I didn't mean for this to happen. I tried to save him. I'm sorry. Please Anna, please forgive me. Oh God, Anna, I'm sorry, I'm sorry."

So Anna May dreamed of those final moments of a six-year-old life. And it stunned her that she wasn't there to see him die when she had been there to see him come into life.

Anna May stayed dry but she found herself looking into cupboards at odd times. Looking for something. Looking for something to drink. She thought of ways to buy wine and hide it, taking a drink when she needed it. But there was Catherine. Catherine would know and Catherine's face, already so lined and tired and old, would become more so. Anna May looked at her own face in the mirror. She was thirty-six and looked twenty years older. Her black hair had gray streaks she hadn't noticed before. Her forehead had deep lines carved into the flesh, and her eyes—her eyes that had cried so many tears—were a faded and washed-out blue. Her mouth was wrinkled, the lips parched and chapped. She and Catherine were aged and ghostlike figures walking through a dead house.

Anna May thought about the bottle of wine. It look on large proportions in her mind. A bottle of wine, just one, that she could drink from and never empty. A bottle of wine—that sweet, red kind that would take away the dryness, the wrinkled insides of her. She went to meetings but never spoke, only saying her name and "I'll pass tonight." Catherine wanted to talk, but Anna May had nothing to say to this woman she loved, who slept beside her, who shared the same dream. Anna May thought about the bottle of wine. The bottle, the red liquid inside, the sweet taste gathering in her mouth, moving down her throat, hitting her bloodstream, warming her inside, killing the deadness.

She arranged time off work and told Catherine she was going away for a few days—she needed to think, to be alone. Catherine watched her face, the framing of the words out of her mouth, her washed-out eyes. Catherine said, "I understand."

"Will you be all right?" Anna May asked of her.

"I'll be fine," Catherine said. "I'll see friends. We haven't seen our friends in so long, they are concerned about us. I'll be waiting when you get back. I love you so much."

Anna May got in the car and drove up 401, up 19, over to 8 and the motel, the shower, the dream.

Anna May smoked her cigarettes and drank coffee until daylight. She made her plans to buy the bottle of wine. After that, she had no plans, other than the first drink and how it would taste and feel.

She found a meeting in Goderich and sat there, ashamed and angered with herself to sit in a meeting and listen to the stories and plan her backslide. She thought of speaking, of talking about Simon, about the bottle of wine, but she was afraid they would stop her or say something that would make her stop. Anna May didn't want to be stopped. She wanted to drink and drink and drink until it was all over. "My name is Anna May and I'll just pass." Later, she hung around for coffee, feeling like an infiltrator, a spy, and a woman took hold of her arm and said, "Let's go out and talk. I know what you're planning. Don't do it. Let's talk." Anna May shrugged off the woman's hand and left. She drove to a liquor outlet, *vins et spiriteaux.*"Don't do it." She found the wine, one bottle, that was all she'd buy. "Don't do it." One bottle, that was all. She paid and left the store, the familiar curve of the bottle wrapped in brown paper. "Don't do it." Only one bottle. It wouldn't hurt and she laughed at the excuses bubbling up in her mouth like wine. Just one. She smoked a cigarette sitting in the parking lot, wondering where to go, where to stop and turn the cap that would release the red, sweet smell of the wine before the taste would overpower her and she wouldn't have to wonder anymore.

She drove north on 21 heading for the Bruce Peninsula, Lake Huron on her left, passing the little resort towns, the cottages by the lake. She stopped for a hamburger and without thinking, got her thermos filled with coffee. This made her laugh, the bottle sitting next to her, almost a living thing. She drank the coffee, driving north along 21, thinking not of Simon, not of Catherine, but thinking of her father. Charles, her mother had called him. Everyone else had called him Charley. Good old Charley. Good-time Charley. Injun Charley. Charles was a hard worker, working at almost anything, construction being his best and favorite. He worked hard, he drank hard. He attempted to be a father, a husband, but the work and the drink took his attempts away. Anna May's mother never complained, never left him. She cooked and kept house and raised the children and always called him Charles. When Anna May grew up, she taunted her mother with the fact that *her Charles* was a drunk and why didn't she care more about her kids than her drunken husband? Didn't her mother know how ashamed they were to have such a father, to hear people talk about him, to laugh at him, to laugh at them—the half-breeds of good-old-good-time-Injun-Charley?

Anna May laughed again, the sound ugly inside the car. Her father was long dead and, she supposed, forgiven in some way by her. He was a handsome man back then, and her mother a skinny, pale girl, an orphan girl, something unheard of by her father. How that must have appealed to the romantic that was her father. Anna May didn't know how her mother felt about the life she'd had with Charles. Her mother never talked about those things. Her mother, who sobbed and moaned at Simon's death as she never had at her husband's. Anna May couldn't remember her father ever being mean. He just went away when he drank. Not like his daughter, who'd fight anything in her way when she was drunk. The bottle bounced beside her as she drove.

Anna May drove north and her eyes began to see the colors of the trees. They looked like they were on fire, the reds and oranges competing with the yellows and golds. She smoked her cigarettes and drank from the thermos and remembered this was her favorite season. She and Catherine would be cleaning the garden, harvesting the beets, turnips, and cabbage. They would be digging up the gladioli and letting them dry before packing the bulbs away. They would be planting more tulips because Catherine could never get enough of tulips. It was because they had met in the spring, Catherine always said. "We met in the spring and the tulips were blooming in that little park. You looked so beautiful against the tulips, Simon on your lap. I knew I loved you."

Last autumn Simon had been five and had raked leaves and dug holes for the tulip bulbs. Catherine had made cocoa and cinnamon toast and Simon had declared that he liked cinnamon toast better than pie.

Anna May tasted the salt tears on her lips. She licked the wet salt, imagining it was sweet wine on her tongue. "It's my fault," she said out loud. She thought of all the things she should have done to prevent Simon's leaving. She should have placated Tony, she should have lived alone, she should have pretended to be straight, she should have never become an alcoholic, she should have never loved, she should have never been born. Let go! she cried somewhere inside her. Let go! Isn't that what she learned? But how could she let go of Simon and the hate she had for Tony and for herself? How could she let go of that? If she let go, she'd have to forgive—the forgiveness Tony begged of her now that Simon was gone. Even Catherine, even the woman she loved, asked her to forgive Tony. "It could have happened when he was with us," Catherine cried at her. "Forgive him, then you can forgive yourself." But Catherine didn't know what it was to feel the baby inside her, to feel him pushing his way out of her, to feel his mouth on her breast, to feel the sharp pain in her womb every time his name was mentioned. Forgiveness was for people who could afford it. Anna May was poverty-struck.

The highway turned into a road, the trees crowding in on both sides of her, the flames of the trees almost blinding her. She was entering the Bruce Peninsula, a sign informed her. She pulled off the road, consulting her map. Yes, she would drive to the very tip of the peninsula and it would be there she'd open the bottle and drink her way to whatever she imagined was there. The bottle rested beside her. She touched the brown paper, feeling soothed, feeling a hunger in her stomach.

She saw another sign—SAUBLE FALLS. Anna May thought this would be a good place to stop, to drink the last of the coffee, to smoke another cigarette. She pulled over onto the gravel lot. There was a small path leading down onto the rocks. Another sign: ABSOLUTELY NO FISHING. WATCH YOUR STEP—ROCKS ARE SLIPPERY. She could hear the water before she saw it.

She stepped out of the covering of trees and onto the rock shelf. The falls were narrow, spilling out on various layers of rock. She could see the beginnings of Lake Huron below her. She could see movement in the water going away from the lake and moving toward the rocks and the falls. Fish tails flashed, catching lights from the sun. Hundreds of fish tails moving upstream. She walked across a flat slab of rock and there, beneath her in the shallow water, salmon slowly moving their bodies, their gills expanding and closing as they rested. She looked up to another rock slab and saw a dozen fish congregating at the bottom of a water spill—waiting. Her mind barely grasped the fact that the fish were migrating, swimming upstream, when a salmon leapt and hurled itself over the rushing water above it. Anna May stepped up to another ledge and watched the salmon's companions waiting their turn to jump the flowing water and reach the next plateau. She looked down toward the mouth of the lake. There were other people, like her, standing and silently watching the struggle of the fish. No one spoke, as if to speak would be blasphemous in the presence of this. She looked again into the water, the fish crowding each resting place before resuming the leaps and the jumps. Here and there on the rocks, dead fish, a testimony to the long and desperate struggle that had taken place. They lay, eyes glazed, sides open and bleeding, food for the gulls that hovered over Anna May's head. Another salmon jumped, its flesh torn and gaping, its body spinning and hurtling until it made it over the fall. Another one, its dorsal fin torn, leapt and was washed back by the power of the water. Anna May watched the fish rest, its open mouth like another wound. The fish was large, the dark body undulating in the water. She watched it begin a movement of tail. Churning the water, it shot into the air, twisting its body, shaking and spinning. She saw the underbelly, pale yellow and bleeding from the battering against the rocks, the water. He made it. Anna May wanted to clap, to shout with elation at the sheer power of such a thing happening before her. She looked around again. The other people had left. She was alone with the fish, the only sound besides the water was her breath against the air. She walked farther upstream, her sneakers getting wet from the splashing of the fish. She didn't feel the wet, she only waited and watched for the salmon to move. She had no idea of time, of how long she stood waiting for the movement, waiting for the jumps, the leaps, the flight. Anna May watched for Torn Fin, wanting to see him move against the current in his phenomenal swim of faith.

Anna May reached a small dam, the last hurdle before the calm waters and the blessed rest. She sat on a rock, her heart beating fast, the adrenaline pouring through her at each leap and twist of the fish. There he was, Torn Fin, his last jump ahead of him. She watched, then closed her eyes, almost ashamed to be a spectator at this act of faith, this primal movement to get to the place of all beginning—only knowing he had to get there. He had to push his bleeding body forward, believing in his magic to get him there. Believing, believing he would get there. No thoughts of death, no thoughts of food, no thoughts of rest, no thoughts but the great urging and wanting to get there, get *there*. Anna May opened her eyes and saw him, another jump before being pushed back. She held her hands together, her body willing Torn Fin to move, to push, to jump, to fly! Her body rocked forward and back, her heart beating madly inside her breast. She rocked, she shouted, "Make it, damn it, make it!" The fish gathered at the dam. She rocked and held her hands tight, her fingers twisting together, nails scratching her palms. She whispered, "Simon. Simon." She rocked. She rocked and watched Torn Fin's fight to reach his home. She rocked and whispered the name of her son into the water, "Simon. Simon." Like a chant, "Simon. Simon. Simon," into the water, as if the very name of her son was magic and could move the salmon to their final place. She rocked. She chanted. "Simon. Simon." Anna May rocked and put her hands in the water, wanting to lift the fish over the dam and to life. Just as the thought flickered through her brain, Torn Fin slapped his tail against the water and jumped. He battled the current. He twisted and arced into the air, his great mouth gaping and gasping, his wounds standing out in relief against his body, the fin discolored and shredded. With a push, he turned a complete circle and made it over the dam.

"Simon!" Torn Fin gave one more slap of his tail and was gone, the dark body swimming home. She thought . . . she thought she saw her son's face, his black hair streaming behind him, a look of joy transfixed on his little face before the image disappeared.

Anna May stood on the rock, hands limp at her sides, watching the water, watching the salmon, watching. She watched as the sun fell behind the lake and night came closer to her. She walked to the path and back to her car. She looked at the bottle sitting next to her, the brown paper rustling as she put the car in gear. She drove south, stopping at a telephone booth.

She could still hear the water in her ears.

Elizabeth Cook-Lynn (Crow Creek Dakota)

A Good Chance

I

When I got to Crow Creek I went straight to the Agency, the place they call "the Fort," and it was just like it always has been to those of us who leave often and come home now and then: mute, pacific, impenitent, concordant. I drove slowly through the graveled streets until I came to a light blue HUD house.

"I'm looking for Magpie," I said quietly to the little boy who opened the door at Velma's place and looked at me steadily with clear brown eyes. We stood and regarded one another until I, adultlike, felt uncomfortable, and so I repeated, "Say, I'm looking for Magpie. Do you know where he is?"

No answer.

"Is your mother here?"

After a few moments of looking me over, the little boy motioned me inside.

"Wait here," he said.

He went down the cluttered hallway and came back with a young woman wearing jeans and a cream-colored ribbon shirt and carrying a naked baby covered only with rolls of fat. "I'm Amelia," she said, "do you want to sit down?"

The small, shabby room she led me into was facing east, and the light flooded through the window, making everything too bright, contributing to the uneasiness we felt with each other as we sat down.

"I need to find Magpie," I said, "I've really got some good news for him, I think," and I pointed to the briefcase I was carrying. "I have his poems and letter of acceptance from a University in California where they want him to come and participate in the fine arts program they have started for Indians."

"You know, then, that he's on parole, do you?" she asked, speaking quickly, with assurance. "I'm his wife, but we haven't been together for a while." She looked at the little boy who had opened the door, motioned for him to go outside, and after he had left, she said softly, "I don't know where my husband is, but I've heard that he's in town somewhere."

"Do you mean in Chamberlain?"

"Yes. I live here at the Agency with his sister, and she said that she saw him in town . . . quite a while ago."

I said nothing.

"Did you know that he was on parole?"

"Well, no . . . not exactly," I said hesitantly. "I haven't kept in touch with him, but I heard that he was in some kind of trouble. In fact, I didn't know about you. He didn't tell me that he was married, though I might have suspected that he was."

She smiled at me and said, "He's gone a lot. It's not safe around here for him, you know. His parole officer really watches him all the time, and so, sometimes, it is just better for him not to come here. Besides," she said, looking down, absentmindedly squeezing the rolls of fat on the baby's knees, "we haven't been together for a while."

Uncomfortably, I folded and unfolded my hands and tried to think of something appropriate to say. The baby started to cry as though, bored with all this, he needed to hear his own voice. It was not an expression of pain or hunger. He rolled his tongue against his gums and wrinkled his forehead, but when his mother whispered something to him, he quieted immediately and lay, passive, in her lap.

"But Magpie would not go to California," she said, her eyes somehow masking something significant that she thought she knew of him. "He would never leave here now, even if you saw him and talked to him about it."

"But he did before," I said, not liking the sound of my own positive, defensive words. "He went to the university in Seattle."

"Yeah, but . . . well, that was before," she said as though to finish the matter.

"Don't you want him to go?" I asked.

Quickly, she responded, "Oh, it's not up to me to say. He is gone from me now," and she moved her hand to her breast, "I'm just telling you that you are in for a disappointment. He no longer needs the things that people like you want him to need," she said positively.

When she saw that I didn't like her reference to "people like you" and the implication that I was interested in the manipulation of her estranged husband, she stopped for a moment and then put her hand on my arm. "Listen," she said, "Magpie is happy now, finally; he is in good spirits, handsome and free and strong. He sits at the drum and sings with his brothers, and he's okay now. When he was saying all those things against the government and against the council he became more and more ugly and embittered, and I used to be afraid for him. But I'm not now. Please, why don't you just leave it alone now?"

She seemed so young to know how desperate things had become for her young husband in those days and I was genuinely moved by her compassion for him and for a few moments neither of us spoke. Finally, I said, "But I have to see him. I have to ask him what he wants to do. Don't you see that I have to do that?"

She leaned back into the worn, dirty sofa and looked at me with cold hatred. Shocked at the depth of her reaction, I got up and went outside to my car. The little boy who had opened the door for me appeared at my elbow, and as I opened the car door, he asked, "If you find him, will you come back?"

"No," I said, "I don't think so."

I had the sense that the little boy picked up a handful of gravel and threw it after my retreating car as I drove slowly away. When I pulled around the corner, I glanced over my shoulder and saw that he was still standing there, watching my car leave the street: he was small, dark, closed in that attitude of terrible resignation I recognized from my own childhood, and I knew that resignation to be the only defense, the only immunity in a world where children are often the martyrs. That fleeting glimpse of my own past made me even more certain that Magpie had to say yes or no to this thing, himself . . . that none of us who knew and loved him could do it for him.

II

Home of the Hunkpati, proclaimed a hand-lettered sign hanging over the cash register at the café. It could not be said to be an inaccurate proclamation, as all of us who perceived the movement of our lives as emanating from this place knew, only an incomplete one. For as surely as the Hunkpati found this their home, so did the Isianti, the Ihanktowai, even the Winnebagoes, briefly, and others. Even in its incompleteness, though, it seemed to me to be ne plus ultra, the superstructure of historiography which allows us to account for ourselves, and I took it as an affirmation of some vague sort. In a contemplative mood, now, I sat down in a booth and ordered a cup of what turned out be the bitterest coffee I'd had since I left Santa Fe. "*Aa-a-eee-e, pe juta sapa,*" I could hear my uncle saying.

I thought about the Hunkpati and all the people who had moved to this place and some who were put in prison here as great changes occurred and as they maintained an accommodation to those changes. The magic acts of white men don't seem to work well on Indians, I thought, and the stories they tell of our collective demise have been greatly exaggerated; or, to put it into the vernacular of the myth tellers of my childhood, "*Heha yela owi hake,*" this the appropriate ending to the stories which nobody was expected to believe anyway.

I was thinking these things so intently I didn't notice the woman approaching until she was standing behind the booth, saying, "They gave me your note at the Bureau of Indian Affairs office. You wanted to see me?"

"Yes," I said from the great distance of my thoughts, having nearly forgotten my search for the young poet I wished to talk to about his great opportunity. As I looked up into her sober, intent face it all seemed unimportant, and for a moment I felt almost foolish.

Remembering my mission, I said solicitously, "Thank you for coming," and asked her to sit down across the table from me.

"Are you Salina?"

"Yes."

"This place here didn't even exist when I was a child," I told her, "the town that we called 'the Fort' in those days lay hidden along the old creek bed, and this prairie above here was the place where we gathered to dance in the summer sun."

"I know," she said, "my mother told me that we even had a hospital here then, before all this was flooded from the Oahe Dam. She was born there in that hospital along the Crow Creek."

We sat in thoughtful remembrance, scarcely breathing, with twenty years' difference in our ages, and I thought: Yes, I was born there, too, along that creek bed in that Indian hospital which no longer exists, in that Agency town which no longer exists except in the memories of people who have the capacity to take deeply to heart the conditions of the past. And later my uncle offered me to the four grandfathers in my grandmother's lodge, even though it was November and the snow had started and I was taken into the bosom of a once large and significant, now dwindling family; a girl-child who, in the old days, would have had her own name.

Abruptly, she said, "I don't know where Magpie is. I haven't seen him in four days."

"I've got his poems here with me," I said, "and he has a good chance of going to a fine arts school in California, but I have to talk with him and get him to fill out some papers. I know that he is deeply interested . . ."

"No, he isn't," she broke in. "He doesn't have those worthless, shitty dreams anymore."

"Don't say that, Salina. This is a good chance for him."

"Well, you can think what you want," and she turned her dark eyes on me, "but have you talked to him lately? Do you know him as he is now?"

"I know he is good. I know he has such talent . . ."

"He's Indian," she said as though there was some distinction I didn't know about. "And he's back here to stay this time."

She sat there all dressed up in her smart gray suit and her black, shiny fashion boots, secure in the GS-6 bureau secretarial position, and I wondered what she knew about "being Indian" that accounted for the certainty of her response. Was it possible that these two women with whom I had talked today, these two lovers of Magpie, one a wife and the other a mistress, could be right about all of this? I wondered silently. Is it possible that the drama of our personal lives is so quiescent as to be mere ceremony, whose staging is predictable, knowable? In the hands of those who love us are we mere actors mouthing their lines? Magpie, I thought, my friend, a brother to me, who am I, who are they, to decide these things for you?

Near defeat in the face of the firm resolve of these two women, almost resigned, with folded hands on the table, I looked out the window of the café and saw the lines of HUD houses, row upon row, the design of government bureaucrats painted upon the surface of this long-grassed prairie and I remembered the disapproving look of the little boy who threw gravel at my car and I found the strength to try again.

"Would you drive into Chamberlain with me?" I asked.

She said nothing.

"If he is Indian as you say, whatever that means, and if he is back here to stay this time, and if he tells me that, himself, I'll let it go. But, Salina," I urged, "I must talk to him and ask him what he wants to do. You see that, don't you?"

"Yes," she said finally, "he has a right to know about this . . . but you'll see . . ."

Her heels clicked on the brief sidewalk in front of the café as we left, and she became agitated as she talked. "After all that trouble he got into during the protest at Custer when the courthouse was burned, he was in jail for a year. He's still on parole, and he will be on parole for another five years . . . and they didn't even prove anything against him! Five years! Can you believe that? People, these days, can commit murder and not get that kind of a sentence."

She stopped to light a cigarette before she opened the car door and got in.

As we drove out of "the Fort" toward town, she said, "Jeez, look at that," and she pointed with her cigarette to a huge golden eagle tearing the flesh from some carcass which lay in the ditch alongside the road.

I thought, As many times as I've been on this road in my lifetime, I've never seen an eagle here before. I've never seen one even near this place . . . *ma tuki* . . .

III

Elgie was standing on the corner near the F & M Bank as we drove down the main street of Chamberlain, and both Salina and I knew, without speaking, that this man, this good friend of Magpie's, would know of his whereabouts. We looked at him as we drove past, and he looked at us, neither giving any sign of recognition. But when we went to the end of the long street, made a U-turn, and came back and parked the car, Elgie came over and spoke: "I haven't seen you in a long time," he said as we shook hands.

"Where you been?" he asked as he settled himself in the back seat of the car, "New Mexico?"

"Yes."

"I seen the license plates on your car," he said, as if in explanation. There might have been more he wanted to say, but a police car moved slowly to the corner where we were parked and the patrolman looked at the three of us intently and we pretended not to notice.

I looked down at my fingernails, keeping my face turned away, and I thought, This is one of those towns that never changes. You can be away twenty minutes or twenty years and it's the same here. I remembered a letter that I had read years before, written by a former mayor of this town, revealing his attitude toward Indians. He was opposing the moving of the Agency, flooded out by the Fort Randall Power Project, to his town:

April 14, 1954

Dear U.S. Representative:

I herewith enclose a signed resolution by the city of Chamberlain and a certified copy of a resolution passed by the Board of County Commissioners of Brule County, So. Dak. The County Commissioners are not in session so I could not get a signed resolution by them. As I have advised you before, we have no intentions of making an Indian comfortable around here, especially an official. We have a few dollar diplomats that have been making a lot of noise and trying to get everyone that is possible to write you people in Washington that they wanted the Indians in here, but the fact is that 90 percent of the people are strongly opposed to it and will get much more so, if this thing comes in. Anybody who rents them any property will have to change his address and I wouldn't want the insurance on this building. We do not feel that this town should be ruined by a mess like this and we do not intend to take it laying down irregardless of what some officials in Washington may think.

H.V.M., Mayor

That same spring my uncle Narcisse, thirty-seven years old, affable, handsome, with a virtuous kind of arrogance that only Sioux uncles can claim, was found one Sunday morning in an isolated spot just outside of town with "fatal wounds" in his throat. This city's coroner and those investigating adjudged his death to be an "accident," a decision my relatives knew to be ludicrous and obscene. Indians killing and being killed did not warrant careful and ethical speculation, my relatives said bitterly.

The patrol car inched down the empty street, and I turned cautiously toward Elgie. Before I could speak, Salina said, "She's got some papers for Magpie. He has a chance to go to a writers' school in California."

Always tentative about letting you know what he was really thinking, Elgie said, "Yeah?"

But Salina wouldn't let him get away so noncommittally. "*Ozela,*" she scoffed. "You know he wouldn't go!"

"Well, you know," Elgie began, "one time when Magpie and me was hiding out after that Custer thing, we ended up on the Augustana College campus. We got some friends there. And he started talking about freedom, and I never forgot that, and then, after he went to the pen, it became his main topic of conversation . . . freedom. He wants to be free, and you can't be that, man, when they're watching you all the time. Man, that freak that's his parole officer is some mean watchdog."

"You think he might go for the scholarship?" I asked hopefully.

"I don't know. Maybe."

"Where is he?" I asked.

A truck passed, and we waited until it had rumbled on down the street. In the silence that followed no one spoke.

"I think it's good that you come," Elgie said at last, "because Magpie, he needs some relief from all this," he waved his hand, "this constant surveillance, constant checking up, constant association. In fact, that's what he always talks about: 'If I have to associate with *wasichus,*' he says, 'then I'm not free . . . there's no liberty in that for Indians.' You should talk to him now," Elgie went on earnestly, eyeing me carefully. "He's changed. He's for complete separation, segregation, total isolation from the *wasichus.*"

"Isn't that a bit too radical? Too unrealistic?" I asked.

"I don't know," he said, hostility rising in his voice, angry, perhaps, that I was being arbitrary and critical about an issue we both knew had no answer. "Damn if I know . . . is it?"

"Yeah," said Salina, encouraged by Elgie's response. "And just what do you think it would be like for him at that university in California?"

"But it's a chance for him to study, to write. He can find a kind of satisfying isolation in that, I think."

After a few moments, Elgie said, "Yeah, I think you're right." A long silence followed his conciliatory remark, a silence which I didn't want to break, since everything I said sounded too argumentative, authoritative.

We sat there, the three of us, and I was hoping that we were in some kind of friendly agreement. Pretty soon Elgie got out of the back seat and shut the door; he walked around to the driver's side and leaned his arms on the window.

"I'm going to walk over to the bridge," he said, "it's about three blocks down there. There's an old, white, two-story house on the left side just before you cross the bridge. Magpie's brother, he just got out of the Nebraska State Reformatory and he's staying there with his old lady and that's where Magpie is."

At last! Now I could really talk to him and let him make this decision for himself.

"There's things about this, though," Elgie said. "Magpie shouldn't be there, see, because it's a part of the condition of his parole that he stays away from friends and relatives and ex-cons and just about everybody. But jeez . . . this is his brother."

"Wait until just before sundown, and then come over," he directed. "Park your car at the service station just around the block from there and walk to the back entrance of the house and then you can talk to Magpie about all this."

"Thanks, Elgie" I said.

We shook hands, and he turned and walked down the street, stopping to light a cigarette, a casual window shopper.

IV

Later, in the quiet of the evening dusk, Salina and I listened to our own breathing and the echoes of our footsteps as we walked toward the two-story house by the bridge where Elgie said we could find Magpie. We could see the water of the Missouri River, choppy and dark, as it flowed in a southwesterly direction, and the wind rose from the water, suddenly strong and insistent.

The river's edge, I knew, was the site of what the Smithsonian Institution had called an "extensive" and "major" archaeological "find," as they had uncovered the remains of an old Indian village during the flooding process for the Oahe Dam. The "find" was only about a hundred yards from the house which was now Magpie's hiding place. The remains of such a discovery, I thought, testify to the continuing presence of ancestors, but this thought would give me little comfort as the day's invidious, lamentable events wore on.

Salina was talking, telling me about Magpie's return to Crow Creek after months in exile and how his relatives went to Velma's house and welcomed him home. "They came to hear him sing with his brothers," she told me, "and they sat in chairs around the room and laughed and sang with him."

One old uncle who had taught Magpie the songs felt that he was better than ever, that his voice had a wider range, was deeper, more resonant, yet high-pitched, sharp and keen to the senses at the proper moments. The old uncle, said Salina, had accepted the fact of Magpie's journey and his return home with the knowledge that there must always be a time in the lives of young men when they move outward and away, and in the lucky times, they return.

As she told me about the two great-uncles' plans for the honor dance, I could see that this return of Magpie's was a time of expectation and gratitude. Much later, I could see that this attitude of expectancy, a habit of all honorable men who believe that social bonds are deep and dutiful, was cruelly unrealistic. For these old uncles, and for Magpie, there should be no expectation.

Several cars were parked in the yard of the old house as we approached, and Salina, keeping her voice low, said, "Maybe they're having a party . . . that's all we need."

But the silence which hung about the place filled me with apprehension, and when we walked in the back door, which hung open, we saw people standing in the kitchen, and I asked carefully, "What's wrong?"

Nobody spoke, but Elgie came over, his bloodshot eyes filled with sorrow and misery. He stood in front of us for a moment and then gestured for us to go into the living room. The room was filled with people sitting in silence, and, finally, Elgie said quietly, "They shot him. They picked him up for breaking the conditions of his parole and they put him in jail and . . . they shot him."

"But, why?" I cried. "How could this have happened?"

"They said they thought he was resisting and that they were afraid of him."

"Afraid?" I asked incredulously, ". . . but . . . but . . . was he armed?"

"No," said Elgie, seated now, his arms resting on his knees, his head down. "No, he wasn't armed."

I held the poems tightly in my hands, pressing my thumbs, first one and then the other, against the smoothness of the cardboard folder.

Elizabeth Cook-Lynn (Crow Creek Dakota)
The Power of Horses

The mother and daughter steadied themselves, feet planted squarely, fore-heads glistening with perspiration, and each grasped a handle of the large, steaming kettle.

"Ready?"

"Un-huh."

"Take it, then," the mother said. "Careful." Together they lifted the tub of boiled beets from the flame of the burners on the gas stove and set it heavily on the table across the room. The girl let the towel which had served as a makeshift pot holder drop to the floor as the heat penetrated to the skin, and she slapped her hand against the coolness of the smooth, painted wall and then against her thigh, feeling the roughness of the heavy jeans with tingling fingers. To stop the tingling, she cupped her fingers to her mouth and blew on them, then raised her apologetic eyes and looked at her mother. Without speaking, as if that was the end of it, she sank into the chrome chair and picked up the towel and began wiping the sweat from her face. The sun came relentlessly through the thin gauze curtains, and the hot wind blew gently across the stove, almost extinguishing the gas flames of the burners, making the blue edges turn yellow and then orange and then white. The towel was damp now and stained purple from the beets, and the girl leaned back in the chair and laid the towel across her face, feeling her own hot breath around her nose and mouth.

"Your hands get used to it, Marleen," the mother said, not even glanc-ing at the girl, nor at her own rough, brown hands, "just have to keep at it," saying this not so much from believing it as from the need to stop this feel-ing of futility in the girl and the silence between them. The mother gingerly grasped the bleached stems of several beets and dropped them into a pan of cold water, rolling one and then another of the beets like balls in her hands, pushing the purple-black skins this way and that, quickly, deftly re-moving the peel and stem and tossing the shiny vegetable into another con-tainer. Finishing one, she hurriedly picked up another, as if by hurrying she could forestall the girl's rebellion.

The woman's arms, like her hands, were large, powerful. But, despite the years of heavy work, her sloping shoulders and smooth, long neck were part of a tender femininity only recently showing small signs of decline and age. The dark stains on her dark face might have seemed like age spots or a disfigurement on someone else, but on the woman they spread delicately across her cheeks, forehead, and neck like a sweep of darkened cloud, mak-ing her somehow vulnerable and defenseless.

"Your hands'll get used to it, Marleen," she repeated, again attempting to keep the girl's unwillingness in check, and an avenue to reasonable tol-erance and cooperation open.

The brief rest with the towel on her face seemed to diminish the girl's weariness, and for an instant more she sat silently, breathing peacefully into the damp towel. As the girl drew the towel across her face and away from her eyes, something like fear began to rise in her, and she peered out the window, where she saw her father standing with a white man she had never seen before. Her father was looking straight ahead down the draw where the horses stood near the corral. They always want something from him, she thought, and as she watched the white man put a cigarette in his mouth and turn sideways out of the wind, the flame of his lighter licking toward his bony profile, she wondered what it was this time. She watched the man's quick mannerisms, and she saw that he began to talk earnestly and gesture toward his green pickup truck, which was parked close to the barbed-wire fence encircling the house and yard.

The girl was startled out of her musings at the sound of her mother's "*yu-u-u-u,*" the softly uttered indication of disapproval, insistent, always compelling a change in the girl's behavior. And she turned quickly to get started with her share of the hot beets, handling them inexpertly, but peeling their hot skins away as best she could. After a few minutes, during which the women worked in silence, only the monotonous hiss of the burning gas flame between them, the girl, surprised, thought: her sounds of disapproval aren't because I'm wasting time; instead, they are made because she is afraid my father and the white man will see me watching them. Spontaneously, defensively, she said, "They didn't see me." She looked into the brown-stained face but saw only her mother's careful pretense of being preoccupied with the beets, as she picked up a small knife to begin slicing them. All last winter, every time I came home, I spied on him for you, thought the girl, even riding my horse over to Chekpa's through the snow to see if he was there. And when I came back and told you that he was, you acted as if you hadn't heard anything, like now. So this is not the beginning of the story, nor is it the part of the story that matters, probably, thought the girl, and she started to recognize a long, long history of acrimony between her parents, thinking, in hindsight, that it would have been better if she had stayed at Stephen Mission. But then, she remembered her last talk with Brother Otto at the Mission as he sat before her, one leg languidly draped over the other, his collar open, showing his sparse red chest hairs, his watery, pale eyes looking at her searchingly, and she knew that it wasn't better to have stayed there.

He had sat quivering with sympathy as she had tried to tell him that to go home was to be used by her mother against her father. I rode over to Chekpa's, she told him, hating herself that she was letting out the symptoms of her childish grief, despising him for his delicate white skin, his rapt gaze, the vicariousness of his measly existence, and *Até* was there, cutting wood for the eldest of the Tatiopa women, Rosalie, the one he was supposed to marry, you know, but, instead, he married my mother. My mother sent me there, and when I rode into the yard and saw him, he stood in uncertainty, humiliated in the eyes of Chekpa, his old friend, as well as all of those in the Tatiopa family. Worse yet, she knew, humiliated in the eyes of his nine-year-old daughter.

In her memory of that awful moment, she didn't speak, nor did her father, and so she had ridden out of the yard as abruptly as she had come and home at a dead gallop, standing easily in the stirrups, her face turned toward her right shoulder out of the wind, watching the slush fly behind the horse's hooves. She didn't cut across Archie's field as she usually did, but took the long way, riding as hard as she could alongside the road. When she got to the gate she reined in, dismounted, and led her horse through the gate and then, slowly, down the sloping hill to the tack shed. She stood for a long time with her head against the wide, smooth leather of the stirrup shaft, her eyes closed tightly and the smell of wet horse hair in her nostrils. Much later she had recited the event as fully as she could bear to the mission school priest, much as she had been taught to recite the events of her sinful life: I have taken the Lord's name in vain, I have taken the Lord's name in vain, I have tak . . .

Damn beets, damn all these damn beets, the girl thought, and she turned away from the table back to the stove, where she stirred the second, smaller, pot of sliced beets, and she looked out through the gauze curtains to see if her father and the white man were still there. They had just run the horses into the corral from the small fenced pasture where they usually grazed when they were brought down to the place.

"He must be getting ready to sell them, is he?" she asked her mother.

Her mother said nothing.

"How come? I didn't know he was going to sell," the girl said slowly, noticing that her horse, two quarter-horse brood mares, and a half-Shetland black-and-white gelding she had always called "*Shōta* had been cut out of the herd and were standing at the far corner of the pasture, grazing. The heat shimmered above the long buffalo grass, and the girl's thoughts drifted, and, vaguely, she heard her mother say, "You'd better spoon those sliced ones into these hot jars, Marleen," and then, almost to herself, her mother started talking as if in recognition of what the girl did not know about the factual and philosophical sources from which present life emerges. "I used to have land, myself, daughter," she began, "and on it my grandfather had many horses. What happened to it was that some white men from Washington came and took it away from me when my grandfather died because, they said, they were going to breed game birds there; geese, I think.

"There was no one to do anything about it," she continued, "there was only this old woman who was a mother to me, and she really didn't know what to do, who to see, or how to prevent this from happening.

"Among the horses there on my land was a pair of brood mares just like those two out there." She pointed with her chin to the two bays at the end of the pasture. And, looking at the black-and-white horse called *Shōta,* she said, "And there was also another strange, mysterious horse, *su'ka wak a',*" *i-e-e-e,* she had used the word for "mysterious dog" in the Dakotah language. And the mother and daughter stood looking out the window at the *shōta* horse beside the bays, watching them pick their way through the shimmering heat and through the tall grass, slowly, unhurried. The beets were forgotten, momentarily, and the aging woman remembered the magic of those horses and especially the one that resembled the *shōta* horse, thinking about that time, that primordial time when an old couple of the tribe received a gift horse from a little bird, and the horse produced many offspring for the old man and woman, and the people were never poor after that. Her grandfather, old Bowed Head, the man with many horses, had told her that story often during her childhood when he wished to speak of those days when all creatures knew one another . . . and it was a reassuring thing. "I wish this tribe to be strong and good," the mysterious horse had told the old man, "and so I keep giving my offspring every year and the tribe will have many horses and this good thing will be among you always."

"They were really fast horses," said the mother, musing still, filling in the texture of her imagination and memory, "they were known throughout our country for their speed, and the old man allowed worthy men in the tribe to use them in war or to go on a hunt with them. It is an old story," the woman concluded, as though the story were finished, as though commenting upon its history made everything comprehensible.

As the girl watched her mother's extraordinary vitality, which rose during the telling of these events, she also noted the abruptness with which the story seemed to end and the kind of formidable reserve and closure which fell upon the dark, stained features as the older woman turned again to the stove.

"What happened to the horses?" the girl wanted to know. "Did someone steal them? Did they die?"

After a long silence her mother said, "Yes, I suppose so," and the silence again deepened between them as they fell to filling hot jars with sliced beets and sealing hot lids upon them, wiping and stroking them meticulously and setting them one by one on a dim pantry shelf.

The girl's frustration was gone now, and she seemed mindless of the heat, her own physical discomfort, and the miserableness of the small, squalid kitchen where she and her mother moved quietly about, informed now with the wonder of the past, the awesomeness of the imagination.

The sun moved west and the kitchen fell into shadow, the wind died down, and the mother and daughter finished their tedious task and carried the large tub of hot water out through the entryway a few feet from the door and emptied its contents upon the ground. The girl watched the red beet juice stain the dry, parched earth in which there was no resistance, and she stepped away from the redness of the water, which gushed like strokes of a painter's brush, suddenly black and ominous, as it sank into the ground. She looked up to see the white man's green pickup truck disappear over the rise, the dust billowing behind the heavy wheels, settling gently in the heat.

The nameless fear struck at her again and she felt a knot being drawn tightly inside her and she looked anxiously toward the corral. Nothing around her seemed to be moving, the air suddenly still, the sweat standing out in beads on her face and her hands, oddly, moist and cold. As she ran toward the corral, she saw her mother out of the corner of her eye, still grasping one handle of the boiler tub, strangely composed, her head and shoulders radiant in the sun.

At the corral, moments later, she saw her father's nearly lifeless form lying facedown in the dirt, his long gray hair spread out like a fan above him, pitifully untidy for a man who ordinarily took meticulous care with his appearance. He had his blue cotton scarf which he used as a handkerchief clutched tightly in his right hand, and he was moaning softly.

The odor of whiskey on his breath was strong as she helped him turn over and sit up, and in that instant the silent presence of the past lay monumentally between them, so that he did not look at her nor did he speak. In that instant she dimly perceived her own innocence and was filled with regret that she would never know those times to which *Até* would return, if he could, again and again. She watched as he walked unsteadily toward the house, rumpled and drunk, a man of grave dignity made comic and sad and helpless by circumstances which his daughter could only regard with wonderment.

Keyapi: Late one night, when the old man had tied the horses near his lodge, someone crept through the draw and made ready to steal them; it was even said that they wanted to kill the wonderful horses. The mysterious gift horse called to the sleeping old man and told him that an evil lurked nearby. And he told the old man that since such a threat as this had come upon them and all the people of the tribe, the power of the horses would be diminished, and no more colts would be born and the people would have to go back to their miserable ways.

As her father made his way to the house, walking stiffly past her mother, who pretended to be scrubbing the black residue from the boiler, the girl turned and walked quickly away from the corral in the opposite direction.

I must look: she thought, into the distance, and as she lifted her eyes and squinted into the evening light, she saw the Fort George road across the river, beyond the bend in the river, so far away that it would take most of the day for anyone to get there from where she walked. I must look: at the ground in front of me where my grandmothers made paths to the ti(n)psina beds and carried home with them long braided strands over their shoulders. I must look: she thought, into the past for the horse that speaks to humans.

She took long strides and walked into the deepening dusk. She walked for a long time before returning to the darkened house, where she crept into her bed and lay listening to the summer's night insect sounds, thinking apocalyptic thoughts in regard to what her mother's horse story might have to do with the day's events.

She awoke with a start, her father shaking her shoulder. "You must ride with me today, daughter, before the horse buyer comes back," he said. "I wish to take the horses way out to the far side of the north pasture. I am ready to go, so please hurry."

The girl dressed quickly, and just as dawn was breaking, she and her father, each leading two horses, with the others following, set out over the prairie hills. These were the hills, she knew, to which the people had come when the Uprising was finished and the U.S. Cavalry fell to arguing with missionaries and settlers about the "Indian problem." These were the hills, dark blue in this morning light, which she knew as repositories of sacred worlds unknown to all but its most ancient tenants.

When they reached the ridge above Dry Creek, the girl and her father stopped and let the horses go their way, wildly. The *shōta* horse led them down the steep prairie hills and into the dry creek bed and, one by one, the horses of the herd disappeared into the stand of heavy cottonwood trees which lined the ravine.

She stood beside her father and watched them go. "Why were you going to sell them?" she asked abruptly.

"There are too many," he replied, "and the grass is short this summer. It's been too hot," he said, wiping his face with the blue handkerchief, and he repeated, "The grass is short this summer."

With that, they mounted their horses and rode home together.

Louise Erdrich (Anishinaabe)

The Red Convertible

Lyman Lamartine

I was the first one to drive a convertible on my reservation. And of course it was red, a red Olds. I owned that car along with my brother Henry Junior. We owned it together until his boots filled with water on a windy night and he bought out my share. Now Henry owns the whole car, and his younger brother Lyman (that's myself), Lyman walks everywhere he goes.

How did I earn enough money to buy my share in the first place? My one talent was I could always make money. I had a touch for it, unusual in a Chippewa. From the first I was different that way, and everyone recognized it. I was the only kid they let in the American Legion Hall to shine shoes, for example, and one Christmas I sold spiritual bouquets for the mission door to door. The nuns let me keep a percentage. Once I started, it seemed the more money I made the easier the money came. Everyone encouraged it. When I was fifteen I got a job washing dishes at the Joliet Café, and that was where my first big break happened.

It wasn't long before I was promoted to busing tables, and then the short-order cook quit and I was hired to take her place. No sooner than you know it I was managing the Joliet. The rest is history. I went on managing. I soon became part owner, and of course there was no stopping me then. It wasn't long before the whole thing was mine.

After I'd owned the Joliet for one year, it blew over in the worst tornado ever seen around here. The whole operation was smashed to bits. A total loss. The fryalator was up in a tree, the grill torn in half like it was paper. I was only sixteen. I had it all in my mother's name, and I lost it quick, but before I lost it I had every one of my relatives, and their relatives, to dinner, and I also bought that red Olds I mentioned, along with Henry.

The first time we saw it! I'll tell you when we first saw it. We had gotten a ride up to Winnipeg, and both of us had money. Don't ask me why, because we never mentioned a car or anything, we just had all our money. Mine was cash, a big bankroll from the Joliet's insurance. Henry had two checks—a week's extra pay for being laid off, and his regular check from the Jewel Bearing Plant.

We were walking down Portage anyway, seeing the sights, when we saw it. There it was, parked, large as life. Really as *if* it was alive. I thought of the word *repose,* because the car wasn't simply stopped, parked, or whatever. That car reposed, calm and gleaming, a FOR SALE sign in its left front window. Then, before we had thought it over at all, the car belonged to us and our pockets were empty. We had just enough money for gas back home.

We went places in that car, me and Henry. We took off driving all one whole summer. We started off toward the Little Knife River and Mandaree in Fort Berthold and then we found ourselves down in Wakpala somehow, and then suddenly we were over in Montana on the Rocky Boy, and yet the summer was not even half over. Some people hang on to details when they travel, but we didn't let them bother us and just lived our everyday lives here to there.

I do remember this one place with willows. I remember I laid under those trees and it was comfortable. So comfortable. The branches bent down all around me like a tent or a stable. And quiet, it was quiet, even though there was a powwow close enough so I could see it going on. The air was not too still, not too windy either. When the dust rises up and hangs in the air around the dancers like that, I feel good. Henry was asleep with his arms thrown wide. Later on, he woke up and we started driving again. We were somewhere in Montana, or maybe on the Blood Reserve—it could have been anywhere. Anyway it was where we met the girl.

All her hair was in buns around her ears, that's the first thing I noticed about her. She was posed alongside the road with her arm out, so we stopped. That girl was short, so short her lumber shirt looked comical on her, like a nightgown. She had jeans on and fancy moccasins and she carried a little suitcase.

"Hop on in," says Henry. So she climbs in between us.

"We'll take you home," I says. "Where do you live?"

"Chicken," she says.

"Where the hell's that?" I ask her.

"Alaska."

"Okay," says Henry, and we drive.

We got up there and never wanted to leave. The sun doesn't truly set there in summer, and the night is more a soft dusk. You might doze off, sometimes, but before you know it you're up again, like an animal in nature. You never feel like you have to sleep hard or put away the world. And things would grow up there. One day just dirt or moss, the next day flowers and long grass. The girl's name was Susy. Her family really took to us. They fed us and put us up. We had our own tent to live in by their house, and the kids would be in and out of there all day and night. They couldn't get over me and Henry being brothers, we looked so different. We told them we knew we had the same mother, anyway.

One night Susy came in to visit us. We sat around in the tent talking of this and that. The season was changing. It was getting darker by that time, and the cold was even getting just a little mean. I told her it was time for us to go. She stood up on a chair.

"You never seen my hair," Susy said.

That was true. She was standing on a chair, but still, when she unclipped her buns the hair reached all the way to the ground. Our eyes opened. You couldn't tell how much hair she had when it was rolled up so neatly. Then my brother Henry did something funny. He went up to the chair and said, "Jump on my shoulders." So she did that, and her hair reached down past his waist, and he started twirling, this way and that, so her hair was flung out from side to side.

"I always wondered what it was like to have long pretty hair," Henry says. Well we laughed. It was a funny sight, the way he did it. The next morning we got up and took leave of those people.

On to greener pastures, as they say. It was down through Spokane and across Idaho then Montana and very soon we were racing the weather right along under the Canadian border through Columbus, Des Lacs, and then we were in Bottineau County and soon home. We'd made most of the trip, that summer, without putting up the car hood at all. We got home just in time, it turned out, for the army to remember Henry had signed up to join it.

I don't wonder that the army was so glad to get my brother that they turned him into a Marine. He was built like a brick outhouse anyway. We liked to tease him that they really wanted him for his Indian nose. He had a nose big and sharp as a hatchet, like the nose on Red Tomahawk, the Indian who killed Sitting Bull, whose profile is on signs all along the North Dakota highways. Henry went off to training camp, came home once during Christmas, then the next thing you know we got an overseas letter from him. It was 1970, and he said he was stationed up in the northern hill country. Whereabouts I did not know. He wasn't such a hot letter writer, and only got off two before the enemy caught him. I could never keep it straight, which direction those good Vietnam soldiers were from.

I wrote him back several times, even though I didn't know if those letters would get through. I kept him informed all about the car. Most of the time I had it up on blocks in the yard or half taken apart, because that long trip did a hard job on it under the hood.

I always had good luck with numbers, and never worried about the draft myself. I never even had to think about what my number was. But Henry was never lucky in the same way as me. It was at least three years before Henry came home. By then I guess the whole war was solved in the government's mind, but for him it would keep on going. In those years I'd put his car into almost perfect shape. I always thought of it as his car while he was gone, even though when he left he said, "Now it's yours," and threw me his key.

"Thanks for the extra key," I'd said. "I'll put it up in your drawer just in case I need it." He laughed.

When he came home, though, Henry was very different, and I'll say this: the change was no good. You could hardly expect him to change for the better, I know. But he was quiet, so quiet, and never comfortable sitting still anywhere but always up and moving around. I thought back to times we'd sat still for whole afternoons, never moving a muscle, just shifting our weight along the ground, talking to whoever sat with us, watching things. He'd always had a joke, then, too, and now you couldn't get him to laugh, or when he did it was more the sound of a man choking, a sound that stopped up the throats of other people around him. They got to leaving him alone most of the time, and I didn't blame them. It was a fact: Henry was jumpy and mean.

I'd bought a color TV set for my mom and the rest of us while Henry was away. Money still came very easy. I was sorry I'd ever bought it though, because of Henry. I was also sorry I'd bought color, because with black-and-white the pictures seem older and farther away. But what are you going to do? He sat in front of it, watching it, and that was the only time he was completely still. But it was the kind of stillness that you see in a rabbit when it freezes and before it will bolt. He was not easy. He sat in his chair gripping the armrests with all his might, as if the chair itself was moving at a high speed and if he let go at all he would rocket forward and maybe crash right through the set.

Once I was in the room watching TV with Henry and I heard his teeth click at something. I looked over, and he'd bitten through his lip. Blood was going down his chin. I tell you right then I wanted to smash that tube to pieces. I went over to it but Henry must have known what I was up to. He rushed from his chair and shoved me out of the way, against the wall. I told myself he didn't know what he was doing.

My mom came in, turned the set off real quiet, and told us she had made something for supper. So we went and sat down. There was still blood going down Henry's chin, but he didn't notice it and no one said anything, even though every time he took a bite of his bread his blood fell onto it until he was eating his own blood mixed in with the food.

While Henry was not around we talked about what was going to happen to him. There were no Indian doctors on the reservation, and my mom couldn't come around to trusting the old man, Moses Pillager, because he courted her long ago and was jealous of her husbands. He might take revenge through her son. We were afraid that if we brought Henry to a regular hospital they would keep him.

"They don't fix them in those places," Mom said; "they just give them drugs."

"We wouldn't get him there in the first place," I agreed, "so let's just forget about it."

Then I thought about the car.

Henry had not even looked at the car since he'd gotten home, though like I said, it was in tip-top condition and ready to drive. I thought the car might bring the old Henry back somehow. So I bided my time and waited for my chance to interest him in the vehicle.

One night Henry was off somewhere. I took myself a hammer. I went out to that car and I did a number on its underside. Whacked it up. Bent the tail pipe double. Ripped the muffler loose. By the time I was done with the car it looked worse than any typical Indian car that has been driven all its life on reservation roads, which they always say are like government promises—full of holes. It just about hurt me, I'll tell you that! I threw dirt in the carburetor and I ripped all the electric tape off the seats. I made it look just as beat up as I could. Then I sat back and waited for Henry to find it.

Still, it took him over a month. That was all right, because it was just getting warm enough, not melting, but warm enough to work outside.

"Lyman," he says, walking in one day, "that red car looks like shit."

"Well it's old," I says. "You got to expect that."

"No way!" says Henry. "That car's a classic! But you went and ran the piss right out of it, Lyman, and you know it don't deserve that. I kept that car in A-one shape. You don't remember. You're too young. But when I left, that car was running like a watch. Now I don't even know if I can get it to start again, let alone get it anywhere near its old condition."

"Well you try," I said, like I was getting mad, "but I say it's a piece of junk."

Then I walked out before he could realize I knew he'd strung together more than six words at once.

After that I thought he'd freeze himself to death working on that car. He was out there all day, and at night he rigged up a little lamp, ran a cord out the window, and had himself some light to see by while he worked. He was better than he had been before, but that's still not saying much. It was easier for him to do the things the rest of us did. He ate more slowly and didn't jump up and down during the meal to get this or that or look out the window. I put my hand in the back of the TV set, I admit, and fiddled around with it good, so that it was almost impossible now to get a clear picture. He didn't look at it very often anyway. He was always out with that car or going off to get parts for it. By the time it was really melting outside, he had it fixed.

I had been feeling down in the dumps about Henry around this time. We had always been together before. Henry and Lyman. But he was such a loner now that I didn't know how to take it. So I jumped at the chance one day when Henry seemed friendly. It's not that he smiled or anything. He just said, "Let's take that old shitbox for a spin." Just the way he said it made me think he could be coming around.

We went out to the car. It was spring. The sun was shining very bright. My only sister, Bonita, who was just eleven years old, came out and made us stand together for a picture. Henry leaned his elbow on the red car's windshield, and he took his other arm and put it over my shoulder, very carefully, as though it was heavy for him to lift and he didn't want to bring the weight down all at once.

"Smile," Bonita said, and he did.

That picture. I never look at it anymore. A few months ago, I don't know why, I got his picture out and tacked it on the wall. I felt good about Henry at the time, close to him. I felt good having his picture on the wall, until one night when I was looking at television. I was a little drunk and stoned. I looked up at the wall and Henry was staring at me. I don't know what it was, but his smile had changed, or maybe it was gone. All I know is I couldn't stay in the same room with that picture. I was shaking. I got up, closed the door, and went into the kitchen. A little later my friend Ray came over and we both went back into that room. We put the picture in a brown bag, folded the bag over and over tightly, then put it way back in a closet.

I still see that picture now, as if it tugs at me, whenever I pass that closet door. The picture is very clear in my mind. It was so sunny that day Henry had to squint against the glare. Or maybe the camera Bonita held flashed like a mirror, blinding him, before she snapped the picture. My face is right out in the sun, big and round. But he might have drawn back, because the shadows on his face are deep as holes. There are two shadows curved like little hooks around the ends of his smile, as if to frame it and try to keep it there—that one, first smile that looked like it might have hurt his face. He has his field jacket on and the worn-in clothes he'd come back in and kept wearing ever since. After Bonita took the picture, she went into the house and we got into the car. There was a full cooler in the trunk. We started off, east, toward Pembina and the Red River because Henry said he wanted to see the high water.

The trip over there was beautiful. When everything starts changing, drying up, clearing off, you feel like your whole life is starting. Henry felt it, too. The top was down and the car hummed like a top. He'd really put it back in shape, even the tape on the seats was very carefully put down and glued back in layers. It's not that he smiled again or even joked, but his face looked to me as if it was clear, more peaceful. It looked as though he wasn't thinking of anything in particular except the bare fields and windbreaks and houses we were passing.

The river was high and full of winter trash when we got there. The sun was still out, but it was colder by the river. There were still little clumps of dirty snow here and there on the banks. The water hadn't gone over the banks yet, but it would, you could tell. It was just at its limit, hard swollen, glossy like an old gray scar. We made ourselves a fire, and we sat down and watched the current go. As I watched it I felt something squeezing inside me and tightening and trying to let go all at the same time. I knew I was not just feeling it myself; I knew I was feeling what Henry was going through at that moment. Except that I couldn't stand it, the closing and opening. I jumped to my feet. I took Henry by the shoulders and I started shaking him. "Wake up," I says, "wake up, wake up, wake up!" I didn't know what had come over me. I sat down beside him again.

His face was totally white and hard. Then it broke, like stones break all of a sudden when water boils up inside them.

"I know it," he says. "I know it. I can't help it. It's no use."

We start talking. He said he knew what I'd done with the car. It was obvious it had been whacked out of shape and not just neglected. He said he wanted to give the car to me for good now, it was no use. He said he'd fixed it just to give it back and I should take it.

"No way, " I says. "I don't want it."

"That's okay," he says, "you take it."

"I don't want it, though," I says back to him, and then to emphasize, just to emphasize, you understand, I touch his shoulder. He slaps my hand off.

"Take that car," he says.

"No," I say. "Make me," I say, and then he grabs my jacket and rips the arm loose. That jacket is a class act, suede with tags and zippers. I push Henry backwards, off the log. He jumps up and bowls me over. We go down in a clinch and come up swinging hard, for all we're worth, with our fists. He socks my jaw so hard I feel like it swings loose. Then I'm at his rib cage and land a good one under his chin so his head snaps back. He's dazzled. He looks at me and I look at him and then his eyes are full of tears and blood and at first I think he's crying. But no, he's laughing. "Ha! Ha!" he says. "Ha! Ha! Take good care of it."

"Okay," I says. "Okay, no problem. Ha! Ha!"

I can't help it, and I start laughing, too. My face feels fat and strange, and after a while I get a beer from the cooler in the trunk, and when I hand it to Henry he takes his shirt and wipes my germs off. "Hoof-and-mouth disease," he says. For some reason this cracks me up, and so we're really laughing for a while, and then we drink all the rest of the beers one by one and throw them in the river and see how far, how fast, the current takes them before they fill up and sink.

"You want to go on back?" I ask after a while. "Maybe we could snag a couple nice Kashpaw girls."

He says nothing. But I can tell his mood is turning again.

"They're all crazy, the girls up here, every damn one of them."

"You're crazy too," I say, to jolly him up. "Crazy Lamartine boys!"

He looks as though he will take this wrong at first. His face twists, then clears, and he jumps up on his feet. "That's right!" he says. "Crazier 'n hell. Crazy Indians!"

I think it's the old Henry again. He throws off his jacket and starts springing his legs up from the knees like a fancy dancer. He's down doing something between a grass dance and a bunny hop, no kind of dance I ever saw before, but neither has anyone else on all this green growing earth. He's wild. He wants to pitch whoopee! He's up and at me and all over. All this time I'm laughing so hard, so hard my belly is getting tied up in a knot.

"Got to cool me off!" he shouts all of a sudden. Then he runs over to the river and jumps in.

There's boards and other things in the current. It's so high. No sound comes from the river after the splash he makes, so I run right over. I look around. It's getting dark. I see he's halfway across the water already, and I know he didn't swim there but the current took him. It's far. I hear his voice, though, very clearly across it.

"My boots are filling," he says.

He says this in a normal voice, like he just noticed and he doesn't know what to think of it. Then he's gone. A branch comes by. Another branch. And I go in.

By the time I get out of the river, off the snag I pulled myself onto, the sun is down. I walk back to the car, turn on the high beams, and drive it up the bank. I put it in first gear and then I take my foot off the clutch. I get out, close the door, and watch it plow softly into the water. The headlights reach in as they go down, searching, still lighted even after the water swirls over the back end. I wait. The wires short out. It is all finally dark. And then there is only the water, the sound of it going and running and going and running and running.

Eric Gansworth (Onondaga)
Unfinished Business

I couldn't imagine the fury of my father's moves, the way he drops me to this couch with one kick to the belly, slapping over and over. I manage to block some hits and dodge others, slapping back when I can get a hand up. At one point I get close enough and I bite, sinking into the soft flesh above his collar bone, my canines, ivory thorns, driving deep, nearly meeting below the surface, in the muscle, but he pulls up, and I release him. For the brief second he stands off balance in front of me, I get my foot up and shove him further out.

"Oh, you wanna kick? I'll show you kicking. You'll never dance again, bitch," he shouts, his fingers closing tight around his palms, and he starts in again, punching my thighs down like he is kneading fry bread dough and then stepping on my feet with one heavy work boot, shifting his weight to keep me pinned, kicking my shins with his other foot. I can barely see his face in the dark, but I know he's smiling. He's not going to stop until I'm dead. I use the only weapon I have left.

Blocking his vicious hands with my left arm, driving it up—he keeps going for my face, maybe hoping to slap his features clear off its surface—I simply reach out my other hand and encircle his balls with my fingers. He doesn't even realize my goal until I have his entire small bundle gathered up tightly in my fingers, just before I squeeze a defiant fist. Passing his crumpling form, I run for the bushes and hide. Though I can see myself in the rearview mirror of his Lincoln, my eyes gleaming in the full moonlight, he doesn't seem to see me, shouting in all directions before finally leaving.

I get ahold of Minnie Crews, one of my old friends who will probably retire from dancing now that Bert's gone, from a pay phone across the road, and she rushes right over and takes me to the emergency room. She doesn't ask any questions as we ride to the hospital, and I catch glimpses in her rearview mirror of the new bruises that look conveniently like shadows this night.

Behind the curtain and wearing only this nasty paper gown, after they take pictures and x-rays, I slide the nickel from the pocket of my jeans, which lay crumpled on the floor. I flip the nickel and it lands heads: Indian side up, so I tell the emergency room doctor I fell down a flight of stairs. Not one of my more original stories, but it will have to do; I am in no shape to be creating convincing epics on the spot.

Bert gave me this, my first slice of personal medicine, an Indian-head nickel, when I first moved into her house, four years ago. I gratefully took the coin. The old Indians used to keep four items of personal medicine with them at all times. I saw that in a movie, once. At eighteen, I didn't know too many old Indians on the reservation, and the ones I did talk with were the ones I sat with at the Indian table on bingo night down at the Lewiston Number Two Fire Hall. And I knew Bert, too, of course.

That day four years ago, she reached into her apron pocket and handed me the nickel—her dark and stiff fingers enclosing mine—and told me to keep it at all times, that I'd know who I was with that. "You listen," she said, "when white people mention that kind of nickel, they always call it a buffalo nickel. But you won't call it that."

I looked at the coin. This was the first time I'd ever actually seen one up close, and I was astounded at how much the coin Indian looked like Lee Howard from down on Dog Street. I had always assumed everyone called him "Nickel Man" because he smoked a lot of weed. At one of the bigger powwows in Ottawa the first summer I danced with Bert's group, I had seen a T-shirt with the nickel's image on it; in addition to the nickel itself, there were blurry faded images of its path following its arc across the shirt. The caption read: "IT'S ABOUT TIME FOR THE INDIAN TO COME UP HEADS AGAIN."

I didn't buy that T-shirt, because I had little more than that nickel in my pocket, but I started using the coin to help me make decisions shortly after Bert had given it to me. Once, I read a friend's college book for a course in casino gambling, only to be disappointed to discover it was really a math course on statistics and probabilities, but I read the book, anyway. Once I start something, I can not stop.

The probabilities are fifty/fifty on the coin, and having just moved from my mother's smothering Christian household to Bert's communal traditional one, I was comfortable with those odds. If my coin came up heads, I went the traditional way, and if it landed buffalo side up—the bullshit side, I often called it—I went the white way. So four years and hundreds of flips later, amidst the whirring and whining of emergency room technology and misery, I watch the coin winking in the air, trying to will it against the Indian head. I want so bad to tell them one of the reservation's chiefs beat me because I am his illegitimate daughter.

But it comes up with Lee Howard's stoic face looking sternly into the past. So, I'll take these next few months to heal before I decide what to do with my home.

Even three days later, I ache pretty bad. I've been able to fake normalcy for the most part, wearing my long-sleeve spandex at work, and telling no one but Two-Step what happened, and to be honest, I wouldn't have even done that, but we spend so much time together, there was no avoiding it. My movements are stiff like a robot's as I jam storm window plastic into the couch's cracks, sliding the translucent material across the cushioned surfaces. I heard once that doing this, sealing things in their own little protective sacs, is one way to safeguard furniture that's going to sit unused for long months, furniture that will not know the intimacies of life, of lost dimes and quarters—lost heads and tails—the potential of what those coins could do, the knowledge of what they'd done in the past.

I'm behind. It has taken me these three days just to recover from my father's rage, and as I heal, I know my flipping nickel was right, that I have to respect the traditions, even if those in the power positions are not doing right by the people. Sure as hell not doing right by me, anyway. I can still hardly believe the things he did, but all I have to do is look in a mirror. My body is the map of my father's insanity. Dark purple traces him here, paintings of his steel-toed boot prints and his wicked fingers.

Sweeping the milky sheets across the cushions, I feel as if I am burying Bert's furniture, her belongings, her whole lifestyle, as well as burying the lovely old woman, herself. I sit on the (storm-window covering) and cry for a time. The plastic sobs petite squeaking noises in sympathy as I rock and shake on the couch. I had to spend the entire morning cleaning up the light bulb massacre before I could move on to preparing the trailer for a winter of closure, every shard of glass and ceramic a reminder of what I am up against, just waiting for me to slip so they can work their way in again. I wish I had some Valium or something to get through this week, anything to heal the glaring wound of my present life.

"Here, Trish. I found some more in the back bedroom closet," Two-Step says. Two-Step Harmony, Big Red's twelve year old son, is a born dancer, even in walking, showing the potential his name suggests. He carries a few more rolls of the window-cocooning material bundled in his arms. I lift myself from the couch as he floats into the room on some breeze I can not feel. "Still hurting, huh? I'm telling you, Trish. I was down at the shop visiting Eddie, that night. You remember, my dad and Mason dumped me off at home, but I knew Eddie was covering for my dad and he came and picked me up to keep him company. I could prove Bud was the one that did it. I heard his voice. Why won't you?"

"Who's gonna believe someone named Fiction," I ask him. I shake my head and sit on the couch's arm, looking at the gallery mounted on the wall behind me. The photos are individual shots of Bert's entire group of dancers, captured in mid-performance—thirty years' worth. The earliest are black-and-whites, which over the years have transformed into orange-and-yellows, becoming as fragile and brittle as the dance-prop feathers Bert kept in her store room for new dancers, those who came without tradition of their own. She always said you only need to come with a hunger for tradition, and not just for corn soup and fry bread. This is a future Two-Step has before him, taking on the traditions, and I can't let him risk his future on me. If we lost the case, who knows what might happen to this boy and his father.

"Your picture was supposed to complete this wall. I guess it's still down at Prints Charming. I'll have to go through Bert's things and find the slip. They need the slip at that place."

"Yeah, that would be nice. A shot of my last competition."

"I thought I was the one named Fiction."

"You are. I'm done. It's just not the same. First my ma, now Bert. There's no reason to dance if they're not in the crowd."

"Well, what about your dad?"

"Yeah, I don't know. Maybe I'll change my mind, but I don't think so." He sits down and looks at the last empty spot on the living room wall. Bert just last week rearranged all of the pictures. At Grand River in August, Two-Step had taken First in Young Men's Smoke Dance. Even though his regalia wasn't the greatest, made up of some mismatched pieces, and some beadwork apparently created by a colorblind beader, he had shone through, anyway. The old woman, she had a sense for these things; she told me idly that day, "this time," as she hobbled closer to the main grounds. Bert, she just snapped that image of Two-Step—a resigned tourist preferring the lenses of her own eyes to the distance sites of her Minolta—but I could see the instant smile appear through Two-Step's feathers and movements. Bert knew, and as Two-Step walked away with the prize, she slid the little film canister into her oversize powwow bag.

One night last week, after Bert's bath, while watching the Wheel of Fortune, dancing with the rabbit ears for better reception, as we did almost every night, each trying to shout out the solution before the other, and scolding the clueless contestants for wasting their hard-earned money on vowels—or worse yet, ceramic Dalmatians—Bert, she promptly stood up and pushed the couch away from the wall, not even bothering to let me get off of it. I sincerely doubted this was some sudden bout of cleaning-mania, and jumped from the couch, myself, to see what she was up to; it seemed potentially more interesting than the fabulous Dining Room Showcase from which the cunning puzzlist was ecstatically making purchases. We'd lost the game to static and snow when Bert leapt up, anyway.

She carefully stacked the photos, leaning them upon one another in the proper order on the couch, a cast of forty-nine frozen Indian dominoes, laying spent on her cushions. They had rested on that wall for the five years I'd known Bert, in their seven neat rows of seven photos each. They hadn't always carried seven. Each time Bert received one of her camera messages and added another First Place winner, she had just tacked another nail up, dropping to a new row after seven, as if guided by some sort of photographic typewriter rules.

She pulled all of the nails, coaxing them out gently, harvesting them perfectly straight from the wall. Completing this task, she began renailing them in at seemingly random places. Her hand and mouth finally barren of nails, she picked up the top photo, the most recent, and hung it on the last nail pounded. She followed through and I realized the nails were placed so the photos would hang in concentric circles on the wall. The last photo hung—the first taken—was one of Big Red Harmony, who, in addition to working the late shift at Mason Rollins's Smoke Shop, set up a vendor's table on the powwow circuit when he could swing it. Bert had placed his fragile picture in the very center of the photo rings.

She stepped back, ignoring the staticky ghosts of Pat and Vanna entirely. The outermost circle was empty at the top. It looked like a photographic horseshoe, keeping all the others within its circle of luck. She sat back down and waited for Jeopardy to start.

The day before she died, in the middle of her bath—where she usually made bold statements, I'm guessing to fend off the humiliation of needing someone to help her bathe—she dropped a casual explanation of her new design. She explained, without all that mysticism bullshit so many believe should accompany all Indian acts, that Two-Step's picture would complete the circle started by his father. She would officially have taught two generations of dancers.

"Maybe I'll get up to seven, I got a few more walls," Bert later said, watching TV after her bath. She swept her arm broad to encompass her entire living room. That was the last comment I ever heard Bert utter, regarding dancing.

I look at Two-Step as he walks back down the hall, and wonder what sorts of things are in store for this thin dark boy of twelve with pipe-cleaner arms and long, dense hair. Even though Bert joked about it, every generation of Indians was supposed to look out for the next seven generations, but I have trouble enough worrying about the *next* generation. I wonder who will teach them to dance.

Two-Step drops the rolls of plastic into a chair that vaguely matched the couch, a type that must have been almost generically produced when avocado green was a popular color. You know, we could almost be siblings, though we're not even related by blood. He's a feminine looking sort, sweet, almost, and since this often needs disproving, his wiry limbs are tight, flexible small muscles, rather than the underdeveloped twigs others often misperceived.

He turns and smiles gently, in an apparent effort to comfort me from across the room, and when I smile back, to let him know I appreciate it, he leaves the room, to continue exploring the other areas of Bert's trailer. As happens, my grief eventually passes in wispy clouds and I am able to continue working on the furniture.

The long fingers I inherited from my father have been particularly useful, today. I reach my fingers into the cracks of the padded piece, pressing against the hard coiled springs hidden below its surface. I brush against something metal, flat and circular, a disc. I pull it up and, realizing what it is, I laugh a little, kind of disappointed. The video game token gleams dull in the fall light. It's worn down to its original copper color, the fake gold brassy finish long rubbed off by countless HIGH SCORES and GAME OVERS.

I am just going to throw it out, but I notice something funny about the token. On one side, the twin fish of Pisces chase one another and stare blandly at me—their cold common metal eyes unblinking—which is not unusual iconography for video tokens, but the flipside holds the image of two women, swimming in air, imitating the positions of the Pisceans. The women are naked. I don't know for sure, but I would guess they don't distribute this sort of token at the mall, where the average age of the average customer is fifteen.

I still almost throw it out, but my clan is Eel, and I cannot discard a token meant for me to find, and I feel certain it was. Fish, eel—they're members of the same family, right? I slide it into my front jeans pocket, where I keep my nickel. I itch with the vague notion that I should hang onto these barenaked ladies, at least for a little while. Somehow, Bert meant for me to find it. Otherwise, why would she have willed me the trailer and put me through the horror of what my father did in the name of "The Nation"? Pulling it from my pocket, I flip the token a few times. I'm good at this. I can flip a coin with my right hand and guide it to land on a fingertip on my left. Women swimming, fish swimming, gracefully over and over through the air. I snap the token down on the kitchen table and turn to finish covering the couch in its filmy shroud.

In the steaming whistle of my tea water, Two-Step reappears from the back hallway, his arms filled with three large economy size coffee cans and several Land O' Lakes margarine tubs he found on the floor of Bert's closet. His eyes peek out over the top, so as to not trip on the other possessions that litter the floor.

We shuffle the stuff to the kitchen table, the stove clicking a backbeat for us as the surface coils cool. I have electricity in the trailer for four more days beyond this one, it sings to me. I'll move the trailer when they cut me off. Four more days, can they spare it? My father, though he still fails to acknowledge his seminal role even after his unique christening, passed on the word during our pleasant visit that the Chiefs Council is allowing me a week to get my things in order.

Two-Step sits and we open the lids on the coffee cans. From the first tin, I pull one item, then rummage around inside the can. He frowns as he looks in his tin, and arches his neck to see what mine holds. I wrap a towel around the table's edge as a banking and spill the contents of my can onto the table. He follows immediately with his and the other. The last can empty, the table is covered with over a hundred pill canisters from the reservation clinic.

"So . . . holy shit! I didn't know Bert was that sick." Mason Rollins leans in the trailer door. I saw him coming up the driveway, slid the token into my palm, and flipped: women—exposure, I would tell him the truth, straight out; fish—I'd be slippery, elusive, fish—I'd tell a story. As he stands in the frame, the sun cuts him a long and dark shadow across the living room carpet.

"Oh, yes, barely navigating. We were all amazed she lived this long, not that *you'd* know." Fish. Two-Step gives a slight nod to my wink, almost as if a breeze has somehow caught just his head. "Big Red found her at the table, you know. Her eyes were all bugged right out of her head from years of all that . . ." I glance down at the table, "Digi . . . digitalis." Two-Step shakes his head, slowly with the tragedy my story calls for.

"Jeez. Red told me she looked liked she had just fallen asleep."

"Didn't want to make you feel guilty," I say simply.

"About what?" he asks, frowning.

"Don't know. You got something to feel guilty about?" I have no idea, but usually when I ask that question, regardless of whom I'm asking, I know the answer is yes.

"No . . . so, uh," he says, looking around at the ghostly living room furniture, "you're really gonna do it? You're gonna let the Chiefs pull that shit on you?"

"No choice," I say, clearing another place at the table, and then reaching for another mug from the cupboard. He's going to be here a while, so I might as well invite him to sit down. That's what Bert would have done. He was one of her dancers years ago, even before the powwow circuit took off, when competitions occurred at the National Picnic, county and state fairs, regional field days and the annual border-crossing celebration.

Mason is startled when he notices the framed photo of himself in full regalia on the wall, I guess not knowing a part of him still lived with Bert. He takes the picture down, asking me if he can keep it. It leaves a void in the wall that I don't like, a missing tooth in a perfect smile, but I have no right to keep it from him. The picture he cradles is at least eight years old—when he made the leap from the dancing circles to the ghost circles left under bar room beer glasses.

"Thanks." He sets the photo down on the table and continues. "What do you mean, 'no choice'; I found choices," he says, pointing with his chin out the eastern kitchen window. Though I know what I will find there, I look anyways: the small, bright pink oversized outhouse he has turned, like lightning, into a successful small business.

"Well, maybe you're a little skinny bit smarter than me," I say, hating to admit that, and I turn from his smoke shack, where the lights are shining brightly, even in daylight, despite the Chiefs' order to cut the electricity.

"I don't even have any land, legally, and even if I had what's supposed to be mine, it isn't anywheres near white land, anyway. So I couldn't do what you're doing. Besides, it's what the Nation wants."

"Well, I think you've got options," he replies, and then is silent. What does he know?

"This didn't change *your* life, any. *You're* not 'exploring options,'" I say.

He nods and says he has to go. But before he leaves, he takes the picture and puts it back on the wall, but not in the place he had taken it from. He nods and heads to the door. "By the way, it's kind of dark in here. Don't you have any lamps?" he asks, leaning in the door again.

"The magnetic forces in electricity are slowly pushing people to insanity and causing cancers worldwide. It was in the Sunday supplement."

"Oh," he says and leaves.

"It's no wonder no one believes anything you say, making up shit like that. Why do you do that?" Two-Step says, after Mason is out of hearing range.

"Look. It's right here," I counter, reaching for a magazine featuring power lines and the letters EMF written in a scary design across the top. He flips through the magazine to find the article, as I get up and put the picture back where it belongs. Mason walks up the driveway to the Big House, probably going to see his cousin Eddie. He still seems so positive he's going to score with me, and I don't like that confidence. He's cute, and certainly has a steady income, but something just isn't right about him. I can't place what it is except that it is the one thing really right with Big Red. I don't know what that is, but I place myself back at the moment of Bert's death again for just a moment, to feel Big Red's embrace again. I come back to reality, where there are other, more immediate concerns, anyway— among them, finding some place to stay for the next few months.

Maybe Big Red needs a live-in baby-sitter. The thought of living with him makes me smile at my cleverness for having found a way to keep thinking about him for just a few more minutes, though I'm not sure I'd ever really feel comfortable treating Two-Step as some kind of son. Shit, I've barely been able to take care of myself. If I moved in, it would only be to allow Red to hit the Southwestern powwow circuit in the winter months, anyway, bring in more cash for Two-Step and him, and besides, Two-Step spends most of his time with me, as it is. Red just might go for it. And maybe he'd want to take me with him, but then what would be the reason? Shit, my storytelling skills are slipping. This one is bad, all around. All kinds of gaping holes. Red's struggling like most of the rest of us, out here. If he's working midnights at Mason's shop, things must be pretty bad. That heavy grief and panic seep into me again, a dark mold growing around my insides, weighing me down.

One of the pill bottles from the table idly fills my hand. The neat label reads: "Wampum Purple Shell." Sorting through them randomly, I pick out medicine bottles of "Squash Blossom," "Cornsilk," "Ivory Bone," "Crow Feather," and "Sky Blue Glass."

Setting the others down, I twist the child-proof cap off the "Sky Blue Glass" easily. I am an adult now. I spill a few of the hollow glass pills out into my hand. My palm disappears into the pure blue wide open atmosphere filling in its furrows, my life line, my love line, my death line. I funnel my hand and pour the sky back into its stale medicinal bottle.

"Your gram still beading?" Two-Step scrunches up his face in trying to conjure an answer, but this clearly doesn't help and he smiles, shrugging his shoulders, reveling in his lack of knowledge. Ruby Pem, the late Bev Harmony's mother, is one of the better known beaders from the reservation and was an early proponent of the treaty allowing us to sell beaded souvenirs to tourists at the parks, including Prospect Park, the biggest tourist attraction in the area—the falls, itself. No one else can now do any vending at the park, unless contractually connected with the state parks department.

Now, I don't have any intention of becoming a beadwork vendor; I don't even know how to bead. In fact, I do not know a thing about beadwork. While Bert worked on her beading, the TV was a more interesting draw. She offered to show me time and time again over the years, but my bored eyes always wandered away after a few minutes. Her hands moved too quickly for me to follow, anyway. But none of this means the beads will be entirely useless to me now.

Setting the bottle down, I reach into my pocket for the nickel. My two options are calling me here. I could sell the beads to Ruby, or to any number of people if Ruby doesn't want them. There are plenty enough bottles here to give me a little survival cash. The beads belonged to a dead woman; they hold strong power—the power of the past. They'll be valued by any good beader from the reservation. Reaching the nickel, my fingers hit both coins—more than two options.

The coins slide easily onto my thumbs to flip. I've never tried a double flip before. As I cast them into the air, I realize my probabilities are shot. We watch my future spin out of control in the afternoon sun. Traditional ways. Fabrication. Outside ways. Truth. Lee Howard, fish, buffalo, and naked women blur, become one, flying and falling, as gravity pulls them in.

I bring my hands up as the two coins pass one another before me, clapping their paths shut prematurely. The coins, sliding back into my pocket, will mingle forever. The surest bet is one in which you have a stake in all aspects. Like that, I am suddenly complete. It is not a matter of probabilities; it's a matter of balance. In the four coin sides, I have my four medicines. Learning to balance their influences will be the trick.

"I knew you couldn't do a double flip," Two-Step says. "Hey, are we gonna do any more, tonight?" My future has just been decided, and all of the enshrouding we spent the afternoon involved in doesn't matter, anymore. "I'm gonna go see if I can catch a ride at least to Snakeline and Dog Street from someone at the shop. You want I should ask my dad if Gram still beads? He might know." Big Red should know. He still takes his mother-in-law's work and other pieces on consignment to powwows from almost anyone else who had goods to sell. After a minute, I shake my head. If I need Ruby, I'll have to go see her in person, anyway. "If you wanna take it to court, I'm here," he says.

I nod. Two-Step ducks out the door and heads up to the Big House as I flick the fluorescent ring on over the table—the only light that survived my father's tirade—and open one of the larger margarine tubs with a label marked UNFINISHED BUSINESS on its side. As I suspected, the tub contains a partially completed piece of beadwork. It is a gauntlet.

Its black velvet background traces my touches, afterimages of the place I try to connect with Bert. My fingertips ride rough over the raised, three dimensional leaves and roses making up the design. Strangely, no thorns exist here. Maybe that was what hadn't been completed. A needle and thread protrude from the lower end of the beaded stem.

Bert would have wanted all of her business affairs completed. Slipping the needle back through the work, I begin a slow healing dance with the gauntlet, unraveling and reconstructing, watching and feeling the beads and the weave. As the night grows long, I stubbornly make the war glove's designs vanish and reappear, learning in confidence its secrets, its web of supports, its strengths, its weaknesses, following its ghosts, becoming more fluid with every row. I can feel the repetitious movements of Bert's dance instruction as they permeate the troupe of hollow glass globes. I absorb the gauntlet, row by row, into my long fingers, warmly replacing the aches and bruises.

I stop for a short time to grab some food, but even while cooking, I memorize patterns I see in the work. Outside the kitchen window, the moon blooms and withers, while Mason's lights remain, beacons of things to come. I do not sleep—there will be time for that later—but I do pause briefly to rip the shrouds of plastic from the furniture and for the moment, smile, sitting on the resurrected couch.

At one point—it occurs to me that it must be past midnight—I look out. Big Red's truck is out behind the smoke shack and then I glance into the living room, where a teenage Red balances perfectly still, his left leg arched high in the air while his right arm arced fiercely from behind, Thunder Dance, in the center of a small Indian universe. He's still carrying on that warrior tradition, providing for the future, working the midnight shift at the smoke shop for his boy, and still as good looking as when he was eighteen, better looking, actually. Life has worn some nice creases into his face, like the comfort of clothes you have worn for years into perfection.

I put the gauntlet down and head for the back bedroom. There, I find Bert's various purses and rummage through them, finally finding what I'm looking for. The Prints Charming receipt was in Bert's powwow bag, where I should have looked first, if I'd really thought about it. I slide the tag onto the nail at the photo horseshoe's top where, tomorrow, I make myself promise, Two-Step's picture will complete the circle in the place Bert meant for him. This done, I return to my work at the table.

I have four days to pull off a future and preserve the past. Bert tried to insure I would carry on, passing on the trailer, the beads, the pictures, and everything else. She would not have expected her things to be wrapped in cold storage. The two coins sit comfortably in my jeans pocket, polishing one another—Lee Howard caressed by the naked women, and maybe even smiling for the first time ever, warming his cold metal cheeks and showing his silvery teeth. Tradition can not work without truth. Before the four days are up, I am betting my father will know this. The courts aren't my only option for truth.

I take up a needle as my own for the first time and look at the beads. I can see Bert's gauntlet in my mind, somehow knowing how to complete it, adding my own touches, adding myself. I select two of the amber bottles and set them close beside me. "Ivory Bone" will come a little later, for my thorns, and bring serious weight, but I need to begin with something to carry me through. The gauntlet rose sits dark and obscure nestled in its black velvet garden. It needs some sunlight, needs to be exposed in the open air, to dance in the freedom of breezes. I crack the lid of the sky and jab my needle in. Piercing myself a line of it, I begin to rise.

Diane Glancy (Cherokee)

Aunt Parnetta's Electric Blisters

Some stories can be told only in winter.
This is not one of them
because the fridge is for Parnetta
where it's always winter.

Hey chekta! All this and now the refrigerator broke. Uncle Filo scratched the long gray hairs that hung in a tattered braid on his back. All that foot stomping and fancy dancing. Old warriors still at it.

"But when did it help?" Aunt Parnetta asked. The fridge ran all through the cold winter when she could have set the milk and eggs in the snow. The fish and meat from the last hunt. The fridge had walked through the spring when she had her quilt and beading money. Now her penny jar was empty, and it was hot, and the glossy white box broke. The coffin! If Grandpa died, they could put him in it with his war ax and tomahawk. His old dog even. But how would she get a new fridge?

The repairman said he couldn't repair it. Whu chutah! Filo loaded his rifle and sent a bullet right through it. Well, he said, a man had to take revenge. Had to stand against civilization. He watched the summer sky for change as though the stars were white leaves across the hill. Would the stars fall? Would Filo have to rake them when cool weather came again? Filo coughed and scratched his shirt pocket as though something crawled deep within his breastbone. His heart maybe, if he ever found it.

Aunt Parnetta stood at the sink, soaking the sheets before she washed them.

"Dern't nothin' we dude ever work?" Parnetta asked, poking the sheets with her stick.

"We bought that ferge back twenty yars," Filo told her. "And it nerked since then."

"Weld, dernd," she answered. "Could have goned longer til the frost cobered us. Culb ha' set the milk ertside. But nowd. It weren't werk that far."

"Nope," Filo commented. "It weren't."

Parnetta looked at her beadwork. Her hands flopped at her sides. She couldn't have it done for a long time. She looked at the white patent-leathery box. Big enough for the both of them. For the cow if it died.

"Set it out in the backyard with the last one we had."

They drove to Tahlequah that afternoon. Filo's truck squirting dust and pinging rocks. They parked in front of the hardware store on Muskogee Street. The regiments of stoves, fridges, washers, dryers, stood like white soldiers. The Yellow Hair Custer was there to command them. Little Big Horn. Whu chutah! The prices! Three hundred crackers.

"Some mord than thad," Filo surmised. His flannel shirt-collar tucked under itself. His braid sideways like a rattler on his back.

"Filo, I dern't think we shulb decide terday."

"No," the immediate answer stummed from his mouth like a roach from under the baseboard in the kitchen.

"We're just lookin'."

"Of course," said Custer.

They walked to the door, leaving the stoves, washers, dryers, the televisions all blaring together, and the fridges lined up for battle.

Filo lifted his hand from the rattled truck.

"Surrender," Parnetta said. "Izend thad the way id always iz?"

The truck spurted and spattered and shook Filo and Aunt Parnetta before Filo got it backed into the street. The forward gear didn't buck as much as the backward.

When they got home, Filo took the back off the fridge and looked at the motor. It could move a load of hay up the road if it had wheels. Could freeze half the fish in the pond. The minute coils, the twisting intestines of the fridge like the hog he butchered last winter, also with a bullet hole in its head.

"Nothin' we dude nerks." Parnetta watched him from the kitchen window. "Everythin' against uz," she grumbled to herself.

Filo got his war feather from the shed, put it in his crooked braid. He stomped his feet, hooted. Filo, the medicine man, transcended to the spirit world for the refrigerator. He shook each kink and bolt. The spirit of cold itself. He whooped and warred in the yard for nearly half an hour.

"Not with a bullet hole in it." Parnetta shook her head and wiped the sweat from her face.

He got his wrench and hack saw, the ax and hammer. It was dead now for sure. Parnetta knew it at the sink. It was the thing that would be buried in the backyard. "Like most of us libed," Aunt Parnetta talked to herself. "Filled with our own workings, not doint what we shulb."

Parnetta hung the sheets in the yard, white and square as the fridge itself.

The new refrigerator came in a delivery truck. It stood in the kitchen. Bought on time at a bargain. Cheapest in the store. Filo made sure of it. The interest over five years would be as much as the fridge. Aunt Parnetta tried to explain it to him. The men set the fridge where Parnetta instructed them. They adjusted and leveled the little hog feet. They gave Parnetta the packet of information, the guarantee. Then drove off in victory. The new smell of the gleaming white inside as though cleansed by cedar from the Keetowah fire.

Aunt Parnetta had Filo take her to the grocery store on the old road to Tahlequah. She loaded the cart with milk and butter. Frozen waffles. Orange juice. Anything that had to be kept cool. The fridge made noise, she thought, she would get used to it. But in the night, she heard the fridge. It seemed to fill her dreams. She had trouble going to sleep, even on the clean white sheets, and she had trouble staying asleep. The fridge was like a giant hog in the kitchen, rutting and snorting all night. She got up once and unplugged it, waking early the next morn to plug it in again before the milk and eggs got warm.

"That ferge bother yeu, Filo?" she asked.

"Nord."

Aunt Parnetta peeled her potatoes outside. She mended Filos's shirts under the shade tree. She didn't soak anything in the kitchen sink anymore, not even the sheets or Filo's socks. There were things she just had to endure, she grumped. That's the way it was.

When the grandchildren visited, she had them run in the kitchen for whatever she needed. They picnicked on the old watermelon table in the backyard. She put up the old teepee for them to sleep in.

"Late in the summer fer that?" Filo quizzed her.

"Nert. It waz nert to get homesick for the summer that's leabing us like the childurn." She gratified him with her keen sense. Parnetta could think up anything for what she wanted to do.

Several nights Filo returned to their bed, with its geese-in-flight-over-the-swamp pattern quilt, but Aunt Parnetta stayed in the teepee under the stars.

"We bined muried thurdy yars. Git in the house," Filo said one night under the white leaves of the stars.

"I can't sleep 'cause of that wild hog in the kitchen," Aunt Parnetta said. "I tald yeu that."

"Hey chekta!" Filo answered her. "Why didn't yeu teld me so I knowd whad yeu said?" Filo covered the white box of the fridge with the geese quilt and an old Indian blanket he got from the shed. "Werd yeu stayed out thar all winder?"

"'Til the beast we got in thar dies."

"Hawly gizard," Filo spurted. "Thard be anuther twendy yars!"

Aunt Parnetta was comforted by the bedroom that night. Old Filo's snore after he made his snorting love to her. The gray-and-blue-striped wallpaper with its watermarks. The stovepipe curling up to the wall like a hog tail. The bureau dresser with a little doily and her hairbrush. Pictures by their grandchildren. A turquoise coyote and a ghostly figure the boy told her was Running Wind.

She fell into a light sleep where the white stars blew down from the sky, flapping like the white sheets on the line. She nudged Filo to get his rake. He turned sharply against her. Parnetta woke and sat on the edge of the bed.

"Yeu wand me to cuber the furge wid something else?" Filo asked from his sleep.

"No," Aunt Parnetta answered him. "Nod unless id be the polar ice cap."

Now it was an old trip to Minnesota when she was a girl. Parnetta saw herself in a plaid shirt and braids. Had her hair been that dark? Now it was streaked with gray. Everything was like a child's drawing. Exaggerated. The way dreams were sometimes. A sun in the left corner of the picture. The trail of chimney smoke from the narrow house. It was cold. So cold that everything creaked. She heard cars running late into the night. Early mornings. Steam growled out of the exhaust. The pane of window glass in the front door had been somewhere else. Old lettering showed up in the frost. Bones remembered their aches in the cold. Teeth, their hurt. The way Parnetta remembered every bad thing that happened. She dwelled on it.

That cold place was shriveled to the small upright rectangle in her chest, holding the fish her grandson caught in the river. That's where the cold place was. Right inside her heart. No longer pumping like the blinker lights she saw in town. She was the Minnesota winter she remembered as a child. The electricity it took to keep her cold! The energy. The moon over her like a ceiling light. Stars were holes where the rain came in. The dripping buckets. All of them like Parnetta. The *hurrrrrrrrr* of the fridge. Off. On. All night. That white box. Wild boar! Think of it. She didn't always know why she was disgruntled. She just was. She saw herself as the fridge. A frozen fish stiff as a brick. The Great Spirit had her pegged. Could she find her heart, maybe, if she looked somewhere in her chest?

Hurrrrrrr. Rat-tat-at-rat. *Hurrr.* The fridge came on again, and startled, she woke and teetered slightly on the edge of the bed while it growled.

But she was a stranger in this world. An Indian in a white man's land. "Even the ferge's whate," Parnetta told the Great Spirit.

"Wasn't everybody a stranger and pilgrim?" The Great Spirit seemed to speak to her, or it was her own thoughts wandering in her head from her dreams.

"No," Parnetta insisted. Some people were at home on this earth, moving with ease. She would ask the Great Spirit more about it later. When he finally yanked the life out of her like the pin in a grenade.

Suddenly Aunt Parnetta realized that she was always moaning like the fridge. Maybe she irritated the Great Spirit like the white box irritated her. Did she sound that way to anyone else? Was that the Spirit's revenge? She was stuck with the cheapest box in the store. In fact, in her fears, wasn't it a white boar which would tear into the room and eat her soon as she got good and asleep?

Hadn't she seen the worst in things? Didn't she weigh herself in the winter with her coat on? Sometimes wrapped in the blanket also?

"Filo?" She turned to him. But he was out cold. Farther away than Minnesota.

"No. Just think about it, Parnetta," her thoughts seemed to say. The Spirit had blessed her life. But inside the white refrigerator of herself—inside the coils, an ice river surged. A glacier mowed its way across a continent. Everything frozen for eons. In need of a Keetowah fire. Heat. The warmth of the Great Spirit. Filo was only a spark. He could not warm her. Even though he tried.

Maybe the Great Spirit had done her a favor. Hope like white sparks of stars glistened in her head. The electric blisters. *Temporary!* She could shut up. She belonged to the Spirit. He had just unplugged her a minute. Took his rifle right through her head.

The leaves growled and spewed white sparks in the sky. It was a volcano from the moon. Erupting in the heavens. Sending down its white sparks like the pinwheels Filo used to nail on trees. It was the bright sparks of the Keetowah fire, the holy bonfire from which smaller fires burned, spreading the purification of the Great Spirit into each house. Into each hard, old pine-cone heart.

Paula Gunn Allen (Laguna Pueblo, Sioux)

Deer Woman

Two young men were out snagging one afternoon. They rode around in their pickup, their Ind'in Cadillac, cruising up this road and down that one through steamy green countryside, stopping by friends' places here and there to lift a few beers. The day was sultry and searing as summer days in Oklahoma get, hot as a sweat lodge.

Long after dark they stopped at a tavern twenty or thirty miles outside of Anadarko, and joined some skins gathered around several tables. After the muggy heat outside, the slowly turning fan inside felt cool. When they'd been there awhile, one of the men at their table asked them if they were headed to the stomp dance. "Sure," they said, though truth to tell, they hadn't known there was a stomp dance that night in the area. The three headed out to the pickup.

They drove for some distance along narrow country roads, turning occasionally at unmarked crossings, bumping across cattle guards, until at length they saw the light of the bonfire, several unshaded lights hanging from small huts that ringed the danceground, and headlights from a couple of parking cars.

They pulled into a spot in the midst of a new Winnebago, a Dodge van, two Toyotas, and a small herd of more battered models, and made their way to the danceground. The dance was going strong, and the sound of turtle shell and aluminum can rattles and singing, mixed with occasional laughter and bits of talk, reached their ears. "All right!" Ray, the taller and heavier of the two exclaimed, slapping his buddy's raised hand in glee. "Gnarly!" his pal Jackie responded, and they grinned at each other in the unsteady light. Slapping the man who'd ridden along with them on the back, the taller one said, "Man, let's go find us some snags!"

They hung out all night, occasionally starting a conversation with one good-looking woman or another, but though the new brother who had accompanied them soon disappeared with a long-legged beauty named Lurine, the two anxious friends didn't score. They were not the sort to feel disheartened, though. They kept up their spirits, dancing well and singing even better. They didn't really care so much about snagging as it gave them something to focus on while they filled the day and night with interesting activity. They were among their own, and they were satisfied with their lives and themselves.

Toward morning, though, Ray spotted two strikingly beautiful young women stepping onto the danceground. Their long hair flowed like black rivers down their backs. They were dressed out in traditional clothes, and something about them—something elusive—made Ray shiver with a feeling almost like recognition, and at the same time, like dread. "Who are they?" he asked his friend, but Jackie shrugged silently. Ray could see his eyes shining for a moment as the fire near them flared suddenly.

At the same moment, they both saw the young women looking at them out of the corners of their eyes as they danced modestly and almost gravely past. Jackie nudged Ray and let out a long, slow sigh. "All right," he said in a low, almost reverent voice. "All right!"

When the dance was ended, the young women made their way to where the two youths were standing, "Hey, dude," one of them said. "My friend and I need a ride to Anadarko, and they told us you were coming from there." As she said that she gestured with her chin over her left shoulder toward a vaguely visible group standing across the danceground.

"What's your friend's name?" Ray countered.

"Linda," the other woman said. "Hers is Junella."

"My friend's name's Jackie," Ray said, grinning. "When do you want to take off?"

"Whenever," Junella answered. She held his eyes with hers. "Where are you parked?"

They made their way to the pickup and got in. It was a tight fit, but nobody seemed to mind. Ray drove, backing the pickup carefully to thread among the haphazardly parked vehicles that had surrounded theirs while they were at the dance. As he did, he glanced down for a second, and thought he saw the feet of both women as deer hooves. Man, he thought. I gotta lay off the weed. He didn't remember he'd quit smoking it months before, and hadn't had a beer since they'd left the tavern hours before. The women tucked their feet under their bags, and in the darkness he didn't see them anymore. Besides, he had more soothing things on his mind.

They drove companionably for some time, joking around, telling a bit about themselves, their tastes in music, where they'd gone to school, when they'd graduated. Linda kept fiddling with the dial, reaching across Junella to get to the knob. Her taste seemed to run to hard-core country and western or what Ray privately thought of as "space" music.

She and Linda occasionally lapsed into what seemed like a private conversation, or joke; Ray couldn't be sure which. Then, as though remembering themselves, they'd laugh and engage the men in conversation again.

After they'd traveled for an hour or so, Linda suddenly pointed to a road that intersected the one they were on. "Take a left," she said, and Ray complied. He didn't even think about it, or protest that they were on the road to Anadarko already. A few hundred yards further, she said "Take a right." Again he complied, putting the brake on suddenly as he went into the turn, spilling Junella hard against him. He finished shifting quickly and put his arm around her. She leaned into him, saying nothing, and put her hand on his thigh.

The road they had turned onto soon became gravel, and by the time they'd gone less than a quarter of a mile, turned into hard-packed dirt. Ray could smell water, nearby. He saw some trees standing low on the horizon and realized it was coming light.

"Let's go to the water," Linda said. "Junella and I are kind of traditional, and we try to wash in fresh running water every morning."

"Yeah," Junella murmured. "We were raised by our mother's grandmother, and the old lady was real strict about some things. She always made sure we prayed to Long Man every day. Hope it's okay."

Jackie and Ray climbed out of the truck, the women following. They made their way through the thickest of scrub oak and bushes and clambered down the short bank to the stream, the men leading the way. They stopped at the edge of the water, but the young women stepped right in, though still dressed in their dance clothes. They bent and splashed water on their faces, speaking the old tongue softly as they did so. The men removed their tennis shoes and followed suit, removing their caps and tucking them in the hip pockets of their jeans.

After a suitable silence, Junella pointed to the opposite bank with her uplifted chin. "See that path," she asked the men. "I think it goes to our old house. Let's go up there and see."

"Yes," Linda said, "I thought it felt familiar around here. I bet it is our old place." When the women didn't move to cross the shallow river and go up the path, the men took the lead again. Ray briefly wondered at his untypical pliability, but banished the thought almost as it arose. He raised his head just as he reached the far bank and saw that the small trees and brush were backed by a stone bluff that rose steeply above them. As he tilted his head back to spot the top of the bluff, he had a flashing picture of the small round feet he'd thought he'd seen set against the floorboard of the truck. But as the image came into his mind, the sun rose brilliantly just over the bluff, and the thought faded as quickly as it had come, leaving him with a slightly dazed feeling and a tingling that climbed rapidly up his spine. He put on his cap.

Jackie led the way through the thicket, walking as rapidly as the low branches would allow, bending almost double in places. Ray followed him, and the women came after. Shortly, they emerged from the trees onto a rocky area that ran along the foot of the bluff like a narrow path. When he reached it, Jackie stopped and waited while the others caught up. "Do you still think this is the old homestead?" he quipped. The women laughed sharply, then fell into animated conversation in the old language. Neither Ray nor Jackie could talk it, so they stood waiting, admiring the beauty of the morning, feeling the cool dawn air on their cheeks and the water still making their jeans cling to their ankles. At least their feet were dry, and so were the tennies they'd replaced after leaving the river.

After a few animated exchanges, the women started up the path, the men following. "She says it's this way," Linda said over her shoulder. "It can't be far." They trudged along for what seemed a long time, following the line of the bluff that seemed to grow even higher. After a time Junella turned into a narrow break in the rock and began to trudge up its gradual slope, which soon became a steep rise.

"I bet we're not going to Grandma's house," Jackie said in quiet tones to his friend.

"I didn't know this bluff was even here," Ray replied.

"It's not much farther," Junella said cheerfully. "What's the matter? You dudes out of shape or something?"

"Well, I used to say I'd walk a mile for a camel," Jackie said wryly, "but I didn't say anything about snags!" He and Ray laughed, perhaps more heartily than the joke warranted.

"This is the only time I've heard of Little Red Riding Hood leading the wolves to Grandma's," Ray muttered.

"Yah," Linda responded brightly. "And wait'll you see what I'm carrying in my basket of goodies." Both women laughed, the men abashedly joining in.

"Here's the little creek I was looking for," Junella said suddenly. "Let's walk in it for a while." Ray looked at Jackie quizzically.

"I don't want to walk in that," Jackie said quickly. "I just got dry from the last dip." The women were already in the water walking upstream.

"Not to worry," Junella said. "It's not wet; it's the path to the old house."

"Yeah, right," Ray mumbled, stepping into the water with a sigh. Jackie followed him, falling silent. But as they stepped into what they thought was a fast-running stream of water their feet touched down on soft grass. "Hey!" Ray exclaimed. "What's happening?" He stopped abruptly and Jackie plowed into him.

"Watch it, man," the smaller man said. He brushed past Ray and made after the women who were disappearing around a sharp turn.

Ray stood rooted a moment, then hurried after him. "Wait up," he called. His voice echoed loudly against the cliff.

As Ray turned the corner he saw Linda reaching upward along the cliff where a tall rock slab leaned against it. She grasped the edge of the slab and pulled. To the men's astonishment it swung open, for all the world like an ordinary door. The women stepped through.

Ray and Jackie regarded each other for long moments. Finally, Ray shrugged and Jackie gestured with his outspread arm at the opening in the cliff. They followed the women inside.

Within, they were greeted with an astonishing scene. Scores of people, perhaps upward of two hundred, stood or walked about a green land. Houses stood scattered in the near distance, and smoke arose from a few chimneys. There were tables spread under some large trees, sycamore or elm, Ray thought, and upon them, food in large quantities and tantalizing variety beckoned to the men. Suddenly aware they hadn't eaten since early the day before, they started forward. But before they'd taken more than a few steps Linda and Junella took their arms and led them away from the feast toward the doorway of one of the houses. There sat a man who seemed ancient to the young men. His age wasn't so much in his hair, though it hung in waist-long white strands.

It wasn't even so much in his skin, wrinkled and weathered though it was beneath the tall crowned hat he wore. It was just that he seemed to be age personified. He seemed to be older than the bluff, than the river, than even the sky.

Next to him lay two large mastiffs, their long, lean bodies relaxed, their heads raised, their eyes alert and full of intelligence. "So," the old one said to the women, "I see you've snagged two strong young men." He shot a half-amused glance at the young men's direction. "Go, get ready," he directed the women, and at his words they slipped into the house, closing the door softly behind themselves.

The young men stood uneasily beside the old man who, disregarding them completely, seemed lost in his own thoughts as he gazed steadily at some point directly before him.

After maybe half an hour had passed, the old man addressed the young men again. "It's a good thing you did," he mused, "following my nieces here. I wonder that you didn't give up or get lost along the way." He chuckled quietly as at a private joke. "Maybe you two are intelligent men." He turned his head suddenly and gave them an appraising look. Each of the young men shifted under that knowing gaze uncomfortably. From somewhere, the ground, the sky, they didn't feel sure, they heard thunder rumbling. "I have told everybody that they did well for themselves by bringing you here."

Seeing the surprised look on their faces, he smiled. "Yes, you didn't hear me, I know. I guess we talk different here than you're used to where you come from. Maybe you'll be here long enough to get used to it," he added. "That is, if you like my nieces well enough. We'll feed you soon," he said. "But first there are some games I want you to join in." He pointed with pursed lips in the direction of a low hill that rose just beyond the farthest dwelling. Again the thunder rumbled, louder than before.

A moment later the women appeared. Their long, flowing hair was gone, and their heads shone in the soft light that filled the area, allowing distant features to recede into its haze. The women wore soft clothing that completely covered their bodies, even their hands and feet. It seemed to be of a bright, gleaming cloth that reflected the light at the same intensity as their bald heads. Their dark eyes seemed huge and luminous against skin that somehow gave off a soft radiance. Seeing them, both men were nearly overcome with fear. They have no hair at all, Ray thought. Where is this place? He glanced over at Jackie, whose face mirrored his own unease. Jackie shook his head almost imperceptibly, slowly moving it from side to side in a gesture that seemed mournful, and at the same time, oddly resigned.

Linda and Junella moved to the young men, each taking the hand of one and drawing him toward the central area nearby. In a daze Ray and Jackie allowed themselves to be led into the center of the area ringed by heavily laden tables, barely aware that the old man had risen from his place and with his dogs was following behind them. They were joined by a number of other young men, all wearing caps like the ones Ray and Jackie wore. Two of the men carried bats, several wore gloves, and one was tossing a baseball in the air as he walked. Slowly the throng made their way past the tables and came to an open area where Jackie and Ray saw familiar shapes. They were bases, and the field that the soft light revealed to them was a baseball diamond.

The old man took his place behind first base, and one of the young men crouched before him as a loud peal of thunder crashed around them. "Play ball!" the old man shouted, and the men took up their places as the women retired to some benches at the edge of the field behind home plate where they sat.

The bewildered young men found their positions and the game was on. It was a hard-played game, lasting some time. At length, it reached a rowdy end, the team Jackie and Ray were on barely edging out the opposition in spite of a couple of questionable calls the old man made against them. Their victory was due in no small measure to a wiry young man's superb pitching. He'd pitched two no-hit innings and that had won them the game.

As they walked with the other players back toward the houses the old man came up to them. Slapping each on the back a couple of times, he told them he thought they were good players. "Maybe that means you'll be ready for tomorrow's games," he said, watching Jackie sharply. "They're not what you're used to, I imagine, but you'll do all right."

They reached the tables and were helped to several large portions of food by people whose faces never seemed to come quite into focus but whose goodwill seemed unquestionable. They ate amid much laughter and good-natured joshing, only belatedly realizing that neither Linda nor Junella was among the revelers. Ray made his way to Jackie, and asked him if he'd seen either woman. Replying in the negative, Jackie offered to go look around for them.

They agreed to make a quick search and rendezvous at the large tree near the old man's house. But after a fruitless hour or so Ray went to the front of the house and waited for his friend, who didn't come. At last, growing bored, he made his way back to the tables where a group had set up a drum and were singing lustily. A few of the younger people had formed a tight circle around the drummers and were slowly stepping around in it , their arms about each others' waists and shoulders. All right! Ray thought, cheered. "49's." He joined the circle between two women he hadn't seen before, who easily made way for him, and smoothly closed the circle about him again as each wrapped an arm around his waist. He forgot all about his friend.

When Ray awoke the sun was beating down on his head. He sat up, and realized he was lying near the river's edge, his legs in the thicket, his head and half-turned face unshielded from the sun. It was about a third of the way up in a clear sky. As he looked groggily around, he discovered Junella sitting quietly a few yards away on a large stone. "Hey," she said, smiling.

"How'd I get here?" Ray asked. He stood and stretched, surreptitiously feeling to see if everything worked. His memory seemed hesitant to return clearly, but he had half-formed impressions of a baseball game and eating and then the 49. He looked around. "Where's Jackie and, uh—"

"Linda?" Junella supplied as he paused.

"Yeah, Linda," he finished.

"Jackie is staying there," she told him calmly. She reached into her bag and brought out a man's wristwatch. "He said to give you this," she said, holding it out to him.

Ray felt suddenly dizzy. He swayed for a moment while strange images swept through him. Junella with no hair and that eerie light; the one that was some pale tan but had spots or a pattern of soft gray dots that sort of fuzzed out at the edges to blend into the tan. The old man.

He took a step in her direction. "Hey," he began. "What the hell's—" but broke off. The rock where she sat was empty. On the ground next to it lay Jackie's watch.

When Ray told me the story, about fifteen months afterward, he had heard that Jackie had showed up at his folks' place. They lived out in the country, a mile or so beyond one of the numerous small towns that dot the Oklahoma landscape. The woman who told him about Jackie's return, Jackie's cousin Ruth Ann, said he had come home with a strange woman who was a real fox. At thirteen, Ruth Ann had developed an eye for good looks and thought herself quite a judge of women's appearance. They hadn't stayed long, he'd heard. Mainly they packed up some of Jackie's things and visited with his family. Ray had been in Tulsa and hadn't heard Jackie was back until later. None of their friends had seen him either. There had been a child with them, he said, maybe two years old, Ruth Ann had thought, because she could walk by herself.

"You know," Ray had said thoughtfully, turning a Calistoga slowly between his big hands, a gesture that made him seem very young and somehow vulnerable, "one of my grandma's brothers, old Jess, used to talk about the little people a lot. He used to tell stories about strange things happening around the countryside here. I never paid much attention. You know how it is. I just thought he was putting me on, or maybe he was pining away for the old days. He said that Deer Woman would come to dances sometimes, and if you weren't careful she'd put her spell on you and take you inside the mountain to meet her uncle. He said her uncle was really Thunder, one of the old gods or supernaturals, whatever the traditionals call them."

He finished his drink in a couple of swallows and pushed away from the table we were sitting at. "I dunno," he said, and gave me a look that I still haven't forgotten, a look that was somehow wounded and yet with a kind of wild hope mixed in. "Maybe those old guys know something, eh?"

It was a few years before I saw him again. Then I ran into him unexpectedly in San Francisco a couple of years ago. We talked for a while, standing on the street near the Mission BART station. He started to leave when my curiosity got the better of my manners. I asked if he'd ever found out what happened to Jackie.

Well, he said that he'd heard that Jackie came home off and on, but the woman—probably Linda, though he wasn't sure—was never with him. Then he'd heard that someone had run into Jackie, or a guy they thought was him, up in Seattle. He'd gone alcoholic. Later, they'd heard he'd died. "But you know," Ray said, "the weird thing is that he'd evidently been telling someone all about that time inside the mountain, and that he'd married her, and about some other stuff, stuff I guess he wasn't supposed to tell." Another guy down on his luck, he guessed. "Remember how I was telling you about my crazy uncle, the one who used to tell about Deer Woman? Until I heard about Jackie, I'd forgotten that the old man used to say that the ones who stayed there were never supposed to talk about it. If they did, they died in short order."

After that, there didn't seem to be much more to say. Last time I saw Ray, he was heading down the steps to catch BART. He was on his way to a meeting and he was running late.

Gordon Henry (Anishinaabe)

Sleeping in Rain

I

Wake chants circle, overhead, like black crows watching her will stumble through weak moments. Like when she heard the carriage outside and went to the window with his name on her lips. Or when she looked over in the corner and saw him sleeping, with his mouth open, in the blue chair, next to the woodstove. She saw them, dissembled reflections, on the insides of her black glasses. Moments passed, etched, like the lines of age in the deep brown skin of her face. She's somewhere past ninety now; bent over, hollow boned, eyes almost filled. She lives in a room. A taken care of world. Clean sheets, clean blankets, wall-to-wall carpeting, a nightstand, and a roommate who, between good morning and good night, wanders away to card games in other rooms. Most of her day is spent in the chair, at the foot of the bed. Every now and then, she leaves and takes a walk down one of the many hallways of the complex. Every now and then, she goes to the window and looks out, as if something will be there.

II

Motion falls apart in silence, tumbling, as wind turns choreographed snow through tangents of streetlights. I am alone; to be picked up at the Saint Paul bus terminal. I fucked up. Dropped out. Good, it's not what I wanted. What is a quasar? The tissue of dreams. Fuck no, there are no secrets. There is nothing hard about astronomy, sociology, calculus, or Minnesota winters. Those are just reasons I used to leave. To go where? To go watch my hands become shadows over assembly lines?

A voice clicks on in the darkness. "We are now in Saint Paul and will be arriving at the Saint Paul terminal." Let me guess. In five minutes. "In ten minutes," the driver says. It figures.

III

My uncle's eyes have long since fallen from the grasp of stars. Now, they are like the backends of factories; vague indications of what goes on beneath the tracks of comb in his thick black hair. He was waiting when I arrived. Waiting, entranced in existence. A series of hypnotic silences, between words, that had to be spoken. Silences leading me to a beat-up car in a dark parking lot. I am too far away from him; too far away to be leaving for something further. I don't believe he doesn't like me. No, that's not quite what I'm getting at. It's something I saw when his shadow exploded into a face as he bent down, over the steering wheel, to light his cigarette.

IV

The cold white moon over houses too close together. Front windows, where shadows pass in front of blue lights of televisions. I am one of them now; a sound on wood stairs. There is a sanctuary of dreams waiting for my footsteps to fade.

V

The old woman dreams she is up north, on the reservation. It is autumn. Pine smoke hanging over the tops of houses, leaves sleepwalking in gray wind, skeletal trees scratching ghost gray sky. She is in the old black shack. At home. Stirring stew in the kitchen. The woodstove snaps in the next room. Out the window, he lifts the axe. He is young. She watches as it splits a log on the tree stump. He turns away and starts toward the house. He is old. He takes out his pipe and presses down tobacco. She goes to the door to meet him. She opens the door. She tries to touch him. He passes through her, like a cold shiver, and walks into a photograph on the wall.

VI

The mind bends over, in the light through a window, down and across the body of Jesus Christ as he stumbles through the sixth station of the cross. It comes to me sometimes, when I close my eyes. September sun in the old church. Smoke of sweet grass in stained glass light. Red, blue and yellow light. Prisms of thought behind every eye. Chippewa prayers stumbling through my ears. Old Ojibwa chants fading away in the walk to the cemetery. I look at the hole in the ground. I look at the casket beside it. I look at the hole, I look at the casket. At the hole, at the casket, at the hole, at the casket, at the hole.

The clock glows red across the room; a digital 2:37. My cousin lies in darkness. Another figure covered up in sleep.

VII

Dust swims in sunlight of an open door as dreams evaporate in the face of a clock.

VIII

"Get up, I said. It's raining. It's raining and you, lying there. Get up, old man, I said." It is my uncle talking. He found the old man where he lay in the rain. He had fallen asleep and fallen down from his seat on an old bench I tried to set on fire when I was ten or eleven. The next week they buried him in the coolness of Autumn coming. Weeks after, the old woman thought she heard his carriage outside the window of her new room in the city.

IX

Cities of snow melt, blurred in liquid between wiper blades. We are waiting for the light to change. My uncle is driving. The old woman is waiting. Not really for us. Not for us, but waiting. I will see her this morning. This afternoon I will be gone. Another bus. Home. The light changes in the corner of my eye turning away.

X

The room never moves for her. It is not like snow falling, like leaves falling, like stones through water. It is a window, a bed, and a chair.

XI

As the old woman touches me it is like air holding smoke. I am something else. Vestiges of prayer, gathered in a hollow church. Another kind of reflection. A reflection on the outsides of her black glasses. A reflection that cries when eyes leave it.

As the old woman touches me it is like air holding smoke. I am something else. Fleet anguish, like flying shadows. A moment vanishing. A moment taken, as I am being.

As the old woman touches me it is like air holding smoke. It spins it. It grasps it. It shapes it in a wish. After that there is a mist too fine to see.

Linda Hogan (Chickasaw)

Aunt Moon's Young Man

That autumn when the young man came to town, there was a deep blue sky. On their way to the fair, the wagons creaked into town. One buckboard, driven by cloudy white horses, carried a grunting pig inside its wooden slats. Another had cages of chickens. In the heat, the chickens did not flap their wings. They sounded tired and old, and their shoulders drooped like old men.

There was tension in the air. Those people who still believed in omens would turn to go home, I thought, white chicken feathers caught on the wire cages they brought, reminding us all that the cotton was poor that year and that very little of it would line the big trailers outside the gins.

A storm was brewing over the plains, and beneath its clouds a few people from the city drove dusty black motorcars through town, angling around the statue of General Pickens on Main Street. They refrained from honking at the wagons and the white, pink-eyed horses. The cars contained no animal life, just neatly folded stacks of quilts, jellies, and tomato relish, large yellow gourds, and pumpkins that looked like the round faces of children through half-closed windows.

"The biting flies aren't swarming today," my mother said. She had her hair done up in rollers. It was almost dry. She was leaning against the window frame, looking at the ink-blue trees outside. I could see Bess Evening's house through the glass, appearing to sit like a small, hand-built model upon my mother's shoulder. My mother was a dreamer, standing at the window with her green dress curved over her hip.

Her dress was hemmed slightly shorter on one side than on the other. I decided not to mention it. The way she leaned, with her abdomen tilted out, was her natural way of standing. She still had good legs, despite the spidery blue veins she said came from carrying the weight of us kids inside her for nine months each. She also blamed us for her few gray hairs.

She mumbled something about "the silence before the storm" as I joined her at the window.

She must have been looking at the young man for a long time, pretending to watch the sky. He was standing by the bushes and the cockscombs. There was a flour sack on the ground beside him. I thought at first it might be filled with something he brought for the fair, but the way his hat sat on it and a pair of black boots stood beside it, I could tell it held his clothing, and that he was passing through Pickens on his way to or from some city.

"It's mighty quiet for the first day of fair," my mother said. She sounded far away. Her eyes were on the young stranger. She unrolled a curler and checked a strand of hair.

We talked about the weather and the sky, but we both watched the young man. In the deep blue of sky his white shirt stood out like a light. The low hills were fire-gold and leaden.

One of my mother's hands was limp against her thigh. The other moved down from the rollers and touched the green cloth at her chest, playing with a flaw in the fabric.

"Maybe it was the tornado," I said about the stillness in the air. The tornado had passed through a few days ago, touching down here and there. It exploded my cousin's house trailer but it left his motorcycle, standing beside it, untouched. "Tornadoes have no sense of value," my mother had said. "They are always taking away the saints and leaving behind the devils."

The young man stood in that semi-slumped, half-straight manner of fullblood Indians. Our blood was mixed like Heinz 57, and I always thought of purebloods as better than us. While my mother eyed his plain moccasins, she patted her rolled hair as if to put it in order. I was counting the small brown flowers in the blistered wallpaper, the way I counted ceiling tiles in the new school, and counted each step when I walked.

I pictured Aunt Moon inside her house up on my mother's shoulder. I imagined her dark face above the yellow oilcloth, her hands reflecting the yellow as they separated dried plants. She would rise slowly, as I'd seen her do, take a good long time to brush out her hair, and braid it once again. She would pet her dog, Mister, with long slow strokes while she prepared herself for the fair.

My mother moved aside, leaving the house suspended in the middle of the window, where it rested on a mound of land. My mother followed my gaze. She always wanted to know what I was thinking or doing. "I wonder," she said, "why in tarnation Bess's father built that house up there. It gets all the heat and wind."

I stuck up for Aunt Moon. "She can see everything from there, the whole town and everything."

"Sure, and everything can see her. A wonder she doesn't have ghosts."

I wondered what she meant by that, everything seeing Aunt Moon. I guessed by her lazy voice that she meant nothing. There was no cutting edge to her words.

"And don't call her Aunt Moon." My mother was reading my mind again, one of her many tricks. "I know what you're thinking," she would say when I thought I looked expressionless. "You are thinking about finding Mrs. Mark's ring and holding it for a reward."

I would look horrified and tell her that she wasn't even lukewarm, but the truth was that I'd been thinking exactly those thoughts. I resented my mother for guessing my innermost secrets. She was like God, everywhere at once knowing everything. I tried to concentrate on something innocent. I thought about pickles. I was safe; she didn't say a word about dills or sweets.

Bess, Aunt Moon, wasn't really my aunt. She was a woman who lived alone and had befriended me. I liked Aunt Moon and the way she moved, slowly, taking up as much space as she wanted and doing it with ease. She had wide lips and straight eyelashes.

Aunt Moon dried medicine herbs in the manner of her parents. She knew about plants, both the helpful ones and the ones that were poisonous in all but the smallest of doses. And she knew how to cut wood and how to read the planets. She told me why I was stubborn. It had to do with my being born in May. I believed her because my father was born a few days after me, and he was stubborn as all get out, even compared to me.

Aunt Moon was special. She had life in her. The rest of the women in town were cold in the eye and fretted over their husbands. I didn't want to be like them. They condemned the men for drinking and gambling, but even after the loudest quarrels, ones we'd overhear, they never failed to cook for their men. They'd cook platters of lard-fried chicken, bowls of mashed potatoes, and pitchers of creamy flour gravy.

Bess called those meals "sure death by murder."

Our town was full of large and nervous women with red spots on their thin-skinned necks, and we had single women who lived with brothers and sisters or took care of an elderly parent. Bess had comments on all of these: "They have eaten their anger and grown large," she would say. And there were the sullen ones who took care of men broken by the war, women who were hurt by the men's stories of death and glory but never told them to get on with living, like I would have done.

Bessie's own brother, J.D., had gone to the war and returned with softened, weepy eyes. He lived at the veterans hospital and he did office work there on his good days. I met him once and knew by the sweetness of his eyes that he had never killed anyone, but something about him reminded me of the lonely old shacks out on cotton farming land. His eyes were broken windows.

"Where do you think that young man is headed?" my mother asked.

Something in her voice was wistful and lonely. I looked at her face, looked out the window at the dark man, and looked back at my mother again. I had never thought about her from inside the skin. She was the mind reader in the family, but suddenly I knew how she did it. The inner workings of the mind were clear in her face, like words in a book. I could even feel her thoughts in the pit of my stomach. I was feeling embarrassed at what my mother was thinking when the stranger crossed the street. In front of him an open truck full of prisoners passed by. They wore large white shirts and pants, like immigrants from Mexico. I began to count the flowers in the wallpaper again, and the truckful of prisoners passed by, and when it was gone, the young man had also vanished into thin air.

Besides the young man, another thing I remember about the fair that year was the man in the bathroom. On the first day of the fair, the prisoners were bending over like great white sails, their black and brown hands stuffing trash in canvas bags. Around them the children washed and brushed their cows and raked fresh straw about their pigs. My friend Elaine and I escaped the dust-laden air and went into the women's public toilets, where we shared a stolen cigarette. We heard someone open the door, and we fanned the smoke. Elaine stood on the toilet seat so her sisters wouldn't recognize her shoes. Then it was silent, so we opened the stall and stepped out. At first the round dark man, standing by the door, looked like a woman, but then I noticed the day's growth of beard at his jawline. He wore a blue work shirt and a little straw hat. He leaned against the wall, his hand moving inside his pants. I grabbed Elaine, who was putting lipstick on her cheeks like rouge, and pulled her outside the door, the tube of red lipstick still in her hand.

Outside, we nearly collapsed by a trash can, laughing. "Did you see that? It was a man! A man! In the women's bathroom." She smacked me on the back.

We knew nothing of men's hands inside their pants, so we began to follow him like store detectives, but as we rounded a corner behind his shadow, I saw Aunt Moon walking away from the pigeon cages. She was moving slowly with her cane, through the path's sawdust, feathers, and sand.

"Aunt Moon, there was a man in the bathroom," I said, and then remembered the chickens I wanted to tell her about. Elaine ran off. I didn't know if she was still following the man or not, but I'd lost interest when I saw Aunt Moon.

"Did you see those chickens that lay the green eggs?" I asked Aunt Moon.

She wagged her head no, so I grabbed her free elbow and guided her past the pigeons with curly feathers and the turkeys with red wattles, right up to the chickens.

"They came all the way from South America. They sell for five dollars, can you imagine?" Five dollars was a lot for chickens when we were still recovering from the Great Depression, men were still talking about what they'd done with the CCC, and children still got summer complaint and had to be carried around crippled for months.

She peered into the cage. The eggs were smooth and resting in the straw. "I'll be" was all she said.

I studied her face for a clue as to why she was so quiet, thinking she was mad or something. I wanted to read her thoughts as easily as I'd read my mother's. In the strange light of the sky, her eyes slanted a bit more than usual. I watched her carefully. I looked at the downward curve of her nose and saw the young man reflected in her eyes. I turned around.

On the other side of the cage that held the chickens from Araucania was the man my mother had watched. Bess pretended to be looking at the little Jersey cattle in the distance, but I could tell she was seeing that man. He had a calm look on his face and his dark chest was smooth as oil where his shirt was opened. His eyes were large and black. They were fixed on Bess like he was a hypnotist or something magnetic that tried to pull Bess Evening toward it, even though her body stepped back. She did step back, I remember that, but even so, everything in her went forward, right up to him.

I didn't know if it was just me or if his presence charged the air, but suddenly the oxygen was gone. It was like the fire at the Fisher Hardware when all the air was drawn into the flame. Even the chickens clucked softly, as if suffocating, and the cattle were more silent in the straw. The pulse in everything changed.

I don't know what would have happened if the rooster hadn't crowed just then, but he did, and everything returned to normal. The rooster strutted and we turned to watch him.

Bessie started walking away and I went with her. We walked past the men and boys who were shooting craps in a cleared circle. One of them rubbed the dice between his hands as we were leaving, his eyes closed, his body's tight muscles willing a winning throw. He called me Lady Luck as we walked by. He said, "There goes Lady Luck," and he tossed the dice.

At dinner that evening we could hear the dance band tuning up in the makeshift beer garden, playing a few practice songs to the empty tables with their red cloths. They played "The Tennessee Waltz." For a while, my mother sang along with it. She had brushed her hair one hundred strokes and now she was talking and regretting talking all at the same time. "He was such a handsome man," she said. My father wiped his face with a handkerchief and rested his elbows on the table. He chewed and looked at nothing in particular. "For the longest time he stood there by the juniper bushes."

My father drank some coffee and picked up the newspaper. Mother cleared the table, one dish at a time and not in stacks like usual. "His clothes were neat. He must not have come from very far away." She moved the salt shaker from the end of the table to the center, then back again.

"I'll wash," I volunteered.

Mother said, "Bless you," and touched herself absently near the waist, as if to remove an apron. "I'll go get ready for the dance," she said.

My father turned a page of the paper.

The truth was, my mother was already fixed up for the dance. Her hair looked soft and beautiful. She had slipped into her new dress early in the day, "to break it in," she said. She wore nylons and she was barefoot and likely to get a runner. I would have warned her, but it seemed out of place, my warning. Her face was softer than usual, her lips painted to look full, and her eyebrows were much darker than usual.

"Do you reckon that young man came here for the rodeo?" She hollered in from the living room, where she powdered her nose. Normally she made up in front of the bathroom mirror, but the cabinet had been slammed and broken mysteriously one night during an argument so we had all taken to grooming ourselves in the small framed mirror in the living room.

I could not put my finger on it, but all the women at the dance that night were looking at the young man. It wasn't exactly that he was handsome. There was something else. He was alive in his whole body while the other men walked with great effort and stiffness, even those who did little work and were still young. Their male bodies had no language of their own in the way that his did. The women themselves seemed confused and lonely in the presence of the young man, and they were ridiculous in their behavior, laughing too loud, blushing like schoolgirls, or casting him a flirting eye. Even the older women were brighter than usual. Mrs. Tubby, whose face was usually as grim as the statue of General Pickens, the Cherokee hater, played with her necklace until her neck had red lines from the chain. Mrs. Tens twisted a strand of her hair over and over. Her sister tripped over a chair because she'd forgotten to watch where she was going.

The men, sneaking drinks from bottles in paper bags, did not notice any of the fuss.

Maybe it was his hands. His hands were strong and dark.

I stayed late, even after wives pulled their husbands away from their ball game talk and insisted they dance.

My mother and father were dancing. My mother smiled up into my father's face as he turned her this way and that. Her uneven skirt swirled a little around her legs. She had a run in her nylons, as I predicted. My father, who was called Peso by the townspeople, wore his old clothes. He had his usual look about him, and I noticed that faraway, unfocused gaze on the other men too. They were either distant or they were present but rowdy, embarrassing the women around them with the loud talk of male things: work and hunting, fights, this or that pretty girl. Occasionally they told a joke, like "Did you hear the one about the traveling salesman?"

The dancers whirled around the floor, some tapping their feet, some shuffling, the women in new dresses and dark hair all curled up like in movie magazines, the men with new leather boots and crew cuts. My dad's rear stuck out in back, the way he danced. His hand clutched my mother's waist.

That night, Bessie arrived late. She was wearing a white dress with a full gathered skirt. The print was faded and I could just make out the little blue stars on the cloth. She carried a yellow shawl over her arm. Her long hair was braided as usual in the manner of the older Chickasaw women, like a wreath on her head. She was different from the others with her bright shawl. Sometimes she wore a heavy shell necklace or a collection of bracelets on her arm. They jangled when she talked with me, waving her hands to make a point. Like the time she told me that the soul is a small woman inside the eye who leaves at night to wander new places.

No one had ever known her to dance before, but that night the young man and Aunt Moon danced together among the artificial geraniums and plastic carnations. They held each other gently like two breakable vases. They didn't look at each other or smile the way the other dancers did; that's how I knew they liked each other. His large dark hand was on the small of her back. Her hand rested tenderly on his shoulder. The other dancers moved away from them and there was empty space all around them.

My father went out into the dark to smoke and to play a hand or two of poker. My mother went to sit with some of the other women, all of them pulling their damp hair away from their necks and letting it fall back again, or furtively putting on lipstick, fanning themselves, and sipping their beers.

"He puts me in the mind of a man I once knew," said Mrs. Tubby.

"Look at them," said Mrs. Tens. "Don't you think he's young enough to be her son?"

With my elbows on my knees and my chin in my hands, I watched Aunt Moon step and square when my mother loomed up like a shadow over the bleachers where I sat.

"Young lady," she said in a scolding voice. "You were supposed to go home and put the children to bed."

I looked from her stern face to my sister Susan, who was like a chubby angel sleeping beside me. Peso Junior had run off to the gambling game, where he was pushing another little boy around. My mother followed my gaze and looked at Junior. She put her hands on her hips and said, "Boys!"

My sister Roberta, who was twelve, had stayed close to the women all night, listening to their talk about the fullblood who had come to town for a rodeo or something and who danced so far away from Bessie that they didn't look friendly at all except for the fact that the music had stopped and they were still waltzing.

Margaret Tubby won the prize money that year for the biggest pumpkin. It was 220.4 centimeters in circumference and weighed 190 pounds and had to be carried on a stretcher by the volunteer firemen. Mrs. Tubby was the town's chief social justice. She sat most days on the bench outside the grocery store. Sitting there like a full-chested hawk on a fence, she held court. She had watched Bess Evening for years with her sharp gold eyes. "This is the year I saw it coming," she told my mother, as if she'd just been dying for Bess to go wrong. It showed up in the way Bess walked, she said, that the woman was coming to a no good end just like the rest of her family had done.

"When do you think she had time to grow that pumpkin?" Mother asked as we escaped Margaret Tubby's court on our way to the store. I knew what she meant, that Mrs. Tubby did more time with gossip than with her garden.

Margaret was even more pious than usual at that time of year when the green tent revival followed on the heels of the fair, when the pink-faced men in white shirts arrived and, really, every single one of them was a preacher. Still, Margaret Tubby kept her prize money to herself and didn't give a tithe to any church.

With Bess Evening carrying on with a stranger young enough to be her son, Mrs. Tubby succeeded in turning the church women against her once and for all. When Bessie walked down the busy street, one of the oldest dances of women took place, for women in those days turned against each other easily, never thinking they might have other enemies. When Bess appeared, the women stepped away. They vanished from the very face of earth that was named Comanche Street. They disappeared into the Oklahoma red-stone shops like swallows swooping into their small clay nests. The women would look at the new bolts of red cloth in Terwilligers with feigned interest, although they would never have worn red, even to a dog fight. They'd purchase another box of face powder in the five and dime, or drink cherry phosphates at the pharmacy without so much as tasting the flavor.

But Bessie was unruffled. She walked on in the empty mirage of heat, the sound of her cane blending in with horse hooves and the rhythmic pumping of oil wells out east.

At the store, my mother bought corn meal, molasses, and milk. I bought penny candy for my younger sisters and for Peso Junior with the money I earned by helping Aunt Moon with her remedies. When we passed Margaret Tubby on the way out, my mother nodded at her, but said to me, "That pumpkin grew fat on gossip. I'll bet she fed it with nothing but all-night rumors." I thought about the twenty-five-dollar prize money and decided to grow pumpkins next year.

My mother said, "Now don't you get any ideas about growing pumpkins, young lady. We don't have room enough. They'd crowd out the cucumbers and tomatoes."

My mother and father won a prize that year, too. For dancing. They won a horse lamp for the living room. "We didn't even know it was a contest," my mother said, free from the sin of competition. Her face was rosy with pleasure and pride. She had the life snapping out of her like hot grease, though sometimes I saw that life turn to a slow and restless longing, like when she daydreamed out the window where the young man had stood that day.

Passing Margaret's post and giving up on growing a two-hundred-pound pumpkin, I remembered all the things good Indian women were not supposed to do. We were not supposed to look into the faces of men. Or laugh too loud. We were not supposed to learn too much from books because that kind of knowledge was a burden to the soul. Not only that, it always took us away from our loved ones. I was jealous of the white girls who laughed as loud as they wanted and never had rules. Also, my mother wanted me to go to college no matter what anyone else said or thought. She said I was too smart to stay home and live a life like hers, even if the other people thought book learning would ruin my life.

Aunt Moon with her second sight and heavy breasts managed to break all the rules. She threw back her head and laughed out loud, showing off the worn edges of her teeth. She didn't go to church. She did a man's work, cared for animals, and chopped her own wood. The gossiping women said it was a wonder Bessie Evening was healthy at all and didn't have female problems—meaning with her body, I figured.

The small woman inside her eye was full and lonely at the same time.

Bess made tonics, remedies, and cures. The church women, even those who gossiped, slipped over to buy Bessie's potions at night and in secret. They'd never admit they swallowed the "snake medicine," as they called it. They'd say to Bess, "What have you got to put the life back in a man? My sister has that trouble, you know." Or they'd say, "I have a friend who needs a cure for the sadness." They bought remedies for fever and for coughing fits, for sore muscles and for sleepless nights.

Aunt Moon had learned the cures from her parents, who were said to have visited their own sins upon their children, both of whom were born out of wedlock from the love of an old Chickasaw man and a young woman from one of those tribes up north. Maybe a Navajo or something, the people thought.

But Aunt Moon had numerous talents and I respected them. She could pull cotton, pull watermelons, and pull babies with equal grace. She even delivered those scrub cattle, bred with Holsteins too big for them, caesarean. In addition to that, she told me the ways of the world and not just about the zodiac or fortune cards. "The United States is in love with death," she would say. "They sleep with it better than with lovers. They celebrate it on holidays, the Fourth of July, even in spring when they praise the loss of a good man's body."

She would tend her garden while I'd ask questions. What do you think about heaven? I wanted to know. She'd look up and then get back to pulling the weeds. "You and I both would just grump around up there with all those righteous people. Women like us weren't meant to live on golden streets. We're Indians," she'd say as she cleared out the space around a bean plant. "We're like these beans. We grew up from mud." And then she'd tell me how the people emerged right along with the crawdads from the muddy female swamps of the land. "And what is gold anyway? Just something else that comes from mud. Look at the conquistadors." She pulled a squash by accident. "And look at the sad women of this town, old already and all because of gold." She poked a hole in the ground and replanted the roots of the squash. "Their men make money, but not love. They give the women gold rings, gold-rimmed glasses, gold teeth, but their skin dries up for lack of love. Their hearts are little withered raisins." I was embarrassed by the mention of making love, but I listened to her words.

This is how I came to call Bessie Evening by the name of Aunt Moon: She'd been teaching me that animals and all life should be greeted properly as our kinfolk. "Good day, Uncle," I learned to say to the longhorn as I passed by on the road. "Good morning, cousins. Is there something you need?" I'd say to the sparrows. And one night when the moon was passing over Bessie's house, I said, "Hello, Aunt Moon. I see you are full of silver again tonight." It was so much like Bess Evening, I began to think, that I named her after the moon. She was sometimes full and happy, sometimes small and weak. I began saying it right to her ears: "Auntie Moon, do you need some help today?"

She seemed both older and younger than thirty-nine to me. For one thing, she walked with a cane. She had developed some secret ailment after her young daughter died. My mother said she needed the cane because she had no mortal human to hold her up in life, like the rest of us did.

But the other thing was that she was full of mystery and she laughed right out loud, like a Gypsy, my mother said, pointing out Bessie's blue-painted walls, bright clothes and necklaces, and all the things she kept hanging from her ceiling. She decorated outside her house, too, with bits of blue glass hanging from the trees, and little polished quartz crystals that reflected rainbows across the dry hills.

Aunt Moon had solid feet, a light step, and a face that clouded over with emotion and despair one moment and brightened up like light the next. She'd beam and say to me, "Sassafras will turn your hair red," and throw back her head to laugh, knowing full well that I would rinse my dull hair with sassafras that very night, ruining my mother's pans.

I sat in Aunt Moon's kitchen while she brewed herbals in white enamel pans on the woodstove. The insides of the pans were black from sassafras and burdock and other plants she picked. The kitchen smelled rich and earthy. Some days it was hard to breathe from the combination of wood-stove heat and pollen from the plants, but she kept at it and her medicine for cramps was popular with the women in town.

Aunt Moon made me proud of my womanhood, giving me bags of herbs and an old eagle feather that had been doctored by her father back when people used to pray instead of going to church. "The body divines everything," she told me, and sometimes when I was with her, I knew the older Indian world was still here and I'd feel it in my skin and hear the night sounds speak to me, hear the voice of water tell stories about people who lived here before, and the deep songs came out from the hills.

One day I found Aunt Moon sitting at her table in front of a plate of un-touched toast and wild plum jam. She was weeping. I was young and did-n't know what to say, but she told me more than I could ever understand. "Ever since my daughter died," she told me, "my body aches to touch her. All the mourning has gone into my bones." Her long hair was loose that day and it fell down her back like a waterfall, almost to the floor.

After that I had excuses on the days I saw her hair loose. "I'm putting up new wallpaper today," I'd say, or "I have to help Mom can peaches," which was the truth.

"Sure," she said, and I saw the tinge of sorrow around her eyes even though she smiled and nodded at me.

Canning the peaches, I asked my mother what it was that happened to Aunt Moon's daughter.

"First of all," my mother set me straight, "her name is Bess, not Aunt Moon." Then she'd tell the story of Willow Evening. "That pretty child was the light of that woman's eye," my mother said. "It was all so fast. She was playing one minute and the next she was gone. She was hanging on to that wooden planter and pulled it right down onto her little chest."

My mother touched her chest. "I saw Bessie lift it like it weighed less than a pound—did I already tell you that part?"

All I had seen that day was Aunt Moon holding Willow's thin body. The little girl's face was already gone to ashes and Aunt Moon blew gently on her daughter's skin, even though she was dead, as if she could breathe the life back into her one more time. She blew on her skin the way I later knew that women blow sweat from lovers' faces, cooling them. But I knew nothing of any kind of passion then.

The planter remained on the dry grassy mound of Aunt Moon's yard, and even though she had lifted it, no one else, not even my father, could move it. It was still full of earth and dead geraniums, like a monument to the child.

"That girl was all she had," my mother said through the steam of boiling water. "Hand me the ladle, will you?"

The peaches were suspended in sweet juice in their clear jars. I thought of our lives—so short, the skin so soft around us that we could be gone any second from our living—thought I saw Willow's golden brown face suspended behind glass in one of the jars.

The men first noticed the stranger, Isaac, when he cleaned them out in the poker game that night at the fair. My father, who had been drinking, handed over the money he'd saved for the new bathroom mirror and took a drunken swing at the young man, missing him by a foot and falling on his bad knee. Mr. Tubby told his wife he lost all he'd saved for the barber shop business, even though everyone in town knew he drank it up long before the week of the fair. Mr. Tens lost his Mexican silver ring. It showed up later on Aunt Moon's hand.

Losing to one another was one thing. Losing to Isaac Cade meant the dark young man was a card sharp and an outlaw. Even the women who had watched the stranger all that night were sure he was full of demons.

The next time I saw Aunt Moon, it was the fallow season of autumn, but she seemed new and fresh as spring. Her skin had new light. Gathering plants, she smiled at me. Her cane moved aside the long dry grasses to reveal what grew underneath. Mullein was still growing, and holly.

I sat at the table while Aunt Moon ground yellow ochre in a mortar. Isaac came in from fixing the roof. He touched her arm so softly I wasn't sure she felt it. I had never seen a man touch a woman that way.

He said hello to me and he said, "You know those fairgrounds? That's where the three tribes used to hold sings." He drummed on the table, looking at me, and sang one of the songs. I said I recognized it, a song I sometimes dreamed I heard from the hill.

A red handprint appeared on his face, like one of those birthmarks that only show up in the heat or under the strain of work or feeling.

"How'd you know about the fairgrounds?" I asked him.

"My father was from here." He sat still, as if thinking himself into another time. He stared out the window at the distances that were in between the blue curtains.

I went back to Aunt Moon's the next day. Isaac wasn't there, so Aunt Moon and I tied sage in bundles with twine. I asked her about love.

"It comes up from the ground just like corn," she said. She pulled a knot tighter with her teeth.

Later, when I left, I was still thinking about love. Outside where Bess had been planting, black beetles were digging themselves under the turned soil, and red ants had grown wings and were starting to fly.

When I returned home, my mother was sitting outside the house on a chair. She pointed at Bess Evening's house. "With the man there," she said, "I think it best you don't go over to Bessie's house anymore."

I started to protest, but she interrupted. "There are no ands, ifs, or buts about it."

I knew it was my father who made the decision. My mother had probably argued my point and lost to him again, and lost some of her life as well. She was slowed down to a slumberous pace. Later that night as I stood by my window looking toward Aunt Moon's house, I heard my mother say, "God damn them all and this whole damned town."

"There now," my father said. "There now."

"She's as dark and stained as those old black pans she uses," Margaret Tubby said about Bess Evening one day. She had come to pick up a cake from Mother for the church bake sale. I was angered by her words. I gave her one of those "looks could kill" faces, but I said nothing. We all looked out the window at Aunt Moon. She was standing near Isaac, looking at a tree. It leapt into my mind suddenly, like lightning, that Mrs. Tubby knew about the blackened pans. That would mean she had bought cures from Aunt Moon. I was smug about this discovery.

Across the way, Aunt Moon stood with her hand outstretched, palm up. It was filled with roots or leaves. She was probably teaching Isaac about the remedies. I knew Isaac would teach her things also, older things, like squirrel sickness and porcupine disease that I'd heard about from grandparents.

Listening to Mrs. Tubby, I began to understand why, right after the fair, Aunt Moon had told me I would have to fight hard to keep my life in this town. Mrs. Tubby said, "Living out of wedlock! Just like her parents." She went on, "History repeats itself."

I wanted to tell Mrs. Tubby a thing or two myself. "History, my eye," I wanted to say. "You're just jealous about the young man." But Margaret Tubby was still angry that her husband had lost his money to the stranger, and also because she probably still felt bad about playing with her necklace like a young girl that night at the fair. My mother said nothing, just covered the big caramel cake and handed it over to Mrs. Tubby. My mother looked like she was tired of fools and that included me. She looked like the woman inside her eye had just wandered off.

I began to see the women in Pickens as ghosts. I'd see them in the library looking at the stereopticons, and in the ice cream parlor. The more full Aunt Moon grew, the more drawn and pinched they became.

The church women echoed Margaret. "She's as stained as her pans," they'd say, and they began buying their medicines at the pharmacy. It didn't matter that their coughs returned and that their children developed more fevers. It didn't matter that some of them could not get pregnant when they wanted to or that Mrs. Tens grew thin and pale and bent. They wouldn't dream of lowering themselves to buy Bessie's medicines.

My mother ran hot water into the tub and emptied one of her packages of bubble powder in it. "Take a bath," she told me. "It will steady your nerves."

I was still crying, standing at the window, looking out at Aunt Moon's house through the rain.

The heavy air had been broken by an electrical storm earlier that day. In a sudden crash, the leaves flew off their trees, the sky exploded with lightning, and thunder rumbled the earth. People went to their doors to watch. It scared me. The clouds turned green and it began to hail and clatter.

That was when Aunt Moon's old dog, Mister, ran off, went running like crazy through the town. Some of the older men saw him on the street. They thought he was hurt and dying because of the way he ran and twitched. He butted right into a tree and the men thought maybe he had rabies or something. They meant to put him out of his pain. One of them took aim with a gun and shot him, and when the storm died down and the streets misted over, everything returned to heavy stillness and old Mister was lying on the edge of the Smiths' lawn. I picked him up and carried his heavy body up to Aunt Moon's porch. I covered him with sage, like she would have done.

Bess and Isaac had gone over to Alexander that day to sell remedies. They missed the rain, and when they returned, they were happy about bringing home bags of beans, ground corn, and flour.

I guess it was my mother who told Aunt Moon about her dog.

That evening I heard her wailing. I could hear her from my window and I looked out and saw her with her hair all down around her shoulders like a black shawl. Isaac smoothed back her hair and held her. I guessed that all the mourning was back in her bones again, even for her little girl, Willow.

That night my mother sat by my bed. "Sometimes the world is a sad place," she said and kissed my hot forehead. I began to cry again.

"Well, she still has the burro," my mother said, neglecting to mention Isaac.

I began to worry about the burro and to look after it. I went over to Aunt Moon's against my mother's wishes, and took carrots and sugar to the gray burro. I scratched his big ears.

By this time, most of the younger and healthier men had signed up to go to Korea and fight for their country. Most of the residents of Pickens were mixed-blood Indians and they were even more patriotic than white men. I guess they wanted to prove that they were good Americans. My father left and we saw him off at the depot. I admit I missed him saying to me, "The trouble with you is you think too much." Old Peso, always telling people what their problems were. Margaret Tubby's lazy son had enlisted because, as his mother had said, "It would make a man of him," and when he was killed in action, the townspeople resented Isaac, Bess Evening's young man, even more since he did not have his heart set on fighting the war.

Aunt Moon was pregnant the next year when the fair came around again, and she was just beginning to show. Margaret Tubby had remarked that Bess was visiting all those family sins on another poor child.

This time I was older. I fixed Mrs. Tubby in my eyes and I said, "Mrs. Tubby, you are just like history, always repeating yourself."

She pulled her head back into her neck like a turtle. My mother said, "Hush, Sis. Get inside the house." She put her hands on her hips. "I'll deal with you later." She almost added, "Just wait till your father gets home."

Later, I felt bad, talking that way to Margaret Tubby so soon after she lost her son.

Shortly after the fair, we heard that the young man inside Aunt Moon's eye was gone. A week passed and he didn't return. I watched her house from the window and I knew, if anyone stood behind me, the little house was resting up on my shoulder.

Mother took a nap and I grabbed the biscuits off the table and snuck out.

"I didn't hear you come in," Aunt Moon said to me.

"I didn't knock," I told her. "My mom just fell asleep. I thought it'd wake her up."

Aunt Moon's hair was down. Her hands were on her lap. A breeze came in the window. She must not have been sleeping and her eyes looked tired. I gave her the biscuits I had taken off the table. I lied and told her my mother had sent them over. We ate one.

Shortly after Isaac was gone, Bess Evening again became the focus of the town's women. Mrs. Tubby said, "Bessie would give you the shirt off her back. She never deserved a no good man who would treat her like dirt and then run off." Mrs. Tubby went over to Bess Evening's and bought enough cramp remedy from the pregnant woman to last her and her daughters for the next two years.

Mrs. Tens lost her pallor. She went to Bessie's with a basket of jellies and fruits, hoping in secret that Bess would return Mr. Tens's Mexican silver ring now that the young man was gone.

The women were going to stick by her; you could see it in their squared shoulders. They no longer hid their purchases of herbs. They forgot how they'd looked at Isaac's black eyes and lively body with longing that night of the dance. If they'd had dowsing rods, the split willow branches would have flown up to the sky, so much had they twisted around the truth of things and even their own natures. Isaac was the worst of men. Their husbands, who were absent, were saints who loved them. Every morning when my mother said her prayers and forgot she'd damned the town and everybody in it, I heard her ask for peace for Bessie Evening, but she never joined in with the other women who seemed happy over Bessie's tragedy.

Isaac was doubly condemned in his absence. Mrs. Tubby said, "What kind of fool goes off to leave a woman who knows about tea leaves and cures for diseases of the body and the mind alike? I'll tell you what kind, a card shark, that's what."

Someone corrected her. "Card *sharp*, dearie, not *shark*."

Who goes off and leaves a woman whose trees are hung with charming stones, relics, and broken glass, a woman who hangs sage and herbs to dry on her walls and whose front porch is full of fresh-cut wood? Those women, how they wanted to comfort her, but Bess Evening would only go to the door, leave them standing outside on the steps, and hand their herbs to them through the screen.

My cousins from Denver came for the fair. I was going to leave with them and get a job in the city for a year or so, then go on to school. My mother insisted she could handle the little ones alone now that they were bigger, and that I ought to go. It was best I made some money and learned what I could, she said.

"Are you sure?" I asked while my mother washed her hair in the kitchen sink.

"I'm sure as the night's going to fall." She sounded lighthearted, but her hands stopped moving and rested on her head until the soap lather began to disappear. "Besides, your dad will probably be home any day now."

I said, "Okay then, I'll go. I'll write you all the time." I was all full of emotion, but I didn't cry.

"Don't make promises you can't keep," my mother said, wrapping a towel around her head.

I went to the dance that night with my cousins, and out in the trees I let Jim Tens kiss me and promised him that I would be back. "I'll wait for you," he said. "And keep away from those city boys."

I meant it when I said, "I will."

He walked me home, holding my hand. My cousins were still at the dance. Mom would complain about their late city hours. Once she even told us that city people eat supper as late as eight o'clock P.M. We didn't believe her.

After Jim kissed me at the door, I watched him walk down the street. I was surprised that I didn't feel sad.

I decided to go to see Aunt Moon one last time. I was leaving at six in the morning and was already packed and I had taken one of each herb sample I'd learned from Aunt Moon, just in case I ever needed them.

I scratched the burro's gray face at the lot and walked up toward the house. The window was gold and filled with lamplight. I heard an owl hooting in the distance and stopped to listen.

I glanced in the window and stopped in my tracks. The young man, Isaac, was there. He was speaking close to Bessie's face. He put his finger under her chin and lifted her face up to his. He was looking at her with soft eyes and I could tell there were many men and women living inside their eyes that moment. He held her cane across the back of her hips. With it, he pulled her close to him and held her tight, his hands on the cane pressing her body against his. And he kissed her. Her hair was down around her back and shoulders and she put her arms around his neck. I turned to go. I felt dishonest and guilty for looking in at them. I began to run.

I ran into the bathroom and bent over the sink to wash my face. I wiped Jim Tens's cold kiss from my lips. I glanced up to look at myself in the mirror, but my face was nothing, just shelves of medicine bottles and aspirin. I had forgotten the mirror was broken.

From the bathroom door I heard my mother saying her prayers, fervently, and louder than usual. She said, "Bless Sis's Aunt Moon and bless Isaac, who got arrested for trading illegal medicine for corn, and forgive him for escaping from jail."

She said this so loud, I thought she was talking to me. Maybe she was. Now how did she read my mind again? It made me smile, and I guessed I was reading hers.

All the next morning, driving through the deep blue sky, I thought how all the women had gold teeth and hearts like withered raisins. I hoped Jim Tens would marry one of the Tubby girls. I didn't know if I'd ever go home or not. I had Aunt Moon's herbs in my bag, and the eagle feather wrapped safe in a scarf. And I had a small, beautiful woman in my eye.

E. Pauline Johnson (Mohawk)
As It Was in the Beginning

They account for it by the fact that I am a Redskin, but I am something else, too—I am a woman.

I remember the first time I saw him. He came up the trail with some Hudson's Bay trappers, and they stopped at the door of my father's tepee. He seemed even then, fourteen years ago, an old man; his hair seemed just as thin and white, his hands just as trembling and fleshless as they were a month since, when I saw him for what I pray his God is the last time.

My father sat in the tepee, polishing buffalo horns and smoking; my mother, wrapped in her blanket, crouched over her quill-work, on the buffalo-skin at his side; I was lounging at the doorway, idling, watching, as I always watched, the thin, distant line of sky and prairie; wondering, as I always wondered, what lay beyond it. Then he came, this gentle old man with his white hair and thin, pale face. He wore a long black coat, which I now know was the sign of his office, and he carried a black leather-covered book, which, in all the years I have known him, I have never seen him without.

The trappers explained to my father who he was, the Great Teacher, the heart's Medicine Man, the "Blackcoat" we had heard of, who brought peace where there was war, and the magic of whose black book brought greater things than all the Happy Hunting Grounds of our ancestors.

He told us many things that day, for he could speak the Cree tongue, and my father listened, and listened, and when at last they left us, my father said for him to come and sit within the tepee again.

He came, all the time he came, and my father welcomed him, but my mother always sat in silence at work with the quills; my mother never liked the Great "Blackcoat."

His stories fascinated me. I used to listen intently to the tale of the strange new place he called "heaven," of the gold crown, of the white dress, of the great music; and then he would tell of that other strange place—hell. My father and I hated it; we feared it, we dreamt of it, we trembled at it. Oh, if the "Blackcoat" would only cease to talk of it! Now I know he saw its effect upon us, and he used it as a whip to lash us into his new religion, but even then my mother must have known, for each time he left the tepee she would watch him going slowly away across the prairie; then when he was disappearing into the far horizon she would laugh scornfully, and say:

"If the white man made this Blackcoat's hell, let him go to it. It is for the man who found it first. No hell for Indians, just Happy Hunting Grounds. Blackcoat can't scare me."

And then, after weeks had passed, one day as he stood at the tepee door he laid his white, old hand on my head and said to my father: "Give me this little girl, chief. Let me take her to the mission school; let me keep

her, and teach her of the great God and His eternal heaven. She will grow
to be a noble woman, and return perhaps to bring her people to the Christ."

My mother's eyes snapped. "No," she said. It was the first word she ever
spoke to the "Blackcoat." My father sat and smoked. At the end of a half-
hour he said:

"I am an old man, Blackcoat. I shall not leave the God of my fathers. I
like not your strange God's ways—all of them. I like not His two new places
for me when I am dead. Take the child, Blackcoat, and save her from hell."

The first grief of my life was when we reached the mission. They took
my buckskin dress off, saying I was now a little Christian girl and must dress
like all the white people at the mission. Oh, how I hated that stiff new cal-
ico dress and those leather shoes! But, little as I was, I said nothing, only
thought of the time when I should be grown, and do as my mother did, and
wear the buckskins and the blanket.

My next serious grief was when I began to speak the English, that they
forbade me to use any Cree words whatever. The rule of the school was that
any child heard using its native tongue must get a slight punishment. I never
understood it, I cannot understand it now, why the use of my dear Cree
tongue could be a matter for correction or an action deserving punishment.

She was strict, the matron of the school, but only justly so, for she had
a heart and a face like her brother's, the "Blackcoat." I had long since
ceased to call him that. The trappers at the post called him "St. Paul," because, they told me, of his self-sacrificing life, his kindly deeds, his rarely
beautiful old face; so I, too, called him "St. Paul," though oftener "Father
Paul," though he never liked the latter title, for he was a Protestant. But as
I was his pet, his darling of the whole school, he let me speak of him as I
would, knowing it was but my heart speaking in love. His sister was a
widow, and mother to a laughing yellow-haired little boy of about my own
age, who was my constant playmate and who taught me much of English
in his own childish way. I used to be fond of this child, just as I was fond
of his mother and of his uncle, my "Father Paul," but as my girlhood
passed away, as womanhood came upon me, I got strangely wearied of
them all; I longed, oh, God, how I longed for the old wild life! It came
with my womanhood, with my years.

What mattered it to me now that they had taught me all their ways?—
their tricks of dress, their reading, their writing, their books. What mattered
it that "Father Paul" loved me, that the traders at the post called me pretty,
that I was a pet of all, from the factor to the poorest trapper in the service?
I wanted my own people, my own old life, my blood called out for it, but
they always said I must not return to my father's tepee. I heard them talk
amongst themselves of keeping me away from pagan influences; they told
each other that if I returned to the prairies, the tepees, I would degenerate,
slip back to paganism, as other girls had done; marry, perhaps, with a
pagan—and all their years of labor and teaching would be lost.

I said nothing, but I waited. And then one night the feeling overcame me. I was in the Hudson's Bay store when an Indian came in from the north with a large pack of buckskin. As they unrolled it a dash of its insinuating odor filled the store. I went over and leaned above the skins a second, then buried my face in them, swallowing, drinking the fragrance of them, that went to my head like wine. Oh, the wild wonder of that wood-smoked tan, the subtilty [sic] of it, the untamed smell of it! I drank it into my lungs, my innermost being was saturated with it, till my mind reeled and my heart seemed twisted with a physical agony. My childhood recollections rushed upon me, devoured me. I left the store in a strange, calm frenzy, and going rapidly to the mission house I confronted my Father Paul and demanded to be allowed to go "home," if only for a day. He received the request with the same refusal and the same gentle sigh that I had so often been greeted with, but *this* time the desire, the smoke-tan, the heart-ache, never lessened.

Night after night I would steal away by myself and go to the border of the village to watch the sun set in the foothills, to gaze at the far line of sky and prairie, to long and long for my father's lodge. And Laurence—always Laurence—my fair-haired, laughing, child playmate, would come calling and calling for me: "Esther, where are you? We miss you; come in, Esther, come in with me." And if I did not turn at once to him and follow, he would come and place his strong hands on my shoulders and laugh into my eyes and say, "Truant, truant, Esther; can't *we* make you happy?"

My old child playmate had vanished years ago. He was a tall, slender young man now, handsome as a young chief, but with laughing blue eyes, and always those yellow curls about his temples. He was my solace in my half-exile, my comrade, my brother, until one night it was, "Esther, Esther, can't *I* make you happy?"

I did not answer him; only looked out across the plains and thought of the tepees. He came close, close. He locked his arms about me, and with my face pressed up to his throat he stood silent. I felt the blood from my heart sweep to my very finger-tips. I loved him. O God, how I loved him! In a wild, blind instant it all came, just because he held me so and was whispering brokenly, "Don't leave me, don't leave me, Esther; *my* Esther, my child-love, my playmate, my girl-comrade, my little Cree sweetheart, will you go away to your people, or stay, stay for me, for my arms, as I have you now?"

No more, no more the tepees; no more the wild stretch of prairie, the intoxicating fragrance of the smoke-tanned buckskin; no more the bed of buffalo hide, the soft, silent moccasin; no more the dark faces of my people, the dulcet cadence of the sweet Cree tongue—only this man, this fair, proud, tender man who held me in his arms, in his heart. My soul prayed his great white God, in that moment, that He let me have only this. It was twilight when we re-entered the mission gate. We were both excited, feverish. Father Paul was reading evening prayers in the large room beyond the hallway; his soft, saint-like voice stole beyond the doors, like a benediction upon us. I went noiselessly upstairs to my own room and sat there undisturbed for hours.

The clock downstairs struck one, startling me from my dreams of happiness, and at the same moment a flash of light attracted me. My room was in an angle of the building, and my window looked almost directly down into those of Father Paul's study, into which at that instant he was entering, carrying a lamp. "Why, Laurence," I heard him exclaim, "what are you doing here? I thought, my boy, you were in bed hours ago."

"No, uncle, not in bed, but in dreamland," replied Laurence, arising from the window, where evidently he, too, had spent the night hours as I had done.

Father Paul fumbled about a moment, found his large black book, which for once he seemed to have got separated from, and was turning to leave, when the curious circumstance of Laurence being there at so unusual an hour seemed to strike him anew. "Better go to sleep, my son," he said simply, then added curiously, "Has anything occurred to keep you up?"

Then Laurence spoke: "No, uncle, only—only, I'm happy, that's all."

Father Paul stood irresolute. Then: "It is—?"

"Esther," said Laurence quietly, but he was at the old man's side, his hand was on the bent old shoulder, his eyes proud and appealing.

Father Paul set the lamp on the table, but, as usual, one hand held that black book, the great text of his life. His face was paler than I had ever seen it—graver.

"Tell me of it," he requested.

I leaned far out of my window and watched them both. I listened with my very heart, for Laurence was telling him of me, of his love, of the new-found joy of that night.

"You have said nothing of marriage to her?" asked Father Paul.

"Well—no; but she surely understands that—"

"Did you speak of *marriage?*" repeated Father Paul, with a harsh ring in his voice that was new to me.

"No, uncle, but—"

"Very well, then; very well."

There was a brief silence. Laurence stood staring at the old man as though he were a stranger; he watched him push a large chair up to the table, slowly seat himself; then mechanically following his movements, he dropped on to a lounge. The old man's head bent low, but his eyes were bright and strangely fascinating. He began:

"Laurence, my boy, your future is the dearest thing to me of all earthly interests. Why, you *can't* marry this girl—no, no, sit, sit until I have finished," he added, with raised voice, as Laurence sprang up, remonstrating. "I have long since decided that you marry well; for instance, the Hudson's Bay factor's daughter."

Laurence broke into a fresh, rollicking laugh. "What, uncle," he said, "little Ida McIntosh? Marry that little yellow-haired fluff ball, that kitten, that pretty little dolly?"

"Stop," said Father Paul. Then, with a low, soft persuasiveness, "She is *white,* Laurence."

My lover started. "Why, uncle, what do you mean?" he faltered.

"Only this, my son: poor Esther comes of uncertain blood; would it do for you—the missionary's nephew, and adopted son, you might say—to marry the daughter of a pagan Indian? Her mother is hopelessly uncivilized; her father has a dash of French somewhere—half-breed, you know, my boy, half-breed." Then, with still lower tone and half-shut, crafty eyes, he added: "The blood is a bad, bad mixture, *you* know that; you know, too, that I am very fond of the girl, poor dear Esther. I have tried to separate her from evil pagan influences; she is the daughter of the Church; I want her to have no other parent; but you never can tell what lurks in *a caged animal that has once been wild.* My whole heart is with the Indian people, my son; my whole heart, my whole life, has been devoted to bringing them to Christ, *but it is a different thing to marry with one of them.*"

His small old eyes were riveted on Laurence like a hawk's on a rat. My heart lay like ice in my bosom.

Laurence, speechless and white, stared at him breathlessly.

"Go away somewhere," the old man was urging; "to Winnipeg, Toronto, Montreal; forget her, then come back to Ida McIntosh. A union of the Church and the Hudson's Bay will mean great things, and may ultimately result in my life's ambition, the civilization of this entire tribe, that we have worked so long to bring to God."

I listened, sitting like one frozen. Could those words have been uttered by my venerable teacher, by him whom I revered as I would one of the saints in his own black book? Ah, there was no mistaking it. My white father, my life-long friend who pretended to love me, to care for my happiness, was urging the man I worshipped to forget me, to marry with the factor's daughter—because of what? Of my red skin; my good, old, honest pagan mother; my confiding French-Indian father. In a second all the care, the hollow love he had given me since my childhood, were as things that never existed. I hated that old mission priest as I hated his white man's hell. I hated his long, white hair; I hated his thin, white hands; I hated his body, his soul, his voice, his black book—oh, how I hated the very atmosphere of him!

Laurence sat motionless, his face buried in his hands, but the old man continued, "No, no; not the child of that pagan mother; you can't trust her, my son. What would you do with a wife who might any day break from you to return to her prairies and her buckskins? *You can't trust her.*" His eyes grew smaller, more glittering, more fascinating then, and leaning with an odd, secret sort of movement towards Laurence, he almost whispered, "Think of her silent ways, her noiseless step; the girl glides about like an apparition; her quick fingers, her wild longings—I don't know why, but with all my fondness for her, she reminds me sometimes of a strange—*snake.*"

Laurence shuddered, lifted his face, and said hoarsely: "You're right, uncle; perhaps I'd better not; I'll go away, I'll forget her, and then—well, then—yes, you are right, it *is* a different thing to marry one of them." The old man arose. His feeble fingers still clasped his black book; his soft white hair clung about his forehead like that of an Apostle; his eyes lost their peering, crafty expression; his bent shoulders resumed the dignity of a minister of the living God; he was the picture of what the traders called him—"St. Paul."

"Good-night, son," he said.

"Good-night, uncle, and thank you for bringing me to myself."

They were the last words I ever heard uttered by either that old arch-fiend or his weak, miserable kinsman. Father Paul turned and left the room. I watched his withered hand—the hand I had so often felt resting on my head in holy benedictions—clasp the door-knob, turn it slowly, then, with bowed head and his pale face wrapped in thought, he left the room—left it with the mad venom of my hate pursuing him like the very Evil One he taught me of.

What were his years of kindness and care now? What did I care for his God, his heaven, his hell? He had robbed me of my native faith, of my parents, of my people, of this last, this life of love that would have made a great, good woman of me. God! how I hated him!

I crept to the closet in my dark little room. I felt for a bundle I had not looked at for years—yes, it was there, the buckskin dress I had worn as a little child when they brought me to the mission. I tucked it under my arm and descended the stairs noiselessly. I would look into the study and speak good-bye to Laurence; then I would—

I pushed open the door. He was lying on the couch where a short time previously he had sat, white and speechless, listening to Father Paul, I moved towards him softly. God in heaven, he was already asleep. As I bent over him the fullness of his perfect beauty impressed me for the first time; his slender form, his curving mouth that almost laughed even in sleep, his fair, tossed hair, his smooth, strong-pulsing throat. God! how I loved him!

Then there arose the picture of the factor's daughter. I hated her. I hated her baby face, her yellow hair, her whitish skin. "She shall not marry him," my soul said. "I will kill him first—kill his beautiful body, his lying, false heart." Something in my heart seemed to speak; it said over and over again, "Kill him, kill him; she will never have him then. Kill him. It will break Father Paul's heart and blight his life. He has killed the best of you, of your womanhood; kill *his* best, his pride, his hope—his sister's son, his nephew Laurence." But how? how?

What had that terrible old man said I was like? A *strange snake*. A snake? The idea wound itself about me like the very coils of a serpent. What was this in the beaded bag of my buckskin dress? this little thing rolled in tan that my mother had given me at parting with the words, "Don't touch much, but some time maybe you want it!" Oh! I knew well enough what it was—a small flint arrow-head dipped in the venom of some *strange snake*.

I knelt beside him and laid my hot lips on his hand. I worshipped him, oh, how, how I worshipped him! Then again the vision of *her* baby face, *her* yellow hair—I scratched his wrist twice with the arrow-tip. A single drop of red blood oozed up; he stirred. I turned the lamp down and slipped out of the room—out of the house.

I dream nightly of the horrors of the white man's hell. Why did they teach me of it, only to fling me into it?

Last night as I crouched beside my mother on the buffalo-hide, Dan Henderson, the trapper, came in to smoke with my father. He said old Father Paul was bowed with grief, that with my disappearance I was suspected, but that there was no proof. Was it not merely a snake bite?

They account for it by the fact that I am a Redskin.

They seem to have forgotten I am a woman.

Thomas King (Cherokee)

Borders

When I was twelve, maybe thirteen, my mother announced that we were going to go to Salt Lake City to visit my sister who had left the reserve, moved across the line, and found a job. Laetitia had not left home with my mother's blessing, but over time my mother had come to be proud of the fact that Laetitia had done all of this on her own.

"She did real good," my mother would say.

Then there were the fine points to Laetitia's going. She had not, as my mother liked to tell Mrs. Manyfingers, gone floating after some man like a balloon on a string. She hadn't snuck out of the house, either, and gone to Vancouver or Edmonton or Toronto to chase rainbows down alleys. And she hadn't been pregnant.

"She did real good."

I was seven or eight when Laetitia left home. She was seventeen. Our father was from Rocky Boy on the American side.

"Dad's American," Laetitia told my mother, "so I can go and come as I please."

"Send us a postcard."

Laetitia packed her things, and we headed for the border. Just outside of Milk River, Laetitia told us to watch for the water tower.

"Over the next rise. It's the first thing you see."

"We got a water tower on the reserve," my mother said. "There's a big one in Lethbridge, too."

"You'll be able to see the tops of the flagpoles, too. That's where the border is."

When we got to Coutts, my mother stopped at the convenience store and bought her and Laetitia a cup of coffee. I got an Orange Crush.

"This is real lousy coffee."

"You're just angry because I want to see the world."

"It's the water. From here on down, they got lousy water."

"I can catch the bus from Sweetgrass. You don't have to lift a finger."

"You're going to have to buy your water in bottles if you want good coffee."

There was an old wooden building about a block away, with a tall sign in the yard that said "Museum." Most of the roof had been blown away. Mom told me to go and see when the place was open. There were boards over the windows and doors. You could tell that the place was closed, and I told Mom so, but she said to go and check anyway. Mom and Laetitia stayed by the car. Neither one of them moved. I sat down on the steps of the museum and watched them, and I don't know that they ever said anything to each other. Finally, Laetitia got her bag out of the trunk and gave Mom a hug.

I wandered back to the car. The wind had come up, and it blew Laetitia's hair across her face. Mom reached out and pulled the strands out of Laetitia's eyes, and Laetitia let her.

"You can still see the mountain from here," my mother told Laetitia in Blackfoot.

"Lots of mountains in Salt Lake," Laetitia told her in English.

"The place is closed," I said. "Just like I told you."

Laetitia tucked her hair into her jacket and dragged her bag down the road to the brick building with the American flag flapping on a pole. When she got to where the guards were waiting, she turned, put the bag down, and waved to us. We waved back. Then my mother turned the car around, and we came home.

We got postcards from Laetitia regular, and, if she wasn't spreading jelly on the truth, she was happy. She found a good job and rented an apartment with a pool.

"And she can't even swim," my mother told Mrs. Manyfingers.

Most of the postcards said we should come down and see the city, but whenever I mentioned this, my mother would stiffen up.

So I was surprised when she bought two new tires for the car and put on her blue dress with the green and yellow flowers. I had to dress up, too, for my mother did not want us crossing the border looking like Americans. We made sandwiches and put them in a big box with pop and potato chips and some apples and bananas and a big jar of water.

"But we can stop at one of those restaurants, too, right?"

"We maybe should take some blankets in case you get sleepy."

"But we can stop at one of those restaurants, too, right?"

The border was actually two towns, though neither one was big enough to amount to anything. Coutts was on the Canadian side and consisted of the convenience store and gas station, the museum that was closed and boarded up, and a motel. Sweetgrass was on the American side, but all you could see was an overpass that arched across the highway and disappeared into the prairies. Just hearing the names of these towns, you would expect that Sweetgrass, which is a nice name and sounds like it is related to other places such as Medicine Hat and Moose Jaw and Kicking Horse Pass, would be on the Canadian side, and that Coutts, which sounds abrupt and rude, would be on the American side. But this was not the case.

Between the two borders was a duty-free shop where you could buy cigarettes and liquor and flags. Stuff like that.

We left the reserve in the morning and drove until we got to Coutts.

"Last time we stopped here," my mother said, "you had an Orange Crush. You remember that?"

"Sure," I said. "That was when Laetitia took off."

"You want another Orange Crush?"

"That means we're not going to stop at a restaurant, right?"

My mother got a coffee at the convenience store, and we stood around and watched the prairies move in the sunlight. Then we climbed back in the car. My mother straightened the dress across her thighs, leaned against the wheel, and drove all the way to the border in first gear, slowly, as if she were trying to see through a bad storm or riding high on black ice.

The border guard was an old guy. As he walked to the car, he swayed from side to side, his feet set wide apart, the holster on his hip pitching up and down. He leaned into the window, looked into the back seat, and looked at my mother and me.

"Morning, ma'am."

"Good morning."

"Where you heading?"

"Salt Lake City."

"Purpose of your visit?"

"Visit my daughter."

"Citizenship?"

"Blackfoot," my mother told him.

"Ma'am?"

"Blackfoot," my mother repeated.

"Canadian?"

"Blackfoot."

It would have been easier if my mother had just said "Canadian" and been done with it, but I could see she wasn't going to do that. The guard wasn't angry or anything. He smiled and looked towards the building. Then he turned back and nodded.

"Morning, ma'am."

"Good morning."

"Any firearms or tobacco?"

"No."

"Citizenship?"

"Blackfoot."

He told us to sit in the car and wait, and we did. In about five minutes, another guard came out with the first man. They were talking as they came, both men swaying back and forth like two cowboys headed for a bar or a gunfight.

"Morning, ma'am."

"Good morning."

"Cecil tells me you and the boy are Blackfoot."

"That's right."

"Now, I know that we got Blackfeet on the American side and the Canadians got Blackfeet on their side. Just so we can keep our records straight, what side do you come from?"

I knew exactly what my mother was going to say, and I could have told them if they had asked me.

"Canadian side or American side?" asked the guard.

"Blackfoot side," she said.

It didn't take them long to lose their sense of humor, I can tell you that. The one guard stopped smiling altogether and told us to park our car at the side of the building and come in.

We sat on a wood bench for about an hour before anyone came over to talk to us. This time it was a woman. She had a gun, too.

"Hi," she said. "I'm Inspector Pratt. I understand there is a little misunderstanding."

"I'm going to visit my daughter in Salt Lake City," my mother told her. "We don't have any guns or beer."

"It's a legal technicality, that's all."

"My daughter's Blackfoot, too."

The woman opened a briefcase and took out a couple of forms and began to write on one of them. "Everyone who crosses our border has to declare their citizenship. Even Americans. It helps us keep track of the visitors we get from the various countries."

She went on like that for maybe fifteen minutes, and a lot of the stuff she told us was interesting.

"I can understand how you feel about having to tell us your citizenship, and here's what I'll do. You tell me, and I won't put it down on the form. No-one will know but you and me."

Her gun was silver. There were several chips in the wood handle and the name "Stella" was scratched into the metal butt.

We were in the border office for about four hours, and we talked to almost everyone there. One of the men bought me a Coke. My mother brought a couple of sandwiches in from the car. I offered part of mine to Stella, but she said she wasn't hungry.

I told Stella that we were Blackfoot and Canadian, but she said that that didn't count because I was a minor. In the end, she told us that if my mother didn't declare her citizenship, we would have to go back to where we came from. My mother stood up and thanked Stella for her time. Then we got back in the car and drove to the Canadian border, which was only about a hundred yards away.

I was disappointed. I hadn't seen Laetitia for a long time, and I had never been to Salt Lake City. When she was still at home, Laetitia would go on and on about Salt Lake City. She had never been there, but her boyfriend Lester Tallbull had spent a year in Salt Lake at a technical school.

"It's a great place," Lester would say. "Nothing but blondes in the whole state."

Whenever he said that, Laetitia would slug him on his shoulder hard enough to make him flinch. He had some brochures on Salt Lake and some maps, and every so often the two of them would spread them out on the table.

"That's the temple. It's right downtown. You got to have a pass to get in."

"Charlotte says anyone can go in and look around."

"When was Charlotte in Salt Lake? Just when the hell was Charlotte in Salt Lake?"

"Last year."

"This is Liberty Park. It's got a zoo. There's good skiing in the mountains."

"Got all the skiing we can use," my mother would say. "People come from all over the world to ski at Banff. Cardston's got a temple, if you like those kinds of things."

"Oh, this one is real big," Lester would say. "They got armed guards and everything."

"Not what Charlotte says."

"What does she know?"

Lester and Laetitia broke up, but I guess the idea of Salt Lake stuck in her mind.

The Canadian border guard was a young woman, and she seemed happy to see us. "Hi," she said. "You folks sure have a great day for a trip. Where are you coming from?"

"Standoff."

"Is that in Montana?"

"No."

"Where are you going?"

"Standoff."

The woman's name was Carol and I don't guess she was any older than Laetitia. "Wow, you both Canadians?"

"Blackfoot."

"Really? I have a friend I went to school with who is Blackfoot. Do you know Mike Harley?"

"No."

"He went to school in Lethbridge, but he's really from Browning."

It was a nice conversation and there were no cars behind us, so there was no rush.

"You're not bringing any liquor back, are you?"

"No."

"Any cigarettes or plants or stuff like that?"

"No."

"Citizenship?"

"Blackfoot."

"I know," said the woman, "and I'd be proud of being Blackfoot if I were Blackfoot. But you have to be American or Canadian."

When Laetitia and Lester broke up, Lester took his brochures and maps with him, so Laetitia wrote to someone in Salt Lake City, and, about a month later, she got a big envelope of stuff. We sat at the table and opened up all the brochures, and Laetitia read each one out loud.

"Salt Lake City is the gateway to some of the world's most magnificent skiing.

"Salt Lake City is the home of one of the newest professional basketball franchises, the Utah Jazz.

"The Great Salt Lake is one of the natural wonders of the world."

It was kind of exciting seeing all those color brochures on the table and listening to Laetitia read all about how Salt Lake City was one of the best places in the entire world.

"That Salt Lake City place sounds too good to be true," my mother told her.

"It has everything."

"We got everything right here."

"It's boring here."

"People in Salt Lake City are probably sending away for brochures of Calgary and Lethbridge and Pincher Creek right now."

In the end, my mother would say that maybe Laetitia should go to Salt Lake City, and Laetitia would say that maybe she would.

We parked the car to the side of the building and Carol led us into a small room on the second floor. I found a comfortable spot on the couch and flipped through some back issues of *Saturday Night* and *Alberta Report*.

When I woke up, my mother was just coming out of another office. She didn't say a word to me. I followed her down the stairs and out to the car. I thought we were going home, but she turned the car around and drove back towards the American border, which made me think we were going to visit Laetitia in Salt Lake City after all. Instead she pulled into the parking lot of the duty-free store and stopped.

"We going to see Laetitia?"

"No."

"We going home?"

Pride is a good thing to have, you know. Laetitia had a lot of pride, and so did my mother. I figured that someday, I'd have it, too.

"So where are we going?"

Most of that day, we wandered around the duty-free store, which wasn't very large. The manager had a name tag with a tiny American flag on one side and a tiny Canadian flag on the other. His name was Mel. Towards evening, he began suggesting that we should be on our way. I told him we had nowhere to go, that neither the Americans nor the Canadians would let us in. He laughed at that and told us that we should buy something or leave.

The car was not very comfortable, but we did have all that food and it was April, so even if it did snow as it sometimes does on the prairies, we wouldn't freeze. The next morning my mother drove to the American border.

It was a different guard this time, but the questions were the same. We didn't spend as much time in the office as we had the day before. By noon, we were back at the Canadian border. By two we were back in the duty-free shop parking lot.

The second night in the car was not as much fun as the first, but my mother seemed in good spirits, and, all in all, it was as much an adventure as an inconvenience. There wasn't much food left and that was a problem, but we had lots of water as there was a faucet at the side of the duty-free shop.

One Sunday, Laetitia and I were watching television. Mom was over at Mrs. Manyfingers's. Right in the middle of the program, Laetitia turned off the set and said she was going to Salt Lake City, that life around here was too boring. I had wanted to see the rest of the program and really didn't care if Laetitia went to Salt Lake City or not. When Mom got home, I told her what Laetitia had said.

What surprised me was how angry Laetitia got when she found out that I had told Mom.

"You got a big mouth."

"That's what you said."

"What I said is none of your business."

"I didn't say anything."

"Well, I'm going for sure, now."

That weekend, Laetitia packed her bags, and we drove her to the border.

Mel turned out to be friendly. When he closed up for the night and found us still parked in the lot, he came over and asked us if our car was broken down or something. My mother thanked him for his concern and told him that we were fine, that things would get straightened out in the morning.

"You're kidding," said Mel. "You'd think they could handle the simple things."

"We got some apples and a banana," I said, "but we're all out of ham sandwiches."

"You know, you read about these things, but you just don't believe it. You just don't believe it."

"Hamburgers would be even better because they got more stuff for energy."

My mother slept in the back seat. I slept in the front because I was smaller and could lie under the steering wheel. Late that night, I heard my mother open the car door. I found her sitting on her blanket leaning against the bumper of the car.

"You see all those stars," she said. "When I was a little girl, my grandmother used to take me and my sisters out on the prairies and tell us stories about all the stars."

"Do you think Mel is going to bring us any hamburgers?"

"Every one of those stars has a story. You see that bunch of stars over there that look like a fish?"

"He didn't say no."

"Coyote went fishing, one day. That's how it all started." We sat out under the stars that night, and my mother told me all sorts of stories. She was serious about it, too. She'd tell them slow, repeating parts as she went, as if she expected me to remember each one.

Early the next morning, the television vans began to arrive, and guys in suits and women in dresses came trotting over to us, dragging microphones and cameras and lights behind them. One of the vans had a table set up with orange juice and sandwiches and fruit. It was for the crew, but when I told them we hadn't eaten for a while, a really skinny blonde woman told us we could eat as much as we wanted.

They mostly talked to my mother. Every so often one of the reporters would come over and ask me questions about how it felt to be an Indian without a country. I told them we had a nice house on the reserve and that my cousins had a couple of horses we rode when we went fishing. Some of the television people went over to the American border, and then they went to the Canadian border.

Around noon, a good-looking guy in a dark blue suit and an orange tie with little ducks on it drove up in a fancy car. He talked to my mother for a while, and, after they were done talking, my mother called me over, and we got into our car. Just as my mother started the engine, Mel came over and gave us a bag of peanut brittle and told us that justice was a damn hard thing to get, but that we shouldn't give up.

I would have preferred lemon drops, but it was nice of Mel anyway.

"Where are we going now?"

"Going to visit Laetitia."

The guard who came out to our car was all smiles. The television lights were so bright they hurt my eyes, and, if you tried to look through the windshield in certain directions, you couldn't see a thing.

"Morning, ma'am."

"Good morning."

"Where you heading?"

"Salt Lake City."

"Purpose of your visit?"

"Visit my daughter."

"Any tobacco, liquor, or firearms?"

"Don't smoke."

"Any plants or fruit?"

"Not any more."

"Citizenship?"

"Blackfoot."

The guard rocked back on his heels and jammed his thumbs into his gun belt. "Thank you," he said, his fingers patting the butt of the revolver. "Have a pleasant trip."

My mother rolled the car forward, and the television people had to scramble out of the way. They ran alongside the car as we pulled away from the border, and, when they couldn't run any farther, they stood in the middle of the highway and waved and waved and waved.

We got to Salt Lake City the next day. Laetitia was happy to see us, and, that first night, she took us out to a restaurant that made really good soups. The list of pies took up a whole page. I had cherry. Mom had chocolate. Laetitia said that she saw us on television the night before and, during the meal, she had us tell her the story over and over again.

Laetitia took us everywhere. We went to a fancy ski resort. We went to the temple. We got to go shopping in a couple of large malls, but they weren't as large as the one in Edmonton, and Mom said so.

After a week or so, I got bored and wasn't at all sad when my mother said we should be heading back home. Laetitia wanted us to stay longer, but Mom said no, that she had things to do back home and that, next time, Laetitia should come up and visit. Laetitia said she was thinking about moving back, and Mom told her to do as she pleased, and Laetitia said that she would.

On the way home, we stopped at the duty-free shop, and my mother gave Mel a green hat that said "Salt Lake" across the front. Mel was a funny guy. He took the hat and blew his nose and told my mother that she was an inspiration to us all. He gave us some more peanut brittle and came out into the parking lot and waved at us all the way to the Canadian border.

It was almost evening when we left Coutts. I watched the border through the rear window until all you could see were the tops of the flagpoles and the blue water tower, and then they rolled over a hill and disappeared.

Thomas King (Cherokee)
A Seat in the Garden

Joe Hovaugh settled into the garden on his knees and began pulling at the wet, slippery weeds that had sprung up between the neat rows of beets. He trowled his way around the zucchini and up and down the lines of carrots, and he did not notice the big Indian at all until he stopped at the tomatoes, sat back, and tried to remember where he had set the ball of twine and the wooden stakes.

The big Indian was naked to the waist. His hair was braided and wrapped with white ermine and strips of red cloth. He wore a single feather held in place by a leather band stretched around his head, and, even though his arms were folded tightly across his chest, Joe could see the glitter and flash of silver and turquoise on each finger.

"If you build it, they will come," said the big Indian.

Joe rolled forward and shielded his eyes from the morning sun.

"If you build it, they will come," said the big Indian again.

"Christ sakes," Joe shouted. "Get the hell out of the corn, will ya!"

"If you build it . . ."

"Yeah, yeah. Hey! This is private property. You people ever hear of private property?"

". . . they will come."

Joe struggled to his feet and got his shovel from the shed. But when he got back to the garden, the big Indian was gone.

"All right!" Joe shouted, and drove the nose of the shovel into the ground. "Come out of that corn!"

The cornstalks were only about a foot tall. Nevertheless, Joe walked each row, the shovel held at the ready, just in case the big Indian tried to take him by surprise.

When Red Mathews came by in the afternoon, Joe poured him a cup of coffee and told him about the big Indian and what he had said. Red told Joe that he had seen the movie.

"Wasn't a movie, Red, damn it. It was a real Indian. He was just standing there in the corn."

"You probably scared him away."

"You can't let them go standing in your garden whenever they feel like it."

"That's the truth."

The next day, when Joe came out to the garden to finish staking the tomatoes, the big Indian was waiting for him. The man looked as though he were asleep, but as soon as he saw Joe, he straightened up and crossed his arms on his chest.

"You again!"

"If you build it . . ."

"I'm going to call the police. You hear me. The police are going to come and haul you away."

". . . they will come."

Joe turned around and marched back into the house and phoned the RCMP, who said they would send someone over that very afternoon.

"Afternoon? What am I supposed to do with him until then? Feed him lunch?"

The RCMP officer told Joe that it might be best if he stayed in his house. There was the chance, the officer said, that the big Indian might be drunk or on drugs, and if that were the case, it was better if Joe didn't antagonize him.

"He's walking on my corn. Does that mean anything to you?"

The RCMP officer assured Joe that it meant a great deal to him, that his wife was a gardener, and he knew how she would feel if someone walked on her corn.

"Still," said the officer, "it's best if you don't do anything."

What Joe did do was to call Red, and when Red arrived, the big Indian was still in the garden, waiting.

"Wow, he's a big sucker, all right," said Red. "You know, he looks a little like Jeff Chandler."

"I called the police, and they said not to antagonize him."

"Hey, there are two of us, right?"

"That's right," said Joe.

"You bet it's right."

Joe got the shovel and a hoe from the shed, and he and Red wandered out into the garden, as if nothing were wrong.

"He's watching us," said Red.

"Don't step on the tomatoes," said Joe.

Joe walked around the zucchini, casually dragging the shovel behind him. Red ambled through the beets, the hoe slung over his shoulder.

"If you build it, they will come," the Indian said.

"Get him!" shouted Joe. And before Red could do anything, Joe was charging through the carrots, the shovel held out in front like a lance.

"Wait a minute, Joe," yelled Red, the hoe still on his shoulder. But Joe was already into the tomatoes. He was closing on the big Indian, who hadn't moved, when he stepped on the bundle of wooden stakes and went down in a heap.

"Hey," said Red. "You okay?"

Red helped Joe to his feet, and when the two men looked around, the big Indian was gone.

"Where'd he go?" said Joe.

"Beats me," said Red. "What'd you do to get him so angry?"

Red helped Joe to the house, wrapped an ice pack on his ankle, and told him to put his leg on the chair.

"I saw a movie a couple of years back about a housing development that was built on top of an ancient Indian burial mound," Red said.

"I would have got him, if I hadn't tripped."

"They finally had to get an authentic medicine man to come in and appease the spirits."

"Did you see the look on his face when he saw me coming?"

"And you should have seen some of those spirits."

When the RCMP arrived, Joe showed the officer where the Indian had stood, how he had run at him with the shovel, and how he had stumbled over the bundle of stakes.

After Joe got up and brushed himself off, the RCMP officer asked him if he recognized the big Indian.

"Not likely," said Joe. "There aren't any Indians around here."

"Yes, there are," said Red. "Remember those three guys who come around on weekends every so often."

"The old winos?" said Joe.

"They have that grocery cart, and they pick up cans."

"They don't count."

"They sit down there by the hydrangea and crush the cans and eat their lunch. Sometimes they get to singing."

"You mean drink their lunch."

"Well, they could have anything in that bottle."

"Most likely Lysol."

The RCMP officer walked through the garden with Joe and Red and made a great many notes. He shook hands with both men and told Joe to call him if there was any more trouble.

"Did you ever wonder," said Red, after the officer left, "just what he wants you to build or who 'they' are?"

"I suppose you saw a movie."

"Maybe we should ask the Indians."

"The drunks?"

"Maybe they could translate for us."

"The guy speaks English."

"That's right, Joe. God, this gets stranger all the time. Ed Ames, that's who he reminds me of."

On Saturday morning, when Joe and Red walked out on the porch, the big Indian was waiting patiently for them in the corn. They were too far away to hear him, but they could see his mouth moving.

"Okay," said Red. "All we got to do is wait for the Indians to show up."

They showed up around noon. One Indian had a green knapsack. The other two pushed a grocery cart in front of them. It was full of cans and bottles. They were old, Joe noticed, and even from the porch, he imagined he could smell them. They walked to a corner of the garden behind the hydrangea where the sprinklers didn't reach. It was a dry, scraggly wedge that Joe had never bothered to cultivate. As soon as the men stopped the cart and sat down on the ground, Red got to his feet and stretched.

"Come on. Can't hurt to talk with them. Grab a couple of beers, so they know we're friendly."

"A good whack with the shovel would be easier."

"Hey, this is kind of exciting. Don't you think this is kind of exciting?"

"I wouldn't trip this time."

When Joe and Red got to the corner, the three men were busy crushing the cans. One man would put a can on a flat stone and the second man would step on it. The third man picked up the crushed can and put it in a brown grocery bag. They were older than Joe had thought, and they didn't smell as bad as he had expected.

"Hi," said Red. "That's a nice collection of cans."

"Good morning," said the first Indian.

"Getting pretty hot," said the second Indian.

"You fellows like a drink," said the third Indian, and he took a large glass bottle out of the knapsack.

"No thanks," said Red. "You fellows like a beer?"

"Lemon water," said the third Indian. "My wife makes it without any sugar so it's not as sweet as most people like."

"How can you guys drink that stuff?" said Joe.

"You get used to it," said the second Indian. "And it's better for you than pop."

As the first Indian twisted the lid off the bottle and took a long drink, Joe looked around to make sure none of his neighbors were watching him.

"I'll bet you guys know just about everything there is to know about Indians," said Red.

"Well," said the first Indian, "Jimmy and Frank are Nootka and I'm Cree. You guys reporters or something?"

"Reporters? No."

"You never know," said the second Indian. "Last month, a couple of reporters did a story on us. Took pictures and everything."

"It's good that these kinds of problems are brought to the public's attention," said Red.

"You bet," said the third Indian. "Everyone's got to help. Otherwise there's going to be more garbage than people."

Joe was already bored with the conversation. He looked back to see if the big Indian was still there.

"This is all nice and friendly," said Joe. "But we've got a problem that we were hoping you might be able to help us with."

"Sure," said the first Indian. "What's the problem?"

Joe snapped the tab on one of the beers, took a long swig, and jerked his thumb in the direction of the garden. "I've got this big Indian who likes to stand in my garden."

"Where?" asked the second Indian.

"Right there," said Joe.

"Right where?" asked the third Indian.

"If you build it, they will come," shouted the big Indian.

"There, there," said Joe. "Did you hear that?"

"Hear what?" said the first Indian.

"They're embarrassed," said Red under his breath. "Let me handle this."

"This is beginning to piss me off," said Joe, and he took another pull on the beer.

"We were just wondering," Red began. "If you woke up one day and found a big Indian standing in your cornfield and all he would say was, 'if you build it, they will come,' what would you do?"

"I'd stop drinking," said the second Indian, and the other two Indians covered their faces with their hands.

"No, no," said Red. "That's not what I mean. Well . . . you see that big Indian over there in the cornfield, don't you?"

The Indians looked at each other, and then they looked at Joe and Red.

"Okay," said the first Indian. "Sure, I see him."

"Oh yeah," said the second Indian. "He's right there, all right. In the . . . beets?"

"Corn," said Joe.

"Right," said the third Indian. "In the corn. I can see him, too. Clear as day."

"That's our problem," said Red. "We think maybe he's a spirit or something."

"No, we don't," said Joe.

"Yes, we do," said Red, who was just getting going. "We figure he wants us to build something to appease him so he'll go away."

"Sort of like . . . a spirit?" said the first Indian.

"Hey," said the second Indian, "remember that movie we saw about that community that was built . . ."

"That's the one," said Red. "What we have to figure out is what he wants us to build. You guys got any ideas?"

The three Indians looked at each other. The first Indian looked at the cornfield. Then he looked at Joe and Red.

"Tell you what," he said. "We'll go over there and talk to him and see what he wants. He looks . . . Cree. You guys stay here, okay?"

Joe and Red watched as the three Indians walked into the garden. They stood together, facing the beets.

"Hey," shouted Joe. "You guys blind? He's behind you."

The first Indian waved his hand and smiled, and the three men turned around. Red could see them talking, and he tried to watch their lips, but he couldn't figure out what they were saying. After a while, the Indians waved at the rows of carrots and came back over to where Joe and Red were waiting.

"Well," said Red. "Did you talk to him?"

"Yes," said the first Indian. "You were right. He is a spirit."

"I knew it!" shouted Red. "What does he want?"

The first Indian looked back to the cornfield. "He's tired of standing, he says. He wants a place to sit down. But he doesn't want to mess up the garden. He says he would like it if you would build him a . . . a . . . bench right about . . . here."

"A bench?" said Joe.

"That's what he said."

"So he can sit down?"

"He gets tired standing."

"The hell you say."

"Do you still see him?" asked the second Indian.

"You blind? Of course I still see him."

"Then I'd get started on the bench right away," said the third Indian.

"Come on, Red," said Joe, and he threw the empty beer can into the hydrangea and opened the other one. "We got to talk."

Joe put the pad of paper on the kitchen table and drew a square. "This is the garden," he said. "These are the carrots. These are the beets. These are the beans. And this is the corn. The big Indian is right about here."

"That's right," said Red. "But what does it mean?"

"Here's where those winos crush their cans and drink their Lysol," Joe continued, marking a spot on the pad and drawing a line to it.

"Lemon water."

"You listening?"

"Sure."

"If you draw lines from the house to where the big Indian stands and from there to where the winos crush their cans and back to the house . . . Now do you see it?"

"Hey, that's pretty good, Joe."

"What does it remind you of?"

"A bench?"

"No," said Joe. "A triangle."

"Okay, I can see that."

"And if you look at it like this, you can see clearly that the winos and the big Indian are there, and the house where you and I are is here."

"What if you looked at it this way, Joe," said Red, and he turned the paper a half turn to the right. "Now the house is there and the old guys and the big Indian are here."

"That's not the way you look at it. That's not the way it works."

"Does that mean we're not going to build the bench?"

"It's our battle plan."

"A bench might be simpler," said Red.

"I'll attack him from the house along this line. You take him from the street along that line. We'll catch him between us."

"I don't know that this is going to work."

"Just don't step on the tomatoes."

The next morning, Red waited behind the hydrangea. He was carrying the hoe and a camera. Joe crouched by the corner of the house with the shovel.

"Charge!" yelled Joe, and he broke from his hiding place and lumbered across the lawn and into the garden. Red leapt through the hydrangea and struggled up the slight incline to the cornfield.

"If you built it, they will come," shouted the Indian.

"Build it yourself," shouted Joe, and he swung the shovel at the big Indian's legs. Red, who was slower, stopped at the edge of the cornfield to watch Joe whack the Indian with his shovel and to take a picture, so he saw Joe and his shovel run right through the Indian and crash into the compost mound.

"Joe, Joe . . . you all right? God, you should have seen it. You ran right through that guy. Just like he wasn't there. I got a great picture. Wait till you see the picture. Just around the eyes, he looks a little like Sal Mineo."

Red helped Joe back to the house and cleaned the cuts on Joe's face. He wrapped another ice pack on Joe's ankle and then drove down to the one-hour photo store and turned the film in. By the time he got back to the house, Joe was standing on the porch, leaning on the railing.

"You won't believe it, Joe," said Red. "Look at this."

Red fished a photograph out of the pack. It showed Joe and the shovel in mid-swing plunging through the corn. The colors were brilliant.

Joe looked at the photograph for a minute and then he looked at the cornfield. "Where's the big Indian?"

"That's just it. He's not there."

"Christ!"

"Does that mean we're going to build the bench?"

The bench was a handsome affair with a concrete base and a wooden seat. The Indians came by the very next Saturday with their knapsack and grocery cart, and Red could tell that they were impressed.

"Boy," said the first Indian, "that's a good-looking bench."

"You think this will take care of the problem?" asked Red.

"That Indian still in the cornfield?" said the second Indian.

"Of course he's still there," said Joe. "Can't you hear him?"

"I don't know," said the third Indian, and he twisted the lid off the bottle and took a drink. "I don't think he's one of ours."

"What should we do?"

"Don't throw your cans in the hydrangea," said the first Indian. "It's hard to get them out. We're not as young as we used to be."

Joe and Red spent the rest of the day sitting on the porch, drinking beer, and watching the big Indian in the garden. He looked a little like Victor Mature, Red thought, now that he had time to think about it, or maybe Anthony Quinn, only he was taller. And there was an air about the man that made Red believe—believe with all his heart—that he had met this Indian before.

D'Arcy McNickle (Métis)

The Hawk Is Hungry

My sister had come to spend the summer at my Montana ranch. It was a long ten years since I had seen her, I was fond of her, and I was hoping to keep her in the West. I wasn't subtle about it. I was bragging shamelessly about our advantages, I was ready to lie if need be.

My sister is an attractive person. She is young, she will always be young, she is pleasing to look at, and she enjoys herself. Her name is Anne Elizabeth, after a great-grandmother, whom she resembles, if the painting which hung in the library of our Connecticut home is to be trusted.

As I say, I wasn't being subtle in my campaign of persuasion. Every day I thought up something for the purpose.

"You laugh when you hear mention of the 'great open spaces,' but the fact remains, this is the place to live." I would make such a remark during our morning's ride—she likes horses and I had done everything to cultivate this interest.

"I know—splendid air—open-hearted people."

My fondness for Anne runs to such foolish lengths that she may take any sort of liberty with me—she always ends by regretting it and treating me with tender regard.

"Nonsense!" After one of her digs I tried to be stern. "We are really a free people out here. The American spirit is making its last stand here. Every man is his master. He believes in himself. We don't know anything about tenement life, ward politics, the factory system—all that. . . ."

Then she would smile, and I would know that she was ready to squash me once more. "Yes, you know so little about these things that you've let the Easterners get control of your power sites, your mines, and your politics. As for tenement life, look at your farmers. . . ."

"Ranchers, Anne!"

She gave me her broadest smile, in which, I suspected, was hidden a good bit of amused tolerance. We had reached home after the ride and we were hungry. We smelled our breakfast coffee as we came near the ranch house. If I have not already given myself away, I will make it clear that I am a bachelor, and that I keep a man and wife to cheer me up and to do the hard work. And after smelling the coffee, who could continue the argument? For once she did not wind up by calling me a romancer, a hopeless romancer, her pet term for me.

On that day I had promised to take Anne to visit the Brown sisters, Matilda and Beth. I had counted on the Browns to help me persuade Anne about the freedom of the West. They, like Anne, had been teaching school in one of those New York beehives; they had wearied of it, as her letters told me she had; and they had struck for freedom, coming here and taking up a homestead. They had talked to me about that. "We needed a change," they had said during one of our first conversations. "The city was stifling us and we needed a little free movement—needed to get our hands in the dirt." I had remembered their words. It wasn't any of my romancing. I had admired their courage. My coming to the West had been forced upon me by a physical and nervous system which had collapsed without much warning. The Browns had come by choice. That was what mattered.

Their homestead is high on a hillside. Some people have been unkind enough to speak of this as a piece of stupidity. "Who in hell would try to farm a hilltop, if he was in his right mind!" I've heard people say it. That wasn't fair. There wasn't much homestead land left when the girls came, and their choice was not the worst they might have made.

Their only water is a sluggish spring, and the soil up there is coarse and thirsty. In a dry summer—most of our summers are dry—they have the tedious task of carrying water to their garden. But what prejudiced people was the fact that the Browns had planted, and watered, a flower garden as well as the indispensable vegetable plot.

I told Anne about this and was surprised by my own vehemence in defending them against the harsh comments I had heard. These I put down to ignorance laughing at what it could not understand. High art in low company is nonsense. "You can see why they were misunderstood," I appealed to Anne.

I don't know what I had expected of her. A nod of the head, if it had been sympathetic, would have sufficed. All she said was, "You must take me to see them sometime."

That cooled me. I believe I changed the subject. At least I didn't tell her any more stories about the Browns, and there were more. There was one about the time Matilda washed the two pigs they had just bought, because "pigs are naturally clean" if given a chance, as their books on agricultural science informed them. And there was the time they were taken in by a rustic wag and on his advice had tried to buy "side-hill cattle," the kind with legs shorter on one side to make side-hill grazing more convenient. Without investigating these stories, I had dismissed them as fabrications; but the fact that I withheld them from Anne would indicate, I suppose, that I wasn't sure.

Still, I had introduced the subject of the visit and I wasn't permitted to let it drop. I suspect that Anne thought she might have some fun out of me. She had said, "I would like to see that flower garden built in defiance of the laws of nature, to say nothing of realistic neighbors."

Laughter and scepticism lay behind those words, and I shied. "All right, Anne. But I warn you, you may not enjoy them."

At that she did laugh. "I believe you're afraid to show them off!" I protested that I was nothing of the sort.

We drove the ten miles behind my fast bay team, setting out right after breakfast. On the way we talked about our childhood Connecticut, always a safe topic.

　　I am now coming to the part of this record which decidedly I do not like to recall. Our visit went so suddenly from a commonplace friendly call to—well, let's call it ridiculous and let it go at that.

　　The Brown place looked especially forlorn that morning. I had been there before, but I must admit that I had not noticed details. I suppose I was always full of thoughts about their independence of spirit and their making their own fate.

　　Their house was built of slab siding, refuse which most mills either burn or throw away, and the roof of a single slope was covered with tar-paper. Beside the house there was a shed for the chickens, which but for being smaller was equal to their own living quarters. The chicken house was shaded by a growth of wild elderberry bushes, around the roots of which the hens dusted themselves in holes worn by their bodies. There was a shed for the cow, a plain cow, no fantastic "side-hill" beast. Then there was a berry patch, with many dead bushes, the vegetable garden which gave them sustenance, and finally the flowers—against the walls of the house, in a round bed in the center of the yard, and a perfect nest of hollyhocks against the outhouse.

　　The eye took all this in in a single glance. I saw Anne look, and then look at me. I looked dead ahead. "This," she was saying silently (in my mind, of course), "you call superior to tenement conditions? It's true there is an abundance of fresh air! What a lot of fresh air!"

　　I had managed to get word to the sisters by calling their nearest neighbor on the telephone. So they were expecting us that Saturday morning. When they came out of the house a minute or two after we drew up, they had tidy aprons over their freshly ironed gingham dresses.

　　Anne slides very easily into any situation, and I should have known that there would be no difficulty in getting acquainted and settling ourselves. But I had become so apprehensive about Anne and the impression she would get of my prize exhibits that I did nothing but fidget.

　　"You've been here three years now, if I remember correctly," I observed at the first opportunity. I don't know what I expected them to say. I suppose Anne knew. I suppose it was written all over my face and in my manner, my eagerness to hear the Brown girls get rapturous over their manner of life. The words would not matter.

　　That was when things began to get ridiculous.

　　Matilda, the younger and the more quick-spoken, snapped me up. "Three of the dreariest years mortals ever endured. If you called it half a century it wouldn't seem wrong."

　　Her voice was absolutely flat. For a moment we all only stared at her, Anne and I—more especially I—trying to get at her meaning. How seriously did she intend her words?

　　"Really," I said, trying to ignore that flatness in her voice, "it hasn't been that bad! Whenever I've seen you, you've both looked cheery—I would say happy. Always some new thing happening. . . ."

"Mr. Buck, you've seen very little of us—and you've never seen us after a broiling day when we've come in broken-backed from carrying water to our garden—you've never seen me get raving mad when that murderous chicken hawk carries off one of our precious few hens. . . ."

I was ready to drop the subject. It was the elder sister, Beth, who made the shift and got us back on safe ground.

I had noticed before that if at any time Matilda failed to make herself understood, or if one questioned her reasoning in a discussion, Beth came to her aid, perhaps not consciously. Matilda of course resented intrusions of that sort, and I had seen her contradict herself, apparently simply to embarrass her sister. Beth was mild and warm and devoted; Matilda was lean-faced, impetuous, argumentative, caustic, demanding.

"Everybody tells us we arrived in the driest years this country has ever seen. This hill, they tell us, used to be green all summer through. Maybe they're right. We only know what we've seen." She let it go at that and got Anne to talking about Connecticut, which was their homeland as well as ours. They came from Meriden, we from Hartford. Since they had been teaching in New York City not so many years before, it soon turned out that Anne and they had common acquaintances. After that, things went along pleasantly, almost gaily, for a while.

Matilda shook off the gloom which had resulted from our first exchange and was most eager in her questioning about life "back there."

"You've no idea what a treat it is to hear you talk," she said suddenly, her eyes shining.

The simple luncheon they served was made an occasion for bringing out their linen (they had a few pieces buried in a trunk) and silver, nice old-fashioned flatware. While the sisters worked at setting things in place and getting the food served up, Anne and I tossed words at them, never looking at each other. I saw her examine the surroundings in quick, shielded glances. I looked about too and felt depressed. The house inside lacked the shabbiness of the yard and garden, and it was scrubbed clean, but it was depressing.

The room in which we sat was hardly more than ten feet square and it was full of evidence of that rejected world (I could see now, realistically, that what had been left behind was more real, better understood, and better loved, than what they had come to)—an album of photographs, framed etchings and prints, a plaster cast of the Apollo Belvedere, Breton earthenware on a plate rail, and of course books, shelved against every vacant wall. I also saw a bookcase in the small room adjoining, the bedroom, and no doubt there were books stored away in boxes.

We looked at these things, Anne and I, and tried to make conversation. She avoided my eyes. She smiled gently when she caught the glances of the sisters. She was moved to tenderness. In fact, her reactions were what mine should have been, since I am supposed to be the more feeling person and she the more rational. And there I was, glum and depressed.

The table was set in the doorway, but it might as well have been on top of the stove. There was no shade outside but there even the noon sun was sufferable. As for that cabin, with its thin walls, low roof and small square windows, it was a perfect heat trap. We sat about the table and perspired, eating making it worse, and only slavish obedience to social custom kept us fully clothed and amiable.

Matilda took command of the conversation at the table. It seemed that we had all been in Brittany, at different times, and the talk turned first to the Quimper plates on the rack.

"We did get about," Matilda was saying. "Our two salaries combined meant an occasional summer in Europe, Christmas with our Connecticut folks, Easter in Bermuda. It wasn't bad, teaching."

I squirmed, not looking at Anne.

"There was that time we made an excursion in the Hautes Alpes. Motorbus trip. Remember, Beth? Like today, there were heat waves, layer on layer, and the peasants were on the mountainside above us, scything hay. We were in the last seat of the autobus, watching them. It was intolerable when we stopped, heat and dust, and burnt petrol. We wondered if the peasants did not hate us for carrying that smell into their mountains. Remember? We watched them, like brown moles on the mountainside, swinging their scythes. We said something like 'How patient and enduring. . . .' I often think of that when we're blistering on our hillside. Not very enduring, I'd say."

We laughed a little, without gaiety.

As we sat there I noticed a hen, a grouchy-looking bird of a dirty brown color, walk or rather stroll across the yard, obviously intent on looking us over. Coming near, she cocked her head at us and stood with one foot raised.

Beth saw me look. "That's Molly, the boss of the hencoop. She heard strange voices and has come round to investigate. None of the others, not even Tom the rooster, would stir about in this heat."

When Beth tossed out a crumb, Molly the hen showed some of her quality. If she had run excitedly for the tidbit, she would have attracted attention in the hencoop. Instead, she walked quietly toward the crumb, looked back once to make sure she was unobserved, then deftly clipped it with her beak and turned once more toward the humankind.

We all commented.

"A creature of sense."

"You could call it insight."

"Oh, Molly," Beth exclaimed. "She never makes a false move!"

It was left for Matilda to make the wry comment. "You see what we have come to. The neighbors think us fantastic, so they avoid us. Result, we're reduced to making conversations with the barnyard folk. You should hear us carry on. Some days you'd think we were a family of ten, the way we call out names. 'Tom, get out of the garden this minute! Susiebell—that's the guinea-hen—stop that racket!' "

Beth looked a little stung. "But they are like people! We've known people just like Molly. Bossy, fussy, always wanting her way, and getting it. Even Tom the old rooster has a way of giving in. The young rooster positively avoids her. He has his younger set. But that Molly—she'll even fight off the chicken hawk! The others, with old Tom in the lead, the silly thing, run at the first sight of his shadow."

That left us wondering what to say next. A kind of embarrassment had come upon me and I supposed that Anne shared it. I felt that under the surface of this neighborly visit were many quirky currents of meaning, hidden eddies of the subject which somehow one must avoid, deep pools of resentment and frustration. I began to wish we could be on our way—and we hadn't yet reached the dessert course.

Now it was Touraine, the château at Loches, and the little blue room with fleur-de-lys on the walls where Anne of Brittany had sat looking out upon the Loire flowing toward the sea—as the guide told it.

"At Chenancoux we stood in the room of that Medici woman. It was so different from Anne's little blue room . . .," Matilda chanted, remembering more of her guidebook. "When we got bored by French chatter, we had tea at Thomas Cook's, upstairs. The English make those snug upstairs tea shops all over France."

If we could have kept to France and Bermuda and teaching in New York, all would have been well, and at the proper moment Anne and I would have started for home. Instead, we were swept suddenly into the full current of their hidden, complex lives.

It began when a shadow drifted across the yard. But before that, the rooster, with some of his hens in tow, had wandered out to share whatever entertainment Molly had found. They were together in a group, midway across the parched yard. Their beaks hung open. It was wretchedly hot just then. The sun blast withered every living thing, blinding animal eyes and giving a droop to green leaves. The utter quiet of the willows at the spring showed how breathless was the air. The faint piping whistle of a threshing machine in the valley announced the end of the noon rest. There was work to do. We at the table were wilted.

Molly the hen suddenly jerked her head erect. She looked toward the cabin, then off to the spring. Then a quick step of alarm. A moment later all the chickens had caught her awareness. Heads poked high. The rooster gave a throaty warning.

From my position at the table I had the best view of the yard and had seen that first stir of alarm. Matilda must have seen it almost as soon as I, for she reacted before the others. Her breath caught on a half-uttered sound.

The shadow streaked across the yard, was lost, then drifted back again from a different angle. It came to a pause. The hawk was directly overhead, descending.

Matilda reared up, on the point of screaming, but no sound coming. Her face, when I glanced up, was intense with pain. It chilled me.

The outcry of the chickens was shrill and wild. Wings fluttered, feathered bodies hurtled through the air, stirring small whirls of dust. The noontime stillness was suddenly loud with terror.

Molly gave ground slowly, backing away, wings spread and head lowered, scolding loudly. And then the bolt of death struck her, sprawling in the dust. A shower of feathers and scattering pebbles marked her last fight. Great wings flapped again. The sky raider was struggling upward. The hapless Molly screeched despairingly, her scolding tone beaten out of her. She rasped weakly. The sound rose higher and higher, and before any of us moved, it had stopped altogether. A few feathers floated earthward.

Matilda in this moment of stress was incoherent. She was the first to reach the yard, where she grabbed up a few stray brown feathers. The hawk was already out of sight.

"The beast! The—the beast!" It was as much as she could pronounce.

Beth had reached her by then, stretched out a hand to her floundering sister, thought better of it. For a moment she stood there empty-handed. Then her trick of explaining her sister asserted itself. She turned to us.

"It is hard to make you understand, I suppose, how terrible this is. Molly was so much—almost a person. We've been so alone here. And so, this, well. . . ."

That effort of Beth's to explain the situation finally aroused Matilda. She came at us fiercely, fairly shouting. She was oblivious of us, of course. Her quarrel was with that miserable hillside shack, with the years of dreariness. But she explained it better.

"Damnation! It was more than that! You make us seem like two old maids talking to ourselves. I say *no* to that and damn the notion! That hen was an idea. The idea of personal integrity. Standing alone and damn the consequences. Men try to live like that. Few do. Very few. The hen did. Did you see her? And this hawk, he's the witless brute force that insults us all. The best of us! We put ourselves above the beast, but when the hawk is hungry he comes for us. And what are we then?

"We liked Molly because we fancied ourselves her kind of a person. That's the truth of the matter. Birds of her feather! How do you like that?"

With an expression of disgust, she stopped short and snapped her head earthward, letting fall the few feathers which old Molly had lost in her fatal encounter.

I heard Anne's soft voice and when I looked up from a study of the ground at my feet, I saw that she had approached Matilda, put her hand out to her.

"Why don't you come home, to Connecticut? That's what you want to do, isn't it? Come home with me."

The sisters seemed to fold up at that. Perhaps it had been in their minds for a long time and they had never spoken of it aloud. Perhaps. I don't know. They seemed to get limp, Matilda and Beth together, and they slumped into chairs at the table. Neither spoke until they had sat reflecting for moments. Brittany, peasants on the mountainside, the Bermuda sands, winter in the Connecticut hills—it must all have been in their minds. Perspiration poured down their faces without distracting their thought.

"But we couldn't," Matilda spoke her thought aloud. "We couldn't—any more than Molly could run from the hawk."

She spoke a great deal more, beginning slowly and reflectively. A little unsure of herself, it seemed, but gradually warming to the idea and adding intensity to her words. Soon she was glowing, her eyes looking at us brightly. Beth began to catch some of her conviction.

"Oh, we haven't given up. Only the other day we were talking about renting a place down in the valley where the soil is better. We saw a place we could get at a small rental."

Hours later, as the afternoon was cooling, we started home, Anne and I. The girls, by then, seemed cheerful and full of prospects.

Anne stirred one sceptic thought, however, which has stayed in my mind ever since. She said, "I wonder—was it worth it—if that's the way the West was settled?"

I don't like to carry that question around with me, but I confess it has lodged in my mind and I can't get rid of it.

Jim Northrup (Anishinaabe)

Veterans' Dance

Don't sweat the small shit, Lug thought; it's all small shit unless they're shooting at you.

The tall, skinny Shinnob finished changing the tire on his car. It took longer than usual because he had to improvise with the jack. Summer in Minnesota and Lug was on his way to a powwow.

The powwow was on its second day. The dancers were getting ready for their third grand entry. Singers around the various drums had found their rhythm. Old bones were loosening up. The emcee was entertaining the crowd with jokes. Some of the jokes brought laughs and others brought groans. Kids were weaving through the people that circled the dance arena. The drum-sound knitted the people together.

Lug brushed his long hair away from his face as he looked in the sky for eagles. He had been away from home a long time and was looking forward to seeing his friends and relatives again.

He really enjoyed powwows, although he didn't dance. Lug was content to be with his people again. Ever since the war he had felt disconnected from the things that made people happy.

The first time he walked around the arena he just concentrated on faces. He was looking for family. While walking along he grazed at the food stands. He smelled then sampled the fry bread, moose meat, and wild rice soup.

The Shinnobs walking around the dance arena looked like a river that was going in two directions. Groups of people would stop and talk. Lug smiled at the laughing circles of Shinnobs. He looked at faces and eyes.

That little one there, she looked like his sister Judy did when she was that age. Lug wondered if he would see her here. Judy was a jingle-dress dancer and should be at this powwow. After all, she only lived a mile away from the powwow grounds.

The guy walking in front of him looked like his cousin that went to Vietnam. Nope, couldn't be him. Lug had heard that he died in a single-car accident last fall.

Sitting in a red and white striped powwow chair was an old lady that looked like his grandma. She wore heavy brown stockings that were held up with a big round knot at the knees. She chewed Copenhagen and spit the juice in a coffee can just like his gram. Of course, Lug's grandma had been dead for ten years, but it was still a good feeling to see someone who looked like her.

Lug recognized the woman walking toward him. She was his old used-to-be girlfriend. He hoped she didn't want to talk about what went wrong with them. She didn't, just snapped her eyes and looked away. Lug knew it was his fault he couldn't feel close to anyone. His face was a wooden mask as they passed each other. He could feel her looking up at him out of the corner of her eyes. Maybe, he thought, just maybe.

He stopped at a food stand called Stand Here. Lug had black coffee and a bag of mini-donuts. The sugar and cinnamon coating stuck to his fingers when he finished. He brushed off his hands and lit a smoke. Lug watched the snaggers 8 to 68 cruising through the river of Shinnobs.

That jingle-dress dancer walking toward him looked like his sister Judy. Yup it was her. The maroon dress made a tinkling, jingling sound as she came closer. She looks healthy, Lug thought. A few more gray hairs, but she moves like she was twenty years younger. They both smiled just hard as their eyes met. Warm brown eyes reached for wary ones.

She noticed the lines on his face were deeper. The lines fanned out from the edges of his eyes. He looked like he had lost some weight since the last time she saw him. His bluejean jacket just hung on him, she thought.

Lug and Judy shook hands and hugged each other. Her black-beaded bag hit him on the back as they embraced. They were together again after a long time apart. Both leaned back to get a better look at each other.

"C'mon over to the house when they break for supper," she said.

"Got any cornbread?" he asked.

"I can whip some up for you," she promised.

"Sounds good," he said.

Eating cornbread was a reminder of when they were young together. Sometimes it was the only thing to eat in the house. Cornbread was the first thing she made him when he came back from Vietnam.

"I have to get in line for the grand entry so I'll see you later. I want to talk to you about something," she said.

"Okay, dance a round for me," Lug said.

"I will, just like I always do."

Lug watched the grand entry. He saw several relatives in their dance outfits. He nodded to friends that were standing around the dance arena. Lug sipped hot coffee as the grand entry song was sung. He saw Judy come dancing by. Lug turned and looked at his car.

He walked to it as the flag song started. He almost moved in time to the beat as he walked. Lug decided to get his tire fixed at the truck stop. He got in and closed the car door as the veterans' song came over the public address system.

Lug left the powwow grounds and slipped a tape in his cassette player. The Animals singing "Sky Pilot" filled the car. Lug sang along with the vintage music.

He drove to the truck stop and read the newspaper while the mechanic fixed his tire. Lug put the tire in his trunk, paid the guy and drove to his sister's house. He listened to the Righteous Brothers do "Soul and Inspiration" on the way.

Judy's car was in the driveway, so he knew she was home. He parked and walked up to the front door. He rang the doorbell and walked in. He smelled cornbread.

She was in the kitchen making coffee. He sat at the kitchen table as she took the cornbread out of the oven. The steaming yellow bread made his mouth moist. Judy poured him a cup of coffee and sat down at the table.

"How have you been?" she asked.

"Okay, my health is okay."

"Where have you been? I haven't heard from you in quite a while."

"Oh you know, just traveling here and there. I'd work a little bit and then move on. For a while there I was looking for guys I knew in the war."

"Where was that you called from last March?" she asked.

"D.C., I was in Washington D.C. I went to the Wall and after being there I felt like I had to talk to someone I knew."

"You did sound troubled about something."

"I found a friend's name on the Wall. He died after I left Vietnam. I felt like killing myself."

"I'm glad you didn't."

"Me too, we wouldn't be having this conversation if I had gone through with it."

She got up, cut the cornbread and brought it to the table. He buttered a piece and began taking bites from the hot bread. She refilled his cup.

"Remember when we used to have to haul water when we were kids? I was thinking about it the other day, that one time it was thirty below and the cream cans fell off the sled? You somehow convinced me it was my fault. I had to pump the water to fill the cans again. You told me it was so I could stay warm. I guess in your own way you were looking out for me," she said.

"Nahh, I just wanted to see if I could get you to do all the work." Lug smiled at his sister.

"I thought it was good of you to send the folks money from your first military paycheck so we could get our own pump. We didn't have to bum water from the neighbor after that."

"I had to, I didn't want you to break your back lugging those cream cans around."

"Yah, I really hated wash days. Ma had me hauling water all day when she washed clothes."

She got up and got a glass of water from the kitchen faucet. As she came back to the table she said, "I've been talking to a spiritual leader about you. He wants you to come and see him. Don't forget to take him tobacco."

"That sounds like a good idea. I've been wanting to talk to someone," he said.

"What was it like in the war? You never talked much about it."

Lug stared deep into his black medicine water as if expecting an answer to scroll across. He trusted his sister, but it was still difficult talking about the terrible memories.

His eyes retreated into his head as he told her what happened to him, what he did in the war. She later learned that this was called the thousand yard stare. His eyes looked like he was trying to see something that was that far away. The laugh lines were erased from his face.

"Sometimes I'd get so scared I couldn't get scared anymore," he said, hunched over his coffee cup.

Judy touched his arm. Her face said she was ready to listen to her brother.

"One night they were shooting at us. No one was getting hurt. It got to be a drag ducking every time they fired. The gunfire wasn't very heavy, just a rifle round every couple of minutes. We didn't know if it was the prelude to a big attack or just one guy out there with a case of ammo and a hard on. We laid in our holes, counted the rounds going by and tried to shrink up inside our helmets. The bullets went by for at least a half hour. I counted seventeen of them. The ones that went high made a buzzing noise as they went by. The close ones made a crack sound. First you'd hear the bullet go by then the sound of where it came from."

"I got tired of that shit. I crawled up out of my hole and just stood there. I wanted to see where the bad guy was shooting from. The guys in the next hole told me to get down, but I was in a fuck-it mood. I didn't care what happened, didn't care if I lived or died."

Lug stood up to show his sister what it was like standing in the dark. He was leaning forward trying to see through the night. His hands clutched an imaginary rifle. Lug's head was swiveling back and forth as he looked for the hidden rifleman. He jerked as a rifle bullet came close to him. He turned his head toward the sound.

Judy watched Lug. She could feel her eyes burning and the tears building up. Using only willpower she held the tears back. Judy somehow knew the tears would stop the flood of memories coming out of her brother. She waited.

"I finally saw the muzzle flash. I knew where the bastard was firing from. After he fired the next time we all returned fire. We must have shot 500 rounds at him. The bad guy didn't shoot anymore. We either killed him or scared the shit out of him. After the noise died down I started getting scared. I realized I could have been killed standing up like that."

He paused before speaking again.

"That shows you how dangerous a fuck-it attitude is. I guess I have been living my life with a fuck-it attitude."

Lug sat back down and reached for another piece of cornbread. He ate it silently. When he finished the cornbread he lit a cigarette.

She touched his shoulder as she poured more coffee. Lug accepted this as permission to continue fighting the war. Judy sat down and lit her own cigarette.

"It was really crazy at times. One time we were caught out in this big rice paddy. They started shooting at us. I was close to the front of the formation so I got inside the treeline quick. The bad guys couldn't see me.

When I leaned over to catch my breath I heard the snick, snick, bang sound of someone firing a bolt-action rifle. The enemy soldier was firing at the guys still out in the rice paddy. I figured out where the bad guy was from the sound—snick, snick, bang. I fired a three-round burst at the noise. That ass-hole turned and fired at me. I remember the muzzle flash and the bullet going-by noise happened together. I fired again as I moved closer. Through a little opening in the brush I could see what looked like a pile of rags, bloody rags. I fired another round into his head. We used to do that all the time—one in the head to make sure. The 7.62 bullet knocked his hat off. When the hat came off all this hair came spilling out. It was a woman."

Lug slumped at the kitchen table unable to continue his story. He held his coffee cup as if warming his hands. Judy sat there looking at him. Tears were running down her cheeks and puddling up on the table.

Lug coughed and lit a cigarette. Judy reached for one of her own and Lug lit it for her. Their eyes met. She got up to blow her nose and wipe her eyes. Judy was trembling as she came back and sat at the table. She wanted to cradle her brother but couldn't.

"Her hair looked like grandma's hair used to look. Remember her long, black shiny hair? This woman had hair like that. I knew killing people was wrong somehow but this made it worse when it turned out to be a woman."

Lug was slowly rocking his head back and forth.

When it looked like Lug was not going to talk anymore Judy got up and opened the back door. She poured more coffee and sat there looking at him. He couldn't meet her eyes.

"Tell me how you got wounded. You never did talk about it. All we knew was that you had won a Purple Heart," she probed.

After a long silence, Lug answered. "Ha, won a Purple Heart? We used to call them Idiot Awards. It meant that you fucked up somehow. Standing in the wrong place at the wrong time, something like that."

Lug's shoulders tightened up as he began telling her about his wounds. He reached down for his leg. "I don't know what happened to my leg. It was a long firefight, lots of explosions. After it was over, after the medivac choppers left, we were sitting around talking about what happened.

"I looked down and noticed blood on my leg. I thought it was from the guys we carried in from the listening post. The pain started about then. I rolled up my pants and saw a piece of shrapnel sticking out. Doc came over and pulled it out. He bandaged it up and must have written me up for a Heart. I remember that it took a long time to heal because we were always in the water of the rice paddies."

Lug was absently rubbing his leg as he told his sister about his wound.

He suddenly stood up and changed the subject. He didn't talk about his other wounds. He drained his cup.

"I gotta go, I think I talked too much already. I don't want you to think I am crazy because of what I did in the war. I'll see you at the powwow," said Lug, walking to the door.

As she looked at his back she wished there was something she could do to ease his memories of the war. "Wait a minute," Judy told her brother.

She lit some sage and smudged him with an eagle feather. He stood there with his eyes closed, palms facing out.

He thanked her and walked out the door.

While cleaning up after her brother left, Judy remembered hearing the ads on TV for the Vet's Center. She looked the number up in the book and called. Judy spoke to a counselor who listened. The counselor suggested an Inpatient Post-Traumatic Stress Disorder program.

The closest one was located in southern Minnesota. Judy got the address for her brother.

She went back to the powwow and found Lug standing on the edge of the crowd. "They have a program for treating PTSD," she told Lug.

"Yah, I saw something on TV about PTSD."

"What did you think of it? What do you think of entering a treatment program?"

"It might do some good. I was talking to a guy who went through it. He said it helped him. It might be worth a shot," Lug said.

"I talked to a counselor after you left. She said you can come in anytime."

"How about right now? Do you think they are open right now?"

"Sure, they must keep regular hours."

When she saw him walking to his car she thought it didn't take much to get him started.

Lug left the powwow and drove to the Vet's Center. On the way he listened to Dylan singing "Blowing in the Wind."

At the Vet's Center Lug found out he could enter the program in a couple of days. His stay would be about a month.

Lug talked to the spiritual man before he went in for the program. He remembered to bring him a package of Prince Albert tobacco and a pair of warm socks.

In talking with the man, Lug learned that veterans were respected because of the sacrifices they had made in the war. He told Lug he would pray for him. The spiritual man told Lug to come back and see him when he got out of the Veterans Hospital.

Lug went to see the counselor and she helped him fill out the paperwork. He thanked her and drove to his sister's house. He parked his car and went inside. She showed him where he could leave his car parked while he was gone.

Judy drove Lug to the brick hospital. He took his bag of clothes and walked up the steps. Judy waved from her car. As he turned and looked, he noticed she was parked under an American flag.

He walked into the building. The smell of disinfectant reminded him of other official buildings he had been through.

He was ready for whatever was to come. Don't sweat the small shit, he thought.

Lug quickly learned that he was not the only one having trouble coping with memories of the war. He felt comfortable talking with other vets who had similar experiences.

Living in the Vet's Hospital felt like being in the military again. He slept in a warm bed and ate warm food. He spent most of his time with guys his age who had been to Vietnam. His time was structured for him.

In the group therapy sessions they told war stories at first. After being together a while they began to talk about feelings. Lug became aware that he had been acting normal in what was an abnormal situation. He felt like he was leaving some of his memories at the hospital.

In spite of the camaraderie he felt, Lug was anxious to rejoin his community. He wanted to go home. He knew he would complete the program but didn't expect to spend one extra minute at the hospital.

While he was gone Judy was busy. She was making Lug a pair of moccasins. The toes had the traditional beaded floral design. Around the cuffs she stitched the colors of the Vietnam campaign ribbon. She had called the counselor at the Vet's Center to make sure the colors were right. It was green, then yellow with three red stripes, yellow then green again. The smoke-tanned hide smell came to her as she sewed.

The hardest part was going down in the basement for the trunk her husband had left when he went to Vietnam. The trunk contained the traditional dance outfit he used to wear. It had been packed away because he didn't come back from the war.

Judy drove to the hospital and picked Lug up when he had completed the PTSD program. Looked like he put on some weight she thought when she first saw him.

She drove to the spiritual man's house, and listened to a powwow tape while driving. Lug tapped his hand on his knee in time to the drum. On the way Lug told hospital stories. She could see his laugh lines as he talked about the month with the other vets.

At the house Judy waited outside while the two men talked and smoked. She listened to both sides of the tape twice before Lug came out. He had a smile and walked light on his feet. Lug got in the car.

Judy drove to her house. They listened to the powwow on the way. She could see that Lug was enjoying the music.

"I've got that extra bedroom downstairs. You can stay there until you get your own place," she told him.

"Sounds like a winner. Cornbread every day?"

"Nope, special occasions only."

"I might be eligible for a disability pension, but I'd rather get a job," Lug said.

"Do what you want to do," she said.

"Where are we going now?" Lug asked.

"We're going to a powwow. I got my tent set up already and I want to dance in the first grand entry."

"Okay, it'll feel good to see familiar faces again."

"Did the hospital do anything for you?" she asked.

"I think so, but it felt better talking to the spiritual man," he answered.

When they got to the powwow grounds Judy drove to her tent. Lug perched on the fender when she went inside to change into her jingle dress.

Sure the hospital was nice but it felt better being here with his relatives, Lug thought. He breathed deep in the cool air. He could hear his sister's jingle dress begin to make sounds as she got dressed. He was trying to decide which food stand to start with when his sister came out.

"Tie this up for me, will you?" she asked.

Judy handed him the eagle fluff and medicine wheel. He used rawhide to tie it to her small braid. After she checked to make sure it was the way she wanted it, Judy said, "Go in the tent and get your present."

"Okay," he said, jumping off the fender and unzipping the tent.

Inside the tent he saw a pair of moccasins on top of a traditional dance outfit. The colors of the campaign ribbon on the moccasins caught his eye. He took off his sneakers and put on the moccasins.

"Hey, thanks a lot, I needed some moccasins," said Lug.

"The rest of the outfit belongs to you too," she said.

"Really?" he recognized the dance outfit. He knew who used to own it. He thought of his brother-in-law and the Vietnam war.

"Hurry up and put it on. It is almost time for grand entry," Judy told him.

Lug put on the dance outfit and walked out for the inspection he knew she would give. He did a couple of steps to show her how it fit. She smiled her approval.

They walked to where the people were lining up. He was laughing as he joined the traditional dancers. He saw his cousin Fuzzy who was a Vietnam vet.

"Didja hear? They got a new flavor for Vietnam vets," Lug said.

"Yah, what is it?" asked the guy who had been in Khe San in '68.

"Agent Grape," said Lug.

They both laughed at themselves for laughing.

Lug danced the grand entry song with slow dignity; he felt proud. He moved with the drum during the flag song.

When the veteran's song began Lug moved back to join his sister. Both of them had tears showing as they danced the veteran's honor song together.

Simon J. Ortiz (Acoma Pueblo)

The Killing of a State Cop

Felipe was telling me how it happened. I was then twelve years old. They would get him, he knew, he said. And he was scared. He looked around nervously all the time that we sat on the trough which ran around the water tank.

Felipe wasn't a bad guy. Not at all. A little wild maybe. He had been in the marines and he could have gotten kicked out if he had wanted to, he said. But he hadn't because he could play it pretty straight like a good guy, too.

He used to tell me a lot of things, about what he had seen, about what he had done, about what he planned to do, and about what other people could do to you. That was one trouble with him. He was always thinking about what other people could do to you. Not the people around our place, the Indians, but other people.

How that state policeman died was like this (Felipe wanted me to remember what he said always, and he talked very seriously and sometimes sadly, and again he said they would get him anyway):

"What the hell. He deserved to die, the bastard."

It was the wine, Felipe said. And that thing he had about people, I guess. He didn't say, but I knew.

"It makes you warm in the head and other things like that," he said.

He had gone to town from the reservation with Antonio, his brother. They drove their pickup truck to town where they bought the wine from a bootlegger. "From some stupid Mexican bartender. Geesus, I hate Mexicans."

Felipe spat on the ground. Indians were not supposed to drink or buy liquor at that time. It was against the law. Felipe hated the law and broke it whenever he felt he could get away with it.

"One time in Winslow I got off the train when it stopped at the depot and walked into a bar next to the depot to buy a beer. I was still in the marines then and in uniform. This barman, he looked at me very mean and asked if I was Indian. 'Shore,' I said. And he told me to get the hell out before he called the cops. Goddamn, I hated that, and I went around the back and peed on the back door. I don't know why, just because I hated him, I guess."

Felipe and his brother were walking in town, not saying anything much, and maybe looking at things they wanted to buy when they had the money. They stopped in front of the Golden Theater and looked at the pictures of what was in the movies that day and the next day.

"Hey, Indio. Hey, what hell you doing?" It was Luis Baca, a member of the state police who patrolled the state highway near the reservation.

The brothers hated the man. Felipe regarded him with a fierce hate because he had been thrown in jail by him once. He had been beaten, and he feared the cop because of that. They did not answer.

"Hey, goddammey Indio, get the hell away from there. Get out of town."

For no reason at all.

"For no reason at all. Goddamn, I got mad and I called him a dirty, fat, lazy good-for-nothing, ugly Mexican."

Felipe looked around him and told me I better learn to be something more than him, a guy who would probably die in the electric chair up at Santa Fe.

Felipe told Antonio he was going to kill the Mexican, but Antonio said that it was no good talk and persuaded him to leave town.

They left, followed by the curses and jeers of Luis Baca. When they got back to the pickup truck, they opened another bottle of wine and drank.

"It makes a noise in your head, and you want to do something," Felipe told me.

They decided to go home. Almost out of town, they heard a siren scream behind them and saw a black police car with Baca driving it. Felipe told Antonio not to stop. They did not go faster, though. Luis Baca drove alongside and laughed at the brothers, who were frightened and suspicious.

Antonio stepped on the brake then, and he let the policeman pass them. They were past the town limits.

"Antonio, my brother, he is a kind of a funny guy," Felipe said. "He doesn't get mad like me. I mean yell or cuss. He just kind of looks mean or sad. He told me to give him the wine and he drank some and put it on the seat between his legs."

The police car leading and pickup truck following were heading toward the reservation.

Suddenly, a few miles out of town, Antonio pressed his foot down on the gas pedal and the pickup truck picked up speed. It seemed that the policeman did not see the truck bearing down on him until it was almost too late.

"Antonio wasn't trying to run into the car. I thought he was going to, but he was only trying to scare the bastard."

Luis Baca swerved off the road anyway, and there was a cloud of dust as his car skidded into a shallow ditch.

Felipe and Antonio didn't stop. Looking through the rear window, they saw the cop get out of the car. Antonio stopped the pickup truck. He started up again and made a U-turn. Passing by the police car, they saw that the policeman was trying to get his car out. The tires kept spinning and throwing gravel. A few miles down the road, they turned around and headed back toward the police car again.

"Wine makes you do stupid things. Son-of-a-bitch. Sometimes you think about putting your hand between a girl's legs or taking money from somebody or even killing somebody."

They slowed down as they approached the police car. It was slowly coming out of the ditch.

"I drank the wine left in the bottle, and as we passed I threw the bottle against the window of the car and I made a dirty sign with my hand at the Mexican," Felipe said.

Antonio speeded the truck up. They kept looking back, and soon they saw the police car following them and heard the siren. They turned into the road that led into the reservation. It was a dirt road, and the truck bounced and jolted as they sped along it. The police car turned off the highway and followed them.

Felipe reached behind the seat of the truck and brought out a .30-30 Winchester rifle which was wrapped in a homemade case of denim from old Levis. He took the rifle out of the denim case and pulled down the lever so that the chamber was open. There was nothing in there, and he closed the lever and lowered the hammer very carefully as usual. He opened the truck compartment and brought out an almost full box of cartridges.

"You remember that .30-30 I was using when I went deer hunting last year? The one I let you shoot even though you aren't supposed to before you shoot at a deer with it. That one. My father bought it when he was working for the railroad. That one."

They followed the road that led to the village, but turned off to another road before they got there. The road climbed a hill and led toward Black Mesa, several miles to the south. At the top of the hill they stopped and watched to see if the police car was still following them. It was at the bottom of the hill and coming up.

The dirt road led through a forest of juniper and piñon. This was near the heart of the reservation. They sped by a scattered herd of sheep tended by a boy who looked at them as they passed by. The sheep dogs barked at them and ran alongside for a while.

"The road is very rough and sometimes sandy, and we couldn't go too fast. No one uses it except sheepherders and people going for wood in their wagons. We stopped on a small hill to see if Luis Baca was still coming after us. We couldn't see him because of the forest, so I told my brother to shut off the engine so I could listen. It was real quiet in the forest like it always is, and you can hear things from a long ways away. I could hear the cop car still coming, about a half-mile back. I told Antonio to go on."

They passed the windmill which was a mile from Black Mesa. The one road branched there into several directions. The one that led east of Black Mesa into some rough country and canyons was the one they chose.

Antonio slowed the truck and drove slowly until they saw that the policeman could see which road they had taken, and then he speeded up again.

"Aiee, I can see stupidity in a man. Sometimes even my own. I can see a man's drunkenness making him do crazy things. And Luis Baca, a very stupid son-of-a-bitch, was more than I could see. He wanted to die. And I, because I was drunken and *muy loco* like a Mexican friend I had from Nogales used to say about me when we would play with the whores in Korea and Tokyo, wanted to make him die. I did not care for anything else except that Luis Baca who I hated was going to die."

Directly to the east of Black Mesa is a plain which runs for about two miles in all directions. There is grass on the plain, and there are many prairie dogs. At the edge of the grassy plain is a thin forest of juniper and piñon. A few yards beyond the edge of the forest there is a deep ravine which is the tail end of a deep and wide canyon which runs from the east toward Black Mesa. The ravine comes to a point almost against one edge of Black Mesa. There is only a narrow passage, which crumbles away each year with erosion, between the ravine and the abruptly rising slopes of the mesa. The road passes this point and goes around the mesa and to a spring called Spider Spring.

The brothers passed through the narrow passage and stopped fifty yards away. Felipe got out with the rifle and bullets, and Antonio parked the pickup truck behind a growth of stunted juniper growing thickly together.

"I took some bullets out of the box and put them into the rifle. Six of them, I think, the kind with soft points. I laid down the rifle for a while and waited for Antonio. He didn't come right away from the truck and I called to him. We laid down behind a small mound of sand and rocks; the ground was hot from the sun. We could hear the police car coming.

" 'Are we just going to scare him so he won't bother us no more?' Antonio asked me.

"I looked at Antonio, and he looked like he used to when we were kids and he used to pretend not to be scared of rattlesnakes.

" 'I don't know,' I said. I was going to shoot the man. I don't know why, but I was going to. Maybe I was kind of scared then.

"When the car came out of the trees, it was not coming very fast. It approached the narrow place and slowed down. I thought Luis Baca would see me, so I slid down until I could barely see over the edge of the mound behind which we lay.

"He had slowed down because of the narrow place, and I thought he would stop and turn back. But he didn't. He shifted into first and came on very slowly. That's when I put my rifle on a flat rock and aimed it. Right at the windshield where the steering wheel is. The sun was shining on the windshield very brightly and I could not see very well."

Felipe relaxed a bit, took a breath, opened and closed the lever on the rifle.

The bullet made a hole right above where the metal and glass were joined by a strip of rubber in front of the steering wheel. It made an irregular pattern in the windshield glass. The shot echoed back and forth in the ravine and was followed by another shot. The bullet made a hole a few inches to the upper right of the first. Another shot followed and it was wild. It ricocheted off the top and into some rocks on the mesa slope.

"Four times I shot, and I could see the holes almost in the spot where I wanted them to be. One wasn't though. But the car didn't stop or go crooked. It kept coming and crossed the narrow place. It stopped then, and Luis Baca got out very slowly. He called something like he was crying. '*Compadre*,' he said. He held up his right hand and reached to us. There was blood on his neck and shoulder."

Felipe settled himself into place and aimed very carefully. Luis Baca tried to unbuckle his pistol belt, but the bullet tore into his belly and he leaned against the car as he was knocked back a step. A last shot whipped his head around violently, and he dropped to the ground. Felipe started to put more bullets into the rifle but decided not to.

The two brothers walked to the car and stood over the still-moving body of Luis Baca. Antonio reached down and slid the police revolver out of the holster, took aim, and pulled the trigger.

"Luis Baca, the poor fool, made a feeble gurgle like a sick cat and went to hell.

"They will catch me, I know. There were people who saw us being chased by the cop. Antonio went to Albuquerque and he took the pistol. He will get caught too."

That was what he told me that night when we were sitting at the water tank. He used to tell me all kinds of things because I would listen. I liked those stories he told about the Korean war. That was where he learned how to drive a truck, and he had saved up his money so that he could buy a truck after he got out of the marines. Felipe and I used to go hunting and fishing too.

I sort of believed him, about the killing of Luis Baca the state cop, but not really, until a few days later when I heard my mother talking about it with my father. I asked something about it, and they told me to forget it and said that Felipe would probably die in the electric chair. Every night, for quite a while, I prayed a rosary or something for him.

Louis Owens (Choctaw, Cherokee)

Blessed Sunshine

Nora Miriam Bailey, six years old, woke in darkness, lost and terrified until she felt the thick river shift beneath her. The raft sighed and settled, and she heard the brittle kree of a kingfisher pass by in the night. She remembered then. In her brief life, she'd known different brown waters, but nothing like this Texas river or this raft with its load of death. On the other side of the cold barrel stove and tin chimney, in a wooden box of a bed, the man breathed so hard she could feel the rancid air moving in the tiny room. The small woman in the bed with him made no sound at all, and Nora thought how the woman had looked like a white-breasted bird in the gray daylight. River dampness rose through wood floor and corn shuck mattress and pasted the flour-sack nightgown to her skinny thighs. She hugged the patchwork comforter closer to her chin, hoping to hear the kingfisher again in the night but hearing only the man's breathing now and the quiet slap of water. The heavy air, which bore the weight of fried fish, well used lard, the extinguished kerosene lantern, fleshed animal hides, unwashed human bodies, and the rotting river below them, pressed her to the limp mattress and floor. She understood that her life had been given over to unknown forces and strangeness yet unnamed, and she determined with all the cunning of her years to live through this too. "Waddo," the man had said to Mr. Timmons, "Thank you" in Indian. She was a thing given, and thus was sown the seed of her own giving scant years later.

Atop the raft house, beyond her sight even had she been able to penetrate that darkness, were coon skins scraped and stretched on stick frames like death's wings, and the bloated body of a wildcat laid casually on the roof's edge. This had been her first vision when she'd arrived the day before, and it remained with her in the complete darkness of the little room. If a wind came up, she knew the skin sails would carry the raft down that black river of ghosts where her mother and granma waited. This was her terror and her consolation.

They'd traveled a week to get there in the wagon, Mr. Timmons with his thin, serious face coaxing and threatening the mules every step of the way. "This here country's Texas," he'd said on the second afternoon. "Yeller rose." He'd smiled at her with his crooked teeth. "How'd you like to be the yeller rose, little Nora Myrum, the yeller rose o' Texas?" On the splintery seat beside him, she looked away toward the big horseflies swirling about the poor mules. She'd seen a yellow rose in Nakey Waters' yard the week Nakey died of fever. Mr. Timmons began to mutter a song about the "yeller rose o' Texas" that was the only gal for him. She heard "diamunts" and something like "Roserlee." His sudden voice after so much silence was frightening, like a ghost or an owl call at night.

"A owl called that night granma died," she said, looking at the backs of the mules' heads. "A screech owl."

Mr. Timmons stopped his song and nodded his long head once, acknowledging the gravity of what she'd said. Then they were both quiet for a long time, watching the horseflies and the ragged country they were passing through.

Blackjack oaks ranged the low hills on either side of the road, and ravens kept darting shadows over the wagon so she had to close her eyes not to see. Sometimes, when she opened her eyes and brushed her thin hair back, she saw squirrels moving in the woods, and she thought of her granma's biscuits and squirrel gravy. In the lard pail, behind the seat with the bedrolls, were still half a dozen of Mrs. Timmons' hard biscuits. The Timmonses were neighbors, their plank-walled cabin just a few miles from the Bailey home. Minnie Timmons was the one that found her and brought her home.

After what seemed like days of silence, when they had left the noisy roads and all towns behind, when only jays called from the brush and hawks and those black buzzards circled the pale sky with motionless wings, he had begun to talk. "They's Cherokees down this way, too, passel of 'em." His dark eyes looked out over the mules toward the dry hills ahead of them, and he lifted and dropped the leather straps gently across the animals' backs. "Old settlers that ain't never moved. You got relatives among this here Trinity River bunch. Don't you worry, little girl, these folks'll keer for you." Still, except that one time he never looked at her and never smiled, and even at six years old she understood the mix of relief and guilt in his voice, tones she'd heard plenty of times. Whoever was there, in that place he was taking her, might not care for her at all. Maybe just like the Timmonses they'd have too many children of their own to take in another one. Or maybe they'd all died or just gone away, the way people did.

A ploughed section of reddish brown earth edged up beside the dirt road, and she watched the furrows sway out of sight toward the woods and wondered what this kind of people planted in the earth, and did such people have children too, and then abruptly they were in a region without ploughed earth or any sign at all of people like them. They had come suddenly into a country like nothing she'd seen before, forests of stumps and splintered brush going away from the road on both sides as far as she could see, all gray and dead, the earth gouged and pocked. No animals moved in the blasted woods, and the sun shone only dimly through the thickened air.

The river, when it rose into view, was starved and brown, its water seeming not to move at all, the broken forest reflected in its surface. Tied to a sliver of stump, in the middle of nothing, the raft with its wood shack looked lost and crazy, and she had to focus on it for a long time to know it was really there. Close to the raft and river, the earth was scraped like a sore, and beyond the scraped place stood dark, splintered trees and heaped

brush, like a world that had been smashed and bruised by powerful lightning. Here the air seemed burned, a gray haze that hung like smoke over
everything, tangling in the fragments of trees. She knew they had found a
place never touched by sun, that they had arrived in the Darkening Land,
the place of nightwalkers and death that her granma had told her of. Then
she understood the black ravens that had shadowed the wagon for two
days, the dark figures that had peopled her nightmares for so long. This was
the Nightland described in stories, where the nightwalkers were.

Mr. Timmons had stopped the wagon atop the long slant to the river,
set the brake, and stared with her at the scene. She could hear him suck air
between his teeth as they sat together, neither moving at all. On the side of
the raft house was a picture of a fish, large and evil, and someone had
painted letters and numbers above the picture. Even she could see that some
of the letters were backwards. "It's a ignorant people," she said to herself so
he couldn't hear. Her granma had taught her letters because ignorance was
of the devil.

When Mr. Timmons spoke, his voice was forced. "Blessed sunshine.
You see them words painted, Nora Myrum? It's your daddy's uncle owns
that boat."

She could feel him taking in the horror of the place, feel even fear emanating from the grown man beside her. She knew that to evoke the sacred
Sunland in such a place was what her granma would call blasphemy. The
fish painted on the boat would devour sunshine like that whale that ate
somebody in the Bible.

"Blessed sunshine. Must be good people would paint that on their
house," Mr. Timmons said, and she knew he was talking not to her.

She'd sat stock still on the wagon seat, eyeing the lightning-burned world and seared earth, in the middle of which was the death raft. The big fish on the side of the raft house scared her. The tall man standing in front of the raft with his moustache, chin whiskers, and fur hat scared her even more, and the little woman stared at her with cocked head, wordless like a bird.

Mr. Timmons had stayed for a supper of fried catfish and cornbread but had begged leave to start back home before dark. She'd gone out with them, down the wood ramp to stand on the shore and watch the wagon go away, his skinny back curved toward home, wanting to call after him but holding to the silence that had mainly kept her all those days. She knew Minnie Timmons would have let her stay. She'd been her mother's friend, and she was Cherokee, too. He wasn't Cherokee. And she'd heard them argue. "Cain't hardly fill the bellies of these six we already got," he'd said. "Them folks down there is her own flesh and blood."

It was like the place after the big flood where all the bones danced. Like everything she had feared since first her mother and then her granma died and for a week she stayed in their cabin alone, eating the cornbread someone had left after they buried Granma Storms.

She had no illusions regarding what lay ahead of her.

At twelve years, she was a scrawny sliver of bone and muscle, small for her age and covered over with taut flesh and flour-sack dress and looked at the world with eyes unchanged since her first vision of the raft. At twelve years she knew the river and the world it creased on both banks, knew the man she now called Uncle and the woman called Aunt Telitha who lay now like wrought iron in the bed. She knew to listen and watch the slightest movements or inclinations of man and animal, air and water, to anticipate and move herself without sound or motion, to act before words. Knew the infinite meaning of Blessed Sunshine.

She watched with the eyes of a fishing bird, poised at the cusp of the raft as her father's uncle spoke.

"You got to imagine it, little Nora, got to jest wrap your mind around all that water. Jest water and air and nary a thing beyond. Brown water like this yere, and nothin but a whole world of it. Look out there." He raised one arm from the pole that pushed the raft upstream and pointed at the sluggish brown river. "The Lord giveth and taketh away. He giveth this world like black woods a night when they ain't no moon nor stars and jest splinters o' lightnin to see and nary a trail and them branches whippin a body's face and He takes those we love, before all others. Before all others."

She knew the river like her own breath. Could read it like the Bible he had taught her to parse. She knew when the hue of the current shifted that there'd been a gully washer somewhere far off and it was coming to them, knew when a bar was forming that no one might ever see or when a submerged tree was making a bad reversal that could jamb the raft tight. Knew the dark places under a cutbank where the huge catfish would lay up and could be grappled out, which under-carved bank would likely deposit a big cottonwood in their path soon, knew which tongues of deep woods held the raccoons he needed to hunt for their cornmeal and coffee and lard. Knew when this old man who cared for her would come back from the shore world drunk on whiskey and crazy.

Those days and nights she would sometimes hide on shore with Aunt Telitha, rolled in a tarp and blankets to keep the cold and chiggers off, hearing him shouting Bible words and Indian words all mixed up that skipped off the river like flat stones. It was one of those nights from which Aunt Telitha had taken sick.

Uncle Jyker pulled the long pole out of the muddy water, leaving a putrid swirl that she followed with her eyes, and then plunged it down again, pushing the raft against the slow current next to the bank. Rains had spilled the river and gathered trees and brush into its current so that the raft moved next to a floating forest. A bloated, newborn calf rocked in tangled branches so close she could have reached out to touch its matted hide, flies rising and settling on the red fur and whitened eyes. She'd seen many dead things along the river, mostly fish like useless gar and an occasional drum, but also dogs and stray livestock. Inside the cabin, the old lady, Aunt Telitha, lay sick in bed for the tenth day, saying nothing but only looking at them the way Nora had seen animals sicken and die. Nora thought she would make tea when the raft was still again.

"And Jehovah saw that the wickedness of man was great in the earth, and he said it repenteth me that I have made them." He turned his brown eyes on her, and she looked away toward a big cottonwood that hung over the river, its roots like snakes exposed by the current. Building midday clouds made bulbous shadows like toads' heads on the water, and flies and gnats swarmed in the still air so she had to wave them away.

"And the earth was filled with violence and corrupted flesh, and God said unto Noah this here is the end of all flesh and I will destroy them all with the earth." He turned and spat tobacco juice into the water and then drove the pole back into the river. The raft edged upstream and she studied the new batch of skins stretched to dry on the roof.

"And the waters prevailed and all flesh died that moved on the earth, both birds and cattle and things that creepeth. And Noah only was left. Imagine that. All alone on that water on a boat like this here. And they must've been trash floatin everwhere since Jehovah drowned all the towns and farms and woods. All them dead people and livestock and wild creatures floatin and rottin on the wide corrupt face of the water like this here river. And the Bible says Noah sent forth a raven, old Raven hisself, and he went forth to and fro and dried up all the waters." He poled the raft into a deep eddy and held it in place for a moment. "And then Old Buzzard come out and flew over the earth, making all these mountains and valleys and rivers ever time his wings touched before Noah went out. Now take the rope and tie it on that tree yonder." He nodded toward an oak ten feet above the waterline and continued as she jumped ashore.

"And Jehovah said I ain't going to smite the earth no more for man's sake, for that the imagination of man is evil from his youth. And the fear of you and the dread of you all shall be upon ever beast of the earth and upon ever bird of the heavens. Ever livin' thing shall be food for you, ever livin' thing, and surely your blood, the blood of your lives, I will require; at the hand of ever beast will I require it: and at the hand of man, even at the hand of ever man's brother, will I require the life of man. Whoso sheddeth man's blood, by man shall his blood be shed. Whoso sheddeth man's blood, by man shall his blood be shed. And be fruitful and multiply. Jehovah said all that and a pile more."

As she wrapped the rope around the trunk with a halfhitch, she considered Jehovah and imagined Old Buzzard touching mountains into being with the delicate tips of his wings. It was after the flood that someone heard all the bones of the drowned people dancing. She heard the rattle of bones inside the cabin and imagined Aunt Telitha dancing a dance of bones.

"Five hundred years, is how old Noah was." He flipped the plank from the raft to shore and walked onto land, immediately testing the knot she had tied and nodding with satisfaction. "Five hundred years." He stopped and cocked his head like a raven. "I ain't but fifty, and my bones hurt like thunder most mornin's. Jest imagine how that old ringworm must of felt." He smiled at her through the beard and reached out to ruffle her short hair. "Ever livin' thing, little Nora. We ain't no more'n a speck of a firefly." She saw his eyes glistening with moisture, and the sight frightened her more than anything ever had.

"I been a preacher and a doctor and a drunk," he said to the river. "And a coon hunter ain't no difference. Skinnin' somebody or somethin' one way or t'other. Your Aunt Telitha is going to die, little Nora."

He sat down suddenly under the oak she'd tied the raft to, and his head fell onto his arms over his overalled knees. She saw the bony body creak and shiver like a snag in a hard current. His voice, when it came, was muffled. "This here is the end of all flesh, little Nora. For out of it thou wast taken. And the eyes of both them was opened."

"You could go for a doctor," Nora said, looking down at him. "A doctor could make her well."

He pushed the fur hat back from his eyes and raised his head and studied the scarred knuckles of both hands, shaking his head. "I been a doctor, little Nora. I seen death come like a thief in the night plenty times. He drove us out from that tree of life, you see, lest we et of it and never died. Me and your aunt been together twenty-three years this summer."

"Maybe a doctor could help Aunt Telitha."

He looked at her, seeming to wake up. "Don't say her name now, little Nora. You can't say that name no more now." His eyes widened. "Ain't you heard it last night? I seen it fly past when I was in the woods comin' down toward the boat, a firey creature leavin' sparks and soundin' all the world like a raven, but no bird ever made a mark in the air like that thing. I run, but when that comes for a body they ain't nothin' to do. He done took her from this corrupt earth. Like a thief in the night."

Thunder sounded abruptly far off above the riparian forest, and she noticed for the first time that black clouds had piled up over the river, casting no reflections at all in the black water.

When she went into the cabin, her father's aunt lay on the floor, as though she had been hurled from the bed, her body as hard and twisted as a piece of knotted stove wood, her face toward the wall. Nora stopped halfway across the tiny room and stared for a moment before she went back outside.

He still sat beneath the oak and watched her. "They move acrost water without no noise nor a ripple, and they get awful lonely."

She stood on the edge of the raft, listening to him and hearing a hawk keening somewhere down river. Nearby a fish jumped heavily on the water, the sound caught up by a new roll of thunder. She became aware of the lap of water between raft and shore, and she felt the raised, splintery grain of the wood against her bare feet. The forest leaned over the river, darkening the cove they lay in, and a light wind had begun to carry the smell of mud in dank ribbons along the shore.

For the thousandth time since she had seen the raft of skin sails six years before, she thought of her granma and then, helplessly, her mother, feeling as though she must be able to see their faces. She had been loved, by a mother whose hair was black and whose brown eyes smiled over her, whose words now were strange, like words spoken under water. By a grandmother who had held her when they buried a mother and daughter at once and whose thin face never smiled. She had been gifted with a childhood of love that was abruptly gone, and now with a childhood as quickly bereft. When she looked back at the great fish and the strange sails now quivering in a growing breeze, she knew she would not set foot on the raft again where, for half her life, she had floated above the immeasurable river.

She would be a traveler by land now for all the days of her life.

Carter Revard (Osage)

Report to the Nation
Repossessing Europe

It may be impossible to civilize the Europeans. When I claimed England for the Osage Nation, last month, some of the English chiefs objected. They said the Thames is not the Thames until it's past Oxford: above Oxford, it is two streams, the Isis and the Cherwell. Forked tongue, forked river I suppose. So even though I'd taken a Thames Excursion boat and on the way formally proclaimed from the deck, with several Germans and some Japanese tourists for witnesses, that all the land this river drained was ours these Oxford chiefs maintained our title was not good, except below their Folly Bridge at most. At least that leaves us Windsor Palace and some other useful properties, and we can deal with the legal hitches later. Also, just in case, I accepted a sheepskin from Oxford with B.A. written on it, and I didn't bother haggling. It will prove I was there; next time if we bring whiskey we can bribe the Oxford chiefs—bourbon only.

So I said the hell with England for this trip and went to France and rented a little Renault in Paris and drove down past the chateaux to Biarritz, stopping only to proclaim that everything the Loire and Seine flowed past was ours. I did this from the filling stations, and I kept the sales-slips for evidence. Oh yes, I waved an arm as I was passing over the Garonne, in Bordeaux, so we now have the area of Aquitaine as I understand the rules of taking possession. The people there talk differently from those in London, but their signs are much the same—they use a lingua franca so to speak—so they recognized my VISA card and gave the Renault gasoline much like that in Oklahoma, globalized enough so they're not completely benighted. Whether they understood that France now belongs to us was not clear, but they were friendly and they fed me well, accepting in return some pieces of beautifully painted paper and metal discs with allegorical figures on them, with which they seemed almost childishly pleased—if they are this credulous we should not have trouble bargaining with them when we come to take the rest of France. It was so easy that I headed on down to Spain.

There, however, some trouble occurred. Everything was crowded because some ceremony that they hold, the first full moon after the spring equinox as I understood it (their shamans appear to differ over this and I believe millions of people have been killed disputing it), had filled their marketplaces and the trails and all their homes away from home—*todas completas,* as the Spanish desk-clerks everywhere kept saying. So it was back to France, the Spanish border-guards restamped our papers, no hassles even though I heard there'd been some bombings, as there had been (I forgot to mention) in England. The Europeans kill each other pretty casually, by natural instinct it seems, not caring whether they blow up women, kids or horses, and next day display the mutilated corpses on front pages or television screens. I mention this so that when we send more expeditions over the people will take care and not assume everything is as friendly and peaceful as the Europeans would like us to think. They can surely be treacherous to us if they treat each other in this way.

After we'd doublecrossed the Spanish border, I thought maybe we'd slip back up a mountain pass at which the Christians once, or so their legends say, had headed off some Saracens. Roland's Pass, they called it, Roncesvalles. Very nice it was, there was a swift clear stream rushing down the gorge and the road went snaking alongside and then got higher and higher, single-lane with bulges (like a snake that had swallowed eggs) for cars to pass each other, till finally we were way up on the side of the pass looking down two thousand feet on apple trees in bloom, and shepherds and white dots of sheep down below ignoring us. I waited to claim the country because I realized this was going to be a watershed and if I waited till the top I could get both France and Spain at once. At the top of the pass there was a giant radar station keeping watch on something, evidently not us though. We climbed out of the Renault, looked along the road to where some young men and women were picnicking on a saddle-back, and decided it would be best to climb all the way to the top of a peak to see what we were claiming. From the top we could see way over into Spain and back to France, a lot of mountain gorges with the mist in some of them, real windy but the sky mostly clear with just a cape of clouds blowing away from the Pyrenees peaks to the south of us. We looked down to where the border guards were stopping cars, checking for Saracens no doubt, and then we looked up and there were a pair of golden eagles circling, back and forth over the border guards, and there was a peregrine falcon that crossed fast from Spain into France, none of the birds showing their passports. So I claimed both sides of the Pyrenees for the Osage Nation, but reserved rights of passage for all hawks and eagles, and decided to include said rights also for doves and sparrows—feathers we may want from them once we go to dance there, no use restricting their crossing rights.

Having claimed this, I went on down to see Carcasonne, where we heard the European "spirit of inquiry" had started in the late twelfth century or so and the instruments of torture which helped in these inquiries were still displayed among the heads of Roman statues etcetera. They had very impressive old walls there, but the wind blowing through loopholes and whirling in the empty towers and chambers was bitter cold. The ramparts, however, gave us a terrific view over orange-tiled roofs and terraced vineyards to villages (walled) on the hills around, each with its castle, pointing, like football fans chanting "We're Number One." I went ahead and claimed those too, you never know when a ruined castle might come in handy, and some day our kids might want to use one for a Forty-Nine Dance, sort of like Cahokia Mounds across the Mississippi from St. Louis. Then we drove down to Narbonne's beach and dipped our toes in the freezing foaming swells, so we could claim all the shores these washed. I am a little worried, though, because these waters touch some lands that we might better sell off to other tribes—water not fit to drink, all kinds of people mad at each other over things done two thousand, or one hundred, or one year ago or maybe yesterday or this morning, all full of land mines and deserts that somebody is always claiming must be made to bloom or sown with salt again.

On the whole, though, this was a profitable trip. We brought back several things of local manufacture showing that the people could be made to clothe and feed us nicely—some dishes, some leather things. If our elders decide it's worth the bother and expense, possibly we could even teach the poor souls our Osage language, although if our faith and goodness can't be pounded into them we may have to kill them all. I hope, though, they will learn—although I concede their history and current attitudes make them look incapable of being civilized. Yet even if they prove intractably savage they can serve as bad examples to our children. They do not know how to use the land, for one thing—they insist on spreading oil and tar all over it. They dry out rocks and reduce them to a powder, transport them hundreds of miles, pour water on it and make it back into rock, and then build their houses out of this stuff. They cut up cliffs and use the pieces to imitate aisles of tall forest trees, and they melt certain rocks and make transparent sheets of it, colored with certain powdered rocks, to imitate the colors of autumn leaves. This shows how ingenious they are, and how they misuse their cleverness, since the stories of their sacred ceremonies that are represented in these colored sheets could be told in the forests among the autumn leaves if they chose, saving the trouble of moving all that rock. I must admit they get some pretty effects this way. It would be nice to have one of these shrines to look at now and then. They certainly have a lot of torture scenes in them, and these are the models for their spiritual life they say. That may explain the bombings that keep happening among them, and the threats of wiping out their enemies with so many different kinds of weapons. We could put together a great museum, if our people wanted, with the skeletons of such victims, and the religious clothes and such—there are plenty of these inside the shrines I mentioned, and even though they seem to object to having these things dug up, I expect a few drinks of firewater will pacify them, and if not we can pacify them with sharper tools. But of course we might not want to collect such barbarous things—it's just a thought. We should, though, have something to remember them by, in case we have to wipe them out as incapable of rising to our level, and it would be easy to convert one of their shrines into such a museum, the Sainte Chapelle in Paris for instance.

In sum—to conclude this part of my report—we have now got much of England, France, and Spain, and a good claim to all the lands with Mediterranean shores. I see no reason why we should not send as many of our people as want to go, and let them take up residence in any of these places. It would at first be a hard and semi-savage life, and there would be much danger from the Europeans who in many cases would not understand our motives. As a chosen people, we would probably have to suppress some opposition, and at times it might be best to temporize. We will, however, as the superior race, triumph in the end.

But hold on a minute: our elders, I realize, don't want to do things the way my report has been suggesting—they think that's too much like the Europeans did our people, and they think we should be more civilized. They do have a point, and we culture-warriors should listen carefully. So I have been wondering—should we even bother with the military side of things? Maybe instead of sending people over to take the land, and drive people off and starve those that won't leave into submission, and show them how to live and worship by force if need be, we'd do better just to transport Europe over to us, and not try to counterpunch Columbus. I have even thought of a way to do this, because I did go on past those late staging areas from which Chris jumped off, and I got back closer to where their power sprang from, first in Rome and then in Greece, and though I did not get to Damascus and Jerusalem and Mecca, or to Peking where what went around is coming around, I saw how we can cram most of Europe into a computer and bring it back to deal with on our own terms, far more efficiently and cheaply than by trying to load all that geography on our backs the way Ameropeans have done. We can turn everything of theirs into electrons dancing around at our fingertips, words or corporations or whatever.

So I've started by looking carefully at Vesuvius and the villas which it saved by destroying, and the fine pornographic walls there, the neat body-casts in volcanic ashes and some of the words left here and there, geographics made out of graffiti. These fitted easily into my preconceptions and cost very little to bring back to Pawhuska, if anybody here should want them. And while we admittedly don't have a volcano handy in Osage country, we do have other things that show us how destroying has been used in theory to save. You may recall my letter in the *Osage Nation News* not long ago, reporting on rock shelters, but in case that's not to hand, here's a copy:

Rock Shelters
(for John Joseph Mathews)

> Up here, bluff-slabs of sandstone
> hang out from the rim,
> painted blue-gray with lichens, sheer
> over dusty level of a
> sheltered place: water sometimes
> down over places worn and knobby drips
> and darkens, softens earth to hold our

lifeprints; buttercup and rock pink
live where the hickory's branches fight
the sun and wind for power, but mostly here's
just humus: leaf-mulch deep and rustling
between great boulders broken from rimrock sliding
invisibly down the steep slope, The walk
down through these to the creek that
runs some of the year below here,
thin and clear over silty sandstone's
edges and angles, is short, steep, shady. Stoop
back beneath this shelter, we're in dust,
but in this damp earth just outside
the overhang are mussel shells—
worn
to flaky whiteness, rainbow of
iridescence long since dead. Here's charcoal too,
deep under the hanging slab. See,
we were
once here.
Moving with Doe Creek down
to where it joins Buck Creek,
down this narrow shallow canyon choked
with rocks you come out where
the trees loom higher, elm and pinoak columns
rise and arch dark over earth
loamy and loose and the creekbanks
of steep sandy clay, roots jutting over pools
muckbottomed winding down to Buck Creek and
mingling where it moves from
sandy shallows down to springfed depths
and darkness. Here, the winter
surrounded deer and turkeys, here lived plenty
of beaver, muskrat, mink and raccoon, fox and
bobcat and cottontail, coyote slinking, quail
and squirrels, mice and weasels all with
small birds watching from the bush or grapevine, berry
tangles, juncoes, waxwings, cardinals like blood on
snow, all sheltered here from
the prairie blizzards north.
And southward, in the bend of
Buck Creek level to the southern ridge a valley
of bluestem bending thigh-deep under
sunflowers nodding, meadowlarks flying and singing with
grazing buffalo, red wolves and coyotes trotting watching
with pricked ears a hunter crawl with

bow and arrows for a shot.
Now crossed
by asphalt road, wire fences, lanes to white farmhouses
where no farming's done, grapes and lettuce and
bananas on the polished table from Texas, from
California, Nicaragua, the orange-fleshed
watermelons that once lay in sandy fields by
Doe Creek gone, as truckloads of melons rumble
past from Louisiana into town where food is
kept. To plant here, you buy. This land
was needed, we were told—it would be used. So oil
is pulsing from beneath it, floats dead
rainbows on Buck Creek and draws brief trails
straight as a Roman road across the sky, where people sit
drinking and eating quietly the flesh of what
has followed buffaloes to winter in
the valleys underneath, on which
sky-travelers look down.
This new world
was endless, centered everywhere, our study
of place and peoples dangerous, surprising, never
completed. Doe Creek
tasted different from Buck Creek and our people still
did not look all alike.
How far, meant counting
the streams that must be crossed.
The reasons why were everywhere, uncircumscribed—
stars twinkle, moon never does, they both
were relative to whippoorwill and owl.
Greenwich did not
keep time for us. Now, the small stars
move fast and send down messages of war
to speech machines or pictures of
pleasure to our living rooms, inviting us out into
a larger endlessness with many
centers. Galaxies, before long, will
be sold for profit, once the first space-ship has
claimed one and the next has come to
kill all those before. Think
of walking on blue stars like
this one, new
plants, new beings, all the rock
shelters where we'll crouch and see
new valleys from.
Here's my

mussel-shell. Here's the charcoal.
We were here.

As you see, it is simple enough to bring Vesuvius and the Roman Empire back, and as for what evaporates in transit, it is easier for our people to go over and enjoy the flavor of it there than send war-dancers over to annex it and have such troubles with the local savages as would be sure to break out. So in case our elders don't want that bother, here's Rome freeze-dried into a poem.

Unfortunately Greece is giving me a little more trouble getting processed. We took a ferry over to Corfu, and then in the town across from Corfu we rented a Volkswagen and drove it across northern Greece, through the Pindus Mountains, to Olympos. We stopped a while in Meteora, to look at that huge rock mountain or tower with all the caves which were lately used by religious hermits. There were great black and white birds sailing in the updrafts around the heights of that place, and I thought they were eagles, but they turned out to be storks. This might explain the guidebook's curious statement about how the medieval hermits became so numerous— they *went into the rocks and multiplied,* it said, and there ARE old Christian legends about storks bringing babies. But what we really wanted to do was drive in the mountains, and I was particularly anxious to get up Mount Olympos, that being the place where Greece's head deity was when Greece was doing things that mattered for a few thousand years. And so I traced the power back up along the Vale of Tempe, under the mountain, and toward its source, since they have a road that lets Volkswagens up clear to the top of Olympos. We got slowed down by a blowout though, and spent the middle part of a sunny chilly spring day beside the green-gray River Peneus, looking up at the great massif of Olympos, and repairing the tire, and eating honey and bread and peanut butter and drinking Coca-Cola. But we found we could drink the spring water around there, showing that the old gods are friendly still, and we filled our empty plastic Coke bottles from Aphrodite's spring, and Apollo's spring, and Dionysus' spring, and the Muses' spring—see, I brought back some in this container, and the water neatly fitted the sides of the cowpond in our bluestem meadow:

To the Muses, in Oklahoma

That Aganippe well was nice, it hit the spot—
sure, this bluestem meadow
is hardly Helicon, we had
to gouge a pond, the mules
dragged a rusty slip scraping
down through dusty topsoil into
dark ooze and muck, grating open
sandstone eggs; but then the thunder

sent living waters down, they filled
the rawness with blue trembling where white
clouds sailed in summer and we
walked upon the water
every winter (truth
is a frozen allomorph of time), though it
was always more fun sliding. We'd go and
chop through six-inch ice by the pond's edge, pry the
ice-slab out onto the pond from its
hole where the dark water welled
up cold to the milk-cows sucking noisily,
snorting their relish; and
when they'd
drunk we shoved the ice-
slab over to where the bank
sloped gently, took
a running chute and leaped atop the slab real
easy and slid,
just glided clear over
the pond riding on ice—
or stretched prone
on the black windowy ice looked
down into darkness where fish dimly
drifted untouchable beneath our fingers.
Ice
makes a whole new surface
within things, keeps
killer whales from seals just long enough to
let new seals be born before they
dive in to feed or be fed upon.
—Come sliding now, and later we'll
go swimming, dive in with the
muskrats, black bass, water moccasins, under
this willow let the prairie wind
drink from our bare skin:
good water
fits every mouth.

I noticed that shepherds in those Greek mountains were very friendly and I
regret missing the chance to cement a relationship when one asked in sign
language for a cigarette I didn't have—they have taken up our discovery of
tobacco's offering-power, but denuminalized it, which makes it hard on their
lungs. This shepherd gave his name as *Aristo-tell-Ace,* and on the whole his
mountain seemed worth claiming since its water (unlike that in Rome, which
is full of Mussolini's Revenge) the gods and muses still approve; so after

changing the blown-out tire we drove from the Vale of Tempe up Mount Olympos. But we did not get all the way to the top, which could be why I have trouble fitting Greece into the word-processor. The blowout cost us quite a bit of sunlight and also reduced the Volkswagen temporarily to four healthy wheels, so we got worried that one of them might be gored by the road, which turned from asphalt to broken stone at about eight thousand feet. Olympos is only something under ten thousand feet but very husky, sprawls a lot with spurs and gorges, and the road keeps winding and zigzagging up one perpendicular ridge and over onto another. It was when we got onto the dirt and rocky road, and from its edge looked down on eagles soaring over several thousand feet of updrafts, and a pine tree had fallen across the road and we had to drive slowly around its tips by the cliff-edge and those on the side next the eagles got nervous, that we decided to claim only as much of Greece as this level of Olympos would allow us to. So we may not have got above the Aonian Mount and this may mean trouble for our epic Osage work at least in English, until the next expedition, but that's for the elders to decide.

What gave me pause when we decided to turn around was the sound of thunder. Since I am of the Thunder people, I wondered whether this was saying to go on up, but then we noticed that some distance out toward the Aegean Sea, on the plains under Olympos, was where the thundering came from, and when I got out of the car and walked over to the rim and listened and looked, it was clear that those were cannons firing, and so I did not believe it was an oracle to go up after all. Later we found that these were army exercises, and tanks firing, near the Greek army's base near Olympos. But at least, in looking for the thunder's source, it was possible to see that the view from Olympos across the Aegean was fine as wine, and the peninsula where Mount Athos is situated was in plain sight over some aquamarine and amethyst distances which darkened to emerald and purple as the light began fading. We dropped back down into the twilight, and joined the tanks going home, and so it would now be possible for any Osages to feel free to use whatever comes down from Olympos, such as epics, tragedies, democracy, either the honey or the honeybees (to misquote Sappho), odes, civil wars of people or gods or both, good water, idealism, all that.

I don't think it is useful to say much more about Greece. Athens we should not bother with; it is too much like Paris and London—everybody tries to be someplace else at the same time, so the paths are all knotted up, covered with asphalt and smog. Like Paris and London and Rome, Athens is full of ruins, but easier to get to than theirs, and on the whole prettier and less cluttered with people living in them. We did go down, also, and had a look at Argos, where Agamemnon took a bath the way Custer took a ride, and then we drove across the Peloponnese to Olympia—by sandy Ladon's lilied banks, the scenic route through Arcadia, where death was the shepherd's friend, and there were redbuds in mauve pink bloom among the fallen marble columns at Olympia—nice to see the Oklahoma state tree there. And there was also a dead European adder, smashed and dried, lying on one of the column-stumps where the lizards were frisking in bright sunlight. I don't know why, in Europe, poison snakes never invented rattles to warn people, but this one evidently did not get in the first strike. On the whole I would be for our claiming all the Peloponnese, including Argos as well as Olympia, because it could be useful to us—what the hell, we might as well have pastoral as well as epic and tragedy if we want to claim Europe for our kids. And it is probably our destiny anyhow, if our elders won't mind such an Ameropean way of putting it, to get the whole subcontinent. I sneaked a piece of the Peloponnese into a lyric as one sample of how it plays on the rez:

As Brer Coyote Said,

> the country's not quite
> all field or fence, blackberries
> root wild on stony soil
> among scrub timber, vines
> thorny still in winter as booted feet thrash
> through hip-high hay, brown and stemmy, after
> the dogs and rabbits running blind
> to blackberry briars until
> they've grabbed and torn, saying
> *this ground is taken for the smaller nations who*
> *live BENEATH, who perch BETWEEN—*
> surviving too spring's burning with the wind swinging
> its gold-crackling scythe across
> the meadow purging
> old nests and vines among rock-croppings
> as dried cow-chips go smoking
> back to the sky or floating
> creekwards with rains and leave the
> marginal things such black clarity to grow in, wild
> plums whiten, chokecherries bloom
> along winding gullies,
> new shoots spring green and fork
> the air like snaketongues coming out
> of eggs to flicker tasting—
> the vines flower loosely as sunburn
> days move in, bare feet
> grow tough enough to walk
> among thorn fringes on the way
> down to the low-water bridge
> (the rock-riffles and pool darkshining
> under arch of elms like a water-floored

cathedral,
brown naked bodies poise,
fly on the ropeswing down from
their high bank and skim
with one heel to rise up, up,
and drop through topwater's warmth into brown
darkness of spring-cold upwellings like waving
tendrils around the thighs)—
and July,
July is BERRIES—
the heaping pans and
handled buckets spilling their black shining
with some a tight
red still
and reaching fingers, even stung
by a hidden wasp to swell
like soft cucumbers, are consoled
by cobblers, whose thick doughs and crusts purple
with juice and flake with sugar under yellow spilling
Jersey cream into blackpurple berries that taste
like nothing else
waiting in roadside ditches,
rockpiles, woodmargins—
FREE
between their thorns.

Well, I am going to end this report for now, only adding that I hope some better fate befalls me than fell on the European conquistadores—you know how Cortez ended up running alongside the chariot of Charles the Fifth, crying about never having been given a piece of the empire he had conquered; and Balboa, Pizarro and the rest got hanged or assassinated. Anyhow Europe, being secondhand and pretty badly used, ought not to be priced so high as Louisiana when Jefferson bought from a French dictator the land on which, as he knew and did not know, our Osage people happened to exist. Freeze-dried as in these words, Europe in any event won't be worth things of serious value. So don't let any of us offer language, traditions, beadwork, religion or even half the Cowboy and Indian myth, let alone our selves, this time. These words, whatever has evaporated, will give its aftertaste, enough for anyone wanting to steal a culture from under the noses of its guardians; they wouldn't let me take the gold mask of Agamemnon, but I did sneak out with his story.

Still, remember that Coyote outsmarted himself and lost his beautiful fur. (Kept his wits though. Wonder how things would have gone if it had been Coyote not Oedipus up against that Sphinx. Europe with a Coyote Complex . . . hey, maybe it WAS Coyote!) Comedy is worth more than tragedy any time where survival is at stake. Always tricky, of course, claiming another continent, especially when you succeed, as I hope we are about to do; and then Sion's hill, and Sinai, though a few hundred years of recycling may be needed first for those. Meantime, keep the oil wells pumping, and let me know if you have any "special" orders for pieces of Russia, China, Japan, or even "India."

Yours ever,
Special Agent Wazhazhe No. 2,230

P.S.—Speaking of Jerusalem, how retroactively can we claim a place? I forgot, in passing through the Dordogne and Spanish areas, to claim the caves at Lascaux and Altamira, etc., but here is a piece of metamorphic rock or maybe a geode that might get them back for us.

Stone Age

Whoever broke a rock first wasn't trying
to look inside it, surely,
just looking for an edge
or meant to hammer something, and it broke.
Then he saw it glitter,
how *bright* inside it was; noticed how things
unseen are fresh. Maybe he said
—it's like the sky, that when the sun has
crashed down through the west
breaks open to the Milky Way, so we see
farther than we are seen for once, as far
as light and time can reach and almost over
the edge of time, its spiral track like agate
swirls in rock from when it still
was water-stains, had not yet found its
non-solution to the puzzle
of dissolution, keeping within its darkness
the traces of its origin as day keeps night and
night keeps stars. Pebbles, headstones, Altamira,
dust-wrinkles over darkness.
What shines within?

Greg Sarris (Miwok-Pomo)

How I Got to Be Queen

I watched Justine across the street. I seen her from the window. Even with Sheldon and Jeffrey asking for lunch, I seen clear enough to know she was up to her old tricks. I said to myself, that queen, she's up to it again. This time it was a boy, a black boy whose name I'd learn in a matter of hours. Justine wastes no time. But just then I pulled away from the window, in case the two little guys might see what I did. Kids have a way of telling things, after all.

Nothing was unpacked. Not even the kitchen this time. I pulled a towel from boxes on the floor and dusted the paper plates left from breakfast. What food we had was on the table. Half loaf of Wonder Bread. Two large jars of peanut butter. Two cans of pie filling. Justine went for another loaf of bread, jam, and a packet of lemonade mix. She got far as the store, which is kitty-corner, just down the street, in plain view from the window.

She stood on one side of the bicycle rack, by the newspaper stand. She stood with a hand on her hip, her head lifted and tilted to the side. Like she was taking a dare, or fixing on some scheme. It makes people notice her. She draws them in that way. She looked black as the boy straddling a bike on the other side of the rack.

I wondered what Mom would do if she seen her there. That's if Mom wasn't at the cannery with Auntie. I think it's bad the way Justine and Mom talk to each other when there's trouble. "Damned black-neck squaw," Mom says. "Dirty fat Indian," Justine says. "You don't even know which Filipino in that apple orchard is my father." On and on it goes. Of course, Mom don't say much any other time. And if Justine goes on long enough, Mom goes out or watches TV. Like nothing was ever started. Like she does with just about anything else.

I took the longest time setting two pieces of bread on each plate. I found things to look for: the aluminum pie tins, the plastic cups left over from Cousin Jeanne's party, the rolling pin. "I'm going to make a pie," I said to the boys standing at the table. "We'll have a party with pie and lemonade." They shifted on their feet with no patience. "All right," I said. "You act like starved rats and you look worse than pigs. Now wash up." I spread peanut butter on the bread, then sprinkled on some sugar. "I don't want no complaining," I told them when they came back.

Justine came in about four, an hour before Mom.

"Now what good's that?" I asked. She put the bag of groceries on the table. "You might as well go back and get the burger and torts for dinner. And get flour. I got canned pumpkin for pies."

"Don't give me no shit, Alice," she said. Times like this she played older sister. She wasn't listening to me. She just shook that silky hair and said, "I'm in love. And he is fine. Ou wee, Sis, the boy is fine."

She was talking like a black person. It's one of her things. I don't mean talking like a black person. Justine does things so you notice. She goes for a response. Like what she started with Jack, the boys' father. Which is behind us coming to Santa Rosa. Mom said it's Justine's fault. I said Jack was old and his family would come for him sooner or later, anyway. Giving Justine credit just fed the fire.

It started with a Social Security check that wandered to the bottom of Mom's purse and stuck itself into something or other. Since a week went by and it didn't come up for air, Jack started to get edgy. "My money, where is it?" he kept asking. He was at the point if his dinner wasn't on time, you was trying to starve him. If a door or window was left open, you wanted him to die of pneumonia. It didn't surprise me he called Clifford, his son.

"What do you mean, you lost it?" Clifford said to Mom.

I heard Jack make the call, so I figured trouble. Clifford and Mom have a history, and Clifford was all along dead against Mom being conservator and signing for Jack. True, Jack wasn't in his right mind half the time, and his insides was shot. Like a sponge that doesn't suck water is what the clinic doctor said. But Mom wasn't no crook. I opened my huckleberry jam. I made toast and set the table. But Clifford, who's more stubborn than a ass and looks worse, seen none of it.

"What's the matter, Mollie, you start on the bottle again?" he asked Mom.

Mom was sitting next to Jack. I looked at the place mats and the food. Anyone could see the old man was cared for and fed.

"Cliff," I said. "Why not put a stop on the check? Go to the Social Security." I felt funny saying Cliff. For a while it was Dad.

"Yeah, and what's my father supposed to eat in the meantime? You kids is using up his money." Then he looked at Mom. "I'm telling you, Mollie, I'm sick of what's going on here."

He brushed past Justine, who stood in the doorway. I said the check would turn up. Justine said, "Who cares?"

But Justine seen how to use the situation to her end. She never liked Jack. "He nags Mom," she said. I said, "How can he give anybody else attention when he's half dead?" Justine didn't see my point. And it was Easter vacation, no school and no work in the orchards, which means you had nothing to do, no one to see. Or, in Justine's case, nowhere else to pull her stunts. So there was time for thinking.

All of a sudden Justine was dressed up. I mean dressed up every day. She found clothes I never knowed existed in that house. She mixed skirts and blouses in different ways. She wore down her eyeliner pencil in a week. Each morning she worked her hair into a hive the size of Sheldon's basketball. And when that was done, she sat at the kitchen table painting her nails the color of a red jelly bean. Then, when Mom went to register at the cannery, she started on how she was going to buy a stereo. "I put down fifty dollars at the Golden Ear," she said.

That got Justine a response.

Clifford made it from the reservation in one hour. And he wasn't alone. His white woman was with him, the woman who opens her mouth only when her nose is plugged and she can't breathe. Her I wasn't afraid of. It was Evangeline, his sister, who just as soon spit than say hello. She hated Mom. She looked at me like I was Mom's bare foot and she wanted to smash it under her work boots.

I knowed the old man went into the bedroom and called someone. I figured one of his kids. I just never put two and two together. And neither did Justine. She never got the pleasure of being falsely accused of stealing.

Clifford left his woman and sister guard. Like we would lift the last penny from Jack's pockets. Then he came back with suitcases and boxes. "Come on, Dad," he said, "Evangeline is going to take care of you. She won't spend the money on *her* kids. Not like this lot of swine."

Mom wasn't legal with Jack. There was nothing she could do. It was agreed about the checks only because he lived with us. Since the car was Jack's, it was gone now, too. Even so, she walked to town, then took the bus to Santa Rosa, and canceled the check at the Social Security. Of course, three days later it floats up from the mess in her purse.

Auntie drove Mom to the res, but it was no use. Evangeline wouldn't let her see Jack. She didn't care about the check. I know what Evangeline said. I heard it before. "You screwed my brother, then went for my father. Dirty whore. I don't believe those two kids are my father's. Now get." I reminded Mom that we are from Lake County. "We're not from that res," I said.

Justine unloaded what I first sent her for, then tore off for the dinner stuff. This time she was back right away. She kept the boys out of my hair. I got busy. My nerves pushed me. Rolling dough for pies, I thought of things. Which is a way I calm my nerves when working won't do it alone. I didn't like what I seen at the store and my imagination started to get the best of me. I thought of Jack. I guess because I hadn't made a pie since we left Healdsburg and came here. I thought how he'd settle down his griping when I cooked. Mom called me whenever he started screeching. He acted drunk, though the hardest thing he took those days was ginger ale. I rolled pie dough and didn't notice when he picked berries or apples or whatever it was out of the bowl. He was quiet. I thought that's what a grandfather would be like.

I set the pies in the oven. Then I got to work on dinner. I turned meat in one skillet and warmed torts in the other. I sent Justine to the store again, this time for cheese and chili sauce. The skillet of meat, a plate of warmed torts, sliced cheese and toast was on the table when Mom got home. Her place was at the head. It's where I put things, like the cheese and chili sauce which she likes on her meat, so you know.

She didn't say nothing. She was tired, I know. She finished eating, then cleaned up and went to play cards with Auntie like she did every night. "Tomorrow, we'll start on the boxes," she told me before she left. She was standing in the kitchen then, combing back her washed hair with Sheldon's pink comb. I kept on with the dishes. It has been two weeks, I thought to myself. Then, with my hands in the greasy water, I resolved to start unpacking myself, no matter what she said. We couldn't wait to see if we was going to stay here or not. Tomorrow, I told myself, first thing. I heard the front door slam.

I was still scrubbing, finishing the damned skillets, when I turned to tell the boys to take a bath before I gave them pie, which I had cooling on the sink. I thought Justine was behind me, seated at the table. But she wasn't. She was standing there with her friend.

"This is Ducker," she said.

First thing I noticed, the boys wasn't there. "They're taking baths," Justine said, seeing how I was looking at the empty seats.

She was referring to them not seeing Ducker. I never heard the door open since it slammed behind Mom. My ears pick up on those things. So I was caught off guard. Justine didn't have to embarrass me. "Close your mouth," she said. "You look like Clifford's wife."

I thought of the boys again. The bathroom door was shut. Then I thought this Ducker might think I'm stupid, or prejudice on account of him being black. My mind was going in several directions at once. I said what made no sense given the circumstances.

"Here, Mister Ducker, sit down and have some pie." I put a pie on the table.

Justine started laughing. I knowed she thought I was in shock seeing this black person in our house.

"It ain't *Mister Ducker*," she said. "It's Ducker. Ducker Peoples."

"Well . . ."

"We don't want pie," she said. She looked toward the bathroom, then to Ducker. "We're going for a walk."

"Nice to meet you . . ." he said, stopping when he got to my name.

"Alice," Justine said.

"Alice," he said.

I was still standing in the same place after they went out the front door. I tore to the window. Then I seen what he looked like. When they was across the street, almost to the store, I remembered who it was in front of me two minutes before. Funny thing about Ducker, he wasn't a man. Well, I mean grown. He was a kid, looked like. Bony arms hanging from flapping short sleeves. His face, shiny smooth, no hair. Like he should be chewing bubblegum and keeping baseball cards. Not holding on to Justine, who was sixteen and looked it.

"Who was here?"

I jumped around, half scared to death. It was Sheldon and Jeffrey out of the bathtub, drying their naked bodies.

"Now dry off in the bathroom," I said.

"Sound like a nigger."

"Hush up, Sheldon."

"Who was here?"

"Nobody."

Next day something concerned me. Mom was in the kitchen, putting things in cupboards. I heard her even before I got up. Even then I didn't think she'd make a day of it.

"It's Tuesday," she said. "Day off."

She finished with the kitchen before I started breakfast. I had to open cupboards to find things. She was in the bedroom by the time I could help her. Her things she put in the closet first. I seen her red dress from where I was standing, opening the boys' boxes. It's crinoline with ruffles. She wears it with her black patent leather shoes with the sides busted out. Like at Great-Auntie's funeral. Or when she came home with Clifford. Same thing with Jack.

"I guess this means we're staying here," I said.

This move was a trial. Ever since we came to Santa Rosa seemed nothing worked for very long. First that house on West Seventh we couldn't afford. Then the one by the freeway which no one told us they was going to tear down for development. Got two months rent from us, anyway. And now this, which Auntie, whose idea it was for us to come here, got from the landlord she knows.

"What choice do we have?" she asked.

The way she said that matched her business putting things away. Like it was nothing. Seemed to me just then, anyway. Like I said, it concerned me. I was the one who most of the time put things away, after all. No matter what she said before or after. It was just this time she made such a big deal about the neighborhood. Then I guess we moved so much. Just three months in Santa Rosa, and three times already.

"Well," I said. "I like it here. It's a change."

"A lot of blacks," Mom said. "Auntie didn't say so much about that."

"Not everybody can be a Pomo Indian," I said. Since Mom had her stuff on the bed, I spread the boys' things on their sleeping bags, which I hadn't rolled up yet. I sorted underwear on my knees. I thought of reminding her that Justine is part Filipino, and that I'm part Mexican. But that is what Justine would do.

"It's nice having Auntie up the street," I said. I liked the way Mom called her cousin "Auntie," which she did for us kids. "I like hearing Auntie tell stories."

"Ah, don't listen to that old Indian stuff."

Auntie cooks good. She's got recipes. And she's classy. Slender-bodied, not like me and Mom. She knows how to talk to social workers, those kind of people.

I got up and put the folded things in the boys' drawers. Mom was hanging up me and Justine's clothes. "Is this okay?" I asked, seeing how she was putting things where she wanted.

"Your sister, I don't know what she'll do here. Run with them kids out there. Niggers, anything."

That made it click. My worries took form in a picture. Justine and Ducker. Still, I wasn't certain, I mean about Mom just then. Did Sheldon or Jeffrey see last night and tell? It's how Mom says things by not saying them. It puts you in a place where you don't know if she's saying something or not. That's far as she'll go. Unless it's with Justine in a fight.

I was caught, trapped, and bothered just the same. Mom kept working, her back to me.

"Don't worry about Justine," I said.

We had a normal family dinner that night. I fixed chops and fried potatoes. I cut celery sticks and carrots. People need greens. But this family don't eat them. Which is one reason there's so much crabbing. They're stopped up.

Mom stayed and helped with the dishes before she went to Auntie's. Of course while things looked peaceful I imagined a disaster. Like Ducker knocking on the door. I wondered if Mom was hanging around in case that happened. I saw loudmouth Sheldon saying, "It's him. It's him." But nothing happened. Even after Mom left.

The boys opened drawers, looking to find where I put their clothes. They kept bugging me about getting the TV fixed and hooked up. Justine moved stuff in the closet to her liking. Me, I only wanted a long enough couch in the living room. I was sleeping on the floor with the boys. I can't sleep in the bed with Mom and Justine. No rest, even with them out like a light.

Next day Mom went fishing to the coast with Auntie. Auntie's Mom and Uncle, they sat in the car when Auntie came in for Mom. The old lady stuck her white head out and said for me to come along. I stood on the front porch to say hello. "I can't," I said. Then she said to me in Indian what men used to say in the old days when they set out fishing. "Get the grill ready, then."

"Damn cannery's so cheap. Got illegals instead of working us extra days," Mom said when she came out.

"Don't think of work, Mollie," Auntie said.

Justine padded up and stood with me to wave good-bye. She was still waving after the car left. I thought she was nuts until I seen it was Ducker she was waving forward. Bold as daylight. He walked right up the front porch.

"Morning, Alice," he said.

I thought of my mouth this time. I kept it closed, not shocked. And I thought what to do. Already the boys seen everything. I got some bread in a plastic bag and headed for the park. I carried Jeffrey part of the way. Sheldon, I just about dragged by the hair.

"What's so big about seeing goldfish?" he said, whining like he does. A sure trait of his father. Proof I would have for Evangeline.

"Shut up," I said. "You damn ass brat."

"You just don't want us there with that—"

I slapped his face. Then he started crying like I tied him to a stake and burned him. Which I wanted to do. We was at the park by then. I put bread in the water for the fish. But nothing worked. Sheldon screamed so the whole park could hear. "I'm telling Mom," he said. Then I thought of the opposite of fire. Water. And I had it right there.

"Shut up," I said, "before I rub your face in dog shit. Now shut up, damn you." Then Jeffrey started crying. "Now see," I said. "Stop it, Sheldon. Please."

I threatened the police. Sheldon quit some, but I knowed what weapon he was harboring, that he'd use against me the minute he seen Mom. I looked at the soggy bread floating on the empty water.

"I'll get the TV fixed," I said. "But not if you act like that, Sheldon."

So I spent what was left in the tobacco tin. It's how I kept Ducker in the house and the boys quiet.

Ducker got to be a regular thing. And more—his friends. The only break I had was Mom's days off. Every night the party was on like clockwork. Soon as Mom was gone to Auntie's ten minutes. Then a worse deal. If Mom went fishing on a day off, the party was all day. I was never one for school, but I wanted this summer over.

Ducker brought his radio. I seen every latest dance. Imagine Justine. She was in her element. She knowed the dances best of anybody and showed it. The boys clapped. It was just boys coming to the house. "Why should girls come here?" Justine said when I asked. "We're the girls."

We had talks, Justine and me. I told her how we couldn't go on like this. She told me not to be so shy. "Don't be afraid to smile," she said. "Don't be worried about your weight."

Then she said how she had a plan for when school started. "I'll show them snobby white girls," she said. "I'll show them Indians from Jack's res, too." She pictured herself walking down the hall with Ducker. She was going to lose fifteen pounds. She was going to wear all kinds of makeup on her face. People would be shocked. They'd be scared of her.

"You already done that plan at Healdsburg," I said, reminding her of how it got her a white boy and a hassle with his family so she hit the mother, knocking her tooth out, and had the cops come and take her to juvee and tell the welfare to take us from Mom.

"Well, everything turned out okay," she said. "You have to see who you are, Alice. Look around and see what you see. See what you can do. How you can be queen. The queen is the baddest. She knows it all. That's how she's queen. Like how I walk at school. Don't be worried about your weight. Some boys like it."

Only thing I was worried about was her plan. I couldn't see the outcome to this one yet. I wasn't a queen. She tried to get certain of Ducker's friends with me. "The kids won't tell, if that's what you're worried about," she said.

This was true. It's not just the TV keeping the boys quiet now. It was Ducker. He took them to the school yard. He showed them all his basketball stuff. After that, I might as well disappear into thin air far as Sheldon cared. I had to get Ducker to make Sheldon mind.

If it was Mom's day off and she went fishing, I took Jeffrey to the park and left Sheldon with Justine. Not that I felt right about it. Another thing I must say, I had a friend. Anthony. Not a boyfriend, not in my mind. Anthony just made himself useful tagging along. "Now don't forget bread for the fish," he said, if we was going to the park. Sometimes we did that, on Mom's day off, all of us. What else Anthony and me talked about I don't know. I got used to him. I didn't even think of him being black. Until we run into Auntie's mom and uncle in the park.

I couldn't get out of it. The two old ones sitting on the park bench seen me five minutes before I seen them. The old lady was looking away the Indian style of looking away. Like you know she seen you and looked away so you don't have to see her. In them situations it's a sign to help yourself and keep walking.

I was hardly fifty feet from them. Anthony with me. He was carrying Jeffrey on his shoulders. I knowed the picture they seen. I took the old lady's cue. I turned straight around, in the direction we came, and went behind the tall cypress trees, out of sight. It wasn't just that Anthony was black. I don't even think it was black people that bothered Mom so much. It was anything disturbing. It was what nobody talked about.

I found the sheets that day. I remember. I had my senses. After what happened in the park, I was thinking. I knowed if I tried to wash the sheets in the sink anybody might see the blood. Anybody could walk in. So I burned them out back in the garbage can. Justine never mentioned a thing, even when I was cleaning up. "Me and Ducker had the most fun," she said, after Mom went to Auntie's that night.

Indians say blood is a sign of the devil. Where it spills will be poison everlasting. That's how a place gets taboo. Auntie told me a story once. It was at Great-Auntie's funeral. It was to explain why Mom didn't cry, why Mom didn't like Great-Auntie who raised Mom and didn't like having to raise her. Great-Auntie got stuck with Mom and her sisters after some man poisoned Mom's mom. But here's what I think of. How Mom and her sisters found their mom in a puddle of salamander eggs and blood.

With Justine the expected worried me much as the unexpected. The expected, I worried when. The unexpected, what. When came like a straight shot, now that I look back at things. Mom came home early from Auntie's that same night. After the park, Justine's episode, and all my cleaning the floors and bed. Why that night? Why at all? I can't believe Mom didn't know what was going on before. Maybe she didn't want us to think she was dumb.

Maybe she had to keep face for Auntie, if the old lady said something to Auntie. I don't know.

By this time our house was party central. It was Justine's party. She was queen. That's what the boys called her. Dance, Justine, dance. The neighborhood knowed Justine. She was dressing again. She was dressed up everyday. Mom saw the party. She stood in the doorway half a minute, then turned around and left.

I unplugged Ducker's radio. I told everyone to get out. Must've been ten guys there. Something came over me so I was fierce. Justine said to shut up. The older sister, again. Usually, I ignored her, kept on about my business. Like Mom with most things. But this time I was Justine and more. I was going to floor her with the weight of my body. She must've seen because she was stopped cold. She tore out the front door with the guys.

Sheldon and Jeffrey, I put in the tub. Sheldon, I slapped in the mouth for no reason. He never made a peep. Neither one of them did. I put them to bed. No TV.

I finished the dishes and put them away. I wiped down the stove and refrigerator with Windex. I did the kitchen table too. Then I put together flour and water for torts. Torts by scratch. Mom's favorite. I was plopping them when Justine snuck past to the bedroom.

I finished. I set the torts on the clean table. I placed a fresh kitchen towel over the pile to keep in the warmth. Then next to a place mat made of paper towels I put a half cube of butter and the sugar bowl with a spoon next to it. Finally, I filled a glass with ice cubes and put it to the left of the place mat, opposite the butter and sugar.

Mom didn't come home until late. Around midnight. I was in the front room. I must've been dozing in the chair because when I opened my eyes, half startled, Mom was past me, turning into the bedroom. I thought of Justine and Mom in that bed together. I didn't hear a sound. Then I dozed again.

It was early morning I heard it. Like two roosters woke up and found themselves in the same pen. It started low in the bedroom, then came at full blast to the kitchen. Really loud. I thought of the boys. I pictured them hiding their heads for cover in their sleeping bags. I didn't move from the chair where I'd been all night.

Mom was hollering. "You're the lowest dirty, black-neck squaw. Chink . . ." And Justine. "Which one is my father? Tell me, you drunk slob, low-life Indian. Prove you're not the whore everyone says you are."

Then I heard the cupboard and something slam on the kitchen table. I couldn't believe my ears. I knowed without seeing what it was. Still, I didn't move. I don't know, it was strange. Then Mom comes out, her hair all wild from sleeping, and takes off, out the front door.

"Look how stupid," Justine said, nodding to the shotgun on the table. It was Jack's, what he forgot. I was still rubbing my eyes, just standing there. I picked it up and put it away.

"Fat bitch thought she was going to scare me with that," Justine said. "Shut up," I said. "Just shut up."

I turned on the oven and warmed the untouched torts for breakfast.

Mom might as well moved to Auntie's. We hardly seen her, except when she came back to sleep. She put so much money in the tobacco tin for me to spend. Like when she was drinking, only now we never seen her, and I didn't have to keep the money in my pockets for fear she'd take it out of the tin. Once, when she was drinking, she accused me of stealing the money. I'd spent it, of course, and gave her what I had left. Five dollars. She went berserk, hollering in the backyard. Just screaming, no words. Someone called the police. She stopped when they got there, then locked herself in the bathroom and cried herself to sleep. Later, to bug Mom, Justine said she called the police.

Mom strayed, like I said. It was me and Justine and the boys. And Ducker and Anthony and whoever else. Seemed nothing I could do.

We walked together, all of us. Who I mentioned. Justine didn't hang back at the house with Ducker so much anymore. She didn't say it, but I knowed she was anxious to try out with other boys what she tried out with Ducker. Certain things she said. The ways she talked to Ducker's friends and looked at them. Especially Kolvey, who was bigger, more grown, like a man. Signs Justine was up to something.

Anyway, I fixed the lunches. Most days we went to the park. Sometimes we walked other places. Like the fairgrounds where they was putting up the rides. Once we took a bus to the mall. Anthony would help me with things. He carried the Koolmate so we'd have cold pop. Another thing he did was the shopping. "What do you need?" he asked me. Like we was a pair. But there was nothing between us. In fact, lots of times at the park I went off by myself. I left him where Justine was pulling her stunts and where the two old ones sat and seen whatever they wanted. I took Jeffrey and went behind the cypress trees. He was the only one obeyed me. "Time to take a nap," I told him. It was cool there, away from everyone, and I pulled him close and slept.

It was Anthony who got me up. He told me something was going on with Justine. I was dead asleep on the grass there, and I felt Jeffrey slip from my arms.

"What?" I asked.

But by this time both Jeffrey and Anthony was looking through the trees. Then I seen it, too. Some skinny black girl and a couple of her friends, small and skinny like her, stood about twenty yards from Justine. Far enough so they was shouting and I could hear. The black girl was sticking out her hand, curling her finger like a caterpillar walking. "Miss Doris say for Mister Ducker Peoples to come right this minute," she was saying.

The boys was still on the ground, setting there. Justine was standing in all her clothes and makeup. Red lips. Nails. "What's this Miss Doris shit?" she said.

The girl shifted her weight to one side and put her hand on her hip. "Miss Doris say for Ducker to come right this minute if he knows what's good for him."

"Justine say Miss Doris eat shit," Justine said.

Then I grabbed Jeffrey. It happened fast. Justine crossed the line. She was face-to-face with that girl, and, with no words, just popped her one upside the head. The girl went over, like she flopped, hitting the ground on her side. Her two friends jumped back, like Justine would go after them next.

"Justine say to eat shit, Miss Doris," Justine said, looking down at that girl who was setting up now holding her face.

"I'm telling you, your sister shouldn't done that," Anthony said.

Something in the way he said that scared me. Like I knowed he told the truth.

"There's your grandparents," he said.

I looked to where Anthony was looking. With the commotion I hadn't seen the old ones on the bench, if they was ever sitting there. They was walking in the opposite direction, away.

"They ain't my grandparents," I said.

It was in the air. Justine's doings filled the rooms of our house, in every cupboard I opened, every potato I sliced. Like you seen the white of the potato and seen Justine when you was doing everything not to. And it was outside. Like fog settling in the streets. It was between the houses, across at the store. You seen it in the way a bird sat still on the telephone wire.

I made macaroni and cheese and potato salad. Macaroni and cheese is easy. Just boil macaroni and melt the cheese. Potato salad, that takes time. Boiling the potatoes, chopping celery and onions. Mayonnaise. All that. I did it. And more. Two pies from scratch. And a cake, even if that was from a box. You'd think we was still on the reservation and I was putting up food for a funeral.

Mom knowed, too. After dinner, she didn't go to Auntie's. How could she explain herself being there when Auntie and them knowed about the trouble here?

I never sat, not once while the others ate. The pies and all that. And I started right in with the dishes. I frosted the cake and set it on the table with a knife and new paper plates. I folded paper towels to make napkins at each place. I put a plastic fork on top of each napkin. I thought of candles and ice cream, but it was too late for that.

I was scrubbing the pots when I heard the first noises and looked over my shoulder and seen the crowd collecting outside on the street. From the sink, if you turned around, you could look through the kitchen door and the front door to the street. I wanted to close the front door, but I didn't move. I mean I kept on in the kitchen. Mom was at the table, kind of peeking out. She had her hands on her knees. Straight arms, like she does when she's going to get up. The boys looked at the cake like they was waiting for me to cut it. I was just about to do that. I thought, what am I doing forgetting about the cake.

Then Justine came out from the bedroom.

She was in Mom's red dress. That's no getup for the occasion, I thought. Not that I lingered on that thought just then. Mom got up and went into the bedroom and the boys followed her. The bedroom door closed.

"Don't do it," I said to Justine.

I guess someone outside seen her, too, because the yelling and name-calling rose up. "Dirty whore. Come out and pick on someone your own size. Slut." All that. I looked once then, and the street was filled with people. Some was near the steps. Young people, old people, kids, filling the air. Shouting.

"You don't have to do it, Justine," I told her again. "Just tell them you didn't mean for them guys to go and say yes."

She looked at me straight. Not like she was mad, or even scared. Kind of like she had a plan. Like she does when she tilts her head and half smiles at you. "I told them, 'yes, I would fight that Miss Doris's sisters,' because I ain't scared of nobody. Not three big-ass mean nigger bitches, nobody. They'll see. I'm the queen, remember?"

That's when I took inventory of her getup. The red dress, too big for Justine, was cinched with a black belt, which matched her pump shoes. And she had nylons on and the delicate gold necklace she found in the girls' gym. Her hair was done up just so. Her face, it was a movie star's. This I was focusing on all the while the people outside came closer and louder. The house was surrounded. I thought girls fight in old clothes. Like the times in Healdsburg when Justine met in the park to fight someone.

"Anyway," I said, "you can't fight in them clothes."

She was still looking at me the same way. Half smiling like I didn't know a thing. And she kept that smiling and looking straight at me when she reached to the table and picked up the knife. She tucked it in the front dress pocket, her hand on the handle, and walked out.

When that many people is surrounding the house and screaming, everything is clattering. The walls, windows. It's like things was going to cave in or blow wide apart. It's where the first rip is you look. And I seen it. A rock through the front window. Glass shattering. A hole wide as a fist.

I was in the doorway between the kitchen and front room. That was far as I got, and when I looked out for Justine, after seeing that rock come through the window, she was gone. Just the crowd screaming and the empty house. Like the boys and Mom wasn't even there. Like they was rolling away, around the corner, out of reach. Everybody. It all just went so fast. The whole place blowing apart. Then I seen the hole again. I was in shock by this time, I guess. I turned around and started putting dishes away. I don't know what. I opened cupboards, and seen the gun. Jack's shotgun. I ran to the front porch and shot it.

I didn't know nothing after that. Just colors. Everybody moving. Voices. People talking to me.

"Dumb ass, bitch. What'd you do that for?"

"Alice, you're the queen now. Nobody's going to mess with you, girl."

"Dumb ass, bitch."

"Hey, Alice. You're bad, girl. Justine never got a lick in."

"Stupid, crazy bitch. Now the cops'll come. Dumb ass, bitch."

They said I just stood there with that gun. Like a statue or something. Like I been there a hundred years.

I thought of that and the other things I heard after, when I started to gain my senses. I was standing in the kitchen, against the sink. Auntie was there by that time, and a good thing. She was talking to two cops in our kitchen. She said the blast wasn't a gun. Some kids who throwed a cherry bomb at our window and made a hole. They believed her, because they never searched the house. She was in official's clothes, the kind that match her voice when she talks to social workers.

"It's a single-parent family," she was saying. "It's an Indian family just moved to town."

I looked at Justine. She was lifting a neat piece of chocolate cake to her mouth with a plastic fork. Her I'd have to reckon with on account I upset her show. I looked at Mom and the boys. They was eating cake, too. Auntie was still talking, painting that picture of us not capable of nothing. I seen the cops looking at the table while she talked. I seen what they seen, what Auntie was saying. But I seen more. I seen everything.

Leslie Marmon Silko (Laguna Pueblo)
The Man to Send Rain Clouds

One

They found him under a big cottonwood tree. His Levi jacket and pants were faded light-blue so that he had been easy to find. The big cottonwood tree stood apart from a small grove of winterbare cottonwoods which grew in the wide, sandy arroyo. He had been dead for a day or more, and the sheep had wandered and scattered up and down the arroyo. Leon and his brother-in-law, Ken, gathered the sheep and left them in the pen at the sheep camp before they returned to the cottonwood tree. Leon waited under the tree while Ken drove the truck through the deep sand to the edge of the arroyo. He squinted up at the sun and unzipped his jacket—it sure was hot for this time of year. But high and northwest the blue mountains were still deep in snow. Ken came sliding down the low, crumbling bank about fifty yards down, and he was bringing the red blanket.

Before they wrapped the old man, Leon took a piece of string out of his pocket and tied a small gray feather in the old man's long white hair. Ken gave him the paint. Across the brown wrinkled forehead he drew a streak of white and along the high cheekbones he drew a strip of blue paint. He paused and watched Ken throw pinches of corn meal and pollen into the wind that fluttered the small gray feather. Then Leon painted with yellow under the old man's broad nose, and finally, when he had painted green across the chin, he smiled.

"Send us rain clouds, Grandfather." They laid the bundle in the back of the pickup and covered it with a heavy tarp before they started back to the pueblo.

They turned off the highway onto the sandy pueblo road. Not long after they passed the store and post office they saw Father Paul's car coming toward them. When he recognized their faces he slowed his car and waved for them to stop. The young priest rolled down the car window.

"Did you find old Teofilo?" he asked loudly.

Leon stopped the truck. "Good morning, Father. We were just out to the sheep camp. Everything is O.K. now."

"Thank God for that. Teofilo is a very old man. You really shouldn't allow him to stay at the sheep camp alone."

"No, he won't do that any more now."

"Well, I'm glad you understand. I hope I'll be seeing you at Mass this week—we missed you last Sunday. See if you can get old Teofilo to come with you." The priest smiled and waved at them as they drove away.

Two

Louise and Teresa were waiting. The table was set for lunch, and the coffee was boiling on the black iron stove. Leon looked at Louise and then at Teresa.

"We found him under a cottonwood tree in the big arroyo near sheep camp. I guess he sat down to rest in the shade and never got up again." Leon walked toward the old man's bed. The red plaid shawl had been shaken and spread carefully over the bed, and a new brown flannel shirt and pair of stiff new Levis were arranged neatly beside the pillow. Louise held the screen door open while Leon and Ken carried in the red blanket. He looked small and shriveled, and after they dressed him in the new shirt and pants he seemed more shrunken.

It was noontime now because the church bells rang the Angelus. They ate the beans with hot bread, and nobody said anything until after Teresa poured the coffee.

Ken stood up and put on his jacket. "I'll see about the gravediggers. Only the top layer of soil is frozen. I think it can be ready before dark."

Leon nodded his head and finished his coffee. After Ken had been gone for a while, the neighbors and clanspeople came quietly to embrace Teofilo's family and to leave food on the table because the gravediggers would come to eat when they were finished.

Three

The sky in the west was full of pale-yellow light. Louise stood outside with her hands in the pockets of Leon's green army jacket that was too big for her. The funeral was over, and the old men had taken their candles and medicine bags and were gone. She waited until the body was laid into the pickup before she said anything to Leon. She touched his arm, and he noticed that her hands were still dusty from the corn meal that she had sprinkled around the old man. When she spoke, Leon could not hear her.

"What did you say? I didn't hear you."

"I said that I had been thinking about something."

"About what?"

"About the priest sprinkling holy water for Grandpa. So he won't be thirsty."

Leon stared at the new moccasins that Teofilo had made for the ceremonial dances in the summer. They were nearly hidden by the red blanket. It was getting colder, and the wind pushed gray dust down the narrow pueblo road. The sun was approaching the long mesa where it disappeared during the winter. Louise stood there shivering and watching his face. Then he zipped up his jacket and opened the truck door. "I'll see if he's there."

Four

Ken stopped the pickup at the church, and Leon got out; and then Ken drove down the hill to the graveyard where people were waiting. Leon knocked at the old carved door with its symbols of the Lamb. While he waited he looked up at the twin bells from the king of Spain with the last sunlight pouring around them in their tower.

The priest opened the door and smiled when he saw who it was. "Come in! What brings you here this evening?"

The priest walked toward the kitchen, and Leon stood with his cap in his hand, playing with the earflaps and examining the living room—the brown sofa, the green armchair, and the brass lamp that hung down from the ceiling by links of chain. The priest dragged a chair out of the kitchen and offered it to Leon.

"No thank you, Father. I only came to ask you if you would bring your holy water to the graveyard."

The priest turned away from Leon and looked out the window at the patio full of shadows and the dining-room windows of the nuns' cloister across the patio. The curtains were heavy, and the light from within faintly penetrated; it was impossible to see the nuns inside eating supper. "Why didn't you tell me he was dead? I could have brought the Last Rites anyway."

Leon smiled. "It wasn't necessary, Father."

The priest stared down at his scuffed brown loafers and the worn hem of his cassock. "For a Christian burial it was necessary."

His voice was distant, and Leon thought that his blue eyes looked tired.

"It's O.K. Father, we just want him to have plenty of water."

The priest sank down into the green chair and picked up a glossy missionary magazine. He turned the colored pages full of lepers and pagans without looking at them.

"You know I can't do that, Leon. There should have been the Last Rites and a funeral Mass at the very least."

Leon put on his green cap and pulled the flaps down over his ears. "It's getting late, Father. I've got to go."

When Leon opened the door Father Paul stood up and said, "Wait." He left the room and came back wearing a long brown overcoat. He followed Leon out the door and across the dim churchyard to the adobe steps in front of the church. They both stooped to fit through the low adobe entrance. And when they started down the hill to the graveyard only half of the sun was visible above the mesa.

The priest approached the grave slowly, wondering how they had managed to dig into the frozen ground; and then he remembered that this was New Mexico, and saw the pile of cold loose sand beside the hole. The people stood close to each other with little clouds of steam puffing from their faces. The priest looked at them and saw a pile of jackets, gloves, and scarves in the yellow, dry tumbleweeds that grew in the graveyard. He looked at the red blanket, not sure that Teofilo was so small, wondering if it wasn't some perverse Indian trick—something they did in March to ensure a good harvest—wondering if maybe old Teofilo was actually at sheep camp corraling the sheep for the night. But there he was, facing into a cold dry wind and squinting at the last sunlight, ready to bury a red wool blanket while the faces of his parishioners were in shadow with the last warmth of the sun on their backs.

His fingers were stiff, and it took him a long time to twist the lid off the holy water. Drops of water fell on the red blanket and soaked into dark icy spots. He sprinkled the grave and the water disappeared almost before it touched the dim, cold sand; it reminded him of something—he tried to remember what it was, because he thought if he could remember he might understand this. He sprinkled more water; he shook the container until it was empty, and the water fell through the light from sundown like August rain that fell while the sun was still shining, almost evaporating before it touched the wilted squash flowers.

The wind pulled at the priest's brown Franciscan robe and swirled away the corn meal and pollen that had been sprinkled on the blanket. They lowered the bundle into the ground, and they didn't bother to untie the stiff pieces of new rope that were tied around the ends of the blanket. The sun was gone, and over on the highway the eastbound lane was full of headlights. The priest walked away slowly. Leon watched him climb the hill, and when he had disappeared within the tall, thick walls, Leon turned to look up at the high blue mountains in the deep snow that reflected a faint red light from the west. He felt good because it was finished, and he was happy about the sprinkling of the holy water; now the old man could send them big thunderclouds for sure.

Leslie Marmon Silko (Laguna Pueblo)

Tony's Story

One

It happened one summer when the sky was wide and hot and the summer rains did not come; the sheep were thin, and the tumbleweeds turned brown and died. Leon came back from the army. I saw him standing by the Ferris wheel across from the people who came to sell melons and chili on San Lorenzo's Day. He yelled at me, "Hey Tony—over here!" I was embarrassed to hear him yell so loud, but then I saw the wine bottle with the brown-paper sack crushed around it.

"How's it going, buddy?"

He grabbed my hand and held it tight like a white man. He was smiling. "It's good to be home again. They asked me to dance tomorrow—it's only the Corn Dance, but I hope I haven't forgotten what to do."

"You'll remember—it will all come back to you when you hear the drum." I was happy, because I knew that Leon was once more a part of the pueblo. The sun was dusty and low in the west, and the procession passed by us, carrying San Lorenzo back to his niche in the church.

"Do you want to get something to eat?" I asked.

Leon laughed and patted the bottle. "No, you're the only one who needs to eat. Take this dollar—they're selling hamburgers over there." He pointed past the merry-go-round to a stand with cotton candy and a snow-cone machine.

It was then that I saw the cop pushing his way through the crowds of people gathered around the hamburger stand and bingo-game tent; he came steadily toward us. I remembered Leon's wine and looked to see if the cop was watching us; but he was wearing dark glasses and I couldn't see his eyes.

He never said anything before he hit Leon in the face with his fist. Leon collapsed into the dust, and the paper sack floated in the wine and pieces of glass. He didn't move and blood kept bubbling out of his mouth and nose. I could hear a siren. People crowded around Leon and kept pushing me away. The tribal policemen knelt over Leon, and one of them looked up at the state cop and asked what was going on. The big cop didn't answer. He was staring at the little patterns of blood in the dust near Leon's mouth. The dust soaked up the blood almost before it dripped to the ground—it had been a very dry summer. The cop didn't leave until they laid Leon in the back of the paddy wagon.

The moon was already high when we got to the hospital in Albuquerque. We waited a long time outside the emergency room with Leon propped between us. Siow and Gaisthea kept asking me, "What happened, what did Leon say to the cop?" and I told them how we were just standing there, ready to buy hamburgers—we'd never even seen him before. They put stitches around Leon's mouth and gave him a shot; he was lucky, they said—it could've been a broken jaw instead of broken teeth.

Two

They dropped me off near my house. The moon had moved lower into the west and left the close rows of houses in long shadows. Stillness breathed around me, and I wanted to run from the feeling behind me in the dark; the stories about witches ran with me. That night I had a dream— the big cop was pointing a long bone at me—they always use human bones, and the whiteness flashed silver in the moonlight where he stood. He didn't have a human face—only little, round, white-rimmed eyes on a black ceremonial mask.

Leon was better in a few days. But he was bitter, and all he could talk about was the cop. "I'll kill the big bastard if he comes around here again," Leon kept saying.

With something like the cop it is better to forget, and I tried to make Leon understand. "It's over now. There's nothing you can do."

I wondered why men who came back from the army were trouble-makers on the reservation. Leon even took it before the pueblo meeting. They discussed it, and the old men decided that Leon shouldn't have been drinking. The interpreter read a passage out of the revised pueblo law-and-order code about possessing intoxicants on the reservation, so we got up and left.

Then Leon asked me to go with him to Grants to buy a roll of barbed wire for his uncle. On the way we stopped at Cerritos for gas, and I went into the store for some pop. He was inside. I stopped in the doorway and turned around before he saw me, but if he really was what I feared, then he would not need to see me—he already knew we were there. Leon was wait-ing with the truck engine running almost like he knew what I would say.

"Let's go—the big cop's inside."

Leon gunned it and the pickup skidded back on the highway. He glanced back in the rear-view mirror. "I didn't see his car."

"Hidden," I said.

Leon shook his head. "He can't do it again. We are just as good as them."

The guys who came back always talked like that.

Three

The sky was hot and empty. The half-grown tumbleweeds were dried-up flat and brown beside the highway, and across the valley heat shimmered above wilted fields of corn. Even the mountains high beyond the pale sandrock mesas were dusty blue. I was afraid to fall asleep so I kept my eyes on the blue mountains—not letting them close—soaking in the heat; and then I knew why the drought had come that summer.

Leon shook me. "He's behind us—the cop's following us!"

I looked back and saw the red light on top of the car whirling around, and I could make out the dark image of a man, but where the face should have been there were only the silvery lenses of the dark glasses he wore.

"Stop, Leon! He wants us to stop!"

Leon pulled over and stopped on the narrow gravel shoulder.

"What in the hell does he want?" Leon's hands were shaking.

Suddenly the cop was standing beside the truck, gesturing for Leon to roll down his window. He pushed his head inside, grinding the gum in his mouth; the smell of Doublemint was all around us.

"Get out. Both of you."

I stood beside Leon in the dry weeds and tall yellow grass that broke through the asphalt and rattled in the wind. The cop studied Leon's driver's license. I avoided his face—I knew that I couldn't look at his eyes, so I stared at his black half-Wellingtons, with the black uniform cuffs pulled over them; but my eyes kept moving, upward past the black gun belt. My legs were quivering, and I tried to keep my eyes away from his. But it was like the time when I was very little and my parents warned me not to look into the masked dancers' eyes because they would grab me, and my eyes would not stop.

"What's your name?" His voice was high-pitched and it distracted me from the meaning of the words.

I remember Leon said, "He doesn't understand English so good," and finally I said that I was Antonio Sousea, while my eyes strained to look beyond the silver frosted glasses that he wore; but only my distorted face and squinting eyes reflected back.

And then the cop stared at us for a while, silent; finally he laughed and chewed his gum some more slowly. "Where were you going?"

"To Grants." Leon spoke English very clearly. "Can we go now?"

Leon was twisting the key chain around his fingers, and I felt the sun everywhere. Heat swelled up from the asphalt and when cars went by, hot air and motor smell rushed past us.

"I don't like smart guys, Indian. It's because of you bastards that I'm here. They transferred me here because of Indians. They thought there wouldn't be as many for me here. But I find them." He spit his gum into the weeds near my foot and walked back to the patrol car. It kicked up gravel and dust when he left.

We got back in the pickup, and I could taste sweat in my mouth, so I told Leon that we might as well go home since he would be waiting for us up ahead.

"He can't do this," Leon said. "We've got a right to be on this highway."

I couldn't understand why Leon kept talking about "rights," because it wasn't "rights" that he was after, but Leon didn't seem to understand; he couldn't remember the stories that old Teofilo told.

I didn't feel safe until we turned off the highway and I could see the pueblo and my own house. It was noon, and everybody was eating—the village seemed empty—even the dogs had crawled away from the heat. The door was open, but there was only silence, and I was afraid that something had happened to all of them. Then as soon as I opened the screen door the little kids started crying for more Kool-Aid, and my mother said "no," and it was noisy again like always. Grandfather commented that it had been a fast trip to Grants, and I said "yeah" and didn't explain because it would've only worried them.

"Leon goes looking for trouble—I wish you wouldn't hang around with him." My father didn't like trouble. But I knew that the cop was something terrible, and even to speak about it risked bringing it close to all of us; so I didn't say anything.

That afternoon Leon spoke with the Governor, and he promised to send letters to the Bureau of Indian Affairs and to the State Police Chief. Leon seemed satisfied with that. I reached into my pocket for the arrowhead on the piece of string.

"What's that for?"

I held it out to him. "Here, wear it around your neck—like mine. See? Just in case," I said, "for protection."

"You don't believe in *that,* do you?" He pointed to a .30-30 leaning against the wall. "I'll take this with me whenever I'm in the pickup."

"But you can't be sure that it will kill one of them."

Leon looked at me and laughed. "What's the matter," he said, "have they brainwashed you into believing that a .30-30 won't kill a white man?" He handed back the arrowhead. "Here, you wear two of them."

Four

Leon's uncle asked me if I wanted to stay at the sheep camp for a while. The lambs were big, and there wouldn't be much for me to do, so I told him I would. We left early, while the sun was still low and red in the sky. The highway was empty, and I sat there beside Leon imagining what it was like before there were highways or even horses. Leon turned off the highway onto the sheep-camp road that climbs around the sandstone mesas until suddenly all the trees are piñons.

Leon glanced in the rear-view mirror. "He's following us!"

My body began to shake and I wasn't sure if I would be able to speak. "There's no place left to hide. It follows us everywhere."

Leon looked at me like he didn't understand what I'd said. Then I looked past Leon and saw that the patrol car had pulled up beside us; the piñon branches were whipping and scraping the side of the truck as it tried to force us off the road. Leon kept driving with the two right wheels in the rut—bumping and scraping the trees. Leon never looked over at it so he couldn't have known how the reflections kept moving across the mirror-lenses of the dark glasses. We were in the narrow canyon with pale sandstone close on either side—the canyon that ended with a spring where willows and grass and tiny blue flowers grow.

"We've got to kill it, Leon. We must burn the body to be sure."

Leon didn't seem to be listening. I kept wishing that old Teofilo could have been there to chant the proper words while we did it. Leon stopped the truck and got out—he still didn't understand what it was. I sat in the pickup with the .30-30 across my lap, and my hands were slippery.

The big cop was standing in front of the pickup, facing Leon. "You made your mistake, Indian. I'm going to beat the shit out of you." He raised the billy club slowly. "I like to beat Indians with this."

He moved toward Leon with the stick raised high, and it was like the long bone in my dream when he pointed it at me—a human bone painted brown to look like wood, to hide what it really was; they'll do that, you know—carve the bone into a spoon and use it around the house until the victim comes within range.

The shot sounded far away and I couldn't remember aiming. But he was motionless on the ground and the bone wand lay near his feet. The tumbleweeds and tall yellow grass were sprayed with glossy, bright blood. He was on his back, and the sand between his legs and along his left side was soaking up the dark, heavy blood—it had not rained for a long time, and even the tumbleweeds were dying.

"Tony! You killed him—you killed the cop!"

"Help me! We'll set the car on fire."

Leon acted strange, and he kept looking at me like he wanted to run. The head wobbled and swung back and forth, and the left hand and the legs left individual trails in the sand. The face was the same. The dark glasses hadn't fallen off and they blinded me with their hot-sun reflections until I pushed the body into the front seat.

The gas tank exploded and the flames spread along the underbelly of the car. The tires filled the wide sky with spirals of thick black smoke.

"My God, Tony. What's wrong with you? That's a state cop you killed." Leon was pale and shaking.

I wiped my hands on my Levis. "Don't worry, everything is O.K. now, Leon. It's killed. They sometimes take on strange forms."

The tumbleweeds around the car caught fire, and little heatwaves shimmered up toward the sky; in the west, rain clouds were gathering.

Leslie Marmon Silko (Laguna Pueblo)

Yellow Woman

One

My thigh clung to his with dampness, and I watched the sun rising up through the tamaracks and willows. The small brown water birds came to the river and hopped across the mud, leaving brown scratches in the alkali-white crust. They bathed in the river silently. I could hear the water, almost at our feet where the narrow fast channel bubbled and washed green ragged moss and fern leaves. I looked at him beside me, rolled in the red blanket on the white river sand. I cleaned the sand out of the cracks between my toes, squinting because the sun was above the willow trees. I looked at him for the last time, sleeping on the white river sand.

I felt hungry and followed the river south the way we had come the afternoon before, following our footprints that were already blurred by lizard tracks and bug trails. The horses were still lying down, and the black one whinnied when he saw me but he did not get up—maybe it was because the corral was made out of thick cedar branches and the horses had not yet felt the sun like I had. I tried to look beyond the pale red mesas to the pueblo. I knew it was there, even if I could not see it, on the sandrock hill above the river, the same river that moved past me now and had reflected the moon last night.

The horse felt warm underneath me. He shook his head and pawed the sand. The bay whinnied and leaned against the gate trying to follow, and I remembered him asleep in the red blanket beside the river. I slid off the horse and tied him close to the other horse. I walked north with the river again, and the white sand broke loose in footprints over footprints.

"Wake up."

He moved in the blanket and turned his face to me with his eyes still closed. I knelt down to touch him.

"I'm leaving."

He smiled now, eyes still closed. "You are coming with me, remember?" He sat up now with his bare dark chest and belly in the sun.

"Where?"

"To my place."

"And will I come back?"

He pulled his pants on. I walked away from him, feeling him behind me and smelling the willows.

"Yellow Woman," he said.

I turned to face him. "Who are you?" I asked.

He laughed and knelt on the low, sandy bank, washing his face in the river. "Last night you guessed my name, and you knew why I had come."

I stared past him at the shallow moving water and tried to remember the night, but I could only see the moon in the water and remember his warmth around me.

"But I only said that you were him and that I was Yellow Woman—I'm not really her—I have my own name and I come from the pueblo on the other side of the mesa. Your name is Silva and you are a stranger I met by the river yesterday afternoon."

He laughed softly. "What happened yesterday has nothing to do with what you will do today, Yellow Woman."

"I know—that's what I'm saying—the old stories about the ka'tsina spirit and Yellow Woman can't mean us."

My old grandpa liked to tell those stories best. There is one about Badger and Coyote who went hunting and were gone all day, and when the sun was going down they found a house. There was a girl living there alone, and she had light hair and eyes and she told them that they could sleep with her. Coyote wanted to be with her all night so he sent Badger into a prairie-dog hole, telling him he thought he saw something in it. As soon as Badger crawled in, Coyote blocked up the entrance with rocks and hurried back to Yellow Woman.

"Come here," he said gently.

He touched my neck and I moved close to him to feel his breathing and to hear his heart. I was wondering if Yellow Woman had known who she was—if she knew that she would become part of the stories. Maybe she'd had another name that her husband and relatives called her so that only the ka'tsina from the north and the storytellers would know her as Yellow Woman. But I didn't go on; I felt him all around me, pushing me down into the white river sand.

Yellow Woman went away with the spirit from the north and lived with him and his relatives. She was gone for a long time, but then one day she came back and she brought twin boys.

"Do you know the story?"

"What story?" He smiled and pulled me close to him as he said this. I was afraid lying there on the red blanket. All I could know was the way he felt, warm, damp, his body beside me. This is the way it happens in the stories, I was thinking, with no thought beyond the moment she meets the ka'tsina spirit and they go.

"I don't have to go. What they tell in stories was real only then, back in time immemorial, like they say."

He stood up and pointed at my clothes tangled in the blanket. "Let's go," he said.

I walked beside him, breathing hard because he walked fast, his hand around my wrist. I had stopped trying to pull away from him, because his hand felt cool and the sun was high, drying the river bed into alkali. I will see someone, eventually I will see someone, and then I will be certain that he is only a man—some man from nearby—and I will be sure that I am not Yellow Woman. Because she is from out of time past and I live now and I've been to school and there are highways and pickup trucks that Yellow Woman never saw.

It was an easy ride north on horseback. I watched the change from the cottonwood trees along the river to the junipers that brushed past us in the foothills, and finally there were only piñons, and when I looked up at the rim of the mountain plateau I could see pine trees growing on the edge. Once I stopped to look down, but the pale sandstone had disappeared and the river was gone and the dark lava hills were all around. He touched my hand, not speaking, but always singing softly a mountain song and looking into my eyes.

I felt hungry and wondered what they were doing at home now—my mother, my grandmother, my husband, and the baby. Cooking breakfast, saying, "Where did she go?—maybe kidnaped," and Al going to the tribal police with the details: "She went walking along the river."

The house was made with black lava rock and red mud. It was high above the spreading miles of arroyos and long mesas. I smelled a mountain smell of pitch and buck brush. I stood there beside the black horse, looking down on the small, dim country we had passed, and I shivered.

"Yellow Woman, come inside where it's warm."

Two

He lit a fire in the stove. It was an old stove with a round belly and an enamel coffeepot on top. There was only the stove, some faded Navajo blankets, and a bedroll and cardboard box. The floor was made of smooth adobe plaster, and there was one small window facing east. He pointed at the box.

"There's some potatoes and the frying pan." He sat on the floor with his arms around his knees pulling them close to his chest and he watched me fry the potatoes. I didn't mind him watching me because he was always watching me—he had been watching me since I came upon him sitting on the river bank trimming leaves from a willow twig with his knife. We ate from the pan and he wiped the grease from his fingers on his Levis.

"Have you brought women here before?" He smiled and kept chewing, so I said, "Do you always use the same tricks?"

"What tricks?" He looked at me like he didn't understand.

"The story about being a ka'tsina from the mountains. The story about Yellow Woman."

Silva was silent; his face was calm.

"I don't believe it. Those stories couldn't happen now," I said.

He shook his head and said softly, "But someday they will talk about us, and they will say, 'Those two lived long ago when things like that happened.'"

He stood up and went out. I ate the rest of the potatoes and thought about things—about the noise the stove was making and the sound of the mountain wind outside. I remembered yesterday and the day before, and then I went outside.

I walked past the corral to the edge where the narrow trail cut through the black rim rock. I was standing in the sky with nothing around me but the wind that came down from the blue mountain peak behind me. I could see faint mountain images in the distance miles across the vast spread of mesas and valleys and plains. I wondered who was over there to feel the mountain wind on those sheer blue edges—who walks on the pine needles in those blue mountains.

"Can you see the pueblo?" Silva was standing behind me.

I shook my head. "We're too far away."

"From here I can see the world." He stepped out on the edge. "The Navajo reservation begins over there." He pointed to the east. "The Pueblo boundaries are over here." He looked below us to the south, where the narrow trail seemed to come from. "The Texans have their ranches over there, starting with that valley, the Concho Valley. The Mexicans run some cattle over there too."

"Do you ever work for them?"

"I steal from them," Silva answered. The sun was dropping behind us and shadows were filling the land below. I turned away from the edge that dropped forever into the valleys below.

"I'm cold," I said; "I'm going inside." I started wondering about this man who could speak the Pueblo language so well but who lived on a mountain and rustled cattle. I decided that this man Silva must be Navajo, because Pueblo men didn't do things like that.

"You must be a Navajo."

Silva shook his head gently. "Little Yellow Woman," he said, "you never give up, do you? I have told you who I am. The Navajo people know me, too." He knelt down and unrolled the bedroll and spread the extra blankets out on a piece of canvas. The sun was down, and the only light in the house came from outside—the dim orange light from sundown.

I stood there and waited for him to crawl under the blankets.

"What are you waiting for?" he said, and I lay down beside him. He undressed me slowly like the night before beside the river—kissing my face gently and running his hands up and down my belly and legs. He took off my pants and then he laughed.

"Why are you laughing?"

"You are breathing so hard."

I pulled away from him and turned my back to him.

He pulled me around and pinned me down with his arms and chest. "You don't understand, do you, little Yellow Woman? You will do what I want."

And again he was all around me with his skin slippery against mine, and I was afraid because I understood that his strength could hurt me. I lay underneath him and I knew that he could destroy me. But later, while he slept beside me, I touched his face and I had a feeling—the kind of feeling for him that overcame me that morning along the river. I kissed him on the forehead and he reached out for me.

When I woke up in the morning he was gone. It gave me a strange feeling because for a long time I sat there on the blankets and looked around the little house for some object of his—some proof that he had been there or maybe that he was coming back. Only the blankets and the cardboard box remained. The .30-30 that had been leaning in the corner was gone, and so was the knife I had used the night before. He was gone, and I had my chance to go now. But first I had to eat, because I knew it would be a long walk home.

I found some dried apricots in the cardboard box, and I sat down on a rock at the edge of the plateau rim. There was no wind and the sun warmed me. I was surrounded by silence. I drowsed with apricots in my mouth, and I didn't believe that there were highways or railroads or cattle to steal.

When I woke up, I stared down at my feet in the black mountain dirt. Little black ants were swarming over the pine needles around my foot. They must have smelled the apricots. I thought about my family far below me. They would be wondering about me, because this had never happened to me before. The tribal police would file a report. But if old Grandpa weren't dead he would tell them what happened—he would laugh and say, "Stolen by a ka'tsina, a mountain spirit. She'll come home—they usually do." There are enough of them to handle things. My mother and grandmother will raise the baby like they raised me. Al will find someone else, and they will go on like before, except that there will be a story about the day I disappeared while I was walking along the river. Silva had come for me; he said he had. I did not decide to go. I just went. Moonflowers blossom in the sand hills before dawn, just as I followed him. That's what I was thinking as I wandered along the trail through the pine trees.

It was noon when I got back. When I saw the stone house I remembered that I had meant to go home. But that didn't seem important any more, maybe because there were little blue flowers growing in the meadow behind the stone house and the gray squirrels were playing in the pines next to the house. The horses were standing in the corral, and there was a beef carcass hanging on the shady side of a big pine in front of the house. Flies buzzed around the clotted blood that hung from the carcass. Silva was washing his hands in a bucket full of water. He must have heard me coming because he spoke to me without turning to face me.

"I've been waiting for you."

"I went walking in the big pine trees."

I looked into the bucket full of bloody water with brown-and-white animal hairs floating in it. Silva stood there letting his hand drip, examining me intently.

"Are you coming with me?"

"Where?" I asked him.

"To sell the meat in Marquez."

"If you're sure it's O.K."

"I wouldn't ask you if it wasn't," he answered.

He sloshed the water around in the bucket before he dumped it out and set the bucket upside down near the door. I followed him to the corral and watched him saddle the horses. Even beside the horses he looked tall, and I asked him again if he wasn't Navajo. He didn't say anything; he just shook his head and kept cinching up the saddle.

"But Navajos are tall."

"Get on the horse," he said, "and let's go."

The last thing he did before we started down the steep trail was to grab the .30-30 from the corner. He slid the rifle into the scabbard that hung from his saddle.

"Do they ever try to catch you?" I asked.

"They don't know who I am."

"Then why did you bring the rifle?"

"Because we are going to Marquez where the Mexicans live."

Three

The trail leveled out on a narrow ridge that was steep on both sides like an animal spine. On one side I could see where the trail went around the rocky gray hills and disappeared into the southeast where the pale sandrock mesas stood in the distance near my home. On the other side was a trail that went west, and as I looked far into the distance I thought I saw the little town. But Silva said no, that I was looking in the wrong place, that I just thought I saw houses. After that I quit looking off into the distance; it was hot and the wildflowers were closing up their deep-yellow petals. Only the waxy cactus flowers bloomed in the bright sun, and I saw every color that a cactus blossom can be; the white ones and the red ones were still buds, but the purple and the yellow were blossoms, open full and the most beautiful of all.

Silva saw him before I did. The white man was riding a big gray horse, coming up the trail toward us. He was traveling fast and the gray horse's feet sent rocks rolling off the trail into the dry tumbleweeds. Silva motioned for me to stop and we watched the white man. He didn't see us right away, but finally his horse whinnied at our horses and he stopped. He looked at us briefly before he loped the gray horse across the three hundred yards that separated us. He stopped his horse in front of Silva, and his young fat face was shadowed by the brim of his hat. He didn't look mad, but his small, pale eyes moved from the blood-soaked gunny sacks hanging from my saddle to Silva's face and then back to my face.

"Where did you get the fresh meat?" the white man asked.

"I've been hunting," Silva said, and when he shifted his weight in the saddle the leather creaked.

"The hell you have, Indian. You've been rustling cattle. We've been looking for the thief for a long time."

The rancher was fat, and sweat began to soak through his white cowboy shirt and the wet cloth stuck to the thick rolls of belly fat. He almost seemed to be panting from the exertion of talking, and he smelled rancid, maybe because Silva scared him.

Silva turned to me and smiled. "Go back up the mountain, Yellow Woman."

The white man got angry when he heard Silva speak in a language he couldn't understand. "Don't try anything, Indian. Just keep riding to Marquez. We'll call the state police from there."

The rancher must have been unarmed because he was very frightened and if he had a gun he would have pulled it out then. I turned my horse around and the rancher yelled, "Stop!" I looked at Silva for an instant and there was something ancient and dark—something I could feel in my stomach—in his eyes, and when I glanced at his hand I saw his finger on the trigger of the .30-30 that was still in the saddle scabbard. I slapped my horse across the flank and the sacks of raw meat swung against my knees as the horse leaped up the trail. It was hard to keep my balance, and once I thought I felt the saddle slipping backward; it was because of this that I could not look back.

I didn't stop until I reached the ridge where the trail forked. The horse was breathing deep gasps and there was a dark film of sweat on its neck. I looked down in the direction I had come from, but I couldn't see the place. I waited. The wind came up and pushed warm air past me. I looked up at the sky, pale blue and full of thin clouds and fading vapor trails left by jets.

I think four shots were fired—I remember hearing four hollow explosions that reminded me of deer hunting. There could have been more shots after that, but I couldn't have heard them because my horse was running again and the loose rocks were making too much noise as they scattered around his feet.

Horses have a hard time running downhill, but I went that way instead of uphill to the mountain because I thought it was safer. I felt better with the horse running southeast past the round gray hills that were covered with cedar trees and black lava rock. When I got to the plain in the distance I could see the dark green patches of tamaracks that grew along the river; and beyond the river I could see the beginning of the pale sandrock mesas. I stopped the horse and looked back to see if anyone was coming; then I got off the horse and turned the horse around, wondering if it would go back to its corral under the pines on the mountain. It looked back at me for a moment and then plucked a mouthful of green tumbleweeds before it trotted back up the trail with its ears pointed forward, carrying its head daintily to one side to avoid stepping on the dragging reins. When the horse disappeared over the last hill, the gunny sacks full of meat were still swinging and bouncing.

Four

I walked toward the river on a wood-hauler's road that I knew would eventually lead to the paved road. I was thinking about waiting beside the road for someone to drive by, but by the time I got to the pavement I had decided it wasn't very far to walk if I followed the river back the way Silva and I had come.

The river water tasted good, and I sat in the shade under a cluster of silvery willows. I thought about Silva, and I felt sad at leaving him; still, there was something strange about him, and I tried to figure it out all the way back home.

I came back to the place on the river bank where he had been sitting the first time I saw him. The green willow leaves that he had trimmed from the branch were still lying there, wilted in the sand. I saw the leaves and I wanted to go back to him—to kiss him and to touch him—but the mountains were too far away now. And I told myself, because I believe it, he will come back sometime and be waiting again by the river.

I followed the path up from the river into the village. The sun was getting low, and I could smell supper cooking when I got to the screen door of my house. I could hear their voices inside—my mother was telling my grandmother how to fix the Jell-o and my husband, Al, was playing with the baby. I decided to tell them that some Navajo had kidnaped me, but I was sorry that old Grandpa wasn't alive to hear my story because it was the Yellow Woman stories he liked to tell best.

Mary TallMountain (Koyukon Athabaskan)

The Disposal of Mary Joe's Children

> Thou hast kept me to be head of the heathen; a people which I know not shall serve me. Strangers shall submit themselves unto me; as soon as they hear, they shall be obedient unto me.
>
> —*2 Samuel 22:44*

Reverend Mother Anne Celesta closed the old bible on the page, softened and curled with the innumerable fingerings. She performed this action each morning. The passage seemed to embody a cryptic message which still baffled her after five years of pondering it in an urgency to discover its relevance to her vocation. "But the heathen are not obedient." She was unsure whether she spoke to herself or to a familiar presence. Again in bitterness she tasted the words: "They are *not* obedient."

The people had appeared docile. At first she considered them ignorant and slow of intelligence. Gradually, she perceived that behind their apparent taciturnity there lay an indecipherable and ancient essence of spirit. She sensed it would remain an enigma. It was exasperating. "A people which I know not shall serve me." She had chosen the boy Innokenty to "serve," after long reflection and with subliminal purpose. His stolid, somehow vulnerable person had come to represent this multifaceted people whose meaning was so elusive.

And still she knew them not.

Into this restive moment she permitted the disorder of her memories. She had arrived at her first mission, far downriver at Holy Cross, wearing the immaculate, long, flowing garments, the white starched coif of the Rule of the Sisters of Saint Anne, unsuited to the rude land where dust, mud, and mosquitoes beset the nuns in summer, paralyzing cold in winter. Her mien was high and proud, befitting the Bride she had been chosen; she carried the idealism of her twenty years like a pennon. She embraced missionary life with ardor. The savage land and the Rule, like stern taskmasters, soon subordinated her young zeal to grueling labor and the demands of hard-won convent ritual. She learned the habit of discipline slowly, harshly, doing herself violence, striving toward perfection. Custody of eyes and tongue—and more particularly, of thoughts and senses. Almost twenty-five years ago, now . . .

Long before, the first nuns of Holy Cross had been hardy women. They had wrested the mission out of the wild new country of Alaska. In a cluster of brown tents they celebrated Mass with the pioneer priests and brothers, said devotions, made their cells. They were forced to wrestle with the emerald-green earth for their meagre garden harvest. The people observed, and sent the children. Then commenced the work for which they had come. By the time Sister Celesta arrived in 1890, there was a completed dormitory building and some eighty children from the river villages, running and shrieking in a makeshift playground. She taught them religion, the Baltimore catechism, and the three R's. Her chief task was the instruction of the older girls in domestic chores: scrubbing, cleaning, waxing; cooking and canning; washing and ironing. She worked side by side with Native children from villages up and down the Yukon. She grew robust of mind and body.

At first it was exciting. She listened to the keening subarctic night song of malamutes and learned to detect their separate personalities, as diverse as the brown, muscular men who drove them. She knew the smells of smoke and salmon. She studied a leaf of alder, knew its green lacquer surface, the veins of its pale, sticky underside. She imagined the powerful presences of wolves circling the great moving dun-colored caribou herd beyond the purple Kaiyuh Mountains. Her eyes reveled to see the harsh, burnt orange sun of spring after the long black winter. She stood whipped by rain, awaiting with fierce joy the monstrous rolling thunder.

Even now, old fragments of beauty returned in the night with such insistence that she wakened with a startled cry, and found the wetness of tears upon her face.

Time brought authority and the blooming of a natural administrative talent; in 1918 she came to Nulato as Reverend Mother Superior. She was in command of the four Sisters and the education of the children. It was, however, her prime duty to serve as exemplar to some 150 Natives. She knew her duty familiarly; she knew their obdurate resistance to duty and to rules.

Now that she lived closer to them, there came on a silent tithing. No fish was caught or game trapped of which a portion did not go into the Mission larder. In lean times, benefactions were given to hungry families. But the proddings of conscience were faint; her mind grew yet more adamant with the intent to carry her vocation to its ultimate perfection.

At last the endless dark days of winter, the paralyzing cold, the enduring toil, entered her very spirit. The pangs were edged bitterly. She gritted her teeth and muttered: "I will not yield," as to a creature locked fast with her in mortal combat. The land had become her personal enemy. There was one solitary outlet. If she became nettled by Father's reticence, surmised a critical flash in a Sister's glance, if she found a child obstinate, the choler lying thin beneath her veneer festered until she found subtle means to mock Innokenty and impress harshly upon him some new bidding. Occasionally a fleet thought struck through: I am unfair to this witless boy. He is my scapegoat.

Even her Sisters did not suspect her strange discontent, and she took great care not to speak harshly to Innokenty in their hearing, so that she thought no one was aware of her strange perversity. In this close proximity, her strong habit of firmness and discipline ensured her safety. She was above reproach.

Now she heard impatiently the shuffling approach of Sister Mary Pacifica in her house slippers. She recalled complaints of a painful old bunion. Sister entered the office, rapping playfully on the door frame. She is remiss in discipline, thought Reverend Mother. Her lips firmed into a thin line, even as she relented, Ah, I am petty. Her fine hazel eyes lifted, and she waited with an air of patience. It was lost on Sister Pacifica.

Sister Mary Pacifica's short figure and wry face affected a look of domesticity. She said, "Little Jim brought up a brace of mallards. You ought to see their glorious green-blue and bronze necklaces!"

"Fine . . . fine . . . How many ducks did he shoot this trip?"

"Why, I don't know. Shall I bake these for Sunday dinner?"

"Cook both, and open two jars of canned duck besides." Why did I ask how many he shot? she thought. We don't need more—thank heaven we've got six dozen jars put by. She determined to curb her curiosity and observe more perfect charity thereby.

"Father Frank will relish it too," Sister said, going out.

Father Frank Galvan. Admittedly, he was a thorn in Reverend Mother's side. His presence filled her with a vague edginess. She had never understood why. To give him his due, he was a rare good man and priest. Ah, his humility, and he with that fiery shock of red hair! Sometimes she believed he saw her clearly, just as she was, from a place far behind his steadfast amber eyes. She felt like a housekeeper, with a clutch of keys at her belt. But I am a good steward, she thought—I have served well these children of God. Why am I constrained to dissemble, to hide my thoughts from him?

Discipline. It was the byword, implicit in the severity of their lives. Such enforced discipline was one matter. The habit of discipline was another, completely different. By now Reverend Mother knew intimately the nature of both. She thought of the coming winter. Wind howling with an obstinate life of its own about the eaves, whining at the white lacery of frost that covered the thin windowpanes, crawling across the Sisters' huddled forms in the ascetic cells which were the only privacy they possessed. It penetrated every crevice with its nagging voice, that voice of loss and want. The voice of discipline.

"And now at last my habit of discipline is beginning to fray," she said aloud. "All because I have not come to know the strangers."

She had closely observed Mary Joe Bolshanin, a most promising pupil at Holy Cross, and was positive the girl would attend normal school after graduation. But in the summer of 1909 when Mary Joe was fourteen she came home to Nulato and her family arranged a marriage to Taria, an older man of the village. She would not graduate. When Reverend Mother went to talk with her mother, Matmiya, she was met with courtesy, a cup of hot tea, and an impassable wall of reserve.

"We have always gotten husbands for the girls. It is the custom," Matmiya said firmly. The tone of her voice ended the discussion.

These were the strangers she had believed she sought to know.

Winged shadows moved over the papers on the desk. She looked out and saw a pair of bank swallows spiraling up from their summer nest under the eaves, tiny bundles of sepia-colored feathers tousled by the wind. Beyond, the river was whipped into a dark green smother, needled with spray. The swallows knew it was time. They spiraled in greater and greater circles, hovered once, and rose high over the village, fluttering and tossing on the vast channels of air. Their courage, their trust in God, she thought, letting themselves ride out on a journey perhaps endless, unknowing, their hearts tiny within them, yet sturdy. So was I once, she thought. The young Celesta would have run and danced in the river wind, celebrating with the swallows.

She shivered. The day had chilled. "They are the last to go," she said.

Ah, yes. Then something had happened. Mary Joe left Taria and returned to her mother's house. After Matmiya's death from consumption, for six years Mary Joe flaunted her affair with Clem Stone, the soldier, appearing with him in the village, he so jaunty in his sauntering manner, she with her black mane of hair tossing under a scarlet band. They were an impudent challenge.

Reverend Mother moved abruptly in her chair. Disturbing images floated out of the deep shadows of her mind: a young girl's forbidden yearnings, slow whispered secrecy in the black folds of confession, earnest repentance, certainty of forgiveness, urgent hasty penance, breathless retreat, dizzied into the light oh free—the child—ah! the chastened children—the children grown, yet fearful—vast nothingness, retribution, dark wings beating—the children . . .

She passed a hand over her eyes. What had she been thinking? Oh. Mary Joe and Clem Stone. It was true, after the first child was born they sought out Father to discuss marriage. He could not request a dispensation. The marriage to Taria had produced a boy, now living with his father in another village. There was no chancery cause for dissolution. Mary Joe was bound. Sister moved jerkily in her chair. Her fingers tapped the arm. Father should have ordered Mary Joe at once to end the impenitent affair. But he would not. He had some strange notion about conscience . . .

Now the people said that because Mary Joe had contracted consumption, the agnostics Doctor and Nellie Merrick would adopt her two children. For Sister, this completed the page of transgressions.

Suddenly she said aloud, "I will put a stop to it."

Quelling her anger with a determined act of the will, she laid her hands upon the breviary. It was the hour of tierce. She would place this knotted sin again into the hands of the Lord. A random page caught her gaze. She was unable to turn it. Her eyes moved inexorably through the passage.

He that ruleth over men must be just, ruling in the fear of God. And he shall be as the light of the morning, when the sun riseth, even a morning without clouds; as the tender grass springing out of the earth by clear shining after rain.

—2 Samuel 23:4.

She read intently and slowly; she read again.

There was no doubt.

Innokenty's flat eyelids oozed open. Like black olives rolling in oil, his eyes shuttled toward the paling square of window. His mind stirred dully, prodded by the knowledge that he had to go again today to council.

It didn't occur to Innokenty to wonder why things were the way they were. Yesterday Big Mike had told him to go to the Dance House. He went. Again today, the other men would talk, going over and over this strange thing about Mary Joe's children. He, Innokenty, would be silent. He hoped the men would believe him wisely thinking.

There was only one reason for him to go there. Sister Celesta wanted him to be there. He never disobeyed her. It had started a long time ago, when he had first seen her in the village. He had been awestruck by her. Over the years, piecemeal, the people had told him he was Eskimo, and that in 1908 when he was a baby he had been bought by a Nulato Indian in a fur deal with an Eskimo trader from Kvih-pak. Later orphaned, he remembered no place besides this village. His life revolved around the Mission, that cluster of buildings between the river and the army barracks, on the land where *Gisakk* lived, a little separate from the native cabins. He did chores for Sister Celesta and gave her his game and fish. Every day at dawn he went to Mass. He was used to her tall muffled presence alone in the front pew. Yesterday morning she had followed him out after Father Galvan's *Ite, missa est.*

She didn't hesitate. "You're going to council today."

His black-olive eyes said yes, he was.

There was a heavy silence.

"Something important is happening." Intently she examined a long splinter at the edge of the last pew. "You're going to help me, Innokenty." She pried away the splinter. "They will ask your opinion. Whatever they say, you must answer *no.*" She looked at him and away; it was as if her face hid behind a thin curtain; and with the word *no,* her hand raised in a cautioning gesture. It clasped again around her shabby black prayer book. He stretched a finger toward the hand. It held steady; his finger moved closer. Then she was gone in a whirl of icy air. The door closed without sound. He peered at it, his look questioning.

The Dance House aroused a different emotion in him that afternoon: the bumpy wooden floor, the four-triangled log roof slanting to the bell tower, noon light lying through to the octagonal, bench-lined wall, dark yet not quite: sparked here by a flash of bright shirt-sleeved arm raised in emphasis, bulked there by the shapes of the others seated in their places in varying attitudes of thought, now and then leaning imperceptibly to each other, closing some intangible separation. The smells of the blue tobacco haze; of garlic on spent breaths; of dead sweat molded into the shapes of pants and jackets; of autumn-ripe forest through the open door; and knifing through it a sometime odor of dissension, wholly living and sharp: these smells distilled and flattened by the sharp-edged and squared spaces of air into the one smell he truly knew: the smell of loneliness.

Himself alone. There had never been anybody else to lean toward, to talk to, to sniff the human odor of, to gaze at, to feel easy with. Around him the talk of the others trickled lazily, exclaimed and surged, rose in agitation, relaxed into slow judicial accents.

He held one idea: Sister had told him to say *no.*

The day stretched into the early dark of fall, and still they talked. It was as if he waited in a hidden place for an animal whose exact whereabouts he knew, as if there were great reaches of time in which to await the animal in patient silence; sensing the least motion of its leisurely approach, whether it was weary or angry, ran or slept, feeling the presence of each insect that disturbed it, each wind that stirred its fur, while he ingested the flow of the oncoming flood of sky and earth curved into vast half-shells: the one brushed by southward wings of geese whose clamor was muted by height; the other belled in colossal rhythms of earthen waves clotted with ancient shining trees and sliding away on the distances to the pale thread of its interface with the first; both speaking in enigmatic tongues born through centuries of unfamiliar dark time—and balancing the movement of these, the reassuring grip of his still tension.

The tension was jolted.

Big Mike rasped, "You ready for the vote?"

Obal Manuska rumbled, "Yes."

"All right, we put it one man at a time. If you want the kids to go, say yes. If not, say no. You got that?" Big Mike spoke as nominal chief of the village, who traditionally acted as mediator at matters of council.

The men nodded in unison. One by one:

Little Jim said quickly, "No."

Steve hung back. "No," he said at length.

Ivan and Floyd's voices in unison said a fast "Yes."

Obal said loudly, "Yes."

They stared at Innokenty. He brushed away a cascade of hair from his face and looked up at the last slim pencils of light lingering in the bell tower. "No," he said.

"Well, God damn it," Big Mike growled, "you men got it all tied up. What the hell."

Everybody talked at once. A nervous laugh was quickly stifled. "Why don't we do it again," someone suggested. The second vote was identical.

Obal frowned directly at Innokenty. "It's late," he said.

"We can't change it tonight," Big Mike said, sending Obal a warning glance. "We'll sleep over it."

The men relaxed. Rising stiffly, rolling cigarettes in their rough fingers, stretching and yawning, they idled out the door and along different paths home. Under the bantering laughter was a sense of the suspension of common matters. They walked with a certain dignity.

Big Mike clasped Innokenty's shoulder. "Come on, young fellow. It's gonna be all right. You get some rest and come back tomorrow." They filed along the boardwalk. Innokenty drifted away to his shack. He wondered what it was that Big Mike had said was all tied up, and whether it could be got loose.

Big Mike and Madeline sat on the ground outside his cabin in the half-light of the crisp early evening.

"Olinga looks good," Big Mike said.

Madeline wrinkled her nose. "Sure—for her age. She was a good-looking woman one time, I guess."

"She still is," he said.

"Oh, Papa, you like all the women."

"Nobody can beat you for looks, daughter."

Olinga came toward them, setting her scruffy boots demurely on the boards. Wisps of bone-colored hair drifted into eyes made ashen by sun and wind. Her face was a red-brown chunk of dry riverbed netted with cracks. Three ample skirts belled out with each of her steps, exhaling the smoky smell of furs and hides that after a lifetime was part of her. She arced a long easy stream of brown Snoose to a hummock of dry grass five feet away. Looking at them humorously she said, *"Do-eennt'a."*

"Aszoon," Madeline said.

Big Mike stood up with a single muscular lunge. Olinga's pale eyes found his face. Clutched under the wrinkles, the cage of bone appeared, clean as a young girl's. Her smile was the color and texture of old ivory. The two stood watching each other with deep and familiar comfort.

"Papa has troubles," Madeline said.

"I know," Olinga said.

Madeline grumbled, "Everybody knows. Now they've got the votes tied up."

Big Mike said, "Them boys—Ivan, Floyd—they're never gonna change. They stick behind Mary Joe a hundred percent." He scratched his chin. "Jimmie and Innokenty won't move an inch either, I know that."

"Never Innokenty," Olinga said. "He'll die to obey Sister, poor dumb child." Faint contempt twisted her lips. "How it happen he got on council anyway?"

"I got to try and keep people peaceful around here," Big Mike answered. "Them boys can't hurt nothing, they balance up . . . This way, we don't shut Sister Celesta out." He grinned.

"Pretty smart, old man," Olinga said. "I hear she want to put Mary Joe and the babies out of the village."

"Hah, shit! not a chance," Big Mike hissed.

"Those boys can't do any harm, least not Innokenty. He have no brains."

"Naw, it's them other two that can't make their mind up," Big Mike grumbled.

"What you think? Steve going to vote no again?" Olinga asked.

"He talks all the time about *Gisakk* ways, education, hygiene," he sniffed, "medical care, new tools and traps and boats. Don't mean a damn thing. It's only in the voice he says it. Him and Missa, they want to stay the same as we are."

Olinga said, "Maybe we won't worry about him." Her lips moved for an instant, and she looked narrowly at Madeline. "I guess it's Obal we're worrying about."

Madeline frowned. "He's got his own mind. Don't you think he loves those kids? His own niece and nephew."

"I know," Big Mike soothed. "He don't want you to get sick, daughter, that's all."

She tossed her long straight mane of hair. "You mean I can't take care of my own sister."

Olinga squatted on the dirt that was stamped solid as a block of stone. She laid her hand on Madeline's knee. "Everybody knows you can," she said. "Obal like Mary Joe's kids same as you do. But he want things right for everybody."

"It don't mean Mary Joe's not gonna have plenty help," Big Mike said. "She trusts in that. She trusts in that better than anybody else does." He chuckled.

Anger formed behind Madeline's eyes. She got up, brushing away Olinga's hand. "Nobody listens to me. My husband won't let me do anything for Sister. I'll shut up. Let it go the way it wants to go. Always it's that way, no matter what I want."

"Hey, daughter, wait a minute." Big Mike sat back down as she walked fast away, stiff and solitary.

"She's too proud," Olinga murmured.

"Sick with nerves," Big Mike said. "What can I do. We got to move on."

Nokinbaa, the Snowy Owl, his feathers already spotted with winter white, flew in silence across Mukluk Creek. His wings lay in a long, still curve. Through the darkening air, the river shone like poured balm. Patterns endlessly formed, dissolved, and reformed. A tranquil watchfulness grasped the two, a waiting ancient as the land.

Tentatively, Olinga said in a half-whisper, "You ever think about giving one child only?"

Startled, Big Mike turned. His teeth gnawed at the edges of his coarse mustache. He pushed back his cap.

"They ask first for Lidwynne. They want her bad," she said.

"Whew!" he breathed.

"Think on it, Mike," she said.

Noon light, sifting through the mist that had swirled all night in the upper air, now paled the open square of the bell tower. Obal, looming tall on the center floor, set a green-enameled gasoline lantern on the floor. He laid a match against the cotton mantle and a mass of glowing specks poured up around it. Flame and fuel hissed steadily together. Brilliance flared on the intent features of the men.

They inspected this new object.

Round-shouldered little Jim Yap stood fascinated. His jaw clenched a wad of Snoose. Inside the sagging seat of his overalls, his buttocks stood loose and skinny. A fringed hole bared his knee, leathery as old moosehide. He blinked at the lantern with the flat, pale-coffee eyes that gave him an incorruptible appearance. "Gee! You got one," he breathed.

"Came in from Sears Roebuck on the barge today," Obal said proudly.

Little Jim's chin sank further into the vee of his wool shirt.

"What's the matter, Jimmie?" Steve asked.

He hawked a lump of phlegm. "No sleep," he said hoarsely. "My woman talks too much."

Innokenty giggled. His front teeth knifed down through a slab of whitefish and his tongue rolled the stony oblong back lumpily in his cheek to the spaces between his molars. Five minutes of slow grinding reduced it to a juicy wad. Smoke oozed around his taste buds; a streak of spit drizzled down his chest.

Floyd muttered, "Always suckin' that goddam fish," and Big Mike lifted a quick palm. Floyd elbowed Ivan. "Lucky we got no woman hollering around like Jimmie's got."

"She's pestering me to death," Little Jim said huskily.

"Talk-talk, they drive you crazy," Ivan agreed, although neither of the young men were yet married.

The other men glanced at Big Mike where he sat a little separated, but he was gazing at the floor and chomping his mustache. They grew serious as they saw that he was preparing to say something.

"Time to go to work," he said, eyeing each man in turn. "You wasted a whole day yesterday. You didn't get no solid opinion. Everybody's too stubborn. How can you men run a village if you can't make up your mind?"

"This one is a big problem," Obal protested. "We can't work it out in a couple days." The other men nodded.

"All right, cancel the whole thing. What I mean, that vote yesterday, it never happened."

They looked questioning at each other and at him. Steve said, "What should we do?" He had a permanent look of worry on his face, its wrinkles deepened now.

"You could start all over again," Big Mike suggested. Seeing their puzzled faces, he grinned. "I got a new idea." He hesitated and took a deep breath. "You should think about separating the two kids. That's what you better talk about today."

"Mike, Mike! Wait a minute," Obal said, "You mean let Doc adopt one and leave the other with Mary Joe?" He rubbed a hand over his chin. "Hell, I never thought about that . . . But which one, which way?"

"That's what I mean. Nobody thought about it, but it might work. Which one. You should talk about that plenty. It's up to you." He looked relieved. There was a jumble of voices and Big Mike leaned back, muttering, "Sweet Jesus. I don't know which one, or how to do what, neither." He had paced the floor of his cabin all night and his face was a mass of tense muscle.

With a grunt, Obal turned off the Coleman lantern. The men's expressions turned harsh in the cold light; sternly facing each other, they seemed to agree that they had reached a point where they might be better able to deal with the matter at hand.

Steve voiced his chief concern: "Lidwynne and Michael are smart kids." He darted a look at Big Mike, who was staring at a point high on the wall. He appeared not to be listening, but the angle of his head said that he would miss nothing. "Both parents come from smart people," Steve said. "Look at Mary Joe. She still remembers how to read."

Obal agreed, "Matmiya done that. She never let up on them kids. Maybe because she didn't learn it herself . . . I remember how she made all her kids, my cousins, go to school and study every night—It was no easy thing. Nobody else much around here bothered."

A smile spread on Big Mike's face.

"Hey, Mary Joe's oldest boy's a smart one, too," Floyd said. "I heard he's good in school down at Kaltag, sings and plays fiddle down there for dances. Ten years old now, that boy. Gee, she got married to Taria young, she was just out of school . . ."

"He's too old for her," Ivan interrupted.

"But she was always like she was on her own," Floyd went on. "She acted different than us, cared about schooling. Even read books when she didn't have to. Old Taria had no care for none of that."

Little Jim said, "*Gisakk* use books to make medicine like shaman. Those books got lot of power."

Obal mused: "It wasn't all work, she had a good time too. Those days she was always laughing, and how she danced."

Steve said, "Clem gets along good with her, he plays his fiddle and makes her dance. I hear them laughing a lot with the kids. Baby Michael has that music in him, he bounces all around and grins when Clem plays the fiddle."

Obal observed, "You can't tell so soon. He might get it from Clem though . . . That Clem's been a good man from the start. Little, but tough. Only *Gisakk* I ever took into Kaiyuh Flats. Made him swear to never tell no other *Gisakk* where our secret hunt grounds was."

Little Jim said, "That poor damn Taria. He tried to get her back, but he was too late."

"Too late? You mean too old," Ivan said.

Big Mike stirred himself and yawned. Warmth of the sun seeped into the chill hall as the men talked.

"What about Sister Celesta?" Ivan said. "She never spoke up till Doc wanted the kids. Right away she runs over to Merricks, wants them herself. Mary Joe refuses, and Sister is her enemy now."

Innokenty threw off his mackinaw and slouched, one boot up, along the bench.

Obal, glancing at the silent Eskimo, said softly, "You know. Grabby, like she's nervous. She wants too much."

"You lie," Innokenty said.

"No, he don't lie," Big Mike said in his calmest voice.

Steve said, "*Gisakk* don't know how to wait, they're not easy in this country. Work too hard when they don't need it. *Gisakk* don't understand Yukon time."

Obal, lighting his corncob pipe, murmured, "That's sure true."

Steve said, "We got to respect the church. Even when the Jesuits want to take away our medicine men, our *yega*, all the old things. But we know they don't mean bad so we go along with that and still follow our ways. It worked out, you bet."

The men nodded; their eyes shone with a tolerance born of years of habit.

"They're not all that way," Steve concluded. He leaned back against the wall, his nervousness settled now that the conversation was going easy.

Little Jim said resentfully, "Mary Joe got Father to baptize them kids when she couldn't stick with the church and Clem both . . . She did what she had to, I don't put no blame on her. Too bad Sister shamed her in front of her little girl, yelling at her in the yard. You ever notice another thing, Sister's got a bad habit, she never look at anybody. People get nervous when some *Gisakk* stare too long or don't look at all."

"All right, now," Innokenty growled, flinging an arm over his eyes and lounging full length on the bench.

"You like Sister real good, don't you," Obal said to him. Innokenty's eyes wavered dreamily. "She's my friend," he muttered, and dozed off.

Obal said, "Some people don't go to Mass regular every day. But we work hard, give Father what help we got. We split his wood, give fish and meat to him. He pays what cash he can turn loose of, he's got the Sisters to feed. Sister Celesta don't do that way. She takes it and offers nothing, like she's entitled. That's all right too, I figure we do the best we can. But if it wasn't for the village, that Mission would starve."

Big Mike rumbled, "Wasn't for the village, that Mission wouldn't be here."

Steve said, "The church expects the missionaries to live off the land, but they don't know how. They're like a bunch of children."

"I thought they were rich, same as Doc," Floyd said.

Obal asked, "What you mean, Doc's rich?"

"Doc's got plenty."

"Hey, he's not rich. Doc and Nellie got enough to eat but he only gets two hundred dollars a month for both of them, place to live, and wood. Fifty cents a day for food. Everything comes in by boat from Uncle Sam, outside. They never want free meat from us, they always buy it, what little fresh meat they get. Most of their meat's in tin cans. We live better than them."

Steve asked, "How long's Nellie been taking care of Mary Joe's kids? I can't remember."

"Off and on maybe three years. When Michael was about a year, she started it. Lidwynne was two then. Doc offered to help Mary Joe. They kept Lidwynne a while, and then kept Michael too. In good weather Mary Joe could get outdoors and fish around here close. She got better and that summer she took Lidwynne to camp at Four Mile, but Nellie sure didn't want to give her up after that. Soft-hearted, that Mary Joe, she let her take her then, right away." Obal laughed self-consciously. "I'm doing all the talking around here."

"Well, you know Doc Merrick better than us," Steve said.

Little Jim said quietly, "Remember they're *Gisakk*. The kids are mostly Indian."

"That's right," Steve said. "It's been on my mind." Worry returned to his face.

The men shuffled their feet and yawned.

Squaring his shoulders, Obal said, "They want those kids bad. They should have my three. Some winters it gets tough, feeding us five."

"I wouldn't care too much," Steve said. "But Missy's crazy for them."

Ivan asked, "You think Nellie could raise them?"

"I'll bet on it," Obal said.

"They'd get education, eat good, and there's Doc right there so they don't get that T.B." Floyd enumerated on his fingers.

"I know, you and Ivan voted to let them both go away," Obal said, "but we got to think about this other. Maybe we got to send one of them kids away." Steve watched Obal intently, the lines deepening in his cheeks.

Innokenty sat up, alert. "Mary Joe gonna be sick a long time?" he questioned.

No one moved.

"Who knows," Obal said at last. "T.B., consumption they call it. Goes different with each person. Might last a year, might be five years. She's a strong woman, she come from good blood." He nodded toward Big Mike, his sturdy Russian body sitting as erectly as any of the younger men.

"Who's gonna take care of her?" Innokenty persisted.

Floyd and Ivan darted looks at each other. A shade of eagerness rippled over Ivan's lean hunter's face. "We already figured that out," he said. "We'll feed her long as she needs, we'll bring wood, sweep her house. Whatever she wants." The young men and Mary Joe were long-time friends; it reached back to babyhood.

"Count me in too," Little Jim said.

"Big Mike knows where I stand," Steve remarked, still carefully observing Obal.

"Now everybody get this straight one time." Obal moved uncomfortably, now being forced into a statement. "I won't let Madeline do it, it's the wrong time, our kids are too young . . . She wants to help Mary Joe, fine, but it's too much work for Madeline, and damn, I—" His bluff voice trailed away.

Quickly Steve said, "It's all right. When the time comes, we can all take care of her, and we can take the kids and raise them . . ." His mouth worked as though he would say more, but he refrained.

"Mary Joe's *kid,* you mean," Obal said. "*One kid.*"

Steve's expression went bleaker than ever. "That's right. We have to split up the children, maybe." He continued to look at Obal covertly, remembering Missa pleading angrily and added, "Big Mike promised those kids to us, long time ago. *Gisakk* can't take them away."

The men eyed each other. They had almost forgotten the old binding promise made by Big Mike, how much depended on keeping promises made. Breaking it this way might bring on the enmities of *yega,* and bring bad luck on everything they tried to do, the whole village. It was as if Steve had thrown a rock at them.

Steve thought he saw why Big Mike had changed things. His son Andy's death last spring had hit hard. He wanted to keep his own family together now. He couldn't take away two of his grandchildren that way, it must be tough, he was so crazy about them. But where had Big Mike got the idea of splitting them up? He had only come up with it this morning. Something had happened during the night, Steve thought. Smart, that Mike, pulling the switch early today so nobody in the village could get to them. Because the people were stirred up and trying to pull council every which way. Like always, Big Mike wanted to please everybody. For him, it was a hell of a spot.

Obal focused on the heart of the problem. "Now, Steve, what if Mary Joe keeps one? It could help her get over losing the other. She could raise the one who stays for a while, anyway."

"What about the agreement, the promise from Big Mike? We can't go against it. It's back luck, you know that."

Obal frowned. "But this means three lives, you see that. I know, Steve, it's a strange thing all the way. We got to bend somewhere, and I got to vote to keep Michael with his mother. Steve, when she gets so she can't look after him you can step in and *then* be keeping the agreement. I know, it's around the bush, but this is a heavy thing."

Steve nodded slowly. "She needs him too. Yeah." Something in the shaping of this idea made some sense to him. It boiled down to a simple thing: the kids had to be separated. Obal wanted to keep Michael and let Lidwynne go. But if he, Steve, let Missa have her way and Steve voted on keeping both, council would be tied up again and they'd be back where they started and likely both kids would have to stay. So he would vote with Obal. He would have to help send Lidwynne away. He felt as heavy as a loaded barge.

His voice was heavy, too, saying, "If we have to pick one, looks to me like Lidwynne should go, I guess. She's used to *Gisakk* ways." This bald utterance already placed a distance between themselves and Lidwynne, a distance which had already entered the hearts of the people, whether recognized or not. They had known that the time of separateness had arrived.

"That's right," Obal said flatly. "It's for everybody's good. There's no way we can help it."

Big Mike's stiff new pants creaked as he crossed his legs. "You men want to talk to my daughter," he stated.

"I guess we should ask her a couple questions," Little Jim said.

It was nearly dark inside. Mary Joe stood against the door, her vision adjusting until she saw the figures and faces of the men. Big Mike pointed to the bench which abutted the one where they sat in a row. She sat down, moving back until she sat erect against the wall, the angle of her body fitting snugly into the corner formed by its jointure with the bench. She glanced quickly at the men and, looking straight ahead, waited.

Their faces turned to her. Innokenty sat up and leaned forward, chin propped on his fists.

"*Snaa'*, they have to ask questions," Big Mike said.

Her head bowed briefly, acknowledging his words. Her look lingered on his face a fraction beyond custom, then turned back.

Each man was reluctant to be the first to speak. Time stretched in a simple waiting. At length Obal broke the pause. "You know what we came here for."

"Yes," she said in her faintly hoarse voice.

"You been sick a long time. You can't take care of the boy and girl. You let Merrick take care of them because you can't."

Her glance flicked over him from the corner of her eye. "He said it was better for me."

"Merricks want to adopt your boy and girl. Yesterday this council couldn't make a decision on that. Now we are thinking it could be done different."

Her eyebrows went up in a question.

"We talked about you giving them one child and keeping one." The words were immovable, hanging on the unmoving air.

Her sharp knuckles pressed each other white. Her face drained to the color of ashes.

"Would it be better if you don't lose both of them?"

"How can that be?"

"It depends on how long Doc Merrick says you will be sick," Obal said.

She moved abruptly. "How can I tell you, he doesn't know, nobody knows. I have to wait." She took a handkerchief from a pocket of the skirt, turned and coughed into it. Returning to him in a long gaze, her eyes were black counters, the lashes ticking off a remote rhythm.

"Doc never told you how long?" Obal asked insistently.

"He said I'm final."

The men turned their dim faces to each other, and heads were shaken.

"How bad is it now?" Steve asked.

"It comes, it goes. When I have hemorrhage I let Merricks keep Lidwynne. She's big. But Michael's still pretty small."

"He depends on you. Now he's running around, you got more work," Big Mike pressed, alert on the edge of the bench.

She didn't answer.

"You hear me?" he questioned.

"Yes, I hear you, Papa."

"Doc don't know how long he gives you," Obal said harshly.

"He can't say. Sometimes I'm strong for work, that helps me. Fresh air, moving around. I might go fast, or I might be a long time."

"Well, I ask you three times how long. Three times you say you don't know. That's enough." Obal's voice softened.

"Could you take care of them by yourself?" Steve asked.

She shuddered lightly. "If I think that, why did I listen to Merrick's wanting to take them?"

"You could handle Michael only?" he asked.

"Maybe so. For a while yet."

"We're going to help you, you understand that."

Her eyes glistened. "I may last long enough so Michael could have a chance—"

Eagerly Floyd interrupted. "That's right, Mary Joe. We bring you what you need and you don't fish, trap, nothing. All you do is keep Michael."

Ivan's large clear eyes bored straight into Mary Joe's, and he nodded, reassuring. Little Jim held out both hands, smiling.

Obal said, "These boys are hunters. Plenty luck. Some other people around here could help out. We'll stick together."

Mary Joe slid to the edge of the bench. "Something I don't understand," she said. "How is it so easy for these fellows to tell me I have to split up my babies. First, I heard they were talking about giving both of them away. That's how I thought it was going to be."

Big Mike cleared his throat.

"Now, I hear these fellows talking about splitting them up," she said, looking intently at the wall.

Big Mike said, "Council couldn't break the tie, *snaa'*, nobody would change their mind. So we had to do something. You have a right to say no. In that case, we can't do nothing. Both kids will stay in Nulato."

"Ahh, already they made up their mind," she said. "Nobody asks me, nobody asks my girl, the whole village decides. I was willing to let them both go. Now my own papa says I can't." Her glittering eyes mirrored the men's faces, looking everywhere except at her. It was the traditional women's scolding, addressed to everyone and no one.

"Now, Mary Joe," Steve said.

"Already Uncle Steve, my friend, is talking too that I should break up my family."

"What do you want, nobody care?" Obal said.

"The people talk about it and don't bother to ask me what I want. Even these men here, I know since I'm a baby."

"You see how it is," Obal said.

"Now what can I say. Have I got a right to say which one stays with me?" she asked Big Mike directly.

"Damn right, you got a right," he said.

She rested her face in her hands for a moment, and they waited. Her arms dropped, palms forward, open. Her eyes were distant, without emotion.

"What are you going to do?" Big Mike asked.

"What am I going to do, he says," she said, stressing each word and examining the ceiling. "What is there to do? My boy is too young. He needs me more than my girl."

"You sure about that?" Obal asked.

She leaned toward the men in a movement of deep reluctance.

"Then you got your mind made up . . . You know we have to vote on it again just the same," Obal said.

"That's right," Big Mike said huskily.

There was no sound as Mary Joe rose and went out.

Luci Tapahonso (Navajo)
All the Colors of Sunset

Even after all this time, when I look back at all that happened, I don't know if I would do anything differently. That summer morning seemed like any other. The sun came up over the mountain around seven or so, and when I went to throw the coffee grounds out, I put the pouch of corn pollen in my apron pocket so that I could pray before I came inside.

During the summers, we sleep most nights in the *chaha'oh,* the shade-house, unless it rains. I remembered early that morning I had heard loud voices yelling and they seemed to come from the north. Whoever it was quieted quickly, and I fell asleep. Right outside the *chaha'oh,* I knew the dogs were alert—their ears erect and eyes glistening. Out here near Rockpoint, where we live, it's so quiet and isolated that we can hear things from a far distance. It's mostly desert and the huge rocks nearby, *tsé ahiłah neeé,* whale rock and the other rocks, seem to bounce noises into the valley. People live far apart and there are no streetlights nearby. The nights are quiet, except for animal and bird noises, and the sky is always so black. In the Navajo way, they say the night sky is made of black jet, and that the folding darkness comes from the north. Sometimes in the evenings, I think of this when the sun is setting, and all the bright colors fall somewhere into the west. Then I let the beauty of the sunset go, and my sadness along with it.

That morning I fixed a second pot of coffee, and peeled potatoes to fry. Just as I finished slicing the potatoes, I thought I heard my grandbaby cry. I went out and looked out toward my daughter's home. She lives across the arroyo a little over a mile away. I shaded my eyes and squinted—the sun was in her direction. Finally, I went inside and finished fixing breakfast. We were going to go into Chinle that afternoon, so I didn't go over to their house.

Later that morning, I was polishing some pieces of jewelry when I heard my daughter crying outside. My heart quickened. I rushed to the door and she practically fell inside the house. She was carrying the baby in her cradleboard and could hardly talk—she was sobbing and screaming so. I grabbed the baby, knowing she was hurt. When I looked at my grand-daughter, I knew the terrible thing that had happened. Her little face was so pale and wet from crying. I could not think or speak—somehow I found my way to the south wall of the hooghan and sat down, still holding my sweet baby. My first and only grandchild was gone.

I held her close and nuzzled her soft neck. I sang over and over the little songs that I always sang to her. I unwrapped her and touched slowly, slowly every part of her little smooth body. I wanted to remember every sweet detail and said aloud each name like I had always done, "*Díí nijáád wolyé, sho'wéé.*" This is called your leg, my baby. I asked her, "*Nits'iiyah sha'?*" and nuzzled the back of her neck like before. "*Jo ka i.*" This time she did not giggle and laugh. I held her and rocked, and sang, and talked to her.

The pollen pouch was still in my pocket, and I put a bit into her mouth as I would have done when her first tooth came in. I put a pinch of pollen on her head as I would have done when she first left for kindergarten. I put a pinch of pollen in her little hands as I would have done when she was given her first lamb, as I would have done when she was given her own colt. This way she would have been gentle and firm with her pets. I brushed her with an eagle feather as I would have done when she graduated from junior high. All this and so much more that could have been swept over me as I sat there leaning over my little grandbaby.

She was almost five months old, and had just started to recognize me. She cried for me to hold her and I tried to keep her with me as much as I could. Sometimes I took her for long walks and showed her everything, and told her little stories about the birds and animals we saw. She would fall asleep on our way home, and still I hummed and sang softly. I couldn't stop singing. For some reason, when she was born, I was given so much time for her. I guess that's how it is with grandparents. I wasn't ever too busy to care for her. When my daughter took her home, my house seemed so empty and quiet.

They said that I kept the baby for four hours that morning. My daughter left and then returned with her husband. They were afraid to bother me in my grief. I don't remember much of it. I didn't know how I acted, or maybe that was the least of what I was conscious of. My daughter said later that I didn't say one word to her. I don't remember.

Finally, I got up and gave the baby to them so they could go to the hospital at Chinle. I followed in my own truck, and there the doctor confirmed her death, and we began talking about what we had to do next. Word spread quickly. When I went to buy some food at Basha's, several people comforted me and helped me with the shopping. My sisters and two aunts were at my home when I returned. They had straightened up the house, and were cooking already. Some of my daughters-in-law were cooking and getting things ready in the *chaha'oh* outside. By that evening, the house and the *chaha'oh* were filled with people—our own relatives, clan relatives, friends from school, church, and the baby's father's kin. People came and held me, comforting me and murmuring their sympathies. They cried with me, and brought me plates of food. I felt like I was in a daze—I hardly spoke. I tried to help cook and serve, but was gently guided back to the armchair that had somehow become "my chair" since that morning.

There were meetings each day, and various people stood up to counsel and advise everyone who was there, including my daughter and her husband. When everything was done, and we had washed our faces and started over again, I couldn't seem to focus on things. Before all this happened, I was very busy each day—cooking, sewing, taking out the horses sometimes, feeding the animals, and often just visiting with people. One of my children or my sisters always came by and we would talk and laugh while I continued my tasks. Last winter was a good year for piñons so I was still cleaning and roasting the many flour sackfuls we had picked. At Many Farms junction, some people from Shiprock had a truckload of the sweetest corn I had ever tasted, so I bought plenty and planned to make *ntsidigodí* and other kinds of cornbread. We would have these tasty delicacies to eat in the winter. We liked to remember summer by the food we had stored and preserved.

When we were little, my mother taught all of us girls to weave, but I hadn't touched a loom in years. When I became a grandmother, I began to think of teaching some of the old things to my baby. Maybe it was my age, but I remembered a lot of the things we were told. Maybe it was that I was alone more than I had ever been—my children were grown. My husband passed on five years ago, and since I was by myself and I had enough on which to live, I stopped working at a paying job.

After all this happened, I resumed my usual tasks and tried to stay busy so that my grandbaby's death wouldn't overwhelm me. I didn't cry or grieve out loud because they say that one can call the dead back by doing that. Yet so much had changed, and it was as if I was far away from everything. Some days I fixed a lunch and took the sheep out for the day and returned as the sun was going down. And when I came back inside, I realized that I hadn't spoken to the animals all day. It seemed strange, and yet I just didn't feel like talking. The dogs would follow me around, wanting attention—for me to throw a stick for them, or talk to them—then after a while they would just lie down and watch me. Once I cleaned and roasted a pan of piñons perfectly without thinking about it. It's a wonder that I didn't burn myself. A few weeks later, we had to brand some colts, and give the horses shots, so everyone got together and we spent the day at the corral in the dust and heat. Usually it was a happy and noisy time, but that day was quieter than usual. At least we had taken care of everything.

Sometimes I dreamt of my grandbaby, and it was as if nothing had happened. In my dreams, I carried her around, singing and talking to her. She smiled and giggled at me. When I awoke, it was as if she had been lying beside me, kicking and reaching around. A small space beside me would be warm, and her scent faint. These dreams seemed so real. I looked forward to sleeping because maybe in sleeping I might see her. On the days following such a dream, I would replay it over and over in my mind, still smiling and humming to her the next morning. By afternoon, the activity and noise had usually worn the dream off.

I heard after the funeral that people were whispering and asking questions about what had happened. It didn't bother me. Nothing anyone said or did would bring my sweet baby back—that was clear. I never asked my daughter how it happened. After the baby's death, she and her husband became very quiet and they were together so much, they seemed like shadows of each other. Her husband worked at different jobs, and she just went with him and waited in the pickup until he was through. He worked with horses, helped build hooghans, corrals, and other construction work. When she came over and spent the afternoon with me, we hardly talked. We both knew we were more comfortable that way. As usual, she hugged me each time before she left. I knew she was in great pain.

Once, when I was at Basha's shopping for groceries, a woman I didn't know said to me, "You have a pretty grandbaby." I smiled and didn't reply. I noticed that she didn't say "*yée*" at the end of "*nitsóíh*" which would have meant "the grandbaby who is no longer alive." That happened at other places, and I didn't respond, except to smile. I thought it was good that people remembered her.

About four months after her death, we were eating at my house when my sisters gathered around me and told me they were very worried about me. They thought I was still too grief-stricken over the baby, and that it was not healthy. "You have to go on," they said, "let her go." They said they wanted the "old me" back, so I agreed to go for help.

We went to a medicine woman near Ganado, and she asked me if I could see the baby sometimes. No, I said, except in dreams.

"Has anyone said they've seen her?" she asked. I said that I didn't think so. Then she said, "Right now, I see the baby beside you." I was so startled that I began looking around for her.

"The baby hasn't left," she said, "she wants to stay with you." I couldn't see my grandbaby. Then I realized that other people could see what the medicine woman had just seen. No wonder, I thought, that sometimes when I woke, I could feel her warm body beside me. She said the baby was wrapped in white.

She couldn't help me herself, but she told me to see another medicine person near Lukaichakai. She said that the ceremony I needed was very old and that she didn't know it herself. The man she recommended was elderly and very knowledgeable and so it was likely that he would know the ceremony, or would at least know of someone who did.

Early in the morning, we went to his house west of Many Farms—word had already been sent that we were coming. The ceremony lasted for four days and three nights, and parts of songs and prayers had such ancient sacred words I wasn't sure if I understood them. When the old man prayed and sang, sometimes tears streamed down my face as I repeated everything after him— word for word, line for line, late into the night—and we would begin again at daybreak the next morning. I was exhausted and so relieved. I finally realized what my grief had done. I could finally let my grandbaby go.

We were lucky that we had found this old man because the ceremony had not been done in almost eighty years. He had seen it as a little boy and had memorized all the parts of it—the songs, the advice, the prayers, and the literal letting go of the dead spirit. Over time, it has become a rare ceremony, because what I had done in holding and keeping the baby for those hours was not in keeping with the Navajo way. I understood that doing so had upset the balance of life and death. When we left, we were all crying. I thanked the old man for his memory, his life, and his ability to help us when no one else could. I understand now that all of life has ceremonies connected with it, and for us, without our memory, our old people, and our children, we would be like lost people in this world we live in, as well as in the other worlds in which our loved ones are waiting.

Anna Lee Walters (Pawnee-Otoe)

The Warriors

In our youth, we saw hobos come and go, sliding by our faded white house like wary cats who did not want us too close. Sister and I waved at the strange procession of passing men and women hobos. Just between ourselves, Sister and I talked of that hobo parade. We guessed at and imagined the places and towns we thought the hobos might have come from or had been. Mostly they were White or Black people. But there were Indian hobos, too. It never occurred to Sister and me that this would be Uncle Ralph's end.

Sister and I were little, and Uncle Ralph came to visit us. He lifted us over his head and shook us around him like gourd rattles. He was Momma's younger brother, and he could have disciplined us if he so desired. That was part of our custom. But he never did. Instead, he taught us Pawnee words. "*Pari* is Pawnee and *pita* is man," he said. Between the words, he tapped out drumbeats with his fingers on the table top, ghost dance and round dance songs that he suddenly remembered and sang. His melodic voice lilted over us and hung around the corners of the house for days. His stories of life and death were fierce and gentle. Warriors dangled in delicate balance.

He told us his version of the story of *Pahukatawa*, a Skidi Pawnee warrior. He was killed by the Sioux, but the animals, feeling compassion for him, brought *Pahukatawa* to life again. "The Evening Star and the Morning Star bore children and some people say that these offspring are who we are," he often said. At times he pointed to those stars and greeted them by their Pawnee names. He liked to pray for Sister and me, for everyone and every tiny thing in the world, but we never heard him ask for anything for himself from *Atius,* the Father.

"For beauty is why we live," Uncle Ralph said when he talked of precious things only the Pawnees know. "We die for it, too." He called himself an ancient Pawnee warrior when he was quite young. He told us that warriors must brave all storms and odds and stand their ground. He knew intimate details of every battle the Pawnees ever fought since Pawnee time began, and Sister and I knew even then that Uncle Ralph had a great battlefield of his own.

As a child I thought that Uncle Ralph had been born into the wrong time. The Pawnees had been ravaged so often by then. The tribe of several thousand when it was at its peak over a century before were then a few hundred people who had been closely confined for more than a hundred years. The warrior life was gone. Uncle Ralph was trapped in a transparent bubble of a new time. The bubble bound him tight as it blew around us.

Uncle Ralph talked obsessively of warriors, painted proud warriors who shrieked poignant battle cries at the top of their lungs and died with honor.

Sister and I were little then, lost from him in the world of children who saw everything with children's eyes. And though we saw with wide eyes the painted warriors that he fantasized and heard their fierce and haunting battle cries, we did not hear his. Now that we are old and Uncle Ralph has been gone for a long time, Sister and I know that when he died, he was tired and alone. But he was a warrior.

The hobos were always around in our youth. Sister and I were curious about them, and this curiosity claimed much of our time. They crept by the house at all hours of the day and night, dressed in rags and odd clothing. They wandered to us from the railroad tracks where they had leaped from slow-moving boxcars onto the flatland. They hid in high clumps of weeds and brush that ran along the fence near the tracks. The hobos usually traveled alone, but Sister and I saw them come together, like poor families, to share a can of beans or a tin of sardines that they ate with sticks or twigs. Uncle Ralph also watched them from a distance.

One early morning, Sister and I crossed the tracks on our way to school and collided with a tall, haggard whiteman. He wore a very old-fashioned pin-striped black jacket covered with lint and soot. There was fright in his eyes when they met ours. He scurried around us, quickening his pace. The pole over his shoulder where his possessions hung in a bundle at the end bounced as he nearly ran from us.

"Looks just like a scared jackrabbit," Sister said, watching him dart away.

That evening we told Momma about the scared man. She warned us about the dangers of hobos as our father threw us a stern look. Uncle Ralph was visiting but he didn't say anything. He stayed the night and Sister asked him, "Hey, Uncle Ralph, why do you suppose they's hobos?"

Uncle Ralph was a large man. He took Sister and put her on one knee. "You see, Sister," he said, "hobos are a different kind. They see things in a different way. Them hobos are kind of like us. We're not like other people in some ways and yet we are. It has to do with what you see and feel when you look at this old world."

His answer satisfied Sister for a while. He taught us some more Pawnee words that night.

Not long after Uncle Ralph's explanation, Sister and I surprised a Black man with white whiskers and fuzzy hair. He was climbing through the barbed-wire fence that marked our property line. He wore faded blue overalls with pockets stuffed full of handkerchiefs. He wiped sweat from his face. When it dried, he looked up and saw us. I remembered what Uncle Ralph had said and wondered what the Black man saw when he looked at us standing there.

"We might scare him," Sister said softly to me, remembering the whiteman who had scampered away.

Sister whispered, "Hi," to the Black man. Her voice was barely audible.

"Boy, it's sure hot," he said. His voice was big and he smiled.

"Where are you going?" Sister asked.

"Me? Nowheres, I guess," he muttered.

"Then what you doing here?" Sister went on. She was bold for a seven-year-old kid. I was older but I was also quieter. "This here place is ours," she said.

He looked around and saw our house with its flowering mimosa trees and rich green mowed lawn stretching out before him. Other houses sat around ours.

"I reckon I'm lost," he said.

Sister pointed to the weeds and brush further up the road. "That's where you want to go. That's where they all go, the hobos."

I tried to quiet Sister but she didn't hush. "The hobos stay up there," she said. "You a hobo?"

He ignored her question and asked his own. "Say, what is you all? You not Black, you not White. What is you all?"

Sister looked at me. She put one hand on her chest and the other hand on me. "We Indians!" Sister said.

He stared at us and smiled again. "Is that a fact?" he said.

"Know what kind of Indians we are?" Sister asked him.

He shook his fuzzy head. "Indians is Indians, I guess," he said.

Sister wrinkled her forehead and retorted, "Not us! We not like others. We see things different. We're Pawnees. We're warriors!"

I pushed my elbow into Sister's side. She quieted.

The man was looking down the road and he shuffled his feet. "I'd best go," he said.

Sister pointed to the brush and weeds one more time. "That way," she said.

He climbed back through the fence and brush as Sister yelled, "Bye now!" He waved a damp handkerchief.

Sister and I didn't tell Momma and Dad about the Black man. But much later Sister told Uncle Ralph every word that had been exchanged with the Black man. Uncle Ralph listened and smiled.

Months later when the warm weather had cooled and Uncle Ralph came to stay with us for a couple of weeks, Sister and I went to the hobo place. We had planned it for a long time. That afternoon when we pushed away the weeds, not a hobo was in sight.

The ground was packed down tight in the clearing among the high weeds. We walked around the encircling brush and found folded cardboards stacked together. Burned cans in assorted sizes were stashed under the cardboards, and there were remains of old fires. Rags were tied to the brush, snapping in the hard wind.

Sister said, "Maybe they're all in the boxcars now. It's starting to get cold."

She was right. The November wind had a bite to it and the cold stung our hands and froze our breaths as we spoke.

"You want to go over to them boxcars?" she asked. We looked at the Railroad Crossing sign where the boxcars stood.

I was prepared to answer when a voice roared from somewhere behind us.

"Now, you young ones, you git on home! Go on! Git!"

A man crawled out of the weeds and looked angrily at us. His eyes were red and his face was unshaven. He wore a red plaid shirt with striped gray and black pants too large for him. His face was swollen and bruised. An old woolen pink scarf hid some of the bruise marks around his neck, and his topcoat was splattered with mud.

Sister looked at him. She stood close to me and told him defiantly, "You can't tell us what to do! You don't know us!"

He didn't answer Sister but tried to stand. He couldn't. Sister ran to him and took his arm and pulled on it. "You need help?" she questioned.

He frowned at her but let us help him. He was tall. He seemed to be embarrassed by our help.

"You Indian, ain't you?" I dared to ask him.

He didn't answer me but looked at his feet as if they could talk so he wouldn't have to. His feet were in big brown overshoes.

"Who's your people?" Sister asked. He looked to be about Uncle Ralph's age when he finally lifted his face and met mine. He didn't respond for a minute. Then he sighed. "I ain't got no people," he told us as he tenderly stroked his swollen jaw.

"Sure you got people. Our folks says a man's always got people," I said softly. The wind blew our clothes and covered the words.

But he heard. He exploded like a firecracker. "Well, I don't! I ain't got no people! I ain't got nobody!"

"What you doing out here anyway?" Sister asked. "You hurt? You want to come over to our house?"

"Naw," he said. "Now you little ones, go on home. Don't be walking round out here. Didn't nobody tell you little girls ain't supposed to be going round by themselves? You might git hurt."

"We just wanted to talk to hobos," Sister said.

"Naw, you don't. Just go on home. Your folks is probably looking for you and worrying bout you."

I took Sister's arm and told her we were going home. Then we said "Bye" to the man. But Sister couldn't resist a few last words, "You Indian, ain't you?"

He nodded his head like it was a painful thing to do. "Yeah, I'm Indian."

"You ought to go on home yourself," 'Sister said. "Your folks probably looking for you and worrying bout you."

His voice rose again as Sister and I walked away from him. "I told you kids, I don't have no people!" There was exasperation in his voice.

Sister would not be outdone. She turned and yelled, "Oh yeah? You Indian ain't you? Ain't you?" she screamed. "We your people!"

His topcoat and pink scarf flapped in the wind as we turned away from him.

We went home to Momma and Dad and Uncle Ralph then. Uncle Ralph met us at the front door. "Where you all been?" he asked looking toward the railroad tracks. Momma and Dad were talking in the kitchen.

"Just playing, Uncle," Sister and I said simultaneously.

Uncle Ralph grabbed both Sister and I by our hands and yanked us out the door. "*Awkuh!*" he said, using the Pawnee expression to show his dissatisfaction.

Outside, we sat on the cement porch. Uncle Ralph was quiet for a long time, and neither Sister nor I knew what to expect.

"I want to tell you all a story," he finally said. " Once, there were these two rats who ran around everywhere and got into everything all the time. Everything they were told not to do, well they went right out and did. They'd get into one mess and then another. It seems that they never could learn."

At that point Uncle Ralph cleared his throat. He looked at me and said, "Sister, do you understand this story? Is it too hard for you? You're older."

I nodded my head up and down and said, "I understand."

Then Uncle Ralph looked at Sister. He said to her, "Sister, do I need to go on with this story?"

Sister shook her head from side to side. "Naw, Uncle Ralph," she said.

"So you both know how this story ends?" he said gruffly. Sister and I bobbed our heads up and down again.

We followed at his heels the rest of the day. When he tightened the loose hide on top of his drum, we watched him and held it in place as he laced the wet hide down. He got his drumsticks down from the top shelf of the closet and began to pound the drum slowly.

"Where you going, Uncle Ralph?" I asked. Sister and I knew that when he took his drum out, he was always gone shortly after.

"I have to be a drummer at some doings tomorrow," he said.

"You a good singer, Uncle Ralph," Sister said. "You know all them old songs."

"The young people nowadays, it seems they don't care bout nothing that's old. They just want to go to the Moon." He was drumming low as he spoke.

"We care, Uncle Ralph," Sister said.

"Why?" Uncle Ralph asked in a hard, challenging tone that he seldom used on us.

Sister thought for a moment and then said, "I guess because you care so much, Uncle Ralph."

His eyes softened as he said, "I'll sing you an *Eruska* song, a song for the warriors."

The song he sang was a war dance song. At first Sister and I listened attentively, but then Sister began to dance the man's dance. She had never danced before and tried to imitate what she had seen. Her chubby body whirled and jumped the way she'd seen the men dance. Her head tilted from side to side the way the men moved theirs. I laughed aloud at her clumsy effort, and Uncle Ralph laughed heartily, too.

Uncle Ralph went in and out of our lives after that. We heard that he sang at one place and then another, and people came to Momma to find him. They said that he was only one of a few who knew the old ways and the songs.

When he came to visit us, he always brought something to eat. The Pawnee custom was that the man, the warrior, should bring food, preferably meat. Then, whatever food was brought to the host was prepared and served to the man, the warrior, along with the host's family. Many times Momma and I, or Sister and I, came home to an empty house to find a sack of food on the table. Momma or I cooked it for the next meal, and Uncle Ralph showed up to eat.

As Sister and I grew older, our fascination with the hobos decreased. Other things took our time, and Uncle Ralph did not appear as frequently as he did before.

Once while I was home alone, I picked up Momma's old photo album. Inside was a gray photo of Uncle Ralph in an army uniform. Behind him were tents on a flat terrain. Other photos showed other poses but only in one picture did he smile. All the photos were written over in black ink in Momma's handwriting. *Ralphie in Korea,* the writing said.

Other photos in the album showed our Pawnee relatives. Dad was from another tribe. Momma's momma was in the album, a tiny gray-haired woman who no longer lived. And Momma's momma's dad was in the album; he wore old Pawnee leggings and the long feathers of a dark bird sat upon his head. I closed the album when Momma, Dad, and Sister came home.

Momma went into the kitchen to cook. She called me and Sister to help. As she put on a bibbed apron, she said, "We just came from town, and we saw someone from home there." She meant someone from her tribal community.

"This man told me that Ralphie's been drinking hard," she said sadly. "He used to do that quite a bit a long time ago, but we thought it had stopped. He seemed to be all right for a few years." We cooked and then ate in silence.

Washing the dishes, I asked Momma, "How come Uncle Ralph never did marry?"

Momma looked up at me but was not surprised by my question. She answered, "I don't know, Sister. It would have been better if he had. There was one woman who I thought he really loved. I think he still does. I think it had something to do with Mom. She wanted him to wait."

"Wait for what?" I asked.

"I don't know," Momma said, and sank into a chair.

After that we heard unsettling rumors of Uncle Ralph drinking here and there.

He finally came to the house once when only I happened to be home. He was haggard and tired. His appearance was much like that of the white-man that Sister and I met on the railroad tracks years before.

I opened the door when he tapped on it. Uncle Ralph looked years older than his age. He brought food in his arms. "*Nowa,* Sister," he said in greeting. "Where's the other one?" He meant my sister.

"She's gone now, Uncle Ralph. School in Kansas," I answered. "Where you been, Uncle Ralph? We been worrying about you."

He ignored my question and said, "I bring food. The warrior brings home food. To his family, to his people." His face was lined and had not been cleaned for days. He smelled of cheap wine.

I asked again, "Where you been, Uncle Ralph?"

He forced himself to smile. "Pumpkin Flower," he said, using the Pawnee name, "I've been out with my warriors all this time."

He put one arm around me as we went to the kitchen table with the food. "That's what your Pawnee name is. Now don't forget it."

"Did somebody bring you here, Uncle Ralph, or are you on foot?" I asked him.

"I'm on foot," he answered. "Where's your Momma?"

I told him that she and Dad would be back soon. I started to prepare the food he brought.

Then I heard Uncle Ralph say, "Life is sure hard sometimes. Sometimes it seems I just can't go on."

"What's wrong, Uncle Ralph?" I asked.

Uncle Ralph let out a bitter little laugh. "What's wrong?" he repeated. "What's wrong? All my life, I've tried to live what I've been taught, but Pumpkin Flower, some things are all wrong!"

He took a folded pack of Camel cigarettes from his coat pocket. His hand shook as he pulled one from the pack and lit the end. "Too much drink," he said sadly. "That stuff is bad for us."

"What are you trying to do, Uncle Ralph?" I asked him.

"Live," he said.

He puffed on the shaking cigarette a while and said, "The old people said to live beautifully with prayers and song. Some died for beauty, too."

"How do we do that, Uncle Ralph, live for beauty?" I asked.

"It's simple, Pumpkin Flower," he said. "Believe!"

"Believe what?" I asked.

He looked at me hard. "*Awkuh!*" he said. "That's one of the things that is wrong. Everyone questions. Everyone doubts. No one believes in the old ways anymore. They want to believe when it's convenient, when it doesn't cost them anything and they get something in return. There are no more believers. There are no more warriors. They are all gone. Those who are left only want to go to the Moon."

A car drove up outside. It was Momma and Dad. Uncle Ralph heard it too. He slumped in the chair, resigned to whatever Momma would say to him.

Momma came in first. Dad then greeted Uncle Ralph and disappeared into the back of the house. Custom and etiquette required that Dad, who was not a member of Momma's tribe, allow Momma to handle her brother's problems.

She hugged Uncle Ralph. Her eyes filled with tears when she saw how thin he was and how his hands shook.

"Ralphie,"she said, "you look awful, but I am glad to see you."

She then spoke to him of everyday things, how the car failed to start and the latest gossip. He was silent, tolerant of the passing of time in this way. His eyes sent me a pleading look while his hands shook and he tried to hold them still.

When supper was ready, Uncle Ralph went to wash himself for the meal. When he returned to the table, he was calm. His hands didn't shake so much.

At first he ate without many words, but in the course of the meal he left the table twice. Each time he came back, he was more talkative than before, answering Momma's questions in Pawnee. He left the table a third time and Dad rose.

Dad said to Momma, "He's drinking again. Can't you tell?" Dad left the table and went outside.

Momma frowned. A determined look grew on her face.

When Uncle Ralph sat down to the table once more, Momma told him, "Ralphie, you're my brother but I want you to leave now. Come back when you're sober."

He held a tarnished spoon in mid-air and put it down slowly. He hadn't finished eating, but he didn't seem to mind leaving. He stood, looked at me with his red eyes, and went to the door. Momma followed him. In a low voice she said, "Ralphie, you've got to stop drinking and wandering— or don't come to see us again."

He pulled himself to his full height then. His frame filled the doorway. He leaned over Momma and yelled, "Who are you? Are you God that you will say what will be or will not be?"

Momma met his angry eyes. She stood firm and did not back down.

His eyes finally dropped from her face to the linoleum floor. A cough came from deep in his throat.

"I'll leave here," he said. "But I'll get all my warriors and come back! I have thousands of warriors and they'll ride with me. We'll get our bows and arrows. Then we'll come back!" He staggered out the door.

In the years that followed, Uncle Ralph saw us only when he was sober. He visited less and less. When he did show up, he did a tapping ritual on our front door. We welcomed the rare visits. Occasionally he stayed at our house for a few days at a time when he was not drinking. He slept on the floor.

He did odd jobs for minimum pay but never complained about the work or money. He'd acquired a vacant look in his eyes. It was the same look that Sister and I had seen in the hobos when we were children. He wore a similar careless array of clothing and carried no property with him at all.

The last time he came to the house, he called me by my English name and asked if I remembered anything of all that he'd taught me. His hair had turned pure white. He looked older than anyone I knew. I marvelled at his appearance and said, "I remember everything." That night I pointed out his stars for him and told him how *Pahukatawa* lived and died and lived again through another's dreams. I'd grown, and Uncle Ralph could not hold me on his knee anymore. His arm circled my waist while we sat on the grass.

He was moved by my recitation and clutched my hand tightly. He said, "It's more than this. It's more than just repeating words. You know that, don't you?"

I nodded my head. "Yes, I know. The recitation is the easiest part but it's more than this, Uncle Ralph."

He was quiet, but after a few minutes his hand touched my shoulder. He said, "I couldn't make it work. I tried to fit the pieces."

"I know," I said.

"Now before I go," he said, "do you know who you are?"

The question took me by surprise. I thought very hard. I cleared my throat and told him, "I know that I am fourteen. I know that it's too young."

"Do you know that you are a Pawnee?" he asked in a choked whisper.

"Yes Uncle," I said.

"Good," he said with a long sigh that was swallowed by the night.

Then he stood and said, "Well, Sister, I have to go. Have to move on."

"Where are you going?" I asked. "Where all the warriors go?" I teased.

He managed a smile and a soft laugh. "Yeah, wherever the warriors are, I'll find them."

I said to him, "Before you go, I want to ask you. . . Uncle Ralph, can women be warriors too?"

He laughed again and hugged me merrily. "Don't tell me you want to be one of the warriors too?"

"No, Uncle," I said, "Just one of yours." I hated to let him go because I knew I would not see him again.

He pulled away. His last words were, "Don't forget what I've told you all these years. It's the only chance not to become what everyone else is. Do you understand?"

I nodded and he left.

I never saw him again.

The years passed quickly. I moved away from Momma and Dad and married. Sister left before I did.

Years later in another town, hundreds of miles away, I awoke in a terrible gloom, a sense that something was gone from the world the Pawnees knew. The despair filled days, though the reason for the sense of loss went unexplained. Finally, the telephone rang. Momma was on the line. She said, "Sister came home for a few days not too long ago. While she was here and alone, someone tapped on the door, like Ralphie always does. Sister yelled, 'Is that you, Uncle Ralphie? Come on in.' But no one entered."

Then I understood that Uncle Ralph was dead. Momma probably knew too. She wept softly into the phone.

Later Momma received an official call confirming Uncle Ralph's death. He had died from exposure in a hobo shanty, near the railroad tracks outside a tiny Oklahoma town. He'd been dead for several days and nobody knew but Momma, Sister, and me.

Momma reported to me that the funeral was well attended by the Pawnee people. Uncle Ralph and I had said our farewells years earlier. Momma told me that someone there had spoken well of Uncle Ralph before they put him in the ground. It was said that "Ralphie came from a fine family, an old line of warriors."

Ten years later, Sister and I visited briefly at Momma's and Dad's home. We had been separated by hundreds of miles for all that time. As we sat under Momma's flowering mimosa trees, I made a confession to Sister. I said, "Sometimes I wish that Uncle Ralph were here. I'm a grown woman but I still miss him after all these years."

Sister nodded her head in agreement. I continued. "He knew so many things. He knew why the sun pours its liquid all over us and why it must do just that. He knew why babes and insects crawl. He knew that we must live beautifully or not live at all."

Sister's eyes were thoughtful, but she waited to speak while I went on. "To live beautifully from day to day is a battle all the way. The things that he knew are so beautiful. And to feel and know that kind of beauty is the reason that we should live at all. Uncle Ralph said so. But now, there is no one who knows what that beauty is or any of the other things that he knew."

Sister pushed back smokey gray wisps of her dark hair. "You do," she pronounced. "And I do, too."

"Why do you suppose he left us like that?" I asked.

"It couldn't be helped," Sister said. "There was a battle on."

"I wanted to be one of his warriors," I said with an embarrassed half-smile.

She leaned over and patted my hand. "You are," she said. Then she stood and placed one hand on her bosom and one hand on my arm. "We'll carry on," she said.

I touched her hand resting on my arm. I said, "Sister, tell me again. What is the battle for?"

She looked down toward the fence where a hobo was coming through. We waved at him.

"Beauty," she said to me. "Our battle is for beauty. It's what Uncle Ralph fought for, too. He often said that everyone else just wanted to go to the Moon. But remember, Sister, you and I done been there. Don't forget, after all, we're children of the stars."

Zitkala-Sa [Gertrude Bonnin] (Sioux)

The Soft-Hearted Sioux

I

Beside the open fire I sat within our tepee. With my red blanket wrapped tightly about my crossed legs, I was thinking of the coming season, my sixteenth winter. On either side of the wigwam were my parents. My father was whistling a tune between his teeth while polishing with his bare hand a red stone pipe he had recently carved. Almost in front of me, beyond the centre fire, my old grandmother sat near the entranceway.

She turned her face toward her right and addressed most of her words to my mother. Now and then she spoke to me, but never did she allow her eyes to rest upon her daughter's husband, my father. It was only upon rare occasions that my grandmother said anything to him. Thus his ears were open and ready to catch the smallest wish she might express. Sometimes when my grandmother had been saying things which pleased him, my father used to comment upon them. At other times, when he could not approve of what was spoken, he used to work or smoke silently.

On this night my old grandmother began her talk about me. Filling the bowl of her red stone pipe with dry willow bark, she looked across at me.

"My grandchild, you are tall and are no longer a little boy." Narrowing her old eyes, she asked, "My grandchild, when are you going to bring here a handsome young woman?" I stared into the fire rather than meet her gaze. Waiting for my answer, she stooped forward and through the long stem drew a flame into the red stone pipe.

I smiled while my eyes were still fixed upon the bright fire, but I said nothing in reply. Turning to my mother, she offered her the pipe. I glanced at my grandmother. The loose buckskin sleeve fell off at her elbow and showed a wrist covered with silver bracelets. Holding up the fingers of her left hand, she named off the desirable young women of our village.

"Which one, my grandchild, which one?" she questioned.

"Hoh!" I said, pulling at my blanket in confusion. "Not yet!" Here my mother passed the pipe over the fire to my father. Then she too began speaking of what I should do.

"My son, be always active. Do not dislike a long hunt. Learn to provide much buffalo meat and many buckskins before you bring home a wife." Presently my father gave the pipe to my grandmother, and he took his turn in the exhortations.

"Ho, my son, I have been counting in my heart the bravest warriors of our people. There is not one of them who won his title in his sixteenth winter. My son, it is a great thing for some brave of sixteen winters to do."

Not a word had I to give in answer. I knew well the fame of my warrior father. He had earned the right of speaking such words, though even he himself was a brave only at my age. Refusing to smoke my grandmother's pipe because my heart was too much stirred by their words, and sorely troubled with a fear lest I should disappoint them, I arose to go. Drawing my blanket over my shoulders, I said, as I stepped toward the entranceway: "I go to hobble my pony. It is now late in the night."

II

Nine winters' snows had buried deep that night when my old grandmother, together with my father and mother, designed my future with the glow of a camp fire upon it.

Yet I did not grow up the warrior, huntsman, and husband I was to have been. At the mission school I learned it was wrong to kill. Nine winters I hunted for the soft heart of Christ, and prayed for the huntsmen who chased the buffalo on the plains.

In the autumn of the tenth year I was sent back to my tribe to preach Christianity to them. With the white man's Bible in my hand, and the white man's tender heart in my breast, I returned to my own people.

Wearing a foreigner's dress, I walked, a stranger, into my father's village.

Asking my way, for I had not forgotten my native tongue, an old man led me toward the tepee where my father lay. From my old companion I learned that my father had been sick many moons. As we drew near the tepee, I heard the chanting of a medicine-man within it. At once I wished to enter in and drive from my home the sorcerer of the plains, but the old warrior checked me. "Ho, wait outside until the medicine-man leaves your father," he said. While talking he scanned me from head to feet. Then he retraced his steps toward the heart of the camping-ground.

My father's dwelling was on the outer limits of the round-faced village. With every heart-throb I grew more impatient to enter the wigwam.

While I turned the leaves of my Bible with nervous fingers, the medicine-man came forth from the dwelling and walked hurriedly away. His head and face were closely covered with the loose robe which draped his entire figure.

He was tall and large. His long strides I have never forgot. They seemed to me then as the uncanny gait of eternal death. Quickly pocketing my Bible, I went into the tepee.

Upon a mat lay my father, with furrowed face and gray hair. His eyes and cheeks were sunken far into his head. His sallow skin lay thin upon his pinched nose and high cheek-bones. Stooping over him, I took his fevered hand. "How, Ate?" I greeted him. A light flashed from his listless eyes and his dried lips parted. "My son!" he murmured, in a feeble voice. Then again the wave of joy and recognition receded. He closed his eyes, and his hand dropped from my open palm to the ground.

Looking about, I saw an old woman sitting with bowed head. Shaking hands with her, I recognized my mother. I sat down between my father and mother as I used to do, but I did not feel at home. The place where my old grandmother used to sit was now unoccupied. With my mother I bowed my head. Alike our throats were choked and tears were streaming from our eyes; but far apart in spirit our ideas and faiths separated us. My grief was for the soul unsaved; and I thought my mother wept to see a brave man's body broken by sickness.

Useless was my attempt to change the faith in the medicine-man to that abstract power named God. Then one day I became righteously mad with anger that the medicine-man should thus ensnare my father's soul. And when he came to chant his sacred songs I pointed toward the door and bade him go! The man's eyes glared upon me for an instant. Slowly gathering his robe about him, he turned his back upon the sick man and stepped out of our wigwam. "Hā, hā, hā! my son, I cannot live without the medicine-man!" I heard my father cry when the sacred man was gone.

III

On a bright day, when the winged seeds of the prairie-grass were flying hither and thither, I walked solemnly toward the centre of the camping-ground. My heart beat hard and irregularly at my side. Tighter I grasped the sacred book I carried under my arm. Now was the beginning of life's work.

Though I knew it would be hard, I did not once feel that failure was to be my reward. As I stepped unevenly on the rolling ground, I thought of the warriors soon to wash off their war-paints and follow me.

At length I reached the place where the people had assembled to hear me preach. In a large circle men and women sat upon the dry red grass. Within the ring I stood, with the white man's Bible in my hand. I tried to tell them of the soft heart of Christ.

In silence the vast circle of bareheaded warriors sat under an afternoon sun. At last, wiping the wet from my brow, I took my place in the ring. The hush of the assembly filled me with great hope.

I was turning my thoughts upward to the sky in gratitude, when a stir called me to earth again.

A tall, strong man arose. His loose robe hung in folds over his right shoulder. A pair of snapping black eyes fastened themselves like the poisonous fangs of a serpent upon me. He was the medicine-man. A tremor played about my heart and a chill cooled the fire in my veins.

Scornfully he pointed a long forefinger in my direction and asked,

"What loyal son is he who, returning to his father's people, wears a foreigner's dress?" He paused a moment, and then continued: "The dress of that foreigner of whom a story says he bound a native of our land, and heaping dry sticks around him, kindled a fire at his feet!" Waving his hand toward me, he exclaimed, "Here is the traitor to his people!"

I was helpless. Before the eyes of the crowd the cunning magician turned my honest heart into a vile nest of treachery. Alas! the people frowned as they looked upon me.

"Listen!" he went on. "Which one of you who have eyed the young man can see through his bosom and warn the people of the nest of young snakes hatching there? Whose ear was so acute that he caught the hissing of snakes whenever the young man opened his mouth? This one has not only proven false to you, but even to the Great Spirit who made him. He is a fool! Why do you sit here giving ear to a foolish man who could not defend his people because he fears to kill, who could not bring venison to renew the life of his sick father? With his prayers, let him drive away the enemy! With his soft heart, let him keep off starvation! We shall go elsewhere to dwell upon an untainted ground."

With this he disbanded the people. When the sun lowered in the west and the winds were quiet, the village of cone-shaped tepees was gone. The medicine-man had won the hearts of the people.

Only my father's dwelling was left to mark the fighting-ground.

IV

From a long night at my father's bedside I came out to look upon the morning. The yellow sun hung equally between the snow-covered land and the cloudless blue sky. The light of the new day was cold. The strong breath of winter crusted the snow and fitted crystal shells over the rivers and lakes. As I stood in front of the tepee, thinking of the vast prairies which separated us from our tribe, and wondering if the high sky likewise separated the soft-hearted Son of God from us, the icy blast from the north blew through my hair and skull. My neglected hair had grown long and fell upon my neck.

My father had not risen from his bed since the day the medicine-man led the people away. Though I read from the Bible and prayed beside him upon my knees, my father would not listen. Yet I believed my prayers were not unheeded in heaven.

"Hā, hā, hā! my son," my father groaned upon the first snowfall. "My son, our food is gone. There is no one to bring me meat! My son, your soft heart has unfitted you for everything!" Then covering his face with the buffalo-robe, he said no more. Now while I stood out in that cold winter morning, I was starving. For two days I had not seen any food. But my own cold and hunger did not harass my soul as did the whining cry of the sick old man.

Stepping again into the tepee, I untied my snow-shoes, which were fastened to the tent-poles.

My poor mother, watching by the sick one, and faithfully heaping wood upon the centre fire, spoke to me:

"My son, do not fail again to bring your father meat, or he will starve to death."

"How, Ina," I answered, sorrowfully. From the tepee I started forth again to hunt food for my aged parents. All day I tracked the white level lands in vain. Nowhere, nowhere were there any other footprints but my own! In the evening of this third fast-day I came back without meat. Only a bundle of sticks for the fire I brought on my back. Dropping the wood outside, I lifted the door-flap and set one foot within the tepee.

There I grew dizzy and numb. My eyes swam in tears. Before me lay my old gray-haired father sobbing like a child. In his horny hands he clutched the buffalo-robe, and with his teeth he was gnawing off the edges. Chewing the dry stiff hair and buffalo-skin, my father's eyes sought my hands. Upon seeing them empty, he cried out:

"My son, your soft heart will let me starve before you bring me meat! Two hills eastward stand a herd of cattle. Yet you will see me die before you bring me food!"

Leaving my mother lying with covered head upon her mat, I rushed out into the night.

With a strange warmth in my heart and swiftness in my feet, I climbed over the first hill, and soon the second one. The moonlight upon the white country showed me a clear path to the white man's cattle. With my hand upon the knife in my belt, I leaned heavily against the fence while counting the herd.

Twenty in all I numbered. From among them I chose the best-fattened creature. Leaping over the fence, I plunged my knife into it.

My long knife was sharp, and my hands, no more fearful and slow, slashed off choice chunks of warm flesh. Bending under the meat I had taken for my starving father, I hurried across the prairie.

Toward home I fairly ran with the life-giving food I carried upon my back. Hardly had I climbed the second hill when I heard sounds coming after me. Faster and faster I ran with my load for my father, but the sounds were gaining upon me. I heard the clicking of snowshoes and the squeaking of the leather straps at my heels; yet I did not turn to see what pursued me, for I was intent upon reaching my father. Suddenly like thunder an angry voice shouted curses and threats into my ear! A rough hand wrenched my shoulder and took the meat from me! I stopped struggling to run. A deafening whir filled my head. The moon and stars began to move. Now the white prairie was sky, and the stars lay under my feet. Now again they were turning. At last the starry blue rose up into place. The noise in my ears was still. A great quiet filled the air. In my hand I found my long knife dripping with blood. At my feet a man's figure lay prone in blood-red snow. The horrible scene about me seemed a trick of my senses, for I could not understand it was real. Looking long upon the blood-stained snow, the load of meat for my starving father reached my recognition at last. Quickly I tossed it over my shoulder and started again homeward.

Tired and haunted I reached the door of the wigwam. Carrying the food before me, I entered with it into the tepee.

"Father, here is food!" I cried, as I dropped the meat near my mother. No answer came. Turning about, I beheld my gray-haired father dead! I saw by the unsteady firelight an old gray-haired skeleton lying rigid and stiff.

Out into the open I started, but the snow at my feet became bloody.

V

On the day after my father's death, having led my mother to the camp of the medicine-man, I gave myself up to those who were searching for the murderer of the paleface.

They bound me hand and foot. Here in this cell I was placed four days ago.

The shrieking winter winds have followed me hither. Rattling the bars, they howl unceasingly: "Your soft heart! Your soft heart will see me die before you bring me food!" Hark! something is clanking the chain on the door. It is being opened. From the dark night without a black figure crosses the threshold. * * * It is the guard. He comes to warn me of my fate. He tells me that tomorrow I must die. In his stern face I laugh aloud. I do not fear death.

Yet I wonder who shall come to welcome me in the realm of strange sight. Will the loving Jesus grant me pardon and give my soul a soothing sleep? or will my warrior father greet me and receive me as his son? Will my spirit fly upward to a happy heaven? or shall I sink into the bottomless pit, an outcast from a God of infinite love?

Soon, soon I shall know, for now I see the east is growing red. My heart is strong. My face is calm. My eyes are dry and eager for new scenes. My hands hang quietly at my side. Serene and brave, my soul awaits the men to perch me on the gallows for another flight. I go.

POETRY

The Possibilities of a Native Poetics

by Kimberly Blaeser

Everyone laughed at the impossibility of it,
but also the truth. Because who would believe
the fantastic and terrible story of all of our survival
those who were never meant

to survive?

"Anchorage"
—Joy Harjo

Of the twenty some poets whose work is included in this volume, all but one is still living and publishing as I write in this the new millennium. American Indian people are not only surviving, but thriving in the richness of their literature and in the vivid memories depicted here. For the poems included give voice not only to the experiences of the contemporary authors themselves, but extend themselves in subject, imagery, and form to forge connections with the literary and cultural history of tribal communities everywhere. From Maurice Kenny's vivid imaginative portrait of the death of "Blackrobe," Father Isaac Joques the seventeenth century Jesuit missionary among the Mohawks, in "Wolf'Aunt,' " to Louise Erdrich's playful trickster account in the narrative poem "Old Man Potchiko," to incantatory selections like Peter Blue Cloud's "Rattle," the poetry constructs its meaning within the continuum of Native reality. And although American Indian poets have firmly established themselves within the larger American and World canons, read together, their works forcefully attest to the possibilities of a Native poetics infused with echoes of the song poems and ceremonial literatures of the tribes, born out of the indigenous revolution, filled with the dialogues of intertextuality, sometimes linked to the cadences and constructions of "an-other" language, frequently self-conscious, and often resistant to genre distinctions and formal structures.

Native poetry's first appearance in print came as the result of a dual translation: from oral to written, from tribal language to English. In many instances the translation required to fully render the meaning and significance was never completed. By this I mean to suggest that many early works were sifted from their cultural context, displayed in a textual and secular nakedness that ignored the performed quality or distorted the sacred layers of ceremonial poetry. Few versions of traditional songs or poems suggested the language, music, ritual, and history of the original. Perhaps in response to this early wrestling of tribal literatures from their cultural contexts, many contemporary writers profess a certain literary sovereignty and self-consciously work to produce a community based poetry.

Still the early interest in American Indian poetry was immense, and our libraries and archives contain a myriad of transcriptions in a variety of forms from those which include musical notation like the work of Frances Densmore to text-only translations like the materials collected in Margot Astrov's *The Winged Serpent*. Perhaps because the publication of original poetry by individuals of Native American ancestry was not great during the first half of the twentieth century, selections from these early translations were reprinted with some regularity in anthologies. Then on the heels of what has come to be called the renaissance of American Indian Literature in the late 1960's, a group of writers, many of whom had already published in fiction, began a small revolution in poetry. First in chapbooks, then in small press anthologies like *Come to Power* (The Crossing Press, 1974), and finally in large press anthologies like *Voices of the Rainbow* (Viking/Seaver Books, 1975) and *Carriers of the Dream Wheel* (Harper, 1975), the voices still associated with Native poetry today began to surface: Duane Niatum, Joseph Bruchac, Leslie Silko, James Welch, Simon Ortiz, Roberta Whiteman, Ray Young Bear, Gerald Vizenor, Wendy Rose, N. Scott Momaday, Lance Henson, Anita Andrezze, Carter Revard. . . . By the time Bruchac edited *Songs from this Earth on Turtle's Back* in 1983, the number represented there had swelled to fifty-two. The Native poetic revolution has continued to grow in both mainstream and small presses and the voices represented in this anthology are only a small number of the contemporary Indian poets publishing today.

Comparatively little in depth interpretation or criticism has been written about Native American poetry. Although articles have been devoted to the work of one or another poet and individual writers have garnered attention for their canon of work (which generally includes several genres), I know of no book length study devoted entirely to the poetic work of a single Native writer. In fact, the first book length analytical discussion of American Indian poetry that I am aware of—*The Heart as a Drum: Continuance and Resistance in American Indian Poetry* (Robin Fast)—was released January 5, 2000.

Despite this apparent dearth of critical analyses, certain facets of Indian-authored poetry have been frequently acknowledged. Most notably, the poems have been recognized to have a significant spiritual and physical landscape, to invest themselves in a political struggle, to search for or attempt to articulate connections with the individual, tribal, or pan-Indian legacy, and—particularly significant to the poetic form—to retain connections to the oral tradition. I would like to suggest at least one other significant facet: the poems are to a greater or lesser degree also engaged in framing a response to the perceived expectations of Native American Literature.

In "How to Write the Great American Indian Novel," Sherman Alexie satirizes the stereotypic expectations of American Indian literature claiming that such a novel must have Indians with tragic features, a half-breed protagonist, visions, alcohol, beautiful Indian women, Indian men from horse cultures, and a requisite tragedy like murder or suicide. We might add war veterans, bits of Native language, ceremony and a wise elder! But in all seriousness, I believe American Indian Literatures (plural) have become aware of the expectations placed upon Indigenous Literature (the single entity) and have responded in some fashion so that what has evolved is what Louis Owens calls metanarratives. There is a certain inevitable self consciousness present, a constant need to respond to or to interrogate the desire for commodification of Native traditions, both literary and non-literary. Geary Hobson and Leslie Silko addressed such issues as early as 1979 in essays dealing with white shamanism in *The Remembered Earth* anthology, Hobson in "The Rise of the White Shaman as a New Version of Cultural Imperialism" and Silko in "An Old Time Indian Attack Conducted in Two Parts." There is a continual attempt, these and other authors suggest, first to simplify Native experiences and to pigeonhole tribal literatures, then to imitate the stereotypical idea of a Native literature. American Indian Literatures find themselves the object of a sometimes desperate search for a certain kind of "authenticity" in literature that borders on the romantic.

The poetry, however, must be allowed its complexity, its multiple layers of connection and reality. The poets and the poems are individual, displaying their own particular voices, methods, themes. Although thematically, and sometimes stylistically, similarities surface, the poems are neither solely wedded to a Native literary aesthetic (however we might define it), nor do they operate completely separately from the Native literary and cultural traditions. The writers in this volume emerge from a range of different physical and physic places on the map of Indian literature. At the same time, the selections from their work do illustrate several important continuities in what I am suggesting might be called a Native poetics. Still these continuities exist simultaneously with deep and significant variations.

It would, for example, be difficult for one to mistake the prose poems of N. Scott Momaday included here in "The Colors of Night" for those say of Joy Harjo as represented here by "Grace." Though both poets are writing in a narrative mode in these instances, the diction, cadence, and timbre of their works distinguish them. When Momaday writes, "One night there appeared a child in the camp," or "Thereafter, wherever the old man ventured, he led a dark hunting horse which bore the bones of his son on its back," the lines have a sparse lyricism and a certain formality or an archaic quality tied to word order and sentence structure which we recognize as characteristic of his style. When Harjo writes, "We had to swallow that town with laughter, so it would go down easy as honey," or "I could say grace was a woman with time on her hands, or a white buffalo escaped from memory. But in that dingy light it was a promise of balance," we likewise recognize a certain informality of phrase, and a power achieved through the accumulation of unusual imagery that we associate with Harjo. Both writers, both poems, invest themselves in a connection with the oral tradition through the process of storytelling, by forging links to older stories, and through their preoccupation with sound. Both authors give important attention in the poems to the rendering of place. Both employ personification (Age, Grace). Both establish a tribal milieu. The similarities are many and many of them might position these poems within the genre of Native poetics. However, the distinctions are likewise great and establish the writers and poems as individual. Gathering an understanding of what might constitute a Native poetics goes a long way in assisting us in the reading of the poems in this volume. It does not take us the full way. The poetry must be allowed its complexity.

Poems like Paula Gunn Allen's "Dear World" and Linda Hogan's "The Truth Is" do deal with the mixedblood reality Alexie playfully recognizes as a prerequisite for "great" Indian literature. So does Alexie's own "13/16." Poems like Simon Ortiz's "Bend in the River" and Carter Revard's "Wazhazhe Grandmother" offer fine examples of the investment in and embodiment of place in American Indian poetry. Wendy Rose's "Three Thousand Dollar Death Song" is written as political protest. Indeed, within this small sampling of Native poetry, we can locate most of the facets associated with the genre. We can also locate the differences, the marks of an individual voice: the arresting imagery tied to dreams in Ray Young Bear's poems, the anecdotal humor in Luci Tapahonso's, the autobiographical strains in Roberta Whiteman's. This intricate weaving of Native traditions and consciousness with individual experiences and identities creates a richness in contemporary Indian poetry. The poems carry history, and therefore perspective, into their encounters with language and life. They also carry the will to survive. Perhaps the most significant facet of a Native Poetics involves the impetus to rise off the page, to teach, to incite continuance. As Linda Hogan writes in "Neighbors," "This is the truth, not just a poem." The questions Chrystos raises in "Today Was a Bad Day Like TB" are not merely rhetorical, they are revolutionary. The threats to ecological survival depicted in Leslie Silko's "Long Time Ago," are not mere fantasy, they are frighteningly prophetic. The poetry finds its place in the realms of literature and life; the poets demand that we grant it both realms. As Linda Hogan also writes: "This is a poem and not just the truth."

Sherman Alexie (Spokane, Coeur d'Alene)

13/16

1.

I cut myself into sixteen equal pieces
keep thirteen and feed the other three
to the dogs, who have also grown

tired of U.S. Commodities, white cans
black letters translated into Spanish.
"Does this mean I have to learn

the language to eat?" Lester FallsApart asks
but directions for preparation are simple:
a. WASH CAN; b. OPEN CAN; c. EXAMINE CONTENTS

OF CAN FOR SPOILAGE; d. EMPTY CONTENTS
OF CAN INTO SAUCE PAN; e. COOK CONTENTS
OVER HIGH HEAT; f. SERVE AND EAT.

2.

It is done by blood, reservation mathematics, fractions:
father (full-blood) + mother (5/8) = son (13/16).

It is done by enrollment number, last name first, first name last:
Spokane Tribal Enrollment Number 1569; Victor, Chief.

It is done by identification card, photograph, lamination:
IF FOUND, PLEASE RETURN TO SPOKANE TRIBE OF INDIANS,
    WELLPINIT, WA.

3.

The compromise is always made
in increments. On this reservation
we play football on real grass
dream of deserts, three inches of rain

in a year. What we have lost:
uranium mine, Little Falls Dam

salmon. Our excuses are trapped
within museums, roadside attractions

totem poles in Riverfront Park.
I was there, watching the Spokane River
changing. A ten-year-old white boy asked
if I was a real Indian. He did not wait

for an answer, instead carving his initials
into the totem with a pocketknife: J.N.
We are what we take, carving my name
my enrollment number, thirteen hash marks

into the wood. A story is remembered
as evidence, the Indian man they found dead
shot in the alley behind the Mayfair.
Authorities reported a rumor he had relatives

in Minnesota. A member of some tribe or another
his photograph on the 11 o'clock news. Eyes, hair
all dark, his shovel-shaped incisor, each the same
ordinary identification of the anonymous.

4.

When my father disappeared, we found him
years later, in a strange kitchen searching
for footprints in the dust: still

untouched on the shelves all the commodity
cans without labels—my father opened them
one by one, finding a story in each.

The Business of Fancydancing

After driving all night, trying to reach
Arlee in time for the fancydance
finals, a case of empty
beer bottles shaking our foundations, we
stop at a liquor store, count out money,
and would believe in the promise

of any man with a twenty, a promise
thin and wrinkled in his hand, reaching into the window of our car. Money
is an Indian Boy who can fancydance
from powwow to powwow. We
got our boy, Vernon WildShoe, to fill our empty

wallets and stomachs, to fill our empty
cooler. Vernon is like some promise
to pay the light bill, a credit card we
Indians get to use. When he reach-
es his hands up, feathers held high, in a dance
that makes old women speak English, the money

for first place belongs to us, all in cash, money
we tuck in our shoes, leaving our wallets empty
in case we pass out. At the modern dance,
where Indians dance white, a twenty is a promise
that can last all night long, a promise reaching into back pockets of unfamiliar Levis. We

get Vernon there in time for the finals and we
watch him like he was dancing on money,
which he is, watch the young girls reaching for him like he was Elvis in braids and an empty
tipi, like Vernon could make a promise
with every step he took, like a fancydance

could change their lives. We watch him dance
and he never talks. It's all a business we
understand. Every drum beat is a promise
note written in the dust, measured exactly. Money
is a tool, putty to fill all the empty
spaces, a ladder so we can reach

for more. A promise is just like money.
Something we can hold, in twenties, a dream we reach.
It's business, a fancydance to fill where it's empty.

Capital Punishment

I prepare the last meal
for the Indian man to be executed

but this killer doesn't want much:
baked potato, salad, tall glass of ice water.

(I am not a witness)

It's mostly the dark ones
who are forced to sit in the chair

especially when white people die.
It's true, you can look it up

and this Indian killer pushed
his fist all the way down

a white man's throat, just to win a bet
about the size of his heart.

Those Indians are always gambling.
Still, I season this last meal

with all I have. I don't have much
but I send it down the line

with the handsome guard
who has fallen in love

with the Indian killer.
I don't care who loves whom.

(I am not a witness)

When it's the warden's stew I don't care
if I add too much salt or pepper.

For the boss I just cook.
He can eat what I put in front of him

but for the Indian man to be executed
I cook just right.

The temperature is the thing.
I once heard a story

about a black man who was electrocuted
in that chair and lived to tell about it

before the court decided to sit him back down
an hour later and kill him all over again.

I have an extra sandwich hidden away
in the back of the refrigerator

in case this Indian killer survives
that first slow flip of the switch

and gets hungry while he waits
for the engineers to debate the flaws.

(I am not a witness)

I prepare the last meal for free
just like I signed up for the last war.

I learned how to cook
by lasting longer than any of the others.

Tonight, I'm just the last one left
after the handsome guard takes the meal away.

I turn off the kitchen lights
and sit alone in the dark

because the whole damn prison dims
when the chair is switched on.

You can watch a light bulb flicker
on a night like this

and remember it too clearly
like it was your first kiss

or the first hard kick to your groin.
It's all the same

when I am huddled down here
trying not to look at the clock

look at the clock, no, don't
look at the clock, when all of it stops

making sense: a salad, a potato
a drink of water all taste like heat.

(I am not a witness)

I want you to know I tasted a little
of that last meal before I sent it away.

It's the cook's job, to make sure
and I was sure I ate from the same plate

and ate with the same fork and spoon
that the Indian killer used later

in his cell. Maybe a little piece of me
lodged in his mouth, wedged between

his front teeth, his incisors, his molars
when he chewed down on the bit

and his body arced like modern art
curving organically, smoke rising

from his joints, wispy flames decorating
the crown of his head, the balls of his feet.

(I am not a witness)

I sit here in the dark kitchen
when they do it, meaning

when they kill him, kill
and add another definition of the word

to the dictionary. America fills
its dictionary. We write down kill and everybody

in the audience shouts out exactly how
they spell it, what it means to them

and all of the answers are taken down
by the pollsters and secretaries

who keep track of the small details:
time of death, pulse rate, press release.

I heard a story once about some reporters
at a hanging who wanted the hood removed

from the condemned's head, so they could look
into his eyes and tell their readers

what they saw there. What did they expect?
All of the stories should be simple.

1 death + 1 death = 2 deaths.
But we throw the killers in one grave

and victims in another. We form sides

have two separate feasts.

(I am a witness)

I prepared the last meal
for the Indian man who was executed

and have learned this: If any of us
stood for days on top of a barren hill

during an electrical storm
then lightning would eventually strike us

and we'd have no idea for which of our sins
we were reduced to headlines and ash.

Defending Walt Whitman

Basketball is like this for young Indian boys, all arms and legs
and serious stomach muscles. Every body is brown!
These are the twentieth-century warriors who will never kill,
although a few sat quietly in the deserts of Kuwait,
waiting for orders to do something, do something.

God, there is nothing as beautiful as a jump shot
on a reservation summer basketball court
where the ball is moist with sweat
and makes a sound when it swishes through the net
that causes Walt Whitman to weep because it is so perfect.

There are veterans of foreign wars here,
whose bodies are still dominated
by collarbones and knees, whose bodies still respond
in the ways that bodies are supposed to respond when we are young.
Every body is brown! Look there, that boy can run
up and down this court forever. He can leap for a rebound
with his back arched like a salmon, all meat and bone
synchronized, magnetic, as if the court were a river,
as if the rim were a dam, as if the air were a ladder
leading the Indian boy toward home.

Some of the Indian boys still wear their military haircuts
while a few have let their hair grow back.
It will never be the same as it was before!
One Indian boy has never cut his hair, not once, and he braids it
into wild patterns that do not measure anything.
He is just a boy with too much time on his hands.
Look at him. He wants to play this game in bare feet.

God, the sun is so bright! There is no place like this.
Walt Whitman stretches his calf muscles
on the sidelines. He has the next game.
His huge beard is ridiculous on the reservation.
Some body throws a crazy pass and Walt Whitman catches it with
    quick hands.
He brings the ball close to his nose
and breathes in all of its smells: leather, brown skin, sweat, black hair,
burning oil, twisted ankle, long drink of warm water,
gunpowder, pine tree. Walt Whitman squeezes the ball tightly.
He wants to run. He hardly has the patience to wait for his turn.
"What's the score?" he asks. He asks, "What's the score?"

Basketball is like this for Walt Whitman. He watches these Indian boys
as if they were the last bodies on earth. Every body is brown!
Walt Whitman shakes because he believes in God.
Walt Whitman dreams of the Indian boy who will defend him,
trapping him in the corner, all flailing arms and legs
and legendary stomach muscles. Walt Whitman shakes
because he believes in God. Walt Whitman dreams
of the first jump shot he will take, the ball arcing clumsily
from his fingers, striking the rim so hard that it sparks.
Walt Whitman shakes because he believes in God.
Walt Whitman closes his eyes. He is a small man and his beard
is ludicrous on the reservation, absolutely insane.

His beard makes the Indian boys laugh righteously. His beard frightens
the smallest Indian boys. His beard tickles the skin
of the Indian boys who dribble past him. His beard, his beard!

God, there is beauty in every body. Walt Whitman stands
at center court while the Indian boys run from basket to basket.
Walt Whitman cannot tell the difference between
offense and defense. He does not care if he touches the ball.
Half of the Indian boys wear T-shirts damp with sweat
and the other half are bareback, skin slick and shiny.
There is no place like this. Walt Whitman smiles.
Walt Whitman shakes. This game belongs to him.

The Exaggeration of Despair

I open the door

(this Indian girl writes that her brother tried to hang himself
with a belt just two weeks after her other brother did hang himself

and this Indian man tells us that, back in boarding school,
five priests took him into a back room and raped him repeatedly

and this homeless Indian woman begs for quarters, and when I ask
her about her tribe, she says she's horny and bends over in front of
    me

and this homeless Indian man is the uncle of an Indian man
who writes for a large metropolitan newspaper, and so now I know
    them both

and this Indian child cries when he sits to eat at our table
because he had never known his own family to sit at the same table

and this Indian woman was born to an Indian woman
who sold her for a six-pack and a carton of cigarettes

and this Indian poet shivers beneath the freeway
and begs for enough quarters to buy pencil and paper

and this fancydancer passes out at the powwow
and wakes up naked, with no memory of the evening, all of his re-
    galia gone)

I open the door

(and this is my sister, who waits years for a dead eagle from the Park
    Service, receives it
and stores it with our cousins, who then tell her it has disappeared

though the feathers reappear in the regalia of another cousin
who is dancing for the very first time

and this is my father, whose own father died on Okinawa, shot
by a Japanese soldier who must have looked so much like him

and this is my father, whose mother died of tuberculosis
not long after he was born, and so my father must hear coughing ghosts

and this is my grandmother who saw, before the white men came,
three ravens with white necks, and knew our God was going to change)

I open the door
and invite the wind inside.

How to Write the Great American Indian Novel

All of the Indians must have tragic features: tragic noses, eyes, and arms.
Their hands and fingers must be tragic when they reach for tragic food.

The hero must be a half-breed, half white and half Indian, preferably
from a horse culture. He should often weep alone. That is mandatory.

If the hero is an Indian woman, she is beautiful. She must be slender
and in love with a white man. But if she loves an Indian man

then he must be a half-breed, preferably from a horse culture.
If the Indian woman loves a white man, then he has to be so white

that we can see the blue veins running through his skin like rivers.
When the Indian woman steps out of her dress, the white man gasps

at the endless beauty of her brown skin. She should be compared to
      nature:
brown hills, mountains, fertile valleys, dewy grass, wind, and clear water.

If she is compared to murky water, however, then she must have a
      secret.
Indians always have secrets, which are carefully and slowly revealed.

Yet Indian secrets can be disclosed suddenly, like a storm.
Indian men, of course, are storms. They should destroy the lives

of any white women who choose to love them. All white women love
Indian men. That is always the case. White women feign disgust

at the savage in blue jeans and T-shirt, but secretly lust after him.
White women dream about half-breed Indian men from horse cultures.

Indian men are horses, smelling wild and gamey. When the Indian man
unbuttons his pants, the white woman should think of topsoil.

There must be one murder, one suicide, one attempted rape.
Alcohol should be consumed. Cars must be driven at high speeds.

Indians must see visions. White people can have the same visions
if they are in love with Indians. If a white person loves an Indian

then the white person is Indian by proximity. White people must carry
an Indian deep inside themselves. Those interior Indians are half-breed

and obviously from horse cultures. If the interior Indian is male
then he must be a warrior, especially if he is inside a white man.

If the interior Indian is female, then she must be a healer, especially if
      she is inside
a white woman. Sometimes there are complications.

An Indian man can be hidden inside a white woman. An Indian
      woman
can be hidden inside a white man. In these rare instances,

everybody is a half-breed struggling to learn more about his or her
      horse culture.

There must be redemption, of course, and sins must be forgiven.

For this, we need children. A white child and an Indian child, gender not important, should express deep affection in a childlike way.

In the Great American Indian novel, when it is finally written,
all of the white people will be Indians and all of the Indians will be
    ghosts.

Crazy Horse Speaks

1.

I discovered the evidence
in a vault of The Mormon Church
3,000 skeletons of my cousins
in a silence so great
I built four walls around it
and gave it a name.
I called it Custer
and he came to me
again in a dream.
He forgave all my sins.

2.

Little Big Horn
Little Big Horn does not belong to me.
I was there
my horse exploded under me.
I searched for Long Hair
the man you call Custer
the man I call My Father.
But it wasn't me who killed him
it was _____
who cut off his head
and left the body for proof.
I dream of him
and search doorways and alleys
for his grave.
General George Armstrong Custer
my heart is beating
survive   survive   survive.

3.

I wear the color of my skin
like a brown paper bag
wrapped around a bottle.
Sleeping between
the pages of dictionaries
your language cuts
tears holes in my tongue
until I do not have strength
to use the word "love."
What could it mean
in this city where everyone is
Afraid-of-Horses?

4.

There are places I cannot leave.
Rooms without doors or windows
the eternal ribcage.
I sat across the fire
from Sitting Bull
shared smoke and eyes.
We both saw the same thing
our futures tight and small
an 8 1/2 by 11 dream
called the reservation.
We had no alternatives
but to fight again and again
live our lives on horseback.
After The Civil War
the number of Indian warriors
in The West doubled
tripled the number of soldiers
but Indians never have shared
the exact skin
never the same home.

5.

History.
History is never the truth.
So much can happen
in the space between
touching and becoming.
I dream custer
walking along the hills

of Little Big Horn
counting blades of grass
trying to find some measurement
of why he fell.
I tell him the exact number
and the story
about the grandmother
the mother and the daughter
who did the counting
each growing larger
and larger with every word.

6.

I am the mirror
practicing masks
and definitions.
I have always wanted to be anonymous
instead of the crazy skin
who rode his horse backwards
and laid down alone.
It was never easy
to be frightened
by the sound of a color.
I can still hear white
it is the sound
of glass shattering.

7.

I hear the verdict
in the museum in New York
where five Eskimo were flown in
to be a living exhibit.
Three died within days
lacking natural immunity
their hearts miles
and miles of thin ice.
The three dead Eskimo
were stuffed and mounted
hunched over a fishing hole
next to the two living
who held their thin hands
close to their chests
mortal and sinless.

8.

> Whenever it all begins again
> I will be waiting.

Paula Gunn Allen (Laguna Pueblo, Sioux)

Dear World

Mother has lupus.
She says it's a disease
of self-attack.
It's like a mugger broke into your home
and you called the police
and when they came they beat up on you
instead of on your attackers,
she says.

I say that makes sense.
It's in the blood,
in the dynamic.
A half-breed woman
can hardly do anything else
but attack herself,
her blood attacks itself.
There are historical reasons
for this.

I know you can't make peace
being Indian and white.
They cancel each other out.
Leaving no one in the place.
And somebody's gotta be there,
to take care of the house,
to provide the food.
And that's gotta be the mother.
But if she's gone to war.
If she's beaten and robbed.
If she's attacked by everyone.
Conquered, occupied, destroyed
by her own blood's diverse strains,
its conflicting stains?

Well, world. What's to be done?
We just wait and see
what will happen next.
The old ways go,
tormented in the fires of disease.
My mother's eyes burn,
they tear themselves apart.
Her skin darkens in her fire's heat,
her joints swell to the point
of explosion, eruption.
And oh, the ache: her lungs
don't want to take in more air,
refuse further oxygenation:
in such circumstances,
when volatile substances are intertwined,
when irreconcilable opposites meet,
the crucible and its contents vaporize.

Kopis'taya, A Gathering of Spirits

Because we live in the browning season
the heavy air blocking our breath,
and in this time when living
is only survival, we doubt the voices
that come shadowed on the air,
that weave within our brains
certain thoughts, a motion that is soft,
imperceptible, a twilight rain,
soft feather's fall, a small body dropping
into its nest, rustling, murmuring, settling
in for the night.

Because we live in the hardedged season,
where plastic brittle and gleaming shine,
and in this space that is cornered and angled,
we do not notice wet, moist, the significant
drops falling in perfect spheres
that are the certain measures of our minds;
almost invisible, those tears,
soft as dew, fragile, that cling to leaves,
petals, roots, gentle and sure,
every morning.

We are the women of the daylight, of clocks
and steel foundries, of drugstores
and streetlights, of superhighways
that slice our days in two. Wrapped around
in plastic and steel we ride our lives;
behind dark glasses we hide our eyes;
our thoughts, shaded, seem obscure.
Smoke fills our minds, whisky husks our songs,
polyester cuts our bodies from our breath,
our feet from the welcoming stones of earth.
Our dreams are pale memories of themselves
and nagging doubt is the false measure
of our days.

Even so, the spirit voices are singing,
their thoughts are dancing in the dirty air.
Their feet touch the cement, the asphalt
delighting, still they weave dreams upon our
shadowed skulls, if we could listen.
If we could hear.
Let's go then. Let's find them.
Let's listen for the water, the careful
gleaming drops that glisten on the leaves,
the flowers. Let's ride
the midnight, the early dawn.
Feel the wind striding through our hair.
Let's dance the dance of feathers,
the dance of birds.

Soundings

I

On such a day as this
something unknown, familiar stirs—
is it a thought? A breeze? A voice gotten through
the great sweep of space between there and here?
There, see just ahead that rise?
The turn in the path, just beneath those boughs
heavy with green, ground piled with needles,
mounds of old leaves, variegated moss,
sky deep with clouds, a-splatter with rain,
its soft sound?

Teeming, tangled growth of sun, riotous, congruent,
like life's unthinking scatterings of deeds, thoughts, wants,
loves, rages, delights, imaginings, and griefs
fallen soft through years onto shadowed,
iron-rich decay, earth spent
in the multitudes of unions, her vital force
shattered, splintering in the air.

How have I come here? Is this a time long told
in English tales about the journey some green knight
takes to find something that gleams with unearthly light,
to find it in some unearthly place?
Is the life-giving girdle something I must penetrate?

And do I now or just recently face
a new rise that when climbed
looks on another country far below
where beings other than the human ones we know
walk, singing spells, calling, eluding sight?

What stirs? A slender branch, heavy with fragrance,
hung with leaf and bud, whose petals
touched by wind, blown and swayed,
ring softly in my ear? Is it leaflight, sunlife,
undone from sky, falling into leaves,
transforming into sullen wood and brooding seed,
falling again into darkening shade, running down
as through successive lives,

to finally come to roost, exhausted, in the soil
to serve at last as mulch and mineral for the trees?
(Can light take root in clay unaided, unalloyed?)

Alone and long among the towering trees
safe in shadow, watching flickering brightness filter
through the narrow ridge of sight among the leaves,
I walk a path that faintly mars the ground,
deer walk, raccoon road, mouse path, snake slither slide,
so faint the track I pick my way along
half by belief, half by fear and rage.
I find a way however tangled, shadowy, brambled,
    overgrown,
seeking as much with fingertip as sight
as much with inward hearing as with outer ear.
I listen to soundings familiar from some other time
water falling, rippling, spray whispering, rising spume:
not a moan, not a sigh, not a sound I can describe
except to say it's the sound of petal fall,
along that line, or swift spray of inward wind
that rises and surrounds,
as though the air had voice to give its thought a form,
and craft to make and fire neurons to its call,
to shape living clay thrown and fired in tune
with another world of needs and tastes, other worldly
    minds.

Listen. Hear it?

It's not exactly water's fall, though it sounds as sweet;
it's not breath of fawn, not murmur of twilight bird
settling her feathers around her for the night;
it's not the sharp goldspray of dawn
presaging full daylight
on earthen place, on mortal lakes or streams.

The sound of which I speak
is not the rustle, soft, of tender new spring's leaves.
It's the voice of something gone forever,
of something over and over returned;
something like the sound of love, enspelling,
runic, tantric, budding, incanting, decanted, spilling,
a certain sound, fallen from another place,
some traveler's tale brought from dreamlike space,
not surreal, not like that sort of case,
but spilled perfume,

taste-of-honey when shimmering in the hive,
sound almost remembered, almost lost, ever alive.

On such a day as this
in a familiar fluster of fresh-sprung air
from somewhere other than here,
I hear the sound again
and stop,
hold my breath close within my chest
like a mother holds a child still
so she might hear some whisper she can't quite hear
and listens, teary-eyed, wonder-filled. So I
awaken once again to something recognized this morning
something at other times forgot.

Is it this that stirs like petals rippling in soft wind,
something neither air nor thought
that sprung from shadow and thick with grace
comes into view, momentarily sharp and dear,
elusive as memory, clear as crystal space,
a radiance exhaled by teeming plenitude,
a half caught vision of a half remembered place,
like yet unlike this where I sit and contemplate
what is so sweet as lightly it emanates
a familiar fragrance that falls,
soft as mist upon my every life,
caught brief for a tangled moment
in a certain kind of light.

Kimberly Blaeser (Anishinaabe)

Living History

Walked into Pinehurst, sunburned, smelling of fish,
Big Indian man paying for some gas and a six pack,
Looking at me hard.
Dreamer, I think. Too old for me.
Heads right toward me.
"Jeez," he says, "You look just like your mom—
You must be Marlene's girl."
Pinches my arm, but I guess it's yours
he touches.
Hell, wasn't even looking at me.
Wonder if I'm what they call living history?

Rewriting Your Life

not just the part
that matters the most,

but those haunting scenes
that make anger and panic rise in your throat
at the domestic quarrels of strangers.
The same sort
that make my pulse pound in my ears
to drown out that saccharine alcohol voice
of the women two booths away.

Erasing, replacing
the longings that arose from want
the causes
of your jacket fetish
the causes
of the bathtub in my parents' yard
the causes
of all old patterns stumbling on to renew themselves
of personal quirks
and other small tortures.

The children we were
we are.

I've added
a child with chink eyes
to those
bruised souls
whose lives
I rewrite
on my bluest days
and in the midst of my happiest moments
some part that seems physical
surges
with a longing
to repair
the past.

The aches in our bones are memories I'm told.
The tearing and stitching of our flesh
not the physical wear of age
really small but impossible hopes
dreamed endlessly
in smoke-filled pool halls
in one-room cold-water flats
dreams of grease splattered arms
taking shorthand
legs crossed at the ankles
just above a pair of black patent leather pumps.

The little tug in our voices
we wash down with complimentary water
at public podiums and in banquet halls
it is the pull of the small store of joy
of a people born poor
studying in school to be ashamed
it is the shiny marbles
our children shot across muddy school yards
and then washed and lined neatly to dry
it is fresh winter snow served with cream and sugar
nickel tent movies
and hurrah for the fourth of july!

It is your memories too now
that raise the flesh on my arms and legs.
And perhaps in time we can write across
that other life with this one,
but never enough to obscure it
just enough to make a new pattern
a new design
pitifully inadequate perhaps
for all that has happened—
but beautiful as only loved pain can be.

And so I write across your life that way
with mine
I write across your life with love
that comes from my own pain
and then, of course,
I write your face across my pain.

Rituals, Yours—and Mine

I.

living by your words
as if i haven't enough of my own
ever
to make them stretch
that long distance
from home to here
from then to now

and all the new words
i've ever read learned
or shelved so neatly
can't explain myself to me
like yours always do

sometimes that one gesture
of your chin and lips
my memory of
the sideways movement of your eyes
are the only words
from that language
i can manage
to put things in their place

II.

walked in on you today
closed the screened door quietly
so you wouldn't notice
just yet
stood watched you
mumbling shuffling about the kitchen
your long yellow-gray braid
hanging heavy down your back

wanted to see you turn
just that way
hear that familiar exclamation
you snapping the dishtowel
landing it just short of me
shame on me for surprising you

you walk toward me laughing
don't change anything I chant silently
wiping your hands on your faded print apron
you lay them gently still damp cool
one on each side of my face
for that long long second

"When'd you come? Sit down, I'm making breakfast."
I watch the wrinkled loose flesh jiggle on your arms
as you reach to wind and pin your braid
hurry to find your teeth behind the water pail
pull up your peanut butter stockings
pull down your flowered house dress
and wet your fingers
to smooth the hair back behind your ears

III.

smoothing away time with the fluid line
of your memory
I am in place at your table
in the morning damp of your still dark kitchen
I wait for you to come
stepping through the curtained doorway
you enter intent on this day
restart the fire
fill place the kettle
pull open the kitchen door
inviting daylight to come
welcoming it into your house—
bringing it into mine.

Where I Was That Day

It wasn't just the pill bugs
gray, many-legged and pulling that stunt
like they always did
closing in on themselves
contracting into the tiny round mass
like an image of the origin circle
And it wasn't the turtle alone either
who became so neatly one half of the earth's sphere

It was partly that day when I stopped at the little creek
and noticed the funny bumps on that floating log
and how they seemed to be looking at me
and how they were really little heads with beady bulging eyes
and how when I came back a half an hour later
the bumps had been rearranged on that log

It was partly the butterflies that would materialize
out of the flower blossoms
and the deer that appeared and disappeared into the forest
while standing stalk still
whose shape would be invisible one minute
and would stand out clearly the next
like the image in one of the connect-the-dot puzzles

It was the stick bugs, the chameleon
the snakes that became branches
the opossum who was dead then suddenly alive
And it was me who fit and saw one minute so clearly
and then stumbled blind the next
that made me think we are all always finding our place
in the great sphere of creation
that made me know I could learn a way
to pull the world around me too
to color myself with earth and air and water
and so become indistinguishable
to match my breath to the one
to pulse in and out with the mystery
to be both still and wildly alive in the same moment
to be strangely absent from myself
and yet feel large as all creation
to know
to know
to know and to belong
while the spell holds
learning to hold it a little longer each time

That's where I was that day
I watched you from the arbor
never blinking
while you looked all about for me
and then turned back home
thinking to find me in another place
when I was there everywhere you looked
I knew then the stories about Geronimo were true
and that he did turn to stone

while the cavalries passed him by
mistook him for just a part of the mountain
when he had really become the whole mountain
and all the air they breathed
and even the dust beneath their horse's hooves

I walk about trying to find the place I was that day
but getting there seems harder now
I feel heavier, my spirit weighted down
and I'm thinking I must shed something
like the animals shed their hair or skin
lose even their antlers annually
while I hold on to everything
and I'm thinking I must change my colors
like the rabbit, the ptarmigan, the weasel
and I'm thinking I must spin a cocoon
grow wings and learn to fly
and I'm thinking I must hibernate and fast
feed off my own excess for a season
and then perhaps emerge
in the place I was that day
and stay there longer this time

And I walk about and watch the creatures
the tree toads becoming and unbecoming a part of the trunk
the rocks in my path that crack open into grasshoppers and fly away
the spider who hangs suspended before me
and then disappears into thin air
and I feel comforted
knowing we are all
in this puzzle together
knowing we are all just learning
to hold the spell
a little longer
each time

Peter Blue Cloud (Mohawk)

Bear: A Totem Dance as Seen by Raven

For Ranoies

The black bear does a strange and shuffling dance
foot to foot slowly, head back, eyes closed
      like that of a man.
Beneath a loosely falling robe,
mouth sewn shut upon protruding tongue
      of red-stained cedar shreddings.
Foot to foot slowly in lumbering
                   shadow dance
within the fog and rain of high, thick ferns,
beneath a dripping, tapping spruce,
      echo of raven
morning cry of night visions unwanted.

A heavy, leaning snag it seems at first
the sound of crashing fall
      suspended
      between ground and lowered sky.
then swirl of fog unveils
      a huge head
carved atop the pole, a silver-grey of cedar.

Gnashing of angry teeth at driftwood shore
and killer whale spews up
      a wreckage
      of pock-infested sailors.

Foot to foot slowly, the totem dance continues,
sky to earth the leaning weight
      of pole
      and people and bear
      and now the drum,
rectangular and fringed with clacking claws.
A chant begins of deep-voiced rumbling,
of the black slate carved
      into bowls now broken
with fragments scattered in despair
      of a death not prophesied.

Great cedar poles in moist earth,
these dwellings speak with dark passages,
   (the rib of a tribe is a brittle section
     of a dugout
  or what is left
    of a stolen house post,
  vast heritage dragged
   into strange museums)

and still, and forever, foot to foot slowly
the strange and shuffling dance continues.
And day after day the mourning chants
and keening voices silence all else
    as dugouts
  with quiet paddles
convey the dead to sacred islands
   in endless procession.

And soil seeps thru roof cracks to fill
the huge and silent dwellings.
And totems lean from which
    great eyes
gaze either up to sky or down to earth,
And the death of a village is a great sorrow,
and the pain of the survivors
   is a great anguish
    never to heal.
Slowly and gently
    foot to foot balanced
and awkward in beauty
    the child dances.
And grandfather taps,
    delicately taps
the drum and his voice is very, very low,
   and the song is a promise
   given a people
in the ancient days of tomorrow.

And grandmother's stiff
    and swollen fingers
weave cedar and fern and spruce,
   and occasionally
   in a far away closeness
her eyes seek the dancing child.

The bear pauses in his quest for food
  to stand and sniff the air

then in a dream like a fasting
              he begins
         to shuffle
            foot to foot slowly
   as the dance continues.

The Old Man's Lazy,

I heard the Indian Agent say,
has no pride, no get up
and go. Well, he came out
here and walked around my
place, that agent. Steps
all thru the milkweed and
curing wormwood; tells me
my place is overgrown
and should be made use
of.

The old split cedar
fence stands at many
angles, and much of it
lies on the ground like
a curving sentence of
stick writing. An old
language, too, black with
age, with different
shades of green of moss
and lichen.
        He always
says he understands us
Indians,
        and why don't
I fix the fence at least;
so I took some fine
hawk feathers fixed
to a miniature woven
shield
        and hung this
from an upright post
near the house.
                He
came by last week
and looked all around

again, eyed the feathers
for a long time.
    He didn't
say anything, and he didn't
smile even, or look within
himself for the hawk.

Maybe sometime I'll
tell him that the fence
isn't mine to begin with,
but was put up by
the white guy who used
to live next door.
    It was
years ago. He built a cabin,
then put up the fence. He
only looked at me once,
after his fence was up,
he nodded at me as if
to show that he knew I
was here, I guess.
    It was
a pretty fence, enclosing
that guy, and I felt lucky
to be on the outside
of it.
    Well, that guy
dug holes all over his
place, looking for gold,
and I guess
    he never
found any. I watched
him grow old for over
twenty years, and bitter,
I could feel his anger
all over the place.
    And
that's when I took to
leaving my place to do
a lot of visiting.
    Then
one time I came home
and knew he was gone
for good.

My children would
always ask me why I
didn't move to town
and be closer to them.

Now, they
tell me I'm lucky to be
living way out here.
            And
they bring their children
and come out and visit me,
and I can feel that they
want to live out here
too, but can't
for some reason, do it.

Each day
a different story is
told me by the fence,
the rain and wind and snow,
the sun and moon shadows,
this wonderful earth,
            this Creation.
I tell my grandchildren
many of these stories,
            perhaps
this too is one of them.

Rattle

When a new world is born, the old
turns itself inside out, to cleanse
and prepare for a new beginning.
            It is
told by some that the stars are
small holes piercing the great
intestine
of a sleeping creature. The earth is
a hollow gourd and earthquakes are
gas rumblings and restless dreaming
of the sleeping creature.
            What
sleeping plant sings the seed
shaken in the globe of a rattle,

Let us shake
the rattle
to call back
a rattlesnake
to dream back
the dancers.

When the wind
sweeps earth
there is fullness
of sound,
we are given
a beat
to dance by

the quick breath of the singer warms
and awakens the seed to life.

The old man rolled fibres of
milkweed across his thigh, softly
speaking to grandchildren, slowly
saying
the thanksgiving to a sacred plant.

His left hand coiled the string as it
grew, thin and very strong; as he
explained the strength of a unity
of threads combined.
                He took his
small basket of cocoons and poured
grains of coarse sand, poured from
his hand the coarse sand like a
funnel
of wind, a cone between hand and
cocoon.

        Then, seven by seven, he bound
these nests to a stick with the
string,
and took the sap of white blood
of the plant, and with a finger,
rubbed
the encircling string.
                And waited, holding
the rattle to the sun for drying. And
when
he shook the first sound, the
children
sucked in their breaths and felt
strange
stirrings in their minds and
stomachs.
And when he sang the first song of
many,
the leaves of the cottonwood joined
in,
and desert winds shifted sand.
                And the
children closed their eyes, the better
    to hear tomorrow.

and drum
now joins us

and flutes
are like gentle
birds and

crickets on
        branches,
swaying trees.
The fan of
winged hawks
brush clouds like
streaks of
white clay upon
a field
of blue sky

water base.
The seeds in

the pod
of a plant

are children
of the sun

of earth
that we sing
we are

a rainfall voice

a plumed

and sacred bird

we are

shadows come back

to protect
the tiny seedlings
we are
a memory in

What sleeping plant sings the seed
in the gourd of night within the
hollow moon, the ladder going down,
down into the core of this good earth
leads to stars and wheeling suns
and
planets beyond count.
                    What sound
is that in the moist womb of the sea;
the softly swaying motion in a
multitude of sleeping seeds.
                Maybe it
is rattlesnake, the medicine singer.
              And
it is gourd, cocoon, seed pod, hollow
horn,
shell of snapping turtle, bark of
birch,
hollowed cedar, intestines of
creatures,
      rattle
is an endless element in sound and
vibration, singing the joys of
awakening,
shushing like the dry stalks of corn
in wind, the cradle songs of night.
    Hail-heavy wind bending upon
a roof of elm bark,
                  the howling song
of a midwinter blizzard heard by
a people sitting in circle close to
the fire. The fire is the sun, is the
burning core of Creation's seed,
sputtering
and seeking the womb of life.

    When someone asked Coyote, why
is there loneliness, and what is the
reason and meaning of loneliness:
Coyote
took an empty gourd and began
shaking
it, and he shook it for a long time.
                Then
he took a single pebble and put it

single dance
which is all
dancing forever.
We are eyes
looking about

for the children
do they
run and play
our echos
our former joys
in today?
Let us shake
the rattle
for the ancients

who dwell

upon this land

whose spirits
joined to ours
guide us

and direct us
that we
may ever walk
a harmony
that our songs
be clear.
Let us shake
the rattle
for the fliers

and swimmers

for the trees
and mushrooms
for tall grasses

blessed by

a snake's passage
for insects
keeping the balance,

into the gourd, and again began to
shake the gourd for many days, and
the pebble was indeed loneliness.
                    Again
Coyote paused to put a handful of
pebbles into the gourd.
                    And the sound
now had a wholeness and a meaning
beyond questioning.

and winds
which bring rain
and rivers
going to sea
and all
things of Creation.
Let us
shake the rattle
        always, forever.

To-ta Ti-om

For an Aunt

my aunt was an herb doctor, one-eyed with crooked yellow
        teeth
        the Christians called her pagan witch
        and their children taunted her
        or ran in fear of their bible lives
            at her approach,
her house of barn lumber leaned into the wind as if toppling
        in winter it grew squat with snow
        and bright sparks from the wood stove
        hissed the snowflakes into steam
            icing the roof,
"when my body dies it will be in winter just in time to see
        the spring"
        she told this while rolling leaves
        to powder between her boney hands
        for her duty as a medicine person
            was to cure,
in early summer grandfather and i would begin planting
        the corn and beans and squash
        just behind my aunt's house
        and she'd hobble over to help
            plant the tobacco,
as the first green shoots emerged into sunlight
        she would sit on the steps
        grating dried roots into a bowl
        stopping every so often to gaze
            at the garden,
when the time of tobacco curing came she'd be there
        feeling and smelling and tasting
        and every season she would approve

then later sit by the woodstove
    smoking her pipe,
"Come," she would say to me, "the time for onanoron is
    here,"
    and she would walk to the pond
    and she would point out strong plants
    for me to wade to and slowly pull
      those medicine roots,
we strung the roots of twisted brown above the woodstove
    to preserve their sacred power
    to be released as needed
    by those who had need
      of such strength,
tiny bundles were made of the roots with bits of string
    then she named the persons
    i was to take onanoron to
    and tied all in a blue bandana
      and said, "go,"
this is for Kaienwaktatse and this for Kaerine
    Lives Close to Town
    and She Bends the Boughs
    a penny or two and bread and jam
      I shyly ate,
the pennies slowly filled the glass jar on the table
    until my aunt went to the store
    a block of salt pork one finger square
    a nutmeg, salt and four candies
      just for me,
sitting there by the woodstove I would steal a glance
    at her tired wrinkled face
    and I'd want to shout loud
    feeling a tightening in my throat
      and maybe cry,
"she was sitting at her table with a bowl in her lap
    and it was just turning Spring,"
    my grandfather wrote this to me
    and i went somewhere to be alone
      and just sat,
it's planting time again and all done except tobacco
    grandfather's leaning on the hoe
    and looking at my aunt's house
    then he smiles and I smile back
      lonely, like crying.

Turtle

The winds are dark passages among the stars,
leading to whirling void pockets
encircled by seeds of thought,
life force of the Creation.
    I am turtle,
and slowly, my great flippers move
propelling my body through space,
and starflowers scatter crystals
which fall as mist upon my lidded eyes.
    I am turtle,
and the ocean of my life swim
is a single chant in the Creation,
as I pass others of my kind,
    my own, unborn, and those,
the holy ancients of my childhood.

My swim is steady and untiring
for great is the burden given me,
the praise and privilege of my eternity
rests upon my back as a single seed
to which I am guardian and giver.
    I am turtle,
and my tribes forever remain countless,
from the day I first raised my head
to gaze back upon the horn of my body,
    and my head was a sun,
    and Creation breathed life upon the seed
    and four times, and again four times,
    I wept for joy the birthing of my tribes,
    and chanted Creation the glory
of all these wondrous days.

The wrinkles and cracks upon this ancient shell
are the natural contours created
by the feel and request of burdened rock
and soil, blood and sustenance to
clans within clans,
    I am turtle,
and the earth I carry is but
a particle in the greater Creation,

my mountains, plains and oceans,
mere reflections in a vaster sea.
>   Turtle, I am called,
>   and breathe clouds of rain,
>   and turn slowly my body to seasons
>   in cycle with my grandchild, Eagle,
>   whose wings enfold thunder pulses,
>   back to back, and
seldom meeting in time.

Patience was given me by Creation,
ancient song on tomorrow's wind,
this chant that was taught my tribes
is now unsung by many clans
of a single tribe,
>   and truly
such pains that exist for this moment,
which slay so many of the innocent
cannot but end in pain repeated
as all are reflected twins to self.
>   I am turtle,
and await the council of my tribes
clan into clan, the merging thought
that evil was never the star path, and
then the chant to the four directions,
>   I am turtle,
and death is not yet my robe,
for drums still throb the many
centers of my tribes, and a young
child smiles me of tomorrow,
>   "and grandparent,"
another child whispers, "please,
tell again my clan's beginning."

Yellowjacket

For Coyote

He rode into town upon a wild-eyed mountain horse
his hat pulled low and down his back and shoulders
swaying and blowing in wind, long black and grey hair,
and no one saw the eyes, but even the soldiers felt
themselves being studied, maybe as coldly as the wind
    blowing downriver,
man and horse, passing through town in silent watching
stirring along small puffs of dust and leaving behind
the strong odors of buckskin and cedar smoke,
"he carries a pistol besides that rifle," someone said,
and a young and respectful voice said, "a real bad one, too,
    I hear."
an old man, a healer who still dared perform the rituals
of curing, but in hiding from the eyes of soldier and
    missionary
hummed and muttered an old mountain song under his
    breath
and whispered, "a spirit rides with him, and he carries
a whole tribe; he is what remains of a tribe, and we, the
    ghosts."
"yes," said the sergeant, "another goddam fence has been
ripped down and dragged until tangled and useless. we give
the heathens a whole valley to live in, but it ain't good
enough for them, should round them up and shoot the lot,
like he was doing before; or at least the real bad ones,
    especially Yellowjacket."
with a half a butchered steer tied to his horse
he approached his sister's tiny shack at the edge of town,
"the deer are moved to the high mountains like me, don't
    like
the smell of oiled leather and iron stoves. here is meat
of a kind best left for the buzzards, but meat at least to eat."
another fence was torn down and three head of cattle
slaughtered, and the meat left at the edge of town, as a dare
to the hungry to take, and to eat and to live a while longer,
and a soldier, too, found with slit throat, a quick and
clean kill and no signs of cruelty or anger, a hunter killed
    by the hunted.
and mounted, the soldiers rode through town
and the people watched and knew a longing,

a feeling for a something lost, just out of reach,
but not a one of them mounted a horse or reached for a
    rifle,
but merely watched and waited, ashamed to raise their eyes
    to one another.
and they saw him, hatless and riding slowly, so slowly
into town, and the clean upriver mountain air wildly
blew his hair about, and as he passed he stared into
the eyes of each with no reproach, and each of them saw
the holes and streaming blood as he rode through their
    midst.
and was never seen again, and the talking, too, stopped
when his sister said to a crowd of them, "don't speak
of him again, you don't deserve his name." and they
watched her saddle up and take her child
and turn her back upon her husband and home and never
    look back.
and on that same evening, a few youngsters, too, saddled
up and for the first time in many seasons, openly
showed their rifles, and some old people joined them
and they rode upriver, up toward the clean air and
naked stone, and the soldiers saw them pass, and dared not
    interfere.

Drum

Badger's Son went to Coyote's winter camp
Where Coyote spent his days and many nights
fashioning drums which were able
        to make very beautiful songs.
"Coyote Old Man, will you teach me
to make those drums that only you can make?"
        asked Badger's Son.
"And what, nephew, will your first song
be about?" And Badger's Son said,
"Why of course it will be about you."
"Nephew, I'm very sorry, but, I've
just forgotten how drums are made,"
        answered Coyote.
And Badger's Son walked slowly, sadly home,
hurt, but not angry. And waited four days,
        and again went to Coyote's camp.
"Coyote Old Man, I must learn to make
those drums that only you can make;

and my first song will be
a thanks to deer for his skin."
Coyote shook his head sadly, "Nephew,
I surely wish I could remember how
to make those drums, so I could teach you."
So Badger's Son left Coyote's camp,
and decided to have a long sweat bath
    and clear his mind of making drums.

On the fourth day of his sweat, he saw a drum,
floating before him, making sounds
    like tapping raindrops.
He followed his vision, and bent a frame
of cedar to a roundness. Now I must
    get some deer hide for the head, he thought.
Then he picked up a stick and pretended
to beat a gentle rhythm on the empty drum.
    He imagined a song.
The song was about the Creation.
All things around him grew silent,
    listening to the song.

Coyote Old Man quietly entered the camp
and sat and listened until the song was done.
    "Nephew," he said, "you have indeed become
a very good drum maker."
Then Badger's Son handed Coyote Old Man
the headless drum, and he, Coyote,
    began to drum and sing.

And all the creatures entered camp
and began to do a round dance.
    "And where," asked someone,
"did such a fine drum come from?"
And Badger's Son said, "Oh, it was
Coyote Old Man who refused to teach me
    to make this fine drum."

Reflections on Milkweed

a twisting, turning
flight above, dry
brown grasses
   pods of milkweed seen.

a glimpse of motion
I perceived in journeying
   mind and eye lent joy.

man's art in fingers
lifting to eyes
the silken
   nesting white seedlings

thoughts of white cloud ribs
drifting the vast
blue sky world
   to swallow a star

or the lone seedling
like a bubble
reflecting
   a current of air.

given these moments
to contemplate
and wonder
   a great peace descends.

man's art in thinking
mind-weaving
singular ties
   is but returning.

the seeds within us
and that which
brought us living
   is an ancient breath.

stone to stone the spark,
fire into dream
into birth,
   we are Creation.

Joseph Bruchac (Abenaki)

Above the Line

Jesse's face stayed dark
despite Northern winters.
So he never went
with us again
on those long migrations,
taken each Easter,
as we drove down
old military roads
Louis Bowman marched
into the South.

Plank trails bordered
by banks of roses
rising mist like smoke
and smoke like mist
eight decades and
two lifetimes gone.

Did my Indian Grampa
remember
his own father's
resurrection?

Four days left for dead
on the wilderness field,
while Thunder beings
rumbled an older chant
than Abenaki drums,
he drank the gift
of rain to survive,
that one who lived
to be my great-grandfather.

So many years
that I did not see,
as I walked
without knowing
above that line.

For though we paused
at Gettysburg,
to my eyes of eight winters

it was only another
glue-eyed attraction,
no more than a roadside
reptile farm
where rattlesnakes struck
at the panes of tapped cases,
pale-fingers safe
from defiant coils,
segregated
by yellow-venomed glass.

Even though
we always drove on deeper
into the heart
of Old Virginia
to the healing springs
of Algonquin stories,
neatly held now
by a century
of resort spa walls
keeping out older dreams
as white-gloved waiters
with mahogany faces
carried trays of food
polished so bright
that the silver became
a mirror clear enough
to reflect the pain
of partial freedom,
I think somewhere
in the back of my mind
I only heard a cartoon bluebird
perched on the shoulders
of old Uncle Remus
beaming a smile so broad
and shallow that it hurt his face
as they sang
a Song of the South.

My grandfather only
went once with us
to visit those places
of his wife's relations.
He could barely read,
but he'd read enough.
The sign on the wall

in a roadside station
was spelled out to him
in large black letters
nothing less
than WHITE.

Those stains of skin
and scarred generations,
never overcame an old knowledge
of remembered waters and healing darkness.
His silence stayed like
a slow river flowing
until it filled my own
innocent heart,
his wordless refusal taught me
the way our old people
alway have known, that
our arms can be raised
to resist or embrace.

Blessing the Waters

There is no blessing older
than the blessing of the waters.
It is in the flow of birth
and the joining of streams.
It is after the end
and before the beginning.
It is the circle
which owns no beginning or end.

As we walk beside the waters
we bless the waters
and they bless us in turn.

As we walk beside the waters,
we carry the rivers within us.
We are rivers walking
we are streams dancing.
We are the oceans
and the deserts joining hands.
We are the clouds and the rain.

As we thank the waters,
the sacred flow of life within us
is blessed by the winds of breath
by words and prayers
moist with the sweetness of water.

As we touch the waters,
as we lift the water to our lips,
as we pour the water over our bodies
as we greet the waters
as we thank the waters
we are equal in blessing
we are equally blessed.

In the flow of tears
in the flow of blood
in the flow of songs
we touch that which is sacred
as only water can be sacred,
for without water
there is neither life
nor the possibility of life.

So, once again
and once again,
we lift our hands to bless the water
knowing it is blessed without our blessing,
knowing it is blessed within our blessing,
and our songs are the surge
of the always returning tide.

Copal, Red Blood

Chiapas, 1998

Copal incense, small figures molded
to sacrifice in the god pot's umbra.
A clearing at the rain forest's edge,
green and a thousand shades of green,
that same riot of verdancy that swallowed
Palenque and more stone-carved cities
than we have words to name.

Orchids, lianas, strangler figs,
philodendron, the buttressed roots
of mahogany and its sister trees
hold thin soil over honeycombed limestone,
hiding the entrances leading down
twisting into Xibalba, a snake's road,
where the hero Twins played ball
with Death and the Children of Death,
died, lost their heads, lived again and won.

Tall cane grass grows at the edge of a grove,
eight harvests after the corn gave way
to trees where fruits hang golden
as the faces of small glowing suns.
Arrow straight cane, arrowshafts pointing
up toward the many layers of Heaven,
the tongue of Creation's Creator.

Here, more than six centuries gone,
briared strings were drawn
through the willing tongues
of the nobly born, great ladies and lords,
offering their own blood from every mouth.

Divination, appeasement, and balance—
before the starving wars of invaders
who threw down the steles, burned the forest paths,
generations ahead of European hunger.

And then there was the second coming
that saw the pale armored shadow
of Quetzelcoatl cross the land.
Some say it was coincidence,
mistaken identity that gave
Hernan Cortez the old brother's name.
But that is not what the Lacandon know,
for that Rabbit Year was not dishonest.
The Conquistador was who he was,
a man so shrunken in memory
so forgetful of the gifts of blood
that now the taking of gold became
the only medicine that could touch
the disease of his shrunken heart,
a disease passed to all those descendents
who demand the people bow to them.
With American jets and machine pistols,
the ghost of Cortez marks his return.

And now, while copal incense burns,
the slow reach to the sacred goes on
long after each apocalypse.

Divination, appeasement, balance
remain before the end of the world,
while the Twins descend to play their game,
return when the world begins again.

Chrystos (Menominee)

Today Was a Bad Day Like TB

FOR AMANDA WHITE

Saw whites clap during a sacred dance
Saw young blond hippie boy with a red stone pipe
    My eyes burned him up
He smiled   *This is a Sioux pipe* he said from his sportscar
    Yes   I hiss   *I'm wondering how you got it*
    & the name is Lakota not Sioux
I'll tell you he said all friendly & liberal as only
    those with no pain can be
    I turned away   Can't charm me   can't bear to know
thinking of the medicine bundle I saw opened up in a glass case
    with a small white card beside it
    naming the rich whites who say they
    "own" it
Maybe they have an old Indian grandma back in time
    to excuse themselves
Today was a day I wanted to beat up the smirking man wearing
a pack with a Haida design from Moe's bookstore
Listen Moe's   How many Indians do you have working there?
How much money are you sending the Haida people
to use their sacred Raven design?
    You probably have an Indian grandma too
    whose name you don't know
    Today was a day like TB
    you cough & cough trying to get it out
        all that comes
           is blood & spit

Nora Dauenhaur (Tlingit)

Salmon Egg Puller—$2.15 an Hour

You learn to dance with machines,
keep time with the header.

Swing your arms,
reach inside the salmon cavity
with your left hand,
where the head was.

Grab lightly
top of egg sack
with fingers,
pull gently, but quick.
Reach in immediately with right hand
for the lower egg sack.
Pull this gently.

Slide them into a chute to catch the eggs.
Reach into the next salmon.
Do this four hours in the morning
with a fifteen minute coffee break.

Go home for lunch.
Attend to the kids, and feed them.
Work four hours in the afternoon
with a fifteen minute coffee break.
Go home for dinner.
Attend to kids, and feed them.

Go back for two more hours,
four more hours.
Reach,
pull gently.

When your fingers start swelling up,
soak them in epsom salts.
If you didn't have time,
stand under the shower
with your hands up under the spray.
Get to bed early if you can.
Next day, if your fingers are sore,
start dancing immediately.
The pain will go away
after icy fish with eggs.

Louise Erdrich (Anishinaabe)

Captivity

"He [my captor] gave me a bisquit, which I
put in my pocket, and not daring to eat it,
buried it under a log, fearing he had put
something in it to make me love him."

> from the narrative of the captivity of
> Mrs. Mary Rowlandson, who was
> taken prisoner by the Wampanoag
> when Lancaster, Massachusetts, was
> destroyed, in the year 1676

The stream was swift, and so cold
I thought I would be sliced in two.
But he dragged me from the flood
by the ends of my hair.
I had grown to recognize his face.
I could distinguish it from the others.
There were times I feared I understood
his language, which was not human,
and I knelt to pray for strength.

We were pursued! By God's agents
or pitch devils I did not know.
Only that we must march.
Their guns were loaded with swan shot.
I could not suckle and my child's wail
put them in danger.
He had a woman
with teeth black and glittering.
She fed the child milk of acorns.
The forest closed, the light deepened.

I told myself that I would starve
before I took food from his hands
but I did not starve.
One night
he killed a deer with a young one in her
and gave me to eat of the fawn.
It was so tender,
the bones like the stems of flowers,
that I followed where he took me.

The night was thick. He cut the cord
that bound me to the tree.

After that the birds mocked.
Shadows gaped and roared
and the trees flung down
their sharpened lashes.
He did not notice God's wrath.
God blasted fire from half-buried stumps.
I hid my face in my dress, fearing He would burn us all
but this, too, passed.

Rescued, I see no truth in things.
My husband drives a thick wedge
through the earth, still it shuts
to him year after year.
My child is fed of the first wheat.
I lay myself to sleep
On a Holland-laced pillowbear.
I lay to sleep.
And in the dark I see myself
as I was outside their circle.

They knelt on deerskins, some with sticks,
and he led his company in the noise
until I could no longer bear
the thought of how I was.
I stripped a branch
and struck the earth,
in time, begging it to open
to admit me
as he was
and feed me honey from the rock.

Indian Boarding School: The Runaways

Home's the place we head for in our sleep.
Boxcars stumbling north in dreams
don't wait for us. We catch them on the run.
The rails, old lacerations that we love,
    shoot parallel across the face and break
just under Turtle Mountains. Riding scars
you can't get lost. Home is the place they cross.

The lame guard strikes a match and makes the dark
less tolerant. We watch through cracks in boards
as the land starts rolling, rolling till it hurts
to be here, cold in regulation clothes.
We know the sheriff's waiting at midrun
to take us back. His car is dumb and warm.
The highway doesn't rock, it only hums
like a wing of long insults. The worn-down welts
of ancient punishments lead back and forth.

All runaways wear dresses, long green ones,
the color you would think shame was. We scrub
the sidewalks down because it's shameful work.
Our brushes cut the stone in watered arcs
and in the soak frail outlines shiver clear
a moment, things us kids pressed on the dark
face before it hardened, pale, remembering
delicate old injuries, the spines of names and leaves.

Jacklight

The same Chippewa word is used both for
flirting and hunting game, while another
Chippewa word connotes both using force in
intercourse and also killing a bear with
one's bare hands.

  R.W. Dunning, *Social and Economic*
  Change Among the Northern Ojibwa (1959)

We have come to the edge of the woods,
out of brown grass where we slept, unseen,
out of knotted twigs, out of leaves creaked shut,
out of hiding.

At first the light wavered, glancing over us.
Then it clenched to a fist of light that pointed,
searched out, divided us.
Each took the beams like direct blows the heart answers.
Each of us moved forward alone.

We have come to the edge of the woods,
drawn out of ourselves by this night sun,
this battery of polarized acids,
that outshines the moon.

We smell them behind it
but they are faceless, invisible.
We smell the raw steel of their gun barrels,
mink oil on leather, their tongues of sour barley.
We smell their mothers buried chin-deep in wet dirt.
We smell their fathers with scoured knuckles,
teeth cracked from hot marrow.
We smell their sisters of crushed dogwood, bruised apples,
of fractured cups and concussions of burnt hooks.

We smell their breath steaming lightly behind the jacklight.
We smell the itch underneath the caked guts on their
    clothes.
We smell their minds like silver hammers

cocked back, held in readiness
for the first of us to step into the open.

We have come to the edge of the woods,
out of brown grass where we slept, unseen,
out of leaves creaked shut, out of our hiding.
We have come here too long.

It is their turn now,
their turn to follow us. Listen,
they put down their equipment.
It is useless in the tall brush.
And now they take the first steps, not knowing
how deep the woods are and lightless.
How deep the woods are.

Old Man Potchikoo

The Birth of Potchikoo

You don't have to believe this, I'm not asking you to. But Potchikoo claims that his father is the sun in heaven that shines down on us all.

There was a very pretty Chippewa girl working in a field once. She was digging potatoes for a farmer someplace around Pembina when suddenly the wind blew her dress up around her face and wrapped her apron so tightly around her arms that she couldn't move. She lay helplessly in the dust with her potato sack, this poor girl, and as she lay there she felt the sun shining down very steadily upon her.

Then she felt something else. You know what. I don't have to say it. She cried out for her mother.

This girl's mother came running and untangled her daughter's clothes. When she freed the girl, she saw that there were tears in her daughter's eyes. Bit by bit, the mother coaxed out the story. After the girl told what had happened to her, the mother just shook her head sadly.

"I don't know what we can expect now," she said.

Well nine months passed and he was born looking just like a potato with tough warty skin and a puckered round shape. All the ladies came to visit the girl and left saying things behind their hands.

"That's what she gets for playing loose in the potato fields," they said.

But the girl didn't care what they said after a while because she used to go and stand alone in a secret clearing in the woods and let the sun shine steadily upon her. Sometimes she took her little potato boy. She noticed when the sun shone on him he grew and became a little more human-looking.

One day the girl fell asleep in the sun with her potato boy next to her. The sun beat down so hard on him that he had an enormous spurt of growth. When the girl woke up, her son was fully grown. He said good-bye to his mother then, and went out to see what was going on in the world.

Potchikoo Marries

After he had several adventures, the potato boy took the name Potchikoo and decided to try married life.

I'll just see what it's like for a while, he thought, and then I'll start wandering again.

How very inexperienced he was!

He took the train to Minneapolis to find a wife and as soon as he got off he saw her. She was a beautiful Indian girl standing at the door to a little shop where they sold cigarettes and pipe tobacco. How proud she looked! How peaceful. She was so lovely that she made Potchikoo shy. He could hardly look at her.

Potchikoo walked into the store and bought some cigarettes. He lit one up and stuck it between the beautiful woman's lips. Then he stood next to her, still too shy to look at her, until he smelled smoke. He saw that she had somehow caught fire.

"Oh I'll save you!" cried Potchikoo.

He grabbed his lady love and ran with her to the lake, which was, handily, across the street. He threw her in. At first he was afraid she would drown but soon she floated to the surface and kept floating away from Potchikoo. This made him angry.

"Trying to run away already!" he shouted.

He leaped in to catch her. But he had forgotten that he couldn't swim. So Potchikoo had to hang on to his wooden sweetheart while she drifted slowly all the way across the lake. When they got to the other side of the lake, across from Minneapolis, they were in wilderness. As soon as the wooden girl touched the shore she became alive and jumped up and dragged Potchikoo out of the water.

"I'll teach you to shove a cigarette between my lips like that," she said, beating him with her fists, which were still hard as wood. "Now that you're my husband you'll do things my way!"

That was how Potchikoo met and married Josette. He was married to her all his life. After she had made it clear what she expected of her husband, Josette made a little toboggan of cut saplings and tied him upon it. Then she decided she never wanted to see Minneapolis again. She wanted to live in the hills. That is why she dragged Potchikoo all the way back across Minnesota to the Turtle Mountains, where they spent all the years of their wedded bliss.

How Potchikoo Got Old

As a young man, Potchikoo sometimes embarrassed his wife by breaking wind during Holy Mass. It was for this reason that Josette whittled him a little plug out of ash wood and told him to put it in that place before he entered Saint Ann's church.

Potchikoo did as she asked, and even said a certain charm over the plug so that it would not be forced out, no matter what. Then the two of them entered the church to say their prayers.

That Sunday, Father Belcourt was giving a special sermon on the ascension of the Lord Christ to heaven. It happened in the twinkling of an eye, he said, with no warning, because Christ was more pure than air. How surprised everyone was to see, as Father Belcourt said this, the evil scoundrel Potchikoo rising from his pew!

His hands were folded, and his closed eyes and meek face wore a look of utter piety. He didn't even seem to realize he was rising, he prayed so hard.

Up and up he floated, still in the kneeling position, until he reached the dark blue vault of the church. He seemed to inflate, too, until he looked larger than life to the people. They were on the verge of believing it a miracle when all of a sudden it happened. Bang! Even with the charm the little ash-wood plug could not contain the wind of Potchikoo. Out it popped, and Potchikoo went buzzing and sputtering around the church the way balloons do when children let go of the ends.

Holy Mass was canceled for a week so the church could be aired out, but to this day a faint scent still lingers and Potchikoo, sadly enough, was shriveled by his sudden collapse and flight through the air. For when Josette picked him up to bring home, she found that he was now wrinkled and dry like an old man.

The Death of Potchikoo

Once there were three stones sitting in a patch of soft slough mud. Each of these stones had the smooth round shape of a woman's breast, but no one had ever noticed this—that is, not until Old Man Potchikoo walked through the woods. He was the type who always noticed this kind of thing. As soon as he saw the three stones, Potchikoo sat down on a small bank of grass to enjoy what he saw.

He was not really much of a connoisseur, the old man. He just knew what he liked when he saw it. The three stones were light brown in color, delicately veined, and so smooth that they almost looked slippery. Old Man Potchikoo began to wonder if they really were slippery, and then he thought of touching them.

They were in the middle of the soft slough mud, so the old man took his boots and socks off. Then he thought of his wife Josette and what she would say if he came home with mud on his clothes. He took off his shirt and pants. He never wore undershorts. Wading toward those stones, he was as naked as them.

He had to kneel in the mud to touch the stones, and when he did this he sank to his thighs. But oh, when he touched the stones, he found that they were bigger than they looked from the shore and so shiny, so slippery. His hands polished them, and polished them some more, and before he knew it that Potchikoo was making love to the slough.

Years passed by. The Potchikoos got older and more frail. One day Josette went into town, and as he always did as soon as she was out of sight, Potchikoo sat down on his front steps to do nothing.

As he sat there, he saw three women walk very slowly out of the woods. They walked across the field and then walked slowly toward him. As they drew near, Potchikoo saw that they were just his kind of women. They were large, their hair was black and very long, and because they wore low-cut blouses, he could see that their breasts were beautiful—light brown, delicately veined, and so smooth they looked slippery.

"We are your daughters," they said, standing before him. "We are from the slough."

A faint memory stirred in Potchikoo as he looked at their breasts, and he smiled.

"Oh my daughters," he said to them. "Yes I remember you. Come sit on your daddy's lap and get acquainted."

The daughters moved slowly toward Potchikoo. As he saw their skin up close, he marveled at how fine it was, smooth as polished stone. The first daughter sank upon his knee and clasped her arms around him. She was so heavy the old man couldn't move. Then the others sank upon him, blocking away the sun with their massive bodies. The old man's head began to swim and yellow stars turned in his skull. He hardly knew it when all three daughters laid their heads dreamily against his chest. They were cold, and so heavy that his ribs snapped apart like little dry twigs.

Dear John Wayne

August and the drive-in picture is packed.
We lounge on the hood of the Pontiac
surrounded by the slow-burning spirals they sell
at the window, to vanquish the hordes of mosquitoes.
Nothing works. They break through the smoke screen for blood.

Always the lookout spots the Indians first,
spread north to south, barring progress.
The Sioux or some other Plains bunch
in spectacular columns, ICBM missiles,
feathers bristling in the meaningful sunset.

The drum breaks. There will be no parlance.
Only the arrows whining, a death-cloud of nerves
swarming down on the settlers
who die beautifully, tumbling like dust weeds
into the history that brought us all here
together: this wide screen beneath the sign of the bear.

The sky fills, acres of blue squint and eye
that the crowd cheers. His face moves over us,
a thick cloud of vengeance, pitted
like the land that was once flesh. Each rut,
each scar makes a promise: *It is
not over, this fight, not as long as you resist.*

Everything we see belongs to us.

A few laughing Indians fall over the hood
slipping in the hot spilled butter.
The eye sees a lot, John, but the heart is so blind.
Death makes us owners of nothing.
He smiles, a horizon of teeth
the credits reel over, and then the white fields
again blowing in the true-to-life dark.
The dark films over everything.
We get into the car
scratching our mosquito bites, speechless and small
as people are when the movie is done.
We are back in our skins.

How can we help but keep hearing his voice,
the flip side of the sound track, still playing:

Come on, boys, we got them
where we want them, drunk, running.
They'll give us what we want, what we need.
Even his disease was the idea of taking everything.
Those cells, burning, doubling, splitting out of their skins.

Turtle Mountain Reservation

The heron makes a cross
flying low over the marsh.
Its heart is an old compass
pointing off in four directions.
It drags the world along,
the world it becomes.

My face surfaces in the green
beveled glass above the washstand.
My handprint in thick black powder
on the bedroom shade.
Home I could drink like thin fire
that gathers
like lead in my veins,
heart's armor, the coffee stains.

In the dust of the double hollyhock,
Theresa, one frail flame eating wind.
One slim candle
that snaps in the dry grass.
Ascending tall ladders
that walk to the edge of dusk.
Riding a blue cricket
through the tumult of the falling dawn.

At dusk the gray owl walks the length of the roof,
sharpening its talons on the shingles,
Grandpa leans back
between spoonfuls of canned soup
and repeats to himself a word
that belongs to a world
no one else can remember.
The day has not come

when from sloughs, the great salamander
lumbers through snow, salt, and fire

to be with him, throws the hatchet
of its head through the door of the three-room house
and eats the blue roses that are peeling off the walls.

Uncle Ray, drunk for three days
behind the jagged window
of a new government box,
drapes himself in fallen curtains, and dreams that the odd
beast seen near Cannonball, North Dakota,
crouches moaning at the door to his body. The latch
is the small hook and eye

of religion. Twenty nuns
fall through clouds to park their butts
on the metal hasp. Surely that
would be considered miraculous almost anyplace,

but here in the Turtle Mountains
it is no more than common fact.
Raymond wakes,
but he can't shrug them off. He is looking up
dark tunnels of their sleeves,
and into their frozen armpits,
or is it heaven? He counts the points
of their hairs like stars.

One by one they blink out,
and Theresa comes forth
clothed in the lovely hair
she has been washing all day. She smells
like a hayfield, drifting pollen
of birch trees.
Her hair steals across her shoulders
like a postcard sunset.

All the boys tonight, goaded from below,
will approach her in The Blazer, The Tomahawk,
The White Roach Bar where everyone
gets up to cut the rug, wagging everything they got,
as the one bass drum of The Holy Greaseballs
lights a depth
charge through the smoke.

Grandpa leans closer to the bingo.
The small fortune his heart pumps for
is hidden in the stained, dancing numbers.
The Ping-Pong balls rise through colored lights,
brief as sparrows
God is in the sleight of the woman's hand.

He walks from Saint Ann's, limp and crazy
as the loon that calls its children
across the lake
in this broke, knowing laughter.
Hitchhiking home from the Mission, if he sings,
it is a loud, rasping wail
that saws through the spine
of Ira Comes Last, at the wheel.

Drawn up through the neck ropes,
drawn out of his stomach
by the spirit of the stones that line
the road and speak
to him only in their old agreement.
Ira knows the old man is nuts.
Lets him out at the road that leads up
over stars and the skulls of white cranes.

And through the soft explosions of cattail
and the scattering of seeds on still water,
walks Grandpa, all the time that there is in his hands
that have grown to be the twisted doubles
of the burrows of mole and badger,
that have come to be the absence
of birds in a nest.
Hands of earth, of this clay
I'm also made from.

Joy Harjo (Muskogee)
She Had Some Horses

She had some horses.

She had horses who were bodies of sand.
She had horses who were maps drawn of blood.
She had horses who were skins of ocean water.
She had horses who were the blue air of sky.
She had horses who were fur and teeth.
She had horses who were clay and would break.
She had horses who were splintered red cliff.

She had some horses.

She had horses with long, pointed breasts.
She had horses with full, brown thighs.
She had horses who laughed too much.

She had horses who threw rocks at glass houses.
She had horses who licked razor blades.

She had some horses.

She had horses who danced in their mothers' arms.
She had horses who thought they were the sun and their
bodies shone and burned like stars.
She had horses who waltzed nightly on the moon.
She had horses who were much too shy, and kept quiet
in stalls of their own making.

She had some horses.

She had horses who liked Creek Stomp Dance songs.
She had horses who cried in their beer.
She had horses who spit at male queens who made
them afraid of themselves.
She had horses who said they weren't afraid.
She had horses who lied.
She had horses who told the truth, who were stripped
bare of their tongues.

She had some horses.
She had horses who called themselves, "horse."
She had horses who called themselves, "spirit," and kept
their voices secret and to themselves.
She had horses who had no names.
She had horses who had books of names.

She had some horses.

She had horses who whispered in the dark, who were afraid
to speak.
She had horses who screamed out of fear of the silence, who
carried knives to protect themselves from ghosts.
She had horses who waited for destruction.
She had horses who waited for resurrection.

She had some horses.

She had horses who got down on their knees for any savior.
She had horses who thought their high price had saved
    them.
She had horses who tried to save her, who climbed in her
bed at night and prayed as they raped her.

She had some horses.

She had some horses she loved.
She had some horses she hated.

These were the same horses.

Transformations

This poem is a letter to tell you that I
have smelled the hatred you have tried
to find me with; you would like to destroy me.
Bone splintered in the eye of one you choose
to name your enemy won't make it better for you
to see. It could take a thousand years if you name it
that way, but then, to see after that time never
could anything be so clear. Memory has many forms.
When I think of early winter I think of a blackbird
laughing in the frozen air; guards a piece of light.
I saw the whole world caught in that sound. The sun
stopped for a moment because of tough belief. I don't
know what that has to do with what I am trying to tell
you, except that I know you can turn a poem into something
else. This poem could be a bear treading the far northern
tundra, smelling the air for sweet alive meat. Or a piece
of seaweed stumbling in the sea. Or a blackbird, laughing.
What I mean is that hatred can be turned into something
else, if you have the right words, the right meanings
buried in that tender place in your heart where
the most precious animals live. Down the street
an ambulance has come to rescue an old man who is slowly
losing his life. Not many can see that he is already
becoming the backyard tree he has tended
for years, before he moves on. He is not sad, but
compassionate for the fears moving around him.
That's what I mean to tell you. On the other side
of the place you live stands a dark woman.
She has been trying to talk to you for years.
You have called the same name in the middle of a
nightmare, from the center of miracles.
She is beautiful.
This is your hatred back. She loves you.

I Give You Back

I release you, my beautiful and terrible
fear. I release you. You were my beloved
and hated twin, but now, I don't know you
as myself. I release you with all the
pain I would know at the death of
my daughters.

You are not my blood anymore.

I give you back to the white soldiers
who burned down my home, beheaded my children,
raped and sodomized my brothers and sisters.
I give you back to those who stole the
food from our plates when we were starving.

I release you, fear, because you hold
these scenes in front of me and I was born
with eyes that can never close.

I release you, fear, so you can no longer
keep me naked and frozen in the winter,
or smothered under blankets in the summer.

I release you
I release you
I release you
I release you

I am not afraid to be angry.
I am not afraid to rejoice.
I am not afraid to be black.
I am not afraid to be white.
I am not afraid to be hungry.
I am not afraid to be full.
I am not afraid to be hated.
I am not afraid to be loved.
to be loved, to be loved, fear.

Oh, you have choked me, but I gave you the leash.
You have gutted me but I gave you the knife.
You have devoured me, but I laid myself across the fire.
You held my mother down and raped her,
         but I gave you the heated thing.

I take myself back, fear.
You are not my shadow any longer.
I won't hold you in my hands.
You can't live in my eyes, my ears, my voice
my belly, or in my heart my heart
my heart   my heart

But come here, fear
I am alive and you are so afraid
                        of dying.

Call It Fear

There is this edge where shadows
and bones of some of us walk
                      backwards.
Talk backwards. There is this edge
call it an ocean of fear of the dark. Or
name it with other songs. Under our ribs
our hearts are bloody stars. Shine on
shine on, and horses in their galloping flight
strike the curve of ribs.
                   Heartbeat
and breathe back sharply. Breathe
                     backwards.
There is this edge within me
          I saw it once
an August Sunday morning when the heat hadn't
left this earth. And Goodluck
sat sleeping next to me in the truck.
We had never broken through the edge of the
singing at four a.m.
             We had only wanted to talk, to hear
any other voice to stay alive with.
             And there was this edge—
not the drop of sandy rock cliff
bones of volcanic earth into
               Albuquerque.
Not that,
        but a string of shadow horses kicking
and pulling me out of my belly,
       not into the Rio Grande but into the music
barely coming through

Sunday church singing
from the radio. Battery worn-down but the voices
talking backwards.

Eagle Poem

To pray you open your whole self
To sky, to earth, to sun, to moon
To one whole voice that is you.
And know there is more
That you can't see, can't hear
Can't know except in moments
Steadily growing, and in languages
That aren't always sound but other
Circles of motion.
Like eagle that Sunday morning
Over Salt River. Circled in blue sky
In wind, swept our hearts clean
With sacred wings.
We see you, see ourselves and know
That we must take the utmost care
And kindness in all things.
Breathe in, knowing we are made of
All this, and breathe, knowing
We are truly blessed because we
Were born, and die soon, within a
True circle of motion,
Like eagle rounding out the morning
Inside us.
We pray that it will be done
In beauty.
In beauty.

The Woman Hanging from the Thirteenth Floor Window

She is the woman hanging from the 13th floor
window. Her hands are pressed white against the
concrete molding of the tenement building. She
hangs from the 13th floor window in east Chicago,
with a swirl of birds over her head. They could
be a halo, or a storm of glass waiting to crush her.

She thinks she will be set free.

The woman hanging from the 13th floor window
on the east side of Chicago is not alone.
She is a woman of children, of the baby, Carlos,
and of Margaret, and of Jimmy who is the oldest.
She is her mother's daughter and her father's son.
She is several pieces between the two husbands
she has had. She is all the women of the apartment
building who stand watching her, watching themselves.

When she was young she ate wild rice on scraped down
plates in warm wood rooms. It was in the farther
north and she was the baby then. They rocked her.
She sees Lake Michigan lapping at the shores of
herself. It is a dizzy hole of water and the rich
live in tall glass houses at the edge of it. In some
places Lake Michigan speaks softly, here, it just sputters
and butts itself against the asphalt. She sees
other buildings just like hers. She sees other
women hanging from many-floored windows
counting their lives in the palms of their hands
and in the palms of their children's hands.

She is the woman hanging from the 13th floor window
on the Indian side of town. Her belly is soft from
her children's births, her worn levis swing down below
her waist, and then her feet, and then her heart.
She is dangling.

The woman hanging from the 13th floor hears voices.
They come to her in the night when the lights have gone
dim. Sometimes they are little cats mewing and scratching

at the door, sometimes they are her grandmother's voice,
and sometimes they are gigantic men of light whispering
to her to get up, to get up, to get up. That's when she wants
to have another child to hold onto in the night, to be able
to fall back into dreams.

And the woman hanging from the 13th floor window
hears other voices. Some of them scream out from below
for her to jump, they would push her over. Others cry softly
from the sidewalks, pull their children up like flowers and
    gather
them into their arms. They would help her, like themselves.

But she is the woman hanging from the 13th floor window,
and she knows she is hanging by her own fingers, her
own skin, her own thread of indecision.
She thinks of Carlos, of Margaret, of Jimmy.
She thinks of her father, and of her mother.
She thinks of all the women she has been, of all
the men. She thinks of the color of her skin, and
of Chicago streets, and of waterfalls and pines.
She thinks of moonlight nights, and of cool spring storms.
Her mind chatters like neon and northside bars.
She thinks of the 4 a.m. lonelinesses that have folded
her up like death, discordant, without logical and
beautiful conclusion. Her teeth break off at the edges.
She would speak.

The woman hangs from the 13th floor window crying for
the lost beauty of her own life. She sees the
sun falling west over the grey plane of Chicago.
She thinks she remembers listening to her own life
break loose, as she falls from the 13th floor
window on the east side of Chicago, or as she
climbs back up to claim herself again.

Grace

FOR WIND AND JIM WELCH

I think of Wind and her wild ways the year we had nothing to lose
and lost it anyway in the cursed country of the fox. We still talk

about that winter, how the cold froze imaginary buffalo on the stuffed
horizon of snowbanks. The haunting voices of the starved and mutilated
broke fences, crashed our thermostat dreams, and we couldn't stand it
one more time. So once again we lost a winter in stubborn memory,
    walked
through cheap apartment walls, skated through fields of ghosts into
a town that never wanted us, in the epic search for grace.

Like Coyote, like Rabbit, we could not contain our terror and
    clowned
our way through a season of false midnights. We had to swallow
that town with laughter, so it would go down easy as honey. And one
morning as the sun struggled to break ice, and our dreams had found us
with coffee and pancakes in a truck stop along Highway 80,
we found grace.

I could say grace was a woman with time on her hands, or a white
buffalo escaped from memory. But in that dingy light it was a promise
of balance. We once again understood the talk of animals, and spring
was lean and hungry with the hope of children and corn.

I would like to say, with grace, we picked ourselves up and walked
into the spring thaw. We didn't; the next season was worse. You went
home to Leech Lake to work with the tribe and I went south. And, Wind,
I am still crazy. I know there is something larger than the memory
of a dispossessed people. We have seen it.

The Woman Who Fell from the Sky

Once a woman fell from the sky. The woman who fell from the sky was neither a murderer nor a saint. She was rather ordinary, though beautiful in her
walk, like one who has experienced freedom from earth's gravity. When I
see her I think of an antelope grazing the alpine meadows in mountains
whose names are as ancient as the sound that created the first world.

Saint Coincidence thought he recognized her as she began falling toward
him from the sky in a slow spin, like the spiral of events marking an ascension of grace. There was something in the curve of her shoulder, a familiar
slope that led him into the lightest moment of his life.

He could not bear it and turned to ask a woman in high heels for a quarter.
She was of the family of myths who would give everything if asked. She looked
like all the wives he'd lost. And he had nothing to lose anymore in this city of
terrible paradox where a woman was falling toward him from the sky.

The strange beauty in heels disappeared from the path of Saint Coincidence, with all her money held tightly in her purse, into the glass of advertisements. Saint Coincidence shuffled back onto the ice to watch the woman falling and falling.

Saint Coincidence, who was not a saint, perhaps a murderer if you count the people he shot without knowing during the stint that took his mind in Vietnam or Cambodia—remembered the girl he yearned to love when they were kids at Indian boarding school.

He could still see her on the dusty playground, off in the distance, years to the west past the icy parking lot of the Safeway. She was a blurred vision of the bittersweet and this memory had forced him to live through the violence of fire.

There they stood witness together to strange acts of cruelty by strangers, as well as the surprise of rare kindnesses.

The woman who was to fall from the sky was the girl with skinned knees whose spirit knew how to climb to the stars. Once she told him the stars spoke a language akin to the plains of her home, a language like rocks.

He watched her once make the ascent, after a severe beating. No one could touch the soul masked by name, age and tribal affiliation. Myth was as real as a scalp being scraped for lice.

Lila also dreamed of a love not disturbed by the wreck of culture she was forced to attend. It sprang up here and there like miraculous flowers in the cracks of the collision. It was there she found Johnny, who didn't have a saint's name when he showed up for school. He understood the journey and didn't make fun of her for her peculiar ways, despite the risks.

Johnny was named Johnny by the priests because his Indian name was foreign to their European tongues. He named himself Saint Coincidence many years later after he lost himself in drink in a city he'd been sent to to learn a trade. Maybe you needed English to know how to pray in the city. He could speak a fractured English. His own language had become a baby language to him, made of the comforting voice of his grandmother as she taught him to be a human.

Johnny had been praying for years and had finally given up on a god who appeared to give up on him. Then one night as he tossed pennies on the sidewalk with his cousin and another lost traveler, he prayed to Coincidence and won. The event demanded a new name. He gave himself the name Saint Coincidence.

His ragged life gleamed with possibility until a ghost-priest brushed by him as he walked the sidewalk looking for a job to add to his stack of new luck. The priest appeared to look through to the boy in him. He despaired. He would always be a boy on his knees, the burden of shame rooting him.

Saint Coincidence went back to wandering without a home in the maze of asphalt. Asphalt could be a pathway toward God, he reasoned, though he'd always imagined the road he took with his brothers when they raised sheep as children. Asphalt had led him here to the Safeway where a woman was falling from the sky.

The memory of all time relative to Lila and Johnny was seen by an abandoned cat washing herself next to the aluminum-can bin of the grocery story.

These humans set off strange phenomena, she thought and made no attachment to the thought. It was what it was, this event, shimmering there between the frozen parking lot of the store and the sky, something unusual and yet quite ordinary.

Like the sun falling fast in the west, this event carried particles of light through the trees.

Some say God is a murderer for letting children and saints slip through his or her hands. Some call God a father of saints or a mother of demons. Lila had seen God and could tell you God was neither male nor female and made of absolutely everything of beauty, of wordlessness.

This unnameable thing of beauty is what shapes a flock of birds who know exactly when to turn together in flight in the winds used to make words. Everyone turns together though we may not see each other stacked in the invisible dimensions.

This is what Lila saw, she told Johnny once. The sisters called it blasphemy.

Johnny ran away from boarding school the first winter with his two brothers, who'd run away before. His brothers wrapped Johnny Boy, as they called him, with their bodies to keep him warm. They froze and became part of the stars.

Johnny didn't make it home either. The school officials took him back the next day. To mourn his brothers would be to admit an unspeakable pain, so he became an athlete who ran faster than any record ever made in the history of the school, faster than the tears.

Lila never forgot about Johnny, who left school to join the army, and a few years later as she walked home from her job at Dairy Queen she made a turn in the road.

Call it destiny or coincidence—but the urge to fly was as strong as the need to push when at the precipice of any birth. It was what led her into the story told before she'd grown ears to hear, as she turned from stone to fish to human in her mother's belly.

Once, the stars made their way down stairs of ice to the earth to find mates. Some of the women were angry at their inattentive husbands, bored, or frustrated with the cycle of living and dying. They ran off with the stars, as did a few who saw their chance for travel and enlightenment.

They weren't heard from for years, until one of the women returned. She dared to look back and fell. Fell through centuries, through the beauty of the night sky, made a hole in a rock near the place Lila's mother had been born. She took up where she had left off, with her children from the stars. She was remembered.

This story was Lila's refuge those nights she'd prayed on her knees with the other children in the school dorms. It was too painful to miss her mother.

A year after she'd graduated and worked cleaning house during the day, and evenings at the Dairy Queen, she laughed to think of herself wearing her uniform spotted with sweets and milk, as she left on the arms of one of the stars. Surely she could find love in a place that did not know the disturbance of death.

While Lila lived in the sky she gave birth to three children and they made her happy. Though she had lost conscious memory of the place before, a song climbed up her legs from far away, to the rooms of her heart.

Later she would tell Johnny it was the sound of destiny, which is similar to a prayer reaching out to claim her.

You can't ignore these things, she would tell him, and it led her to the place her husband had warned her was too sacred for women.

She carried the twins in her arms as her daughter grabbed her skirt in her small fists. She looked into the forbidden place and leaped.

She fell and was still falling when Saint Coincidence caught her in his arms in front of the Safeway as he made a turn from borrowing spare change from strangers.

The children crawled safely from their mother. The cat stalked a bit of flying trash set into motion by the wave of falling—

or the converse wave of gathering together.

I traveled far above the earth for a different perspective. It is possible to travel this way without the complications of NASA. This beloved planet we call home was covered with an elastic web of light. I watched in awe as it shimmered, stretched, dimmed and shined, shaped by the collective effort of all life within it. Dissonance attracted more dissonance. Harmony attracted harmony. I saw revolutions, droughts, famines and the births of new nations. The most humble kindnesses made the brightest lights. Nothing was wasted.

I understood love to be the very gravity holding each leaf, each cell, this earthy star together.

Linda Hogan (Chickasaw)

Blessing

Blessed
are the injured animals
for they live in his cages.
but who will heal my father,
tape his old legs for him?

Here's his bird with the two broken wings
and her feathers are white as an angel
and she says goddamn stirring grains
in the kitchen. When the birds fly out
he leaves the cages open
and she kisses his brow for such
good works.

  Work he says
  all your damned life
  and at the end
  you don't own even a piece of land.

Blessed are the rich
for they eat meat every night.
They have already inherited the earth.

For the rest of us, may we just live
long enough
and unwrinkle our brows,
may we keep our good looks
and some of our teeth
and our bowels regular.

Perhaps we can go live in places
a rich man can't inhabit,
in the sunfish and jackrabbits,
in the cinnamon colored soil,
the land of red grass
and red people
in the valley
of the shadow of Elk
who aren't there.

  He says the old earth
  wobbles so hard, you'd best hang on
  to everything. Your neighbors
  steal what little you got.

Blessed are the rich
for they don't have the same old
Everyday to put up with
like my father
who's gotten old,
      Chickasaw
        chikkih asachi, which means
they left as a tribe not a very great while ago.
They are always leaving, those people.

Blessed
are those who listen
when no one is left to speak.

Song for My Name

Before sunrise
think of brushing out an old woman's
dark braids.
Think of your hands,
fingertips on the soft hair.

If you have this name,
your grandfather's dark hands
lead horses toward the wagon
and a cloud of dust follows,
ghost of silence.

That name is full of women
with black hair
and men with eyes like night.
It means no money
tomorrow.

Such a name my mother loves
while she works gently
in the small house.
She is a white dove
and in her own land
the mornings are pale,
birds sing into the white curtains
and show off their soft breasts.

If you have a name like this,
there's never enough water.

There is too much heat.
When lightning strikes, rain
refuses to follow.
It's my name,
that of a woman living
between the white moon
and the red sun, waiting to leave.
It's the name that goes with me
back to earth
no one else can touch.

Bamboo

First woman was made of slender bones
like these that stand upright together
in the rich, green world of daylight.

At night, they are a darkened forest
of sisters who grow quickly
in moving water
and talk in the clattering breeze
as if each is an open throat, rising
to speak.

I tell a man about this beautiful,
creaking world, how it flowers all
at once. He has been to war. He says
with bamboo they do terrible things
to men and women.

I look at this bamboo.
It did not give permission to soldiers.
It is imprisoned in its own skin.
The stalks are restless about this.
They have lived too long in the world of men.
They are hollow inside.

Lord, are you listening to this?
Plants are climbing to heaven
to talk to you.

Celebration: Birth of a Colt

When we reach the field
she is still eating
the heads of yellow flowers
and pollen has turned her whiskers
gold. Lady,
her stomach bulges out,
the ribs have grown wide.
We wait, our bare feet dangling
in the horse trough,
warm water
where goldfish brush
our smooth ankles.
We wait
while the liquid breaks
down Lady's dark legs
and that slick wet colt
like a black tadpole
darts out
beginning at once
to sprout legs.
She licks it to its feet,
the membrane still there,
red,
transparent
the sun coming up shines through,
the sky turns bright with morning
and the land
with pollen blowing off the corn,
land that will always own us,
everywhere it is red.

Drought

Once we said thunder
was the old man of sky snoring,
lightning was the old man
striking a match,
but now we only want him to weep
so we tell him our stories
in honest tongues.

The New Apartment, Minneapolis

The floorboards creak.
The moon is on the wrong side of the building,

and burns remain
on the floor.

The house wants to fall down
the universe when earth turns.

It still holds the coughs of old men
and their canes tapping on the floor.

I think of Indian people here before me
and how last spring white merchants hung an elder

on a meathook and beat him;
he was one of The People.

I remember this war
and all the wars

and relocation like putting the moon in prison
with no food and that moon was a crescent

but be warned, the moon grows full again
and the roofs of this town are all red

and we are looking through the walls of houses
at people suspended in air.

Some are baking, with flour on their hands,
or sleeping on floor three, or getting drunk.

I see the businessmen who hit their wives
and the men who are tender fathers.

There are women crying or making jokes.
Children are laughing under beds.

Girls in navy blue robes talk on the phone all night
and some Pawnee is singing 49s, drumming the table.

Inside the walls
world changes are planned, bosses overthrown.

If we had no coffee,
cigarettes or liquor,

says the woman in room 12,
they'd have a revolution on their hands.

Beyond walls are lakes and plains,
canyons and the universe;

the stars are the key
turning in the lock of night.

Turn the deadbolt and I am home.
I have walked to the dark earth,

opened a door to nights where there are no apartments,
just drumming and singing;

The Duck Song, The Snake Song,
The Drunk Song.

No one here remembers the city
or has ever lost the will to go on.

Hello aunt, hello brothers, hello trees
and deer walking quietly on the soft red earth.

The Truth Is

In my left pocket a Chickasaw hand
rests on the bone of the pelvis.
In my right pocket
a white hand. Don't worry. It's mine
and not some thief's.
It belongs to a woman who sleeps in a twin bed
even though she falls in love too easily,
and walks along with hands
in her own empty pockets
even though she has put them in others
for love not money.

About the hands, I'd like to say
I am a tree, grafted branches
bearing two kinds of fruit,

apricots maybe and pit cherries.
It's not that way. The truth is
we are crowded together
and knock against each other at night.
We want amnesty.

Linda, girl, I keep telling you
this is nonsense
about who loved who
and who killed who.

Here I am, taped together
like some old civilian conservation corps
passed by from the great depression
and my pockets are empty.
It's just as well since they are masks
for the soul, and since coins and keys
both have the sharp teeth of property.

Girl, I say,
it is dangerous to be a woman of two countries.
You've got your hands in the dark
of two empty pockets. Even though
you walk and whistle like you aren't afraid
you know which pocket the enemy lives in
and you remember how to fight
so you better keep right on walking.
And you remember who killed who.
For this you want amnesty
and there's that knocking on the door
in the middle of the night.

Relax, there are other things to think about.
Shoes for instance.
Now those are the true masks of the soul.
The left shoe
and the right one with its white foot.

Elk Song

We give thanks
to deer, otter,
the great fish
and birds that fly over

and are our bones and skin.
Even the yelping dog at our heels
is a hungry crow
picking bones wolf left behind.
And thanks to the corn and trees.
The earth
is a rich table
and a slaughterhouse
for humans as well.

But this is for the elk,
the red running one
like thunder over hills,
a saint with its holy hoof dance
an old woman whose night song
we try not to hear.

This song is for the elk
with its throat whistling
and antlers
above head and great hooves
rattling earth.

One spring night, elk
ran across me
while I slept on earth
and every hoof missed
my shaking bones.

That other time, I heard elk run
on earth's tight skin,
the time I was an enemy
from the other side of the forest.
Didn't I say the earth is a slaughterhouse
for humans as well?

Some nights in town's cold winter,
earth shakes.
People say it's a train full of danger
or the plane-broken barriers of sound,
but out there
behind the dark trunks of trees
the gone elk have pulled the hide of earth
tight and they are drumming
back the woodland,
tall grass and days we were equal
and strong.

Geraniums

Life is burning
in everything, in red flowers
abandoned in an empty house,
the leaves nearly gone,
curtains and tenants gone,
but the flowers red and fiery
are there and singing,
let us out.

Even dying they have fire.
Imprisoned, they open,
so like our own lives blooming,
exploding, wanting out,
wanting love,
water,
wanting.

And you, with your weapons and badges
and your fear about what neighbors think
and working overtime
as if the boss will reward you,
you can't bloom that way
so open the door,
break the glass. There's fire
in those flowers. Set off the alarm.
What's a simple crime of property
when life, breath, and all
is at stake?

Heritage

From my mother, the antique mirror
where I watch my face take on her lines.
She left me the smell of baking bread
to warm fine hairs in my nostrils,
she left the large white breasts that weigh down
my body.

From my father I take his brown eyes,
the plague of locusts that leveled our crops,
they flew in formation like buzzards.

From my uncle the whittled wood
that rattles like bones
and is white
and smells like all our old houses
that are no longer there. He was the man
who sang old chants to me, the words
my father was told not to remember.

From my grandfather who never spoke
I learned to fear silence.
I learned to kill a snake
when you're begging for rain.

And grandmother, blue-eyed woman
whose skin was brown,
she used snuff.
When her coffee can full of black saliva
spilled on me
it was like the brown cloud of grasshoppers
that leveled her fields.
It was the brown stain
that covered my white shirt,
my whiteness a shame.
That sweet black liquid like the food
she chewed up and spit into my father's mouth
when he was an infant.
It was the brown earth of Oklahoma
stained with oil.
She said tobacco would purge your body of poisons.
It has more medicine than stones and knives
against your enemies.

That tobacco is the dark night that covers me.

She said it is wise to eat the flesh of deer
so you will be swift and travel over many miles.
She told me how our tribe has always followed a stick
that pointed west
that pointed east.
From my family I have learned the secrets
of never having a home.

It Must Be

I am an old woman
whose skin looks young
though I ache
and have heard the gravediggers call me
by name.

The pathologists come
with their forceps and gowns.
It must be a disease, they say,
it must be.

It must be, they say,
over there in the joints
that her grandmothers refuse to bend
one more time
though her face smiles at the administrators
taking reports.

The doctors come
with their white coats and masks.
It must be
her heart, let us cut her open with knives.

Doctor, did you hear the singing in my heart?
Or find the broken-off love, the lost brother?
Surely you witnessed all the old women
who live in the young house of this body
and how they are full of black wool
and clipped nails.

They make me carry on
under my jeans and sweater,
traditions and complaints about the sad
state of the nation.

They have big teeth
for biting through leather and birch bark
and lies
about the world.
They have garlic in their pockets
to protect us from the government.

The nurses arrive with pink nails
and the odor of smoke. They arrive
from lifting the hips of old men
as if they were not old men.

One of the old women inside
lashes out at the nurses
and all who remain girls,
and at bankers and scholars.
But despite that old woman,
there are days I see my girlish hands
and wonder which banker owns them
and there are nights I watch the wrong face
in the mirror, and afternoons
I hold that face down to the floor by its neck
with those banker's hands,
those scholar's hands
that wish to silence the old woman inside
who tells the truth
and how it must be.

And there are days
the old women gossip and sing,
offering gifts of red cloth and cornbread
to one another.
On those days I love the ancestors
in and around me,
the mothers of trees and deer
and harvests, and that crazy one
in her nightgown
baring herself to the world,
daring the psychiatrists to come
with their couches and theories and rats.
On those days the oldest one is there,
taking stock
in all her shining
and with open hands.

Map

This is the world
so vast and lonely
without end, with mountains

named for men
who brought hunger
from other lands,
and fear
of the thick, dark forest of trees
that held each other up,
knowing fire dreamed of swallowing them
and spoke an older tongue,
and the tongue of the nation of wolves
was the wind around them.
Even ice was not silent.
It cried its broken self
back to warmth.
But they called it
ice, wolf, forest of sticks,
as if words would make it something
they could hold in gloved hands,
open, plot a way
and follow.

This is the map of the forsaken world.
This is the world without end
where forests have been cut away from their trees.
These are the lines wolf could not pass over.
This is what I know from science:
that a grain of dust dwells at the center
of every flake of snow,
that ice can have its way with land,
that wolves live inside a circle
of their own beginning.
This is what I know from blood:
the first language is not our own.

Morning: The World in the Lake

Beneath each black duck
another swims
shadow
joined to blood and flesh.

There's a world beneath this one.
The red-winged blackbird calls
its silent comrade down below.

The world rises
and descends
in the black eyes of a bird,
its crescent of fire
crossing lake and sky,
its breast turning up on water.

The sun burns behind dark mountains.

My daughter rises at water's edge.
Her face lies down on water
and the bird flies through her.
The world falls
into her skin
down to the world beneath,
the fiery leap of a fish
falling into itself.

And then it rises, the blackbird
above the world's geography of light and dark
and we are there, living
in that revealed sliver of red
living in the black
something of feathers,
daughters, all of us,
who would sleep as if reflected
alongside our mothers,
the mothers of angels and shadows,
the helix and spiral of centuries
twisting inside.
The radiant ones are burning
beneath this world.
They rise up
the quenching water.

Maurice Kenny (Mohawk)

Akwesasne

partridge drum in the land of the elm
Akwesasne
partridge drum in the land of white roots
Akwesasne

wampum
wampum is carried, the runner carries

the wampum
>   for the still of the forest
>   for the quiet of the valleys
wampum
partridge drum in the land of the elm

Dekanawidah broke arrows
>   in the land of the elm
Akwesasne

morning raised clear and blue
as the sun poured into the mountain
the runner carried the wampum
from village to village, from sachem to sachem
in the land of the north
>   the land of the elm
>   where the partridge drum

the Wolf and the Bear and the Turtle
dance in the land of the Mohiks
the Deer and the Snipe and the Heron
dance in the land of the Seneca
the Beaver and Eagle dance in the land of the Onondaga
>   in the land of the younger brothers
>   Cayuga, Oneida
where the partridge drums
as the runner carries the wampum
from Dekanawidah to the sachems
in the land of the north and the elm
and the sky remained clear

Hiawatha spoke to Atotarho
where the partridge drums

one morning the sky burst red
like the early star that so often frightens
the hunter and the women taking water
one morning the sky burst red
and the arrows were fitted together
as the runner carried the wampum
from village to village, from sachem to sachem
in the land of the north and the elm
where the partridge drums

words spilled over hills, spread over cedar
rolled onto paper, folded for draws, weapons, for fat judges
who never heard the partridge drum
never heard Dekanawidah

nor saw him break the arrows
never spoke with Hiawatha
as he walked through the land of the elm
never heard Handsome Lake
nor saw him break the arrows
as he walked through the land of the elm
where the partridge drums
Akwesasne

rolled into paper, folded into draws,
weapons for fat judges
who never spoke with Dekanawidah
in the land of the north
in the land of the elm
where the strawberry ripens
under the sun, under the sky
                    blue and clear
by the running rivers of the valleys
where the partridge drums
the runner carries the wampum
Akwesasne

Legacy

my face is grass
                color of April rain;
arms, legs are the limbs
                of birch, cedar;
my thoughts are winds
                which blow;
pictures in my mind
                are the climb up hill
                to dream in the sun;
                hawk feathers, and quills
                of porcupine running
                the edge of the stream
                which reflects stories
                of my many mornings
                and the dark faces of night
                mingled with victories
                of dawn and tomorrow;
corn of the fields and squash . . .

the daughters of my mother
who collect honey
and all the fruits;
meadow and sky are the end of my day,
the stretch of my night
yet the birth of my dust;
my wind is the breath of a fawn
the cry of the cub
the trot of the wolf
whose print covers
the tracks of my feet;
my word, my word,
loaned
legacy, the obligation I hand
to the blood of my flesh
the sinew of the loins
to hold to the sun
and the moon
which direct the river
that carries my song
and the beat of the drum
to the fires of the village
which endures.

Sweetgrass

For Jerome and Diane Rothenberg

Seeded in the mud on turtle's back
Greened in the breath of the west wind
Fingered by the children of the dawn
Arrowed to the morning sun
Blessed by the hawk and sparrow
Plucked by the many hands in the laughter
of young girls and the art of old women

You hold the moments of the frost and the thaw
You hold the light of the star and the moon
You hold the darkness of the moist night
and the music of the river and the drum
You are the antler of the deer

You are the watery fire of the trout
You are the dance of the morning
You are the grunts and the groans
 the whimpers and whistles of the forest

You are the blood of the feet
 and the balm for the wound
You are the flint and the spark
You are the child of the loins
 and the twin of the armpit
You are the rock of the field
 and the great pine of the mountain
You are the river that passes in the burnt afternoon
You are the light on the beak and the stump
 and the one-legged heron in the marsh
You are the elk in the snow
You are the groundhog and the bear
You are the claw of the muskrat

You are the ache in the spine
 yet the scent of summer
You are the plum and the squash and the gooseberry
 the flower of the bean
You are the bark of the house

You are the rainbow
 and the parched corn in your woven basket
You are the seed of my flesh
 and I am the flesh of your seed

They Tell Me I Am Lost

For Lance Henson

 my feet are elms, roots in the earth
 my heart is the hawk
 my thought the arrow that rides
  the wind across the valley
 my spirit eats with eagles on the mountain crag
  and clashes with the thunder
 my grass is the breath of my flesh
  and the deer is the bone of my child
 my toes dance on the drum
  in the light of the eyes of the old turtle

my chant is the wind
my chant is the muskrat
my chant is the seed
my chant is the tadpole
my chant is the grandfather
   and his many grandchildren
   sired in the frost of March
   and the summer noon of brown August
my chant is the field that turns with the sun
   and feeds the mice
   and the bear red berries and honey
my chant is the river
   that quenches the thirst of the sun
my chant is the woman who bore me
   and my blood and my flesh of tomorrow
my chant is the herb that heals
   and the moon that moves the tide
   and the wind that cleans the earth
      of old bones singing in the morning dust
my chant is the rabbit, skunk, heron
my chant is the red willow, the clay
   and the great pine that bulges the woods
   and the axe that fells the birch
   and the hand that breaks the corn from the stalk
   and waters the squash and catches stars
my chant is a blessing to the trout, beaver
   and a blessing to the young pheasant
      that warms my winter
my chant is the wolf in the dark
my chant is the crow flying against the sun
my chant is the sun
   sleeping on the back of the grass
      in marriage
my chant is the sun
   while there is sun I cannot be lost
my chant is the quaking of the earth
   angry and bold

although I hide in the thick forest
   or the deep pool of the slow river
   though I hide in a shack, a prison
   though I hide in a word, a law
   though I hide in a glass of beer
      or high on steel girders over the city
      or in the slums of that city

> though I hide in a mallard feather
>> or the petals of the milkwort
>> or a story told by my father

> though there are eyes that do not see me
>> and ears that do not hear my drum
>> or hands that do not feel my wind
>> and tongues which do not taste my blood
> I am the shadow on the field
>> the rain on the rock
>> the snow on the limb
>> the footprint on the water
>> the vetch on the grave
> I am the sweat on the boy
>> the smile on the woman
>> the paint on the man
> I am the singer of songs
>> and the hunter of fox
> I am the glare on the sun
>> the frost on the fruit
>> the notch on the cedar
> I am the foot on the golden snake
> I am the foot on the silver snake
> I am the tongue of the wind
>> and the nourishment of grubs
> I am the claw and the hoof and the shell
> I am the stalk and the bloom and the pollen
> I am the boulder on the rim of the hill
> I am the sun and the moon
>> the light and the dark
> I am the shadow on the field

> I am the string, the bow and the arrow

Wild Strawberry

For Helene

And I rode the Greyhound down to Brooklyn
where I sit now eating woody strawberries
grown on the backs of Mexican farmers
imported from the fields of their hands,
juices without color or sweetness

my wild blood berries of spring meadows
sucked by June bees and protected by hawks
have stained my face and honeyed
my tongue . . . healed the sorrow in my flesh

vines crawl across the grassy floor
of the north, scatter to the world
seeking the light of the sun and innocent
tap of the rain to feed the roots
and bud small white flowers that in June
will burst fruit and announce spring
when wolf will drop winter fur
and wrens will break the egg

my blood, blood berries that brought laughter
and the ache in the stooped back that vied
with dandelions for the plucking,
and the wines nourished our youth and heralded
iris, corn and summer melon

we fought bluebirds for the seeds
armed against garter snakes, field mice;
won the battle with the burning sun
which blinded our eyes and froze our hands
to the vines and the earth where knees knelt
and we laughed in the morning dew like worms
and grubs; we scented age and wisdom

my mother wrapped the wounds of the world
with a sassafras poultice and we ate
wild berries with their juices running
down the roots of our mouths and our joy

I sit here in Brooklyn eating Mexican
berries which I did not pick, nor do
I know the hands which did, nor their stories . . .
January snow falls, listen . . .

Wolf "Aunt"

For Rochelle Ratner

They came to the lodge door
and called him by name.
Blackrobe, they called.
Blackrobe, come out.

Foolish and determined.
Obstinate, adamant.
Oh! He'll save these children
all right, but from the throne of his god.

I tried to persuade him
to return to the Hurons, his friends.
I told him not to carry that cross
when he walked alone in the village . . .

holding it, flaunting it in the faces
of both the chiefs and clan mothers.
I told him to stop mumbling
over the sick children,

that the duties of curing
belonged to our doctors
who have centuries of service
and the herbs to heal.

Would he listen! No!
At hearing of an illness
he would drop his bowl of food
and rush out into a blizzard

that cross before him, those beads
clanking on the wind.
I gave him a warm place to sleep,
and deer meat my brother killed.

With my own hands I sewed him moccasins.
I thought he would learn our ways.
All he learned was our language
so he could "speak to the people."

I threatened him
and told him the false-faces
would come when walking
in the woods, they would

bite his flesh and suck
out his spirit. Did he
listen! No, of course not.
Instead he made signs

over me, always smiling what others
thought a smirk, a leer, but he was
smiling. He was too dumb to smirk.
No, not dumb, but foolish.

I was positive that one day the Bear
would grow tired of his posturing,
that some doctor or other would become
jealous, fearful of his powers,

that a clan mother would envy his
living within my lodge,
that some boy would resent his stares,
and that a child would hear his

mumblings and scream out to his
uncle for help. I told him this
every morning of his life
and every night that predicted his death.

And finally they came to the door,
called him by name.
Blackrobe, they called.
Blackrobe, come out!

The moon was very beautiful that night.
Full and yellow. The shadows cast
were long, ominous.
The air was bright, sky blue.

He barely placed his foot on the earth
outside the lodge
when I heard a thump and I knew
his body crumpled under the club.

I will be searching
his bones for years . . .
bone by bone.

Joyce carlEtta Mandrake (Anishinabee)

Who I Am

You must be an Indian, you have a braid.
One single braid flowing down my back.
This white woman staring at me says it again,
You must be an Indian, you have a braid.

If my hair was balanced on my head in a bun,
Would anyone say you must be old, you have a bun.
If my hair was short with a pink bow on the side,
Would anyone say you must be young, you have a bow.

After all is said and done,
I am just a forty-year old dame wondering,
I must be an Indian, I have a braid.

N. Scott Momaday (Kiowa)

Angle of Geese

How shall we adorn
Recognition with our speech?—
Now the dead firstborn
Will lag in the wake of words.

Custom intervenes;
We are civil, something more:
More than language means,
The mute presence mulls and marks.

Almost of a mind,
We take measure of the loss;
I am slow to find
The mere margin of repose.

And one November
It was longer in the watch,
As if forever,
Of the huge ancestral goose.

So much symmetry!—
Like the pale angle of time
And eternity.
The great shape labored and fell.

The Bear

What ruse of vision,
escarping the wall of leaves,
rending incision
into countless surfaces,

would cull and color
his somnolence, whose old age
has outworn valor,
all but the fact of courage?

Seen, he does not come,
move, but seems forever there,
dimensionless, dumb,
in the windless noon's hot glare.

More scarred than others
these years since the trap maimed him,
pain slants his withers,
drawing up the crooked limb.

Then he is gone, whole,
without urgency, from sight,
as buzzards control,
imperceptibly, their flight.

At Risk

I played at words.
It was a long season.

Soft syllables,
Images that shimmered,
Intricate etymologies.

They cohered in wonder.
I was enchanted.

My soul was at risk.
I struggled

Towards hurt,
Towards healing,
Towards passion,
Towards peace.

I wheeled in the shadow of a hawk.
Dizziness came upon me;
The turns of time confined and confounded me.

I lay in a cave,
On a floor cured in blood.

Ancient animals danced about me,
Presenting themselves formally,
In masks.

And there was I, among ancient animals,
In the formality of the dance,
Remembering my face in the mirror of masks.

December 29, 1890

Wounded Knee Creek

In the shine of photographs
are the slain, frozen and black

on a simple field of snow.
They image ceremony:

women and children dancing,
old men prancing, making fun.

In autumn there were songs, long
since muted in the blizzard.

In summer the wild buckwheat
shone like fox fur and quillwork,

and dusk guttered on the creek.
Now in serene attitudes

of dance, the dead in glossy
death are drawn in ancient light.

The Colors of Night

1. White

An old man's son was killed far away in the Staked Plains. When the old man heard of it he went there and gathered up the bones. Thereafter, wherever the old man ventured, he led a dark hunting horse which bore the bones of his son on its back. And the old man said to whomever he saw: "You see how it is that now my son consists in his bones, that his bones are polished and so gleam like glass in the light of the sun and moon, that he is very beautiful."

2. Yellow

There was a boy who drowned in the river, near the grove of thirty-two bois d'arc trees. The light of the moon lay like a path on the water, and a glitter of low brilliance shone in it. The boy looked at it and was enchanted. He began to sing a song that he had never heard before; only then, once, did he hear it in his heart, and it was borne like a cloud of down upon his voice. His voice entered into the bright track of the moon, and he followed after it. For a time he made his way along the path of the moon, singing. He paddled with his arms and legs and felt his body rocking down into the swirling water. His vision ran along the path of light and reached across the wide night and took hold of the moon. And across the river, where the path led into the shadows of the bank, a black dog emerged from the river, shivering and shaking the water from its hair. All night it stood in the waves of grass and howled the full moon down.

3. Brown

On the night before a flood, the terrapins move to high ground. How is it that they know? Once there was a boy who took up a terrapin in his hands and looked at it for a long time, as hard as he could look. He succeeded in memorizing the terrapin's face, but he failed to see how it was that the terrapin knew anything at all.

4. Red

There was a young man who had got possession of a powerful medicine. And by means of this medicine he made a woman out of sumac leaves and lived with her for a time. Her eyes flashed, and her skin shone like pipestone.

But the man abused her, and so his medicine failed. The woman was caught up in a whirlwind and blown apart. Then nothing was left of her but a thousand withered leaves scattered in the plain.

5. Green

A young girl awoke one night and looked out into the moonlit meadow. There appeared to be a tree; but it was only an appearance; there was a shape made of smoke; but it was only an appearance; there was a tree.

6. Blue

One night there appeared a child in the camp. No one had ever seen it before. It was not bad-looking, and it spoke a language that was pleasant to hear, though none could understand it. The wonderful thing was that the child was perfectly unafraid, as if it were at home among its own people. The child got on well enough, but the next morning it was gone, as suddenly as it had appeared. Everyone was troubled. But then it came to be understood that the child never was, and everyone felt better. "After all," said an old man, "how can we believe in the child? It gave us not one word of sense to hold on to. What we saw, if indeed we saw anything at all, must have been a dog from a neighboring camp, or a bear that wandered down from the high country."

7. Purple

There was a man who killed a buffalo bull to no purpose, only he wanted its blood on his hands. It was a great, old, noble beast, and it was a long time blowing its life away. On the edge of the night the people gathered themselves up in their grief and shame. Away in the west they could see the hump and spine of the huge beast which lay dying along the edge of the world. They could see its bright blood run into the sky, where it dried, darkening, and was at last flecked with flakes of light.

8. Black

There was a woman whose hair was long and heavy and black and beautiful. She drew it about her like a shawl and so divided herself from the world that not even Age could find her. Now and then she steals into the men's societies and fits her voice into their holiest songs. And always, just there, is a shadow which the firelight cannot cleave.

N. Scott Momaday (Kiowa)

The Eagle-Feather Fan

The eagle is my power,
And my fan is an eagle.
It is strong and beautiful
In my hand. And it is real.
My fingers hold upon it
As if the beaded handle
Were the twist of bristlecone.
The bones of my hand are fine
And hollow; the fan bears them.
My hand veers in the thin air
Of the summits. All morning
It scuds on the cold currents;
All afternoon it circles
To the singing, to the drums.

Simon J. Ortiz (Acoma Pueblo)

Bend in the River

Flicker flies by.
His ochre wing
is tied to prayer sticks.
Pray for mountains,
the cold strong shelter.

Sun helps me to see
where Arkansas River
ripples over pebbles.
Glacial stone moves slowly;
it will take a while.

A sandbank cuts sharply
down to a poplar log
buried in damp sand.
Shadow lengths tell me
it is afternoon.

There are tracks
at river's edge, raccoon,

coyote, deer, crow,
and now my own.

My sight follows
the river upstream
until it bends.
Beyond the bend
is more river
and, soon, the mountains.
We shall arrive,
to see, soon.

The Creation, According to Coyote

"First of all, it's all true."
Coyote, he says this, this way,
humble yourself, motioning and meaning
what he says.

You were born when you came
from that body, the earth;
your black head burst from granite,
the ashes cooling,

until it began to rain.
It turned muddy then,
and then green and brown things
came without legs.

They looked strange.
Everything was strange.
There was nothing to know then,

until later, Coyote told me this,
and he was b.s.-ing probably,
two sons were born,
Uyuyayeh and Masaweh.

They were young then,
and then later on they were older.

And then the people were wondering
what was above.
They had heard rumors.

But, you know, Coyote,
he was mainly bragging
when he said (I think),
"My brothers, the Twins then said,
'Let's lead these poor creatures
and save them.' "

And later on, they came to light
after many exciting and colorful
and tragic things of adventure;
and this is the life, all these, all these.

My uncle told me all this, that time.
Coyote told me too, but you know
how he is, always talking to the gods,
the mountains, the stone all around.

And you know, I believe him.

Dry Root in a Wash

The sand is a fine grit
and warm to the touch.
An old juniper root
lies by the cutbank of sand;
it lingers, waiting
for the next month of rain.

I feel like saying,
It will rain, but you know
better than I these centuries
don't mean much
for anyone to be waiting.

Upstream, towards the mountains,
the Shiwana work for rain.

They know we're waiting.

Underneath the fine sand
it is cool
with crystalline moisture,
the forming rain.

My Father's Song

Wanting to say things,
I miss my father tonight.
His voice, the slight catch,
the depth from his thin chest,
the tremble of emotion
in something he has just said
to his son, his song:

We planted corn one spring at Acu—
we planted several times
but this one particular time
I remember the soft damp sand
in my hand.

My father had stopped at one point
to show me an overturned furrow;
the plowshare had unearthed
the burrow nest of a mouse
in the soft moist sand.

Very gently, he scooped tiny pink animals
into the palm of his hand
and told me to touch them.
We took them to the edge
of the field and put them in the shade
of a sand moist clod.

I remember the very softness
of cool and warm sand and tiny alive mice
and my father saying things.

A Story of How a Wall Stands

At Acu, there is a wall almost 400 years old which supports hundreds of tons
of dirt and bones—it's a graveyard built on a steep incline—and it looks like
it's about to fall down the incline but will not for a long time.

My father, who works with stone,
says, "That's just the part you see,
the stones which seem to be

just packed in on the outside,"
and with his hands puts the stone and mud
in place. "Underneath
what looks like loose stone,
there is stone woven together."
He ties one hand over the other,
fitting like the bones of his hands
and fingers. "That's what is
holding it together."

"It is built that carefully,"
he says, "the mud mixed
to a certain texture," patiently
"with the fingers," worked
in the palm of his hand. "So that
placed between the stones, they hold
together for a long, long time."

He tells me those things,
the story of them worked
with his fingers, in the palm
of his hands, working the stone
and the mud until they become
the wall that stands a long, long time.

The Boy and Coyote

for a friend, Ed Theis,
met at VAH, Ft. Lyons, Colorado,
November and December 1974

You can see the rippled sand rifts
shallow inches below the surface.
I walk on the alkalied sand.
Willows crowd the edges of sand banks
sloping to the Arkansas River.

I get lonesome for the young afternoons
of a boy growing at Acoma.
He listens to the river,
the slightest nuance of sound.

Breaking thin ice from a small still pool,
I find Coyote's footprints.
Coyote, he's always somewhere before you;
he knows you'll come along soon.
I smile at his tracks which are not fresh
except in memory and say a brief prayer
for goodluck for him and for me and thanks.

All of a sudden, and not far away,
there are the reports of a shotgun,
muffled flat by saltcedar thickets.
Everything halts for several moments,
no sound; even the wind holds to itself.
The animal in me crouches, poised immobile,
eyes trained on the distance, waiting
for motion again. The sky is wide;
blue is depthless; and the animal
and I wait for breaks in the horizon.

Coyote's preference is for silence
broken only by the subtle wind,
uncanny bird sounds, saltcedar scraping,
and the desire to let that man free,
to listen for the motion of sound.

Carter Revard (Osage)

And Don't Be Deaf to the Singing Beyond

You never could tell what my deaf Uncle Arthur heard.
That Sunday when the black storm-cloud came at us
He sat there churning butter in a bedroom window.
We saw this strange cloud way off west on the hills,
A little dark funnel with specks dancing round.
"It's only a big whirlwind," he said with a smile.
Well, pretty soon we saw the specks were trees
And heard this rumble like freight trains on a trestle,
But Uncle Arthur was deaf and wouldn't believe us.
We ran like hell to the car and drove off east;
When hail and rain came blasting after to blind us.
He still sat up in his window, churning away.
Of course the storm passed before we got to the school
And ran down steps to stand in its flooded cellar;

So, after fifteen minutes, we drove back home.
When we got in, he had two pounds of butter
All worked, salted, and molded onto dishes.
The funnel had passed a half-mile north and west—
Its swath, a quarter-mile wide of levelled blackjacks,
Went up and over the valley's northern rim.
We drove up north to find out who'd been killed,
But in the dirt yard of the paintless two-room house
Our Holy Roller friends were standing unharmed.
"We knelt and prayed; God turned his wrath aside,"
                                they said.
Which tasted sweeter'd be hard to say, by now,
That Jersey butter from Uncle Arthur's churn
Or the name of God in Mrs. Parks' mouth.
I still get peeved, thinking of what missed them
So close they saw the lightning up in its blackness,
And what we missed, down in our scorpion-filled cellar.
Well, when my Uncle Arthur died years later
He was way the hell out in California
And Aunt Jewel, my Uncle Woody's wife,
Saw him collapse there with his coronary
And when she ran up he lay there on his back
Turned his eyes to her, smiled, closed them, was dead.
"He was so deaf," she said, "and he saw my mouth
Just calling and calling, and seemed to think it was funny."

Driving in Oklahoma

On humming rubber along this white concrete
    lighthearted between the gravities
of source and destination like a man
        halfway to the moon
    in this bubble of tuneless whistling
at seventy miles an hour from the windvents
            over prairie swells rising
    and falling, over the quick offramp
    that drops to its underpass and the truck
            thundering beneath as I cross
with the country music twanging out my windows,
        I'm grooving down this highway feeling
technology is freedom's other name when
        —a meadowlark

comes sailing across my windshield
with breast shining yellow
and five notes pierce
the windroar like a flash
of nectar on mind
gone as the country music swells up and
drops me wheeling down
my notch of cement-bottomed sky
between home and away
and wanting
to move again through country that a bird
has defined wholly with song
and maybe next time see how
he flies so easy, when he sings.
lunges, glides,
spins upside down and turns
to butterfly! that stops precisely underneath
an image of white larkspur nodding upon
the water's surface so it seems
that dimly there
among cruising crawdads a
butterfly of shadows tastes
sweet light again.

In Kansas

The '49 dawn set me high on a roaring yellow tractor,
slipping the clutch or gunning a twenty-foot combine
to spurt that red-gold wheat into Ceres' mechanical womb:
I'd set her on course and roll for a straight two miles
before turning left, and that got monotonous as hell,
at first all the roar and dust and the jiggling stems
collapsing
to whisk up that scything platform and be stripped of
their seed,
then even the boiling from under of rats and rabbits
scrambling
to hide again in their shrinking island of tawny grain
as the hawks hung waiting their harvest of torn fur
and blood.
So I'd play little god with sunflowers drooping
their yellow heads;

see a clump coming and spin the wheel left, right,
                straight.
The shuddering combine swiveled on its balljoint hitch
first right, then left, its great chatter of blades
                swinging
so the tip barely brushed those flowers and left
                their clump standing
like a small green nipple out from the golden breastline
and next time past
reversing wheel-spins cut free a sinuous lozenge left
                for the bumblebees
with butter-and-black-velvet tops limp-nodding over
                wilted leaves.
But sunflowers weren't enough. I left on the slick stubble
                islets
of blue-flowered chicory, scarlet poppies, and just
for the hell of it cockleburrs:
"From now on, kid, you run that sumbitch straight,"
                the farmer said.
Hell's bells, out on that high prairie I bet goldfinches,
bobwhites, and pheasants still are feasting
                in that farmer's fields
on the flower seeds I left out, summer, fall, and
                winter harvests
that make the bread I eat taste better
                by not being ground up with it,
                        then or now.

An Eagle Nation

For the Camp/Jump brigades

You see, I remember this little Ponca woman
    who turned her back to the wall and placed her palms
        up over her shoulders flat on the wall
and bent over backwards and walked her hands down the wall
    and placed them flat on the floor behind her back—that's
        how limber she was, Aunt Jewell,
            when I was a boy.
And FAST! you wouldn't BELIEVE how she could sprint:
    when an Osage couple married, they would ask Aunt Jewell
        to run for the horses for them.
Now she's the eldest in her clan, but still the fastest

to bring the right word, Ponca or English, sacred or
profane, whatever's needed to survive she brings it, sometimes in
a wheelchair, since her heart
alarms the doctors now and then.
So one bright day we loaded
the wheelchair, and ourselves, and lots of chicken
barbecued and picnic stuff
into our cars and zoomed away
from Ponca City and White Eagle, *Southward Ho!*
To the Zoo, we said, the Oke City Zoo—we'd picnic there!
Grandchildren, see, they love the zoo,
and has she got GRANDchildren? well, maybe
one of her children knows how many, the rest of us
stopped counting years ago, so there were quite a few
with serious thoughts of chicken barbecue and we all rolled in
to the Zoo and parked, and we walked, and scrambled, and rolled,
we scuttled and sprinted, we used up all the verbs
in English, she'd have to get those Ponca words
to tell you how we made our way,
but somehow we ALL of us got in, and found
the picnic tables, and we feasted there and laughed
until it was time to inspect the premises, to see just what
the children of Columbus had prepared for us.
Snow leopards and black jaguars, seals and dolphins, monkeys and
baboons, the elephants and tigers looked away
thinking of Africa, of Rome, oceans, dinnertime, whatever—
and as for us, we went in all directions,
grandchildren rolled and bounced like marbles up and down
the curving asphalt ways, played hide and seek, called me to look
at camels maybe. And then we were all
getting tired and trying to reassemble, when Casey
came striding back to where we were wheeling Aunt Jewell
and said "Mom,
there's this eagle over here you should see,"
and we could tell it mattered. So we wheeled along
to this cage set off to itself with a bald eagle sitting,
eyes closed and statue-still,
on the higher perch inside, and there was a couple
standing up next to the cage and trying
to get its attention.
A nice white couple, youngish, the man
neatly mustached and balding, the woman
white-bloused and blondish: the man clapped hands
and clicked his tongue and squeaked, and whistled. The eagle

was motionless. Casey wheeled Aunt Jewell
a little to the side. The man stopped making noises.
He and the woman looked at each other, then at us, and
looked away.
There was a placard on the cage's side that said:
This bald eagle was found wounded, and
although its life was saved, it will never fly again,
so it is given this cage to itself.
Please do not feed him.
Aunt Jewell, from her wheelchair, spoke in Ponca to him,
so quietly that I could hardly hear
the sentences she spoke.
Since I know only
a few words of Ponca, I can't be sure
what she said or asked, but I caught the word
Kahgay:
Brother, she said.
The eagle opened his eyes and turned his head.
She said something else. He partly opened his beak
and crouched and looked head-on toward her,
and made a low shrill sound.
The white couple were kind of dazed, and so was I.
I knew she was saying good things for us.
I knew he'd pass them on.
She talked a little more, apologizing
for all of us, I think.
She put one hand up to her eyes and closed them for a while
till Casey handed her a handkerchief,
and she wiped her eyes.
"I guess we're 'bout ready to go now," Aunt Jewell said,
so we wheeled along back to the car, and we gathered all
the clan and climbed aboard
and drove from the Zoo downtown to where
the huge *Red Earth* powwow was going on, because
her grandson Wesley, Mikasi, was dancing there.
We hadn't thought Aunt Jewell's heart
was up to Zoo and Powwow in one day, but as usual she
knew better. They CHARGED ADMISSION, and that really
outraged my Ponca folks, for whom
a powwow should be free. Worse than that,
the contest DANCERS had to pay a fee.
"That's not our way," Aunt Jewell said.
But once inside we found our way,
wheelchair and all, up to the higher tiers,

where we and thousands of Indian people looked down
to the huge Arena floor where twelve drums
thundered and fourteen hundred dancers spun and eddied round,
and dancing in his wolfskin there
was Mikasi where Casey pointed, and we saw
his Grampa Paul Roughface gliding
with that eagle's calm he has,
and I saw how happy Casey and Mike were then
that their eldest son was dancing down there, and I felt
what the drum did for Aunt Jewell's heart and ours, and she told us
of seventy years ago when she was a little girl and her folks
would load the wagons up there in White Eagle and go
and ford the Arkansas into the Osage country and drive all day
and camp at night on the prairie and then drive on
to the Grayhorse Osage Dances, or those in Pawhuska even.
I remembered how Uncle Woody Camp had told me
of going to the Osage dances later and seeing her
for the first time and asking:
"Who IS that beautiful Ponca girl over there?"
and someone said,
"Oh that's McDonald's girl,"
and they met that way.
And he and Uncle Dwain would tell
of the covered wagon in which they rode,
my Irish and Scotch-Irish mother's folks, from Missouri out
to the Kansas wheat harvest, and then on down
to the Osage Reservation in Oklahoma, where mules were needed,
and our grandfather hauled the bricks to build
the oil-boom Agency town of Pawhuska, where the million-dollar
lease sales, and the Osage Dances, were held.
So I was thinking how the eagles soared,
in their long migration flights, over all these places,
how they looked down on the wagons moving
westward from Missouri, eastward from Ponca lands
to meet in Pawhuska, how all the circles
had brought us into this Oklahoma time and what
had passed between cage and wheelchair before
we mounted up to view on this huge alien floor the long-ago drum
in its swirling rainbow of feathers and
bells and moccasins lifting up here
the songs and prayers from long before cars or wagons,
and how it all has changed and the ways are strange but
the voices still
are singing, the drum-heart

still beating here, so whatever the placards on
their iron cages may have to say, we the people,
as Aunt Jewell and Sun Dancers say,
are an EAGLE NATION, now.

What the Eagle Fan Says

For Bob and Evelyne Voelker, Dale and Arlene Besse,
and the St. Louis Gourd Dancers

I strung dazzling thrones   of thunder beings
on a spiraling thread   of spinning flight,
beading dawn's blood   and blue of noon
to the gold and dark   of day's leaving,
circling with Sun   the soaring heaven
over turquoise eyes   of Earth below,
her silver veins,   her sable fur,
heard human relatives   hunting beneath
calling me down,   crying their need
that I bring them closer   to Wakonda's ways,
and I turned from heaven   to help them then.
When the bullet came   it caught my heart,
the hunter's hands   gave earth its blood,
loosened light beings   and let us float
toward the sacred center   of song in the drum,
but fixed us first   firm in tree-heart
that green light-dancers   gave to men's knives,
ash-heart in hiding where   a deer's heart had beat,
and a one-eyed serpent   with silver-straight head
strung tiny rattles   around white softness
in beaded harmonies   of blue and red—
now I move lightly   in a man's left hand,
above dancing feet   follow the sun
around old songs   soaring toward heaven
on human breath,   and I help them rise.

This poem offers thanks for the honor of being given eagle feathers which
were then set into a beaded fan. It tells how the eagle in flight pierces clouds
just as a beadworker's needle goes through beads and buckskin, spiraling
round sky or fan-handle—and how the eagle flies from dawn to sunset, linking day and night colors as they are linked on a Gourd Dancer's blanket

(half crimson, half blue), and as they are linked in the beading of the fan's handle. The poem's form is the alliterative meter used by the Anglo-Saxon tribes, and its mode is the Anglo-Saxon "riddle," in which mysterious names are given to ordinary things: here, tree leaves are *green light-dancers,* wood is *tree-heart* or *ash-heart,* clouds are *thrones of thunder beings.* I hope the one-eyed serpent will find its ordinary name in the reader's memory.

Wazhazhe Grandmother

—i-ko-eh, tha-gthi a tho

(HO-e-ga, literally "bare spot": the center of the forehead of the mythical elk ... a term for an enclosure in which all life takes on bodily form, never to depart therefrom except by death ... the earth which the mythical elk made to be habitable by separating it from the water ... the camp of the tribe when ceremonially pitched ... life as proceeding from the combined influences of the cosmic forces.

—Francis LaFlesche, A Dictionary of the Osage Language, 1932)

They chose their allotted land
    out west of the Agency
            at the prairie's edge,
      where the Osage Hills begin thcy built
        their homestead, honeymooned there
near Timber Hill,
      where Bird Creek meanders in
from the rolling grassy plains with their prairie chicken
           dancing in spring,
  built in a timbered hollow where deer came down
    at dusk with the stars
to drink from the deep pools
    near Timber Hill
       and below the
    waterfall that seemed
  so high to me the summer
when I was six and walked up near its clearness gliding
    some five or six feet down from the flat
      sandstone ledge to its pools,
        she called it in Osage, *ni-xe ga-thpe,*
where the dark water turning into
    a spilling of light
        was a curtain clear and flowing, under
    the blue flash of a kingfisher's diving
    into the pool above the falls

and his flying up
again to the dead white branch of his willow—
the whole place was so quiet,
in the way Grandma was quiet,
it seemed a place to be still,
seemed waiting for us,
though no one lived there by then
since widowed during the war she'd moved
to the place south of Pawhuska,
and why we had driven down there from Timber Hill, now,
I can't quite remember—
was it a picnic, or some kind
of retreat or vacation time
out of the August heat of Pawhuska?
The pictures focus sharp-edged:
a curtain of dark green ivy ruffled
a bit by breeze and water beside
the waters falling there
and a dirt road winding red and rocky
across tree-roots, along which, carefully,
my mother eased our rumbling Buick Eight
in that Depression year when Osage oil
still poured to float us into
a happy future—

but whether I dreamed, or saw real things in time,
their road, their house, the waterfall back in the
woods are all
at the bottom of Lake Bluestem now,
because Bird Creek,
blessed with a dam,
is all psyched out
of its snaggly, snaky self into a
windsparkling lake
whose deep blue waters, the politicians promise, will soon
come piped into Pawhuska pure and drinkable,
filling with blue brilliance municipal pools
and sprinkling the lawns to green or pouring freshets
down asphalt gutters to cool the shimmering
cicada-droning fevers of August streets
even as
in Bird Creek's old channel under Lake Bluestem big
catfish grope slowly in darkness
up over the sandstone ledge of the drowned

waterfall, or
scavenge through the ooze of
the homestead and along the road where
the bride and groom came riding one special day
and climbed down from the buggy in all their
best finery
to live in their first home.

Wendy Rose (Miwok-Hopi)

I Expected My Skin and My Blood to Ripen

*When the blizzard subsided four days later [after the massacre in 1890 at
Wounded Knee], a burial party was sent ... a long trench was dug. Many of
the bodies were stripped by whites who went out in order to get the Ghost
shirts and other accoutrements the Indians wore ... the frozen bodies were
thrown into the trench stiff and naked ... only a handful of items remain in
private hands ... exposure to snow has stiffened the leggings and moccasins,
and all the objects show the effects of age and long use ... [items pictured for
sale] moccasins $140; hide scraper $350; buckskin shirt $1200; womens'
leggings $275; bone breastplate $1000...*

—*Kenneth Canfield's 1977 Plains Indian
Art Auction Catalog*

I expected my skin and my blood
to ripen, not be ripped from my bones;
like fallen fruit I am peeled, tasted,
discarded. My seeds open
and have no future.
Now there has been no past.
My own body gave up the beads,
my own hands gave the babies away
to be strung on bayonets,
to be counted one by one
like rosary stones and then
tossed to the side of life
as if the pain of their birthing
had never been.
My feet were frozen to the leather,
pried apart, left behind—bits of flesh
on the moccasins, bits of paper deerhide
on the bones. My back was stripped
of its cover, its quilling intact,
was torn, was taken away.
My leggings were taken like in a rape
and shriveled to the size
of stick figures
like they had never felt the push
of my strong woman's body

walking in the hills.
It was my own baby
whose cradleboard I held—
would've put her in my mouth like a snake
if I could, would've turned her into a bush
or rock if there'd been magic enough
to work such changes. Not enough magic
to stop the bullets, not enough magic
to stop the scientists, not enough magic
to stop the money.

If I Am Too Brown or Too White for You

remember I am a garnet woman
whirling into precision
as a crystal arithmetic
or a cluster and so

why the dream
in my mouth,
the flutter of blackbirds
at my wrists?

In the morning
there you are
at the edge of the river
on one knee

and you are selecting me
from among polished stones
more definitely red or white
between which tiny serpents swim

and you see
that my body is blood
frozen into giving birth
over and over, a single motion,

and you touch the matrix
shattered in winter
and begin to piece together
the shape of me

wanting the curl in your palm
to be perfect

and the image less clouded,
less mixed

but you always see
just in time
working me around
the last hour of the day

there is a small light
in the smoke, a tiny sun
in the blood, so deep
it is there and not there,

so pure
it is singing.

Three Thousand Dollar Death Song

"19 American Indian skeletons valued at $3,000;
please pay from this invoice ...."—museum invoice, 1975.

Is it
in cold hard cash? the kind
that dusts the insides of mens' pockets
laying silver-polished surface
along the cloth?   Or in bills?
papering wallets of they who go about
threading the night with dark words.
Or checks? paper promises
that weigh the same as words spoken once
between the grown grass of our history and
the hidden water in the clouds.
However it goes, it goes:

through my body it goes. Assessing each nerve,
running its edges along my arteries, planning ahead
for whose hands will rip me into pieces
of dusty red paper, whose hands will
smooth and smatter me into traces of rubble.
It's invoiced now:

how our bones are valued.
Our bones that stretch out pointing
to sunrise or are flexed into one last
foetal bend; our bones—removed

piece by piece and knocked about, catalogued,
numbered with black ink on
their newly-white foreheads. We come apart
as we were formed
having gone together to laughter
of white soldiers, white students,
all the same in our fleshless prison.
From this distant point
we watch our bones   auctioned
with our careful beadwork, our
quilled medicine bundles, even the bridles
of our shot-down horses.

How
have you priced us? At what cost
removed us?
What price the pits
where our bones share a single word:
      remembering . . . still
we don't see how one century
has turned our dead
into something else, what you call
"specimens." Our blindness
might be catching, you know . . . picture the mortars,
the arrowheads, the labrets
standing up and shaking off their labels
like animals suddenly awake to find
the world went on while they slept;
watch them touch each other, become as one,
march together out the door, walk
into the wind searching for us.
Watch our bones rise to meet them.

At what cost then
our sweet-grass-smelling having-been?
Is it to be paid
in clam shell beads or steatite,
dentalia shells or turquoise,
or blood?

Leslie Marmon Silko (Laguna Pueblo)

Indian Song: Survival

We went north
      to escape winter
climbing pale cliffs
          we paused   to sleep at the river.
Cold water   river from the north
I sink my body in the shallow
          sink into sand and cold river water.

You sleep in the branches of
          pale river willows above me.
I smell you in the silver leaves, mountain lion man
          green willows aren't sweet enough to hide you.

I have slept with the river   and
          he is warmer than any man.
At sunrise
    I heard ice on the cattails.

Mountain lion, with dark yellow eyes
          you nibble moonflowers
          while we wait.
I don't ask why do you come
          on this desperation journey north.

I am hunted for my feathers
I hide in spider's web
          hanging   in a thin gray tree.
          above the river.
In the night   I hear music
         song of branches   dry leaves scraping the moon.

Green spotted frogs sing to the river
          and I know he is waiting.
Mountain lion shows me the way
        path of mountain wind
        climbing higher
           up
          up to Cloudy Mountain.

It is only a matter of time, Indian
          you can't sleep with the river forever.
Smell winter and know.

I swallow black mountain dirt
while you catch hummingbirds
trap them with wildflowers
pollen and petals
fallen from the Milky Way.

You lie beside me in the sunlight
warmth around us and
you ask me if I still smell winter.
Mountain forest wind travels east and I answer:
taste me,
I am the wind
touch me,
I am the lean gray deer
running on the edge of the rainbow.

(Untitled)

The Laguna people
always begin their stories
with "humma-hah":
that means "long ago."
And the ones who are listening
say "aaaa-eh"

This story took place
somewhere around Acoma
where there was a lake,
a lake with pebbles along the edges.
It was a beautiful lake
and so a little girl and her sister
went there one day.
The older girl never liked to take care of her sister
but this day
she seemed to be anxious to take care of her sister.
So she put the little sister
on her back
That was the traditional way
of carrying babies, you know,
strapped on their back—

And so they went off to this lake
and this lake had shells around it
and butterflies and beautiful flowers—
they called it Shell Lake

shells and other pretty pebbles
where she amused her little sister
all day long.
And finally
toward evening
they came home to their village home.
And all was quiet in the village
there seemed to be no one stirring around or left,
and then
when they got to their house
which was a two-story house
traditional home of the Keres
she called "*Deeni!* Upstairs!"
because the entrance was generally from the top.

No one answered
until an old man came out
decrepit and he says
"You poor children—
nobody is here.
All our people have gone to Maúhuatl."
That was the name
of the high place
where they all went that day
to escape the flood that was coming.

He says
"Today the earth is going to be
filled with water.
And everyone has gone
to Maúhuatl
that high mesa land
to escape drowning.
Your mother is not here.
She left early in the day
to go with the rest of the people.
Only the old people
who cannot travel
are left.
And if you and your little sister
follow the rest
you can tell by their foot tracks.
But be sure and walk fast—
make haste
because the flood may be coming up
before you reach the mesa."

So she said they would.
She started off with her little sister on her back and
pretty soon they began to cry
and what they cried
is a song that is sung.
Their crying became this little song.
It goes like this:

> Little sister go to sleep, go to sleep.
> I suppose our mother didn't think much
> of us
> so she left us behind. Go to sleep. Go to sleep.
> By luck we might catch up to the crowd. Go to sleep.
> We might catch up to our mother who has gone
> ahead to Maúhuatl. Go to sleep.

That is how the song goes.
And so the little girl kept walking
faster and faster.
By that time
the water was coming up to her ankles.
She was wading along
and as they went along
her little sister on her back
began to cry again.
She sang

> Go to sleep little sister, go to sleep.
> I suppose our mother didn't think much of us
> Or she wouldn't have left us behind.

By that time
the water had come up her legs
almost to her knees
and finally they reached the bottom
of Maúhuatl which was a mesa.
And there was a trail up there
and finally the older girl
walked up the mesa steps—
stone formations like steps.
They got to the top
before the flood really reached the top
and they looked around and
saw the people—
all the people up there
who had gone before.
They looked around
but they didn't see anything

of their mother.
They sat down,
the older girl did.
She saw the rest of them sitting around
holding their babies
and holding their little ones on their laps
so she thought she would sit down too
and hold her little sister on her lap.
Which she did.
She sat there for a little while
and then they all turned into stone.

The story ends there.
Some of the stories
Aunt Susie told
have this kind of ending.
There are no explanations.

(Untitled; from *Ceremony*)

Long time ago
in the beginning
there were no white people in this world
there was nothing European.
And this world might have gone on like that
except for one thing:
witchery.
This world was already complete
even without white people.
There was everything
including witchery.

Then it happened.
These witch people got together.
Some came from far far away
across oceans
across mountains.
Some had slanty eyes
others had black skin.
They all got together for a contest
the way people have baseball tournaments nowadays
except this was a contest
in dark things.

So anyway
they all got together

witch people from all directions
witches from all the Pueblos
and all the tribes.
They had Navajo witches there,
some from Hopi, and a few from Zuni.
They were having a witches' conference,
that's what it was
Way up in the lava rock hills
north of Cañoncito
they got together
to fool around in caves
with their animal skins.
Fox, badger, bobcat, and wolf
they circled the fire
and on the fourth time
they jumped into that animal's skin.

But this time it wasn't enough
and one of them
maybe a Sioux or some Eskimos
started showing off.
"That wasn't anything,
watch this."

The contest started like that.
Then some of them lifted the lids
on their big cooking pots,
calling the rest of them over
to take a look:
dead babies simmering in blood
circles of skull cut away
all the brains sucked out.
Witch medicine
to dry and grind into powder
for new victims.

Others untied skin bundles of disgusting objects:
dark flints, cinders from burned hogans where the
dead lay
Whorls of skin
cut from fingertips
sliced from the penis end and clitoris tip.

Finally there was only one
who hadn't shown off charms or powers.
The witch stood in the shadows beyond the fire
and no one ever knew where this witch came from

which tribe
or if it was a woman or a man.
But the important thing was
this witch didn't show off any dark thunder charcoals
or red ant-hill beads.
This one just told them to listen:
"What I have is a story."

At first they all laughed
but this witch said
Okay
go ahead
laugh if you want to
but as I tell the story
it will begin to happen.

Set in motion now
set in motion by our witchery
to work for us.

Caves across the ocean
in caves of dark hills
white skin people
like the belly of a fish
covered with hair.

Then they grow away from the earth
then they grow away from the sun
then they grow away from the plants and animals.
They see no life
When they look
they see only objects.
The world is a dead thing for them
the trees and rivers are not alive
the mountains and stones are not alive.
The deer and bear are objects
They see no life.

They fear
They fear the world.
They destroy what they fear.
They fear themselves.

The wind will blow them across the ocean
thousands of them in giant boats
swarming like larva
out of a crushed ant hill.

They will carry objects
which can shoot death
faster than the eye can see.

They will kill the things they fear
all the animals
the people will starve.

They will poison the water
they will spin the water away
and there will be drought
the people will starve.

They will fear what they find
They will fear the people
They kill what they fear.

Entire villages will be wiped out
They will slaughter whole tribes.

Corpses for us
Blood for us
Killing killing killing killing.

And those they do not kill
will die anyway
at the destruction they see
at the loss
at the loss of the children
the loss will destroy the rest.

Stolen rivers and mountains
the stolen land will eat their hearts
and jerk their mouths from the Mother.
The people will starve.

They will bring terrible diseases
the people have never known.
Entire tribes will die out
covered with festered sores
shitting blood
vomiting blood.
Corpses for our work

Set in motion now
set in motion by our witchery
set in motion
to work for us.

They will take this world from ocean to ocean
they will turn on each other
they will destroy each other
Up here
in these hills
they will find the rocks,
rocks with veins of green and yellow and black.
They will lay the final pattern with these rocks
they will lay it across the world
and explode everything.

Set in motion now
set in motion
To destroy
To kill
Objects to work for us
objects to act for us
Performing the witchery
for suffering
for torment
for the stillborn
the deformed
the sterile
the dead.

Whirling
Whirling
Whirling

Whirling
set into motion now
set into motion.

So the other witches said
"Okay you win; you take the prize,
but what you said just now—
it isn't so funny
It doesn't sound so good.
We are doing okay without it
we can get along without that kind of thing.
Take it back.
Call that story back."

But the witch just shook its head
at the others in their stinking animal skins, fur
and feathers.
It's already turned loose.
It's already coming.
It can't be called back.

Storytelling

You should understand
the way it was
back then,
because it is the same
even now.

Long ago it happened
that her husband left
to hunt deer
before dawn
And then she got up
and went to get water.
Early in the morning
she walked to the river
when the sun came over
the long red mesa.

He was waiting for her
that morning
in the tamarack and willow
beside the river.

Buffalo Man
in buffalo leggings.
"Are you here already?"
"Yes," he said.
He was smiling.
"Because I came for you."
She looked into the
shallow clear water.
"But where shall I put my water jar?"
"Upside down, right here," he told her,
"on the river bank."

"You better have a damn good story,"
her husband said,
"about where you been for the past
ten months and how you explain these
twin baby boys."

"No! That gossip isn't true.
She didn't elope

She was *kidnapped* by
that Mexican
at Seama feast.
You know
my daughter
isn't
that kind of girl."

It was
in the summer
of 1967.
T.V. news reported
a kidnapping.
Four Laguna women
and three Navajo men
headed north along
the Rio Puerco river
in a red '56 Ford
and the F.B.I. and
state police were
hot on their trail
of wine bottles and
size 42 panties
hanging in bushes and trees
all along the road.

"We couldn't escape them," he told police later.
"We tried, but there were four of them and
only three of us."

Seems like
it's always happening to me.
Outside the dance hall door
late Friday night
in the summertime,
and those
brown-eyed men from Cubero,
smiling.
They usually ask me
"Have you seen the way stars shine
up there in the sand hills?"
And I usually say "No. Will you show me?"

It was
that Navajo
from Alamo,
you know,

the tall
good-looking
one.

He told me
he'd kill me
if I didn't
go with him
And then it
rained so much
and the roads
got muddy.
That's why
it took me
so long
to get back home.

My husband
left
after he heard the story
and moved back in with his mother.
It was my fault and
I don't blame him either.
I could have told
the story
better than I did.

Story from Bear Country

You will know
when you walk
in bear country
By the silence
flowing swiftly between the juniper trees
by the sundown colors of sandrock
all around you.

You may smell damp earth
scratched away
from yucca roots
You may hear snorts and growls
slow and massive sounds
from caves
in the cliffs high above you.

It is difficult to explain
how they call you
All but a few who went to them
left behind families
      grandparents
      and sons
      a good life.

The problem is
you will never want to return
Their beauty will overcome your memory
like winter sun
melting ice shadows from snow
And you will remain with them
locked forever inside yourself
      your eyes will see you
      dark shaggy and thick.

We can send bear priests
loping after you
their medicine bags
bouncing against their chests
Naked legs painted black
bear claw necklaces
rattling against
their capes of blue spruce.

They will follow your trail
into the narrow canyon
through the blue-gray mountain sage
to the clearing
where you stopped to look back
and saw only bear tracks
behind you.

When they call
faint memories
will writhe around your heart
and startle you with their distance.
But the others will listen
because bear priests
sing beautiful songs
They must
if they are ever to call you back.

They will try to bring you
step by step
back to the place you stopped
and found only bear prints in the sand
where your feet had been.

Whose voice is this?
You may wonder
hearing this story when
after all
you are alone
hiking in these canyons and hills
while your wife and sons are waiting
back at the car for you.

But you have been listening to me
for some time now
from the very beginning in fact
and you are alone in this canyon of stillness
not even cedar birds flutter.
See, the sun is going down now
the sandrock is washed in its colors
Don't be afraid
        we love you
        we've been calling you
        all this time
Go ahead
turn around
see the shape
of your footprints
in the sand.

Toe'osh:
A Laguna Coyote Story

For Simon Ortiz, July, 1973

1

In the wintertime
at night
we tell coyote stories
           and drink Spanada by the stove.

How coyote got his
ratty old fur coat
>> bits of old fur
>> the sparrows stuck on him
>> with dabs of pitch.
That was after he lost his proud original one in a poker game.
anyhow, things like that
are always happening to him,
that's what she said, anyway.

And it happened to him at Laguna
and Chinle
and at Lukachukai too, because coyote got too smart for his own
> good.

2

But the Navajos say he won a contest once.
It was to see who could sleep out in a
snow storm the longest
and coyote waited until chipmunk badger and skunk were all
curled up under the snow
and then he uncovered himself and slept all night
inside
and before morning he got up and went out again
and waited until the others got up before he came
in to take the prize.

3

Some white men came to Acoma and Laguna a hundred years ago
and they fought over Acoma land and Laguna women, and even now
some of their descendants are howling in
the hills southeast of Laguna.

4

Charlie Coyote wanted to be governor
and he said that when he got elected
he would run the other men off
the reservation
and keep all the women for himself.

5

> One year
> the politicians got fancy
> at Laguna.
> They went door to door with hams and turkeys
> and they gave them to anyone who promised
> to vote for them.
> On election day all the people
> stayed home and ate turkey
> and laughed.

6

> The Trans-Western pipeline vice president came
> to discuss right-of-way.
> The Lagunas let him wait all day long
> because he is a busy and important man.
> And late in the afternoon they told him
> to come back again tomorrow.

7

> They were after the picnic food
> that the special dancers left
> down below the cliff.
> And Toe'osh and his cousins hung themselves
> down over the cliff
> holding each other's tail in their mouth making a coyote chain
> until someone in the middle farted
> and the guy behind him opened his
> mouth to say "What stinks?" and they
> all went tumbling down, like that.

8

> Howling and roaring
> Toe'osh scattered white people
> out of bars all over Wisconsin.
> He bumped into them at the door
> until they said
>   "Excuse me"
> And the way Simon meant it
> was for 300 or maybe 400 years.

When Sun Came to Riverwoman

June 10, 1973

that time
    in the sun
    beside the Rio Grande.

voice of the mourning dove
    calls
       long ago   long ago
    remembering the lost one
    remembering the love.

Out of the dense green
      eternity of springtime
    willows rustle in the blue wind
      timeless
    the year unknown
      unnamed.

The muddy fast water
    warm around my feet
    you move into the current slowly

    brown skin   thighs
    deep intensity
    flowing water.

Your warmth penetrates
      yellow sand and sky.

Endless eyes shining always
    for green river moss
    for tiny water spiders.
Crying out   the dove
      will not let me forget
    it is ordained
    in swirling brown water
        and it carries you away,
      my lost one
      my love,
        the mountain.

man of Sun
      came to riverwoman
      and in the sundown wind
   he left her
       to sing
         for rainclouds swelling in the northwest sky
         for rainsmell on pale blue winds
            from China

Mary TallMountain (Koyukon, Athabaskan)

Good Grease

The hunters went out with guns
at dawn.
We had no meat in the village,
no food for the tribe and the dogs.
No caribou in the caches.

All day we waited.
At last!
As darkness hung at the river
we children saw them far away.
Yes! They were carrying caribou!
We jumped and shouted!

By the fires that night
we feasted.
The old ones clucked,
sucking and smacking,
sopping the juices with sourdough bread.
The grease would warm us
when hungry winter howled.

Grease was beautiful,
oozing,
dripping and running down our chins,
brown hands shining with grease.
We talk of it
when we see each other
far from home.

Remember the marrow
sweet in the bones?
We grabbed for them like candy.
Good.
Gooooood.

Good grease.

Mary TallMountain (Koyukon, Athabaskan)

The Last Wolf

the last wolf hurried toward me
through the ruined city
and I heard his baying echoes
down the steep smashed warrens
of Montgomery Street and past
the few ruby-crowned highrises
left standing
their lighted elevators useless

passing the flicking red and green
of traffic signals
baying his way eastward
in the mystery of his wild loping gait
closer the sounds in the deadly night
through clutter and rubble of quiet blocks
I heard his voice ascending the hill
and at last his low whine as he came
floor by empty floor to the room
where I sat
in my narrow bed looking west, waiting
I heard him snuffle at the door and
I watched
he trotted across the floor

he laid his long gray muzzle
on the spare white spread
and his eyes burned yellow
his small dotted eyebrows quivered

Yes, I said.
I know what they have done.

There Is No Word for Goodbye

Sokoya,[1] I said, looking through
        the net of wrinkles into
        wise black pools
        of her eyes.

---

[1]*Sokoya*—aunt (mother's sister).

What do you say in Athabaskan
>when you leave each other?
>What is the word
>for goodbye?

A shade of feeling rippled
>the wind-tanned skin.
>Ah, nothing, she said,
>watching the river flash.

She looked at me close.
>We just say, Tlaa. That means,
>See you.
>We never leave each other.
>When does your mouth
>say goodbye to your heart?

She touched me light
>as a bluebell.
>You forget when you leave us;
>you're so small then.
>We don't use that word.

We always think you're coming back,
>but if you don't,
>we'll see you someplace else.
>You understand.
>There is no word for goodbye.

Matmiya

For my grandmother

I see you sitting
Implanted by roots
Coiled deep from your thighs.
Roots, flesh red, centuries pale.
Hairsprings wound tight
Through fertile earthscapes
Where each layer feeds the next
Into depths immutable.

Though you must rise, must
Move large and slow
When it is time, O my
Gnarled mother-vine, ancient

As vanished ages,
Your spirit remains
Nourished,
Nourishing me.

I see your figure wrapped in skins
Curved into a mound of earth
Holding your rich dark roots.
Matmiya,
I see you sitting.

Lucí Tapahonso (Navajo)

Blue Horses Rush In
For Chamisa Bah Edmo, Shisóí 'aláájí' naaghígíí

Before the birth, she moved and pushed inside her mother.
Her heart pounded quickly and we recognized
the sound of horses running:
      the thundering of hooves on the desert floor.

Her mother clenches her fists and gasps.
She moans ageless pain and pushes: This is it!

Chamisa slips out, glistening wet, and takes her first breath.
      The wind outside swirls small leaves
      and branches in the dark.
Her father's eyes are wet with gratitude.
He prays and watches both mother and baby—stunned.

This baby arrived amid a herd of horses,
      horses of different colors.

White horses ride in on the breath of the wind.
White horses from the east
where plants of golden chamisa shimmer in the moonlight.

She arrived amid a herd of horses.

Blue horses enter from the south
bringing the scent of prairie grasses
from the small hills outside.

She arrived amid a herd of horses.

Yellow horses rush in, snorting from the desert in the south.
It is possible to see across the entire valley to Niist'áá from Tó.
Bah, from here your grandmothers went to war long ago.

She arrived amid a herd of horses.

Black horses came from the north.
They are the lush summers of Montana and still white winters of Idaho.

Chamisa, Chamisa Bah. It is all this that you are.
You will grow: laughing, crying,
and we will celebrate each change you live.

You will grow strong like the horses of your past.
You will grow strong like the horses of your birth.

In Praise of Texas

So many times I've rushed into airports frazzled,
my hair everywhere as I lugged bags along,
my face flushed from hurrying,
and my breathing loud and raspy.

But I will never be seen like that in Texas.

Because George Strait lives in Texas.
A friend saw him once at Gate 29 at Dallas-Fort Worth.
He is so nice, she said, and to prove it,
she handed me a picture.
George Strait had his arm around her. He was smiling.
I struggled so to share her happiness.

Though that was years ago, I believe that unending faith
precedes glittering possibilities.
I believe that the world is basically good,
and so I am certain that one day
I will just happen to run into George Strait in Texas.
Maybe he'll be buying the *Dallas Morning News* at a Circle K.
Maybe as I'm having a salad, he'll walk into the same cafe,
like an ordinary person, and order a medium Diet Coke.®

Each time I am in Texas,
my hair shines radiant,
I won't allow dark thoughts to mar my face even for an instant,
my hat has been steamed and re-shaped,
my clothes are smooth and coordinated,
and I am never rushed.

Once as we dined alongside the Riverwalk in San Antonio, my
husband smiled at me and said, "You sure are pretty."
"Thanks honey," I said, "but do you really mean it,
or are you just saying that?"
"I really mean it," he said.
I removed my sunglasses and searched his face
in the evening light,
but I couldn't tell if he really meant it.
In any case, I glanced around very discreetly to see
if anyone else (maybe a country western singer)
shared his sentiment. Just in case, I reminded
myself to sit up straight.

No way.
You'll never see me looking frazzled
or the least bit scuzzy in Texas.
Whether we drive through Dalhart, visit Fort Worth
for a few days, take in a Rangers game,
or whether I have a brief layover at Houston-Hobby,
I believe that one has to be prepared
for whatever Texas has to offer.

Sometimes as the plane glides over that vast, plain state,
above scattered herds of horses, I can see the luster
sparkling off their broad backs like intense hope and I am
reassured that dreams can blossom without any urging on our part.

Light a Candle

For Hector Torres

The other night thunder shook the house
and lightning slashed brilliant blue across the bed.
I slept in bits, my heart raced with each explosion of noise and rain.
And though he held me, my breathing was ragged and exhausted.
I may never sleep through these storms.

Hector, light a candle for me.

Last week we returned to our birth place,
and as we drove through southern Colorado,
we were stunned by the beauty of autumn leaves,
the deep cool mountain canyons,
and twice, deer stood beside the road.

They watched as we passed through their land.
Their eyes glistened black softness.
Misty said, "Isn't it neat that we saw them on our way home?"

Hector, light a candle for her.

In a small reservation town, a little boy shakes his mother.
She has passed out on the floor and he is hungry.
"Mama," he says, "can you make some potatoes?"
She stirs, "Leave me alone, damn it!"
He climbs up on the counter, takes down a box of Cheerios
and sits back down to watch TV.
The noise he makes eating dry cereal is steady and quiet.

Hector, light a candle for him.

Some evenings Leona just wants to sit with her sisters and mother
around the kitchen table and talk of everything and nothing.
Instead, she sits in the quiet kitchen, and outside
leaves blow against the window—the wind is cold and damp.
In front of Leona, the table stretches out clean and shiny.

Hector, light a candle for her.

North of here, the Kaw rushes westward, a wide muted roar.
The trees alongside sway and brush against each other,
dry, thin leaves swirl in the cold wind.
The river smell and heavy wind settle in my hair,
absorbing the dull thundering water,
            the rolling waves of prairie wind.

This time I have walked among the holy people:
the river, the wind, the air swirling down from the hills,
the exhilaration of the biggest catch,
the smooth grace of eagles as they snatch their prey,
the silent pleas of those who drowned here.

Hector, light a candle for me.
            Light a candle for me.

Raisin Eyes

I saw my friend Ella
with a tall cowboy at the store
the other day in Shiprock.

Later, I asked her
Who's that guy anyway?

Oh Luci, she said (I knew what was coming).
It's terrible. He lives with me.
And my money and my car.
But just for a while.
He's in AIRCA and rodeos a lot.
And I still work.

This rodeo business is getting to me
you know and I'm going to leave him
because I think all this I'm doing now
will pay off better somewhere else
but I just stay with him and it's hard
because

he just smiles that way you know
and then I end up paying entry fees
and putting shiny Tony Lamas on lay-away again.
It's not hard.

But he doesn't know when
I'll leave him and I'll drive across the flat desert
from Red Rock in blue morning light
straight to Shiprock so easily.

And anyway
my car is already used to humming
a mourning song with Gary Stewart
complaining again of aching and breaking
down-and-out love affairs.

Damn.
These Navajo cowboys with raisin eyes
and pointed boots are just bad news
but it's so hard to remember that
all the time.

She said with a little laugh.

James Welch (Blackfeet, Gros Ventre)

Christmas Comes to Moccasin Flat

Christmas comes like this: Wise men
unhurried, candles bought on credit (poor price
for calves), warriors face down in wine sleep.
Winds cheat to pull heat from smoke.

Friends sit in chinked cabins, stare out
plastic windows and wait for commodities.
Charlie Blackbird, twenty miles from church
and bar, stabs his fire with flint.

When drunks drain radiators for love
or need, chiefs eat snow and talk of change,
an urge to laugh pounding their ribs.
Elk play games in high country.

Medicine Woman, clay pipe and twist tobacco,
calls each blizzard by name and predicts
five o'clock by spitting at her television.
Children lean into her breath to beg a story:

Something about honor and passion,
warriors back with meat and song,
a peculiar evening star, quick vision of birth.
Blackbird feeds his fire. Outside, a quick 30 below.

Surviving

The day-long cold hard rain drove
like sun through all the cedar sky
we had that late fall. We huddled
close as cows before the bellied stove.
Told stories. Blackbird cleared his mind,
thought of things he'd left behind, spoke:

"Oftentimes, when sun was easy in my bones,
I dreamed of ways to make this land."
We envied eagles easy in their range.
"That thin girl, old cook's kid, stripped naked
for a coke or two and cooked her special stew
round back of the mess tent Sundays."
Sparrows skittered through the black brush.

That night the moon slipped a notch, hung
black for just a second, just long enough
for wet black things to sneak away our cache
of meat. To stay alive this way, it's hard. . . .

Thanksgiving at Snake Butte

In time we rode that trail
up the butte as far as time
would let us. The answer to our time
lay hidden in the long grasses
on the top. Antelope scattered

through the rocks before us, clattered
unseen down the easy slope to the west.
Our horses balked, stiff-legged,
their nostrils flared at something unseen
gliding smoothly through brush away.

On top, our horses broke, loped through
a small stand of stunted pine, then jolted
to a nervous walk. Before us lay
the smooth stones of our ancestors, the fish,
the lizard, snake and bent-kneed

bowman—etched by something crude,
by a wandering race, driven by their names
for time: its winds, its rain, its snow
and the cold moon tugging at the crude figures
in this, season of their loss.

Snow Country Weavers

A time to tell you things are well.
Birds flew south a year ago.
One returned, a blue-wing teal
wild with news of his mother's love.

Mention me to friends. Say
wolves are dying at my door,
the winter drives them from their meat.
Say this: say in my mind

I saw your spiders weaving threads
to bandage up the day. And more,
those webs were filled with words
that tumbled meaning into wind.

Riding the Earthboy 40

Earthboy: so simple his name
should ring a bell for sinners.
Beneath the clowny hat, his eyes
so shot the children called him
dirt, Earthboy farmed this land
and farmed the sky with words.

The dirt is dead. Gone to seed
his rows becoming marker to a grave
vast as anything but dirt.
Bones should never tell a story
to a bad beginner. I ride
romantic to those words,

those foolish claims that he
was better than dirt, or rain
that bleached his cabin
white as bone. Scattered in the wind
Earthboy calls me from my dream:
Dirt is where the dreams must end.

Roberta Hill (Oneida)

Dream of Rebirth

We stand on the edge of wounds, hugging canned meat,
waiting for owls to come grind
nightsmell in our ears. Over fields,
darkness has been rumbling. Crows gather.
Our luxuries are hatred. Grief. Worn-out hands
carry the pale remains of forgotten murders.
If I could only lull or change this slow hunger,
this midnight swollen four hundred years.

Groping within us are cries yet unheard.
We are born with cobwebs in our mouths
bleeding with prophecies.

Yet within this interior, a spirit kindles
moonlight glittering deep into the sea.
These seeds take root in the hush
of dusk. Songs, a thin echo, heal the salted marsh,
and yield visions untrembling in our grip.

I dreamed an absolute silence birds had fled.
The sun, a meager hope, again was sacred.
We need to be purified by fury.
Once more eagles will restore our prayers.
We'll forget the strangeness of your pity.
Some will anoint the graves with pollen.
Some of us may wake unashamed.
Some will rise that clear morning like the swallows.

For Heather, Entering Kindergarten

She tests the curb with a chubby boot,
lolls around the door,
then offers a smile before she walks
down halls that smell of crayon.

When the bell rings, each chart clings
to another from the day before.
Too willing to be wrong, she knows our clock
doesn't tock the same as theirs, and I'm afraid

she'll learn the true length of forlorn,
the quotient of the quick
who claim that snowflakes never speak,
that myths are simply lies.

Aware of each minute and its death,
I scrubbed my Catholic
desk with nubs of tissue and piqued
the sister's early prayers.

Some, bullied into disbelief,
want clues to the terrible cutting
taking place as we race to reason.
I want to gather shreds of bark

and press them in my forehead.
I want to stand near curbs and sing:
The stars can hear. In what season
will you send a message?

Sixth graders scorn my truth. Heather walks away,
sways in delightful idleness while somewhere
mountain flowers in a sudden gust of wind
openly send word to Algol and Procyon.

In the Longhouse, Oneida Museum

House of five fires, you never raised me.
Those nights when the throat of the furnace
wheezed and rattled its regular death,
I wanted your wide door,

your mottled air of bark and working sunlight,
wanted your smokehole with its stars,
and your roof curving its singing mouth above me.
Here are the tiers once filled with sleepers,

and their low laughter measured harmony or strife.
Here I could wake amazed at winter,
my breath in the draft a chain of violets.
The house I left as a child now seems

a shell of sobs. Each year I dream it sinister
and dig in my heels to keep out the intruder
banging at the back door. My eyes burn
from cat urine under the basement stairs

and the hall reveals a nameless hunger,
as if without a history, I should always walk
the cluttered streets of this hapless continent.
Thinking it best I be wanderer,

I rode whatever river, ignoring every zigzag,
every spin. I've been a fragment, less than my name,
shaking in a solitary landscape,
like the last burnt leaf on an oak.

What autumn wind told me you'd be waiting?
House of five fires, they take you for a tomb,
but I know better. When desolation comes,
I'll hide your ridgepole in my spine

and melt into crow call, reminding my children
that spiders near your door
joined all the reddening blades of grass
without oil, hasp or uranium.

Ray A. Young Bear (Mesquakie)
Black Eagle Child Quarterly

The fall 1965 issue of the *Black Eagle Child Quarterly*
contained the sad news that the state legislature had reneged
on its long-held promises of twenty new houses
with indoor plumbing. The prominent headline read:
"Youthman Throws Cantaloupes at State Officials."
The caption and text below the photograph
of the splattered cantaloupes read:

"All Hope of Flushing Toilets Down the Drain
for Twenty BEC Households:
Claude Youthman, 35, of Cutfoot Crossing,
walked out the courtroom on August 14,
Tuesday, under the assumption he was acquitted
of charges of deadly assault with a 'round-shaped
projectile' levied against him by the state.
When the prosecuting attorney proclaimed,
'Your Honor, we submit,' in reference
to the visual evidence of the weapon,
Youthman misinterpreted 'we submit'
to mean the attorney had given up.
He was subsequently apprehended
for serious assault and terrorism
before he stepped off the courthouse
lawn.

"During Farmers Market in downtown Why Cheer
a month previous, Youthman contended 'a mean group'
of white men 'in good, clean clothes were listening
when theys weren't suppose ta' when his wife Henrietta
was accosted by a farmer with lewd suggestions.
'She knows little language. The white man's. Yours,'
he said to Judge Manez. 'When farmer say "put it in,"
she ran away and told me. I get mad and go ask farmer
why talk dirty? To get soap and wash mouth.
But they laugh, the farmer and men in the long
black car. I not know he (farmer) mean a sack
to put cantaloupe in.'

"Representing the state was the county attorney,
Tom Katz, who based the case on a series
of photographs taken at the scene.

One photograph of split cantaloupes
was enlarged to the size of a blackboard,
and another showed the open-mouths of a crowd
in dismay. 'This is a mockery of the good
relations we have with our Indians,'
testified the mayor, who later said
he wasn't anywhere near Farmers Market
where the event transpired. 'Whether I was
there or not is irrelevant. I came to tell
the folks at the capital we are genuinely
sorry for what happened. We vow to take better
care of our natives. We'll drive them home,
if necessary, when we detect telltale breath.'
When Judge Manez asked the mayor if he felt
the subject was under the influence at the time,
he said, 'When are they not? He probably was.
They are no different than children who need
strict supervision. The sad part is, they're
full-grown A-dults who oughta know better than
to act out their frustrations in a public forum.
That's why they're overly dependent on us.
They need to be more appreciative of what
they acquired from us thus far and not be
a burden to us good, tax-paying folks.'
The jury and courtroom audience applauded
the mayor's words of wisdom . . ."

Getting arrested proved to be the most audacious
thing that ever happened to Claude Youthman.
But he had this queer, nagging feeling
a monumental change was taking place.
Where it would take him and when
and how he would unboard he did not know.
All his life he had taken precautions
to maintain a mile's distance from
the type of inhumanity represented
in the county. In his wildest fears
Youthman never anticipated becoming
an innocent passenger aboard a train
of outcasts. Being away for five years
was, therefore, an unnerving experience.
He now knew where the two railroad tracks
that diagonally crisscrossed the Settlement
went. He was enlightened. The trains were
capable of stealing breath from those

he knew and dearly loved, but the rails
also led to federal prisons.

Abandoned as a child—the stories of his origins
were purposely kept vague—he grew up under
the care and attention of his grandfather,
Jim Percy, a kind-hearted leader
of the Star-Medicine Society.
Never quite understanding his
purpose, Youthman became hermitlike
after dropping out from Weeping Willow
Elementary in the fifth grade. He could
not stand the prospect of one day being
questioned about his mother and father.
They were unknown; he knew of none.
This blank spot had a frightening
effect on his psyche.

If there were doings sponsored
by his grandfather, he would lock himself
in the attic with his magazines of sensational
crime and jubilant Hollywood personalities—
Audie Murphy, the war hero, and the exquisite
Elizabeth Taylor. Those who came up the hill
to participate in ceremonies never sought
him out of curiosity, for all were aware
the darting figure or a creaking tree branch
was indication he was nearby. If by chance
someone accidentally caught him around
a corner or in a closet, he would look
down, stumble out sideways, and not look up
until he maneuvered his way to the staircase.
In spite of his introvertedness, the visitors
found him pleasing in appearance. He had oily,
jet-black hair that graced his classic slanted
eyes and high cheekbones, and he wore brown
summer shirts and gray baggy denims.
What did bother people was the fact
they only saw a profile. Even though
Youthman would tense up around strangers,
he remained photogenic. The people glanced
at his visage and then politely looked away.
Hunching his bony back over his tightly folded
arms, he brought his jaw to one of the shoulders
and kept it there. When addressed directly
the young man would pucker his large lips

and speak in a deep voice. He was his own
ventriloquist and wooden dummy. Ed Sullivan.
He made speech without facial gestures
an art form. A renowned spearfisherman once
equated the "young hermit's" lips to the lips
of a walleye in its last throes of life
over the frozen river. "As the walleye dies
from the puncture wounds of the barbed tines
and the subzero weather, it stiffens
and every fiber and nerve can be seen on
its lips. This is the way I see Claude when
he talks. He grits his parched mouth so much
the only movement you see is his quivering
lip muscles. Why does he do that anyway?"
The grandfather of the recluse usually
had no explanations.

Enclosed in the subhuman surroundings
of a Kansas prison, Youthman completely
reversed his outlook and philosophy.
By scooping up triangular edges
of his facial skin with a jagged piece
of glass he sewed himself with carpet
thread and curved needle to the iron bars.
Satisfied the exterior mask would peel
cleanly at the end of a backward run,
he severed himself from the hunchbacked
figure—and was born. From the musty
compartments of his paranoia the black-
and-yellow wings broke out, extended,
and dried out in the red prairie wind.

He took advantage of the prison's exemplary
reeducation program to acquire an art history
degree with an emphasis in Postimpressionism.
The numbness that came with incarceration,
a condition he felt was as close to death
as anything, prompted his obsession
with school and eventual survival
in prison. More important, he pledged
to forever understand the English language,
to avoid finding himself in dire circumstances
again. The world would not be right without
a walleye-lipped, oily-haired hunchback
who kept a shriveled image of his aboriginal
self in a Kinney's shoebox. In the dark before

dawn, he would unravel the tanned, glossy face
and suspend it on a wire hanger. Growing tired
of holding it at arm's length, he would hang
the mask on the gray wall and stare at it.
By so doing he was able to train the wings
to flex from their shoulder harnesses.
At first light the butterfly's hold on
the ceiling weakened, and Claude Youthman,
who long concerned himself with aspects
of aerodynamics, flew.

By the fourth year he was writing editorials
for the *Wichita Times-Republican,* the exclusive
Sunday issues. He penned treatises on the redundancy
of corporal punishment of American Indians.
"It is noteworthy to keep in mind," wrote one editor
as part of a series introduction, "that while Youthman
is a convicted felon, his arguments on federal law
vs. state law vs. tribal sovereignty issues deserve
consideration. What is especially startling
is the fact he is one person who benefited
from the penal system. Without the ridiculous
'cantaloupe' crime for which he was unjustly indicted
Youthman was destined to merely live out his life
as a woodsman and illiterate dreamer."
(July 6, 1970)

Throughout internment Youthman balanced
social concerns with neck-deep studies
in cathedral structures and ancient marble
sculptures. In those years in Grandfather's attic,
listening to Perry Como and the McGuire Sisters,
he chipped and gouged his way with a sharpened
spoon and rusty penknife, producing thornwood
statues of "Audie" and "National Velvet."

It was then that a Father Jeff Caster heard
of his skills and gave him an art history book
and a set of expensive oils and brushes.
Of the art that Youthman could duplicate
on canvas and thumbtack to the attic wall,
it was the works of Toulouse-Lautrec and Seurat.
Youthman's late interest had complications.
The *A tta i ka na ni,* Sioux tipis, he did
in pointillism resembled cone-shaped bubblegum
vending machines. He longed for exact reproduction,

images you could almost touch, like Christ's crown
of thorns he made for Grandfather or the duplicates
of Elizabeth's horse, but there he remained,
right on through college, with a painting
technique he was comfortable with and stuck with.

Taken by postcard renditions one day of what
an incarcerated Indian sees in a glance,
he initiated the "Gray Indian Series."
The act itself was controversial.
Using large canvases made of layered
newspaper and flour paste, he depicted
365 days of the color of imprisoned light.
On each of the twelve canvases
he divided the days as geometric shapes—
octagons, diamonds, circles, rectangles,
and stripes. Into each shape was filled
an intense or subtle degree of gray.
That was all. There wasn't any kind
of humanness. Just a different shape
of gray he saw each day. The Goslin Art
Institute of Omaha, Nebraska, upon seeing
photographs that accompanied the editorials,
sponsored the first exhibition. *LIFE* magazine
followed with an interview with the celebrated
"American Indian Artist and Self-proclaimed
Revolutionary: From Cantaloupes to Cathedral
Buttresses." The Honorable Governor was obligated
to attend, and he sat at the reception table
with Youthman. "Then what does the 'Gray Series'
have to do with Postimpressionism?" opened Youthman
rhetorically upon his introduction, shaking
the silver chains and the wrist of a federal
marshal he was shackled to in protest.
"This is what I was asked by the warden
when the Goslin Institute first proposed
the exhibit. The warden's no dummy,
I told myself, but I'd be a darn fool
to believe he came up with the question.
He was coached, and all in an effort
to stifle my notoriety. He knows I will
speak of deplorable conditions, maggot-
infested food, and the urinal stench
of my living quarters. Simply posing
an 'art' question carries little weight.

Studying Postimpressionism was the best choice,
and it is a tranquil place from where
abstract visions are shaped—today."

National celebrities are made daily,
and their reigns end just as quickly.
The world is full of actors who weep
at footage of old but famous movies.
It pains them to remember the short-lived
glory. For artists and revolutionaries nothing
remains but laminated clippings and embossed
invitations with signatures of dignitaries
who later became unknown themselves.
And so it was for Claude.
The good people of Kansas wrote a total
of four replies to his editorials
from a circulation of four million.
From the publicity of *LIFE* he received
$10,000 for the paintings
and invitations to sit on several prominent
boards in the East. He also obtained permission
to purchase art supplies for prisoner-artists,
but a few found ways to inhale the paints,
thinners, and aerosols, killing the project.
Upon hearing this, museums and galleries
ceased communication. The public television
crew from WITC who had stated categorically
they'd be there to film his prison release
and drive him back to Iowa never showed.
It was only after he had been waiting four hours
that an apologetic telephone message arrived:
"Mr. Youthman: We are sorry but WITC has changed
priorities midstream and has opted to do
a piece on Molly Dolly, chosen this year
as the loveliest artist by People of America.
We are sending a taxi instead and will be
glad to pay for the first twenty miles
to the interstate." Claude Youthman took
the taxi ride, got off at an overpass,
and hitchhiked the rest of the way
to Black Eagle Child.

Henrietta, Mrs. Youthman, the ingenuous one
whose honor Claude was defending on that day
of infamy at Farmers Market, cried at the sight
of her husband as he limped up the hill
past the water tower. She dropped the plate

of beads and rushed out to the porch. She stood
and waited while the miniature souvenirs
of moccasins and canoes (what would have been
Claude's bus fare) dangled from her blouse.

Claude's homecoming was largely uneventful.
Except for the brief hugs and touches
he received from his wife and grown children,
nothing had changed: the front door still
had one hinge missing; the same greasy curtains
were there, held by a stone-smooth yarn string;
and the tribe was still without indoor plumbing.
While impermanence was not a reality they knew,
he became embittered. When his family made
the first physical contact with him ever,
he openly wept. Indians never needed to touch
each other to demonstrate love and affection.
More so if you were once a recluse like Claude.
You could touch or kiss someone in the family
all your life—or you could not. In the end,
when someone's presence was no longer,
the pain of their loss or absence
was the same. He planned to rest
before venturing back to society
to pick up where he left off—
or would he?

He had learned to fight the establishment
from behind the prison walls, to correct
injustice. He hoped he could do the same
for his home. "To make this a better place
to live" as the billboard on Highway 63 read.
At first, he was welcomed with a community dance,
and the BEC Business Council congratulated him
with pithy sentences. The tribe knew about his
exploits, for Henrietta had submitted his editorials
to the *BEC Quarterly*. The neighbors were amazed
how "an illiterate woodsman" was able to circumvent
disaster. After that, getting rides into Why Cheer
for groceries and typing paper was easy.
The people were glad to chat with a notable.
But they couldn't fathom his intellect.
Instead of listening and responding
to what he planned to do with health,
education, and socioeconomics, they spoke
about family spats and burned food.

Claude Youthman had taken five years off
from social or family responsibility.
The small benign things began to take
precedent. He wanted to savor lost moments
with Henrietta and their grown children.
From afar, however, he began to jot notes why
the tribe could not prosper economically.
Later, he read them aloud to himself,
Henrietta, and admirers who visited:

"Politics here are comparable to a birthday party
attended by a dozen robust children on a hot summer
afternoon. There is excitement, as well as apprehension. The fun and honor of it is simply being
invited to the affair; the reality is that only
one birthday occurs per child per year. Picture
this, if you will. After the party has swiftly
gone past the food, dessert, and the unwrapping
of presents, the children sit back, digest,
and exchange idle chitchat. Soon, even before
the parents are finished cleaning and clearing
the tables, some children demand the games
commence. The parents smile kindly before
wiping their sweaty brows. The children
giggle uncontrollably as balloons are inflated
and attached to their ankles with string.
They are then herded to the center
of the room where everyone can see them.
One concerned parent leans down and gives
last-second instructions. The object,
of course, is to bust as many balloons
as possible while keeping yours intact.
Those who cannot stand the thought
of losing 'jump the gun' by stomping
on the balloons of unsuspecting participants
before the countdown is given. The game stalls
and new balloons are inflated. When the game
finally starts there is chaos. In the same
vein, the tribe will cooperate to a certain
degree. Food and pleasantries will be shared
and exchanged. The trouble starts when a novel
proposal is submitted for consideration.
Someone will become outraged for not
having thought of it before. And that person
will instigate the first trampling, and others

(relatives and loyal band members) will follow
suit. Without evaluating if the novelty could
benefit the tribe, the balloon-busters begin
jumping up and down without really knowing
why. How does this tribe function then?
People are not apprised of anything that
may affect them. All is done without
their knowledge and approval by false
leaders. That means you, Lardass . . ."

As the years progressed, the rebellious
vigor he acquired in prison began to diminish.
Stirring changes he once shared with people on
rides to town were next to zero. He began
to realize why no one ever paid attention:
few possessed the voracity to follow through
with their own ideas.

By the time he secured a part-time position
as "tribal arts instructor" at Weeping Willow
Elementary in 1988—a program which had been
written by a former teacher, Lorna Bearcap,
(another success story)—he had a master's
in art history. He should have been content
with published articles on the "Post-Gray
Indian Series," but insights as to why
the tribe was an inept, bureaucratic
monstrosity were formulated. He concluded
the people who were running the tribe
were the real "illiterate dreamers."
The BEC Business Council allowed its
welfare, health, education, and commerce
committees to promote a greed or help thy-
self system. This is what Lorna Bearcap
had desperately tried to convey shortly
before she was dismissed from Weeping Willow.
As the only BEC college-educated teacher,
she had been instrumental in developing
programs whereby students were taken beyond
the barbed-wire fence. But her feats drew
the ire of the retarded advisory board.
After she had obtained grants in excess
of half a million dollars, she was accused
of "exploiting the school's singers and dancers."
The funds were then embezzled or shifted

to baseball diamond restoration (located
on a known floodplain), intertribal basketball
tournament trips (party time), or (rigged)
dance competitions. Nepotism brought about
a school principal with a degree in mechanical
drafting and welding. There were embarrassing
audits that made the lead-ins on television news.

Lorna Bearcap's last memo to the advisory
board chairman (who was reportedly caught
lollipopping one of the Hyena brothers) read:
"When a true genius appears in the world,
you may know [her] by this sign, that the dunces
are all in confederacy against [her]—Jonathan Swift."
Thus ended the extraordinary efforts of a person
who crawled out from the brewery ditches
and made a drastic change for herself—
and for students whom she deeply cared about.
Like Claude, Lorna took the highway sign
seriously. Because her employers could not,
she was viewed as an obstructionist.

"The school has been relegated for years
with a monumental task of being the last carrier
and bastion of identity. To this end a unique
bilingual/bicultural curriculum has been
written and adopted. Unfortunately,
it is a disgrace. The school tries
in vain to convey the most rudimentary
skills, yes, but the students' retentive
abilities—to think, speak, and write
in our language and to recall precepts,
myths, and rules to live by—are far
from exemplary . . .

"We perceive the antiquated institution
as a gleaming aircraft whose defective
nuts and bolts are about to pop in flight
eight miles above. With all due respect
to our alma mater, unless the craft
can be completely 'overhauled,'
administration and direction-wise,
it faces further structural and academic
deterioration. There is something deeply
disturbing about a child who cannot begin
a conversation in our mother tongue,

and even more if a proper sentence
cannot be composed in English . . ."

The tribe patched itself back up by shinnying
up a tree, licking its wounds, and forgetting
anyone ever took the thousands of dollars.
Disguises were poor: new trucks were driven
and satellite dishes installed, but the children
of the suspects wore ragged clothes. Unfortunately,
the state and federal agencies chose not to file
charges, which gave a green light for repetition.
The commodity surplus cheese and flour supplies
were depleted by various committees for Indian
taco sales; clothing items that had been donated
and trucked in by wealthy Boston people
were resold to the tribe; gas and clothing
assistance through the welfare department
were distributed among the working people
at the BEC tribal center; Social Security
checks and ADC checks were channeled,
skimmed, and reissued; monetary or land
donations were kept a secret and divided
by the Business Council. The list
of improprieties grew, and Bingo
Extravaganza was just around the corner.

Claude Youthman forgot about enlightening
the "Outside World." He set aside his paints
and brushes, and he sat down to write a letter
of complaint to a reputable Republican.
He detailed the despicable goings-on
in the *BEC Quarterly*. "Before we can
even begin to focus on the future we
must dispose of our own pretentious scum."
Before the Weeping Willow advisory board
had a chance to fire him, he resigned
under the lights of a press conference.
Lorna Bearcap was there also. Here they were,
the only people who had miraculously educated
themselves and remained. Now they were being
ostracized for revealing ugly truths.

But the infighting was far from over. In fact,
it had just begun. The common BEC man or woman
had no right to define and dictate policy.
They sought the advice of hereditary leaders

in absentia, and they grew more determined
than ever that all problems were attributable
to the lack of divine leadership.
In their opinion elections were over with.
With divine leadership, the Black Eagle Child
Nation would grow strong again.

Even though the blood which coursed
through the veins of the true Chieftains
coursed through theirs vicariously,
Claude Youthman and Lorna Bearcat sat
together at the kitchen table and penned
the first of their diatribes,
the WEEPING WILLOW MANIFESTO.
There was no other resolution.
There had to be an immediate
return to the Old Ways
beginning from the bottom
up.

The First Dimension of Skunk

It is the middle of October
and frosted leaves
continue to introduce
their descent as season
and self-commentary.
On the ground yellow-jacket
bees burrow themselves
into the windfall apples.
On the house the empty body shells
of locusts begin to rattle with
the plastic window covering
torn loose the night previous
in the first sudden gusts of wind.
South of the highway bridge
two extinct otters are seen
by Selene's father while
setting traps.
"Mates swimming;
streamlined and playing
games along the Iowa River."
In the midst of change

all it takes is one anachronism,
one otter whistle.

For us, it began with the healthy-
looking salamander who stopped our car.
So last night we stood in the cold
moonlight waiting for the black
coyote. No animal darted
from tree to tree, encircling us.
There was a time in an orange grove
next to the San Gabriel mountains
when I was surrounded by nervous
coyotes who were aware
of the differences
between thunder
and an earth tremor.
Selene motioned for me to stand
still, and the moonlit foothills
of Claremont disappeared.
An owl began to laugh.
I remained quiet and obliged
her gesture not to mimic its laugh,
for fear we might accidentally trigger
the supernatural deity it possesses
to break this barrier—
and once again find ourselves
observing a ball of fire
rise from an abandoned garden
which separates into four fireflies
who appear like four distant jets
coming into formation
momentarily
before changing into one intense
strobe light,
pulsating inside an appletree,
impervious to hollow-point bullets,
admissions of poverty and carlights.
We stood without response
and other thoughts came.
From the overwhelming sound
of vehicles and farm machinery,
together with the putrid odor
of a beef slaughterhouse,
such anticipation

seemed inappropriate.
Whoever constructed
the two railroad tracks
and highways through Indian land
must have planned and known
that we would be reminded daily
of what is certainty.
In my dream the metal
bridge plays an essential part
and subsequent end of what
was intended to occur.
I would speak to the heavy
glass jar, telling it
the paper bullet
was useless underwater.

Three days ago, in the teeth
of Curly and Girl, a skunk
was held firmly and shook
until lifeless.
The first evening
we hear its final death call.
At the same hour the second night
we hear it again. The third night-
sound is more brave and deliberate;
it waits to blend with the horn
of an oncoming Northwestern train,
forcing us to step backward,
taking random shots at objects
crashing through the brush.
We have a theory that Destiny
was intercepted, that the Executioner
ran elsewhere for appeasement.
We also think the skunk's
companion returned on these nights
to mourn a loved one,
but all had to be deleted,
leaving us more confused.
Yesterday, we examined the dead
skunk and were surprised to find it
three times less the size I first
saw it with Mr. D.
My parents offered an explanation.
"A parrot or a pelican on their
migratory route."

With our surroundings
at someone else's disposal,
all we have are the embers
and sparks from our woodstove
and chimney: the fragrance
to thwart the supernatural.

Winter of the Salamander

i've waited through my wife's eyes
in the time of death. although we have peeled
the masks of summer away from our faces
we have each seen the badger encircle itself
to a star, knowing that a covenant with his spirit
is always too much to ask for.

unlike us, her birth-companions have gone before us,
resembling small jittery waterbugs who keep
bumping into each other, unable to perceive
the differences between the eyes of their
children, the light-colored seals
camouflaged with native tongue
and beaded outfits.

we'd like to understand why we breathe
the same air, why the dead grow
in number, the role i play in speaking
to mouths that darken blur with swollen
gunpowder burns, chapped lips, and alcohol.
we keep wondering whether or not we'll ever
leave in the form of eight sticks.
we have waited until morning to turn off
the lights, hoping to catch a glimpse
of light chasing light.

there was a man whose name was k.
there was another whose name was m.
they knew they shared the same father.
the car of their killer sits within
the fresh snow. their grandfather sits
within the thought of a hummingbird,
women arriving at his request,
the mistake in the deaths of his grandsons,
the spell that came back.

they say: the mixbloods know of one
chance to be a people.
some of us, knowing of little dispute
in our past, forget and we assume life
will go well for us, life after death
being automatic. they are told
to absorb themselves into religion,
to learn and to outdo some drunken
fullblood's life. and me: like a dim star
i shine on and off in the midst of many
who have sat repeatedly within this line
of seated men, singing into the ears of leaves,
fresh twigs of the fresh green bean.

alfred and pete are still godless.
the morning has shown itself through
the windows of their houses, dissolving
the peyote in their stomachs, mixing
into the meal of sweetened meat and coffee,
half-man, half-horse, the green shirt
and the lamb.

turning eagle and i sit in the roomlight
of the salamander's two houses.
within the third house the windows frost.
at the beginning and end of each winter
we sit here before a body the size of our hand.
we made ourselves believe that no one
was responsible. we took the sound it made
from its last breath and we imagined a dwarf
hanging from the rafters with a lighted
cigarette in his mouth, reminding us
of the midpoint in the day.

the black kettle in the corner changes
into my young wife and she walks over

The Language of Weather

The summer rain isn't here yet,
but I hear and see the approaching
shadow of its initial messenger:
Thunder.

The earth's bright horizon
sends a final sunbeam directly
toward me, skimming across the tops
of clouds and hilly woodland.
All in one moment, in spite
of my austerity, everything
is aligned: part land, part cloud,
part sky, part sun and part self.
I am the only one to witness
this renascence.
Before darkness replaces the light
in my eyes, I meditate briefly
on the absence of religious
importunity; no acknowledgment
whatsoever for the Factors
which make my existence possible.
My parents, who are hurrying
to overturn the reddish-brown dirt
around the potato plants, begin to talk
above the rumbling din.
"Their mouths are opening.
See that everyone in the household
releases parts of ourselves
to our Grandfathers."
While raindrops begin to cool
my face and arms, lightning
breaks a faraway cottonwood
in half; small clouds of red
garden dust are kicked into
the frantic air by grasshoppers
in retreat.
I think of the time I stood
on this same spot years ago,
but it was under moonlight,
and I was watching this beautiful
electrical force dance above
another valley.
In the daylight distance,
a stray spirit whose guise
is a Whirlwind, spins and attempts
to communicate from its ethereal
loneliness.

morning talking mother

tonight, i encircle myself to a star
and my love for the earth shimmers
like schools of small rainbow-colored fish,
lighting the drowned walnut trees inside
the brown flooded rivers
swelling birth along the woods.
i think of each passing day when time expands
bringing the land against my chest
and the birds keep walking as they
sing wildly over our house:
be in this daylight with me.
push yourself from the walls.
let me see you walk beneath me.
let me see your head sway.
let me see you breathe.
everyone has been up into the daylight.

i walk over her head and remember
of being told that no knives
or sharp objects must pierce
inside her hair.
this is her hair.
another grandmother whose hair
i am combing.
there are paths winding over her face
and every step is the same:
the feeling of one who is well known,
one who knows the warmth rising
as morning talking mother.

in her hands she prepares snow for the visitor.
she sprinkles the snow into the bare hills
and valleys where in the spring
after the plants have grown
people with medicine eyes come
to lift the plants from her head
taking them home to the sick.

i remember as i was looking out
from my eyes that my eyes were like windows
smeared and bent out of proportion,

that the earth was curved from where
i was sitting. cars came and disappeared.
it was summer and i sat on a blanket.
i watched my grandmother as she came to me,
holding a skillet. she set it down beside me
and she fanned the smoke which came from medicine
crackling over the hot coals
towards me.

The Significance of a Water Animal

Since then I was
the North.
Since then I was
the Northwind.
Since then I was nobody.
Since then I was alone.

The color of my black eyes
inside the color of King-
fisher's hunting eye
weakens me, but sunlight
glancing off the rocks
and vegetation strengthens me.
As my hands and fingertips
extend and meet,
they frame the serene
beauty of bubbles and grain—
once a summer rainpool.

A certain voice of *Reassurance*
tells me a story of a water animal
diving to make land available.
Next, from the Creator's
own heart and flesh
Ukimau was made:
the progeny of divine
leaders. And then
from the Red Earth
came the rest of us.

"To believe otherwise,"
as my grandmother tells me,

"or to simply be ignorant,
Belief and what we were given
to take care of,
is on the verge
of ending . . ."

Nothing Could Take Away the Bear-King's Image

At first I thought I would feel
guilty in not missing you,
that despite its unfortunate
occurrence,
I would see you again
(exactly the way you were
before a hunter's arrow
glanced off some willows—
lodging near the pulsating song
of the Red Earth heart)
either here,
or towards that memorable direction
near the oily air of Los Angeles
where once a Zuni Indian companion
peered into a telescope aimed
at the Orion constellation:
"These three faint stars
are known for their parallel
formation rather than by four
of the bright stars which
frame them."
While we were sitting
on a manicured knoll
positioned above a Greek theatre,
we heard the distant skirling
sound of Scottish bagpipes
coming through the eucalyptus trees.
We went to them, and there,
the astronomer-physicist
invited us to share his interest
in the night skies he was playing for.
He told a story of this Greek hunter
composed of stars;

The "Three-Stars-In-A-Row"
were his belt.
"I think that's me, Grandfather,"
responded my Zuni companion,
"but I will believe you more
if you sell us your scotch whiskey—
and consider the magnitude of my belief
if I told you the bubbles of my Creator's
saliva made the stars, Grandson."
"Grandfather? Grandson? In the same
sentence? I am not related to you
in any way!" demurred the scholarly man.
The two Hispanics, Sergio & Camacho,
who were with us reaffirmed the Zuni's
request by bumping the academician
with their expanded chests.
"Grandfather, Grandson,"
they repeated.
Later, with erratic wind-notes
and chinking necklace shells,
my companion tripped and fell on
the professor's bagpipes
as he was completing
his third revolution
around the observatory.
He rolled down the sandy incline
breaking the instrument
into several pieces.
Suddenly, the professor's eyes
possessed a wild gleam:
a distant fire we hadn't seen before;
a nebula of sorts.
He knelt next to the dead instrument
and began to weep.
"My dear chanter! My drone!"
Like gentlemen, Sergio & Camacho
offered to pay for the irreplaceable
parts, but it was too late.
We left (no, we fled from)
the observatory.

Back at the Greek theatre,
we found solace by the singing
of round and grass dance songs

with three white friends:
one jeweler, one ROTC student,
and one KSPC disc jockey,
until we were greeted
by Sioux voices from the dark.
There was immediate silence,
and then the Sioux National Anthem:
"The United States flag will stand forever.
As long as it stands the people will live
and grow; therefore, I am doing this
say the Indian soldier boys."
The radio announcer advised us
the voice was amplified,
possibly by a handheld system.
Pretty soon, we were surrounded
by figures wearing bronze helmets.
The jeweler whispered to us.
"They look like Mudheads with metallic paint."
The military student observed and commented
on their evenly-spaced formation.
Several descended the stone steps
and their boot heels echoed
onto the stage.
When they got close
with their glistening visors,
nightsticks and badges,
we were bewildered.
The police officer explained
that he was a boy scout leader
and learning Siouan was essential.
"Would you boys consider singing
for our troop in Pomona?"
he queried before stating
the purpose of his visit.
"What disturbance?" we asked
in regard to bagpipes and walked back
to our individual dormitory rooms.
We called each other on the phone,
laughing at times, exchanging crazy
warhoops in a warm California night;
that ancient but comical time and place
where we hypothesized the draft
which lifted Marilyn Monroe's dress
came from the San Andreas Fault.
When it shifted, Orozco's murals

in Frary Hall actually moved,
responding to the land wave
and the force of the Pacific Ocean.

We are endless like the Midwestern
breeze in winter which makes the brittle
oak leaves whisper in unison of this
ethereal confidence.
Nothing could take away
the Bear-King's own image
who is human and walks.
There remains a bottle of champagne
beside the charred concrete block;
the half-smoked cigarette
of corn husk and Prince Albert tobacco
which was propped next
to the green bottle
has disappeared
into the snowdrift.
The Bow Priest hasn't been summoned.
In the tribal gymnasium, exercise
equipment is marked by the greasy
handprints of a phantom infant.
The caretaker's two bows
and their arrows lie unpropelled.
The crooked snakelike arm doesn't
have the strength to draw back
the taut string, which would
have triggered an old time
message to the brain.
On top of a moonlit hill
stands a boy whose lithe body
has been painted black
with numerous light-blue spots.
He signals us to follow him,
and he lights small fires
along the way.
Inside the earth-mound,
a small man in a bright-red headband
places an arrow in the bowstring
of his left hand which is bent
like a bow.
He explains the meaning
of the arrow's crest.
"From birds the bison dreams about.

This shaft of wood tipped with sharpened flint,
together with the wolfskin draped over the hunter
crouching low against the salty earth . . ."

DRAMA

Harold of Orange: A Screenplay

Gerald Vizenor (Anishinaabe)

Introduction to the Film

> Harold and the Warriors of Orange
> are descendants of the great trickster
> who created the new earth after the flood.

> But the trickster was soon word-driven
> from the land by the white man,
> who claimed the earth as his own
> and returned to the trickster
> only what he couldn't use.

> Now, Harold and the Warriors of Orange,
> tribal tricksters determined to reclaim
> their estate from the white man,
> are challenging his very foundations.

Trickster Song

> In the great tradition of faith and con,
> The trickster's way is the magic one.
> If you can believe, then it can be done.

> Trickster Hi! Hi! Lo!   Trickster Hi! Hi! Lo!

> Let's reroute some of that money green,
> Move the banks and you move the stream.
> Trickster change how everything seem.

> Trickster lying in a bed at night,
> Lying, lying, lying.
> Thinking up schemes to put you right.

Trickster Hi! Hi! Lo!   Trickster Hi! Hi! Lo!

Trickster on the run.
If you believe, then it will be done.

Trickster Hi! Hi! Lo!   Trickster Hi! Hi! Lo!

(final verse used at the end of the film)

If you get to thinking in the first degree,
It's an inspiration to you and me.
Miracles are there for all who see.

Buffy Sainte-Marie

1 Exterior: Harold of Orange Coffee House—Sunrise

Harold Sinseer rumbles down a dirt road on the reservation in his damaged car, assembled from multicolored parts, and stops in front of a row of small commercial buildings. A bald tire rolls up to the screen; a car door squeaks open, and a foot touches the road. Harold has a round brown face and black hair. His cheeks are full and his relaxed stomach behind the wheel folds over his wide beaded belt about two inches. He is dressed in a ribbon shirt and brown leather vest. He gestures with his lips in the tribal manner when he speaks. The sign "Harold of Orange Coffee House" is painted over the front of the building. Another sign, printed on a pine board, "The New School of Socioacupuncture," is suspended in the window of the storefront. Harold wears well-worn moccasins.

HAROLD (*to the camera*):   Over there, deep in the brush, the Orange River runs through this reservation as fast as it can down to the wild sea . . . We live at the best loop in the river, a natural high rise on the earth . . .

Harold pauses and then he climbs out of his car. He expands his chest and continues speaking to the camera.

HAROLD: We are the Warriors of Orange, tricksters in the new school of socioacupuncture where a little pressure fills the purse . . . We run a clean coffee house, tend to our miniature oranges, and talk about mythic revolutions on the reservation . . .

Harold pauses; he smiles, an ironic gesture, and then he continues talking to the camera.

HAROLD: Com'on in for a pinch of coffee . . .

1A Interior: View of Harold Through the Coffee House Window

Harold walks to the back of his car, pries open the trunk, removes several bags of plastic cups and dozens of neckties, and then he turns toward the coffee house. Mongrels sit near the front door as he approaches. There is a small sign near the front door: "What This Country Needs Is a Good Injun Tuneup." The sign is weathered and curled at the corners.

2 Int: Harold of Orange Coffee House—Morning

The screen is filled with a large photographic silhouette of Harold and Fannie posed like the statue of Hiawatha and Minnehaha. Harold walks into the screen, across the silhouette, and the camera follows him around the coffee house. An aluminum coffee urn rests on top of the table or woodstove in the center of the room. Front and rear doors are open. Mongrels move in and out. Light pours in. The walls and ceiling are covered with photographs and radical broadsides. The Warriors of Orange are seated on boxes and chairs, alone and in pairs, drinking coffee and eating fast food. There are two large pots in the corner, an orange tree in one, and a coffee shrub in the other. Several warriors wear hats, one a painter hat. One warrior is reading The Wall Street Journal. *Snow shoes are stacked in the corner of the room.*

PLUMERO: My god, here he is on mythic time . . .

HAROLD: You got the first part right.

PLUMERO: Where to this mornin, chief?

HAROLD: To the Bily Foundation with our pinch beans . . .

NEW CROWS: Not the old pinch bean scheme?

HAROLD: Nothin but the best. Hand picked in the traditional way . . .

Harold unloads the cups and neckties on the table next to the woodstove. The cups bear the pinch bean coffee label. Son Bear sees the neckties and removes his earphones. Powwow music can be heard through the earphones around his neck.

NEW CROWS: Who'd believe in pinch beans?

PLUMERO: The same people who fell for miniature oranges.

SON BEAR: Potted oranges?

Plumero picks an orange from the tree in the pot and throws it to Son Bear. Several warriors turn and laugh.

HAROLD: Our orchard grows in tax free bonds . . .

SON BEAR: Orange bonds?

HAROLD: The source of your allowance.

NEW CROWS: From these trees?

New Crows points toward the potted orange tree in the corner.

PLUMERO: We ordered eight crates from an organic farmer in the southwest . . .

HAROLD: Eight? Thought it was fifteen?

PLUMERO: Too expensive, eight's enough for the foundation directors . . .

Harold pours a cup of coffee into his special orange mug and then he walks backwards around the table as he speaks in a dramatic tone of voice. He picks an orange from the miniature tree.

HAROLD: Now, with miniature oranges in hand, we return with a proposal to open coffee houses on reservations around the world.

Plumero reaches into a large bin and pulls out a handful of coffee beans.

PLUMERO: And from these pinch beans comes our mythic revolution . . .

Plumero throws the coffee beans into the air.

SON BEAR: What revolution?

HAROLD: Where there are coffee houses there are tricksters and revolutions . . .

NEW CROWS: Coffee never made no warrior . . .

PLUMERO: Maybe not, but there's more tricksters in Berkeley than Beejimee . . .

HAROLD: Bemidji, Bemidji!

PLUMERO: There too.

Harold sorts through the neckties on the table. Coffee beans crunch under foot. Son Bear points at the neckties.

SON BEAR: What're these for?

HAROLD: The uniform for our foundation pinch bean show . . .

NEW CROWS: Nothin doin . . . Not around my neck.

SON BEAR: The whiteman got white from neckties, stopped the blood to his brains . . .

PLUMERO: You got nothin to lose . . .

NEW CROWS: He cut short more than that . . .

Harold holds up several neckties and admires them with a smile.

Son Bear: Man, ties'll turn us white . . .

Plumero: Those white designer shorts you got never cut short your blood supply.

Son Bear: But mixedbloods run a higher risk . . .

The warriors laugh and tease the neckties on the table. One warrior finds a bow tie in the pile; he examines it.

Harold: Come on, choose a necktie . . . Loose knots for the mixed-bloods.

New Crows: We never did this for the orange money.

Harold: The stakes are much higher this time around . . . No one can resist a skin in a necktie.

Harold takes the bow tie from the warrior near the table; he clips it on and continues talking.

Harold: When we show up in neckties that foundation pack won't remember nothin we tell them but the truth . . .

Plumero: What was that again?

Harold: Nothin but the truth . . .

Harold throws neckties to the other warriors.

Harold: Wear these neckties with pride, the pride of a trickster . . .

Son Bear refuses a necktie; others scorn the selection. Powwow music can be heard from the earphones around his neck. Son Bear picks up the two oranges on the table, picks a third from the miniature tree, and juggles them.

Son Bear: We are Warriors of Orange, not white heads . . .

Plumero catches one orange; Harold tucks a necktie in Son Bear's back pocket. The warriors hoot and trill.

Plumero: So, where's the meetin?

Harold: Board room at the Bily Foundation . . .

Plumero: *Bored* room for sure . . .

Harold: This time they want something personal . . .

Plumero: Like a name ceremony.

Harold: Something serious . . .

Plumero: Like a ghost dance.

A school bus rattles to a stop in front of the storefront. "The Warriors of Orange" is painted on the side over a cameo portrait of a whiteman, a brand label for miniature oranges. A bus horn honks.

HAROLD: Something active . . .

PLUMERO: Like a softball game in the park.

HAROLD: Right . . .

2A Int: Breakfast Meeting at the Board Room— Morning

Kingsley Newton cuts a sliver of strawberry and pushes it back on his fork. Breakfast meeting. Fannie Mason attends the first meeting of the executive committee of the board of directors. She is eager to please. Marion Quiet and Andrew Burch are seated opposite Fannie and Kingsley. One place is vacant, set for Ted Velt, who is late for the meeting. Kingsley is mannered, elite, formal, a romantic about tribal cultures. He is dressed in light colored clothing. The other directors are dressed in dark business suits. Fannie wears casual, expensive clothing. Kingsley cuts a strawberry as Fannie speaks, strawberry on the screen.

FANNIE: D. H. Lawrence wrote that "The most unfree souls go west, and shout of freedom. . . . Men are freest when they are most unconscious of freedom. . . ."

MARION: Like American Indians?

FANNIE: Yes . . .

MARION: Have you lived with them?

FANNIE: Not on a reservation . . . You see, my real interest in Indians was stimulated in college . . .

Andrew leans forward, over his plate, to speak to Fannie.

ANDREW: As you must know, my father was in the timber business . . . We shared numerous adventures with some of the finest native woodsmen . . .

FANNIE: Yes, I have studied the . . .

MARION: Pulp cutters?

FANNIE: The exploitation . . . The, ahh, corporate development of resources on the reservation.

Kingsley attempts to direct the conversation.

KINGSLEY: Fannie studied American Indian folklore . . .

FANNIE: Literature, which is a much larger subject than folklore.

MARION: Do Indians have a written language?

FANNIE: No, they have *oral* traditions.

KINGSLEY: Which reminds me . . . Harold of Orange will make his special presentation to the board this afternoon . . .

MARION: That little orange man?

Marion laughs too hard; she does not notice the silence of the other directors.

ANDREW: Have we not already approved his proposal?

KINGSLEY: Yes, informally as the executive committee.

MARION: Does he know?

KINGSLEY: No . . . Even if he did he would still insist on an oral presentation . . .

MARION: The oral tradition seems so natural to him.

FANNIE: Harold of Orange? Is that his name?

KINGSLEY: Fannie has not yet read his unusual proposal . . .

Marion leans forward to speak to Fannie.

MARION: Harold Sinseer . . .

Marion laughs too hard. Fannie blinks several times when she hears the name. She turns her head from side to side, a nervous tic. She remembers an affair, one night in the park, with Harold ten years earlier.

MARION: Sinseer, if you can believe that as a surname.

Ted Velt, the other member of the executive committee, seems to leap into the board room. He is a small man, breathless, with a forceful personality.

TED: Better late than sorry . . . The scissors were too dull at the ribbon cutting . . .

KINGSLEY: Nice of you to show . . .

Ted is seated; he folds his hands over his plate, breaks into a wide smile, and looks from face to face around the table. Kingsley leans toward Fannie to speak.

KINGSLEY: Watch out for Ted Velt, he made his fortune on tricks and games.

Ted extends his hand across the table to Fannie.

TED: Call me Veltie . . .

FANNIE: Call me Fannie, Veltie . . .

Fannie shakes his hand. Still holding her hand, Ted turns his wrist to show his digital watch. He points to his watch with his other hand, across the table.

TED: Watch this . . .

Ted pushes a button on his watch, still holding onto Fannie's hand, and a tune, the theme music from The Lone Ranger, fills the board room.

3 Int: The Warriors of Orange Bus—Morning

The warriors are seated on the bus as they chant the lines of a poem. The bus is running. Harold enters last and when he takes his seat the warriors begin their chant.

PLUMERO: Oranges and darkness . . .

NEW CROWS: Oranges and light . . .

SON BEAR: Orangewood and promises . . .

NEW CROWS: Oranges and delight . . .

PLUMERO: Orange warriors . . .

SON BEAR: Oranges for Christ . . .

NEW CROWS: Oranges in magical flight . . .

PLUMERO: We are orange tricksters . . .

HAROLD: And Lawrence is white.

The bus lurches forward; voices change from surreal to conversational.

SON BEAR: Lawrence of Arabia?

HAROLD: No, Lawrence of New Mexico . . . David Herbert Lawrence of the red and the white . . .

NEW CROWS: Did you tell him about the oranges?

HAROLD: No, but I told him he was right.

PLUMERO: White about what?

HAROLD: How he loves to hate the dark and how we love to hate the white . . .

3A Ext: Bus Moving Down a Dirt Road—Morning

The bus rumbles down a dirt road as the warriors continue their conversation. The question by Son Bear, the answer by Harold, and the song "Our women are poisoned part white ho ho ho ho . . ." are heard as the bus passes. Guitar music with the song. The song voice carries over into the next scene where Harold and Fannie are intimate in the board room. Guitar music continues to the next scene.

SON BEAR: Did Lawrence of New Mexico wear a necktie?

HAROLD: He wore it so tight he faded in the bright light . . .

WARRIORS' SONG: Our women are poisoned part white ho ho ho ho peeled part white ho ho ho ho buried deep down where the dead turn around . . .

4 Int: Carpeted Board Room at the Foundation— Afternoon

Harold and Fannie are seen in an intimate, private embrace. The camera circles close. Fannie remembers; the past is revealed on her face as she begins to resist the passion of the moment. The resistance is slow, develops in silence, in subtle facial gestures. She turns away, avoids his eyes, his lips; we see her face as Harold speaks to her.

HAROLD: Tell me you're not still sore.

FANNIE: *No,* I mean yes . . . Forget it. You are ten years too late . . .
Forget it.

Fannie breaks from his embrace. The board room is decorated with original works of art by tribal artists, placed for the occasion.

HAROLD: Have you forgotten the oral tradition?

FANNIE: Yes, *and* the interruptions.

Fannie turns from Harold and moves around the table as she speaks, placing materials on the table for the board meeting. Harold follows her as he speaks.

HAROLD: The shaman called me back to the reservation.

FANNIE: You told me your grandmother had died.

HAROLD: Well, she did.

FANNIE: She died four times that year, right?

Harold follows Fannie around the table.

HAROLD: Hey, Fannie, bend a little, turn with the stories . . . You know me, short on apologies.

FANNIE: Do you have a grandmother?

HAROLD: We buried our relatives in college to avoid exams . . . We survived, didn't we?

FANNIE: On fake funerals and borrowed money.

Harold is distracted, nervous. He expands his chest. Fannie touches his arm, affection with a purpose. She smiles, tilts her head, gestures of dominance.

FANNIE: Remember that thousand you borrowed from me?

HAROLD: What thousand?

FANNIE: That thousand you said you needed to bury your grandmother for the fourth time . . .

Harold looks around the room; he is anxious, cornered in his own game. When he turns back to Fannie he is more aggressive.

HAROLD: Listen, we need your money . . . I mean, we need your support for this pinch bean proposal . . . Can we count on you for that much?

Fannie looks down in silence. She turns her ring.

HAROLD: Come on, this proposal is not for me alone.

Fannie looks up and smiles.

FANNIE: Of course not, your proposal is for the traditional elders on the reservation who cannot speak for themselves . . .

HAROLD: You know the old foundation game, we get the money and the foundation gets the good name . . .

FANNIE: No I don't know that . . .

Harold is more dramatic; he raises his voice in poetic anger.

HAROLD: The Warriors of Orange are not victims to please the white man . . . We never cheat people, we are not corrupt politicians with medicine bundles stuffed with false promises . . . We are imaginative survivors, we cross the world in the middle of the block . . .

FANNIE: Save the rest for the foundation directors . . . Listen to me now.

Harold gestures with his lips; he exhales and smiles.

HAROLD: My ears are to the daffodils.

Fannie is more aggressive, at the edge of anger.

FANNIE: You owe me one thousand dollars.

HAROLD: The check is in the mail . . .

FANNIE: No, no, this afternoon, return my money this afternoon before the
directors make their final decision on your proposal . . .

*Kingsley Newton enters the board room. He pulls the drapes open and then
walks toward Fannie and Harold. The room is filled with light, white.
Foundation directors and warriors also enter the room. The warriors are
carrying crates of miniature oranges. The directors admire the new tribal art
on the walls. Harold notices an affectionate gesture between Fannie and
Kingsley. Harold thrusts his chest forward, smiles, and moves close to Fannie's
ear to speak.*

HAROLD: This afternoon then, on my grandmother's grave . . .

4A: Carpeted Board Room at the Foundation— Afternoon

*Kingsley stands in front of a podium. The directors are seated around the
conference table. Harold stands next to Kingsley. Fannie is seated near the
front of the table. The warriors stand in the back of the board room. Kingsley
spreads his arms as he speaks.*

KINGSLEY: Now it is my pleasure to present Harold Sinseer, one proud
American Indian from the Watteau Point Reservation in beautiful
northern Minnesota . . . Some of you know him as Harold of Orange
because we funded his last proposal to cultivate an orchard of
miniature oranges . . . In a secret place to avoid pests and competition
. . . And this afternoon we will have our first taste of the oranges.

*Ted Velt arrives late; he bursts through the door into the board room. He
notices the crates of oranges, points at them, comments on the portrait on the
label, and then greets the warriors, slaps them on the back, and moves to his
seat at the table. The warriors are uncomfortable with his attention. Velt takes
his seat, stacks his hands on the table, and smiles to each director. His watch
fills the screen while Kingsley continues his introduction.*

TED: Oranges overnight? How about that . . . Hey chief, good to see a little
color here for a change . . .

KINGSLEY: Harold has challenged us in the private foundation field to meet
his proposal in places around the cities, a removal, as it were, from the
carpets . . .

MARION: Not removed too far . . .

ANDREW: Not too long, I trust . . .

KINGSLEY: Where we will experience something serious and
ceremonial . . .

Three warriors move forward to the front of the board room and stand with their arms folded, stoical postures. Kingsley is nervous.

KINGSLEY: But first, allow me to introduce his workers, warriors, from the orange orchards . . .

Kingsley makes a sign to each of the warriors.

KINGSLEY: We welcome you one and all, and we celebrate your desire to better yourselves in a miniature orchard of your own on the reservation . . .

Kingsley pauses and then gestures to Harold.

KINGSLEY: My friend, Harold Sinseer . . .

Harold rises to the podium. Guitar music. Harold speaks like an evangelist. He leans forward and turns his head as he speaks.

HAROLD: Once we climbed into church basements to better ourselves with heavy hearts and empty pocketbook speeches . . . The money was good then, but the guilt has changed and so have we . . . So here we are dressed in neckties with oranges and pinch beans . . .

MARION: Mister Sinseer, we have heard so much about your oral traditions . . .

Fannie clears her throat and turns the rings on her fingers.

HAROLD: Listen, first we told you about miniature oranges and now with two hundred thousand dollars we will serve you pinch bean coffee with the oral tradition . . .

Several warriors loosen their neckties and examine the art on the walls.

MARION: Miniature oranges, and now pinch beans, what ever will be next?

HAROLD: Truffles and cashews.

MARION: Truffles? Can you be serious?

HAROLD: Red Lake truffles . . .

Harold pauses in silence. The foundation directors laugh, in short and practiced bursts. Harold clears his throat.

HAROLD: Grand Portage cashews . . . Not to mention White Earth caviar . . .

Harold steps forward to the conference table; he speaks in a secretive tone of voice. The directors lean forward to listen. Fannie examines her fingernails.

HAROLD: Now follow me down the great white road to the orange bus for the first *red* pinch . . .

5 Int: Orange Bus on the Road in the City—Afternoon

The bus moves through the city, down Franklyn Avenue, on the way to the first stop, the Naming Ceremony. The foundation directors are not comfortable, seated next to the warriors, but their manners compel them to speak and to raise questions about culture and the weather. Points of view out the window include several scenes of tribal people. Son Bear has his earphones on; he moves in his seat to the beat of powwow music. Harold stands, moves from seat to seat.

MARION: How many Indians live on *your* reservation?

PLUMERO: Seventeen hundred and thirty-nine . . .

Plumero loosens his necktie and flashes a thin smile. Marion turns to comment on the view out the window.

ANDREW: I have considered the origin theories of the American Indians . . . Some are *quite* interesting. I find the Bering Strait migration theory to be the most credible . . . How about you then, what are your thoughts on the subject?

NEW CROWS: Which way, east or west?

ANDREW: Which *way?* What do you mean?

NEW CROWS: Which way across the Bering Strait, *then?*

ANDREW: Yes, I see . . . Well, I hadn't really thought about it that way. Which way do *you* think?

NEW CROWS: From here to there, we emerged from the flood here, the first people, unless you think we are related to the panda bear.

ANDREW: Oh, not at all, not at all . . . Actually, What you say makes a great deal of sense, but the problem I seem to have, you see, is that there is so little evidence to support your idea . . .

NEW CROWS: Jesus Christ was an American Indian . . .

ANDREW: Was he now, who would have guessed?

Andrew examines his fingernails and then looks out the window of the bus. New Crows watches him and smiles. Point of view is outside the moving bus: scene of tribal people. Harold takes a seat next to Kingsley. Fannie is at the front of the bus, seated alone.

KINGSLEY: Your warriors certainly are knowledgeable. The directors seem quite impressed . . .

HAROLD: The Warriors of Orange are trained in the art of socioacupuncture . . . We imagine the world and cut our words from the centerfolds of histories . . .

KINGSLEY: Is that a tribal tradition?

Harold cocks his head to the side, smiles; he appears pensive.

HAROLD: We are wild word hunters, tricksters on the run . . .

KINGSLEY: We are impressed . . . You seem to know so much about so many things, from orange trees to linguistics . . .

HAROLD: Not to mention pinch beans . . .

KINGSLEY: Yes, of course . . . I have asked our new associate Fannie Mason to pay particular attention to your oral proposal . . .

Harold turns to the camera and smiles. Cut to Kingsley.

HAROLD: I have a problem which I hesitate to share with you at this time, but you are an understanding person . . .

KINGSLEY: *Yes,* please continue . . .

HAROLD: Well, the problem is money . . . We have none and we wondered if the foundation could advance us about a thousand dollars to cover our expenses for this presentation . . .

KINGSLEY: It would be highly irregular to advance money on your proposal which the full board has not yet approved . . .

HAROLD: We are hard pressed for cash or else I wouldn't think about asking . . .

KINGSLEY: Of course, we will forget that you asked.

Harold moves forward on the bus to direct the driver to the first stop for the Naming Ceremony. The warriors and directors continue talking. Kingsley brushes his suit coat sleeves and tightens his necktie. Son Bear lowers his earphones around his neck; the powwow music can still be heard.

TED: I was reading about American Indian populations in the *National Geographic* magazine . . .

SON BEAR: Where, in the doctor's office?

TED: We have a subscription . . . The article mentions the revisions of the population estimates of American Indians at the time of Columbus . . .

SON BEAR: Who? Who was that?

TED: Christopher Columbus, when he discovered the New World . . . Well, actually an island . . . How many Indians were there then, here I mean, on this continent?

SON BEAR: None.

TED: None? What do you mean *none?*

SON BEAR: None, not one. Columbus never discovered anything, and when he never did he invented us as Indians because we never heard the word before he dropped by by accident . . .

TED: Of course, I see what you mean . . . Well, let me phrase the question in a different way then. How many tribal people were there here then, ahh, before Columbus invented Indians?

Ted smiles, pleased with his question. He looks out the bus window. Point of view, scene of tribal people. The voice of Son Bear is over the point of view scene: tradition at a bus stop.

SON BEAR: Forty-nine million, seven hundred twenty-three thousand, one hundred and ninety-six on this continent, including what is now Mexico . . .

TED: Really, that many then?

6 Ext: Fry Bread Cart in a Parking Lot—Afternoon

The Warriors of Orange bus rumbles to a stop in a parking lot at Franklyn Circle. The warriors, directors, and others, gather around a large cart on wheels:

THE LAST STAND
Oral Traditional Food
FRY BREAD AND COOL AIDE
THE EDIBLE MENU
miniature orange marmalade
pinch bean espresso
mild moose burgers
totem crackers
COMMODITIES FOR THE RESERVATION BLUES

The directors and warriors gather around The Last Stand where they are each served a piece of fry bread with miniature orange marmalade. The warriors take deep soul bites, but the directors are hesitant; they nibble at their fry bread. The directors are polite and carry their fry bread to the next scene.

HAROLD: This is a special name feast prepared by the Warriors of Orange in honor of all the founders and foundations in the New World . . .

PLUMERO: And a few fakes and fools.

Loud music. An audience of white and tribal shoppers, with their bags and carts, gather around the bus and the fry bread cart. Plumero bears a cigar box with a cigar store Indian on the label. New Crows carries a fist full of orange chicken feathers.

HAROLD: Kingsley Newton . . . The urban spirits have directed me in a dream to select your new name from the cigar box.

Harold closes his eyes as he reaches into the box. Kingsley is nervous. He looks around and tightens his tie.

KINGSLEY: Are you serious?

HAROLD: Who could be serious about anything in a parking lot at a shopping center . . . use your imagination.

KINGSLEY: By all means . . .

HAROLD: Your new name speaks to me from the cigar store Indian box . . .

Harold reaches into the box and selects a property card from a monopoly game. Loud music. More people gather, move closer.

HAROLD: Your new name is . . . Baltic, your urban dream name is Baltic . . . Congratulations, bear your name with pride . . .

Harold hands the monopoly car to Kingsley. The warriors hoot and trill; the audience cheers and applauds. Baltic unbuttons his suit coat and swallows a nervous smile. The keeper of the Last Stand hands him another piece of fry bread. He has fry bread in both hands. He nibbles at both. Plumero moves close to Kingsley, whispers in his ear.

PLUMERO: Fry bread is white on the inside, you know.

Kingsley examines both pieces of fry bread, looks up and smiles.

HAROLD: Who will be our next contestant . . . Who will seek a fortune as a founder with a new name? Step forward into an urban dream . . .

Marion is volunteered by the other directors. She is applauded and she applauds herself as she steps forward, but her smile does not relieve her tension. Marion stands next to Plumero.

MARION: Should the oral tradition be a public affair?

PLUMERO: Close your eyes when the shaman calls your name . . .

MARION: Never . . .

HAROLD: The great urban shaman who directs all the interstates has given me your name in a dream . . . Where is the card . . .

Harold closes his eyes and selects a card from the box.

MARION: This better be good . . .

HAROLD: Your name is . . . Connecticut . . .

The audience applauds and the warriors hoot and trill.

HAROLD: Now, one more dream name for the lady over there with the
  sweet daffodil . . .

*The audience looks around. Fannie tries to avoid attention, but her gestures
attract attention. She shakes her head and avoids the event. Harold slides his
hand into the cigar box, a sensuous gesture. Ted's watch sounds the theme of
The Lone Ranger.*

HAROLD: My fingers are searching the box, I have a name, the name is
  chance, chance . . . But wait, the name card reads: "Good for one
  thousand dollars."

*The audience applauds and the warriors hoot and trill. Harold hands the card
to Fannie; she returns it, puts it in his pocket. Strangers from the audience step
forward to receive an urban dream name but the warriors close the box. The
remaining feathers are presented to the audience.*

HAROLD: The box is closed for the afternoon; all the proud cigar store
  Indians have retired in the west . . .

7 Int: Orange Bus Moving Down Summit Avenue—Afternoon

*Bus moves down Summit Avenue. Points of view of the affluent white world.
Focus on a personal license plate that reads: "Indian" or "Savage." Harold is
sitting next to Andrew. Fannie is behind them; she overhears their
conversation.*

ANDREW: One is still not certain how your pinch bean trees survive the
  winter?

HAROLD: Coffee shrubs . . .

ANDREW: Shrubs then . . . Are the beans frost resistant?

*Andrew is distracted when Harold points out the window of the bus at a
white couple with a white child who wears a feather headdress and carries
a rubber tomahawk.*

HAROLD: Were you in the war?

ANDREW: The great war?

HAROLD: Yes, the great wars . . . Do you remember those little packets of instant coffee?

ANDREW: Not with pleasure, to be sure . . .

HAROLD: We supplied the great war with the first instant coffee from woodland beans . . . Our tribal children gathered the beans in winter and then we pinched them for the war.

ANDREW: Indeed, your stories seem convincing enough, but will we have the pleasure of meeting the live shrubs?

Harold looks out the window of the bus. Point of view: an attractive blonde is washing her car.

HAROLD: That depends on how you see the oral tradition.

ANDREW: I see, well then, please explain.

Harold removes a large red felt-tip pen from his pocket, holds open his left hand, and draws two crude shrubs on the palm of his hand to illustrate his explanation. Fannie leans forward between them, sees the drawings, hears the explanation, and then rolls her eyes and falls back into her seat.

HAROLD: A logical positivist would demand cold clear data to be sure, while a mythic trickster in the oral tradition, on the other hand, would be satisfied with a handful of beans . . . Either way, as you can see, there are still two shrubs . . .

Harold reaches into his pocket and offers Andrew a handful of coffee beans. The director is nonplussed; he holds out both of his hands to receive the beans. Andrew examines the beans; he tries to pinch them, as Harold continues talking.

HAROLD: Remember those code talkers who spoke tribal languages to confuse the enemies?

Harold watches Andrew pinching the beans. Harold takes one bean from his hand and pinches it as he continues to talk. The bean becomes powder. Andrew is amazed.

HAROLD: Well, we maintained an elaborate pinch bean exchange in military units throughout the great war . . .

ANDREW: How did you do that?

HAROLD: That, sir, is a tribal secret . . .

Fannie leans forward and tries to pinch a bean. Andrew continues pinching beans without success. Harold moves back to sit with Kingsley.

HAROLD: Are you still interested in that reservation tour you once asked me about?

KINGSLEY: Yes, that would be interesting . . .

HAROLD: I could make arrangements to hunt wild rice, whatever interests you the most . . . But of course I would need some money in advance to cover the expenses . . . you understand.

KINGSLEY: Of course, let me get back to you on that.

HAROLD: I could make the arrangements today . . .

KINGSLEY: I should check my schedule first.

Point of view outside the bus: sunbathers on a balcony.

8 Int: Anthropology Department Artifact Cases— Afternoon

Scene begins with a photographic slide of the ghost dance. Harold steps into the slide; the ghost dance figures are projected on his face and body; he appears to be in the dance. Harold stands in light on an artifact case in an anthropology department. Plumero operates the slide projector. The warriors and directors are gathered near the case. Harold speaks in a deep dramatic tone of voice. Sound of a rattle.

HAROLD: The earth will rise to cover these sacred bones in the ghost dance vision . . . Time will run behind and white people will soon disappear . . .

MARION: What about the mixedbloods?

HAROLD: Mixedbloods will be buried as deep as their white blood . . . The more the deeper . . . Fullbloods will levitate in a sacred dance at the treelines . . .

Several anthropologists, dressed in western attire, string ties, turquoise are alarmed that the artifacts might be seized by militants. Harold points toward the nervous group of professors. Sound of a rattle. Slide change: death scene from Wounded Knee.

HAROLD: Those anthropologists over there will be buried upside down with their toes exposed like mushrooms . . .

PLUMERO: Poison mushrooms . . .

Ted is nervous; he checks his watch and wrinkles his face.

TED: Get on with the pitch, I mean pinch.

HAROLD: The rivers are dead near the universities, the fish are poisoned, even the carp yawn near shore . . . Birds are stalled in flight . . . Interstates uproot our families . . .

PLUMERO: And we hold the secrets of survival in a tribal pinch bean . . .

Harold seems surprised. His mood changes; he is less serious. He smiles and becomes an evangelist. Slide change: Wild West Show broadside.

HAROLD: Resurrection on a pinch bean.

Two university police officers push through the crowd, followed by a student newspaper reporter. The foundation directors move back to avoid trouble. The anthropologists are relieved. Flash photographs. Harold smiles and steps down from the cases.

POLICE OFFICER: Is this an authorized assembly?

HAROLD: Yes, sir, from the president himself . . .

POLICE OFFICER: Which president?

HAROLD: The university president . . . The Warriors of Orange, he said, are always welcome to examine these tribal artifacts.

The students cheer and applaud the warriors.

FANNIE: Sir, perhaps I could explain . . . You see, he is presenting his proposal for . . .

The students boooo and hisssss.

POLICE OFFICER: Who are you?

FANNIE: Fannie Mason, and this is Harold Sinseer . . .

POLICE OFFICER: Sincere?

HAROLD: Sinseer, yes, my name is on this letter . . .

Harold unfolds a letter from a small square and hands it to the police officer. The police officer examines the letter; he turns it upside down, sideways, then smiles. Sound of rattles.

POLICE OFFICER: Sincerely, is that it there?

The police officer points to the bottom of the letter.

HAROLD: Sinseer on the top, sincerely on the bottom, sir . . .

The students, even the anthropologists, laugh.

POLICE OFFICER: Right . . . Are you an Indian?

HAROLD: Right . . . Are you an Irish?

The students appreciate the humorous confrontation.

POLICE OFFICER: Right . . . Could you examine these artifacts while standing on the floor?

HAROLD: I was dancing how high the earth will be come the ghost dance vision.

POLICE OFFICER: The ghost dance?

HAROLD: When all this disappears . . .

POLICE OFFICER: Right . . . Keep your feet on the floor.

The students applaud while the police officer refolds the letter into a small square; he looks around and then returns the letter to Harold. Sound of a rattle. The anthropologists are embarrassed; the foundation directors are relieved. Slide change to a photograph of Paul Newman in Buffalo Bill and the Indians.

NEWS REPORTER: What did you say about the ghost dance?

HAROLD: I said that the river is dead below the brain trust . . .

NEWS REPORTER: What brain trust?

HAROLD: The university faculties . . .

NEWS REPORTER: Are you serious?

HAROLD: Come the ghost dance vision the brain trust will become the brain drain . . .

NEWS REPORTER: That I can believe, but is this a protest against the anthropology department?

HAROLD: The cultures that anthropologists invent never complain about anything . . .

NEWS REPORTER: What are you doing here then?

HAROLD: We are pinching a foundation for grants to establish coffee houses on reservations . . .

NEWS REPORTER: Coffee houses?

HAROLD: Coffee houses foster revolutions.

NEWS REPORTER: I see . . . Here's my card, let me know when the revolution is served . . . Make mine with cream.

Harold smiles and then folds the card into a small square. He turns toward the students and continues his stories. His voice is more dramatic.

HAROLD: We come to the cities from our tribal past and pace around our parts here like lost and lonesome animals . . .

Harold continues talking while Kingsley and a foundation director discuss the merits of his proposal. The two are standing at the end of the cases. Guitar music. Slide changes to a portrait of Buffalo Bill Cody.

HAROLD: In the beginning there were words and pinch beans and when the first flood came the great trickster saved a few beans to create a new earth . . . Then the trickster was word-driven from the land the second time, but he saved the secret of the pinch beans and now we come to a foundation with a plan to create coffee houses on reservations . . .
The great spirit created the frost tolerant pinch beans and gave them to the trickster for the tribes . . . The pinch shrubs flower late in the spring and then red berries appear in the summer . . . Late in winter under a whole moon the berries are harvested in birch bark containers . . . The secret is that there is no processing . . .

While Harold is telling stories in the background, Kingsley and the foundation director are discussing the merits of his proposal:

ANDREW: Kingsley, tell me, is he serious?

KINGSLEY: Harold insists that he is a trickster . . .

ANDREW: A confidence man?

KINGSLEY: No, a tribal trickster is not the same . . . He is rather sincere, even innocent, artless at times . . . He believes that he can stop time and change the world through imagination.

Andrew is nonplussed; he pulls his ear and frowns.

ANDREW: With a foundation grant of course . . .

KINGSLEY: Of course . . . Who could change the world without a foundation grant?

Kingsley and Andrew smile; they share the same secret.

ANDREW: Quite right, for a proponent of the oral tradition that letter from the president was a smart move.

KINGSLEY: He seems to have a word or a letter for all occasions . . .

The class bell rings and most of the students leave. Slide change: scene of Harold bearing Fannie in his arms, like the pose of the statue of Hiawatha and Minnehaha.

9 Ext: Statue of Hiawatha and Minnehaha—Afternoon

The statue is on the screen as the bus approaches and stops. The warriors leave the bus dressed in "Anglo" shirts, the name of their softball team; the directors leave the bus with "Indian" shirts, the name of their team. Fannie and Harold walk toward the field together. He carries the bats and gloves; she carries the softball. Kingsley, who is the umpire, does not wear a team shirt. The directors have removed their suit coats and loosened their ties. Kingsley remains formal, suit coat buttoned. Harold and Fannie are heard speaking, voiceover from a distance as they walk away from the statue.

HAROLD: Is it true that Indians are great lovers?

FANNIE: Sometimes, when you catch one with his mouth closed in an "Anglo" shirt . . .

10 Ext: Softball Diamond—Afternoon

The "Indians" and the "Anglos" are huddled in separate teams, Harold in a huddle with the warriors who are the "Anglos."

HAROLD: Listen gang, we are the "Anglos" and we're here to win and win big . . . Play by the rules if you must, but rape and plunder to win the game . . . When the "Indians" talk about the earth and their sacred ceremonies, steal a base, win the game like we stole their land, with a smile . . . Score, score, score, in the name of god, win, and send those "Indians" back to the reservation as victims, where the slow grass grows . . . We'll mine the resources later.

PLUMERO: But if you should lose, you can't count on a job with the Bureau of Indian Affairs to get even . . .

Harold pulls off his "Anglos" shirt and walks over to the "Indians" team huddle. The directors are stoical.

HAROLD: We are in the cities now and we must never forget what the missionaries said our elders said around the fires . . .

TED: Lead me to the foundations?

HAROLD: That was much earlier; we dropped the first grant proposal with the pilgrims . . . The elders said we should never enter the game to win but to dream . . . We are made in dreams and the white man is the one who must win . . . When we help him win we are free and soon the white man will want to be like us, and when that happens we can leave him, once and for all times, a winner, on the reservations he made for us . . .

MARION: Who invented that game?

HAROLD: Boy Scouts and anthropologists.

ANDREW: The Order of the Arrow, you will be pleased to know, still whistles in the dark.

HAROLD: Competition is not our curse, but we are the best tricksters in town to let the white man win with pride . . .

TED: Trick the white devils to win? . . . That defies all reason.

Harold puts on his "Anglos" shirt and returns to his team, which is first at bat. Fannie is the pitcher for the "Indians" and Harold, who is the first at the plate for his team, is the pitcher for the "Anglos." Harold dances at the plate. The first ball rolls across the plate, ball one. The second rolls behind him, ball two.

HAROLD: Throw the ball, this is not a treaty conference . . .

Ball three rolls over the plate.

HAROLD: Come on, just *one* high enough to hit and you can be my Indian guide forever . . .

Fannie pitches a fast ball, strike one; strike two. Then she rolls the fourth ball over the plate and Harold walks to first base. Ted is an "Indian" at first base. Harold talks to Ted.

HAROLD: This is my first visit to a real reservation . . . Where is your bingo hall?

TED: Behind the smoke shop, honkie . . .

Harold steals to second base. Harold talks to Andrew on second base.

HAROLD: My great grandmother was an Indian princess once . . .

ANDREW: Cherokee, no doubt . . . Listen, my grandmother was a French Duchess . . .

Harold steals to third base. Harold talks with Marion on third base; he removes a moccasin and hands it to Marion.

HAROLD: An old Indian guide gave these moccasins to my grandfather . . . I was wondering if you could tell me what tribe made them . . .

Marion, of the "Indians" team, sniffs the toe of the moccasin; she ponders the smell, and then sniffs it again.

MARION: Yes, these were worn by an old gambler who lived three miles north of Bad Medicine Lake . . .

HAROLD: What tribe is that?

MARION: Mixedblood Nacirema . . .

Harold seems to move from base to base, inning to inning, in magical flight. He appears and disappears in fast cuts of the game. Fannie comes to bat; Harold teases her with a fast ball, strike one, but she hits the second pitch out of the park. Harold dances on the mound.

HAROLD: White people always want to be better Indians than the Indians . . . The missionaries never translated the meaning of a "home run."

MARION: We blame everything on the Bureau of Indian Affairs . . . Even when we win.

The players ad lib from base to base; the "Indians" win the game.

11 Int: Carpeted Board Room at the Bily Foundation—Afternoon

The directors and warriors return to the board room, exhausted, for the conclusion of the proposal; all are seated around the conference table still wearing their team shirts from the softball game.

KINGSLEY: Thank you for remaining to the end of this most unusual oral traditional ball game . . .

MARION: The pretend Indians won again . . .

PLUMERO: So did the pretend "Anglos."

TED: Most unusual, most unusual, but I do have one last question before we adjourn . . .

HAROLD: Your questions are my very answers.

Kingsley frowns. Ted twists his face as he speaks.

TED: The Warriors of Orange, all of you, have been perfect gentlemen . . . Calm and mannered throughout, which makes my question all the more difficult to construct without appearing . . .

HAROLD: Without sounding like a racist?

Harold removes his "Anglos" shirt and throws it on the table.

TED: Exactly . . . You understand then?

HAROLD: Perhaps we could help you find the first unracist words . . . Does your question have anything to do with our proposal?

TED: Not at all . . . Pinch beans will give us all a good name.

Ted waves his arms wide. Harold smiles and then gestures with his lips to the warriors.

HAROLD: Savagism, the question must be about savagism and civilization.

TED: Well, yes, in the broadest sense of the word.

PLUMERO: How broad can a savage be?

HAROLD: Would you like to meet a beautiful tribal woman?

TED: No . . . Well, of course, but not in an improper manner . . .

PLUMERO: How about a hunting guide?

TED: No, that's not it at all, but that would be interesting now that you mention it . . .

PLUMERO: Sweat lodge ceremonies . . . Purification?

TED: No, not that either . . . Well, what I mean is that I am too sensitive to the heat . . .

PLUMERO: A shaman, an herbal healing then?

Ted is more relaxed; he takes pleasure in being the center of attention; the pursuit of the question.

TED: What does a shaman do?

Harold and Plumero and the other warriors become more aggressive. Plumero pulls his "Anglos" shirt off and throws it on the table.

PLUMERO: Leather and beadwork?

The warriors are restless, they rise and move around the room, they remove their "Anglos" shirts and stop from time to time to stare at the directors. Ted clears his throat.

TED: No, not beadwork . . . My wife bought too much, dozens of beautiful objects for practically nothing from an old Indian woman who was in the hospital . . . What I mean is that my wife was a volunteer and she took care of this woman . . . No, not beads this time.

Ted thrusts his head back like a bird. He pinches his lips with his two fingers and then expands his chest as he buttons his suit coat. He clears his throat. The warriors circle his chair. Sound of a rattle. Plumero raises his voice and bangs the table with his fist.

PLUMERO: Indian alcoholism . . .

Kingsley stiffens and looks over to Fannie. Fannie rolls her head and looks at the ceiling. Ted is pleased; the warriors have discovered his question.

TED: That's it! Yes, thank you, yes, my question is about Indian drinking, but it bothered me to say the word . . .

Ted examines his watch.

HAROLD: The old firewater thesis, of course, we should have known . . .

Kingsley is uncomfortable and interrupts the conversation.

KINGSLEY: What he means to say is that he has worked with American Indians who have had serious drinking problems and he appreciates how sensitive the subject can be . . . Even in the best of times, we all have had some problem with spirits . . .

HAROLD: The "Indians" seemed sober to me during the ball game . . .

PLUMERO: Even the "Anglos" . . .

The board room is silent. The warriors and directors all look off in different directions.

TED: That's what I mean . . . That's exactly what I wanted to ask you about . . . You are all so sober, and you should be *proud* that you are . . .

The warriors turn on their heels. Harold interrupts the director with a harsh tone of voice. Ted still enjoys the attention.

HAROLD: What *is* your question?

TED: My question is, ahh, how did all of you overcome the need and temptation to use alcohol? You are so sober, a credit to your race . . .

Fannie and Kingsley cover their eyes with their hands. Faces are frozen in time and place. Harold begins to smile. He claps his hands.

HAROLD: Pinch beans, pinch beans my friend are the cure . . .

The warriors hoot and trill. Ted seems confused.

TED: Pinch beans?

HAROLD: Pinch beans are the perfect booze blocker; the beans block the temptation to take alcohol from evil white men . . . Our proposal to establish coffee houses will lead to a sober, as well as a mythic, revolution . . .

TED: Fantastic, indeed this is fantastic, you've got my vote for sure . . .

KINGSLEY: And not a minute too soon, I hasten to add . . .

HAROLD: Let me explain how our pinch beans will . . .

Kingsley stands and interrupts Harold; he raises his voice.

KINGSLEY: Harold, we congratulate you and your warriors on a fine presentation . . . something personal and ceremonial . . .

ANDREW: Ever so memorable . . .

HAROLD: Pinch seven beans once a day into warm water while looking at a tree and your delusions of progress and domination will dissolve . . .

The directors smile and applaud. The warriors have removed their "Anglos" shirts, but the directors still wear their "Indians" shirts. Harold moves closer to Kingsley at the end of the table.

HAROLD: Listen, I have been avoiding the real reason I need the thousand dollars . . . I did not want to trouble you with my personal problems.

KINGSLEY: Please, trust me . . .

HAROLD: My traditional grandmother died last week.

KINGSLEY: Harold, I am so sorry . . .

HAROLD: She lived a full and wonderful life; she cared for me during the hard times on the reservation, and now, well, we don't have the money to bury her . . . She is at home now laid out in the kitchen waiting to enter the spirit world . . . Do you suppose you could borrow me one thousand dollars to bury her?

KINGSLEY: Borrow? Oh, yes, of course . . . Harold, you should have come to me sooner . . .

Kingsley writes a check and hands it to Harold.

HAROLD: Thank you, you are most generous . . . Please keep this to yourself because I am embarrassed to ask my friends for money . . .

KINGSLEY: My lips are sealed . . . Could I attend the funeral?

HAROLD: Ahh, this is a traditional burial . . . But we will invite you up to the reservation in about a week.

Harold crosses the board room; he looks back to be sure he is not being watched and then endorses the check. He looks around again, sees that Kingsley is involved in a conversation, and then hands the check to Fannie.

HAROLD: At last, we are even . . .

Fannie examines the check, rolls her head, looks toward Kingsley, and then to Harold. She crumples the check in her fist.

12 Ext: Orange Bus Moving Past on the Interstate— Late Afternoon

Harold and the warriors smile and wave from the windows of the bus as it passes in slow motion on the interstate. Harold speaks, voiceover as the bus passes, in a poetic tone of voice. Guitar and sound of a rattle.

HAROLD: We are the Warriors of Orange and we move in mythic time . . . We are elusive birds in borrowed nests, animals at the treelines in late winter . . . We are thunderclouds on the run . . . We are tricksters in the best humor, we leave no culture stains from separations, nothing so cruel as civilization and loneliness . . .

The bus disappears in the distance.

13 Ext: Harold of Orange Coffee House—Sunset

The bus stops in front of the building. The warriors stumble out and walk into the building. The lights are turned on in the coffee house, and the sign is illuminated. Harold is the last to leave the bus. Near the bus, with the coffee house in the background, he speaks to the camera for the last time.

HAROLD (*to the camera*):   This is where the revolution starts, on a gravel road in the brush . . . At a reservation coffee house in the softwoods . . . Remember, you were here with some of the best trickster founders of this new earth . . .

Harold smiles and turns from the camera. He walks toward the coffee house. In the last shot Harold is seen through the front window of the coffee house with other warriors. Harold and the warriors burst into wild laughter and the scene fades.

SELECTED LIST OF INDIAN LITERATURE AND HISTORICAL EVENTS

By American Indians	By Non-Indians	Historical Events	
		1492	Columbus's first encounters Bahamas, Cuba, Haiti
		1493	Columbus encounters Puerto Rico, Dominica, Jamaica
		C1500	Formation of Iroquois Confederacy
		1513	Juan Ponce de Leon arrives in Florida
		1526	San Miguel de Guadalupe (first European Settlement in U.S.)
	1608 *A True Relation of Virginia*—Captain John Smith	1607	Jamestown, Va. (first English settlement)
		1614	Pocahontas marries John Rolfe
		1619	First slaves in North America arrived in Virginia
		1620	Plymouth Colony
		1637	Pequot War In New England
		1680	Pueblo Revolt
1772 Sermon preached at the execution of Moses Paul— Samson Occom (Mohigan)		1682	LaSalle claims Louisiana Territory for France
		1754–63	French and Indian War

By American Indians	By Non-Indians	Historical Events
		1812 War of 1812 (U.S. and Britain)
	1826 *Last of the Mohicans*—James F. Cooper	
1827 *Sketches of Ancient History of the Six Nations*— David Cusik		
1829 *Son of the Forest*— William Apes (Pequot)	1828 *Biography of Columbus*— Washington Irving	
		1830 Removal Act
		1831 *Cherokee v. Georgia*
		1832 Bureau of Indian Affairs (BIA) established in War Department
1833 *Black Hawk, an Autobiography*— Black Hawk (Sauk)		
	1835 *The Yemassee*— William Gilmore Simms	1835–42 Seminole War
		1838–39 Trail of Tears
	1840 *The Pathfinder*— James F. Cooper	
1847 *Life, History, and Travels of Kah-Ge-Ga-Gah-Bowh*— George Copway (Ojibwa)		1848 Treaty of Guadalupe Hidalgo
		1848 Gold Rush
		1849 Office of Indian Affairs transferred to Department of the Interior
1850 *The Ojibway Conquest*—George Copway (Ojibwa)		
1854 *The Life and Adventures of Joaquin Murieta*— John Rollin Ridge (Cherokee)	1855 *Song of Hiawatha*—H. W. Longfellow	
		1862 Emancipation Proclamation
		1863 Kit Carlson invades Navajo territory: Long Walk
		1864 Massacre at Sand Creek
		1865 Civil War ends
		1869 Red River Rebellion in Canada
		1871 End of treaty-making period
		1876 Custer's defeat at Little Big Horn
1883 *Life Among the Paiutes*—Sarah Winnemucca Hopkins (Paiute)	1884 *Ramona*—Helen Hunt Jackson	1883 W. F. Cody (Buffalo Bill) organizes "Wild West Show"
		1883 Indian Rights Association founded

By American Indians	By Non-Indians	Historical Events
		1886 Geronimo surrenders
		1887 Dawes Act (Allotment)
	1890 *The Delight Makers*—Adolph Bandelier	1890 Massacre at Wounded Knee
1891 *Wynema*—S. Alice Callahan (Cherokee)		
1899 *Queen of the Woods*—Simon Pokagan (Potawatomi)		
1900 *The Middle Five*—Francis LeFlesche (Omaha)		
1901 *Old Indian Legends*—Zitkala Sa (Sioux)	1901 *Zuni Folk Tales*—Frank Cushing	
1902 *Indian Boyhood*—Charles A. Eastman (Sioux)	1907 *Indian's Book*—Natalie Curtis	1907 Oklahoma becomes a state
1910 *Collected Poems*—Alex Posey (Creek)	1910 *Winnetou*—Karl May	
1911 *Soul of the Indian*—Charles A. Eastman (Sioux)		1912 Arizona and New Mexico become states
		1912 Jim Thorpe wins Olympic gold medal
1916 *From Deep Woods to Civilization*—Charles A. Eastman (Sioux)		1914–18 World War I
1917 *Flint and Feather*—Pauline Johnson (Mohawk)	1918 *The Path on the Rainbow*—George Cronyn	
	1923 *The American Rhythm*—Mary Austin	1924 Indian Citizenship Act (Snyder Act)
1925 *Wild Harvest*—John Milton Oskison (Cherokee)		
1926 *Black Jack Davy*—John Milton Oskison (Cherokee)	1926 *The American Indians and Their Music*—Frances Densmore	
1927 *Co-Ge-We-A: The Half Blood*—Hum-ishu-Ma (Okanogan)		1928 Merriam Report
	1929 *Laughing Boy*—Oliver LaFarge	
		1930s New Deal
1932 *Wah'Kon-Tah*—John Joseph Mathews (Osage)	1932 *Black Elk Speaks*—John Neihardt	

By American Indians	By Non-Indians	Historical Events
1932 *Flaming Arrow's People*—James Paytiamo (Acoma)		
1933 *Land of the Spotted Eagle*—Chief Luther Standing Bear (Sioux)		
1934 *Sundown*—John Joseph Mathews (Osage)		1934 Indian Reorganization Act (Wheeler-Howard)
1935 *Brothers Three*—John Milton Oskison (Cherokee)		
1936 *The Surrounded*—D'Arcy McNickle (Cree/Salish)		
1936 *The Autobiography of a Papago Woman*—Maria Chona (Papago)	1937 *People of the Earth*—Edwin Lorles	
	1938 *Singing for Power*—Ruth Underhill	1939–45 WWII
	1942 *The Man Who Killed the Deer*—Frank Waters	
1944 *Speaking of Indians*—Ella C. Deloria (Sioux)		1944 National Congress of American Indians founded
1945 *Talking to the Moon*—J. J. Mathews (Osage)	1946 *The Winged Serpent*—Margot Astrov	1946 Indian Claims Committee established
	1951 *The Sky Clears*—A. Grove Day	1948 Indians granted right to vote in Arizona and New Mexico
	1953 *Cheyenne Autumn*—Mari Sandoz	
1954 *Runner in the Sun*—D'Arcy McNickle (Cree/Salish)		1954 Termination Policy passed
		1961 National Indian Youth Council
	1963 *When the Legends Die*—Hal Borland	1964 Indian fish-ins
	1964 *Little Big Man*—Thomas Berger	
	1964 *The Morphology of North American Folktales*—Alan Dundes	
	1965 *Savagism and Civilization*—Roy Harvey Pearce	1966 Alaska Federation of Natives founded
1967 *Wintercount*—Dallas Chief Eagle (Sioux)		

By American Indians	By Non-Indians	Historical Events
1968 *House Made of Dawn*—N. Scott Momaday (Kiowa)		1968 Indian Civil Rights Act
		1968 American Indian Movement founded
1969 *Custer Died for Your Sins*—Vine Deloria, Jr. (Sioux)	1969 *Shaking the Pumpkin*—Jerome Rothenberg	1969 Alcatraz Island takeover
	1969 *Indians: A Play*—Arthur Kopit	1969 Navajo Community College founded
1970 *Harpoon of the Hunter*—Markoosie (Inuit)	1970 *The Man Who Killed the Deer*—Frank Waters	1970 National Indian Education Association founded
1970 *The Way to Rainy Mountain*—N. Scott Momaday (Kiowa)	1970 *Bury My Heart at Wounded Knee*—Dee Brown	1970 Native American Rights Fund
		1970 Blue Lake returned to Taos Pueblo
		1970 Americans for Indian Opportunity founded
	1971 *The Magic World*—William Brandon	
	1971 *In the Trail of the Wind*—John Bierhorst	
	1971 *Indian Oratory*—W. C. Vanderwerth	
1972 *We Talk, You Listen*—Vine Deloria, Jr. (Sioux)	1972 *Finding the Center*—Dennis Tedlock	1972 Trail of the Broken Treaties
1972 *Tsali*—Denton R. Bedford (Munsee)		1972 Indian Education Act
1972 *Seven Arrows*—Hyemeyohsts Storm (Cheyenne)		1972 Menominee Restoration Act
1972 *The Song of Heyoekhah*—Hyemeyohsts Storm (Cheyenne)		
1973 *God Is Red*—Vine Deloria, Jr. (Sioux)	1973 *The Portable North American Reader*—Frederick W. Turner III	1973 A.I.M. Takeover at Wounded Knee, S.D., Pine Ridge
1973 *Halfbreed*—Maria Campbell (Métis)		
1973 *Navajo Stories of the Long Walk Period*—Ruth Roessel (Navajo)	1973 *I Heard the Owl Call My Name*—Margaret Craven	
1974 *Winter in the Blood*—James Welch (Blackfeet)		1974 International Indian Treaty Council founded
1974 *The Owl's Song*—Janet Campbell Hale (Coeur D'Alene)		1974 Indian Financing act passed

By American Indians	By Non-Indians	Historical Events
1975 *Indian's Summer*—Nasnaga (Shawnee)	1975 *Literature of the American Indian*—Abraham Chapman	1974 Public Law 94-531—Navajo/Hopi joint use area partitioned
1975 *The Last Song*—Joy Harjo (Creek)	1975 *The Ignoble Savage: American Literary Racism 1790–1890*—Louise K. Barnett	1975 Indian Self-Determination and Ed. Assist. Act
1975 *Bobbie Lee: Indian Rebel*—Lee Maracle (Metis)	1975 *The Literature of the American Indian*—T. Sanders and W. Peek, Eds.	1975 Confrontation at Pine Ridge results in death of two FBI agents; Leonard Peltier is convicted
	1975 *The Man to Send Rain Clouds: Contemporary Stories by American Indians*—Kenneth Rosen	1975 Council of Energy Resources Tribes
1976 *The Names*—N. Scott Momaday (Kiowa)		1976 Indian Health Care Improvement Act
1976 *The Reservation*—Ted C. William (Tuscarora)		1977 Indian Law Resource Center
1976 *Going for the Rain*—Simon Ortiz (Acoma)		
1977 *Nightwing*—Martin Cruz Smith (Senucu del Sur/Yaqui)	1977 *Giving Birth to Thunder Sleeping with His Daughter*—Barry Lopez	
1977 *Then Badger Said This*—Liz Cook-Lynn (Sioux)		
1977 *Ceremony*—Leslie M. Silko (Laguna)		
1978 *Wordarrows*—Gerald Vizenor (Ojibwa)	1978 *American Indian Fiction*—Charles Larson	1978 American Indian Religious Freedom Act
1978 *Wind from an Enemy Sky*—D'Arcy McNickle (Métis)	1978 *The White Man's Indian: Images of the American Indian from Columbus to the Present*	1978 Indian Child Welfare Act
1978 *The Dreams of Jesse Brown*—Joseph Bruchac (Abenaki)		1978 The Longest Walk (San Francisco to D.C.)
1978 *Darkness in Saint Louis Bearheart*—Gerald Vizenor (Ojibwa)		1978 American Indian Sciences and Engineering Society founded
1979 *The Death of Jim Loney*—James Welch (Blackfeet)	1979 *American Indian Literature: An Anthology*—Alan Velie, Ed.	

By American Indians	By Non-Indians	Historical Events
1979 *The Remembered Earth*—Geary Hobson Ed (Cherokee/Chicka-saw)	1979 *Hanta Yo*—Ruth Beebe Hill	1979 U.S. Department of Health, Education, and Welfare issues regulations prohibiting sterilization of Indian women
1980 *The Autobio-graphy of a Yaqui Poet*—Refugio Savala (Yaqui)	1980 *Facing West—* Richard Drinnon	1979 U.S. Supreme Court upholds Boldt decision on fishing rights
1980 *The Ways of My Grand-Mothers—* Beverly Hungry Wolf (Blackfeet)	1980 *The Third Women: Minority Women Writers of the U.S.*—Dexter Fisher	
1980 *New Native American Drama*—Hanay Geiogamah (Kiowa)		
1981 *Winter of the Salamander*—Ray Young Bear (Mesquakie)		1981 *Lakota Times,* later *Indian Country Today,* begins publication
1981 *Earthdivers: Tribal Narratives on Mixed Descent*—Gerald Vizenor (Ojibwa)		
1981 *Storyteller*—Leslie M. Silko (Laguna)		
1981 *Wahanee—* Waheenee (Itidatsa)		
1982 *Petroglyphs—* Barney Bush (Shawnee/Cayuga)	1982 *The Wishing Bone Cycle: Narrative Poems of the Swampy Creek Indians*—Howard A. Norman	1982 Gay American Indians founded in New York
	1982 *Smoothing the Ground: Essays on Native American Literature*—Brian Swann	1982 Tribal Government Tax Status Act
		1982 Jim Thorpe's medals returned to his family
1983 *Eclipse*—Linda Hogan (Chickasaw)	1983 *Native American Renaissance—* Kenneth Lincoln	
1983 *The Women Who Owned the Shadows*—Paula Gunn Allen (Laguna)		

By American Indians	By Non-Indians	Historical Events
1983 *Studies in American Indian Literature*—Paula Gunn Allen (Laguna/Sioux)		
1984 *Love Medicine*—Louise Erdrich (Chippewa)	1984 *Lonesome Dove*—Larry McMurtry	
1984 *American Indian Myths and Legends*—Richard Erdoes and Alfonso Ortiz	1984 *American Indian Women Telling Their Lives*—Gretchen Bataille and Kathleen Sands	
1984 *The Sun Is Not Merciful*—Anna Lee Walters (Pawnee/Otoe)		
1985 *The Jailing of Cecelia Capture*—Janet Campbell Hale (Coeur d'Alene)	1985 *Critical Essays on Native American Literature*—Andrew O. Wiget	1986 (July 7) Deadline for Navajo relocation (later extended)
1986 *Stallion Gate*—Martin Cruz Smith (Senecu Del Sur/Yaqui)		
1986 *The Sacred Hoop*—Paula Gunn Allen (Laguna)		
1986 *Fools Crow*—James Welch (Blackfeet)		
1986 *Beet Queen*—Louise Erdrich (Ojibwa)		
1987 *A Yellow Raft on Blue Water*—Michael Dorris (Modoc)	1987 *Recovering the Word*—Brian Swann and Arnold Krupat, Eds.	
1987 *Yaqui Deer Songs: Maso Bwikam*—Larry Evers and Felipe S. Molina (Yaqui)		
1987 *Touchwood*—Gerald Vizenor (Ojibwa)		
1987 *A Breeze Swept Through*—Luci Tapahonso (Navajo)		
1987 *Survival This Way*—Joseph Bruchac (Abenaki)		

By American Indians	By Non-Indians	Historical Events
1987 *Griever: An American Monkey King in China*—Gerald Vizenor (Ojibwa)		
1988 *Tracks*—Louise Erdrich (Ojibwa)	1988 *A Thief in Time*—Tony Hillerman	1988 Navajo Families file First Amendment lawsuit to challenge relocation
1988 *Waterlily*—Elia C. Deloria (Sioux)		
1988 *Ghost Singer*—Anna Lee Waters (Otoe/Pawnee)		
1989 *Spider Woman's Granddaughters*—Paula Gunn Allen (Laguna)	1989 *Native American Literatures*—Laura Coltelli	1989 Smithsonian Institution policy on ancestral remains in museums
1989 *Baptism of Desire*—Louise Erdrich (Ojibwa)	1989 *The Voice in the Margin*—Arnold Krupat	1989 National Museum of the American Indian established by U.S. Congress as part of the Smithsonian Institution
1989 *The Ancient Child*—N. Scott Momaday (Kiowa)	1989 *Ancestral Voice: Conversations with N. Scott Momaday*—Charles L. Woodard	
1989 *Narrative Chance: Postmodern Discourse on Native American Indian Literatures*—Gerald Vizenor (Ojibwa)		
1989 *The Broken Cord*—Michael Dorris (Modoc)		
1990 *Mean Spirit*—Linda Hogan (Chickasaw)	1990 *American Indian Literatures*—A. LaVonne Brown Ruoff	1990 Native American Grave Protection and Repatriation Act
1990 *The Indian Lawyer*—James Welch (Blackfoot)	1990 *Winged Words: American Indian Writers Speak*—Laura Coltelli	1990 U.S. Supreme Court rules that states are allowed to outlaw the use of peyote
1990 *Lakota Woman*—Mary Crow Dog (Lakota) and Richard Erdoes	1990 *Landmarks of Healing*—Susan Scarberry-Garcia	1990 Native American Languages Act passed
1990 *Interior Landscapes*—Gerald Vizenor (Ojibwa)	1990 *Dancing on the Rim of the World*—Andrea Lerner, Ed.	
1990 *In Mad Love and War*—Joy Harjo (Creek)		
1990 *Medicine River*—Thomas King (Cherokee)		
1990 *Food and Spirits*—Beth Brant (Mohawk)		1991 Over 3,000 Native

By American Indians	By Non-Indians	Historical Events
1991 *The Crown of Columbus*—Louise Erdrich (Ojibwa) and Michael Dorris (Modoc)	1991 *American Indian Women: A Guide to Research*—Gretchen Bataille and Kathleen M. Sands	Americans serve in Persian Gulf War (Desert Storm)
1991 *Heirs of Columbus*—Gerald Vizenor (Ojibwa)	1991 *Sacajawea & Co.*—Asebrit Sandquist	1991 Little Big Horn memorial authorized by U.S. Congress
1991 *Almanac of the Dead*—Leslie M. Silko (Laguna)		
1991 *Wolfsong*—Louis Owens (Choctaw/ Cherokee)		
1991 *From the River's Edge*—Elizabeth Cook-Lynn (Sioux)		
1991 *Grandmothers of the Light*—Paula Gunn Allen (Laguna)		1992 First "Returning the Gift": hundreds of Native authors gather in Norman, Oklahoma
1992 *Other Destinies: Understanding the Native American Novel*—Louis Owens (Choctaw/ Cherokee)		1992 Columbus Quincentenary
1992 *The Sharpest Sight*—Louis Owens (Choctaw/ Cherokee)		1992 Pentagon honors Navajo "code talkers"
1992 *The Sharpest Sight*—Louis Owens (Choctaw/ Cherokee)		
1992 *Talking Indian*—Anna Lee Walters (Pawnee/Otoe)		
1992 *Sending My Heart Back Across the Years*—Hertha Dawn Wong (Creek)		
1992 *Claiming Breath*—Diane Glancy		1993 Wordcraft Circle of Native Writers and Storytellers is incorporated in Virginia
1993 *Green Grass, Running Water*—Tom King	1993 "Yellow Woman"—Melody Graulich (Cherokee)	
1993 *Saanii Dahataal*—Luci Tapahonso (Navajo)		

By American Indians		By Non-Indians		Historical Events
1993	*Keeping Slug Woman Alive*— Greg Sarris (Coast Miwok/Pomo)	1993	*Native American Women: A Biographical Dictionary*— Gretchen M. Bataille (Cherokee)	
1993	*Ohitika Woman*— Mary Brave Bird (Lakota) and Richard Erdoes	1993	*New Voices in Native American Criticism*—Arnold Krupat	
1993	*Bloodlines*—Janet Campbell Hale (Coeur d'Alene)			
1993	*The Lone Ranger and Tonto Fistfight in Heaven*—Sherman Alexie (Spokane/Coeur D'Alene)			
1993	*Full Moon on the Reservation*— Gloria Bird (Spokane)			
1993	*Mankiller: A Chief and Her People*— Wilma Mankiller (Cherokee)			
1993	*The Book of Medicines*—Linda Hogan (Chickasaw)			
1993	*An Eagle Nation*— Carter Revard (Osage)			
1994	*Bone Dance*— Wendy Rose (Hope/Miwok)	1994	*Dictionary of Native American Literature*— Andrew Wiget, Ed.	
1994	*Ohitika Woman*— Mary Brave Bird (Lakota)	1994	*Native America: Portrait of the Peoples*—Duane Champagne	
1994	*The Bingo Palace*—Louise Erdrich (Chippewa)	1994	*Native American Autobiography*— Arnold Krupat	
1994	*Returning the Gift*—Joe Bruchac (Abneki)			
1994	*Grand Avenue*— Greg Sarris (Miwok)			
1995	*Smoke Rising*—Joe Bruchac (Abneki)			
1995	*Dwellings*—Linda Hogan (Chickasaw)			

By American Indians	By Non-Indians	Historical Events
1995 *Solar Storms—* Linda Hogan (Chickasaw)	1995 *Coming to Light: Contemporary Translations of the Native Literatures of North American—*Brian Swann	
1995 *Eye Killers—*A. A. Carr (Navajo/Laguna Pueblo)		
1995 *All My Sins Are Relatives—*W. S. Penn (Nez Percé/Osage)	1995 *Mediation in Contemporary Native American Fiction—*James Ruppert	
1995 *Catch Colt—* Sidner Larson (Gros Ventre)	1995 *Messengers of the Wind: Native American Women Tell Their Stories—* Jane Katz, Ed.	
1995 *Completing the Circle—*Virginia Driving Hawk Sneve (Sioux)		
1995 *Reservation Blues—*Sherman Alexie (Spokane)		
1996 *Yellow Woman and a Beauty of the Spirit—*Leslie M. Silko (Laguna)		
1996 *Tales of Burning Love—*Louise Erdrich (Chippewa)		
1996 *Native Time—*Lee Francis (Laguna)		
1996 *Reclaiming the Vision—*Lee Francis (Laguna) and James Bruchac (Abenaki)		
1996 *Indian Killer—* Sherman Alexie (Spokane)		
1997 *Reinventing the Enemy's Language—*Joy Harjo (Creek) and Gloria Bird (Spokane)	1997 *Native American Writers of the U.S.—*Kenneth Roemer, Ed.	
1997 *Cloud Chamber—* Michael Dorris (Modoc)		
1998 *Power—*Linda Hogan (Chickasaw)		

By American Indians	By Non-Indians	Historical Events
1998 *The Antelope Wife*—Louise Erdrich (Chippewa)		

Note: This list is only partial. Few biographies or collections of poetry are included. Historical events are included to place the works in the context of American Indians' relationship to U.S. society and government.

Compiled by:
Gretchen M. Bataille
Washington State University
January 1999

CREDITS

Sherman Alexie, "The Approximate Size of My Favorite Tumor" and "This Is What It Means to Say Phoenix, Arizona" from *The Lone Ranger and Tonto Fistfight in Heaven.* Copyright © 1993 by Sherman Alexie. Reprinted with the permission of Grove/Atlantic, Inc. "13/16" and "The Business of Fancydancing" from *The Business of Fancydancing.* Copyright © 1992 by Sherman Alexie. Reprinted with the permission of Hanging Loose Press. "Capital Punishment," "Defending Walt Whitman," "The Exaggeration of Despair," and "How to Write the Great American Indian Novel" from *The Summer of Black Widows.* Copyright © 1996 by Sherman Alexie. Reprinted with the permission of Hanging Loose Press. "Crazy Horse Speaks" from *Old Shirts & New Skins* (Los Angeles: UCLA American Indian Studies Center, 1993). Copyright © 1993 by Sherman Alexie. Reprinted with the permission of the author.

Paula Gunn Allen, "Deer Woman" from *Talking Leaves: Contemporary Native American Short Stories,* edited by Greg Lesley (New York: Dell Publishing, 1991). "Soundings" from *Harper's Anthology of 20th Century Native American Poetry,* edited by Duanne Niatum (New York: HarperCollins Publishers, 1988). Copyright by Paula Gunn Allen. All reprinted with the permission of the author. "Dear World" and "Kopis'taya, a Gathering of Spirits" from *Life Is a Fatal Disease: Selected Poems, 1964–1994.* Copyright © 1994 by Paula Gunn Allen. Reprinted with the permission of West End Press. "The Sacred Hoop: A Contemporary Perspective" from *The Sacred Hoop: Recovering the Feminine Side in American Indian Traditions.* Copyright © 1986 by Paula Gunn Allen. Reprinted with the permission of Beacon Press, Boston.

Kimberly Blaeser, "Living History," "Where Was I That Day," "Rewriting Your Life," and "Rituals, Yours—and Mine" from *Trailing You* (Greenfield Center, NY: Greenfield Review Press, 1995). Copyright © 1995 by Kimberly Blaeser. Reprinted with the permission of the author.

Peter Blue Cloud, "Bear: A Totem Dance As Seen By Raven," "The Old Man's Lazy," "To-ta Ti-om," "Turtle," and "Yellowjacket." from *Clans of Many Nations: Selected Poems 1969–1994* (Fredonia, N.Y.: White Pine Press, 1995). "Drum." "Reflections on Milkweed" from *Wounds Beneath the Flesh,* edited by Maurice Kenny (New York: White Pine Press, 1987). All reprinted with the permission of the author.

Beth Brant, "Swimming Upstream" from *Food & Spirits.* Copyright © 1991 by Beth Brant. Reprinted with the permission of Firebrand Books, Ithaca, New York.

Joseph Bruchac, "Above the Line," "Blessing the Waters," and "Copal, Red Blood." Copyright © by Joseph Bruchac. Reprinted with the permission of the author.

Susan Pérez Castillo, "Postmodernism, Native American Literature and the Real: The Silko-Erdrich Controversy" from *The Massachusetts Review* 32, no. 1. Copyright © 1991 by The Massachusetts Review. Reprinted by permission.

Chrystos, "Today Was a Bad Day Like TB" from *Not Vanishing.* Copyright © 1988 by Press Gang. Reprinted with the permission of the author, c/o Wales Literary Agency.

Elizabeth Cook-Lynn, "A Good Chance" and "The Power of Horses" from *The Power of Horses and Other Stories* (New York: Arcade, 1990). Copyright © 1990 by Elizabeth Cook-Lynn. Reprinted with the permission of the author. "The American Fiction Writers: Cosmopolitanism, Nationalism, the Third World, and First Nation Sovereignty" from *Why I Can't Read Wallace Stegner and Other Essays: A Tribal Voice.* Copyright © 1996. Reprinted with the permission of The University of Wisconsin Press.

Nora Dauenhauer, "Salmon Egg Puller—$2.15 an Hour" from *Wicazo Sa Review* 5, no. 1 (Spring 1989), as found in *Raven Tells Stories: An Anthology of Alaskan Native Writing,* edited by Joseph Bruchac (Greenfield Center: The Greenfield Review, 1991). Reprinted with permission.

Vine Deloria, Jr., "Indian Humor" from *Custer Died for Your Sins: An Indian Manifesto.* Copyright © 1969 by Vine Deloria, Jr. Reprinted with the permission of Scribner, a division of Simon & Schuster, Inc.

Louise Erdrich, "The Red Convertible" from *Love Medicine: New and Expanded Version.* Copyright © 1993 by Louise Erdrich. "Captivity," "Indian Boarding School: The Runaways," "Jacklight," "Old Man Potchikoo," "Turtle Mountain Reservation," and "Dear John Wayne" from *Jacklight,* edited by Louise French. Copyright © 1984 by Louise Erdrich. All reprinted with the permission of Henry Holt and Company, LLC.

Eric Gansworth, "Unfinished Business." Reprinted with permission.

Diane Glancy, "Aunt Parnetta's Electric Blisters" from *Trigger Dance* (Boulder: Fiction Collective Two, 1991). Copyright © 1991 by Diane Glancy. Reprinted with the permission of the author.

Joy Harjo, "Call It Fear," "I Give You Back," "She Had Some Horses," and "The Woman Hanging from the Thirteenth Floor Window" from *She Had Some Horses.* Copyright © 1983, 1997 by Thunder's Mouth Press. Reprinted with the permission of the publisher, Thunder's Mouth Press. "Transformations." Reprinted with the permission of the author. "Grace" and "Eagle Poem" from *In Mad Love and War.* Copyright © 1990 by Joy Harjo. Reprinted with the permission of the University Press of New England. "The Woman Who Fell from the Sky" from *The Woman Who Fell from the Sky.* Copyright © 1994 by Joy Harjo. Reprinted with the permission of W. W. Norton & Company, Inc.

Gorden Henry, "Sleeping in Rain" from *Earth Power Coming: Short Fiction in Native American Literature,* edited by Simon J. Ortiz (Tsaile, Ariz.: Navajo CCP, 1993). Reprinted with the permission of the author.

Linda Hogan, "Aunt Moon's Young Man" from *Talking Leaves: Contemporary Native American Short Stories,* edited by Greg Lesley (New York: Dell Publishing, 1991). Reprinted with the permission of the author. "Blessing," "Song for My Name," "Heritage," and "Celebration: Birth of a Colt" from *Red Clay: Poems and Stories* Copyright © 1994 by Linda Hogan. Reprinted with the permission of Greenfield Review Press. "Elk Song," "The New Apartment, Minneapolis," and "It Must Be" from *Savings.* Copyright © 1988 by Linda Hogan. Reprinted with the permission of Coffee House Press. "Map" from *The Book of Medicines.* Copyright © 1993 by Linda Hogan. Reprinted with the permission of Coffee House Press. "Morning: The World in the Lake" and "The Truth Is" from *Seeing Through the Sun.* Copyright © 1985 by The University of Massachusetts Press. Reprinted with the permission of the publishers.

Maurice Kenny, "Akwesasne" from *North: Poems of Home* (Marvin, South Dakota: Blue Cloud Press, 1977). Copyright © 1977 by Maurice Kenny. "Legacy," "Sweetgrass," "They Tell Me I Am Lost," "Wild Strawberry," and "Wolf 'Aunt' " from *Harper's Anthology of 20th Century Native American Poetry,* edited by Duanne Niatum (New York: HarperCollins Publishers, 1988). Copyright © by Maurice Kenny. All reprinted with the permission of the author. Thomas King, "Borders" and "A Seat in the Garden" from *One Good Story, That One* (Toronto: HarperCollins, 1993). Copyright © 1993 by Dead Dog Cafe Productions, Inc. Reprinted with the permission of the author c/o Westwood Creative Artists.

Joyce carlEtta Mandrake, "Who I Am." Reprinted with the permission of the author.

D'Arcy McNickle, "The Hawk Is Hungry" from *The Hawk Is Hungry and Other Stories,* edited by Birgit Hans (Tucson: The University of Arizona Press, 1992). Reprinted with the permission of The Newberry Library.

N. Scott Momaday, "The Bear," "Angle of Geese," "At Risk," "The Colors of the Night," and "December 29, 1980: Wounded Knee Creek" from *In the Presence of the Sun: Stories and Poems, 1961–1991.* Copyright © 1992 by N. Scott Momaday. Reprinted with the permission of St. Martin's Press, LLC. "The Eagle-Feather Fan" from *The Gourd Dancer* (New York: Harper & Row, 1976). Copyright © 1976 by N. Scott Momaday. Reprinted with the permission of the author.

Jim Northrup, "Veteran's Dance." Reprinted with the permission of the author.

Simon J. Ortiz, "The Killing of a State Cop" from *The Man to Send Rain Clouds: Contemporary Stories by American Indians,* edited by Kenneth Rosen (New York: Viking, 1974). "Bend in the River," "The Creation, According to Coyote," "Dry Root in a

Wash," "My Father's Song," "A Story of How a Wall Stands," and "The Boy and Coyote" from *Woven Stone* (Tucson: University of Arizona Press, 1992). Copyright © 1992 by Simon J. Ortiz. All reprinted with the permission of the author. "Towards a National Indian Literature: Cultural Authenticity in Nationalism" from *MELUS: The Journal of the Society for the Study of Multi-Ethnic Literature of the United States* 8, no. 2 (Summer 1981). Reprinted with permission.

Lewis Owens, "Blessed Sunshine." Reprinted with the permission of the author.

Carter Revard, "Report to the Nation: Repossessing Europe" from *Family Matters, Tribal Affairs.* Originally published as "Report to the Nation: Reclaiming Europe" from *Earth Power Coming: Short Fiction in Native American Literature,* edited by Simon J. Ortiz (Tsaile, Ariz.: Navajo CCP, 1993). Reprinted with permission. "History, Myth, and Identity Among Osages and Other Peoples" from *Family Matters, Tribal Affairs.* Copyright © 1998 by Carter Revard. Reprinted with the permission of The University of Arizona Press. "And Don't Be Deaf to the Singing Beyond," "Driving in Oklahoma," and "In Kansas" from *Harper's Anthology of 20th Century Native American Poetry,* edited by Duanne Niatum (New York: HarperCollins Publishers, 1988). Reprinted with the permission of the author. "An Eagle Nation" from *An Eagle Nation.* Copyright © 1993 by Carter Revard. Reprinted with the permission of The University of Arizona Press. "What the Eagle Fan Says" from *An Eagle Nation* (Tucson: The University of Arizona Press, 1993). Originally published in *Poetry East,* #32 (1991). Reprinted with permission. "A Powwow Story," "Skins as Old Testament," and "Wazhazhe Grandmother." Copyright © 1993 by Carter Revard. Reprinted with the permission of the author.

Wendy Rose, "For the Complacent College Student" and "If I Am Too Brown or Too White for You" from *Going to War With All My Relations: New and Selected Poems* (Flagstaff: Entrada Books/The Northland Press, 1993). Copyright © 1993 by Wendy Rose. Reprinted with the permission of the author. "I Expected My Skin and My Blood to Ripen" and "Three Thousand Dollar Death Song" from *Lost Copper.* Copyright © 1980 by Malki Museum, Inc. Reprinted with the permission of Malki Museum Press.

Greg Sarris, "How I Got to Be a Queen" from *Talking Leaves: Contemporary Native American Short Stories,* edited by Greg Lesley (New York: Dell Publishing, 1991). Reprinted with the permission of the author. "The Woman Who Loved a Snake: Orality in Mabel McKay's Stories" from *Keeping Slug Woman Alive: A Holistic Approach to American Indian Texts.* Copyright © 1993 by The Regents of the University of California. Reprinted with the permission of University of California Press.

Leslie Marmon Silko, "The Man to Send Rain Clouds," "Tony's Story," "Yellow Woman," "Indian Song: Survival," "Long Time Ago," "Storytelling," and "Toe'osh: A Laguna Coyote Story" from *Storyteller.* Copyright © 1981 by Leslie Marmon Silko. "When Sun Came to Riverwoman" and "Story from Bear County." Copyright © 1979 by Leslie Marmon Silko. "An Old-Time Indian Attack Conducted in Two Parts: Part One: Imitation 'Indian' Poems/Part Two: Gary Snyder's Turtle Island" from *Shantih* 4, no. 2 (1979). Copyright © 1979 by Leslie Marmon Silko. All reprinted with the permission of The Wylie Agency, Inc. "Language and Literature from a Pueblo Perspective" from *Yellow Woman and a Beauty of the Spirit: Essays on a Native American Life Today.* Copyright © 1996 by Leslie Marmon Silko. Reprinted with the permission of Simon & Schuster, Inc.

Mary TallMountain, "The Disposal of Mary Joe's Children" from *Spider Woman's Granddaughters: Traditional Tales and Contemporary Writing by Native American Women,* edited by Paula Gunn Allen (New York: Fawcett Columbine, 1989). "Good Grease," "The Last Wolf," "There Is No Word for Goodbye," and "Matmiya" from *There Is No Word for Goodbye* (Marvin, South Dakota: Blue Cloud Quarterly, 1981). All reprinted with the permission of M. Catherine Costello, TallMountain Literary Executor.

Luci Tapahonso, "Blue Horses Rush In," "In Praise of Texas," and "All the Colors of Sunset" from *Blue Horses Rush In: Poems and Stories.* Copyright © 1997 by Luci Tapahonso. "Light a Candle" from *Sáanii Dahataal, the Women Are Singing: Poems and Stories.* Copyright © 1993 by Luci Tapahonso. All reprinted with the permission of The University of Arizona Press. "Raisin Eyes" from *A Breeze Swept Through.* Copyright © 1987 by Luci Tapahonso. Reprinted with the permission of West End Press.

Gerald Vizenor, *Harold of Orange: A Screenplay* from *Studies in American Indian Literatures* 5:3 (Fall 1993). Reprinted with the permission of the author.

Anna Lee Walters, "The Warriors" from *The Sun Is Not Merciful.* Copyright © 1985 by Anna Lee Walters. Reprinted with the permission of Firebrand Books, Ithaca, New York.

James Welch, "Christmas Comes to Moccasin Flat," "Riding the Earthboy 40," "Snow Country Weavers," "Surviving," and "Thanksgiving at Snake Butte" from *Riding the Earthboy 40* (Pittsburgh: Carnegie-Mellon University Press, 1998). Copyright © 1998 by James Welch. Reprinted with permission.

Roberta Hill Whiteman, "Dream of Rebirth," "For Heather, Entering Kindergarten," and "In the Longhouse, Oneida Museum" from *Star Quilt* (Duluth, Minn.: Holy Cow! Press, 1994). Copyright © 1994. Reprinted with the permission of the publisher. All rights reserved.

Ray Young Bear, "Black Eagle Child Quarterly" from *Black Eagle Child: The Facepaint Narratives.* Copyright © 1992 by Ray A. Young Bear. Reprinted with the permission of the University of Iowa Press. "The First Dimension of a Skunk," "The Language of Weather," "Nothing Could Take Away the Bear-King's Image," and "The Significance of a Water Animal" from *The Invisible Musician* (Duluth: Holy Cow! Press, 1990). Copyright © 1990. Reprinted with the permission of the publisher. "Morning Talking Mother" and "Winter of the Salamander" from *Winter of the Salamander: The Keeper of Importance* (New York: Harper & Row, 1980). Copyright © 1980 by Ray A. Young Bear. Reprinted with the permission of the author, c/o Carlisle & Company, New York.

INDEX